Linguistic Forms at the Border of Lexis and Grammar:

Grammaticalization of Adpositions across Languages

Omnia vincit amor, et in aeternum stat.

Linguistic Forms at the Border of Lexis and Grammar:
Grammaticalization of Adpositions across Languages

ⓒ 이성하 (Seongha Rhee), 2021

1판 1쇄 인쇄__2021년 11월 20일
1판 1쇄 발행__2021년 11월 29일

지은이__이성하 (Seongha Rhee)
펴낸이__홍정표 (Jeongpyo Hong)
펴낸곳__글로벌콘텐츠 (Global Contents Publishing)
　　　　등록__제25100-2008-000024호

공급처__(주)글로벌콘텐츠출판그룹
　　　　대표_홍정표 이사_김미미 편집_하선연 권군오 최한나 홍명지 문방희 기획·마케팅_김수경 이종훈 홍민지
　　　　주소__서울특별시 강동구 풍성로 87-6, 201호
　　　　전화__02) 488-3280 팩스__02) 488-3281
　　　　홈페이지__http://www.gcbook.co.kr
　　　　이메일__edit@gcbook.co.kr

값 38,000원
ISBN 979-11-5852-358-9 93740

Linguistic Forms at the Border of Lexis and Grammar:
Grammaticalization of Adpositions across Languages

Seongha Rhee

2021

This work was supported by the National Research Foundation of Korea Grant
funded by the Korean Government
(NRF-2014S1A5B1065578).

이 저서는 2014년 정부(교육부)의 재원으로 한국연구재단의 지원을 받아 수행된 연구임
(NRF-2014S1A5B1065578).

Preface

A noun in a sentence is an island.[1] Not in the sense of constraints of extraction but in the sense of its inability to connect with others without help of its supporters. These supporters are, among others, adpositions. Adpositions serve a noun by signaling its diverse roles in the sentence. They are the bridges for the nouns, whereby the nouns can properly relate to other sentential constituents. Figuratively speaking, the *raison d'être* of a nominal is made explicit by the adpositions that host it. Thus, as a signal of syntactic and semantic role of nominals, adpositions constitute an interesting grammatical category.

My interest in English prepositions began while I was a college student. It was primarily because of their wide spectrum of meaning. While I was a graduate student at the University of Texas at Austin (1991-1996), I attended the 1995 Summer Institute by the Linguistic Society of America, in Albuquerque, New Mexico, with financial support arranged by my supervisor, Prof. Dr. Manfred Krifka. Taking the courses taught by leading scholars, I was greatly intrigued by grammaticalization theory. The theory shows that the emergence of functions of grammatical forms and their inexplicably complex functions can be systematically explained by tracing their developmental paths and relating them to human cognition. That was a life-changing experience and I became a grammaticalizationist. I greatly owe to the LSA LI-1995

---

[1] John Ross (1967) in his MIT doctoral dissertation suggested a rule, famously known among formal syntacticians as the Complex NP Constraint, which disallows extraction of a constituent out of a complex noun phrase.

instructors, Prof. Bernd Heine, Prof. Joan Bybee, Prof. Paul Hopper, Prof. Scott DeLancey, among others.

I was fortunate to have the opportunity to pursue my five-year crosslinguistic research through the funding of the Korean Government, National Research Foundation of Korea (NRF-2014S1A5B1065578) from 2014. I am thankful for their generous support. I was greatly helped by my collaborative research experience with Prof. Heiko Narrog and Prof. John Whitman on Korean and Japanese grammaticalization; with Prof. Kyunghee Kim on Korean and Spanish grammaticalization; with Prof. Kyungeun Park on Korean and Thai grammaticalization; with Prof. Tania Kuteva and Prof. Sunhee Yae on Korean, English, German, and Bulgarian grammaticalization; and Prof. Bernd Heine, Prof. Tania Kuteva, Prof. Heiko Narrog, Prof. Bo Hong, and Prof. Haiping Long for crosslinguistic research. I am also thankful to Prof. Elizabeth Traugott, Prof. Ad Foolen, Prof. Christa König, Prof. Martine Robbeets, Prof. Miriam Locher, Prof. Xinren Chen, Prof. Kaoru Horie, Prof. Yo Matsumoto, Prof. Sung-Ock Sohn, Prof. Minju Kim, Prof. Jinho Park, Prof. Iksoo Kwon, Prof. Jungran Chin, Dr. Jiin Kim, Prof. Hyun Sook Lee, Prof. Mikyung Ahn, Prof. Junghye Baik, Dr. Sujin Eom, Dr. Kyou-Dong Ahn, Dr. Eunmi Kim, Dr. Hye-Won Yi, Prof. Kingkarn Thepkanjana, and my colleagues at Hankuk University of Foreign Studies.

Many colleagues kindly provided support either by reading the manuscript, or by responding to my occasional queries, or by painstakingly collecting and analyzing the data from corpora. My thanks go to Prof. Dongkyu Kim, Prof. Reijirou Shibasaki, Prof. Yuko Higashiizumi, and Soohyun Pae for Japanese; Prof. Kyunghee Kim and Heeran Lee for Spanish; Prof. Xiao He, Prof. Yeon Jin Ahn, Dr. Seon-A Kwun, Dr. Eun-Joo Lee, and Lin Zhang for Chinese; and Prof. Kyungeun Park, Prof. Kewalin Simuang, Prof. Supakit Buakhao, Prof. Kultida Khammee, Bo-Eun Kim, and Ji-Eun Park for Thai. Despite their valuable assistance, all errors in interpretation of data and argumentation are solely mine.

I am deeply indebted to my life-time mentor, Prof. Dr. Bernd Heine, for his constant support. My special thanks go to Prof. Hyun Jung Koo for her never-failing support and encouragement throughout my research career. The insights she kindly shared with me were invaluable inspirations. It has been a true privilege to have worked with her and I am deeply grateful.

My heart-felt thanks go to my long-time, faithful colleague and friend, Prof. Shaun Manning. He has provided me with all the help needed by kindly reading and commenting on my manuscripts. I am also thankful to Dr. Jeongpyo Hong at Global Contents Publishing for kindly agreeing to publish this monograph.

Last but not least, my thanks go to my family: Amy, Eunice, Sam, Joshua, Elijah, and Micah for their moral support.

September 29, 2021

Seongha Rhee
Hankuk University of Foreign Studies
Seoul, Korea

Contents

1. Introduction

2. Preliminaries: Space and Adposition

3. Grammaticalization of Postpositions in Korean

4. Grammaticalization of Postpositions in Japanese

7. Grammaticalization of Adpositions in Chinese

8. Grammaticalization of Prepositions in Thai

9. Grammaticalization Principles and Hypotheses Revisited

10. Typology and Beyond

11. Conclusion

List of Tables

List of Abbreviations

a	adjective			Español
ABL	ablative		CSJ	Corpus of Spontaneous
ACC	accusative			Japanese, the
ad	adverb		D-0	zero dimension
ADD	additive		D-1	first dimension
ADJ/adj	adjective		D-2	second dimension
ADN	adnominal		D-3	third dimension
ADV/adv	adverb		DAT	dative
ALL	allative		DEC	declarative
ATMP	attemptive		DIR	directional
BEN	benefactive		DISJ	disjunctive
C	Chinese		DIST	distributive
CCL	Center for Chinese Linguistics		E	English
	at Peking University, the		EMPH	emphatic
CLS	classifier		END	sentence-ender
CMPX	complex adposition		ENUM	enumerative
CMST	composite adposition		ESS	essive
CNTP	contempt		EXTR	extreme
CNTR	contrast		EXTT	extent
COCA	Corpus of Contemporary		FDMC	*Frequency Dictionary of*
	American English, the			*Modern Chinese*
COM	comitative		FOC	focus
COMP	complementizer		Fr	French
comp	comparative		GEN	genitive
CONJ	conjunctive		HON	honorific
CONN	connective		INST	instrumental
Conv	converb		IP	inflectional phrase
CREA	Corpus de Referencia de		It	Italian

J	Japanese
K	Korean
KU-CKD	*Korea University Chinese-Korean Dictionary*
L	Latin
L1	first language
L2	second/foreign language
Lat	Latin
LMT	limitive
LOC	locative
LP	léxico + preposición
M	masculine
N/n	noun
-n	suffix noun
n=	number (count)
NEG	negative
NF	non-finite
NGLE	*Nueva Gramática de la Lengua Española*
NJ	native Japanese
NK	native Korean
NOM	nominative
NP	noun phrase
NPI	negative polarity item
OE	Old English
OED	*Oxford English Dictionary, the*
p	preposition; postposition
P_1	first preposition; first postposition
P_2	second preposition; second postposition
PART	particle
P(D)NP	preposition-(determiner)-noun-

	-preposition
PDNP	preposition-determiner-noun-preposition
PEJ	pejorative
PERF	perfective
pJ	Proto-Japanese
pK	Proto-Korean
PL/pl	plural
PMW/pmw	per million word
PNP	preposition-noun-preposition; postposition-noun-postposition
P-N-P	preposition-noun-preposition; postposition-noun-postposition
POL	polite
POS	part of speech
$Post_1$	first postposition
$Post_2$	second postposition
pp	past participle
PP	prepositional phrase; postpositional phrase
pref	prefix
PREP/prep	preposition
$Prep_1$	first preposition
$Prep_2$	second preposition
PRES	present
PRIM	primary adposition
PROG	progressive
PROH	prohibitive
PROL	prolative
prp	present participle
PST	past
pTg	Proto-Tungusic
P-V	postposition-verb

Q	question (interrogative)	super	superlative
-q	prefix	SVO	subject–verb–object
QUOT	quotative	T	Thai
RAE	Real Academia Española	T.	temporal
RES	resultative	TAM	tense–aspect–modality
RN	relational noun	THM	theme
S	Spanish	TNC	Thai National Corpus
Sc	Scandinavian	TOP	topic
SEQ	sequential	ULT	ulterior
sg	singular	V/v	verb
SJ/sj	Sino-Japanese	vn	verbal noun
SK/sk	Sino-Korean	VP	verb phrase
SOV	subject-object-verb	WALS	*World Atlas of Language Structures, the*
Sp	Spanish		
suf	suffix		

Introduction

1.1 Objectives

Presumably all languages have one or more means, explicit or implicit, to signal the syntactic and thematic roles of nominal constituents occurring in a sentence. Implicit means may be largely based on the pragmatic interpretations of the string with the assumption that linguistic representation will reflect the states of the affairs in the reality and be consistent with the common expectations about the world (cf. 'pragmatically-oriented grammar', Enfield 2009; 'emergentist' view of grammar, Ellis 1998, Elman 1999, MacWhinney 1999, O'Grady 2005, 2008).[1] Such languages, labeled as 'zero-marking languages', are admittedly of a low proportion.[2] In such languages, the argument roles tend to be marked by means of syntactic configuration (Andrews 2007[1985]: 142). A far more frequent pattern, however, is to use explicit morphological markers (Iggesen 2005: 206).

Nominal morphologies for signaling the function of the nominal constituent may

---

[1] For instance, in Dakota, the word order determines the thematic role (e.g., The man killed a bear vs. A bear killed the man) but in instances where the interpretation cannot be ambiguous from the world knowledge (e.g., The man saw a rock), the word order is free (Andrews 2007[1985]: 142).

[2] According to Iggesen (2005: 206), 81 languages (out of 261 languages) do not have morphological case marking. See also Iggesen (2008: 246-257).

appear as bound morphemes (i.e., as case inflection) either at the beginning or the end of the host. Such functional signals may also take the form of loosely bound particles (i.e., adpositions) either before or after the host noun. Their functions may widely vary depending on the language but it seems that they still belong to a limited set across languages (see 2.2.1). Among diverse types, we focus on adpositions, and among those diverse functions, we focus on spatial adpositions in the present volume.

It is also widely known that grammaticalization scenarios often exhibit remarkably similar patterns across languages but also systematically different patterns across language types (see works in Bisang and Malchukov (eds.) 2020a,b). The similarity may be largely due to the universal properties of human cognitive operations, and the systematic differences may be due to the language structures that impose mechanical constraints. Thus, typological features play a significant role in language change and language development.

The objectives of this book are manifold: to describe the contemporary adpositional systems in typologically and genealogically diverse language samples; to analyze the spatial adpositions with respect to their functional salience and grammaticalization patterns; to identify crosslinguistic commonalities and differences arising from variable typological features; and to discuss theoretically important issues in the light of the grammaticalization scenarios exhibited by the sampled languages.

In order to achieve these objectives, this book is organized in the following way. We will first describe, from Chapters 3 to 8, the adpositional systems in general in six typologically and genealogically diversified languages, i.e., Korean, Japanese, English, Spanish, Chinese, and Thai, and then analyze the spatial adpositions with respect to their distribution and their lexical sources. Among the spatial adpositions, we select a subset of adpositions consisting of those that are supposedly undergoing grammaticalization with reasonable viability, and compare them with those of similar functions that have advanced to a greater extent of grammaticalization on the one hand, and those that have not undergone much grammaticalization process on the other. Grammaticalization mechanisms and functional extension patterns are reviewed in the light of grammaticalization scenarios of the adpositions in each language.

Further, based on the description of grammaticalization of adpositions in each language, we discuss in Chapter 9, a number of important grammaticalization principles and hypotheses, i.e., divergence, persistence, source determination, unidirectionality, universal path, reanalysis and reinterpretation. We also discuss in Chapter 10, from a typological perspective, some of the observed crosslinguistic commonalities as well as the issues related to word classes, influence of morphological typology, and language contact.

1.2 Research Methods

This research adopts a quantitative method. Quantitative methods subscribe to the tenet that the frequency of a linguistic formant in use directly reflects the degree of its conceptual salience (cf. 'lexical strength' Bybee 1985: 117-123, Eom 2020). We selected six languages with diverse morphological typology and genealogy (see 1.3 below) and collected adpositions in those languages from existing literature with the help of consultants, who are trained linguists in the language concerned.

Using frequency information to examine the functional strengths is well justified by the truism that the linguistic system is affected and formed by use, as is well articulated in the usage-based models of grammar (cf. Barlow and Kemmer 2000). Frequency yields entrenchment (Langacker 1987, 1991, 2000, Haiman 1994), and humans have the capacity to abstract more schematic structural patterns from recurring specific but similar instances (Rohde 2001). With these theoretical underpinnings, we used corpora in individual languages for frequency analyses. The information about the corpus for individual languages is provided in each chapter. In cases where no part of speech distinction is available from parameter settings in the search engine, we used random samples as deemed appropriate and made projections based on the proportions in the sample.

1.3 Language Typology and Language Samples

Languages may fall under different classifications according to their typological attributes. Morphological typology makes use of such concepts as synthetic vs. analytic languages, depending on the way the language combines morphemes. Synthetic languages may combine a noun with discrete particles or fuse the grammatical concepts with the host noun, whereas analytic languages may primarily rely on auxiliary words or word order leaving the host noun intact. The type of synthetic language utilizing particles is called an agglutinative language, whereas one utilizing fusion is called an inflectional language. Thus, typologists generally use a three-way classification, i.e., isolating, fusional, and agglutinative types (Schwegler 1990). Such morphological typologies are generally believed to be dominant in certain language families and regions, e.g., analytic languages are found in the Sino-Tibetan family and some Germanic languages; agglutinative languages are widely spread in Koreanic, Japonic, Turkic, Dravidian, Bantu families, among others; and fusional languages are found in most Indo-European and Semitic families, among others.

Linguistic typological features of a language may change over time. For instance, English, a Germanic language, was a heavily inflected language as its close genealogical relatives still are. Over the last 1,200 years, however, English has lost nearly all of its inflection and has become a weakly inflected language (cf. Allen 2006, Fischer 2010, Sims-Williams and Baerman 2021). The extent of inflection loss is such that, overall, contemporary English is classifiable as an analytic language.

In the present study, we have chosen six languages to diversify their typological features, across agglutinative, fusional, and isolating languages. Since many adpositions are historically old grams, we decided to include English under the fusional (inflectional) language group. A large number of English prepositions developed while the language had a fully inflectional system, and thus English presents a unique case in which old grams date back to times when the language was fusional, whereas new grams are being innovated while the language has analytic typological features. The languages under discussion, thus, are as follows:

(1)   a. Korean: Agglutinative (Koreanic)

　　　b. Japanese: Agglutinative (Japonic)

　　　c. English: Inflectional, Fusional (formerly) (Germanic, Indo-European)

　　　d. Spanish: Inflectional, Fusional (currently) (Romance, Indo-European)

　　　e. Chinese (Mandarin): Isolating, Analytic (Sinitic, Sino-Tibetan)

　　　f. Thai: Isolating, Analytic (Tai, Kra-Dai)

A brief information on each language along with their typological characteristics are given below. Also provided is the information on the corpora used for statistical analyses of adpositions.

1.3.1 Korean

Korean is spoken by about 81.5 million people (*Ethnologue*; Eberhard et al. 2021) in and around the Korean peninsula: South Korea, North Korea, China, Japan, and other Korean communities around the world.[3] It was formerly regarded as an Altaic language since eminent Finnish Altaic linguist Gustaf Ramstedt proposed it in 1939 (Ramstedt 1997[1939]), but in the modern linguistic research tradition the Altaic hypothesis is contested (see N Kim 1992, H Sohn 1999, J Song 2005, among others, for discussion of the issue). *Ethnologue* (Eberhard et al. 2021) lists it as a 'Koreanic' language. Most recently it is frequently discussed under the geographically motivated classificatory term 'Transeurasian languages' (Johanson and Robbeets 2010, Robbeets 2015, Robbeets and Savelyev 2020), often along with Japanese since the two languages share many structural characteristics (Narrog and Rhee 2013, Narrog et al. 2018).[4]

　　　Typologically Korean is an agglutinating, head-final, SOV language. In line with the SOV word order characteristics in morphology, it is suffixal and postpositional (see Robbeets 2020). Prepositions do not exist and prefixes are relatively unproductive. Therefore, in most grammaticalization scenarios independent

---

[3] This description is modified from S Rhee (2020b: 575-577).

[4] *Ethnologue* (Eberhard et al. 2021) states that scholars differ as to whether or not Korean is related to Japanese.

lexemes develop into suffixes and postpositions as bound morphemes. Multiple suffixes and postpositions may occupy slots of a relatively fixed order. Argument NPs are often omitted and NPs may occur without their postpositional particles, especially in speech, and the interpretive flexibility thus created often affects grammaticalization. NPs are strictly head-final, thus all nominal modifiers occur before the modified noun. Further, there is no article among the nominal modifiers, and plural marking is optional. Syntactic and thematic functions of NPs are marked with case markers and postpositions. With these role markers NPs may occur rather freely without functional confusion, even though there is a canonical and preferred word order.

The data source for quantitative analyses is a 24-million word Drama & Movies Corpus, a collection of 7,454 scenarios of dramas, sitcoms, and movies dating from 1992 through 2015 (see 3.1 for more information).

1.3.2 Japanese

Japanese is spoken by 126.4 million speakers, mostly in Japan (*Ethnologue*; Eberhard et al. 2021). It is a 'Japonic' language (Serafim 1985, 2003, Bentley 2008: 23, Vovin 2008: 5), but its ultimate derivation and relation to other languages are unlcear, even though its shared ancestry with Korean has often been hypothesized.[5] It was formerly thought to be an Altaic language, but has since been discredited. In recent research, Japanese is discussed as a 'Japanic' language (Janhunen 1996: 77-81, 1999: 2, Robbeets 2015: 22-23), belonging to Transeurasian languages (Johanson and Robbeets 2010, Robbeets 2015, Robbeets and Savelyev (eds.) 2020), often along with Korean since the two languages share many structural characteristics (Narrog and Rhee 2013, Narrog et al. 2018, cf. works in McClure and Vovin (eds.) 2018; see Y Matsumoto 1998 for phonological features; see also works in Robbeets and Savelyev 2020 for diverse shared features from a broader perspective).

---

[5] *Ethnologue* (Eberhard et al. 2021) also notes that Japanese is possibly related to Korean. Japanese and Korean share the same etyma in a number of words (Whitman 1985, Pellard 2018, Robbeets and Savelyev 2020).

Japanese has been a strictly head-final SOV language with accusative alignment, and with frequent omission of argument NPs, throughout its documented history.[6] Morphologically, Japanese is agglutinating, and given the head-final nature of the language, clear cases of grammaticalization typically lead to the suffixation of formerly independent morphemes (i.e. lexemes) (Robbeets 2020). Prefixation is much less common, confined to a small number of categories, mostly honorification and negation. It has been noted in Narrog et al. (2018) that many of the structural characteristics of Japanese (and Korean) are shared across Transeurasian languages as well as Nivkh, Yukaghir, and for the most part Ainu (see Robbeets 2015, Robbeets and Savelyev 2020 and works therein).

The data source for quantitative analyses of Modern Japanese is the Corpus of Spontaneous Japanese (CSJ), a 7.52 million word POS-tagged corpus, about 650 hours of spontaneous speech, developed by the National Institute for Japanese Language and Linguistics and its partner institutions (1999–2003).

1.3.3 English

English is spoken by 1,348 million people widely spread around the world, with 370 million L1 speakers and 978 million L2 speakers (*Ethnologue*; Eberhard et al. 2021). It is the most spoken language in the world, even though its L1 population is exceeded by Mandarin Chinese and Spanish. It is an Indo-European language belonging to the West Germanic group of Germanic languages.

Typologically, it is a non-tonal, head-initial language, having the SVO word order, articles, and prepositions. Its lexical similarity with German is 60%, with French 27%, and with Russian 24% (*Ethnologue*; Eberhard et al. 2021). Even though it is classified as a Germanic language as it shares some characteristics such as division of strong verbs and weak verbs in their inflection, as indicated above, it has lost much of inflectional complexity and has become a weakly inflecting language classifiable as an analytic language.

---

[6] This description is modified from Narrog et al. (2018: 166-168 –357P).

The data source for quantitative analyses of Modern English is the Corpus of Contemporary American English (COCA) (formerly known as BYU Corpora), a 1-billion word, genre-balanced corpus, consisting of the texts from 1990 through 2019.

1.3.4 Spanish

Spanish is spoken by 543 million people, with 471 million L1 speakers and 72 million L2 speakers around the world (*Ethnologue*; Eberhard et al. 2021). It is spoken by the people in Spain and many countries in the Americas. It is a Romance language, belonging to the Ibero-Romance group of the Indo-European language family.

Typologically, Spanish is a non-tonal, head-initial language, having the SVO word order, articles, and prepositions. As a descendant of Latin, it has a great level of similarity with Latin, with 75% of its vocabulary derived from it (Pei 1949, Camacho Becerra et al. 2004[1998], Comparán Rizo 2006). Its lexical similarity with Portuguese is 89% and with French 75% (*Ethnologue*; Eberhard et al. 2021). As we shall see in 10.4, its high resemblance to Latin and French and the influence of French on English result in the great similarity between Spanish and English complex prepositions.

The data source for quantitative analyses is the corpus CREA (Corpus de Referencia de Español Actual) developed by Real Academia Española. It is a 170-million word corpus, consisting of a large collection of records, from varied sources dated between 1975 and 2004, the data from 1975 to 1999 accounting for 85% of the entire corpus.

1.3.5 Chinese (Mandarin)

Mandarin Chinese, also known as *Pǔtōnghuà* (普通话), is spoken by 1,120 million people around the world, with 921 million L1 speakers and 199 million L2 speakers (*Ethnologue*; Eberhard et al. 2021). Mandarin Chinese ranks first in the number of native speakers. It belongs to the group of Sinitic languages, natively spoken across northern and southwestern China, and belongs to the Sino-Tibetan family.

Typologically, Chinese is a tonal, noun head-final language, having the SVO word order, with no articles or inflection. It is a strongly analytic, isolating language, thus one word is typically one morpheme (see 7.2, however, for the character–word relations). Since nouns are not marked for grammatical case and rarely for number, the functional resolution usually relies on word order and particles. Thus, the adpositional concepts are usually signaled by these particles, which we will call prepositions and postpositions depending on their location relative to the host noun. As we note in 7.2, Chinese had spelling reforms in the 1950s, simplifying the classical characters. Thus, in this book we use either both or one of them, as deemed appropriate in the context.

The data for quantitative analyses is taken from the modern Chinese section of the CCL (The Center for Chinese Linguistics at Peking University) online corpus, consisting of 581,794,456 characters, without word segmentation or POS tagging (see 7.2 for more detail).

1.3.6 Thai

Thai is spoken by 60.7 million speakers around the world, with 20.7 million L1 speakers and 40 million L2 speakers (*Ethnologue*; Eberhard et al. 2021). It is a Tai language of the Kra-Dai language family, and is spoken by Central Thai people and vast majority of Thai Chinese.

Typologically, Thai is a head-initial, tonal language, having the SVO word order, no articles, and prepositions. It is an analytic, isolating language lacking any form of inflectional morphology. Arguments in a sentence, including the subject, can be, and are often, omitted. Thus, encoding the functions of the arguments relies on the word order and separate particles. Accordingly, adpositional functions are marked by particles, which we call prepositions. The status of these prepositions has often been a topic of scholarly debate (see 8.2 for more discussion).

The data source for quantitative analyses is the Thai National Corpus (TNC), an online searchable, 33.4 million word corpus, developed by Chulalongkorn University. The corpus texts are mostly dated from 1988 through 2017, accounting for 75.8%, but the corpus data also includes the texts of unknown date (18.6%) and pre-1988 texts (5.7%).

1.4 Grammaticalization

Based on the quantitative data from the corpus, we analyze the development of adpositions from a grammaticalization perspective. According to this framework, language change reveals the conceptual and cognitive mechanisms operating in a unidirectional way, a process named grammaticalization. Grammaticalization theory has greatly aided language scientists in understanding diverse aspects of language, especially with respect to the formative forces in grammar. Antoine Meillet (1865-1935) took interest in the origin of grammatical categories as he noticed that the secondary linguistic forms, *mots accessoires*, historically originated from the primary linguistic forms, *mots principaux*. He proposed the term 'grammaticalisation' to describe the process of attributing grammatical character to an erstwhile autonomous word ("[l']attribution du caractère grammatical à un mot jadis autonome") (Meillet 1912: 133). Jerzy Kuryłowicz (1895-1978) defined grammaticalization as "the increase of the range of a morpheme advancing from a lexical to a grammatical and from a less grammatical to a more grammatical status" (Kuryłowicz, 1975[1965]: 52).

Christian Lehmann (2015[1982]) proposed an elegant set of parameters that can be used as diagnostics of grammaticalization. The parameters are based on the two major distinctions, i.e. autonomy-grammaticality on the one hand and paradigm-syntagma on the other. By applying three components, i.e. weight, cohesion, and variability, to paradigm and syntagma, he proposed six parameters altogether, i.e., integrity, scope, paradigmaticity, bondedness, paradigmatic variability, and syntagmatic variability.

More recently, Hopper and Traugott (2003[1993]) defined grammaticalization as "the change whereby lexical items and constructions come in certain linguistic contexts to serve grammatical functions and, once grammaticalized, continue to develop new grammatical functions" (p. xv). They emphasize that grammaticalization is an ongoing process in which earlier forms may coexist with later ones and earlier meanings may constrain later meanings and/or structural characteristics (Hopper and Traugott, 2003[1993]: 16). Grammaticalizationists investigate the omnipresent change of a linguistic form from the starting point, the path, and the end point from its lexical source to the resultant grammatical function (S Rhee, 2016[1998]: 24).

Language change, from the perspective of grammaticalization, occurs in such a systematic way that it can be explained by resorting to a set of principles and mechanisms. For instance, Hopper (1991) proposes five principles of grammaticalization, widely subscribed to by the grammaticalization researchers, i.e., layering, divergence, specialization, persistence, and decategorialization. Bybee et al. (1994) propose seven hypothesis, i.e. source determination, unidirectionality, universal paths, parallel reduction, relevance, semantic retention, and layering. A more recent proposal is found in Heine and Kuteva (2002; revised as Kuteva et al., 2019), in which desemanticization, decategorialization, extension, and erosion are proposed as the major operating principles. Many of these mechanisms and principles are discussed in chapters addressing individual languages and collectively in Chapter 9.

1.5 Scope of Research

Grammaticalization of adpositions has been investigated in a large number of studies in and across languages, e.g., Bowden (1992, Oceanic languages), Giacalone Ramat (1994, Italian), Peyraube (1994, Chinese), T Ohori (1995, Japanese), J Chung (1996, Korean), J Ahn (1997, Korean), Y Matsumoto (1998, Japanese), Davy (2000), Di Meola (2000, German), S Rhee (2003a, 2004c, 2006b, Korean), Cifuentes (2003, Spanish), De Mulder (2003, French), J Baik (2004, English), Hoffmann (2005, English), H Jung (2006, Thai), Fagard and De Mulder (2007, French), Chappell and Peyraube (2008, Chinese), Fagard (2008, French), Yae (2008, 2018, English), F Wu (2008, Chinese), M Ahn (2009a, English), Maeng and Kwun (2009, Chinese), Esseesy (2010, Arabic), Y Jang (2010, Korean), H Park (2012, Chinese), W Park (2012, Chinese), Choi and Kwun (2012, 2013, Chinese), S Yae (2012, 2015, Korean), S Park (2013, Japanese), J Wang (2014, Chinese), J Park (2014, English), K Ahn (2015, English), Hoelbeek (2017, French and Italian), K Park (2017, Thai), Eom (2018, English), K Kim (2018, 2019, Spanish), J Ha (2018, Japanese), Park and Rhee (2018, Thai), Y Jung (2018, Korean), and a number of crosslinguistic studies e.g., Heine et al. (1991a,b), Svorou (1994), Fagard (2006), Fagard and Mardale (2012), among many others.

Drawing upon the insights from these earlier studies, this book addresses grammaticalization scenarios of adpositions in six languages, i.e., Korean, Japanese, English, Spanish, Chinese, and Thai. Of these, Korean and Japanese are exclusively postpositional; English, Spanish, and Thai are (nearly) exclusively prepositional; and Chinese is prepositional and, to a lesser extent, postpositional. From the typological view, Korean and Japanese are synthetic and agglutinative; English and Spanish are, or was in history, synthetic and inflectional; and Chinese and Spanish are analytic and isolating. Genealogically, all these six languages are unrelated: Korean and Japanese are isolates (in Koreanic and Japonic, respectively); English is a Germanic language; Spanish is a Romance language; Chinese is a Sinitic language; and Thai is a Tai (Kra-Dai) language. Even though the language samples are deliberately chosen to diversify typological and genealogical distribution, it is difficult, due to the inherent complexity of linguistic structure, to establish representative validity of each of them for the type they are meant to represent. More indepth studies will complement the present analysis.

The primary objective of our research is to gain insight on the adpositional system, especially on spatial adpositions. In order to facilitate the crosslinguistic comparison, certain aspects that may be also important in individual languages could not be addressed in earnest. Furthermore, our immediate interest is on those adpositions that have not yet fully grammaticalized but have sufficient viability as reflected in use frequency, i.e., those that may be regarded as currently undergoing grammaticalization. Therefore, those that are either fully grammaticalized as primary adpositions or have very low strengths as reflected by the low token frequency are not given due attention. More comprehensive and multi-dimensional studies are needed for a fuller understanding of the grammaticalization of adpositions.

2

Preliminaries:
Space and Adposition

2.1 Space in Language

Since humans, like all organisms, exist in space, the notion of space, its perception, and its linguistic representation have long been the topic of interest in linguistics (Leech 1969, Fillmore 1971, Clark 1973, Lyons 1977, Johnston and Slobin 1979, Svorou 1986, 1994, Heine et al. 1991a, Levinson 1994, 2004[2003], Bloom et al. (eds.) 1999, Heine 1997, Bowerman and Choi 2001, Hickmann and Robert (eds.) 2006, Tenbrink et al. (eds.) 2013, and many others). Levinson (1996b: 358) notes that space, as a pretheoretical notion, covers "at least location and motion, and arguably shape as well - in fact much of what we talk about." Indeed, spatial cognition and conceptual structure are inseparably connected (cf. Jackendoff 1999). Despite there being many different approaches to the concept of space, it is widely agreed upon that space is a basic category of human thinking, a basic metaphor of conceptualization. Brisard (1991), for instance, notes that:

"The same schemas that structure our experience of space structure concepts themselves. [...] [T]he spatial aspect is the basic organizing principle of human experience, and for this reason it should be obvious that we find this situation reflected in language." (Brisard 1991, as cited in Broschart 1992: 44)

It has also been shown that spatial conceptualization is fundamentally grounded in human experiential basis, and thus is revealed in other, non-linguistic, modalities, e.g., pointing, eye-movement, drawing, etc. (see works in Paradis et al. (eds.) 2013).

However, space perception in detail and its representation is not uniform, as discussed in depth in Levinson (2004[2003]), works in Bloom et al. (eds.) (1999), Hickmann and Robert (2006a) and works therein.[1] The perception of space depends on the relative position of the observer, i.e., from the perspective (Lessau 1994), and therefore, it has the potential of being intrinsically subjective (see for example, S Rhee 2002c, 2004a, 2004b). In addition to this dependency on the individual perceiver, there is also a variation across languages, i.e., different languages may have different frames of spatial reference, such as Absolute, Relative, and Intrinsic frames (Levinson 1992, 1997, 2004[2003], Haviland 1992, Brown 1994). Furthermore, different languages may develop spatial grams from different models, such as the anthropomorphic model, the zoomorphic model, the landmark model, and the relational concepts model (Heine et al. 1991a, Heine 1997, cf. Svorou 1986). Talmy (1988: 171) noted that all closed-class spatial morphemes tend to be topological in character, being neutral over shape, material or medium, angle and magnitude, and that the nature of cognitive structure underlying spatial morphemes is "largely relativistic or topological rather than absolute or Euclidean." Levinson (2002), however, based on crosslinguistic observations, refutes the idea and contends that axial and angular properties are common across languages (e.g. English *across, opposite, on, over,* etc.), and shape discriminations are rarer but attested (e.g. Karuk adpositions; Levinson 2004[2003]: 63, Mithun 1999: 142).

As has been observed in the foregoing exposition, the crosslinguistic variations are such that a crosslinguistic one-to-one mapping is myth. However, there does exist

---

[1] See Creissels (2006), in particular, for discussion of Subsaharan African languages that are peculiar in that their locative adpositions or case affixes never participate in the encoding of the distinction between localization, source of motion, and destination of motion. This finding points to the broad diversity of spatial marking in languages.

a meaningful level of correspondence and the correspondence is not at all erratic. For example, spatial grams may be organized by differing yet crosslinguistically valid axes, as has been suggested by Svorou (1994). Spatial grams may also be organized in terms of their major variables that make the grams distinct by virtue of occupying different locations along the continuum of ground-marking, such as Goal, Location, and Source (Levinson 2004[2003]).

In this light, the present study looks at patterns of encoding spatial relationship between entities, in six languages, with special focus on adpositions signaling diverse ground-marking and the axial location marking with polar distinction.

2.2 Adposition

2.2.1 Adposition as a Grammatical Category

The World Atlas of Language Structures (WALS; Haspelmath et al. 2005: 346) defines adpositions as a form which "combines with a noun phrase and indicates the grammatical or semantic relationship of the noun phrase to the verb in the clause." Adpositions have been investigated in a large number of studies. With the advent of cognitive linguistics, and grammaticalization theory in particular, adpositions crosslinguistically have been among the most frequently studied areas in recent years because research turned up interesting universalities across languages in recruitment patterns of adpositional sources, and the paths of the development with similar motivating forces (see e.g. Heine et al. 1991a, Svorou 1994, Kuteva and Sinha 1994, among others).

On the lexicality-grammaticality continuum, adpositions are largely located close to the end of the grammaticality pole, even though they do not exhibit intracategorial homogeneity (Heine et al. 1991a, Hopper and Traugott 2003[1993], Lehmann 2015[1982], Y Matsumoto 1998, S Rhee 2003a). It needs to be noted, however, that there is a controversy in the generative paradigm over the theoretical status of prepositions ranging from the position that prepositions are lexical (Jackendoff 1973), one that they are intermediate (Abney 1987), one that they are functional (Grimshaw 1991), and one that they are heterogeneous (Riemsdijk 1990, Zwarts 1995). In a discussion on German postpositions, Di Meola (2003) notes that German postpositions constitute a fuzzy category between lexical and function words, and Grünthal (2003) shows that there are no clear boundaries between Finnic adpositions on the one hand and nouns and adverbs on the other. The proximity to lexical category seems to be generally applicable to most secondary adpositions, i.e., composite adpositions and complex adpositions. Many adpositions across languages exhibit categorial fluidity. Most English prepositions, for instance, have cross-categorial uses, notably with adverbs and conjunctions (S Rhee 2002b; see Svorou 1986, 1994, Heine 1989, Bowden 1992 for adverb-adposition connection). The notion of 'adprep' with three way distinction of particle, preposition, and adprep in Bolinger (1971), Sroka (1972), O'Dowd (1998) also shows the intercategorial fluctuations.

When we consider that adpositions are located toward the grammaticality pole, as suggested by Heine et al. (1991a: 167): [lexical > (adverbs >) adpositions > case affixes > zero], we can assume that adpositions have undergone the grammaticalization process to a reasonable extent, and thus they would tend to be polysemous. This polysemy again suggests their high level semantic generality, which makes them increasingly susceptible to erosive grammaticalization process even to a point of loss and renewal. Indeed, in English, for example, an extremely small number of prepositions are actively used as compared to the number of historically attested prepositions (S Rhee 2003b).

Since adpositions as a grammatical category comprise numerous members with diverse nature, individual studies set typology of adpositions based on their semantics. For example, Bennett (1975), in his study of English prepositions, divides the usage into spatial uses and temporal uses; S Nam (1995) classifies locative prepositions in English into topological invariants, symmetric locatives, orientational locatives, and directional locatives based on their semantic characterization; and Tyler and Evans (2003) divide English prepositions into those making use of the vertical axis, spatial particles of orientation, and those of bounded landmarks. Vandeloise (1991), in his analysis of French prepositions, differentiates geometric, logical, and functional description of spatial prepositions.

Undoubtedly, adpositions are closely related to case and the boundary is ill-defined, since they are often functionally indistinguishable. Blake (2004[2003]: 9) states that "[a]dpositions can be considered to be analytic case markers as opposed to synthetic case markers". In comparison with Japanese (analytic) and Latin (synthetic), Blake further remarks that the main difference in case marking is that languages like Japanese have no case suffixes, just the postpositions, whereas languages like Latin have case suffixes as well as adpositions (p. 9).

The number of grammatical cases varies across languages. For instance, there are eight cases in Sanskrit, i.e., Nominative, Accusative, Instrumental, Dative, Ablative, Genitive, Locative, Vocative, six cases in Turkish, i.e., Nominative, Accusative, Genitive, Dative, Locative, Ablative, and also six cases in Latin, i.e., Nominative, Vocative, Accusative, Genitive, Dative, Ablative (Blake 2004[2003]: 2, 4, 64). According to Blake (2004[2003]: 156ff), languages may have as few as two cases (e.g., Uto-Aztecan), three cases (e.g., Semitic), four cases (e.g., Germanic), six cases (e.g., Slavic), up to as many as a dozen or so (Blake 2004[2003]: 155). These classifications are largely based on the inflectional (Eurocentric) languages, and König (2004, as cited in J Song 2008: 13) expands the definition to include adpositional languages. In a comprehensive elaboration of case notions, Haspelmath (2009:508) presents different ways of classifying case, i.e., grammatical vs. semantic cases (Blake 1994), relational vs. adverbial cases (Bergsland 1997), grammatical vs. concrete cases (Jespersen 1924), core vs. peripheral cases (Blake 1994), abstract vs. concrete cases (Lyons 1968). The complexity of case functions seem to be overwhelming. Thus, Malchukov and Narrog (2009) analyze them through a semantic map approach to show how diverse functions in fact form a network and how different case encoding is realized through different segmentation of space in the map.

The distinction between grammatical case and adposition, as indicated above, is often unclear, and the classification and membership crucially depend on the researcher (for terminological issue, see Haspelmath 2009). For instance, in discussion of case in Korean, H Choe (1989[1929]) suggests a six case system whereas H Lee (1949) suggests as many as 18 cases (as cited in K Song 2008: 12). In this context of unsettled classification of case and adpositions, the classifications by Lehmann

(2004: 1845-1851), Blake (2004[1994]), Sylak-Glassman et al. (2015: 83) are intuitively useful, with the three subclassificatory terms, i.e., 'grammatical cases' (e.g., Nominative, Accusative, Dative, etc.), 'local cases' (e.g., Ablative, Allative, etc.), and '(non-local) cases' (e.g., Instrumental, Vocative, etc.).[2] Thus, in the context of discussing adpositions, all these three types of cases will be included, with an expanded membership for the local and (non-local) cases, in particular.

2.2.2 Terminological Issues

Adpositions are not uniform in form. Such heterogeniety led to diverse terms to refer to adpositions and the kindred forms. For instance, Libert (2013: 1-29), in his review of literature, introduces the works using such terms as fake adposition, true adposition, quasi-adposition, semi-adposition, pseudo-adposition, impure adposition, etc. Hagège (2010: 103-105) also lists alternative terms used in research, e.g., adposition, relator, case-marker, flag, functeme.

Many researchers have discussed their formal and functional differences. For instance, Lehmann (2015 [1982]), Y Matsumoto (1998), and S Rhee (2002a,b) for discussion of different status of individual prepositions and postpositions, which motivates the distinction of primary and secondary, or simplex and complex adpositions. Bolinger (1971) and O'Dowd (1998) also discuss the fluid categorial issue, and propose a category 'adprep', the intermediate category between prepositions and particles.

In grammaticalization studies, the distinction between primary and secondary adpositions has been often used. For instance, Lehmann (1985: 304) show a grammaticalization path from relational nouns to fusional case affixes, as in (1):

---

[2] Grammatical cases seem to constitute basic categories as has often been discussed across languages. Despite the large number of prepositions and case markers in Greek, for example, Accusative (marking object), Dative (marking indirect-object), and Genitive (marking possession) may occur without explicit prepositions (Luraghi 2003: 49-73).

(1)   relational noun ⟩ secondary adposition ⟩ primary adposition ⟩ agglutinative affix ⟩ fusional case affix

Similarly, in an analysis of Hungarian, Traugott and Trousdale (2013: 97) present the following grammaticalization continuum involving relational nouns:

(2)   N- [relational N + directional case marker ⟩ N + primary (coalesced) adposition ⟩ N + fusional case affix

With respect to primary vs. secondary adpositions, Lehmann (2015[1982]: 102) notes that the primary adpositions are often all monosyllabic, while the secondary ones may be polysyllabic (cf. also Kahr 1976: 138).

Similarly, some authors use the distinction between simple adpositions and complex adpositions. This distinction is based on the number of words involved, i.e., prepositions in English such as *of, in, to, for,* etc. are simple prepositions, whereas those like *in spite of, by virtue of, thanks to, with respect to,* etc. are complex prepositions (Quirk and Mulholland 1964, Quirk et al. 1985: 655-673, Huddleston and Pullum 2005: 146-47). Complex adpositions, consisting of multiple words, act like a single word and have conceptual unity. Since they have an internal structure following the syntactic rules, the distinction between complex adpositions and freely composed syntactic constructions is often not straightforward. Individual complex adpositions may have differential degrees of fossilization, often involving differential degrees of loss of phonetic volume as well as morphosyntactic flexibility. Thus, Quirk et al. (1985: 669ff) discuss diverse morphosyntactic behavior, which varies depending on the level of fossilization, by means of a battery of diagnostic tests. Quirk et al. (1985) include 'two-word sequences' and 'three-word sequences' in the complex prepositions.

In this book, following Kurzon (2008), Hagège (2010: 103-105), Libert (2013), Givón (2021), and others, we use 'adposition' as a cover term for prepositions, postpositions, and case markers. Further, in order to classify adpositions with respect to their gradient nature, we will employ a three-way classification, i.e., primary, composite, and complex adpositions, based on their formal shapes and structural characteristics.

Primary adpositions are those that are short in form (monomorphemic) and synchronically opaque with respect to their source construction. Therefore, if an adposition historically involved multiple morphemes that are synchronically not recognizable, it is included in the primary adpositions. For instance, the English preposition *about* is historically trimorphemic, i.e., *on* 'in, on' + *be* 'by, near' + *ut* 'out' (see 5.2), but its composition is no longer recognizable in Contemporary English, and thus it is regarded as a primary preposition. Similarly, the Korean postposition *-pwuthe* 'from' is historically bimorphemic, i.e., *puth-* 'adhere' and the linker *-e* (see 3.3.3.2), which is no longer recognizable in Contemporary Korean, and thus it is regarded as a primary postposition.

Composite adpositions are those that consist of two words or two morphemes. In agglutinative languages like Korean and Japanese, composite adpositions are relatively short in form but their sources are relatively visible synchronically or are perceived as consisting of more than one morpheme even though the functions of each morpheme cannot sometimes be straightforwardly identified. In analytic languages, composite adpositions are simply those that consist of two words or characters, e.g., the Chinese postposition *shàngmiàn* (上面) 'above, on top of' consists of two characters/words *shàng* (上) 'top' and *miàn* (面) 'side' (see 7.2), and the Thai preposition *hây kàp* (ให้กับ) 'with' consists of *hây* (ให้) 'for' and *kàp* (กับ) 'with' (see 8.2). In English and Spanish, the criterion involves the number of words, instead of morphemes in a strict sense, and thus the English preposition *following,* despite its analyzability as consisting of *follow* and *-ing* (see 5.2), is counted as a primary preposition. Likewise, the Spanish preposition *durante* 'during' is analyzable as bimorphemic, i.e. *durar* v. 'last' and the participle *-ante* (see 6.2), but is classified as a primary preposition.

Complex forms, on the other hand, are visibly polymorphemic and polylexemic, often indistinguishable from syntactic constructions. For Korean and Japanese, if a form involves a syntactic template such as [P–N–P] or [P–V–linker] it is classified as a complex postposition. For English, Spanish, and Thai, if a form involves three or more words, it is regarded as a complex preposition. Complex prepositions are typically of the [P(D)NP] structure in English and Spanish. Chinese two-word forms are classified either as a composite form or a complex form. If they simply consist of two words they are categorized as composite forms but if they involve a syntactic linker such as *zhī*(之) 'of', *de* (的) 'of', or *yǐ* (以) 'from', they are classified as complex adpositions. Thus, the category of complex adpositions is meant to be a group of adpositions having syntactically derived structures, whose constructional makeup is still visible.

2.2.3 Grammatical Functions of Adpositions

When adpositions are conceived of as a cover term to encompass case markers and nominal morphology that designate the relationship between the noun (phrase) and other sentential elements, the functions of adpositions are truly vast. Their functions include marking spatial, temporal, and other diverse abstract relationship.

When adpositions signal spatial relationship, the types of spatial expressions may be applicable. For instance, Levinson and Wilkins (2006) note that spatial description can be divided conceptually into place (i.e., static location) and motion (i.e., dynamic location). Further, Levinson and Wilkins (2006: 531-533) argue that there are also different styles of conceptualization of motion events crosslinguistically, i.e., durative and non-durative motions. For durative motion event, motion is conceived of as 'translocation', i.e., as a durative displacement of the figure along a continuous trajectory over time, e.g., the verb of translocation 'go'. For non-durative motion event, motion is solely thought of as a change of state without transitional phases, i.e., change of location or change of locative relation. In the non-durative conceptualization, change of state typically involves boundary-crossing such as the verb of ingressive motion 'enter'. In analogy of these general spatial expression types, the functions of adpositions can also be classified as static adpositions, e.g., 'on', 'behind', 'below', 'inside', etc. and dynamic adpositions, e.g., 'from', 'towards', 'until', etc. (Smessaert et al. 2014).

Luraghi (2003), in her intensive study of Greek prepositions and cases, lists diverse semantic roles, e.g., Space, Time, Comitative, Causal semantic roles, Recipient, Beneficiary, Experiencer, Possessor, Purpose, Patient, Manner, and Area (pp. 17-48), and Greek cases, e.g., Genitive, Ablative, Dative, Locative, and

Instrumental. Of these, she notes, Accusative, Genitive, and Dative may occur without explicit prepositions, suggesting their primacy in grammar.

Similarly, in their seminal work on English, Quirk et al. (1985: 673-709) observe that prepositions have various types of relational meaning, including Space and Time, which are relatively easier to describe, as well as Instrument and Cause, which are difficult to describe systematically. Their classification of space-marking functions can be summarized as follows (pp. 673-685):

(3) a.   Spatial relations by dimensions 0~3: D-0 (point) *at,* D-1 (Line) *on,* D-2 (Area) *on, in,* D-3 (Enclosed space) *in*

     b.   Positive position and destination: *at, to, on, onto, in, into*

     c.   Source or negative position: *away from, off, out of*

     d.   Relative position: *over, before, in front of, under, below, above, behind,* etc.

     e.   Space: *by, beside, with, near (to), close to, opposite*

     f.   Space: *between, among, amongst, amid, amidst*

     g.   Space: *around, round, about*

     h.   Relative destination: *over, under, behind,* etc.

     i.   Passage: *over, under, behind,* etc.

     j.   Passage: *across, through, past*

     k.   Movement with reference to a directional path: *up, down, along, across,* etc.

     l.   Orientation: *beyond, over, past, up, across,* etc.

     m.   Resultative meaning: *from, out of, over, past,* etc.

     n.   Pervasive meaning: *over, throughout, with,* etc.

Creissels (2009), in his discussion of spatial cases, use a different way of classification, e.g., unidimensional, bidimensional, tridimensional spatial case systems, among others. The functions of these spatial markers can be extended to non-spatial marking as well.

Undoubtedly, these classificatory systems in the literature are helpful in understanding cases and adpositions in one way or another. This book is intended to compare various spatial functions marked by adpositions in typologically and genealogical diversified language. In order to facilitate the comparison, this book will use the following division of functions:

(4) A. Non-axial spatial marking
    a.   Regional: 'at'
    b.   Directional: 'towards'
    c.   Source: 'from'
    d.   Path: 'through'
    e.   Goal: 'to'
    f.   Medial: 'between, among'
    g.   Ulterior: 'over, beyond, across'
    h.   Association: 'with' 'along with'
    i.   Adjacency: 'near, around'
    j.   Separation: 'apart from'
    k.   Contiguity: 'contiguous to'
    l.   Opposite: 'facing, opposite'

   B. Axial spatial marking
    a.   Interior: 'in, within'
    b.   Exterior: 'outside'
    c.   Superior: 'on, above'
    d.   Inferior: 'below, under'
    e.   Anterior: 'before, in front of'
    f.   Posterior: 'behind, after'
    g.   Lateral: 'beside, right to, left to'

It is to be noted, however, that the conceptual categories of adpositions do not form exclusive classes. Thus, a form may have multiple membership in this categorization, e.g., Directional and Goal; Adjacency, Contiguity, and Association; Medial and Interior, etc. may be marked by an identical form (cf. Kittilä and Ylikoski 2011). Also to be noted is that the category label may be coarse-grained and thus a category can be further divided into subgroups if a finer-grained analysis is required.

3

Grammaticalization of Postpositions in Korean

3.1 Introduction

As we noted in 2.3, adpositions arise from various sources and develop into markers of diverse functions, and Korean, having a rich postpositional system, is not an exception in this respect. Korean postpositions share some of these characteristics but they also exhibit interesting differences from the adpositional systems of other languages. This chapter describes, from a grammaticalization perspective, the paradigm of Korean postpositions denoting diverse concepts, focusing on the spatial postpositions that are actively undergoing grammaticalization in Modern Korean. Further, it will discuss some noteworthy aspects of grammaticalization scenarios from typological and comparative linguistic perspectives.

The frequency information is based on the 24-million word Drama & Movies Corpus, a collection of 7,454 scenarios of dramas, sitcoms, and movies dating from 1992 through 2015, developed by Min Li of Tsinghua University and the search engine, UNICONC, developed by Jinho Park.[1] The number of words in Korean

---

[1] Special thanks go to the developers of the corpus and the search tools for their generosity of granting their use for research.

corpora is based on Korean writing conventions which dictate inter-lexical spacing, according to which nominal particles (e.g., postpositions) should occur with the host noun without spacing, and verbal particles (e.g., TAM, connective, speech-act type markers, etc.) should occur with the host verb without spacing. When multiple particles are used, they are stacked without spacing among them (note that Korean is an agglutinative language). Therefore, a unit separated from another unit by an orthographic space contains more than a 'word' in a normal sense with respect to some Western languages such as English, and thus these units are often called an *ecel* '(lit.) speech joint' in Korean linguistics. According to empirical studies, one *ecel* contains about two morphemes/words (2.19 in J Choe et al. 2008: 91).[2] The corpus used in this research contains 24 million *ecel* units, which can be translated as 53,129,400 morphemes/words.[3] A direct comparison with other languages using word-based spacing, e.g., English and Spanish, is not appropriate because in these languages the number of words cannot be equated with the number of morphemes.

3.2 Postpositions in Korean

Korean has a large inventory of postpositional particles that carry diverse grammatical and semantic functions. There is no agreement as to the exact number of such particles among linguists who have different criteria for the status of individual items and for the definition of the category '(postpositional) particle'. It is largely agreed, however, that the particles consist of two subcategories: case particles (격조사; *kyekcosa*) and auxiliary particles (보조사; *pocosa*). The distinction separates those that mark the grammatical relationship among sentential arguments with respect to the state or event denoted by the predicate and those that participate in information structuring and/or scalarity marking. Since postpositions are constantly in flux, with some existing forms undergoing formal and functional change and new

---

[2] In J Kim (2005), one *ecel* is equal to 1.98. The *ecel*-morpheme ratio is variable.

[3] For convenience, the 24-million *ecel* corpus is treated as 53-million 'word' corpus and all statistical figures are in relation to this figure.

forms continually being innovated, postpositions do not form a homogeneous category with respect to form and function.

Postpositions may be categorized into primary, composite, and complex forms, based on their formal shapes and structural characteristics. According to our working definition, as briefly discussed in 2.2.2, primary forms are short in form and synchronically opaque with respect to their source construction (e.g., Nominatives -*i* (이) and -*ka* (가)), and composite forms are relatively short in form but their sources are relatively visible synchronically (e.g., Dative -*hanthey* (한테) analyzable as *han* (한) 'one' and *tey* (데) 'place') or are perceived as consisting of more than one morpheme even though the functions of each morpheme cannot sometimes be straightforwardly identified (e.g., Dative -*eykey* (에게) derived from Locative -*ey* (에) and the place noun *key* (게), the latter not commonly known by many). However, the distinction between primary and composite postpositions is not straightforward, since they form gradient categories. Complex forms, on the other hand, are visibly polymorphemic and polylexemic, often indistinguishable from syntactic constructions. There are fuzzy boundaries among these three groups, because the morphological devices used to create the syntactic constructions developing into complex postpositions (e.g., Accusative -*(l)ul* (를), or Locative -*ey* (에), etc.) are often elided and then the resultant forms are readily interpretable either as the primary postposition or composite postposition depending on their further analyzability.

The classificatory difficulties notwithstanding, we present 24 primary and 15 composite postpositions, listed with their major functions in Modern Korean. Complex postpositions are more numerous, numbering around 165, and more complex in makeup and will be discussed later in the exposition, and the list is presented separately in Appendix 1.

Primary/Composite POSTs	Meaning/Function
-*i*	Nominative
-*ka*	Nominative
-*kkeyse*	Nominative [+Honorific]
-*(l)ul*	Accusative

-uy	Genitive
-eykey	Dative
-kkey	Dative [+Honorific]
-hanthey	Dative
-ey	Essive/Allative/Causative/Enumerative
-eyse	Essive/Ablative/Agentive
-lo	Allative/Instrumental/Translative/Status
-kkaci	Allative, Focus/extreme example 'even'
-wa/kwa	Comitative, Enumerative
-hako	Comitative, Enumerative
-pwuthe	Ablative
-eykeyse	Ablative
-losse	Instrumental
-kacko	Instrumental
-hamye	Enumerative
-pota	Comparative
-mankhum	Similative
-chelem	Similative
-kathi	Similative
-(y)a	Vocative
-lose	Status
-(n)un	Topic
-to	Additive focus 'also'
-man	Exclusive focus 'only'
-pakkey	Exclusive focus 'only' (NPI)
-ppwun	Exclusive focus 'only'
-cocha	Focus/extreme example 'even'
-mace	Focus/extreme example 'even'
-mata	Distributive 'each'
-ssik	Distributive 'each', Limitative 'as much'
-taylo	Prolative 'according to'
-khenyeng	Unexpected 'let alone' (NPI)

-chiko	Hypothetical topic
-sekken	Inclusive 'together with'
-ttala	Adversative ('on, among, etc.)

Table 3.1 Primary and composite postpositions in Modern Korean

Apart from those listed in Table 3.1, there are other primary and composite particles addressed in studies of particles. One particular class is directly affixed to nouns, and thus appears to be postpositional particles hosting a noun. However, these particles are in fact simply variant forms of verbal particles in special phonological environments, specifically if the host noun ends with an open syllable and the following verb is the copula *i-* (이), e.g., N-*i-na* 〉 N-*na*; N-*i-nama* 〉 N-*nama*, etc., where *-na* (나) and *-nama* (나마) are markers of enumerated options. In such phonological environments the copula *i-* (이) becomes phonologically weak and is susceptible to deletion. This phenomenon merits separate research in that the developmental path may eventually constitute a grammaticalization channel into nominal particles via verbal particles, but since they are not nomimal particles *per se,* they are not listed here (see Rhee and Koo 2015, for discussion of the emergence of the tepidity marker *-na* (나)).

It is obvious from the list in Table 3.1 that many primary and composite postpositions in Korean signal 'grammatical cases' (e.g., Nominative, Accusative, Dative, etc.), 'local cases' (e.g., Ablative, Allative, etc.), and '(non-local) cases' (e.g., Instrumental, Vocative, etc.), following the classifications by Lehmann (2004: 1845-1851), Blake (2004[1994]), Sylak-Glassman et al. (2015: 83), among others, with minor modifications. As is evident from the fact that primary and composite postpositions are relatively shorter and etymologically often obscure, they have undergone grammaticalization processes extensively. More interesting for our purposes are the local case markers that designate the spatial location of an entity with respect to its referenced entity since they are relatively less well-established and often exhibit ongoing grammaticalization (see 3.3 below).

Even though a large number of grammatical forms are classified as postpositions (as shown in Table 3.1 above), the members of the category of postpositions exhibit a great variation in terms of their functional strengths, as reflected in use frequency. The 39 primary and composite postpositions are listed in the order of descending frequency in Table 3.2.

Frequency Range	Primary/Composite Postpositions	Meaning/Function	PMW
High (1,000~ pmw) (n=12)	-(l)ul	Accusative	17,164
	-ka	Nominative	11,103
	-i	Nominative	10,438
	-ey	Essive/Allative/Causative/Enumerative	9,197
	-to	Additive focus 'also'	8,270
	-uy	Genitive	6,500
	-(n)un	Topic	5,671
	-man	Exclusive focus 'only'	2,669
	-eyse	Essive/Ablative/Agentive	2,111
	-kkaci	Allative, Focus/extreme example 'even'	1,760
	-wa/kwa	Comitative, Enumerative	1,649
	-lo	Allative/Instrumental/Translative/Status	1,309
Medium (100~999 pmw) (n=14)	-pwuthe	Ablative	992
	-hanthey	Dative	977
	-eykey	Dative	897
	-(y)a	Vocative	568
	-chelem	Similative	537
	-taylo	Prolative 'according to'	526
	-pota	Comparative	346
	-pakkey	Exclusive focus 'only' (NPI)	336
	-ssik	Distributive 'each', Limitative 'as much'	223
	-ppwun	Exclusive focus 'only'	208
	-mata	Distributive 'each'	181
	-mankhum	Similative	176
	-kathi	Similative	106
	-hako	Comitative, Enumerative	100

Low (10~99 pmw) (n=8)	-kkey	Dative [+Honorific]	85
	-kkeyse	Nominative [+Honorific]	82
	-cocha	Focus/extreme example 'even'	32
	-lose	Status	30
	-kacko	Instrumental	22
	-eykeyse	Ablative	20
	-chiko	Hypothetical topic	15
	-mace	Focus/extreme example 'even'	12
Very Low (~9 pmw) (n=5)	-khenyeng	Unexpected 'let alone' (NPI)	7
	-losse	Instrumental	3
	-hamye	Enumerative	0
	-sekken	Inclusive 'together with'	0
	-ttala	Adversative ('on, among, etc.)	0

Table 3.2. Frequency of primary and composite postpositions in Modern Korean

The postpositional particles that mark syntactic relations of arguments, i.e., case markers, appear high in the frequency ranking, e.g., Accusative -(l)ul (을/를), Nominatives -i (이), -ka (가), and -kkeyse (께서), Genitive -uy (의), and Topic -(n)un (은/는). A relevant grammatical note is that most postpositions marking grammatical relations have morphophonemically conditioned allomorphs. For instance, Accusative -ul (을) occurs when the preceding syllable of the noun has a coda, and -lul (를), when the syllable is open. Similarly, Topic -un (은) occurs when the preceding syllable of the noun has a coda, and -nun (는), when it does not.[4] Topic markers often resemble Nominative because they often mark the argument that functions as the subject of a sentence, but it is distinct from Nominative for its ability to take an argument with any thematic role, often adding the meaning of 'contrast' (see chapter 4 for a similar situation in Japanese). Nominative has a three-way

---

[4] This correspondence between open vs. closed syllable of the preceding noun and the presence vs. absence of the onset consonant of the allomorphs is generally applicable to all variant forms, except for Comitative -(k)wa (와/과), in which the pattern is reversed.

distinction: *-i* (이), when the preceding syllable has a coda; *-ka* (가), when it does not; and *-kkeyse* (께서), when the host noun is [+Honorific]. When these three Nominatives are considered together, Nominative frequency is 21,623 pmw, far exceeding Accusative, the one with the highest frequency in the list (17,164 pmw).

Another grammatical case to note is Dative for which *-hanthey* (한테), *-eykey* (에게), and *-kkey* (께) are used. They are not allomorphs but their selection is controlled by the genre and interactional context: *-hanthey* (한테) is more colloquial; *-eykey* (에게) is relatively more formal; and *-kkey* (께) is for designating a [+Honorific] person as the goal of the action (see 3.3.3.4 and S Rhee 2021a).

In addition to primary and composite postpositions, there are a large number of complex postpositions. These postpositions are structurally complex, often involving a primary postposition, most notably Locative *-ey* (에), Accusative *-(l)ul* (을/를), and Genitive *-uy* (의), and less commonly Instrumental *-lo* (로) and Dative *-hanthey* (한테). Since complex postpositions are often indistinguishable from syntactic constructions that involve a noun or a verb, the inventory is unavoidably controversial. From the corpus, about 165 items are collected that have relatively established meanings and relative internal cohesion through univerbation (see Appendix 1).

In terms of their structure, complex postpositions take one of the following common patterns, depending on whether the core lexeme in the structure is a noun or a verb.

(1) Noun-based complex postpositions
    a.   *-(uy)* N-*ey(se)*   [GEN N-LOC(EMPH)]
         e.g. *-uy kyeth-ey(se)* (의 곁에(서)) 'beside, by' (*kyeth* (곁) n. 'side')

    b.   *-(ey)* N-*ha-e(se)* [LOC   N-do-CONN(EMPH)]
         e.g. *-ey myen-ha-y(se)* (에 면해(서)) 'facing' (*myen* (면) n. 'face')

(2) Verb-based complex postpositions
    a.   *-(ey)* V-*ko(se)*   [LOC V-CONN(EMPH)]
         e.g. *-ey tay-ko(se)* (에 대고(서)) 'to' (*tay-* (대-) v. 'touch')

b. *-(ul)* V-*e(se)*   [ACC V-CONN(EMPH)]

    e.g. *-ul kenne-e(se)* (을 건너(서)) 'across' (*kenne-* (건너-) v. 'cross')

c. *-(ul)* V-*ko(se)*   [ACC V-CONN(EMPH)]

    e.g. *-ul po-ko(se)* (을 보고(서)) 'to' (*po-* (보-) v. 'see')

Connectives *-e* (어), *-ko* (고), etc. are often named as 'converbs' (Ramstedt 1903, 1997[1939], Haspelmath 1995, Y Ko 2012, 2013, Robbeets 2020, H Chae 2020), and so is the Emphatic particle *-se* (서), which can be affixed to most postpositions.[5] The function of *-se* is adding emphasis and at the same time some sense of temporal separation, thus indicating sequentially preceding events. As a cursory survey of the list would plainly reveal, multiplicity in form is partly due to the addition of Emphatic *-se* in many postpositions. This is also evident in the list of spatial complex postpositions to be discussed below (note that the forms involving *-se* and their *-se*-less counterparts are sometimes listed separately and sometimes together as deemed appropriate in the discussion).

3.3 Spatial Postpositions

3.3.1 Characteristics of Spatial Postpositions

Apart from the 39 primary and composite postpositions listed in Table 3.1, there are also a large number of complex postpositions (165 in total, Appendix 1), which border on syntactic constructions. Among these 204 postpositions are spatial postpositions, inclusive of the primary, composite, and complex forms. Spatial postpositions number 137 in total, as shown in Table 3.2 (note that some forms are listed in more than one conceptual category, e.g., *-eyse* (에서), *-hanthey* (한테), etc., but are not separately counted). Since spatial relations often involve axial

---

[5] The notion of 'converb' was first introduced in Korean linguistics by Ramstedt (1903), and is called *pwutongsa* (K Lee 1998[1961]: 23; B Ahn 1967) among Korean linguists.

configuration, spatial postpositions are listed under the two broad classifications of axial and non-axial categories. The complex postpositions are further divided into two classes depending on their lexical source being native Korean or Sino-Korean (see 3.4.4.1 for discussion on these source differences).

AXIS		PRIMARY (n=7)	COMPOSITE (n=15)	COMPLEX (n=115)	
				NATIVE KOREAN (n=79)	SINO-KOREAN (n=36)
	REGIONAL	*-ey* 'at'	*-eyse* 'at'		
	DIRECTIONAL	*-lo* 'to' *-kkey* 'to'	*-eykey* 'to' *-hanthey* 'to'	*-lo hyanghay* 'toward' *-lo hyanghaye* 'toward' *-(ul) hyanghay* 'toward' *-(ul) hyanghayse* 'toward' *-(ul) hyanghaye* 'toward'	
	SOURCE	*-pwuthe* 'from'	*-eyse* 'from' *-kkeyse* 'from' *-lopwuthe* 'from' *-(ey)sepwuthe* 'from' *-lose* 'from' *-eykeyse* 'from' *-hantheyse* 'from' *-hanthey* 'from'		
	PATH			*-(ul) ttala* 'along, through' *-(ul) ttalase* 'along, through' *-(ul) kalocille* 'across' *-(ul) kalocillese* 'across'	*-(ul) thonghay* 'through' *-(ul) thonghaye* 'through' *-(ul) thonghayese* 'through'
NON-AXIAL	GOAL	*-kkaci* 'to' *-tele* 'to'	*-eykey* 'to' *-hanthey* 'to' *-eykkaci* 'to, till' *-lokkaci* 'to, till' *-hanthey* 'to'	*-(ul)tele* 'to' *-hantheytaka* 'to' *-hantheytayko* 'to' *-hantheytaykose* 'to' *-hantheytakatayko* 'to' *-hantheytakataykose* 'to' *-eytaka* 'to, unto' *-eytakatayko* 'to, unto' *-eytakataykose* 'to, unto' *-lotaka* 'to, unto' *-(ul) poko* 'to' *-(ul) pokose* 'to' *-(ey) tayko* 'to, unto' *-(ey) taykose* 'to, unto' *-(ey)tatayko* 'to' *-(ey)tataykose* 'to'	
	MEDIAL			*-(uy) thumey* 'between' *-(uy) thumeyse* 'between' *-(uy) sayey* 'between' *-(uy) sayeyse* 'between' *-(uy) saiey* 'between' *-(uy) saieyse* 'between'	*-kaney* 'between'
	ULTERIOR			*-(ul) ne.me* 'over' *-(ul) ne.mese* 'over'	

				-(ul) nem.e 'over' -(ul) nem.ese 'over' -(ul) kenne 'across' -(ul) kennese 'across'	
	ASSOCIATION	-wa 'with'	-hako 'with'	-(ey) ttala 'following' -(ey) ttalase 'following' -(ul) ttala 'following' -(ul) ttalase 'following' -(wa) hamkkey '(together) with' -wa kathi '(together) with' -wa tepwule '(together) with' -hako kathi '(together) with' -hako hamkkey '(together) with'	
	ADJACENCY		-kakkai 'near'	-(uy) yephey 'beside, by' -(uy) yepheyse 'beside, by' -(uy) kyethey 'beside, by' -(uy) kyetheyse 'beside, by'	-(uy) cwuwiey 'around' -(uy) cwuwieyse 'around' -(uy) cwupyeney 'around' -(uy) cwupyeneyse 'around'
	SEPARATION		-malko 'except' -ppayko 'except'	-(wa) ttelecye 'apart from' -(wa) ttelecyese 'apart from'	-(ul) kyekhay 'apart from' -(ul) kyekhaye 'apart from' -(ul) kyekhayse 'apart from' -(ul) ceyhako 'except' -(ul) ceyoyhako 'except' -(ul) ceyyohakose 'except'
	CONTIGUITY				-(ey) yenhay 'contiguous to' -(ey) yenhayse 'contiguous to' -(ul) yenhay 'contiguous to' -(ul) yenhayse 'contiguous to'
	OPPOSITE				-(ey) myenhay 'facing' -(ey) myenhayse 'facing'
	INTERIOR			-(uy) aney 'in, within' -(uy) aneyse 'in, within' -(uy) sokey 'in, within' -(uy) sokeyse 'in, within' -(uy) kawuntey 'in, among' -(uy) kawunteyey 'in, among' -(uy) kawunteyse 'in, among'	-nayey 'in, within' -nayeyse 'in, within' -cwungey 'in, among' -cwungeyse 'in, among'
	EXTERIOR			-(uy) pakkey 'outside, except' -(uy) pakkeyse 'outside'	-oyey 'outside, except'
AXIAL	SUPERIOR			-(uy) wiey 'on, above, over' -(uy) wieyse 'on, above, over'	-sangey 'on'
	INFERIOR			-(uy) mithey 'below, under' -(uy) mitheyse 'below, under' -(uy) alay 'below, under' -(uy) alayey 'below, under' -(uy) alayeyse 'below, under' -(uy) alayse 'below, under'	-haey 'under' -haeyse 'under'
	ANTERIOR			-(uy) aphey 'before' -(uy) apheyse 'before'	-ceney 'before'

POSTERIOR	*-(uy) twiey* 'behind, after' *-(uy) twieyse* 'behind' *-(ul) ttala* 'following' *-(ul) ttalase* 'following'	*-hwuey* 'after'
LATERAL	*-(uy) yephey* 'beside, by' *-(uy) yepheyse* 'beside, by' *-(uy) kyethey* 'beside, by' *-(uy) kyetheyse* 'beside, by' *-(uy) palunccokey* 'right to' *-(uy) palunccokeyse* 'right to' *-(uy) olunccokey* 'right to' *-(uy) olunccokeyse* 'right to' *-(uy) oynccokey* 'left to' *-(uy) oynccokeyse* 'left to'	*-(uy) chukmyeney* 'beside' *-(uy) chukmyeneyse* 'beside' *-(uy) wuchukey* 'right to' *-(uy) wuchukeyse* 'right to' *-(uy) cwachukey* 'left to' *-(uy) cwachukeyse* 'left to'

Table 3.3 Spatial postpositions in Modern Korean

The spatial postpositions as a grammatical category in Korean show a number of interesting aspects. Among the prominent aspects is the fact that there are only two Regional postpositions. However, if their use frequency is considered (see Table 3.2 above), their frequencies are very high, which indicates that Regional postpositions are highly specialized (see 3.3.2 below for discussion of frequency).[6]

Another interesting aspect is multiplicity of complex postpositions. Many complex postpositions have already undergone morphosyntactic reduction such as the loss of the particle within the construction, and even some of them have become primary postpositions, of which the source lexical meaning is entirely opaque. However, complex postpositions outnumber the primary postpositions by a large margin. In other words, there are only 22 postpositions (16.1%) that are primary or composite in the sense that their sources are either entirely or relatively opaque with respect to structure and meaning, whereas there are 115 postpositions (83.9%) whose morphosyntactic structures and lexical meanings of the source components are still transparent. These complex postpositions are structurally poly-lexemic and have undergone variable degrees of reduction (see 3.4.3.4 for more discussion).

---

[6] As indicated in Table 3.1, *-eyse* (에서) has the dual functions of marking Regional (Essive) 'at' and Ablative 'from'. An investigation of sample texts shows 63% and 37% for the two functions, respectively (see also 3.4.4.2 for its use as a peripheral Nominative marker as an extended function of Ablative).

3.3.2 Frequencies of Spatial Postpositions

In the preceding exposition we have seen that there are about 137 spatial postpositions (see Table 3.3). However, postpositions are widely variable with respect to their functional strength, which is reflected in their use frequency. The spatial postpositions are listed in the descending order of frequency (note that some of the individually listed forms, which are formal variants from variable reduction, are shown together).

Frequency Range	Spatial Postposition		Meaning	PMW
High (1,000~ pmw) (n=5)	-ey	에	'at, in'	9,197
	-eyse	에서	'at, in, from'	2,111
	-(k)wa	와/과	'with'	1,649
	-lo	로	'to, with'	1,309
	-kkaci	까지	'to, till'	1,306
Medium (100~999 pmw) (n=12)	-pwuthe	부터	'from'	992
	-hanthey(se)	한테(서)	'to (from)'	977
	-eykey(se)	에게(서)	'to, with, from'	897
	-(uy) aphey(se)	(의) 앞에(서)	'before'	365
	-ceney	전에	'before'	173
	-(uy) yephey(se)	(의) 옆에(서)	'beside'	157
	-(uy) wiey(se)	(의) 위에(서)	'on, above, over'	156
	-(uy) aney(se)	(의) 안에(서)	'in, within'	148
	-(ul) hyanghay(e(se))	(을) 향해(서)/향하여(서)	'toward'	141
	-(uy) pakkey(se)	(의) 밖에(서)	'outside, except'	121
	-(uy) sokey(se)	(의) 속에(서)	'in, within'	113
	-hako	하고	'with'	100
Low (10~99 pmw) (n=14)	-kkey	께	'to'	85
	-cwungey(se)	중에(서)	'between, among'	78
	-(ul) ttala(se)	(을) 따라(서)	'following, along'	76
	-(uy) twiey(se)	(의) 뒤에(서)	'behind, after'	63
	-(uy) alayey(se)	(의) 아래에(서)	'below, beneath'	58
	-(ul) thonghay(e(se))	(을) 통해(서)/통하여(서)	'through'	54

	-(ey) tayko(se)	(에) 대고(서)	'to'	33
	-(uy) saiey/sayey(se)	(의) 사이에/새에(서)	'between'	32
	-(ul) poko(se)	(을) 보고(서)	'to'	32
	-(ul) tele	(을) 더러	'to'	24
	-(uy) mithey(se)	(의) 밑에(서)	'below, beneath'	21
	-hwuey(se)	후에(서)	'behind, after'	13
	-(uy) twiey(se)	(의) 뒤에(서)	'behind, after'	12
	-(uy) kyethey(se)	(의) 곁에(서)	'beside'	11
	-(uy) thumey(se)	(의) 틈에(서)	'between'	9
	-(wa/hako) kathi	(와/하고) 같이	'with'	7
	-oyey	외에	'except'	5
	-(ey)taka	(에)다가	'to, unto'	5
	-(ul) kenne(se)	(을) 건너(서)	'across'	4
	-haey(se)	하에(서)	'under'	3
	-nayey(se)	내에(서)	'inside, within'	3
	-(ul) neme(se)	(을) 너머/넘어(서)	'over'	1
	-(uy) kawunteyey(se)	(의) 가운데에(서)	'in, among'	1
Very Low	-kaney	간에	'between'	1
(~9 pmw)	-(ul) kalocille(se)	(을) 가로질러(서)	'across'	1
(n=21)	-(uy) oynccokey(se)	(의) 왼쪽에(서)	'left to'	0
	-(uy) olunccokey(se)	(의) 오른쪽에(서)	'right to'	0
	-(ul) myenhay(e(se))	(을) 면해/면하여(서)	'facing'	0
	-(uy) chukmyeney(se)	(의) 측면에(서)	'beside'	0
	-(uy) wuchukey(se)	(의) 우측에(서)	'right to'	0
	-(uy) cwachukey(se)	(의) 좌측에(서)	'left to'	0
	-(ul) kyekhay(e(se))	(을) 격해/격하여(서)	'apart from'	0
	-(uy) palunccokey(se)	(의) 바른쪽에(서)	'right to'	0
	-(ey/ul) yenhay(e(se))	(에/을) 연해/연하여(서)	'contiguous to'	0
	-sangey(se)	상에(서)	'on'	0

Table 3.4 Sources of Korean spatial postpositions by frequency ranking

It is immediately obvious from the frequency ranking that a handful of spatial postpositions are particularly of high frequency. As briefly indicated in the preceding discussion, the most frequent forms are the 'Regional' postpositions, in the sense of

Svorou (1994: 235), i.e., those without specification with respect to dimensionality, orientation, and shape (thus, a general Locative). The postposition *-ey* (에) 'at, in' occurs at the frequency of 9,197 pmw and its formal and functional relative *-eyse* (에서) 'at, in' occurs at the frequency of 2,111 pmw.[7] The combined frequency of these two top-frequency items exceeds that of all others combined, i.e., *-ey* (에) and *-eyse* (에서) record 11,308 pmw in contrast with 9,236 pmw of all others combined. This is a clear indication of a high level of specialization by the two Regional postpositions.

In the frequency data it is also noteworthy that primary and composite forms are generally toward the top of the list and complex forms are clustered in the lower end. It is particularly intriguing that there are as many as 11 postpositions (in fact, the number is greater if the variably reduced forms are separately counted) that occur at 0 pmw, i.e., fewer than 26 times in the entire corpus.

3.3.3 Grammaticalization Sources

It is widely known that adpositions develop from the primary grammatical categories, i.e., nouns and verbs, hence the notions 'N-adpositions' and 'V-adpositions' (Heine et al. 1991a: 140-147). As Heine et al (1991a: 147) note, N-adpositions tend to retain nominal characteristics and, likewise, V-adpositions tend to retain verbal characteristics. The spatial adpositions and their lexical sources are presented in Table 3.5, arranged in the descending order of frequency in accordance with Table 3.4 above (SK stands for Sino-Korean).

---

[7] As indicated in Table 3.1, *-eyse* has the dual functions of marking Regional (Essive) 'at' and Ablative 'from'. An investigation of sample texts shows 63% and 37% for the two functions, respectively (see also 3.4.4.2 for its use as a peripheral Nominative marker as an extended function of Ablative). The frequency figures given here are projections from the proportion. For discussion of polyfunctionality of a grammatical form, see Koo and Rhee (2006).

Spatial Postposition	Core Lexeme	Lexical Source Meaning	Postpositional Meaning
-ey	*-ey*	(unknown)	'at, in'
-eyse	*iss-*	exist (v)	'at, in, from'
-(k)wa	*-(k)wa*	(unknown)	'with'
-lo	*-lo*	(unknown)	'to'
-kkaci	*kas*	edge (n)	'to, till'
-pwuthe	*puth-*	adhere (v)	'from'
-hanthey(se)	*han tey*	one place (n)	'to, from'
-eykey(se)	*ekuy*	place (n)	'to, with' 'to' 'from'
-(uy) aphey(se)	*aph*	front (n)	'before'
-ceney	*cen* (SK 前)	front (n)	'before'
-(uy) yephey(se)	*yeph*	side (n)	'beside'
-(uy) wiey(se)	*wi*	top (n)	'on, above, over'
-(uy) aney(se)	*an*	inside (n)	'in, within'
-(ul) hyanghay(e(se))	*hyang* (SK 向)	direction (n)	'toward'
-(uy) pakkey(se)	*pakk*	outside (n)	'outside, except'
-(uy) sokey(se)	*sok*	inside (n)	'in, within'
-hako	*ha-*	do/be (v)	'with'
-kkey	*ekuy*	place (n)	'to' (+HON)
-cwungey(se)	*cwung* (SK 中)	middle (n)	'between, among'
-(ul) ttala(se)	*ttalu-*	follow (v)	'following'
-(uy) twiey(se)	*twi*	back (n)	'behind, after'
-(uy) alayey(se)	*alay*	bottom (n)	'below, beneath'
-(ul) thonghay(e(se))	*thong* (SK 通)	pass (n/v)	'through'
-(ey) tayko(se)	*tay-*	touch (v)	'to'
-(uy) saiey/sayey(se)	*sai*	interval (n)	'between'
-(ul) poko(se)	*po-*	see (v)	'to'
-(ul) tele	*tali-*	accompany (v)	'to'
-(uy) mithey(se)	*mith*	bottom (n)	'below, beneath'
-hwuey(se)	*hwu* (SK 後)	back (n)	'behind, after'
-(uy) twiey(se)	*twi*	back (n)	'behind, after'

-(uy) kyethey(se)	*kyeth*	side (n)	'beside'
-(uy) thumey(se)	*thum*	gap (n)	'between'
-(wa/hako) kathi	*kath-*	be same (v)	'with'
-oyey	*oy* (SK 外)	outside (n)	'except'
-(ey) taka	*taku-*	approach (v)	'to, unto'
-(ul) kenne(se)	*kenne-*	cross (v)	'across'
-haey(se)	*ha* (SK 下)	below (n)	'under'
-nayey(se)	*nay* (SK 內)	inside (n)	'inside, within'
-(ul) neme(se)	*nem-*	go over (v)	'over'
-(uy) kawunteyey(se)	*kawuntey*	middle (n)	'in, among'
-kaney	*kan* (SK 間)	gap (n)	'between'
-(ul) kalocille(se)	*kalocilu-*	cross (v)	'across'
-(uy) oynccokey(se)	*oynccok*	left side (n)	'left to'
-(uy) olunccokey(se)	*olunccok*	right side (n)	'right to'
-(ul) myenhay(e(se))	*myen* (SK 面)	face (n)	'facing'
-(uy) chukmyeney(se)	*chukmyen* (SK 側面)	side (n)	'beside'
-(uy) wuchukey(se)	*wuchuk* (SK 右側)	right side (n)	'right to'
-(uy) cwachukey(se)	*cwachuk* (SK 左側)	left side (n)	'left to'
-(ul) kyekhay(e(se)	*kyek* (SK 隔)	separation (n)	'apart from'
_(uy) palunccokey(se)	*palunccok*	right side (n)	'right to'
-(ey/ul) yenhay(e(se))	*yen* (SK 連)	link (n)	'contiguous to'
-sangey(se)	*sang* (SK 上)	top (n)	'on'

Table 3.5 Lexical sources of spatial postpositions in Modern Korean

The lexical sources of three spatial postpositions (i.e., *-ey* (에), *-(k)wa* (와/과), and *-lo* (로)) have not yet been established.[8] Aside from these unknown sources, 12 verbs

---

[8] Even though speculations have been made as to the origin of those particles, most of such speculations tend to stop with determining the probable parts of speech of the items involved, based on the syntagmatic patterns in which they occur. S Kim (1992) speculates that *-ey* (에) 'at, in' might have developed from the noun **(h)Ay* (익/힉) 'middle, center' (p. 283), *-(k)wa* (와/과) 'with' from the

serve as the sources of spatial postpositions, accounting for 24.5%, and nouns constitute the largest source category, i.e., 37 nouns, accounting for 75.5% of all known sources. It is also notable that there are 16 nouns of Chinese origin, indicated as Sino-Korean (SK) in the table, that serve as the lexical sources of spatial postpositions (note that Sino-Korean lexemes are often ambiguous as to their word class in Korean, cf. *thong* (통; 通) n/v 'pass', and their classification in Chinese and Korean are often not identical, cf. S Lee 2021). The postpositions developed from these foreign sources, however, mostly belong to the low frequency range (see 3.4.2 for more discussion on the issue). We now turn to a brief discussion on the source characteristics.

3.3.3.1 Nominal Sources

As shown in Table 3.5 above, the majority of the nouns that participate in the formation of spatial postpositions are relational nouns (RNs) that profile various relationships, notably axial relationships, between two entities, e.g., 'front', 'back', 'top', 'bottom', 'side', etc. Nouns such as 'edge' and 'face' also designate, though non-axial, relationships through different conceptualization of configuration, e.g., center vs. periphery (for 'edge') and directed contiguity vs. discontiguity (for 'face'). The nouns that are used in the development of high-frequency postpositions, e.g., *ekuy* (어긔) 'place' and *han tey* (한 데) 'one place' (< *han* 'one' + *tey* 'place'), are general place nouns, from which Directional 'to' and Source 'from' are developed. As these general place nouns simply designate a location, their source constructions, i.e., [x-place] 'x's place' and [x-one.place] 'one/same place as x', simply mark the location where x is located. The notion of directionality involved in 'to' and 'from' is the product of inference. For instance, sentences like "I go [x's place]" are reinterpreted as "I go to x" and sentences like "A phone call came [x-one.place]", as "A phone call came from x" (and consequently "I got a call from x") (see S Rhee 2010, see also 3.4.4.2 for more discussion).

---

noun **kwa* (과) 'connection' (p. 293), and *-lo* (로) 'to' from the noun **lo* (로) 'cause/reason' (pp. 302-303).

From a crosslinguistic perspective, the use of 'place' with static meaning developing into dynamic adpositions with 'to', 'toward', 'far from', etc. is not entirely uncommon across languages (see Koelle 1968[1854], Westermann 1924 for Vai and Kpelle, Everbroeck 1958 for Lingala, Rapp 1966 for Gurenne, Blake 2004[1994] for Finnish, Narrog and Rhee 2013 for Japanese, Kuteva et al. 2019 for multiple languages, among others), but the preference of this general term over more specific spatial terms, i.e., those having relational/directional meaning, is worth noting. In other words, from a broader perspective, this phenomenon of using PLACE is crosslinguistically less common than using more specific relational terms. Across languages, adpositions denoting relational or directional concepts typically recruit nominals that inherently have relational concepts from either an anthropomorphic or zoomorphic model, prominently body-parts, or verbals that have motional concepts with diverse deictic notions associated with them.

As is shown in the complex postpositions column in Table 3.3 and the sources in Table 3.5, the spatial complex postpositions predominantly make use of relational nouns. These relational nouns often recruit the Genitive marker *-uy* as a connector between the host nominal and the relational nouns. This marker of possession has, in general, a strong tendency to resist assimilating into either the host noun or the relational noun.[9] When the possessive marker is eroded or deleted, it rarely causes any change in the adjacent forms. Consequently, the nominal-derived postpositions tend to maintain formal transparency. This is in sharp contrast with the postpositions, and grammatical markers in general, that develop from the verbal sources. In other words, grammaticalization from verbal sources inevitably involves non-finite markers which often obscure formal transparency and conceptual relatedness between the sources and their resultant postpositions, a process which consequently paves the way to a greater range of semantic change. As indicated, this

---

[9] Rare exceptions are the development of the possessive pronouns *nay* 'my', *cey* 'self's' and *ney* 'your'. The pronoun *nay* 'my' developed from *na-uy* 'I-GEN', a process, despite apparent similarity from the notation, drastic in that the Genitive *-uy* [ɰi] disappeared after changing the preceding vowel [a] to [æ], thus [na] 〉 [næ]. A parallel development occurred to *cey*, i.e., from *ce-uy* [dʑə-ɰi] to *cey* [dʑe] and to *ney*, i.e., from *ne-uy* [nə-ɰi] to *ney* [nɛ].

contrasts with nominal sources in that the source lexemes, especially relational nouns, tend to maintain formal transparency and keep their semantics relatively stable, because the nominal source lexeme remains intact. This may have to do with the relatively static nature of the semantics of the postpositions that developed from spatial nominals. If this reasoning is correct, it can be said that there is a strong connection between the morphosyntactic change of the source structures occurring at the initial and intermediate stages of grammaticalization on the one hand and the semantic-functional change occurring at the later, resultant stage on the other.

We can look into the history of the relational nouns in the complex postpositions. Table 3.6 lists etymologies, taken from a number of historical dictionaries and references (e.g., K Kang 2010, C Yu 2000[1964], Y Cho 2004, K Nam 2007, S Kim 1989, 1992, 2004, W Chae 1990, Y Hong 1990, S Lee 1992[1961], among others). Since many of the proposed etymologies, as noted above, are at the level of speculation, the lexical sources listed in the table are limited to those for which there is sufficient historical evidence.

Relational Noun	Meaning/Function	Lexical Source in Late Middle Korean
aph	front	*alph, alp* (N) 'front', 'south'
twi	back	*twut, twul, twih, twi* (N) 'back, anus' 'north'
wi	top	*wuh* (N) 'top'
alay	below	*alayh* (N) 'bottom, lower region'
mith	bottom	*mith* (N) 'bottom, lower region' *mit, mith* (N) 'core' 'anus' 'buttocks'
sai, say	between	*sAzi, sAi* (N) 'gap'
an	inside	*anh* (N) 'inside, heart, mind'
pakk	outside	*pask* (N) 'outside,
kawuntey	middle	*kavAn-tAy, kaon-tAy* (A+N) 'middle-place'
oynccok	left	*oyn-nyek, oyn-ccok* (A+N) 'left-side' 'wrong-side'
olunccok, palunccok	right	*olhAn-nyek olhAn-ccok* (A+N) 'right-side' 'correct side', *palun-ccok* (A+N) 'correct side'

yeph	side	*nyep* (N) 'loin, armpit, side'
kyeth	side (adjacent region)	*kyes, kyet* (N) 'side area, side'

Table 3.6 Etymology of relational nouns in Modern Korean

As Table 3.6 shows, sources of the relational nouns are mostly body parts ('back', 'anus', 'buttocks'), cardinal directions ('south', 'north'), and place nouns with preceding adjectival modifiers ('middle-place', 'wrong side', 'correct side'). All the nouns presented here had already acquired their spatial meaning by Late Middle Korean, the oldest period with extant data written in the Korean writing system, *Hangeul* (or *Hankul*).

Of special interest are the sources of cardinal directions, as addressed in Narrog and Rhee (2013). According to *Sincungyuhap,* dated from 1576, *alp* (앞) meant 'south' in addition to the primary meaning of 'front'. Likewise, *Hwunmongcahoy* dated from 1527 and *Sincungyuhap* list *twi* (뒤) as denoting 'north' in addition to 'back'. K Kang (2010: 950) suggests a relationship between Korean *oyn* (왼) adj. 'left' and Old Turkish *öŋ* 'east' (citing von Gabain 1950) and written Mongolian *jegün* 'east, left'. Therefore, even though there is no obvious etymological relationship between 'right' and 'west', the historical records sufficiently suggest, at least in part, etymological relations between the deictic and cardinal orientations. Indeed, Heine (1997: 57) states that deictic orientation is among the main sources for cardinal orientation. A peculiarity in Korean, however, is that the reference orientation in this system is a person facing the south. This is a rare system not noted in the cross-linguistic survey of cardinal orientation in 127 languages by Brown (1983). Hock and Joseph (1996: 247-248) only found in a pure form in so-called Altaic languages such as Mongolian and Kalmyk. Robbeets (p.c. with Narrog and Rhee 2013) suggests that it is a Transeurasian feature. Incidentally, the most canonical type is one with a person facing the east (presumably because of its association with sunrise). In contrast, the Hawaiian system is based on a person facing the west (Heine 1997: 52-57).

Another peculiarity is that the sources for 'left' and 'right' have to do with the evaluative judgment of 'wrong' and 'right', respectively. According to Werner (1904: 427f., as cited in Heine 1997: 48-9), this is in fact a very common pattern in the

300-plus Bantu languages. Studies in other languages also strongly suggest that this relationship holds across many languages (see Cienki 1999, Foolen 2017, 2019 for discussion on the right-left asymmetry in language and culture). In terms of morphosyntactic composition, the relational nouns for 'left', 'right' and 'middle' were derived from source constructions consisting of an adnominalized modifier (marked by -n) and a head noun denoting 'side' or 'place'.

3.3.3.2 Verbal Sources

We noted in 3.3.3 that 12 verbs serve as the sources of spatial postpositions, i.e., *is(s)-* 'exist', *puth-* 'adhere', *ha-* 'do/be', *ttalu-* 'follow', *tay-* 'touch', *po-* 'see', *tali-* 'be accompanied by', *kath-* 'be same', *nem-* 'go over', *taku-* 'approach', *kenne-* 'cross', *kalocilu-* 'cross'. Among these, one notable verb is *ha-* 'do/be/say', which is a light verb which participates in grammaticalization of a large number of grammatical markers in Korean (and lexical derivation as well), but often gets reduced or even disappears altogether largely for its lack of phonological prominence. It is also to be noted that some Sino-Korean nouns, such as *hyang* (향 向) 'direction', *myen* 'face', *kyek* (격 隔) 'separation', and *yen* (연 連) 'link', participate in the formation of spatial complex postpositions in conjunction with the native Korean light verb *ha-* (하) 'do/be/say' first, thus, becoming verb forms. If these are to be included in the verbal sources, the number of verbs serving as the lexical sources of spatial complex postpositions will be a little larger.

As is evident from the list of postpositions in Table 3.5, the source verbs are mostly transitive verbs and have diverse meanings, a state of affairs largely consonant with crosslinguistic observations (cf. Heine et al. 1991a, Y Matsumoto 1998, among others), but the postposition of the highest frequency, *-eyse* (에서) 'from', has developed from the static verb *is(s)-* (잇/있) 'exist'. Other source verbs are those denoting some form of directed action to or interaction with an entity, e.g., 'adhere', 'follow', 'touch', 'accompany', 'go over', 'approach', and 'cross'. Considering the fact that the basic function of adpositions is linking two entities, predominant use of such transitive verbs in Korean is in line with expectations. Many of these are transitive verbs and thus often follow a case-marked noun phrase (typically Accusative *-(l)ul* (을

/를)), and are followed by a non-finite marker -*e* (어) and its allomorph -*a* (아) (often termed as the 'converb' marker), as illustrated in (3):

(3) -*ul ttalu-a* 〉 -*ttala* 'along'

해안선을 따라   해안선 따라

*hayansen-**ul**   **ttal-a***   〉〉   *hayansen-**ttala***

coast-ACC   follow-NF   coast-**along**

'follow the coast and'   'along the coast'

We have noted in the preceding discussion that the spatial postpositions that develop from the nominal sources tend to be associated with static meaning (see 3.3.3.1). In contrast, the postpositions that developed from verbal sources, e.g., -*neme* (넘어/너머) 'over' (〈 *nem-* (넘) 'go over'), -*ey tayko* (에 대고) 'at' (〈 *tay-* (대-) v. 'touch'), -*pwuthe* (부터) 'from' (〈 *puth-* (붙-) 'adhere'), -*taka* (다가) 'onto/into' (〈 *tak(ɯ)-* (다그/닥-) 'draw near'), -*ttala* (따라) 'on, along, according to' (〈 *ttalu-* (따르-) 'follow'), -*(ul) kalocille* ((을) 가로질러) (〈 *kalocilu-* (가로지르-) 'cross'), etc., encode dynamic concepts beyond designating simple topographic or relational contour. Many of these also develop into markers of stance, e.g., counterexpectation (known as Mirative), emphasis, etc., which is an instance of subjectification and intersubjectification (Traugott 1982, Traugott and König 1991, Traugott and Dasher 2002, Davidse et al. (eds.) 2010, Narrog 2010, 2017, inter alia; see also H Koo 2019, 2020, Koo and Rhee 2013, S Rhee 2016, Rhee and Koo 2017, 2019, 2020, for Korean). This is also in good contrast with the noun-based postpositions discussed above, because these do not exhibit any notable level of (inter)subjectification. What this phenomenon suggests is that the semantics of the source lexemes determines the dynamicity of the final grammaticalized form. This is in consonance with the principles, such as 'persistence' (Hopper 1991) and 'source determination' (Bybee et al. 1994), which says in effect that the meaning of the source lexemes is largely responsible for the grammaticalization processes in terms of their paths and resultant semantics.

    We also noted that the verbs in the source construction typically occur with a non-finite marker, most frequently -*e*, largely translatable as 'and'. The function of this linker -*e* (어), especially in contrast with another linker -*ko* (고), has long been a research subject. H Koo (1987) characterizes -*e* (어) as the 'consolidating connective' in contrast with -*ko* (고), the 'isolating connective'. Thus, when two verbs are combined with the linker -*e* (어), the two events denoted by the verbs are conceptualized as constituting one coherent event (e.g., *ppaci-e cwuk-* (빠지어 죽-) 'drown' (< 'fall into and die'), see also S Rhee 1996, 2007a, for discussion on the critical role of particles in grammaticalization). When the linker -*e* (어) is attached to a verb in the source construction of spatial postpositions, its effect is significant because it brings forth the effect of scene change. For instance, there has been a controversy as to how the verb *puth-* (붙-) 'adhere to, attach to' could develop into the Ablative -*pwuthe* (부터) 'from', a change in terms of the direction from 'movement toward' to 'movement from'. Some researchers (e.g., S Kim 1992), thus, even hypothesize that the source verb of Ablative -*pwuthe* (부터) might be a different homophonic verb. Considering the role of -*e* (어), however, such a change is a well-motivated one, as shown in (4):

(4) -*ey puth-e*〉 -*pwuthe* 'from'

    집에 붙어   집부터

    *cip-**ey**   puth-**e***   〉〉   *cip-**pwuthe***

    house-DIR   adhere   house-ABL

    'adhere to the house and'   'from the house'

In (4), the source construction carries the meaning of 'adhere to the house and', in which -*e* 'and' forms a juncture with an event that has already occurred (i.e., the subject's coming into contact with the house), and thus sets a scene that what is to follow occurs with the 'house' as the departure point (see S Rhee 2000a, for more discussion on the development of apparent antonyms). Therefore, the perspective change from 'toward' to 'from' is due to the function of -*e* in the source construction which means, in effect, 'x made a contact with the house and then...'.

3.3.3.3 Deictic Sources

The next issue involves the relationship between honorific forms and distal demonstratives. The list of postpositions in Tables 3.1 and 3.2 includes two forms that are inherently marked with honorification, i.e., -*kkey* (께) and -*kkeyse* (께서).[10] These postpositions recruit the speaker-distal demonstrative *ku* (그) 'that', which is incorporated into lexical expression *kuy* (긔) 'that place', as shown in (5) and (6).[11]

(5) X-*s kuy* 'X's that place' 〉 -*kkey* 'to' [+HON]

    a.   아바닚긔와 아ᄌᆞ마닚긔와

       apanim-*s*   *kuy*-wa   acAmanim-*s*   *kuy*-wa

       father:HON-**GEN** **that.place**-and   aunt:HON-**GEN** **that.place**-and

       'to father and aunt' (1447 *Sekposangcel* 6:1)

    a', 아버님께와 아주머님께

       apenim-*kkey*-wa   acwumenim-*kkey*

       father-**DAT:HON**-and   aunt-**DAT:HON**

       'to father and to aunt' (Modern Korean)

(6) X-*s key-sye* 'from X's that place' 〉 -*kkeyse* 'from' [+HON]

    a.   曾祖쩨셔

       CUNGCO-*s*   *key-sye*

       great.grandfather-**GEN**   **that.place**-from

       'from the place of great-grandfather' (1632 *Kalyeyenhay* 1:17)

    a' 증조께서

       cungco-*kkeyse*

       great.grandfather-**NOM:HON**

       'Great grandfather [NOM]' (Modern Korean)

Examples (5) and (6) involve the speaker-distal demonstrative *kuy* (긔) 'that place' (cf.

---

[10] There are two sources that have been generally acknowledged as sources of -*kkeyse* (께서): one is the one presented above; and the other is involving an existence verb *kyesi-* (겨시-) 'to exist' (T Yi 1993[1988], S Rhee 1996, M Kim 2011, among others). For development of demonstrative into personal pronouns, see H Kim (1981).

[11] The Korean historical texts dated before the 20th century do not contain inter-lexical spacing. They are presented with inter-lexical spacing for visual clarity with respect to word boundaries.

S Kim 1992: 388). Lexical expressions involving *kuy* (귀) are used to refer to an honorable person. This is an example of metonymization, i.e., referring to an honorable person by their associated location. This is a strategy to avoid pin-pointing honorable persons in the culture where direct mention or direct pointing of honorable persons is avoided. This time-old custom still survives and is well reflected in that people never utter the names of their parents in full forms (typically two syllables in succession) but, if pronouncing their names is necessitated, they instead present the names syllable by syllable each followed by *-ca* (자) 'character, name', e.g., the first name *Seongha* as [seong-ca ha-ca].[12] This politeness strategy is replicated by courteous service-providers when they use the names of their clients.

On the other hand, this same use of distal demonstrative for honorification is an instance of metaphorization, i.e., respect indicated by maintaining distance (cf. 'negative politeness', Brown and Levinson 1987) is encoded by linguistic expression of distance. Obviously, encoding discourse participant's face-consideration by means of distal demonstrative relates to 'intersubjectification' (Traugott 1982, Traugott and König 1991, Traugott and Dasher 2002, Traugott 2003) of distal expressions. In the cases of *-kkey* (께) and *-kkeyse* (께서), encoding intersubjectification is realized by way of metonymization and metaphorization. As glossed in example (6a') *-kkeyse* (께서) has further developed into a nominative case marker and its association with the space marking function has become nearly imperceivable (see 3.4.4.2 for more discussion).

3.3.3.4 Multiple Sources and Layered Postpositions

Another important aspect is that the distributional patterns of the postpositions do not show the significans-significatum isomorphism, i.e., there is a high degree of

---

[12] An extreme case of this is illustrated in the word *hwica* (휘자) 'avoidable name' to refer to the name of an ancestor or a highly respectable person. During the Koryo Dynasty times (918-1392), various ways of reading such names with substitutes, collectively referred to as *phi-hwi-pep* (피휘법) 'the avoidance and refrainment rule', were widely used, which is similar to the widely known conservative Jewish tradition of not reading God's name *YHWH* (יהוה) but substituting it with *Adonai* (אדוני) 'My Lord', *haShem* (השם) 'The Name', etc. for fear of potential, unintended blasphemy.

many-to-one cardinality between the form and function among the spatial postpositions. For instance, there are multiple terms to encode the grammatical concept of Allative/Dative 'to' and Ablative 'from', among others.[13] There exists a division of labor among the Allative/Dative forms, based on fine-grained semantic and pragmatic distinctions of the goals such as spatiality, animacy, colloquiality, humanness, and honorification, a division of labor as a result of different 'specialization' (Hopper 1991), as listed in (7) and partially exemplified in (8):

(7) a. *-ey* 'to/at' [-Animate]
    b. *-eytaka* 'to' [-Animate], [+Colloquial], [+Emphatic]
    c. *-eytayko* 'to' [-Animate], [+Colloquial], [+Emphatic], [+Pejorative]
    d. *-eytatayko* 'to' [-Animate], [+Colloquial], [+Emphatic], [+Pejorative]
    e. *-eytakatayko* 'to' [-Animate], [+Colloquial], [+Emphatic], [+Pejorative]
    f. *-eykey* 'to' [+Animate]
    g. *-hanthey* 'to' [+Human], largely [+Colloquial]
    h. *-hantheyta* 'to' [+Human], largely [+Colloquial]
    i. *-hantheytaka* 'to' [+Human], largely [+Colloquial]
    j. *-hantheytayko* 'to' [+Human], [+Colloquial], [+Emphatic], [+Pejorative]
    k. *-hantheytatayko* 'to' [+Human], [+Colloquial], [+Emphatic], [+Pejorative]
    l. *-hantheytakatayko* 'to' [+Human], [+Colloquial], [+Emphatic], [+Pejorative]
    m. *-tele* 'to' [+Human]
    n. *-poko* 'to' [+Human]
    o. *-kkey* 'to' [+Human] [+Honorific]
    p. *-kkaci* 'to/until/up.to' [+terminative]

(8) a. 지금 산에 간다.

    *cikum   san-**ey***   *ka-n-ta*
    now   mountain-**ALL**   go-PRES-DEC
    '(I) am going to the mountain.'   (*Wulimalsaym*, entry *-ey*)

---

13) In Old Korean (~917 AD) and Middle Korean (918~1600 AD), even the distinction between Locative and Dative is not clear (J Park 1998, S Choi 2016, D Choi 1996).

b. 누가 술에다가 물을 탔다.

nwu-ka   *swul-**eytaka***   *mwul-ul*   *tha-ss-ta*

someone-NOM   wine-**ALL**   water-ACC   add-PST

'Someone added water to wine (diluted it).'

                             (*Wulimalsaym*, entry *-eytaka*)

c. 영희에게 무슨 일이 생겼을까?

*yenghi-**eykey***   *mwusun*   *il-i*   *sayngky-ess-ul-kka*

[name]-**ALL**   what.kind   matter-NOM   occur-PST-FUT-Q

'What (could have) happened to Younghee?'   (*Wulimalsaym*, entry *-eykey*)

d. 이것은 너한테 주는 선물이다.

ikes-un   *ne-**hanthey***   *cwu-nun*   *senmwul-i-ta*

this-TOP   you-**ALL**   give-ADN   gift-be-DEC

'This is the present for (to be given to) you.'

                             (*Wulimalsaym*, entry *-hanthey*)

e. 어린이한테다가 위험한 물건을 주지 마세요.

*elini-**hantheytaka***   *wihemhan*   *mwulken-ul*   *cwu-ci.ma-seyo*

child-**ALL**   dangerous   thing-ACC   give-PROH-POL.END

'Do not give a dangerous thing to a child.'

                            (*Wulimalsaym*, entry *-hantheytaka*)

f. 그것은 언니더러 물어봐.

kukes-un   *enni-**tele***   *mwul-epw-a*

that-TOP   older.sister-**ALL**   ask-ATMP-END

'For that matter, ask your sister.'   (*Wulimalsaym*, entry *-tele*)

g. 형님께 무슨 일이 생겼나요?

*hyeng-nim-**kkey***   *mwusun*   *il-i*   *sayngky-ess-na-yo*

older.brother-HON-**ALL:HON**   what.kind   matter-NOM   occur-PST-Q-POL

'Has something occurred to my older brother [+HON]?'

                             (*Wulimalsaym*, entry *-kkey*)

h. 동생을 역까지 바래다주었다.

tongsayng-ul   *yek-**kkaci***   *palay-ta.cwu-ess-ta*
younger.sibling-ACC station-**ALL**   see.off-BEN-PST-DEC
'I took my younger brother/sister to the station for him/her.'

(*Wulimalsaym*, entry *-kkaci*)

The functional differentiation indicated in (7) is a schematic generalization glossing over an enormous degree of subtlety. This generalization, however, suggests that linguistic forms that, figuratively speaking, come into acute competition for survival and try to acquire primacy in carrying a grammatical function may divide up the functional territory in a number of subcategories with various semantic properties and settle the conflict with a seemingly peaceful arrangement by distributing the subcategorized functions among them (S Rhee 2021a). An analogous specialization phenomenon is also attested with the reversed directionals, i.e., Ablatives, e.g., *-pwuthe* (부터), *-eyse* (에서), *-eykeyse* (에게서), *-hantheyse* (한테서), *-kkeyse* (께서), *-lose* (로서), etc., as shown in (9):

(9) a. *-pwuthe* 'from'   [+Location]
     b. *-eyse* 'from/at'   [−Animate]
     c. *-eykeyse* 'from'   [+Animate]
     d. *-hantheyse* 'from'   [+Human], largely [+Colloquial]
     e. *-kkeyse* 'from'   [+Human] [+Honorific]
     f. *-lose* 'from'   [+Location]

As shown above, the functional division is based on not only a semantic notion of location, animacy, and humanness but also on pragmatic notions of colloquiality and honorification. As is indicated in the preceding discussion, *-kkeyse* (께서) 'from' is now an honorific Nominative case marker in contemporary Korean (see 3.4.4.2 for more discussion).

3.4 Ongoing Grammaticalization of Spatial Postpositions

One peculiarity associated with the Korean postpositional system is that the primary postpositions are small in number (i.e., 24), though used at a very high frequency, and a large number of the means of encoding relational spatial concepts involves complex postpositions (i.e., 165). Since they exhibit variable degrees of grammaticalization, we will select a subset of spatial postpositions that are supposedly undergoing an active process of grammaticalization and discuss in the following their grammatical status and a number of aspects associated with their grammaticalization.

3.4.1 Selection Criteria

The total number of postpositions in Modern Korean, listed in this chapter, is 204, consisting of 24 primary, 15 composite, and 165 complex postpositions. As indicated above, the frequency of the postpositions is widely variable. Even among the primary postpositions alone, as listed in Table 3.2 above, Accusative -(l)ul (을/를) occurs 17,164 times pmw, whereas three primary postpositions (e.g., Enumerative –hamye (하며), etc.) occur at 0 pmw frequency. Similarly, among the spatial postpositions, Regional –ey (에) occurs at 9,197 tokens pmw, whereas as many as 10 postpositions (e.g., Lateral -(uy) oynccokey(se) ((의) 왼쪽에(서)) 'left to', etc.) in the corpus occur at the frequency of 0 token pmw.

In order to investigate ongoing grammaticalization among postpositions in Korean, further restricting the focus to the markers of spatial relationship, we first need to select optimal postpositions that are currently undergoing grammaticalization. From the entire inventory of 204 postpositions, we select the items that qualify all of the following conditions, with arguably arbitrary cut-off points, as in (10):

(10) (i) It is not in the primary prepositional category in contemporary Korean (180 items);

(ii) It encodes spatial relationship (137 of them);

(iii) It is attested for 10 pmw or more in the corpus (42 of them).

Condition (i) is to rule out the forms firmly established as primary postposition. Condition (ii) is to restrict the scope to our current focus. Condition (iii) is to ensure that the attestations are not chance occurrences attributable to idiolectic styles or that the forms are not at a very incipient stage where the form's viability is yet uncertain. The frequency of 10 pmw is equivalent to 530 occurrences in the 53-million word corpus. As shall be seen in the following chapters, these are the three conditions applied to all languages under discussion. Out of the 204 postpositions, 42 of them (20.6%) meet all the above three criteria, which are listed in Table 3.7 in descending order of token frequency. These 42 postpositions can be said to be actively undergoing grammaticalization in Modern Korean. We will address postpositions in Korean in general but our primary focus will be on these 42 postpositions in the following discussion of grammaticalization.

Spatial Postposition		Meaning	PMW
-eyse	-에서	'at'	2,111
-hanthey(se)	-한테(서)	'to'	977
-eykey	-에게	'to'	897
-eykkaci	-에까지	'to, till'	655
-lokkaci	-로까지	'to, till'	651
-(uy) aphey(se)	-(의) 앞에(서)	'before'	365
-(ey)sepwuthe	-(에)서부터	'from'	340
-lopwuthe	-로부터	'from'	331
-ceney	-전에	'before'	173
-(uy) yephey(se)	-(의) 옆에(서)	'beside, by'	157
-(uy) wiey(se)	-(의) 위에(서)	'on, above, over'	156
-(uy) aney(se)	-(의) 안에(서)	'in, within'	148
-(ul) hyanghay(se)	-(을) 향해(서)	'toward'	141
-(uy) pakkey(se)	-(의) 밖에(서)	'outside, except'	121
-(wa) hamkkey	-(와) 함께	'(together) with'	115
-(uy) sokey(se)	-(의) 속에(서)	'in, within'	113
-hako	-하고	'with'	100
-kkeyse	-께서	'from'	82

-cwungey(se)	–중에(서)	'in, among'	78
-(ul) ttala(se)	–(을) 따라(서)	'following'	76
-(ey) taykose(se)	–(에) 대고(서)	'to, unto'	76
-(uy) twiey(se)	–(의) 뒤에(서)	'behind, after'	63
-(uy) alay(ey(se))	–(의) 아래(에(서))	'below, under'	58
-malko(se)	–말고(서)	'except'	48
-(ey) tayko(se)	–(에) 대고(서)	'to, unto'	33
-(ul) poko(se)	–(을) 보고(서)	'to'	32
-(uy) saiey(se)	–(의) 사이/새에(서)	'between'	32
-lose	–로서	'from'	30
-lo hyanghay(se)	–로 향해(서)	'toward'	28
-(ul) tele	–(을) 더러	'to'	24
-ppayko(se)	–빼고(서)	'except'	22
-(uy) mithey(se)	–(의) 밑에(서)	'below, under'	21
-eykeyse	–에게서	'from'	20
-kakkai(se)	–가까이(서)	'near'	19
-(ul) thonghay(se)	–(을) 통해(서)	'through'	17
-hantheyse	–한테서	'from'	13
-hwuey	–후에	'after'	13
-(uy) cwuwiey(se)	–(의) 주위에(서)	'around'	12
-(uy) cwupyeney(se)	–(의) 주변에(서)	'around'	12
-(uy) kyethey(se)	–(의) 곁에(서)	'beside, by'	11
-hako kathi	–하고 같이	'(together) with'	10
-(ul) neme(se)	–(을) 너머/넘어(서)	'over'	10

Table 3.7 Postpositions undergoing grammaticalization in Modern Korean

3.4.2 General Characteristics

Table 3.7 above lists 15 composite and 27 complex postpositions that are supposedly undergoing grammaticalization with a level of viability. The table shows that *-eyse* (에서) 'at', *-hanthey(se)* (한테(서)) 'to', *-eykey* (에게) 'to', *-eykkaci* (에까지) 'to, till', and

-lokkaci (로까지) 'to, till' are the five most frequent postpositions, which are all composite postpositions. This is in contrast with the complex postpositions, those that are structurally complex, which rank 6th and below.

One of the important generalizations of the grammaticalizing postpositions is that many of these grammaticalizing complex postpositions are developing from nominal sources, as indicated by Genitive *-uy* (의). In terms of the structure, they involve a particle (Genitive *-uy* (의)), a relational noun (RN; e.g., 'front', 'side', 'top', etc.), and a ground marker (mostly Locative *-ey* (에) 'at' or its composite form *-eyse* (에서) 'at, in'). There are also many developing from verbal sources. They involve a case particle (Accusative *-ul* (을) or Locative *-ey* (에) 'at') and the non-finite marker (NF) *-a/e* (아/어). Thus, the grammaticalizing postpositions take the following forms (see 3.4.3.4. for more discussion on formal reduction):

(11) a. Nominal source
    X-uy   *Y-ey*
    X-GEN RN-LOC

  b. 집의 뒤에   집(의)뒤에   집뒤

*cip-**uy** twi-ey*	››	*cip-**(uy)twiey***	››	*cip-**twi***
house-GEN **back-LOC**		house-**behind**		house-**behind**
'at the back of the house'		'behind the house'		'behind the house'

(12) a. Verbal source
    X-ul/ey   *V-e/a*
    X-ACC/LOC V-NF

  b. 산을 넘어   산(을)넘어   산너머

*san-**ul** nem-e*	››	*san-**(ul)neme***	››	*san-**neme***
mountain-ACC **go.over-NF**		mountain-**over**		mountain-**over**
'go over the mountain and'		'over the mountain'		'over the mountain'

It is also notable from the list that the anterior forms, i.e., *-(uy) aphey(se)* ((의) 앞에(서))

'before' (365 pmw) and *–ceney* (전에) 'before' (173 pmw), are of much higher frequency as compared to the posterior forms, i.e., *–(uy) twiey(se)* ((의) 뒤에(서)) 'behind, after' (63 pmw) and *–hwuey* (후에) 'after' (13 pmw). Likewise, the superior form, i.e., *–(uy) wiey(se)* ((의) 위에(서)) 'on, above, over' (156 pmw), is of much higher frequency as compared to the inferior forms, i.e., *–(uy) alay(ey(se))* ((의) 아래(에(서))) 'below, under' (58 pmw) and *–(uy) mith(ey(se))* ((의) 밑(에(서))) 'below, under' (21 pmw). This is consonant with the observation that top and front are the areas suitable for optimal perception and thus are considered 'positive' directions (Andersen 1978: 343; Heine 1997; see other chapters for a similar state-of-affairs in other languages).

Now, we discuss the grammaticalizing postpositions in a few groups by the functions, i.e., Allatives, Ablative, Interior, Proximatives, Inferior, Perlatives, and Medial.

[Allatives (Datives)]

Allatives, also known as, or closely related to, Datives, signal the goal of an action, which may involve locomotion or simply an action that does not involve physical movement, such as speech. Allatives carry, in addition to directionality, a strong emphasis on the terminative nature of the reference point. Allatives in Korean is peculiar for their multiplicity as well as their fine-grained specialization along various factors. Since these markers have been exemplified in (7) and (8), above, we keep the discussion brief at this point. Allatives in Korean are listed in (13) along with their frequency. The postpositions under our focus are highlighted in bold:

(13) Allatives (Dative)

a.	*–ey*	'to'	9,197
b.	*–kkaci*	'to, till'	1,760
c.	***–hanthey(se)***	**'to'**	977
d.	*–eykey*	'to'	897
e.	***–eykkaci***	**'to, till'**	655
f.	***–lokkaci***	**'to, till'**	651
g.	*–(ey) tayko*	'to, unto'	76
h.	***–(ey) taykose***	**'to, unto'**	33

i.	*-(ul) poko(se)*	'to'	32
j.	*-(ul) tele*	'to'	24
k.	*-hantheyta(ka(tayko(se)))*	'to'	0
l.	*-hantheytayko(se)*	'to'	0
m.	*-(ey)ta(ka(tayko(se)))*	'to'	0
n.	*-lotaka*	'to'	0

From the list in (13) it is obvious that the primary postpositions *-ey* (에) and *-kkaci* (까지) 'to, till' are those that have the functional primacy. The exceptionally high frequency of *-ey* (에) is partly due to the fact that it is polyfunctional with other popular concepts, e.g. Regional ('at'). By virtue of being structurally simple, *-kkaci* (까지) far exceeds other competitors in function. It is also to be noted that *-kkaci* (까지) has, in addition to the function of marking space (e.g., *hakkyo-kkaci* (학교까지) [school-to] 'to school', abstract functions such as marking time (e.g., *achim-kkaci* (아침까지) [morning-till] 'until morning') and signaling the speaker's strong subjective stance, i.e., mirative (e.g., *John-kkaci* (존까지) [John-even] 'even John'). Functional generality, then, seems to have contributed to its functional primacy. In addition to the primary *-kkaci* (까지), there are other composite forms involving it as well, i.e., *-eykkaci* (에까지) and *-lokkaci* (로까지), which are also strong Allatives. As noted in (7) and (8) in 3.3.3.4, *-hanthey* (한테) is colloquial, whereas *-eykey* (에게) is register-neutral. A slightly higher frequency of *-hanthey* (한테) may be due to the fact that the data is based on a colloquial corpus. Furthermore, the lower frequency of the forms involving *tay-* (대) and *taka-* (다가) is due to their being emphatic and often pejorative (see (7) and (8) above). In his analysis of these Datives, S Rhee (2021a) states that the source verbs *tay-* (대-) 'touch' and *tak(u)-* (닥/다그-) 'approach' engendered negative meanings due to Korean culture, in which such actions are avoidable. This shows that grammaticalization is intertwined with multiple factors, including culture.

[Ablatives (Sources)]

Ablatives in Korean are also numerous, though not comparable to Datives in number. There are seven Ablatives as listed in (14):

(14) Ablatives

a.	*-pwuthe*	'from'	992
b.	*-(ey)sepwuthe*	*'from'*	*340*
c.	*-lopwuthe*	*'from'*	*331*
d.	*-kkeyse*	*'from'*	*82*
e.	*-lose*	*'from'*	*30*
f.	*-eykeyse*	*'from'*	*20*
g.	*-hantheyse*	*'from'*	*13*

One interesting aspect with Ablatives, plainly observable from the list, is that they have one upper-hand competitor, i.e., the primary postposition *-pwuthe* (부터), but no competitor at the lower end. The strength of *-pwuthe* (부터) is obvious in that the two composite forms involving it are also on the top of the grammaticalizing postpositions. Postposition *-kkeyse* (께서) (14d) is a marked form with the semantic feature [+Honorific], but it is not at all weak as compared to a few others below it. This is due to the Korean idiosyncrasy that honorification is fully grammaticalized, including particle selection and verbal inflection. The postpositions (14d-g) all involve the particle *-se* (서), known as a converb (see 3.2 above), one of the functions of which is to mark sequentiality and thus a starting point. However, these Ablatives are generally weak forms in terms of functional specialization. A side-note in comparison with Datives is that Ablatives surface at a much lower frequency than Datives, which is possibly indicative of the human propensity to pay more attention to a goal than a source (see 10.1.2 for further discussion). Having relatively fewer members may be the reason there are no weaker members among the Ablatives, in contrast with Datives which have as many as four members recording 0 pmw. This means that grammaticalization may be greatly influenced by the number of competitors in the functional domain.

[Interiors]

There are five interiors which are all complex postpositions, as listed in (15):

(15) Interiors

a.	*-(uy) aney(se)*	'in, within'	148
b.	*-(uy) sokey(se)*	'in, within'	113
c.	*-cwungey(se)*	'in, among'	78
d.	*-(uy) nayey*	'in, inside'	3
e.	*-(uy) kawuntey(ey(se))*	'in, among'	2

Interiors grammaticalized from two different sources, i.e., native Korean and Sino-Korean lexemes denoting interiority. The lexemes *an* (안) (15a), *sok* (속) (15b), and *kawuntey* (가운데) (15e) are native Korean nouns denoting 'inside', whereas *cwung* (중; 中) (15c) and *nay* (내; 內) (15d) are Sino-Korean nouns denoting 'inside'. It is evident that the postpositions derived from native Korean lexemes are stronger than those from Sino-Korean lexemes. The reason may be due to the fact that postpositions from Sino-Korean sources largely specialize in denoting abstract notions (see 3.4.4.1 for more discussion). One outlier in this pattern is the Korean relational noun of interiority *kawuntey* (가운데) (15e), which fails to meet the frequency requirement. The reason seems to be that *kawuntey* (가운데) is not only phonetically bulkier but semantically marked in that it tends to mark the right center of a space, such as the bull's eye in a target. This suggests that semantically marked (thus, not sufficiently generalized) forms are disadvantaged in grammaticalization. Other important issues about native vs. Sino-Korean distinction are addressed more in detail in 3.4.4.1.

[Proximatives (Adjacency)]

Proximatives, those that mark adjacency, are peculiar in Korean in that there are five postpositions in the category, but all of them are within the category of actively grammaticalizing postpositions. They are listed in (16):

(16) Proximatives

a.	*-uy yephey(se)*	'beside, by'	157
b.	*-kakkai*	'around, near'	19
c.	*-(uy) cwuwiey(se)*	'around'	12

| d. | -(uy) cwupyeney(se) | 'around' | 12 |
| e. | -uy kyethey(se) | 'beside, by' | 11 |

All Proximatives are deemed to be actively grammaticalizing in Modern Korean, but their functional strengths are widely variable, as indicated in the frequency information. In other words, *-(uy) yephey(se)* ((의) 옆에(서)) (16a) occurring at 157 pmw frequency, is over 14 times as frequent as *-uy kyethey(se)* ((의) 곁에(서)) (16e). The lexical origin also seems to play a role here. The lexemes *yeph* (옆) 'side, loin' (16a), *kakkap-* (가깝-) 'be near' (16b), and *kyeth* (곁) 'side' are native Korean words, whereas *cwuwi* (주위; 周圍) 'surroundings' (16c) and *cwupyen* (주변; 周邊) 'surroundings' (16d) are Sino-Korean words. Evidently, postpositions that developed from native Korean words have gained primacy over those from Sino-Korean words. Since Sino-Korean words tend to belong to the high register, their currency is rather limited, hence leading to weaker grammaticalization (see 3.4.4.1 for more discussion).

[Inferiors]

Inferiors are few in number, i.e., only three postpositions in the category. They are listed in (17):

(17) Inferiors

a.	-(uy) alay(ey(se))	'below, under'	58
b.	-(uy) mithey(se)	'below, under'	21
c.	-haey(se)	'below, under'	3

The situation with Inferiors is similar to many other categories discussed here. That is, there are native Korean lexemes *alay* (아래) 'below' (17a) and *mith* (밑) 'bottom' (17b), and Sino-Korean lexeme *ha* (하; 下) 'bottom, below' (17c), involved in the development of Inferiors. The list clearly shows that the postposition originating from the Sino-Korean lexeme has not acquired the sufficient strength to show strong signs of active grammaticalization.

[Perlatives (Paths)]

Perlatives, or markers of paths, by means of which the trajector travels, are small in number in Korean. They are listed in (18):

(18) Perlatives

a.	*-(ul) ttala(se)*	'along, following'	76
b.	*-ul thonghay(se)*	'through'	17
c.	*-ul kalocille(se)*	'across'	1

The weakest member *-ul kalocille(se)* (을 가로질러(서)) 'across' (18c) is barely attested in the corpus, and the competition seems to exist only between *-(ul) ttala(se)* ((을) 따라 (서)) 'along, following' (18a) and *-ul thonghay(se)* (을 통해(서)) 'through' (18b). Once again, the lexical sources seem to matter: the former is from the native Korean verb *ttalu-* (따르-) 'follow' and the latter is from the Sino-Korean word *thong* (통; 通) 'pass, passage'. The Sino-Korean word has undergone further derivation with the light verb *ha-* (하-) 'do, be'. In addition to the disadvantage in the source, the compositional complexity that resulted from derivation seems to be responsible for its weaker level of grammaticalization. The postposition *-ul kalocille(se)* (을 가로질러(서)) 'across' (18c) is derived from a native Korean verb *kalocilu-* (가로지르-) 'cross' but it is also a compound of the adverbial *kalo* (가로) 'sideways, horizontal' and the verb *cilu-* (지르-) 'dash', thus 'dash horizontally', ultimately developing into the verb 'cross'. This is a strong indication that the structure and meaning of source lexemes play an important role in grammaticalization.

[Medials]

The final category of discussion is Medials, which denote the 'in-between' spatial relationship. Since a trajector requires two entities serving as reference points for its medial positioning, Medials are conceptually marked. There are three Medials in Modern Korean, as listed in (19):

(19) Medials

a.	*-(uy) saiey(se)*	'between'	32
b.	*-uy thumey(se)*	'between'	9
c.	*-kaney*	'between'	1

Among the three Medials in (19), only *-(uy) saiey(se)* ((의) 사이에(서)) 'between' (19a) is deemed to belong to the category of actively grammaticalizing postpositions. The lexemes *sai* (사이) 'gap' of (19a) and *thum* (틈) 'gap' of (19b) are native Korean nouns, whereas *kan* (간; 間) 'interval' of (19c) is Sino-Korean. Thus, the source effect is applicable to this group as well. The disparity between (19a) and (19b), both based on native Korean lexemes, seems to be due to the semantic markedness of the latter, i.e., *thum* (틈) 'gap' tends to be very narrow, thus the presence of which is unintended or undesirable. Therefore, this situation also corroborates the widely subscribed hypothesis that grammaticalization crucially depends on the level of semantic generality (Heine et al. 1991a, Bybee et al. 1994, S Rhee 2000b,c).

3.4.3 Grammaticalization Mechanisms

Since the introduction of grammaticalization theory in modern linguistics, grammaticalization principles and mechanisms have been among the major research interests (Lehmann 2015[1982], Claudi and Heine 1986, Heine et al. 1991a, Hopper and Traugott 2003[1993], Bybee et al. 1994, Heine and Kuteva 2002, S Rhee 2009, Kuteva et al. 2019, among many others). In view of the fact that mechanisms refer to cognitive processes that enable language change, and thus grammaticalization as well, it comes as no surprise then that they have received much attention by grammaticalization researchers. However, there is yet no consensus as to what the precise set of mechanisms in grammaticalization is. An analysis of grammaticalization scenarios may make reference to any set of principles and mechanisms (see Traugott 2011, for a discussion of mechanisms and S Rhee 2009, for a comprehensive review of semantic change mechanisms), but we will use the four mechanisms proposed by Heine and Kuteva (2002: 3) and Kuteva et al. (2019: 3), listed in (20).

(20) Grammaticalization mechanisms
    a. extension (or 'context generalization')
    b. desemanticization (or 'semantic bleaching')
    c. decategorialization
    d. erosion (or 'phonetic reduction')

3.4.3.1 Extension

Extension as a grammaticalization mechanism refers to the increase of the context in which a grammatical form can occur. This mechanism is closely tied to semantic change, because for a form to occur in a heretofore inadequate context, its meaning needs to have changed as well. Spatial postpositions in general retain the original lexical meaning of the relational nouns, and thus the extent of their semantic change tends to be still limited.

With the newly grammaticalizing postpositions, the most prominent aspect of context extension is from their use in spatial designation to signaling temporal or other abstract but related concepts (cf. Haspelmath 1997). In other words, when relational nouns have a lexical meaning, their use is restricted to the function of marking the relation between entities that occupy a physical space. This relation-marking function still survives when they participate in the formation of spatial postpositions. However, once they are grammaticalized, their function may extend from strictly denoting space to other notions, such as time, protection, cause, etc. The most prominent change from space to other abstract notions is exemplified in part in the following constructed examples:

(21) *twi* 'back'

    a. [lexical]

    뒤에 흙이 묻었다.

    twi-ey   *hulk-i*   *mwut-ess-ta*

    back-at   mud-NOM   stain-PST-DEC

    '(Your) back is stained with mud.'

    b. [Spatial postposition]

    집 뒤에 산이 있다.

    cip-twiey   *san-i*   *iss-ta*

    house-**behind**   mountain-NOM   exist-DEC

    'There is a mountain behind the house.'

    c. [Non-spatial postposition]

회의 뒤에 만찬이 있다.

*hoyuy-**twiey***   *manchan-i*   *iss-ta*

meeting-**after**   dinner-NOM   exist-DEC

'There will be a dinner after the meeting.'

(22) *mith* 'bottom'

     a. [lexical]

       독의 밑이 빠졌다.

       tok-uy   **mith**-*i*   *ppaci-ess-ta*

       jug-GEN   **bottom**-NOM   break-PST-DEC

       'The jug has a broken bottom.'

     b. [Spatial postposition]

       산 밑에 마을이 있다.

       *san-**mithey***   *maul-i*   *iss-ta*

       mountain-**below**   village-NOM   exist-DEC

       'There is a village at the foot of the mountain.'

     c. [Non-spatial postposition]

       나는 할머니 밑에 자랐다.

       na-nun   *halmeni-**mithey***   *cala-ss-ta*

       I-TOP   grandma-**under**   grow-PST-DEC

       'I was brought up under the custody of my grandma.'

3.4.3.2 Desemanticization

Desemanticization as a grammaticalization mechanism refers to the loss of meaning content, whereby the meaning of a linguistic form becomes increasingly bleached. Since such loss typically does not involve complete disappearance of former meanings but involves addition of new related meanings by way of the loss of the restriction of semantic domain, desemanticization is tantamount to semantic generalization or even semantic enrichment (see S Rhee 1996 for discussion of convergence of semanticization and desemanticization; see also Lehmann 1978 for discussion of semantic complexity). For instance, a form formerly designating a spatial feature can now designate a temporal feature as well, a process whereby the spatial function is relatively loosened and the temporal function is newly acquired. This is clear in the development of the English *go*-future. When the verb *go* was strictly a verb of locomotion, its use was restricted to spatial movement. When it developed into the future-tense marker *be going to*, however, the form could still be used for spatial movement (*I am going to the library.*), in addition to the innovated future-marking function (*I am going to marry next year.*).

The relation between semantics of a grammatical form and its formal transparency has been often pointed out in literature (Pagliuca 1976, Bybee 1985, Detges and Waltereit 2002, S Rhee 2003b, among others). Likewise, formal transparency is closely tied to formal reduction. It is widely accepted that semantic generalization and formal reduction occur in parallel, hence 'the parallel reduction hypothesis' (Bybee et al. 1994). It has also been pointed out that there exists the effect of the transparency in grammaticalization. For examples, S Rhee (1996), in a discussion of Korean existence verb *kyeysi-* (겨시-) 'exist[+HON]', suggests a series of causal relations of [conservative phonological shape] 〉 [transparent semantics] 〉 [restriction on occurrence] 〉 [limited textual frequency] 〉 [lesser degree of grammaticalization] (S Rhee 1996: 158).

With reference to the spatial postpositions, there is a good contrast between the postpositions of higher frequency and those of lower frequency. In other words, the eight high frequency spatial postpositions, i.e., *-ey* (에) 'at', *-eyse* (에서) 'at, from', *-(k)wa* (와/과) 'with', *-lo* (로) 'to, with', *-kkaci* (까지) 'to, till', *-pwuthe* (부터) 'from', *-hanthey* (한테) 'to', and *-eykey* (에게) 'to', have a high level of opacity, with some entirely unknown (see Table 3.4 for ranked list of spatial postpositions), whereas those of the lower frequency, including *-(uy) aphey* ((의) 앞에) 'before, in front of', *-(uy) yephey* ((의) 옆에) 'beside', *-(uy) wiey* ((의) 위에) 'on, on top of', *-(uy) sokey* ((의) 속에) 'inside', *-(uy) twiey* ((의) 뒤에) 'behind, in the back of', *-(uy) alayey* ((의) 아래에) 'under, below', *-(ul) ttala* ((을) 따라) 'following, through', *-(uy) saiey* ((의) 사이에) 'between', *-(uy) mithey* ((의) 밑에) 'under, below', *-(uy) kyethey* ((의) 곁에) 'beside, next to', *-(ul) neme* ((을) 넘어/너머) 'over', etc., have a high level of lexical source transparency, such as 'front', 'side', 'top', etc. The lexical source transparency is directly related to the morphosyntactic transparency in that most of the lower-frequency items maintain the [*-(uy) X-ey*] '[-(GEN) X-LOC]' structure, in which all elements are identifiable. This state of affairs supports the hypothesis that formal transparency, semantic transparency, and use frequency are closely interrelated in grammaticalization. In other words, formal transparency contributes to semantic persistence, because formal transparency invokes the semantics associated with the source lexeme in the course of language processing. This lends support to the notion 'persistence' as proposed by Hopper (1991) and Hopper and Traugott (2003[1993]).

3.4.3.3 Decategorialization

Decategorialization refers to loss in morphosyntactic properties, characteristic of lexical or other less grammatical forms. Since the lexical category items of the postpositions are predominantly nouns (37 of the 49 known sources) and, to a lesser extent, verbs (12 of the 49 known sources) (see Table 3.5 above), the loss of categorial properties necessarily involve nominal and verbal properties. The nominal and verbal properties in Korean are largely the following:

(23) a. nominal properties: modification by an adjective/adnominal; pluralization
　　　b. verbal properties: inflection by TAM, modification by an adverb

It is to be noted that pluralization or non-pluralization of a noun does not result in grammaticality change since plural marking in Korean is optional. It may only lead to semantic awkwardness when improperly pluralized in view of the context. Also notable is that verbal inflection by TAM is normally applicable to main verbs and thus, verb forms marked by the non-finite *-e* are not subject to such modification for syntactic reasons. Therefore, available tests may largely involve adjective/adnominal modification for nouns and adverb modification for verbs. The results are shown in part in (24):

(24) **-(uy) aphey(se)** 'before'

a. 그들의 앞에서 키스를 나누는 젊은 연인들

kutul-uy apheyse   *khissu-lul*   *nanwu-nun*   *celmun yenin-tul*

they-**before**   kiss-ACC   share-ADN   young   lover-PL

'young lovers kissing before them'

(2002 Drama, Kechimepsnun salang, Episode #10)

a' 그들의 바로 앞에서 키스를 나누는 젊은 연인들

*kutul-uy **palo** apheyse* *khissu-lul*   *nanwu-nun*   *celmun yenin-tul*

they-GEN **right** before   kiss-ACC   share-ADN   young   lover-PL

'young lovers kissing right in front of them'

b. 다른 사람 앞에서 그렇게 웃지 말래는 거지.

talun salam-apheyse   *kulehkey*   *wus-ci.mal-lay-nunkeci*

other person-**before**   like.that   laugh-PROH-QUOT-END

'What I meant is that you should not laugh like that before others.'

(2003 Drama, 1%-uy ettenkes, Episode #25)

b' 다른 사람 바로 앞에서 그렇게 웃지 말래는 거지.

*?talun **salam palo** apheyse*   *kulehkey*   *wus-ci.mal-lay-nunkeci*

other person **right** before   like.that   laugh-PROH-QUOT-END

'What I meant is that you should not laugh like that right in front of others.'

Examples (24a) and (24b) are excerpts from drama scripts and (24a') and (24b') are their modified versions with an inserted modifier. The paired examples show an interesting phenomenon that the longer form (*-uy apheyse*; (의 앞에서)) (24a) is more tolerant of an insertion of a modifier than the shorter form (*-apheyse* (앞에서)) (24b). This seems to have to do with the fact that the longer, thus less developed, form tends to denote an anterior spatial location (e.g., 'in front of') whereas the shorter, thus more developed, form tends to denote a more abstract concept of anteriority (e.g., 'in the presence of', or 'disregarding the presence of'). In other words, examples (24a) and (24a') describe a couple kissing at a close distance to others, whereas example

(24b) describes a man heartily laughing without self-restraint while others are present. Thus, it can be said that there is a variability with respect to the tolerance of modifier insertion depending on the degree of formal reduction, and that the degree of formal reduction is closely related to the degree of semantic abstraction. However, neither sentence is rendered ungrammatical with modifier insertion, which suggests that these spatial postpositions still retain lexical characteristics and have not yet fully grammaticalized.

Modifier insertion can also be tested with the postpositions of verbal sources. The postposition *-(ul) neme* ((을) 넘어/너머) is only weakly grammaticalized, which is based on the verb *nem-* (넘-) 'go over, pass'. One peculiarity in Korean orthography is that when the lexical verb *nem-* (넘-) is followed by the non-finite marker *-e* (어), the word is written with a syllable break between *nem* (넘) and *e* (어) (given the notation *nem.e* (넘어) below) 'go over and', and when the word functions as a spatial postposition, the syllable break is between *ne* (너) and *me* (머) (given the notation *ne.me* (너머) below) 'over, beyond, across'. In reality, however, the two forms are used without strict distinction by many. Incidentally, there is a noun derived from the same verb written as *ne.me* 'the other side'. This state of affairs shows that as a form distances from its lexical source, the formal transparency decreases accordingly. The modifier interpolation test is illustrated in (25):

(25) *-(ul) ne.me* 'over' (⟨ *-(ul) nem.e* [ACC go.over-NF] 'go over and')

    a.   청사 건물 너머 비행기가 착륙하는 모습이 보인다.

        chengsa   *kenmwul-<u>ne.me</u>*   *pihayngki-ka*   *chaklyukha-nun*

        terminal   building-<u>**over**</u>   aircraft-NOM   land-ADN

        mosup   *poi-n-ta*

        scene   be.seen-PRES-DEC

        'Over the terminal building is seen an airplane landing.'

                                     (2007 Drama *Kaywa nuktayuy sikan*, Episode #2)

    a'   청사 건물 바로 너머 비행기가...

        *chengsa   *kenmwul*   **<u>ppalukey</u>**   *ne.me*   *pihayngki-ka...*

        terminal   building   <u>**fast**</u>   over   aircraft-NOM...

'Fast over the terminal building is seen an airplane landing.'

a" 청사 건물을 빠르게 넘어 비행기가...
chengsa   *kenmwul-ul*   **_ppalukey_** *nem.e*   *pihayngki-ka*...
terminal   building-ACC **fast**   go.over-NF aircraft-NOM
'An airplane is seen landing fast flying over the terminal building.'

As shown in (25a'), when a manner adverb *ppalukey* (빠르게) 'fast' is inserted between the bare NP and the postposition *ne.me* (너머), the sentence becomes ungrammatical, whereas the sentence (25a"), in which the same adverb is inserted between the accusative case-marked NP and the NF-marked verb, is grammatical. It is notable, however, that *-ul nem.e* (을 넘어) in (25a") does not have the spatial postposition meaning but the lexical verb meaning 'go over', which served as the basis of the postposition. Thus, the adverb is a manner modifier of the aircraft's motion. In other words, adverbial modifier insertion is not tolerated by the verb-based postpositions, a sign of advanced grammaticalization.

All these findings strongly suggest that the grammaticalizing postpositions have proceeded the decategorialization processes as evidenced by the fact that the lexical items participating in the source construction have lost, though at varying degrees, their nominal and verbal characteristics.

3.4.3.4 Erosion

Erosion as a grammaticalization mechanism refers to the loss in phonetic substance and may involve diverse processes that result in the reduction of the formal shape. With respect to Korean postpositions, erosion may occur notably with particle deletion and orthographic space deletion, even though more subtle reduction such as loss of phonological salience at the suprasegmental level may also occur.

A Korean idiosyncrasy is that arguments and nominal particles are omissible and in speech such omission is even preferable. As was briefly noted in 3.4.2 above, with respect to the noun-based postpositions, the two nominal particles, i.e., Genitive *-uy* (의) and Locative *-ey* (에), are the segments that are susceptible to deletion. There is an asymmetry with the deletion in that the first one is omitted at a much higher frequency than the second. Thus, the degree of formal reduction increases as the number of particles being deleted increases, as shown in the progression from (26a) to (26c), with matching examples (26a') through (26c'):

(26) a. *X-uy*   *Y-ey*   b. *X*   *Y-ey*   c. *X*   *Y*
      [NP]-GEN   [RN]-LOC   [NP]   [RN]-LOC   [NP]   [RN]
      'at Y of X'   'at Y of X'   'at Y of X'

   a' 집의 앞에   b' 집 앞에   c' 집 앞
      cip-__uy__   *__aph-ey__*   *cip*   *__aph-ey__*   *cip*   *__aph__*
      house-**GEN** **front-LOC**   house **front-LOC**   house **front/before**
      'in front of the house'   'in front of the house' 'in front of the house'

In case of the verb-based postpositions, the nominal particles, i.e., Locative *-ey* (에) and Accusative *-(l)ul* (을/를), are also often omitted, whereas the non-finite verbal suffix *-e* (어) (or its allomorph *-a* (아)), also known as a converb, is not omissible since verbal roots cannot stand alone. The reductive pattern is shown in (27a) and (27b), with matching examples (27a') and (27b'), which are reinterpreted and reanalyzed as a postpositional phrase 'across the street':[14]

(27) a. *X-ey/ul*   *Y-e*   b. *X*   *Y-e*
      [NP]-LOC/ACC   V-NF   [NP]   V-NF
      'after V-ing X'   'after V-ing X'

   a'. 길을 건너(어)   b' 길 건너(어)
      kil-__ul__   *__kenne-e__*   *kil*   *__kenne-e__*
      street-**ACC**   **cross-NF**   street **cross-NF**
      'after crossing the street'   'after crossing the street'

---

14) Note that the particles that follow its host that has the identical vowel in its last syllable are deleted as a general rule (e.g., /e/ in (27a') and (27b')).

Furthermore, unlike many Asian languages, Korean makes use of orthographic spacing to set apart words, which comprise a stem and its satellite particles. In grammaticalization research, the spacing convention is very useful in that it reflects writers' perception of the degree of bondedness between linguistic forms. Deletion of spaces between word groups reflects that the language users perceive the two or more adjacent forms as forming a single unit, i.e., an orthographic reflection of morphosyntactic 'coalescence' (Haspelmath 2011) as a way of iconicity. When this orthographic space deletion is coupled with particle deletion, especially in the case of noun-based postpositions, the outcome can be strikingly different from the source structure as illustrated in (28):

(28) a. 산의 아래에   산아래
         san-uy   〈space〉 *alay-ey* 〉〉   *san-alay*
         mountain-GEN   bottom-LOC   mountain-bottom/below
         'at the bottom of a mountain'   'below the mountain'

     b. 강을 따라   강따라
         kang-ul   〈space〉 *ttalu-a*   〉〉   *kang-ttala*
         river-ACC   follow-NF   river-along
         'following the river'   'along the river'

This type of space deletion is characterizable as an example of 'univerbation' (Lehmann 2015[1982]), a process whereby multiple linguistic forms in juxtaposition begin to behave as a single unit (cf. 'cognitive packaging', Givón 1991a).

For noun-based postpositions, the derivational pattern illustrated in (28a) is uniformly, yet optionally, applied to all cases. One aspect relevant to this process is that the formation of the final product (i.e., 'below the mountain') resembles compounding (i.e., 'mountain-bottom'), and in fact, there is no theoretically sound way of separating these two processes, because the resultant form from the above process can be seen as composed of two nouns in juxtaposition, and indeed they can be used as full-fledged nouns instead of prepositional phrases. It is possible that compounding and grammaticalization converge in these instances (see 3.4.4.1 for more discussion).

In this regard, an important aspect in grammaticalization of Korean postpositions is that there are formal variants for a single postposition (note that many forms include elements shown in parenthesis in the lists) and the degree of omission of the parenthetical elements is correlated with the degree of grammaticalization (as reflected in their frequency).[15] For instance, toward the top of the ranked frequency list, the ratios of the shortened forms by way of the deletion of the first nominal particle, which is Genitive *-uy* (의), are consistently high, whereas the ratios decrease as the frequency ranking goes downward. The reduction pattern with the second nominal particle, which is Locative *-ey* (에) and its intensifying particle *-se* (서), is not as clear as the reduction of the first nominal particle. It seems then that, despite the general tendency, there is another factor involved. For instance, some postpositions such as *-(uy) aphey(se)* ((의) 앞에(서)) 'before' and *-(uy) kyethey(se)* ((의) 곁에(서)) 'beside' show a very low rate of Locative deletion, whereas some postpositions such as *-(uy) alayey(se)* ((의) 아래에(서)) 'below, under' show a high rate of deletion as high as 75.5% in the corpus data. Furthermore, in the cases of the relational nouns ending in an open syllable, such as *alay* (아래)'bottom', *wi* (위) 'top', and *sai/say* (사이/새) 'gap', etc., the omission rate of the final locative particle *-ey* (에) is generally higher. This seems to be attributable to the common tendency that Korean speakers delete a segment from a string of successive vowels to economize the articulatory gestures. This tendency of omission of *-ey* (에) after an open syllable (75.5% for *alay* (아래) and 16.4% for *wi* (위)) is in contrast with the relational nouns that end in a closed syllable, notably, *aph* (앞) 'front' and *kyeth* (곁) 'side' (0%).

Another relevant issue is that the morphological/phonological reduction is applicable not only to the particles but also to their stems. The reductive process has operated on some of the relational nouns as *aph* (앞) 'front', *twi* (뒤) 'back', and *wi* (위) 'top'. In historical data the modern *aph* /aph/ (앞) had its predecessors *alp* /alp/ (앒) and *alph* /alph/ (앑) from which the lateral liquid and/or the aspirational feature was deleted. A similar process is replicated with *twi* (뒤), whose historical form is *twih* (뒿).

---

15) For discussion on the correlation between particle omissibility and grammaticalization, see Choi-Jonin (2008).

A slightly different picture emerges with the case of *wi* (위) 'top'. The Middle Korean counterpart of *wi* /wi/ [wi] (위) was *wuh* /uh/ [ut] (운) by itself or /uh/ [uh] (우ㅎ) when followed by a vowel. Therefore, the reductive process occurred in the direction that the final consonant was dropped, and the remaining vowel was compensated by way of diphthongization. Despite the fact that this process is not grammaticalization-specific but of a more general process in Korean historical phonology, it is true that the stem forms under current consideration have undergone phonological reduction over time.

3.4.4 Grammatical Functions

3.4.4.1 Differential Specialization of Native Korean and Sino-Korean Postpositions

As we observed in Table 3.3, some of the complex postpositions have a Chinese origin, i.e., *cen* (전; 前 'front'), *hyang* (향; 向 'direction'), *cwung* (중; 中 'middle'), *thong* (통; 通 'pass'), *hwu* (후; 後 'back'), *oy* (외; 外 'outside'), *nay* (내; 內 'inside'), *ha* (하; 下 'bottom'), *kan* (간; 間 'gap'), *myen* (면; 面 'face'), *chukmyen* (측면; 側面 'side'), *wuchuk* (우측; 右側 'right side'), *cwachuk* (좌측; 左側 'left side'), *kyek* (격; 隔 'separation'), *yen* (연; 連 'link'), and *sang* (상; 上 'top'). It is notable that except for *cen* (전) 'front' and *hyang* (향) 'direction', none of them occur at a frequency higher than 100 pmw (see Table 3.4 above). Furthermore, most, if not all, of these have native Korean counterparts that form postpositions that occur at a frequency high enough to be included in the category of actively grammaticalizing postpositions. This means that the postpositions of the native Korean origin are relatively more productive. This relative primacy seems to be due to functional specialization between the two groups. The postpositions are shown by the relational noun (RN) in Table 3.8 with their spatial and non-spatial meanings. The functions in parentheses are those weakly represented and "T." denotes temporal meanings.

A general observation from the table is that the postpositions based on native Korean relational nouns all carry spatial meaning with some of them also carrying, though weakly, non-spatial meanings, whereas the postpositions based on Sino-Korean relational nouns all carry temporal or other non-spatial meanings with some of them carrying, though weakly, spatial meanings.

	Native Korean RN	Spatial meaning	Non-Spatial meaning	Sino-Korean RN	Spatial meaning	Non-Spatial meaning
INTERIOR	*an* *kawuntey* *sok*	'inside' 'in, among' 'inside'	('within'; T.)	*nay* (內) *cwung* (中)	'inside' 'between'	'within' (T.) 'during' (T.)
EXTERIOR	*pakk*	'outside'	'only'	*oy* (外)		'except'
ANTERIOR	*aph*	'before'		*cen* (前)	('before')	'before' (T.)
POSTERIOR	*twi*	'behind'	('after'; T.)	*hwu* (後)		'after' (T.)
SUPERIOR	*wi*	'on, above'		*sang* (上)	('on')	'based on'
INFERIOR	*alay* *mith*	'below' 'below'		*ha* (下)	('below')	'following'
LATERAL	*yeph* *kyeth* *olunccok* *palunccok* *oynccok*	'beside' 'beside' 'right to' 'right to' 'left to'		*chukmyen* (側面) *wuchuk* (右側) *cwachuk* (左側)	'beside' 'right to' 'left to'	'with respect to'

Table 3.8 Native and Sino-Korean relational nouns in postpositions and their postpositional functions

As we can see in Table 3.8, certain notions are encoded by more than one form (e.g., Interior, Inferior, and Lateral). In such cases, those multiple forms may often be interchangeable, but may also carry subtle differences. For instance, the notion of Inferior ('below, under, beneath') is expressed by two forms involving native Koreans, i.e., *alay* (아래) 'bottom' and *mith* (밑) 'bottom'. A subtle distinction between *-(uy) alayey* ((의) 아래에) and *-(uy) mithey* ((의) 밑에) is that, while both can designate spatially inferior regions, the latter can designate an area immediately contiguous to the referenced entity as English *beneath* does, e.g. *chayk-uy mithey* (책의 밑에) 'beneath the book', whereas the former typically cannot. The Sino-Korean counterpart *ha* (하; 下) 'below', however, is rarely used in spatial postpositions (3 pmw). Instead, it signals more abstract concept as in *cencey-haey* (전제 하에) 'under the premises of', *myenglyeng-haey* (명령 하에) 'under the order of', etc. This pattern of the association of native Korean with spatial postpositions on the one hand and that of Sino-Korean with non-spatial postpositions is a general pattern as shown in part in (29) through (31) (NK denotes native Korean and SK denotes Sino-Korean):

(29) Anterior 'front': NK *aph* vs. SK *cen*

    a.   NK   집(의) 앞에

                cip-(uy) **_aph_**-*ey*   'in front of the house'

    b.   NK   한 시간(의) 앞에

                */? *han.sikan-(uy)* **_aph_**-*ey*   'one hour ago/before' (intended)

    c.   SK   집 전에

                cip-_cen_**-*ey*   'in front of the house' (intended)

    d.   SK   한 시간 전에

                *han.sikan-***_cen_**-*ey*   'one hour ago/before'

(30) Superior 'top': NK *wi* vs. SK *sang*

    a.   NK   다리(의) 위에

                tali-(uy) **_wi_**-*ey*   'on the bridge'

    b.   NK   계약(의) 위에

                kyeyyak-(uy)* **_wi_-*ey*   'according to the contract' (intended)

    c.   SK   다리 상에

                tali-*_sang_**-*ey*   'on the bridge' (intended)

    d.   SK   계약 상에

                *kyeyyak-***_sang_**-*ey*   'according to the contract'

(31) Inferior 'bottom': NK *alay* vs. SK *ha*

    a.   NK   지붕(의) 아래(에)

                cipwung-(uy) **_alay_**(-*ey*)   'under the roof'

    b.   NK   동의 아래(에)

                tonguy-*_alay_**(-*ey*)   'under a consent' (intended)

c. SK   지붕 하에

    *cipwung-**ha**-ey*   'under the roof' (intended)

d. SK   동의 하에

    *tonguy-**ha**-ey*   'under a consent'

In order to understand the lexical semi-diglossic situation more clearly, a brief mention on Chinese influence in Korean is in order. Chinese heavily influenced Korean vocabulary from its supposed introduction in the second century B.C.E. Identifiably Korean texts written in Chinese characters date back to the 5th century C.E. (Nam 2012, Whitman 2015, Narrog et al. 2018, among others). It is supposed that about 60% of the vocabulary is of Chinese origin (Sohn 1999: 13), and in the authoritative dictionary *Phyocwun Kwuke Taysacen* (1992) by the National Institute of the Korean Language, 57.3% of its headwords are of Chinese origin (W Lee 2002).[16] According to quantitative studies, however, a considerably lower percentage of Sino-Korean words are used in daily life. For instance, H Kim (2005) shows that only 19% of the 100 top-frequency words is Sino-Korean words.

It is generally (and correctly) assumed that the roots of grammaticalization are found in conversation, in the interaction of speaker and hearer. For example, in Traugott's model of grammaticalization, pragmatic inferences trigger the process of grammaticalization (cf. Hopper and Traugott 2003[1993]: 81-85). From this perspective, borrowed lexemes are less likely to grammaticalize into grammatical markers since they are often associated with specific genres and styles and consequently have a low frequency of use. This is particularly true with Sino-Korean words because the use of Sino-Korean words tends to belong to the high register, such as philosophical, religious, legal, and scientific texts by the literati class. In Korean, however, we find cases where grammaticalization came through written language, especially through translation, i.e., written language contact. For instance,

---

[16] S Rhee (2006a, 2007c, 2011) hypothesizes that in Korean lexicon the Sino-Korean words account for 55~70%, 80% and 70%, respectively. The hypothetical figures are proven false from statistical research. Hence, the author stands corrected and declares that the earlier statements were incorrect.

Narrog et al. (2018) report the cases of Sino-Korean adverbials carrying grammatical functions, numeral classifiers, mermaid constructions (see J Kim 2013, 2020), and deverbal postpositions as instances of grammaticalization through written language.

A relevant issue in this context is the direction and degree of semantic change. In their seminal work, Heine et al. (1991a: 55) proposed a direction of metaphorization along the ontological continuum as follows:

(32) PERSON 〉 OBJECT 〉 PROCESS 〉 SPACE 〉 TIME 〉 QUALITY

The above continuum shows the direction of metaphorical transfer, i.e., unidirectionally from left to right. This directionality is presumed to have crosslinguistic validity. The directionality can be interpreted that if a grammatical form carries the spatial meaning while another carries the temporal meaning, the latter can be reasonably assumed to have undergone a greater level of grammaticalization processes. This general directionality is well illustrated with English preposition *before* and *in front of*. Historically, *before* had the source construction of something like 'by the fore of', where *fore* meant 'front' (S Rhee 2007b). When this construction underwent a univerbation process with grammaticalization, its meaning became more abstract. As a result, a new periphrastic form *in front of* came into existence to designate physical spatial location. Coexistence of these two forms show that the older gram has the function of marking the more abstract concept, whereas the newer gram has the function of marking the less abstract concept. In a similar line of reasoning, since borrowings are supposedly of a relatively shorter history as compared with the native words, it is natural to suppose that the native Korean relational nouns have longer grammaticalization history and that the native Korean relational nouns would exhibit higher level of abstraction.

It is interesting, however, that the general semantic distinction between the native Korean and Sino-Korean postpositional systems, as shown above, is such that the native Korean system predominantly specializes in spatial concepts whereas the Sino-Korean system largely specializes in temporal concepts, an interesting grammaticalization scenario, described in detail in S Rhee (2005a, 2006b, 2011). This is an anomaly, because, as discussed above, we can reasonably suppose that the native Korean terms should have a longer history of grammaticalization as compared to the borrowed terms from Chinese. In other words, the situation is that the grams having older grammaticalization history are signaling the less developed (i.e., more concrete) semantic notions while the grams having shorter grammaticalization history are signaling the more developed (i.e., more abstract) semantic notions. This situation suggests that the degree of grammaticalization is not in tandem with the temporal length of grammaticalization processes, i.e., each gram may have a different speed of grammaticalization.

This apparent anomaly cannot be easily explained away. Such situations have not been addressed in the grammaticalization literature in other languages, and thus there are no empirically reliable sources of explanation through analogy. However, according to S Rhee (2011), what this situation suggests is that when a new competing system is imported for a certain grammatical paradigm, the extant system may not have to be pushed up to encode more abstract grammatical notions (cf. a 'push-chain' change). Instead, the extant system may specialize in its robust function, giving a new domain to the new system, regardless of the relative degree of the abstraction the semantics of the new domain may have. In other words, there may be no strict rule of division of labor in terms of the level of abstraction, when linguistic forms come into competition and the competitors choose their functions for their specialization.

One potentially relevant point here is that Sino-Korean system exhibits a big difference from the native Korean system. As compared with the postpositions developing from native Korean relational nouns, where the formal variations occur between the full forms and those without the possessive -uy (의), the postpositions developing from Sino-Korean relational nouns have a very strong tendency for use without the possessive -uy (의), thus resembling compounding (see 3.4.3.4 above). That the cognitive mechanisms involved in compounding may be operative in this process is supported by the facts that these Sino-Korean forms prefer the occurrence with Sino-Korean nominals, and that these forms tend to be written without a space in between. Considering that the core elements of the Sino-Korean postpositions are categorically nouns; that Korean compounding exhibits strong preference for native-native or borrowed-borrowed combinations except for rare exceptional cases; and that borrowed-borrowed combinations (typically combination of two or more Sino-Korean words) are normally written without spaces, the use of Sino-Korean postpositions seems to be, or have been, strongly influenced by nominal compounding.

3.4.4.2 Functional Extension of Spatial Postpositions

Korean spatial postpositions exhibit interesting patterns of functional extension. The first one of them is the extension from the Allative to Ablative. For instance, the postposition *-hanthey* (한테), developed from *han tey* (한 데) 'one place' is a directionality marker. Even though the source structure, i.e., 'one place', is absent of any directionality meaning, the Allative meanings seem to have emerged from the pragmatic inference prompted by the context in which it occurred.

(33) 쥐쇠기가 어미흔테 와셔 말흐되

| *cwisAykki-ka* | *emi-hAnthey* | *w-asye* | *malhA-toy* |
| mouse-NOM | mother-to/one.place | come-SEQ | talk-as |

'A mouse comes to its mother and says that...'

(1896 *Sinceng Simsangsohak* 1: L17)

In example (33), the phrases "a mouse comes" and "mother's one/same place" strongly invite the reinterpretation of 'one place' as the end-point of the locomotion, largely due to the presence of the verb 'come', thus, ultimately as a marker of Allative 'to'. Furthermore, the self-same form comes to be used in new contexts as in the following (taken from S Rhee 2010: 584):

(34) a. 아릿 사람흔테 뢰물 바다 먹는 것

| *alAy-s* | *salam-hAnthey* | *loymwul* | *pat-amek-nun* | *kes* |
| below-GEN | person-ABL | bribery | receive-CNTP-ADN | thing |

'receiving bribes from their inferiors' (1923, *Twukyenseng*)

b. 학교에 단일 격에 누구흔테 드르닛가

*hakkyo-ey   tani-l   cyek-ey   nwukwu-**hAnthey*** *tul-uniska*

school-LOC   attend-ADN   time-LOC   someone-**ABL**   hear-as

'As I heard from someone when I was attending the school / what I heard … was'

(1923, Twukyenseng)

c. 총각놈흔데 속아 그 남편을 일어 버리고

*chongkak-nom-**hAntey*** *sok-a* ⋯   *namphyen-ul*   *il-epeli-ko*

bachelor-PEJ-**ABL**   be.deceived-NF   husband-ACC   lose-PERF-and

'(She) was deceived by the wretched bachelor and lost (her) husband, and…'

(1913, Masanglwu)

In (34) above, *hanthey* (한테) in its historical variant forms, functions as a marker of 'the source of transfer' (in (34a)), 'the source of action/stimulus' (in (34b)), and 'the source of force or agency' (in (34c)), all subsumable under the Ablative (see below for more). The emergence of these meanings can also be attributed to pragmatic inferences prompted by the context. In contemporary Korean, even though *hanthey* (한테) is primarily a Dative marker it is also often used as an Ablative, as exemplified by a constructed example:

(35) 너한테 좀 전에 친구한테 전화 왔어.

*ne-hanthey   com   cen-ey   chinkwu-**hanthey*** *cenhwa   w-ass-e*

you-DAT   a.little   before-at   friend-**ABL**   phone   come-PST-END

'There was a phone call for you from your friend moments ago (lit. A phone call from your friend came to you moments ago.)'

Another interesting pattern of functional extension involves Ablative developing into the agency markers, and further into the Nominative case markers. As exemplified in (35) above, Ablative *-hanthey* (한테) developed into markers of sources of different kinds.

In a similar vein, our focus now is on Ablatives *-eyse* (에서) and *-kkeyse* (께서), whose semantic characterization is given in (36):

(36) *-eyse*   ABL   [–Animate]

    -kkeyse   ABL   [+Human] [+Honorific]

Ablative *-eyse* (에서) is often used as an agency marker and Ablative *-kkeyse* (께서) is primarily a marker of Nominative case. The development of nominative from *-kkeyse* (께서) has to do with the crosslinguistic conceptual chain of [Ablative-Status-Instrument-Source-Comitative] (cf. Nichols and Timberlake 1991, S Rhee 1996). Largely due to the conceptual relatedness, Ablatives *-eyse* (에서) and *-kkeyse* (께서) have developed into Nominatives, as exemplified by constructed examples in (37):

(37) a. *-eyse*

경찰에서 그사람을 잡아갔다.

*kyengchal-**eyse***   *kusalam-ul*   *capaka-ss-ta*

police-**NOM**   he-ACC   apprehend-PST-DEC

'The police apprehended him / He was apprehended by the police.'

    b. *-kkeyse*

아버지께서 부르신다.

*apeci-**kkeyse***   *pwulu-si-n-ta*

father-**NOM**   call-HON-PRES-DEC

'Father is calling (you/me).'

Nominative is closely related to the designation of an agent in cases where the predicate requires an agentive argument. Thus, *-kkeyse* (께서) has been fully developed into the marker of Nominative case, whereas *-eyse* (에서) is a peripheral Nominative in contemporary Korean.

3.5 Summary

This chapter addressed grammaticalization of Korean postpositions. Korean has a large number of postpositional particles carrying the function of marking grammatical case, or information structuring and/or scalarity. These particles, heterogeneous in function and formal makeup, are grouped into primary, composite, and complex postpositions, depending on the composition of the postpositions. This chapter addressed a total of 204 postpositions in Modern Korean (24 primary, 15 composite, and 165 complex postpositions). Of these 137 postpositions mark spatial relationship.

The strength of individual postpositions as grammatical markers is widely variable, as reflected in their token frequency, ranging from as high as 17,164 pmw (of Accusative -(l)ul (을/를)) to no attestations at all in the referenced corpus. The spatial postpositions develop predominantly from nominal sources, mostly relational nouns of native Korean and Sino-Korean origins, and a relatively smaller number of them develop from verbal sources. We also noted that there are postpositions that develop from the distal demonstrative, which functions as an iconic representation of distance to encode negative politeness. In terms of form-function mapping, there are multiple forms marking an identical or nearly identical grammatical concept, especially in the categories of Allative, Ablative, etc., where forms have differential specialization.

In order to restrict our focus on the spatial postpositions that are in the process of active grammaticalization, we chose 42 spatial postpositions, based on shape and functional strength. When these actively grammaticalizing postpositions are compared with their functional competitors, some more successful and some less successful, the two common determinants of viability are formal shape (simplicity preferred) are semantics (generality preferred). Also important for Korean postpositions is the source characteristics, i.e., whether the lexeme involved is of native or Chinese origin, because the latter tends to belong to the high register and is used at a lower frequency, thus resulting in lesser degree of grammaticalization.

The grammaticalizing postpositions were examined with respect to the grammaticalization mechanisms, i.e., extension, desemanticization, decategorialization, and erosion. Grammaticalization scenarios of Korean postpositions show extension of use context, which is closely tied to desemanticization, i.e., generalization of meaning. However, we observed that the grammaticalizing postpositions, as compared to the more established, higher-frequency spatial postpositions, are still relatively transparent with respect to their source constructions, mainly due to the presence of relational nouns in most of them. Grammaticalization of postpositions also shows signs of decategorialization when they are tested with modifier insertion. They show, though at variable degrees, resistance to interpolation of nominal or verbal modifiers. If such interpolation is allowed, the meaning of the sentence changes and the postpositions function not as postpositions but as syntactic constructions. Erosion is also prominent with the grammaticalizing postpositions to a variable extent. Noun-based postpositions show a high level of Genitive *-uy* (의) deletion, but most of them tend to retain the Locative *-ey* (에). Our analysis suggests that the Locative particle deletion may be influenced by the syllable structure of the preceding relational noun.

Grammaticalizing postpositions show a marked contrast with their Sino-Korean counterparts in terms of frequency. The postpositions of the native Korean origin tend to mark spatial (i.e., more concrete) notions, whereas the postpositions of the Sino-Korean origin tend to mark temporal or other more abstract notions. The puzzle is that putatively older grams (i.e., native Korean postpositions) show a lesser extent of semantic change, whereas putatively newer grams (i.e., Sino-Korean postpositions) show a greater extent of semantic change, along the metaphorical continuum of ontological categories, proposed by Heine et al. (1991a,b). We suggested that when new competition arises, the existing forms already with well-established functions may cling to the existing functions, whereas the incoming competitors may specialize in other, potentially more abstract, less frequent functions. This division of labor may have been also influenced by the text characteristics of the sources of Sino-Korean lexemes, i.e., elaborate, highly codified, religious, philosophical, scientific texts. Also, Sino-Korean postpositions are invariably used without the Locative *-ey* (에), in contrast with the variable native Korean postpositions. We suggested the possibility of Chinese influence of nominal compounding.

Postpositions typically show functional extension, mostly from spatial meaning to temporal meaning, a common direction widely attested across languages. In addition to such changes, there are instances in which forms denoting location, neutral with respect to directionality of motion, acquired the directionality meaning, e.g., Allative, Ablative, etc., through pragmatic enrichment prompted by the context. We also noted that some Ablatives developed into full-fledged Nominative markers or agency markers, largely due to the association of 'source' or 'departure' of Ablative with 'source of agency' or 'source of force' of Nominative.

Grammaticalization of Postpositions in Japanese

4.1 Introduction

Japanese, sharing many structural and grammatical features with Korean, has a number of commonalities in its postpositional system with the Korean system. It also shares some important properties with the adpositional systems in other languages. This chapter describes the paradigm of Japanese postpositions in contemporary Japanese from a grammaticalization perspective, focusing on the spatial postpositions that are actively undergoing grammaticalization. Further, it will discuss some noteworthy aspects of grammaticalization scenarios from typological and comparative linguistic perspectives.

4.2 Postpositions in Japanese

Japanese has an inventory of well-developed particles that carry diverse grammatical and semantic functions. As is the case with Korean, discussed in Chapter 3, there is no agreement as to the exact number of such particles among linguists who have different criteria for the status of individual items and for the definition of the category '(postpositional) particle'. In Japanese school grammar, the postpositional particles are under the category of *joshi* (助詞) 'auxiliary word', a class to which a number of verbal inflectional endings belong as well. In the Japanese linguistic literature, the class of postpositional particles is referred to as 'postpositions' or 'particles'. These are dependent morphemes with a variety of functions following their host to which they are relatively loosely bound. While the choice of the label may be debatable, we will refer to them as postpositions or, occasionally, postpositional particles.

In the spirit of nomenclature for Korean, Japanese postpositions can be also regarded as comprising primary, composite, and complex prepositions, based on their formal shapes and characteristics. Primary forms are short in form and synchronically opaque with respect to their source composition, thus are felt to be monomorphemic, even though they have be historically polymorphemic. Composite postpositions are also relatively short in form, but their source constructions are relatively transparent, and thus are perceived to be polymorphemic, i.e., compositional. Complex postpositions, on the other hand, are visibly polymorphemic and polylexemic, often indistinguishable from syntactic constructions. Unlike complex postpositions in Korean that involves interlexical spacing by virtue of having more than one word, Japanese complex postpositions are not written with spacing, since interlexical spacing is not practiced in Japanese orthography. Complex postpositions tend to have three or more morphemes in the construction (see Group A in Table 4.3 below) but may have only two morphemes that may be affixed by another primary postposition at the end (see Group B in Table 4.3 below). All complex postpositions, however, contain a primary postposition as its first component in the constructions in the forms of [P-V-Suffix] for verb-based forms or of [P-N-(P)] for noun-based forms.

Notwithstanding categorial fluidity, there are 33 primary postpositions in contemporary Japanese, as shown in Table 4.1, selectively taken from Chino (1991), Katsuki-Pestemer (2003), Narrog and Rhee (2013), Narrog et al. (2018), and elsewhere.

		Form		Function
Case Markers (n=9)	a.	*-ga*	が	NOM
	b.	*-no*	の	GEN 'of'
	c.	*-o (wo)*	を	ACC
	d.	*-e (pye)*	へ	ALL 'to'
	e.	*-ni*	に	DAT/LOC 'to, in'
	f.	*-de*	で	ESS/LOC 'in, on'
	g.	*-kara*	から	ABL 'from'
	h.	*-yori (/yuri/yo/yu)*	より	ABL 'from'
	i.	*-to*	と	COM/QUOT 'and, with, known as'
Information-Structuring/ Scalar Markers (n=24)	j.	*-wa*	は	TOP 'as for'
	k.	*-mo*	も	FOC/ADD 'also'
	l.	*-bakari*	ばかり	FOC/EXTT 'only, just'
	m.	*-dake*	だけ	FOC/EXTT 'only, just'
	n.	*-nomi (nomwi)*	のみ	FOC/EXTT 'only'
	o.	*-hodo*	ほど (程)	FOC/EXTT (large) 'about, as much as'
	p.	*-kurai/gurai*	くらい・ぐらい (位)	FOC/EXTT (small) 'about, approximately'
	q.	*-sika*	しか	FOC/EXTT 'only' (NPI)
	r.	*-sae (sape)*	さえ	FOC/EXTR 'even'
	s.	*-sura*	すら	FOC/EXTR 'even'
	t.	*-dani*	だに	FOC/EXTR 'even'
	u.	*-datte*	だって	FOC/EXTR 'even'
	v.	*-demo*	でも	FOC/EXTR 'even'
	w.	*-koso*	こそ	FOC/CNTR 'precisely'
	x.	*-made*	まで (迄)	LMT 'until, up to, to'
	y.	*-nado*	など	ENUM 'such as, etc.'
	z.	*-toka*	とか	ENUM 'and, such as'
	aa.	*-nari*	なり	ENUM 'or, or something'
	ab.	*-yara*	やら	ENUM 'such as'
	ac.	*-dano*	だの	ENUM 'such as'
	ad.	*-ya*	や	CONJ (non-inclusive) 'or'
	ae.	*-ka*	か	DISJ 'or'
	af.	*-tte*	って	QUOT 'as, as saying'
	ag.	*-zutu*	ずつ	DIST 'each'

Table 4.1 Primary postpositions in Modern Japanese

Despite the difficulties in distinguishing a particle and a noun, 9 postpositions are recognized as case particles in earlier research, e.g., Rickmeyer (1995: 285-316, as cited in Narrog and Rhee 2013: 289). These 9 postpositions are listed from (a) through (i) in Table 4.1, which signal the argument's syntactic role with reference to the state or event denoted by the verb. The 24 postpositions from (j) through (ag) carry a wide range of functions including marking diverse cases, modality, scalarity, etc. As Narrog and Rhee (2013: 288-289) note, they merely constitute a morphological class but not a semantic or functional class.[1]

It is to be noted that some primary postpositions, even though they are not clearly analyzable in contemporary Japanese, may be perceived as having more than one morpheme, for historical reasons or for their appearance. For instance, -demo (でも) 'even' can be phonetically decomposed as -de (で) and -mo (も), each of which is a full-fledged postposition, meaning 'in, on' and 'also', respectively. Since the Focus function with the Extreme example (i.e., 'even') can be conceptually derived from 'in x also', such an analysis is well-motivated.[2]

Many of these postpositions are polyfunctional in that they carry different functions depending on the syntactic and pragmatic contexts. For instance, the genitive -no (の), the most frequent postposition, has a number of different functions, e.g., marking possession, position, category, apposition, authorship, etc. as a postposition, and a nominalizer as a verbal morphology, or even as a sentence-final particle to indicate a question, a mild command, or to 'impart a softer tone to a statement' (Chino 1991: 68-71, see also Horie 1998). Among the information structuring postpositions, -wa (-は), also of a high frequency in the group, is also a noteworthy marker in that its function is often similar to that of a subject marker (a situation similar to Korean), since Japanese (as well as Korean) is a topic-prominent language (Li and Thompson 1976). It also functions as a contrast or emphasis marker (a feature also shared by Korean). The topic marking function is, in fact, carried by a

---

[1] For heterogeneity of the semantics and functions of these markers, Narrog and Rhee (2013) label them as 'particles'. We use 'postpositions' simply to indicate that they are nomimal morphologies placed at the post-nominal position.

[2] Informants, however, take different positions with regard to the issue analyzability of *demo*.

number of markers, as exemplified by Katsuki-Pestemer (2003: 82), e.g., *-wa* (-は), *-nado* (-など), *-nanka* (-なんか), *-nante* (-なんて), *-nanzo* (-なんぞ), *-nazo* (-なぞ), *-tara/ttara* (-たら/ったら), and *-tte* (-って), among which *-wa* (-は) is neutral while all others have additional modality functions such as arrogance, surprise, contempt, scorn, intimacy, etc. Note that some of these are not primary but composite postpositions.

It is also notable in the list that Japanese has many exclusive Extent Focus markers (i.e., 'only'). It is to be noted, however, that *sika* (しか) is a negative polarity item (NPI), and thus not interchangeable with other focus markers. Interchangeability without noticeable semantic change is illustrated in (1), in which *-bakari* (ばかり), *-kurai* (くらい), and *hodo* (ほど) are involved (note that Japanese does not practice inter-lexical spacing, but Japanese data is given with spacing for visual clarity).[3]

(1) 明日から　2日{ばかり, くらい, ほど} 旅行に 行ってきます
    ashita-kara　　　*futsuka-{__bakari, kurai, hodo__}* *ryokō-ni i-tte-ki-masu*
    tomorrow-from　2.days-{**FOC/EXTT**}　　　　　trip-to　go-and-come-END
    'Tomorrow I'll be leaving on a trip for a couple of days.'

    (adapted from Chino 1991: 79)

However, even seemingly synonymous postpositions carry different, delicate shades of meaning. The meaning is often not truth-conditional but pragmatic and affective, as shown in (2), adapted from Chino 1991: 79):

(2) a. 課長は この頃 ウイスキーばかり 飲んでいます ね
       kachō-wa　　　*konogoro uisukī-__bakari__*　　　*non-dei-masu　ne*
       section.chief-TOP　these.days　whiskey-**nothing.but**　drink-PROG-END PART
       'The section chief is drinking nothing but whiskey these days.'

---

[3] Reijirou Shibasaki (p.c.) comments that *dake* and *nomi* are interchangeable with *bakari* in (1) with implied meaning of 'mere', but there are slight differences in naturalness.

b. 課長は この頃 ウイスキーだけ 飲んでいます ね

kachō-wa　　　　*konogoro uisukī-**dake***　　　*non-dei-masu*　　*ne*
section.chief-TOP these.days whiskey-**nothing.but** drink-PROG-END PART
'The section chief is drinking nothing but whiskey these days.'

In (2) *bakari* (ばかり) and *dake* (だけ) both designate exclusive Focus of Extent to mean 'only, just, nothing but', and thus no propositional differences. However, according to Chino (1991: 79), *bakari* (ばかり) carries "a degree of disapproval which *dake* (だけ) does not."

It is also noteworthy that there are multiple Focus markers to indicate Extreme example 'even' often with the mirative overtone or counterexpectation, and Enumerative markers for listing or exemplification (i.e., 'and', 'or', 'such as'). Multiplicity of form in a particular function, however, does not mean complete interchangeability, because they carry different connotations in addition or may have specialization in specific genres or registers.

As is the case with adpositions in other languages, postpositions in Japanese vary widely in their individual frequency of use in contemporary Japanese. The frequency information from Corpus of Spontaneous Japanese (CSJ), a 7.52 million word corpus consisting of the data from 661 hours of spontaneous speech, by the National Institute for Japanese Language and Linguistics shows the frequency ranking of the primary postpositions as in Table 4.2.[4]

---

[4] The figures are based on the random sampling, intended to determine the proportion of postpositional use in the total hits. Sampling and quantification, however, were for selecting postpositions from the total hits only and thus multiple functions of individual postpositions are not differentiated. Since this is a macroscopic study, more microscopic analyses on individual functions should await future research. Special thanks go to Soohyun Pae for her assistance for statistical analyses.

Frequency Range	Postposition		Meaning	PMW
High (1,000~ pmw) (n=14)	*no*	の	'of'	48,043
	ga	が	NOM	25,524
	ni	に	'to, at, in'	22,036
	to	と	'and, with, known as'	21,491
	o (wo)	を	ACC	21,309
	wa	は	TOP 'as for'	20,494
	de	で	'in, on'	12,248
	kara	から	'from, because of'	6,428
	mo	も	'also'	4,142
	tte	って	QUOT 'as, as saying'	3,408
	toka	とか	'and, such as'	2,491
	ka	か	'or'	1,958
	demo	でも	'even, even if, whatever'	1,468
	made	まで (迄)	'until, up to, to'	1,184
Medium (100~999 pmw) (n=9)	*dake*	だけ	'only, just'	955
	ya	や	'or'	774
	kurai/gurai	くらい・ぐらい (位)	'about, approximately'	738
	nado	など	'such as, etc.'	657
	yori	より	'from, than'	576
	e	へ	'to'	474
	sika	しか	'only' NPI	280
	hodo	ほど (程)	'about, as much as'	147
	nomi	のみ	'only'	133
Low (10~99 pmw) (n=9)	*bakari*	ばかり	'only, just'	94
	zutu	ずつ	'each'	86
	koso	こそ	'nothing but, exactly'	58
	datte	だって	'even, even if, whatever'	54
	nari	なり	'or, or something'	39
	sae	さえ	'even'	36

	sura	すら	'even'	12
	dano	だの	'such as'	11
	yara	やら	'such as'	11
Very Low (~9 pmw) (n=1)	*dani*	だに	'even'	1

Table 4.2 Frequency of Japanese primary postpositions

What is immediately noticeable in the frequency information is that case-marking postpositions all belong to the High frequency range. It is also to be noted that the topic marker *-wa* (は) resembles *-ga* (が) in that, as indicated above, it often marks the sentential subject. Since Japanese uses postpositions for core syntactic relations such as subject and object unlike English, which uses the word order, the subject-marking Nominative (and its closely related Topic) and the object-marking Accusative occur at a high frequency in actual use.

Japanese composite prepositions are much smaller in number, i.e., only four, in contrast with other languages. They are listed in (3):

(3) a. *nante*   なんて (何) ENUM 'such as'
     b. *nanka*   なんか (何) ENUM 'such as'
     c. *gotoni*   ごとに   DIST 'each, per'
     d. *dokoroka* どころか   EXTT 'far from'

The postpositions in (3) are not monomorphemic. For instance, *-nante* (なんて) and *-nanka* (なんか) involve the interrogative pronoun *nan* (なん); *-gotoni* (ごとに) is a combination of *goto* (ごと) 'every' and *-ni* (に) 'to, at'; and *-dokoroka* (どころか) consists of the noun *dokoro* (どころ (所)) 'place' and the particle *-ka* (か) 'or'.[5]

---

[5] Since the particle *-ka* (か) functions not only a marker of alternative 'or' but also 'whether' or quotation expressing doubt, its combination *-dokoroka* (どころか) seems to have emerged from the dismissive mention on a hypothetically raised place '(do you mean) the place? - (no!)' to the dismissive Extent marker 'far from (the place)'. If this reasoning correct, a similar strategy is found in

Incidentally, *dokoro* itself is an Extent marker, listed in Narrog and Rhee (2013: 289), but not productive as a postposition in contemporary Japanese.

As compared with composite postpositions, complex postpositions are much larger in number, i.e., 42 in total. These are relatively more transparent with respect to their source composition. They are listed in Table 4.3.

	Complex POST		Meaning	Lexical Source
Group A	*-ni atatte*	にあたって (当)	'in the course of'	*atar-* v. 'hit upon'
	-ni hansite	に反して	'against, contrary to'	*hans-* v. 'go against' (SJ *han* 'opposition')
	-ni itatte	に至って	'coming to, coming at'	*itar-* v. 'arrive'
	-ni kagirazu	に限らず	'not limited to'	*kagir-* v. 'limit'
	-ni kagitte	に限って	'limited to, only'	*kagir-* v. 'limit'
	-ni kakawarazu	に関わらず	'regardless of'	*kakawar-* v. 'relate to'
	-ni kansite	に関して	'concerning'	*kans-* v. 'be related' (SJ *kan* 'relation, gate')
	-ni motoduite	に基づいて	'based on'	*motoduk-* v. 'be based on'
	-ni mukatte	に向かって	'towards'	*mukaw-* v. 'face'
	-ni mukete	に向けて	'towards'	*muke-* v. 'turn towards'
	-ni oite	において (於)	'at, concerning'	*ok-* v. 'put'
	-ni saisite	に際して	'at the occasion of'	*sai* n. 'occasion' (SJ *sai* 'time, occasion')
	-ni sitagatte	にしたがって (従)	'following'	*sitagaw-* v. 'follow'
	-ni site	にして (為)	'only, just because, although, even, at'	*s-* v. 'do'
	-ni taisite	に対して	'towards, against, regarding'	*tais-* v. 'face' (SJ *tai* 'opposition')

the development of some Korean indefinite pronouns and adverbs (S Rhee 2004b).

	-ni tomonatte	にともなって	'in step with, accompanying'	*tomonaw-* v. 'accompany'
	-ni totte	にとって	'as for'	*tor-* 'take'
	-ni tuite	について	'about'	*tuk-* v. 'attach to'
	-ni tuki	につき	'concering'	*tuk-* v. 'attach to'
	-ni turete	につれて	'accompanying'	*ture-* v. 'accompany'
	-ni watatte	にわたって (渡/亙)	'extending over, across'	*watar-* v. 'range, extend over'
	-ni yotte	によって (由/因)	'because of, by (means of)'	*yor-* v. 'come near, depend on'
	-o megutte	をめぐって (巡/廻/回)	'about'	*megur-* v. 'circle around'
	-o motte	をもって (以)	'with'	*mot-* v. 'hold'
	-o toosite	を通して	'through'	*toos-* v. 'pass through' (SJ *too* 'going through')
	-o towazu	を問わず	'regardless of'	*tow-* v. 'question'
	-to site	として	'as'	*s-* v. 'do'
	-no yooni	のように (様)	'like, similar to, as with, in the same way'	*yoo* n. 'appearance, form'
	-no mae	の前	'prior to, before, in front of'	*ma-pe* n. 'location of eye' (SJ *zen*)
	-no ato	の後	'behind, after'	*a[si]-two* n. 'foot-?' (SJ *go*)
Group B	*-no usiro*	の後ろ	'behind, in back of'	*u[ra]-siri* n. 'back-buttocks'; or **mu-siro* n.n. 'body-buttocks'(?) (SJ *go*)
	-no saki	の先	'previous to'	(*saki* n. 'front')
	-no ue	の上	'above, up, over'	**u-pe* ?.n. 'location of ?' (SJ *zyoo*)
	-no sita	の下	'below, beneath, under'	cognate with pK **sta* n. 'ground' (SJ *ge/ka*)
	-no aida	の間	'between, among'	(*aida* n. 'interval') (SJ *kan*)

-no naka	の中	'in, inside of, among, within, during'	(*naka* n. 'inside, center') (SJ *tyuu*)
-no uti	の内 (うち)	'within, inside, among'	(*uti* n. 'inside') (SJ *nai*)
-no soto	の外	'outside (of), exterior to'	**so-t(u)-o(mo)* n. 'back side' (SJ *gai*)
-no yoko	の横	'next to, beside'	(*yoko* 'horizontal, side')
-no gawa	の側	'beside, on the side of'	**kapa* n. 'side, direction'
-no hidari	の左	'to the left of'	**pintari* n. 'where the sun arrives/goes down' (SJ *sa*)
-no migi	の右	'to the right of'	(*migi* n. 'right')

Table 4.3 Complex postpositions in Modern Japanese

As is evident in Table 4.3, most complex postpositions in Group A take the form of [primary preposition + verb + suffix], whereas all complex postpositions in Group B take the form of [primary preposition + noun].

The postpositions in Group A predominantly make use of the preposition marking the general location *-ni* 'to, at, in' and many verbs that are either based on Sino-Japanese words or related to them. When a Sino-Japanese base form is used, e.g., *-ni hansite* (に反して 〈 反 *han* 'opposition'), *-ni kansite* (に関して 〈 関 *kan* 'relation'), *-ni taisite* (に対して 〈 対 *tai* 'facing'), etc., the constructions also involve the light verb *s-* (す-) 'do', which inflects into *site* (して) to perform a conjunctive-like function, i.e., connective (cf. 'converb' Haspelmath 1995, Robbeets 2020). The postposition *-ni saisite* (に際して) 'at the occasion of' is indicated as involving the Sino-Japanese noun *sai* (際) 'occasion' following Narrog and Rhee (2013: 305), but, in fact, *saisite* may also be analyzed as involving the Sino-Japanese-based verb *sai-s-* (際 -す-) 'occasion-do' to mean 'arrive, come to pass, etc.' The Group A postpositions not following this pattern (i.e., not involving the light verb *s-* (す-) 'do') make use of native Japanese verbs. Also, those that do not involve the *-te*-form are those that involve negative inflection, thus ending in *-(a)zu* (ず), as in *-ni kagirazu* (に限らず) 'not limited to', -ni kakawarazu 'regardless of' (にかかわらず), and -o towazu (問わず) 'regardless of'.

The postpositions in Group B are slightly different. They involve the genitive primary postposition -no (の) 'of' as the first primary postposition in the source constructions, followed by a noun, i.e., [-no N]. The nouns in this slot are mostly relational nouns (or 'relator nouns') such as 'front', 'back', 'top', 'down', etc., the only exception being -no yooni (のように (様)) 'like, similar to'.[6] The construction is thus invariably [-no RN], whose semantics can be characterized as taking "a certain relationship as its background concept and defin[ing]... some entity which exists within this relationship in reference to another entity also within this relationship" (Tagashira 1999: 249, as cited in Narrog and Rhee 2013: 294). These structures may further be followed by another primary postposition such as -de 'in, on', e.g., -no mae-de (の 前で) 'at the front of'. Omission of the second primary postposition (e.g., -de in -no mae-de) is variable depending on the context and the semantics of the postposition itself. For instance, postpositions indicating general locations such as -ni (に) 'to, at, in' tend to be more easily omitted, whereas those with more specific information such as -kara (から) 'from', -made (まで) 'up to', etc. tend to resist such omission.

One of the most interesting aspects of these relational noun-based postpositions is that most of them have two words, different in form but nearly identical in meaning, one being of Sino-Japanese pronunciation, the other of native Japanese pronunciation, thus often written interchangeably, e.g., mae (前 n. 'front') in -no mae (の前) is the native Japanese word whose Sino-Japanese word written in the kanji script (Chinese character) is 前 (n. zen 'front'). These Sino-Japanese nouns constituting complex postpositions have been nativized to such an extent that they often diverge in writing from their nominal uses, i.e., they are more often written in the kana script when they are a part of postpositions, and they are written in the kanji script when they are used as full-fledged nouns. Incidentally, some of them only have

---

6) Relational nouns are often viewed as a step in grammaticalization between full lexemic nouns on the one hand and adpositions on the other hand (e.g. Heine et al. 1991a: 143; Blake 2004: 16; DeLancey 2004, 2011; Nichols 2004; Narrog and Rhee 2013).

the postpositional uses with native Japanese pronunciation, and their counterparts in non-postpositional uses have lost their Sino-Japanese pronunciations, e.g., *-no migi* (の右) 'to the right of' which has no nominal use with a Sino-Japanese pronunciation for 右 'right'.

4.3 Spatial Postpositions

4.3.1 Characteristics of Spatial Postpositions

Many, if not most, postpositions in Japanese encode diverse spatial relationships, as is the case with other languages we are addressing in this book. Table 4.4 shows the spatial postpositions across non-axial and axial domains (note that polyfunctional forms are counted only once).

AXIS		PRIMARY (n=7)	COMPOSITE (n=0)	COMPLEX (n=21)
NON-AXIAL	REGIONAL	*-de* *-ni*		*-ni site*
	DIRECTIONAL	*-e*		*-ni mukatte* *-ni mukete* *-ni taisite*
	SOURCE	*-kara* *-yori*		
	GOAL	*-made* *-ni*		
	PATH			*-ni watatte* *-o toosite* *-o totte*
	MEDIAL			*-no aida* *-no naka* *-no uti*
	ULTERIOR			*-ni watatte*
	ASSOCIATION	*-to*		*-ni tomonatte*
	ADJACENCY			*-no yoko* *-no gawa*
	CONTIGUITY			

	SEPARATION		
	OPPOSITE		*-ni taisite* *-ni watatte*
AXIAL	INTERIOR	*-de*	*-no naka* *-no uti*
	EXTERIOR		*-no soto*
	SUPERIOR		*-no ue*
	INFERIOR		*-no sita*
	ANTERIOR		*-no mae* *-no saki*
	POSTERIOR		*-no usiro*
	LATERAL		*-no yoko* *-no gawa* *-no hidari* *-no migi*

Table 4.4 Spatial postpositions in Modern Japanese

The distribution of spatial postpositions in Table 4.4 exhibits a number of notable aspects. First of all, the overall number is much smaller than in other languages being analyzed, i.e., only 28 in total (cf. 137 in Korean, 167 in Spanish, 214 in English, 50 in Chinese, and 91 in Thai). Furthermore, there is no composite postposition that denotes spatial location. This is partly due to the fact that the entire inventory of composite postpositions is significantly smaller than other categories, i.e., only 4.

There are no postpositions specializing in encoding contiguity ('next to', 'in touch with'), separation ('off', 'far from', 'apart from'), etc. even though there are other ways to express such concepts in the language.

The complex prepositions involving relational nouns, i.e., all Group B postpositions in Table 4.3, except for *-no yooni* (のように), encode spatiality (and other concepts in addition, such as temporality, reason, addition, abstract location, etc., in some cases). One exception is *-no ato* (の後) 'behind, after', i.e., the one specializing for temporal encoding, as noted in Narrog and Rhee (2013: 297).

Also notable is the fact that axial notions are almost entirely encoded by complex postpositions involving a relational noun. The only primary postposition denoting an axial notion is *de* (で) 'in', which also marks the general location, Essive and Locative.

4.3.2 Frequencies of Spatial Postpositions

As noted above, there is an inventory of 7 primary and 21 postpositions denoting spatial relationships, totaling 28. They show variability to a great extent in terms of their representational strengths, as reflected in their use frequency. Table 4.5 shows the frequency of the spatial postpositions in four different frequency ranges.

Frequency Range	Form		Function	PMW
High (1,000~ pmw) (n=5)	*-ni*	に	DAT/LOC 'to, at, in'	22,036
	-to	と	COM/QUOT 'with'	21,491
	-de	で	ESS/LOC 'in, on'	12,248
	-kara	から	ABL 'from'	6,428
	-made	まで（迄）	limitative 'until, up to'	1,184
Medium (100~999 pmw) (n=8)	*-no naka*	の中	in, inside of, among, within, during	924
	-yori (/yuri/yo/yu)	より	ABL 'from, than'	576
	-e (pye)	へ	ALL 'to'	474
	-ni site	にして	only, just because, although, even, at	285
	-ni taisite	に対して	towards, against, regarding, in contrast with	509
	-no aida	の間	between, among	183
	-no uti	の内（うち）	within, inside, among	126
	-no ue	の上	above, up, over	109
Low (10~99 pmw) (n=9)	*-no mae*	の前	prior to, before, in front of	83
	-no sita	の下	below, beneath, under	70
	-o toosite	を通して	through, throughout, by way of	44
	-no gawa	の側	beside, on the side of	31
	-ni mukatte	に向かって	towards	30
	-ni watatte	にわたって （渡/亘）	throughout, over a period of, over a span of	17
	-ni mukete	に向けて	towards, for the purpose of	16

	-no usiro	の後ろ	behind, in back of	11
	-no soto	の外	outside (of), exterior to	10
	-no saki	の先	previous to	9
	-ni tomonatte	にともなって (伴)	in step with	8
Very Low (~9 pmw) (n=6)	*-o totte*	を通って	through (physical)	8
	-no yoko	の横	next to, beside	7
	-no hidari	の左	to the left of	3
	-no migi	の右	to the right of	3

Table 4.5 Frequency of spatial postpositions in Modern Japanese

Some notable aspects are apparent in the frequency information in Table 4.5. First of all, there is a big frequency disparity among the five High frequency postpositions. DAT/LOC *-ni* 'to, at, in' and the COM *-to* 'with' are exceptionally high in frequency, and ESS/LOC *-de*, ABL *-kara*, LIM *-made*, though all belonging to the High frequency range, are not comparable to the first two. Considering that *-ni* and *-de* are often functionally synonymous to denote location, the general location-marking postpositions can be said to occur at a very high frequency.[7]

Secondly, the postpositions in the High frequency tier are all primary postpositions, a state of affairs expected from the general patterns of adpositional uses. Also of note are (a) complex postpositions involving relational nouns are generally of lower frequency, and (b) the top/front-related postpositions occur at a higher frequency than the bottom/back-related postpositions. The latter point is consonant with the observation that top and front are the areas suitable for optimal perception and thus are considered 'positive' directions (Andersen 1978: 343; Heine 1997; see other chapters for a similar state-of-affairs in other languages, and 10.1.2 for further discussion).

---

7) It is to be noted, however, that *-ni* (に) and *-de* (で) are not interchangeable in location-marking; *-ni* (に) is used with stative verbs (e.g., *aru* (ある) 'exist, have', *iru* (いる) 'exist, be', *sumu* (住む) 'live', etc.), whereas *-de* (で) is used with action verbs (e.g., *taberu* (食べる) 'eat', *neru* (寝る) 'sleep', *benkyosuru* (勉強する) 'study', etc.).

4.3.3. Grammaticalization Sources

The etymology of a number of Japanese postpositions has not yet been established, but the known cases involve nouns and verbs as their lexical sources. In addition to these two universally common sources, words of Chinese origin constitute an important source category, in which case the Sino-Japanese words involved are nouns, which may be extended to the verbal category by way of using the light verb *s-* (す-) or otherwise. There are also a number of postpositions, the etymologies of which have not yet been established. For convenience, we will address unidentified sources, nominal sources (that are not Sino-Japanese), verbal sources, and Sino-Japanese sources.

4.3.3.1 Unidentified Sources

There are a large number of postpositions, whose lexical origins have not been established. Some of them are listed in (4):

(4)

-ga	が	NOM/GEN	*-koso*	こそ	FOC.CNTR 'precisely'
-no	の	GEN 'of'	*-nado*	など	ENUM 'such as, etc.'
-o	を	ACC	*-nari*	なり	ENUM 'or, or something'
-ni	に	DAT/LOC 'to, at'			
-yori	より	ABL 'from'	*-ka*	か	DISJ 'or'
-wa	は	TOP 'as for'	*-toka*	とか	ENUM 'and, such as'
-mo	も	ADD.FOC 'also'	*-ya*	や	CONJ 'or'
-sika	しか	'only' NPI	*-yara*	やら	ENUM 'such as'
-sae	さえ	FOC.EXTR 'even'	*-dano*	だの	ENUM 'such as'
-sura	すら	FOC.EXTR 'even'	*-tte*	って	QUOT 'as, as saying'
-dani	だに	FOC.EXTR 'even'	*-zutu*	ずつ	DIST 'each, per'
-datte	だって	FOC.EXTR 'even'	*-gotoni*	ごとに	DIST 'each, per'
-demo	でも	FOC.EXTR 'even'			

(5) *-no aida* の間   'between, among' | *-no uti*   の内   'inside, among'
     -no naka の中   'in, among, | *-no yoko* の横   'next to, beside'
                        within' | *-no migi* の右   'to the right of'
     -no saki の先   'previous to'

As is evident from (4) and (5), a large proportion of the primary postpositions is etymologically unidentified. Narrog and Rhee (2013) note that etymological speculations exist for practically every item, but most of them lack consensus among Japanese historical linguists. This suggests that primary postpositions are old grams, whose origins go back to pre-historic times. On the other hand, most composite and complex postpositions have identified lexical sources, which suggests that they are relatively more recent. The complex postpositions in (5) involve nominals whose origins have not yet been identified, unlike those shown in (10) below. Even though the ultimate origins of these nominals are yet unknown, their contemporary nominal meanings denoting relationships between entities, as indicated by the *kanji* script, e.g., 間 'interval', 中 'center', etc., provide clues to their sources.[8] In this respect, Narrog and Rhee (2013: 297) state that Sino-Japanese morphemes are also used for the native Japanese morphemes in writing, which indicates close semantic correspondence. In other words, in order to indicate a medial relationship 'in the middle of', they say *-no aida* (のあいだ; native Japanese) but write *-no kan* (の間; Sino-Japanese).

4.3.3.2 Nominal Sources

There are postpositions that developed from native Japanese nouns. The prominent group comprises of relational nouns, but there are also nominal source lexemes that are not relational nouns. The relational nouns are shown in (5) and the non-relational nouns are listed in (6), mostly taken from Narrog and Rhee (2013: 296) (see also Hino 2000 for grammaticalization of nouns ('pseudonouns') in Japanese):

---

[8] Narrog and Rhee (2013: 296) also present the following as possible source of *yoko*: K *(c)cok* 'row, side' ⟨ pK **cwok* 'side' or **nyekh* 'side' (cf. Robbeets 2005: 321, 404).

(5)   *-no mae*   の前   'prior to, in front of' ⟨ *ma-pe* n. 'location of eye'

    -no ato   の後   'behind, after'   ⟨ **a[si]-two* n.n. 'foot-?'

    -no usiro   の後ろ   'behind, in back of' ⟨ **u[ra]-siri* n.n. 'back-buttocks'(?); or
                                           *mu-siro n.n. 'body-buttocks'(?)

    -no ue   の上   'above, up, over'   ⟨ **u-pe* ?.n. 'location of?'[9]

    -no sita   の下   'below, beneath'   ⟨ cognate with pK **sta-* ⟨ **s(i)ta-* 'ground'?
                                           (Robbeets 2005: 403)

    -no soto   の外   'outside, exterior to' ⟨ pJ **so-t(u)-o(mo)*n. 'back side' (?)

    -no gawa   の側   'beside'   ⟨ pJ **kapa* n. 'side, direction'; cf. pK **kapo-*
                                        'be near' (Robbeets 2005: 403)

    -no hidari   の左   'to the left of'   ⟨ **pintari* ⟨ **pi-n-tari* 'where the sun
                                          arrives/goes down'

(6)   *-e*   ALL 'to'   ⟨ *pye* n. 'place, vicinity'

    -kara   ABL 'from'   ⟨ *kara* n. 'nature/essence'[10]

    -bakari   FOC 'only, just'   ⟨ *hakari* vn. 'measure'

    -dake   FOC 'only'   ⟨ *take* n. 'length, measure'

    -nomi   FOC 'only'   ⟨ *no-mwi* p.n. 'of-body (?)'

    -kurai   EXTT (small) 'about'   ⟨ *kurawi* n. 'rank' ⟨ *kura-wi* n.v. 'platform-sit'

    -made   LMT 'until, up to'   ⟨ *made* n. 'both hands (?)'

    -tokoroka EXTT 'far from'   ⟨ *tokoro* n. 'place'

    -hodo   EXTT (large) 'about'   ⟨ *potwo* n. 'interval'

The relational nouns in (5) make reference to human body parts or involve the terms designating locations, even though some of the sources are still uncertain. The conceptual connection between the source lexical meaning and the target postpositional meaning is well-motivated. The forms listed in (6) involve more heterogeneous nouns with respect to lexical meaning, and the conceptual connection between the source meaning and the grammatical meaning is, in general, less straightforward.

---

9) Narrog and Rhee (2013: 296) also present the following as possible sources of *ue*: **upa*, cognate with pK **wuhu*, pTg **ug-*, etc. (cf. Robbeets 2005: 324); or with K **ugi* ⟩ *ui* ⟩ *ui* (Y Cho 2004); or with K **üge* ⟩ *uhe/ühe* ⟩ *uh/ü* (K Kang 2010), all meaning 'top'.

10) Frellisvig (2005: 9) hypothesizes that the etymology of *-kara* is the noun *kara* 'will, way, extent'.

4.3.3.3 Verbal Sources

One noteworthy aspect of Japanese postpositions is that there are a number of complex postpositions that originate from verbal sources (Y Matsumoto 1998, Honda 1998). Incidentally, there are no primary or composite postpositions that are known to have developed from verbal sources.

(7) -ni atatte 'in the course of'   ⟨ atar- v. 'hit upon'
     -ni itatte 'coming to/at'   ⟨ itar- v. 'arrive'
     -ni kagirazu 'not limited to'   ⟨ kagir- v. 'limit' + (a)zu NEG
     -ni kagitte 'limited to, only'   ⟨ kagir- v. 'limit'
     -ni kakawarazu 'regardless of'   ⟨ kakawar- v. 'relate to' + (a)zu NEG
     -ni motoduite 'based on'   ⟨ motoduk- v. 'be based on'
     -ni mukatte 'towards'   ⟨ mukaw- v. 'face'
     -ni mukete 'towards'   ⟨ muke- v. 'turn towards'
     -ni oite 'at, concerning'   ⟨ ok- v. 'put'
     -ni sitagatte 'following'   ⟨ sitagaw- v. 'follow'
     -ni site 'only, even, at'   ⟨ s- v. 'do'
     -ni tomonatte 'in step with'   ⟨ tomonaw- v. 'accompany'
     -ni totte 'as for'   ⟨ tor- 'take'
     -ni tuite 'about'   ⟨ tuk- v. 'attach to'
     -ni tuki 'concerning'   ⟨ tuk- v. 'attach to'
     -ni turete 'accompanying'   ⟨ ture- v. 'accompany'
     -ni watatte 'extending over, across'   ⟨ watar- v. 'range, extend over'
     -ni yotte 'because of, by means of'   ⟨ yor- v. 'come near, depend on'
     -o megutte 'about'   ⟨ megur- v. 'circle around'
     -o motte 'with'   ⟨ mot- v. 'hold'
     -o towazu 'regardless of'   ⟨ tow- v. 'question'
     -to site 'as'   ⟨ s- v. 'do'

As shown in (7), the verb-based postpositions predominantly take the form of [N-*ni* V-*te*] with the meaning of 'V-ing to N', and less commonly [N-*o* V-*te*], 'V-ing N'. This is a common pattern of grammaticalization in Modern Japanese in which the semantics of the phrase is uniquely determined by the relationship denoted by the first primary postposition and the verb (cf. Muraki 1996: 325-334, Katsuki-Pestemer 2003). When the source meaning is compared with the postpositional meaning, the conceptual connection between them is largely obvious, e.g., [arriving at N] 〉 'coming to/at N'; [not limiting to N] 〉 'not limited to N', etc., thus suggesting that their development is a relatively recent phenomenon.

Narrog and Rhee (2013: 304) note that none of the postpositional verb constructions, except for *to site* (として), have been inherited from Proto-Japanese but are the result of historically documented development from Late Old (Early Middle) Japanese on. They further suggest that the development of the class as a whole has been spurred by the practice of transposing Chinese into Japanese, rendering Chinese monosyllabic function words with short Japanese verb phrases (see 4.3.3.4 below for more discussion).

4.3.3.4 Sino-Japanese Sources

As is evident from the list of Japanese postpositions, there are a number of complex postpositions that are built upon Sino-Japanese morphemes.

(8)   *-ni kansite*   に関して 'in relation to'   〈 *kan*   関 sj.n. 'relation, gate'
    -ni saisite   に際して 'at the time of'   〈 *sai*   際 sj.n. 'time, occasion'
    -ni taisite   に対して 'towards, against'   〈 *tai*   対 sj.n. 'opposite, opposition'
    -ni hansite   に反して 'against'   〈 *han*   反 sj.n. 'going against'
    -o toosite   を通して 'through, by way of'   〈 *too-s-*   通 sj.v. 'pass through'
    -o totte   を通って 'through'   〈 *too-s-*   通 sj.v. 'pass through'

(9)   *-ni atatte*   に當して   'in the course of'
    -ni itatte   に至して   'coming to, at'
    -ni oite   に於して   'at, concerning'
    -ni yotte   に由/因して   'by, because of'
    -o motte   を以して   'with'

(10) *-no yooni*   のように   'like, similar to'   〈 *yoo*   様 sj.n. 'appearance, form'

The complex postpositions listed in (8) involve verbs, thus 'postpositional verbs' in Narrog and Rhee (2013), but these verbs are all derived forms. In other words, they take the form of [*-ni* N-*si-te*], i.e., the primary postposition *-ni* (に) 'at, to', Sino-Japanese noun, the light verb *s-* (す-) 'do' and the converb inflection *-te* (て) (see

Group A complex postpositions in Table 4.3). The postposition *-o toosite* (を通して) 'through, by way of' is slightly different in that it takes the Accusative *-o* (を), instead of the Dative *-ni* (に). The postposition *-o totte* (を通って) 'through' shares the same Sino-Japanese origin as *-o toosite* (を通して), but denotes physical perlative passage, e.g., 'through a shortcut', unlike its relative *-o toosite* (を通して) which tends to denote more abstract ways and means, e.g., 'through an oral tradition'. Evidently, creating such a form, mixed with native Japanese and borrowed Chinese morphemes, seems to have been necessitated while translating Chinese texts. Even the forms in (9), though not directly involving a Chinese borrowing (as evidenced by the Japanese pronunciation), are thought to be influenced by Chinese (as evidenced by the Chinese characters in writing, i.e., kanji). Narrog and Rhee (2013: 304), citing Yamada (1935) and Chen (2005), state that some of those in (9), e.g., *-o motte* (を以して), *-ni oite* (に於して), may be complete calques. The postposition *-no yooni* (のように) in (10) is unique in that it is the only postposition involving a Sino-Japanese source lexeme in the [*-no* X-*ni*] structural template. Semantically, the lexeme *yoo* 'appearance, form' contributes to the similative meaning, a pattern also observed in Korean (e.g., *-n chey* (ㄴ체) 'in pretense of' and *-chelem* (처럼) 'like' both from the Sino-Korean *chey* (체; 體) 'body, form', S Rhee 2005b), English (e.g. *-like* and *-ly* from OE/ME *lician* 'body', OED and E Kim 2011), etc.

In a more extensive study, Narrog et al. (2018) analyze the motivation of the development of these de-verbal postpositions in Japanese and Korean and state that the contact with written Chinese could be the major motivation (cf. Djamouri and Paul 2009). Incidentally, other instances constituting the contact-induced grammaticalization in Japanese and Korean include prolific use of Chinese-based numeral classifiers, development of a large number of 'mermaid constructions' (Tsunoda 2013, 2020) incorporating Chinese borrowings, a sizable inventory of Chinese borrowings used as adverbs (cf. Yamada 1935), among others.

A significant aspect worth considering in this context is the relational nouns of Chinese origin in Japanese. Narrog and Rhee (2013: 298) observe that the majority of Sino-Japanese relational nouns only function as affixes and not as full nouns, and further that Sino-Japanese morphemes do not occur in the general construction [N *no* RN] but are affixed directly to other nouns, especially other Sino-Japanese nouns, such as *tyuusyoku-go* (昼食後) [lunch-after] 'after lunch', *kikan-nai* (期間内) [period.of.time-within] 'within the period of time', *keiken-zyoo* (経験上) [experience-above] 'from experience', etc. (see 4.4.4 for more discussion). As noted by Narrog and Rhee (2013), it is peculiar that borrowing of these forms occurred not at the level of lexemes with literal, spatial meanings, but instead at the level of suffixes, with already abstract, non-spatial meanings. This peculiar situation is also observed with Korean (see 3.4.4.1).

4.3.3.5 Multiple Sources and Layered Postpositions

In studies of emergence of grammatical paradigms it is commonly observed that there are multiple sources. Since different grammaticalization scenarios from multiple sources often lead to the development of a grammatical form of an identical function, the layering phenomenon is commonly observed. As we shall discuss more in detail in Chapter 10, the extent of layering in Japanese postpositions is comparatively limited, not comparable to adpositions in other languages, which is largely due to the fact that Japanese adpositional system is much smaller than those in other languages.

However, there are a sufficient number of cases displaying layering. For instance, as we can see in Table 4.1, there are multiple forms for Ablative (i.e., *-kara* (から) and *-yori* (より)), Extent Focus markers of Extent (i.e., *-bakari* (ばかり), *-dake* (だけ), *-nomi* (のみ), *-hodo* (ほど), *-kurai/gurai* (くらい/ぐらい), and *-sika* (しか)), Focus markers for Extreme examples (i.e., *-sae* (さえ), *-sura* (すら), *-dani* (だに), *-datte* (だって), and *-demo* (でも)), Enumerative (i.e., *-nado* (など), *-toka* (とか), *-nari* (なり), *-yara* (やら), and *-dano* (だの)), Directionals (e.g. *-e* (へ), *-ni mukatte* (に向かって), *-ni mukete* (に向けて), and *-ni taisite* (に対して)), among others (see Table 4.4 above). We have already looked at the Extent Focus markers exemplified in (1) and (2) above, and noted their interchangeability or non-interchangeability due to their different shades of meaning. We will further look into other layered postpositions now.

Ablatives *-kara* (から) and *-yori* (より) both function as temporal starting points, as exemplified in (11), taken (and modified and glossed) from Katsuki-Pestemer (2003: 30):

(11) Ablatives -*kara* and -*yori*

三時から/より 会議が 始まり-ます。

*sanji-**kara/yori***   *kaigi-ga*   *hajimari-masu*

3.o'clock-**ABL**   conference-NOM   begin-END

'The conference begins at three o'clock.'

As shown in (11), the two Ablatives are interchangeable.[11] However, as is obvious from the frequency information in Table 4.2, -*kara* (から) is about 10 times as frequent as -*yori* (より) (6,423 pmw vs. 576 pmw). This is likely to be due to the fact that -*yori* (より) is more stylistically marked, i.e., it is favored in formal styles. The layered postpositions -*kara* and -*yori* (より) are unique in that both of them are old layers and their sources have not been firmly established. According to Frellesvig (2005), in the OJ period, *yori,* in the form of *ywori ~ ywo ~ yuri ~ yu* (originating from the noun *yuri* 'after(wards)', was the "main" Ablative, denoting source of movement, comparison, material and means, whereas -*kara* (から) was "emerging", thus, suggesting that -*yori* (より) is the older layer whereas -*kara* (から) is the younger layer (see also Gruntov and Mazo 2020: 548-551). He further speculates that -*kara* (から) originated from a noun meaning 'will, way, extent' (p. 6).

Directionals/Allatives are numerous as well, which show multiple layers in contemporary Japanese, as listed in (12):

---

11) However, when there are two Ablative-marked constituents in a sentence, the speakers tend to alternate the Ablatives rather than repeating one, as shown in the following example (i), taken and modified from Katsuki-Pestemer (2003:30):

(i) 三時-より この 本-の 五十-ページ-から 読み-ます。

*sanji-**yori***   *kono*   *hon-no*   *goju-ppeji-**kara***   *yomi-masu*

3.oclock-**ABL**   this   book-GEN   50-page-**ABL**   read-END

'Starting at three o'clock we will read the book from page fifty onwards.'

(12)   Directionals/Allatives

a.	*-e.*	〈 *pye*	n. 'place, vicinity'
b.	*-ni mukatte.*	〈 *mukaw-*	v. 'face'
c.	*-ni mukete.*	〈 *muke-*	v. 'turn towards'
d.	*-ni taisite.*	〈 *tais-*	v. 'face' 〈 *tai* SJ.n. 'face'

As shown in (12), Directionals develop from diverse sources. Narrog and Rhee (2013) indicate that *-e* originated from the OJ noun *pye* 'place, vicinity', and evidently it belongs to the oldest layer among the four Directionals/Allatives. Frellesvig (2005) states that the noun *pye* denoting 'side, extent' was nearly obsolete in OJ and was an "emerging" Allative, being grammaticalized at the time but having not attained the grammatical status of the Allative case marker. Directionals/Allatives in the form of complex postpositions are undoubtedly of the newer layers, originating from verbs that designate particular orientation of an entity, most probably a human, by virtue of the directionality of the frontal side, gained by static positioning (e.g., 'face') or dynamic movement (e.g., 'turn around'). It is also to be noted that the verb *tais-* (対す-) 'face' is derived from the Sino-Japanese noun *tai* (対) 'face'. This has to do with the fact that most Sino-Japanese nouns participating in complex postpositions do not function as full nouns.

4.4 Ongoing Grammaticalization of Spatial Postpositions

4.4.1 Selection Criteria

We observed in the foregoing exposition that Japanese has a relatively smaller inventory of postpositions, i.e., 79 in total, than in other languages we address in this book. When the composite category is particularly small, with only 4 members. The entire inventory consists of 79 postpositions, i.e., 33 primary, 4 composite, and 42 complex postpositions. In order to investigate the ongoing grammaticalization among spatial postpositions in Japanese, we use the following criteria to select the target items from the entire inventory of 79 postpositions.

(13) (i) It is not in the primary postpositional category in contemporary Japanese (46 items);

(ii) It encodes spatial relationship (20 items);

(iii) It is attested at least 10 wpm (70 times in the corpus) (15 of them).

As is the case with Korean (Chapter 3), Condition (i) is to ensure that the target postposition is not yet established as a fully grammaticalized postposition. Condition (ii) is to restrict the target items within our research focus, i.e., spatial postposition. Condition (iii) is to ensure that the item is a viable one, not a chance occurrence attributable to idiolectic styles or that the form is not at a very incipient stage where the form's viability is yet uncertain. The cut-off point 10 pmw, which coincides with the cut-off point for Medium Frequency range in Table 4.5 above, is about 70 occurrences in the corpus. The 15 target forms, supposedly actively undergoing grammaticalization, are listed in Table 4.6.

Spatial Postposition		Meaning	PMW
-no naka	の中	'in, inside of, within'	924
-ni taisite	に対して	'towards, against, regarding'	509
-ni site	にして	'only, at, just because'	285
-no aida	の間	'between, among'	183
-no uti	の内うち	'within, inside, among'	126
-no ue	の上	'above, up, over'	109
-no mae	の前	'prior to, in front of'	83
-no sita	の下	'below, beneath, under'	70
-o toosite	を通して	'through'	44
-no gawa	の側	'beside, on the side of'	31
-ni mukatte	に向かって	'towards'	30
-ni watatte	にわたって	'across, extending over'	17
-ni mukete	に向けて	'towards'	16
-no usiro	の後ろ	'behind, in back of'	11
-no soto	の外	'outside (of), exterior to'	10

Table 4.6 Grammaticalizing spatial postpositions in Modern Japanese

4.4.2 General Characteristics

The overall distribution of the 15 grammaticalizing prepositions is such that they are all complex prepositions, a natural consequence of the facts that primary postpositions are excluded in selection and that composite postpositions are extremely small in number. These target items bear special significance in the grammaticalization of Japanese postpositions, which we discuss more in detail below in a few groups by their functions, Regionals, Directionals, Proximatives (Adjacency), Paths, Medials, and Axial postpositions.

[Regionals]
There is only one grammaticalizing postposition in the Regional category, i.e., *-ni site* (にして) 'at, only, even'. Its competing forms, *-ni* (に) and *-de* (で), are all well established as primary postpositions. Their per-million frequencies are compared, with the target item bold-faced, in (14):

(14) Regionals
a.	*-ni*	'in, to'	22,036
b.	*-de*	'in, on'	12,248
c.	***-ni site***	**'at, only, even'**	**285**

It is quite evident from the frequency information that the general location marking is nearly exclusively specialized by *-ni* (に) and *-de* (で). The grammaticalizing form *-ni site* (にして) is very weakly represented. The two well-entrenched forms are highly polyfunctional (cf. Chino 1991, Katsuki-Pestemer 2003), in particular, *-ni* (に) is also a Dative (see below for its difference from *-e* (へ)), and *-de* (で), an Essive. Even as a general Regional, they mark not only spatial but also temporal and other abstract notions related to the locational concept. Since these notions are general, their use frequencies are particularly high. On the other hand, *-ni site* (にして) is quite specific in meaning with a focus meaning 'only at, only when, even', etc. This state of affairs of functional competition well reflects the hypothesis that semantic generalization is on a par with use frequency, and consequently with the level of grammaticalization.

[Directionals]

The situation of Directionals is noteworthy in that there are three actively competing forms currently undergoing grammaticalization with one competitor, as shown in (15):

(15) Directionals (Allatives)

a.	*-ni taisite*	'towards, against, regarding'	509
b.	*-e*	'to'	474
c.	*-ni mukatte*	'towards'	30
d.	*-ni mukete*	'towards'	16

All these four forms are functionally synonymous in that they designate directions. The situation with the Directionals is unique in that one of the grammaticalizing postpositions surpasses its functional counterpart in the primary postposition category. The fact that *-ni taisite* (に対して) is relatively stronger than other Directionals seems to be due to the fact that *-ni taisite* (に対して) carries a wider range of meanings (i.e., direction, opposition, theme, etc.) as compared to the others. A noteworthy aspect concerns the primary postposition *-e* (へ). Japanese postpositions are, in general, highly polysemous in that many of them are interchangeable in certain contexts, but they also exhibit delicately different shades of meaning. For instance, the primary postposition *-e* (へ) is similar to *-ni* (に) in indicating a location but *-e* (へ) has its focus on the path (and direction of the journey), whereas *-ni* (に) has its focus on the destination.

When *-e* (へ) is compared with *-ni taisite* (に対して), the latter, as noted above, is widely polysemous, including even seemingly disparate meanings such as direction and opposition. Incidentally, the conceptual connection between direction and opposition is also attested in English (e.g., *against* is related to straight (line) and opposition; see S Rhee 2002c). It is peculiar that this situation goes against the parallel reduction hypothesis with respect to meaning and form in grammaticalization. In other words, a primary postposition (i.e., shorter in form) is surpassed by a complex postposition (i.e., longer in form) in terms of frequency and a primary postposition (i.e., supposedly of longer grammaticalization history) is surpassed by a complex postposition (i.e., of shorter grammaticalization history) in terms of semantic generality. This situation points to the hypothesis that semantic generality is more crucial than formal simplicity in use frequency.

Another point is that, as is obvious from the formal constructs, the three grammaticalizing Directionals involve the location marker -ni (に) and verb-based inflected forms. The evident reason for the relative primacy of -e over -ni mukatte (に向かって) and -ni mukete (に向けて) seems to be that it is more general in meaning (e.g., encompassing direction, goal, recipient, etc.) and simpler in form (i.e., monolexemic and monosyllabic), whose origin goes back to pre-historic times (see 4.3.3.1 above).

[Proximatives (Adjacency)]

In the category of Proximatives, there is only one postposition that is supposedly actively undergoing grammaticalization, i.e., -no gawa (の側) 'near, next to, beside, on the side of'. Its competitor, -no yoko (の横) 'beside, on the side of', has not attained the strength yet, as shown in (16):

(16) Proximatives (Adjacency)

a. *-no gawa*	'near, next to, beside, on the side of'		31
b. *-no yoko*	'beside, on the side of'		7

The postpositions -no gawa (の側) and -no yoko (の横) are similar in function. They signal adjacency of two referenced entities. Since adjacency is usually perceived on a lateral axis in the environment, they can also mark laterality, as well. However, one notable difference between gawa (側) and yoko (横) is that in the case of the former, the adjacency does not have to involve laterality, whereas the latter does. In other words, gawa (側) may signal closeness along any axes (e.g., up-down, front-back, right-left) but yoko (横) needs to be on the horizontal right-left axis.[12] Thus, the relative primacy of -no gawa (の側) over -no yoko (の横) seems to be due to the fact that the former is semantically less restrictive than the latter, once again supporting the hypothesis that semantic generality is the key in frequency and grammaticalization.

[Perlatives (Paths)]

Perlatives, or markers of paths, are unique in that there are two grammaticalizing postpositions and that there are no functional competitors. Their frequency information is shown in (17):

(17) Paths
    a. *-o toosite*   'through'   44
    b. *-ni watatte* 'across, extending over'   17

It is interesting to note that these two grammaticalizing postpositions do not have functional competitors. Even though they mark paths and temporal duration in common, they have differences in meaning in that *-o toosite* (を通して) tends to encode occupation of temporal duration without regard to homogeneity or heterogeneity of the action or state allowing intermittent repetition of an action or state, whereas *-o watatte* (にわたって) tends to encode sustained occupation of temporal duration in its entirety. Furthermore, *-o toosite* (を通して) can involve abstract paths (e.g., 'through culture', 'through oral tradition', etc.) Thus, the relatively higher frequency of *-o toosite* (を通して) may have to do with relatively less restrictive semantics.

    Another point is that even though there are no functional competitors, these Perlatives do not surface at a high frequency. Even the combined frequencies, i.e., 61 pmw, are very low. This suggests that the concept of Perlative does not have a high

---

12) It is intriguing to note that etymologically Chinese lexemes 側 and 横 both signified 'side' on the horizontal plane, as the former was with reference to human side (cf. the first radical, 亻, signifies the person) and the latter was with reference to the horizonal wooden latch of a gate or door (cf. the first radical, 木, signifies a tree) (Y Ha 2021[2014]: 822, 952). This means that 側 (〉 *gawa*) has undergone more extensive semantic generalization.

mental representation and human construal of events.

[Medials]

A very similar situation is seen with Medials. Signaling that a referenced entity is located at the middle position of another reference entity, Medials have the potential of marking Interior in the axial categories. There are three Medials that are actively grammaticalizing without any functional competitor, as shown in (18):

(18) Medials

    a. *-no naka* (中) 'in, inside of, among, within, during' 924

    b. *-no aida* (間) 'between, among' 183

    c. *-no uti* (內) 'within, inside, among' 126

From the frequency information, it is evident that *-no naka* (の中) is the most highly specialized Medial, many times more so than the other two. The disparity in frequency is also deemed to be from their semantics, i.e., *-no naka* (の中) denotes medial location in a general way, whereas *-no aida* (の間) profiles the interval between two entities in which the reference entity is located (note that *aida* denotes 'interval' or 'gap'), and *-no uti* (の內) tends to signify that the referenced entity is within an enclosing structure or entity, concrete or abstract (e.g., space, candidates, options, etc.), typically in contrast with outside. Thus, the most general *-no naka* (の中) seems to be favored for its semantic unmarkedness.

[Axial Postpositions]

Finally, a mention on the axial postpositions is in order. Unlike other languages, notably Korean, which has much structural affinity with Japanese (chapter 3), as well as other languages, such as English (chapter 5), Spanish (chapter 6), and Thai (chapter 8), Japanese has a much smaller inventory of axial postpositions, as shown in (19):

(19) Axial postpositions

    a. *-no naka* 'inside, within'   INTERIOR 924

    b. *-no ue* 'on, on top of'   SUPERIOR 109

c. *-no mae*	'before, in front of'	ANTERIOR	83
d. *-no sita*	'below, under'	INFERIOR	70
e. *-no gawa*	'on the side of, next to'	LATERAL	31
f. *-no usiro*	'behind, in back of'	POSTERIOR	11
g. *-no soto*	'outside'	EXTERIOR	10

As shown in the list, all axial notions are included. As noted above, *-no naka* (の中) 'inside, within' and *-no gawa* (の側) 'on the side of, next to' can be regarded as Medial and Proximative, respectively. The frequencies of these functionally polysemous postpositions were not counted separately, thus the figures need to be interpreted as approximations (note that individual attestations cannot be effectively divided among polysemous functions). The fact that in the list at least one postposition appears involving each and every axial notion suggests that these notions are conceptually salient. Incidentally, among the axial postpositions those that are not included in the grammaticalizing postpositions are *-no saki* (の先) 'in front of', *-no hidari* (の左) 'on the left of' and *-no migi* (の右) 'on the right of'. The Anterior *-no saki* (の先) 'in front of' yields to *-no mae* (の前) 'in front of' in frequency; the low frequency of *-no hidari* (の左) 'on the left of' and *-no migi* (の右) 'on the right of' seems to be due to the fact that these are highly specific; and, consequently, the more general and polyfunctional *-no gawa* (の側) 'beside, next to' and *-no yoko* (の横) 'beside, next to' seem to be favored (see above for the last two).

4.4.3 Grammaticalization Mechanisms

4.4.3.1 Extension

Extension, or usage context expansion, is well observed with most postpositions whose lexical origins have been identified. This is due to the fact that the meanings of the lexical sources tend to be more concrete whereas the grammatical meanings of the postpositions tend to be more abstract. Thus, desemanticization and extension are closely tied together. Let us look at the following examples:

(20) a. *muke-*   v. 'turn towards'   〉 *-ni mukete* 'towards'
     b. *megur-*   v. 'circle around'   〉 *-o megutte* 'about'
     c. *toos-*   v. 'pass through'   〉 *-o toosite* 'through'

The postposition *-ni mukete* (に向けて) 'towards' developed from the *muke-* (向け) v. 'turn toward'. It is reasonable to suppose that that when *muke-* (向け) was strictly a verb, it could be used to indicate a revolving or semi-revolving motion to assume directionality to some entity. When it developed into a postposition to mean 'towards', any notion of turning around as a physical motion is not part of the postpositional meaning, thus its use context can be extended. Similarly, *megur-* (めぐ-) 'circle around' denotes physical motion around a physical entity, whereas *-o megutte* (をめぐって) 'about' does not need to involve any physical motion and can be used for abstract entities, such as a topic. The verb *toos-* (通す-) 'pass through', based on the Sino-Japanese *too-* (通), referred to a movement going through a physical entity (which is still retained in its formal and functional relative *-o totte* ((を通って)). The postposition developed from it, *-o toosite* (を通して), can be used with respect to abstract passage (see 4.3.3.4 above).

4.4.3.2 Desemanticization

Desemanticization, or semantic bleaching, is frequently observed in the development of postpositions in Japanese. This is particularly true with primary postpositions, as shown in (21):

(21) a. *-tokoroka*   EXTT 'far from'   〈 *tokoro*   n. 'place'
     b. *-e*   ALL 'to'   〈 *pye*   n. 'place, vicinity'

The development of the nouns denoting 'place', i.e., *tokoro* and *pye,* into the postpositions of Extent and Allative, respectively, involves semantic generalization by virtue of losing spatial, locational meaning. Further, the development involves subjectification by virtue of attributing evaluative notion or concessive and insufficiency (e.g., 'far from', cf. Katsuki-Pestemer 2003: 195) and attribution of directionality (e.g., 'to').

Even in the verb-based certain degree of desemanticization is observable, as shown in (22):

(22) a. *-ni atatte*   'in the course of'   ⟨ *atar-* v. 'hit upon'
      b. *-ni oite*   'at, concerning'   ⟨ *ok-* v. 'put'
      c. *-ni sitagatte* 'following'   ⟨ *sitagaw-* v. 'follow'
      d. *-ni site*   'only, even, at'   ⟨ *s-* v. 'do'
      e. *-to site*   'as'   ⟨ *s-* v. 'do'
      f. *-ni yotte*   'because of, by means of' ⟨ *yor-* v. 'come near, depend on'

The postpositions in (22) show that their postpositional meanings are more abstract than the meanings of the lexical items. For instance, the actional and event meaning 'hit upon' (of *atar-* (当た-)) is more physical than than the procedural meaning 'in the course of' (of *-ni atatte* (にあたって)). Similarly, the verb *sitagaw-* (したがう) 'follow' originally denoted physical locomotion behind a referenced entity (typically a human), but the postposition *-ni sitagatte* (にしたがって) 'following' may involve an abstract noun as its reference (e.g., law, tradition, suggestion, etc.). The other cases in (22) also show a certain level of abstraction.

Even though desemanticization is very commonly attested in the course of grammaticalization, the extent of desemanticization in Japanese complex postpositions is very limited. Some such complex postpositions are listed in (23):

(23) a. *-ni itatte*   'coming to/at'   ⟨ *itar-*   v. 'arrive'
     b. *-ni kagitte*   'limited to, only' ⟨ *kagir-*   v. 'limit'
     c. *-ni kagirazu*   'not limited to'   ⟨ *kagir-*   v. 'limit' +*(a)zu* NEG
     d. *-ni motoduite*   'based on'   ⟨ *motoduk-* v. 'be based on'
     e. *-ni kakawarazu* 'regardless of'   ⟨ *kakawar-* v. 'relate' +*(a)zu* NEG
     f. *-ni tomonatte*   'in step with'   ⟨ *tomonaw-* v. 'accompany'
     g. *-ni turete*   'accompanying'   ⟨ *ture-*   v. 'accompany'
     h. *-ni tuite*   'about'   ⟨ *tuk-*   v. 'attach to'
     i. *-ni tuki*   'concerning'   ⟨ *tuk-*   v. 'attach to'
     j. *-o towazu*   'regardless of'   ⟨ *tow-*   v. 'question' +*(a)zu* NEG

k.	*-ni watatte*	'extending over, across' ⟨ *watar-*	v. 'range, extend over'
l.	*-ni totte*	'as for' ⟨ *tor-*	v. 'take'
m.	*-o motte*	'with' ⟨ *mot-*	v. 'hold'

If we compare the source meanings of the postpositions with the grammatical meanings of the complex postpositions, there are often no noticeable differences, as has been observed in Narrog and Rhee (2013). This can be said to go against the parameter of desemanticization, but, conversely, it can be evidence of the relatively lower degree of complex postpositions.

4.4.3.3 Decategorialization

The parameter decategorialization, or loss of the primary category properties, is also commonly found in the development of Japanese postpositions. The following is a partial list of noun-based primary postpositions in Japanese:

(24)	a.	*-kara*	ABL 'from'	⟨ *kara*	n. 'nature/essence'
	b.	*-kurai*	EXTT (small) 'about'	⟨ *kurawi*	n. 'rank' ⟨ *kura-wi* n.v. 'platform-sit'
	c.	*-made*	LMT 'until, up to'	⟨ *made*	n. 'both hands (?)'
	d.	*-hodo*	EXTT (large) 'about'	⟨ *potwo*	n. 'interval'

Since the complete developmental trajectories of the primary postpositions listed in (24) have not been made available, we are unable to examine the gradual loss of nominal properties in the process. However, it is evident that the final products, i.e., postpositions, in contemporary Japanese do not retain any nominal characteristics.

Similarly, postpositions that developed from postpositional verbs show decategorialization. Let us look at the following examples:

(25)	a.	*-ni kagirazu* 'not limited to'	⟨ *kagir-* v. 'limit' + *(a)zu* NEG
	b.	*-ni sitagatte* 'following'	⟨ *sitagaw-* v. 'follow'

The postpositions in (25) are grammaticalized from verbs. The postposition *-ni* *kagirazu* (に限らず) further involves a negation marker *-(a)zu*. Their verbal characteristics, such as adverbial modification can be tested as the following examples:

(26) a. Johnは 女性に 限らず 男性にも 人気が ある。

      *John-wa   zyosei-**ni** **kagirazu**   dansei-ni-mo ninki-ga   aru.*

      John-TOP woman-<u>not.limited.to</u> man-to-also   popularity-NOM exist

      'John is popular not only among women but also among men.' (《 '..not limited to women but..')

   a'. *Johnは 女性に 完全に 限らず 男性にも 人気が ある。

      *John-wa   zyosei-**ni** **kanzenni** kagirazu   dansei-ni-mo*

      John-TOP woman-**completely**.not.limited.to man-to-also

      ninki-ga   aru.

      popularity-NOM exist

      'John is popular not entirely only among women but also among men.'

   b. 私は パソコン 画面の 指示に 従って 実験を した。

      *watasi-wa pasokon gamen-no siji-**ni** sitagatte   zikken-o   sita*

      I-TOP   computer screen-GEN instruction-following experiment-ACC did

      'I carried out the experiment following the instructions on the computer screen.'

   b'. 私は パソコン 画面の 指示を 徹底的に 従って 実験-を した。

      *watasi-wa pasokon   gamen-no   siji-o **tetteiteki-ni**   sitagatte*

      I-TOP   computer screen-GEN screen-<u>ACC **faithfully**   following</u>

      zikken-o   sita.

      experiment-ACC did

      'I carried out the experiment faithfully following the instructions on the computer screen.'

As shown in (26a') the postposition *-ni kagirazu* cannot be extrapolated by an intervening degree modifier *kanzenni* (完全に) 'completely', and, in fact, this modifier cannot be inserted in the sentence because the postposition has grammaticalized and cannot be modified for the verbal component in it, i.e., the verb *kagir-* (かぎる) 'limit'. The situation in (26b') is similar but a little different: the degree modifier *tetteiteki* (徹底的) 'faithfully' cannot be inserted inside *-ni sitagatte* (にしたがって), but it can be placed before it, a situation strongly suggesting the internal cohesion in the form.

The limited flexibility of these complex postpositions has been discussed by Suzuki (1972: 499-500) and T Takahashi (2003: 266-267), who note the impossibility of inserting other elements, e.g., particles, between the noun phrase + case particle and the verb (cf. Miyake 2005: 69), the impossibility of using coordinate structures with each noun being case-marked (cf. Miyake 2005: 69), constraints on verb inflection, and loss of argument structure (as cited in Narrog and Rhee 2013: 303). All these point to a level of decategorialization of the verbal characteristics.

However, postpositions that have relatively shorter historical depth show that the extent of decategorialization exhibited by the development is still limited. The following is a list of more recent postpositions:

(27) a. *-no mae* の前 'prior to, in front of' 〈 *ma-pe* n. 'location of eye'
      b. *-no usiro* の後ろ 'behind, in back of' 〈 **u[ra]-siri* n.n. 'back-buttocks'(?);
                                                   or **mu-siro* n.n. 'body-buttocks'(?)

The postpositions in (27) are instances involving relational nouns, derived from body-part nouns. The head nouns of these complex postpositions in contemporary Japanese, i.e., *mae* (前), *usiro* (後ろ), bear nominal resemblance in form and morphosyntax (note that they are preceded by the Genitive *-no* (の) and that they can be followed by another postposition, such as *-ni* (に) 'to, in', *-kara* (から) 'from', etc.). These nouns, if fully grammaticalized, are expected to have lost their nominal characteristics. However, they do allow a modifier as shown in (28):

(28) a. 公園は 学校の 前に あります。
          koen-wa gakkō-no mae-ni   ari-masu
          park-TOP school-before-LOC   exist-POL.END

'The park is in front of the school.'

a'. 公園は 学校の すぐ 前に あります。
   *koen-wa gakko-<u>no</u>   **<u>sugu</u>** <u>mae</u>-ni   ari-masu*
   park-TOP school-<u>GEN</u> **just** front-LOC   exist-POL.END
   'The park is right in front of the school.'

b. 郵便局は 学校の 後ろに あります。
   yubinkyoku-wa gakkō-<u>no usiro</u>-ni   ari-masu.
   post.office-TOP school-<u>behind</u>-LOC exist-POL.END
   'The post-office is behind the school.'

b'. 郵便局は 学校の すぐ 後ろに あります。
   *yubinkyoku-wa gakko-<u>no</u> **<u>sugu</u>** <u>usiro</u>-ni   ari-masu.*
   post.office-TOP school-<u>GEN</u> **just**   behind-LOC exist-POL.END
   'The post-office is right behind the school.'

As shown in (28), emphatic degree modifier *sugu* (すぐ) 'just' can be inserted before the head noun, which means that the structural 'bondedness' is still weak and 'coalescence' has not fully advanced (Lehmann 2015[1982]: 157ff).

It is noteworthy in this context that Narrog and Rhee (2013) discuss the tricky nature of the grammaticalization of relational nouns in morphosyntactic terms. They discuss the arguments advanced by Tagashira (1999), who, by way of using a number of syntactic tests, claims that relational nouns differ from ordinary nouns, such as inability to take demonstratives, adjectival qualifiers, etc. and invokes the notion of 'index of nominality'. Narrog and Rhee (2013), however, state that many of the differences are in fact not due to grammaticalization but to the inherent semantics of the relational nouns.

The foregoing exposition shows that even though there are postpositions that have lost their primary category characteristics (i.e., nominal and verbal features), the extent of decategorialization in grammaticalization of Japanese postpositions is largely limited. This is in contrast with the states of affairs in other languages discussed in this book.

4.4.3.4 Erosion

Erosion, or loss in phonetic substance, is also observed in the development of Japanese postpositions, especially in the case of primary postpositions. Some of such instances are exemplified in (29):

(29) a. *pi-n-tari* 'where the sun arrives/goes down' ⟩ *pintari* ⟩ *hidari* 'left of'
      b. *u[ra]-siri* 'back-buttocks'(?)/ *mu-siro* 'body-buttocks'(?) ⟩ *usiro* 'behind'
      c. *ma-pye* 'location of eye' ⟩ *mae* 'before, in front of'

As shown in (29), the lexical sources and their phonetic shapes are nearly completely opaque in the contemporary forms. This is largely due to the fact that these, and many other, primary postpositions in Japanese have a long history of grammaticalization. However, the situation is a little different with the complex postpositions, which have a much shorter history of grammaticalization. Some of them are listed in the following:

(30)

-ni atatte	'in the course of'	⟨ *atar-*	v. 'hit upon'
-ni itatte	'coming to/at'	⟨ *itar-*	v. 'arrive'
-ni kagitte	'limited to, only'	⟨ *kagir-*	v. 'limit'
-ni kakawarazu	'regardless of'	⟨ *kakawar-*	v. 'relate to' +(a)zu NEG
-ni motoduite	'based on'	⟨ *motoduk-*	v. 'be based on'
-ni mukatte	'towards'	⟨ *mukaw-*	v. 'face'
-ni mukete	'towards'	⟨ *muke-*	v. 'turn towards'
-ni oite	'at, concerning'	⟨ *ok-*	v. 'put'
-ni site	'only, even, at'	⟨ *s-*	v. 'do'
-ni tomonatte	'in step with'	⟨ *tomonaw-*	v. 'accompany'
-ni totte	'as for'	⟨ *tor-*	v. 'take'
-ni tuite	'about'	⟨ *tuk-*	v. 'attach to'

-ni tuki	'concerning'	⟨ *tuk-*	v. 'attach to'
-ni turete	'accompanying'	⟨ *ture-*	v. 'accompany'
-ni watatte	'extending over, across'	⟨ *watar-*	v. 'range, extend over'
-ni yotte	'because of, by means of'	⟨ *yor-*	v. 'come near, depend on'
-o megutte	'about'	⟨ *megur-*	v. 'circle around'
-o motte	'with'	⟨ *mot-*	v. 'hold'
-o towazu	'regardless of'	⟨ *tow-*	v. 'question'
-to site	'as'	⟨ *s-*	v. 'do'

The complex postpositions listed in (30) take the form of [P-V-*te*], in which *-te* (て) is the inflection of the verb. Narrog and Rhee (2013: 304) note that not only their semantics but also their form exhibit very limited levels of change that their meanings are easily obtainable from the compositional meaning of the individual parts and their formal shapes are straightforward because the verbs participating in complex postpositions can be used in the verb base form and with the *-te* (て) ending without much difference, except *-ni tuite* (について) and *-ni tuki* (につき). The relative transparency of these complex postpositions is due to their short history, as evidenced by the fact that none of them, except for to site, have been inherited from Proto-Japanese but are the result of historically documented developments from Late Old (Early Middle) Japanese on (Narrog and Rhee 2013: 304).

4.4.4 Grammatical Functions

As is the case in many other languages, Japanese postpositions are polyfunctional. Spatial postpositions tend to mark temporal or other abstract notions, presumably by way of metaphorization. Thus, most of them carry spatio-temporal notions, but in certain cases, the spatial function has been lost, e.g., *-o toosite* (を通して) 'through', developed from the verb *toos-* (通す-) 'pass through', denotes non-physical passage, such as abstract ways and means, in contrast with the postposition *-o totte* (を通って) 'through', developed from the same verbal source, denoting physical perlative passage (see 4.3.3.4 above).

In this context a brief mention on an important aspect of Sino-Japanese words and morphemes, the relational nouns, in particular, participating in complex postpositions, is in order. As we noted above (4.2, see also Table 4.3), Japanese has many relational nouns that participate in the grammaticalization of complex postpositions. The Sino-Japanese morphemes in these postpositions carry native Japanese pronunciation, but these self-same morphemes are also used with Chinese-derived pronunciation elsewhere. They are listed in Table 4.7, taken from Narrog and Rhee (2013: 297) (note that N denotes noun; -n, suffix noun; q-, prefix).

Sino-Japanese Morphemes	Character	Meaning/Function	Native Japanese
-zen, zen- (-n, q-)	前	before	*mae*
-go (N, -n)	後	after	*usiro*
-zyoo (-n)	上	on	*ue*
-ge (N, -n); *-ka* (-n)	下	under	*sita*
-nai (-n)	内	among	*uti*
-tyuu (N, -n)	中	inside	*naka*
-gai (-n)	外	outside	*soto*
-kan (N, -n)	間	between	*aida*

Table 4.7 Native Japanese relational nouns and Sino-Japanese counterparts

As shown in Table 4.7, each relational concept is marked by the pair of Sino-Japanese and native Japanese words/morphemes. Despite their similarity in origin, however, they are in general not in competition with their native Japanese counterparts in structure and function. In other words, in structure, as noted above, Sino-Japanese tend to be used as affixes rather than as head nouns in the construction, thus directly affixed to the host noun (i.e., [N-RN]), rather than in the general complex postpositional template involving a Genitive (i.e., [N-*no* RN]). In terms of function in Modern Japanese, as Narrog and Rhee (2013) observe, they are more commonly associated with temporal and abstract than spatial meanings, and thus, they do not create any overlap or competition with the native Japanese, which tend to be associated with spatial meanings.

The extremely rare competition or overlap occurs when the native Japanese relational nouns are used like affixes and can be used for temporal meaning, as shown in (31), in which native Japanese (NJ) is compared with Sino-Japanese (SJ) relational nouns, taken from Narrog and Rhee (2013: 198):

(31) *mae/zen* 'before' and *ato/go* 'after'
    a. (NJ) *is-syuukan-mae* ('one'+ 'week'+ 'before')   – 'one week ago'
    b. (SJ) **is-syuukan-zen* ('one'+ 'week'+ 'before')   – 'one week ago'
    c. (NJ) *?is-syuukan-ato* ('one'+ 'week'+ 'after')   – 'one week later'
    d. (SJ) *is-syuukan-go*   ('one'+ 'week'+ 'after')   – 'one week later'

As the examples show, despite the conceptual comparability between 'before' and 'after', in one case only native Japanese is allowed, whereas in another Sino-Japanese is preferred. Thus, Narrog and Rhee (2013) note that even if there is potential overlap, the competition is usually resolved by convention. This is in exact parallel with Korean complex postpositions involving relational nouns (see 3.4.4.1).

Another point is that some of the Sino-Japanese relational nouns have been recorded from earliest times (e.g., *-zen* 前 'front') but others are relatively new (e.g., *-gai* 外 'outside' from the Edo period). They are thus part of the gradual 'sinification' (cf. Frellesvig 2010: 258-294) of the Japanese language, but still much less entrenched in the language than their Japanese counterparts (Narrog and Rhee 2013: 298-299).

Another aspect bearing significance in function is that there are many instances that exhibit subjectification in the course of development into postpositions. This can be shown, among numerous others, by the following:

(32)   a.   *-bakari*   FOC 'only, just'   < *hakari*   vn. 'measure'
      b.   *-dake*   FOC 'only'   < *take*   n. 'length, measure'

In (32), the nouns denoting 'measure', i.e., *hakari* and *take*, develop into the Focus markers *-bakari* and *-dake*. When these nouns host another noun, the sequence of [N-'measure'] comes to develop into 'only N, just N'. In other words, the noun 'measure' is designating a point in a scale and is making an exclusive reference to the N, e.g., *terebi-bakari* (テレビ-ばかり) 'TV-measure' becoming 'TV-only'; *amaimono-dake*

(甘いもの-だけ) 'sweets-measure' becoming 'sweets-only', etc. Objects, such as TV or sweets are placed in a scale of 'measure' and pinpoint the location of these objects as the reference. Subjective notion of focus or exclusiveness becomes a part of the postpositional meaning through subjectification.

In terms of functional extension, as indicated above, all relational nouns carry the original spatial meaning (note, however, that *ato* (後) 'after' is the only one which is primarily used for temporal, and not spatial meanings), and some of the nouns have developed further figurative, and sometimes grammatical meanings and functions such as the following (cf. *NKD* entries; Tagashira 1999; section 5, as cited in Narrog and Rhee 2013: 296-297):[13]

(33) a. `Abstract location; e.g. social position: *ue* (上) 'top', *sita* (下) 'bottom', *mae* (前) 'front'
   b. Addition: *ue* (上) 'top', *ato* (後) 'after'
   c. Temporal relation: *mae* (前) 'front', *ato* (後) 'after', *aida* (間) 'interval', *uti* (內) 'inside', *sita* (下) 'bottom', *naka* (中) 'in'
   d. Reason: *ue* (上) 'top'

As in Korean, most Japanese relational nouns have Sino-Japanese counterparts, which are presented in Table 4, together with their spelling in Chinese/Japanese. In writing, the character of the Sino-Japanese morpheme is also used for the native Japanese morpheme, which indicates close semantic correspondence.

4.5 Summary

This chapter has dealt with grammaticalization of Japanese postpositions. The inventory of the postpositional system in Modern Japanese comprises 33 primary

---

[13] Incidentally, the space to time extension is commonly observed in the development of Japanese auxiliaries (Hino 2000).

postpositions, 4 composite postpositions, and 42 complex postpositions. This inventory contrasts with those in some of the languages addressed in this book.

The strength of individual forms as grammatical markers is widely variable, as reflected in their token frequency. As expected, primary postpositions are generally more frequent than the composite and complex postpositions.

There are about 28 spatial postpositions denoting diverse axial and non-axial concepts. This number is also considerably smaller as compared to other languages but the forms are generally evenly spread across conceptual domains rather than being concentrated in a large number in a small number of domains. This is also a unique situation as compared with other languages.

Primary postpositions are old grams whose origins are often opaque. Complex postpositions develop from verbal and nominal sources. Noun-based complex postpositions typically take the form of [-P N(-P)] whereas verb-based complex postpositions are usually in the form of [-P V-*te*], in which -*te* is the inflection for connective function. Also notable is the fact that there are a large number of postpositions developed from Sino-Japanese sources, an indication of the influence of contact with written Chinese. When there exist both of the paired forms of Sino-Japanese and native Japanese denoting the same relational concepts, they tend to have differential specialization of functions, with native Japanese typically for spatial meaning and Sino-Japanese for temporal or other abstract meanings, even though the division is not sharply delineated.

About 15 postpositions, all belonging to the complex postposition group, are deemed to be actively undergoing grammaticalization. When they are compared with other competing postpositions outside this group, it was found that semantic generality is closely tied to frequency and consequently to the extent of grammaticalization.

In terms of grammaticalization mechanisms, the development of Japanese postpositions is generally consonant with the notions of extension, desemanticization, decategorialization, and erosion. However, there are a large number of postpositions that do not prominently exhibit such phenomena, largely due to the fact that they have a shallow temporal depth of grammaticalization. The situation of the contemporary Japanese postpositional system is such that there are a few old primary postpositions used at a very high frequency and a few complex postpositions that are spread across diverse conceptual domains without having numerous functional competitors of variable strengths, as often observed in other languages.

Grammaticalization of Prepositions in English

5.1 Introduction

English is among the languages in which a large inventory of prepositions is found. Prepositions as a grammatical category constitute an important element of grammar in English because they are one of the most frequently exploited grammatical exponents ever since they largely replaced the more extensively used case inflectional systems in Old and Middle English. It is for this reason that prepositions encode an array of grammatical notions specifying the semantic and grammatical functions played by the noun phrases they are affixed to.

As we noted in 2.3, and as found in many languages addressed in this book, adpositions arise from various sources and develop into markers of diverse functions, and those characterizations suit English particularly with an impressively large inventory of prepositions. There are many similarities found in English and Spanish (see Ch. 6) for various historical and typological reasons, and other languages as well, but there are also notable language-specific characteristics.

5.2 Prepositions in English

As indicated above, English has a large number of prepositions, and they are used at a very high frequency. Regarding the high frequency of English prepositions, S Rhee (2004d: 399) notes that about 8 of the top 20 high frequency items in English are prepositions. Furthermore, about 20 prepositions, accounting for the majority of the prepositions actively used in Modern English, are in the top 100 high frequency items, exhibiting a high level of semantic polysemy. The English category of prepositions exhibits a great deal of categorial fluidity. S Rhee (2004d) notes that *Oxford English Dictionary* lists 404 items under the preposition category, inclusive of defunct forms in Modern English, and that different sources have different lists, e.g., *Oxford English Dictionary* lists no prepositional use for *as* in its 404 prepositional entries, which ranks the 10th in Johansson and Hofland's (1989) classification. The British National Corpus, on the other hand, does not list *than,* and includes secondary prepositions such as *out of, because of, as well as,* etc. in its 122 prepositional inventory. For these reasons, the inventory of prepositions is debatable.

In addressing English prepositions as a whole, we will conveniently group them according to the number of words involved, i.e., primary for monolexemic prepositions (N.B.: these may be polymorphemic), composite for two-word prepositions, and complex for those involving three or more words.

Based on diverse sources, the primary prepositions used in Modern English, numbering 97 in total, though not conclusive, can be listed alphabetically as in Table 5.1 (* denotes prepositions that can be used intransitively; see below).

*aboard**	*alongside**	*at*
*about**	*amid*	*atop*
*above**	*amidst*	*bar*
abreast	*among*	*barring*
abroad	*amongst*	*before**
*across**	*apropos**	*behind**
afore	*around**	*below**
*after**	*as*	*beneath**
*against**	*aside*	*beside*
*along**	*astride*	*besides**

between*	near*	through*
beyond*	nearer	throughout*
but	nearest	till
by*	notwithstanding*	times
concerning	of	to*
considering	off*	touching
despite	on*	toward
down*	onto	towards
during	opposite	under*
ere	out	underneath*
except	outside*	unlike
excepting	over*	unto
excluding	past*	up*
following	pending	upon
for	per	versus
from	plus	via
in*	re	vis-à-vis
including	regarding	with
inside*	respecting	within*
into	round*	without*
less	saving	worth
like	since*	
minus	than	

Table 5.1 List of primary prepositions in Modern English

The list in Table 5.1 presents a few notable aspects. First of all, there are as many as 22 prepositions that contain an initial *a-*. In many of them, *a-* is a historical remnant of *on* and *an* that were prepositions/prefixes in Old English, with the meaning of 'of local position outside of, but in contact with or close to, a surface' (*Oxford English Dictionary*). The compositions of some of such examples are shown in (1), based on *Oxford English Dictionary,* and partly adapted from S Rhee (2002a: 134):

(1) a. *aboard*   *a* 'on, at' + *board* 'plank, table, shield, ship'
     b. *above*   *a* 'on, at' + *be* 'by, near' + *ufan* 'up, above'
     c. *across*   *a* 'on, at' + *cross* 'cross'
     d. *about*   *on* 'in, on' + *be* 'by, near' + *ut* 'out'
     e. *amid(st)* *on* 'in' + *middan* 'middle (Dative)'

f. *atop*   *a* 'on' + *top* 'top'

However, despite their surface similarity, the prepositions *along(side)*, *after*, *at*, *apropos*, and *as* do not belong to the group. In the case of *along*, according to *Oxford English Dictionary*, *a-* is not a derivative of *an/on* but a historical remnant of *and* that meant 'against, facing, in a direction opposite', which was combined with *lang* 'long' (see also S Rhee 2002a). In the cases of *after* and *at*, they do not contain a separate morpheme but are indivisible lexemes inherited from Germanic. The preposition *apropos* 'fitly' is a 17th century borrowing from French *à propos* 'to the purpose', in which *à* is a preposition 'to', and *as* is a phonetically reduced form of *also* which derives from *eall swa* 'all so' (*Oxford English Dictionary*).

These *a*-derived prepositions carry certain shared characteristics. For instance, many or most of them are based on concrete nouns or nominal concepts, presumably because they are derived forms containing the historical *on/an* which typically made reference to 'a surface' (see above), i.e., a tangible entity. Another characteristic is that many of them can be used intransitively (cf. 'intransitive preposition'; Huddleston and Pullum 2002: 272ff), i.e., they can occur without the prepositional complement (i.e., a noun phrase), in which case the form is often analyzed as an adverb in other frameworks. In fact, this intransitive use is not limited to the *a*-derived prepositions.[1] Among the 98 primary prepositions, as many as 38 can be used intransitively (marked with an asterisk). The 'transitive' and 'intransitive' uses can be shown as in (2):

(2) a. *He put it in the box.*   (transitive)
     b. *He brought the chairs in.*   (intransitive)

                                    (Huddleston and Pullum 2002: 272)

Another aspect in the list is that there are also a group of *be*-derived prepositions

---

[1] See Hagège (2010: 51-57) for discussion on intransitive (adverbial) use of adpositions across languages. Givón (2021: 20-24) also discusses such usage at post-verbal positions in English, labeling them as post-verbal prepositions (and 'particles', p. 31).

(historically *be-* or *bi-*), discussed in S Rhee (2002b). Their composition is illustrated in (3):

(3) a. *before* *be-* 'around' + *fora* 'front'
     b. *behind* *be-/bi-* 'around' + *hindan* 'behind'
     c. *beside* *be* 'around' + *sídan* 'side (Dative:Sg)'
     d. *beyond* *bi-* 'around' + *geondan* 'farther side'

As indicated above, prepositions widely vary in many aspects, e.g., not only their composition but also their frequency is highly variable in contemporary English. Table 5.2 shows the frequency ranking of 97 English primary prepositions, based on the frequency information in COCA, a one-billion word corpus.[2]

Frequency Range	Preposition	PMW
HIGH (1,000~ pmw) (n=13)	*of*	23,159
	in	15,670
	to	9,232
	for	8,195
	with	6,443
	on	6,080
	at	4,024
	from	3,711
	by	3,372
	about	2,428
	as	1,880
	like	1,583
	into	1,462
Medium (100~999 pmw) (n=26)	*through*	752
	after	745

---

[2] Frequency information for certain items is modified because the COCA search algorithm is such that the frequency of a preposition includes that of a multi-word preposition if it is a part of the latter, e.g., *but* including *but for*, *except* including *except for*, etc.

	over	680
	between	559
	against	468
	without	439
	during	424
	before	403
	under	374
	around	319
	among	268
	off	259
	including	245
	within	244
	across	226
	up	209
	behind	203
	toward	181
	upon	141
	per	134
	than	133
	despite	113
	near	112
	beyond	111
	outside	107
	since	105
	along	94
	above	90
	onto	87
	throughout	86
	worth	82
Low (10~99 pmw) (n=30)	inside	78
	down	70
	towards	58
	past	58
	via	51
	plus	47
	regarding	47
	below	38
	beneath	34

	beside	34
	unlike	27
	versus	26
	re	23
	concerning	19
	abroad	18
	except	18
	till	17
	besides	16
	but	16
	alongside	15
	amid	15
	unto	12
	atop	10
	considering	10
	amongst	10
	aboard	9
	underneath	9
	round	9
	minus	6
	following	5
	aside	5
	out	4
	amidst	3
	times	3
Very Low	*opposite*	3
(~9 pmw)	*notwithstanding*	3
(n=28)	*pending*	3
	respecting	2
	less	2
	excluding	2
	vis-à-vis	1
	nearest	1
	abreast	1
	nearer	1
	saving	1
	astride	1

ere	0
excepting	0
bar	0
apropos	0
touching	0
afore	0
barring	0

Table 5.2 Frequency of English primary prepositions

The frequency information in Table 5.2 shows that about a dozen prepositions are highly frequent, occurring more than 1,000 pmw, i.e., they are highly specialized. However, even in that highest tier, the variation is wide (cf. 23,159 tokens pmw of *of* and 1,462 tokens of *into*). Also notable is that the prepositions in the highest tier are mostly monolexemic or, at least they appear to be so (i.e., one would not know the composition of *about* as shown in (1d) above or of *as*, indicated above; the composition of *into*, however, may be more visible). In contrast with the highest tier, those in the Medium frequency group have less opaque composition, especially with *without, before, around, including, across*, etc.

English composite prepositions are also numerous, though not as many as the primary prepositions. From Quirk et al. (1985), Klégr (1997, 2002), and elsewhere, a comprehensive list of composite prepositions, numbering 64 in total, is compiled, granting that the strength of individual items for their membership in this category is variable and inconclusive. They also exhibit great variability in terms of their use frequency. They are listed in Table 5.3:

à la	*as of*	*close to*
according to	*as per*	*contrary to*
across from	*as regards*	*counter to*
ahead of	*as to*	*devoid of*
along with	*aside from*	*down from*
alongside of	*away from*	*due to*
apart from	*back to*	*except for*
as for	*because of*	*exclusive of*
as from	*but for*	*far from*

from among	other than	regardless of
from between	out from	right to
from under	out of	round about
in between	outside of	save for
inside of	over to	subsequent to
instead of	owing to	such as
irrespective of	pertaining to	together with
left to	preliminary to	up against
near to	preparatory to	up to
nearer to	previous to	upwards of
next to	prior to	void of
off of	pursuant to	
opposite of	rather than	

Table 5.3 List of composite prepositions in Modern English

Nearly all composite prepositions end with a primary preposition. The exceptions are *à la* 'in the manner or style of' and *as regards* 'with respect or reference to'. The preposition *à la* is a 16th century borrowing from French *à la* 'to the:FEM', which was used before a feminine noun or the feminine form of an adjective. In Modern English, it is commonly used to indicate a source of information, comparable to 'according to'. The preposition *as regards* is peculiar in that it involves an inflected verb *regard*. According to *Oxford English Dictionary*, there are other related forms *as regarded* and *as regarding*, which, however, are extremely rare in Modern English.

The fact that composite prepositions mostly end with a preposition has to do with the general tendency that the grammatical status of a multi-word expression is largely determined by the grammatical status of the final word (S Rhee 2007a). For this reason, composite prepositions nearly always take a noun phrase as their complement. The extremely rare exceptions are *in between* which is used without a complement for 2,739 times (3 pmw) and *from under*, for 45 times (nearly 0 pmw). In this respect, composite prepositions are clearly different from primary prepositions, many of which can be frequently used intransitively (see above).

Far greater multiplicity of prepositions is found with complex prepositions, i.e., those consisting of three or more words. As is the case with Spanish (see Ch. 6), English complex prepositions are numerous and their categorial boundary is fuzzy.

Complex prepositions as a grammatical category blends into syntactic constructions, which, together, form a continuum, and the crossover from one end to the other cannot be unambiguously identified. Thus, Quirk et al. (1985: 671-672), propose a scale of 'cohesiveness', for which they suggest nine syntagmatic indicators of cohesiveness or conversely separateness between the components (see also Quirk and Mulholland 1964 for diagnostics of complex prepositions).

Klégr's (1997) list contains as many as 513 complex prepositions if the parenthetically indicated forms are all separately counted.[3] Complex prepositions presented in Quirk et al.'s (1985) exposition include 63 prepositions, three of which are not found in Klégr (1997). There are a few more that do not appear in either list but are qualified to be included by virtue of their form, function, and frequency. The total number of complex prepositions thus compiled amounts to 523 (see Appendix 2 for the full list). The ten most frequent complex prepositions are listed in (4), in order of descending frequency:

(4)   a. *in front of*   b. *in terms of*
      c. *in the middle of*   d. *in addition to*
      e. *as part of*   f. *on top of*
      g. *as a result of*   h. *in favo(u)r of*
      i. *in the form of*   j. *with respect to*

When the composition patterns of complex prepositions are analyzed, they have a few common structural patterns. For instance, Quirk et al. (1985: 670-671) present the following patterns (N denotes noun):

(5)   a. *in* N *of*:   *in aid of, in back of, in behalf of...*
      b. *in* N *with*:   *in accordance with, in common with...*
      c. *by* N *of*:   *by dint of, by means of, by way of...*
      d. *on* N *of*:   *on account of, on behalf of, on (the) ground(s) of...*

---

3) Klégr (2002), using a little more expansive criteria, presents as many as 989 items.

Similarly, Klégr (2002: 28) shows in terms of the Prep₁ and Prep₂ combination that the *in*-N-*of* pattern is the most frequent one, accounting for 213 out of 989 (21.5%), the second most frequent one is *at*-N-*of,* accounting for 102 (10.3%), and the third *on*-N-*of,* accounting for 94 (9.5%). He further notes that there is a 54.1% probability that complex preposition will take the form of *in*-N-*of, at*-N-*of, on*-N-*of, under*-N-*of,* or *in*-N-*with*. The prevalence of the *in*-N-*of* pattern has been noted by a number of authors (Quirk and Mulholland 1964, Klégr 1997, K Ahn 2015, S Eom 2018, among others).

5.3 Spatial Prepositions

5.3.1 Characteristics of Spatial Prepositions

Many, if not most, prepositions in English encode diverse spatial relationship, a characteristic shared by adpositions in many other languages. Encoding spatial relationship is a lot more prevalent with primary prepositions. Even though the types of spatial relationships are variable and each preposition's level of specialization is widely variable, the three different subgroups of prepositions show different levels of spatial specialization. In other words, out of 97 primary prepositions 61 of them encode spatial relationship (62.8%), out of 64 composite prepositions 32 of them encode spatial relationship (50.0%), and out of 523 complex prepositions 120 of them (22.9%) encode spatial relationship. This has clearly to do with the facts that the notion of spatial relationship is relatively simpler and more basic (for being topological and schematic in nature) than other more abstract concepts like time and quality (cf. Heine et al. 1991a), and that primary prepositions are formally simpler than composite and complex prepositions, that latter better suiting the circumstance when more elaborate relationships need to be encoded (cf. Rohdenburg's 'complexity principle'; 1996: 152; see 11.1 for more discussion). The list of spatial prepositions is given in Table 5.4.

AXIS		PRIMARY (n=61)	COMPOSITE (n=32)	COMPLEX (n=120)
	REGIONAL	*at*		
NON-AXIAL	DIRECTIONAL	*into* *toward* *towards* *onto* *unto*	*back to*	*in the direction of* *to the front of*
	SOURCE	*of* *from*	*out of* *away from* *out from* *down from* *from under* *from among* *from between*	*from a position of* *from the position of*
	GOAL	*to* *onto* *unto*	*up to*	
	PATH	*through* *throughout* *via*		*on the way to* *en route to* *on the road to* *en route from* *on route to* *on route from*
	MEDIAL	*between* *among* *amid* *amongst* *amidst*	*in between*	*in the middle of* *in the midst of* *in the course of* *in the heart of*
	ULTERIOR	*over* *beyond*	*upwards of*	*beyond the scope of* *beyond the reach of* *beyond the bounds of* *beyond the range of*
	ASSOCIATION	*with* *along* *alongside* *abreast*	*along with* *together with* *alongside of*	*in connection with* *in conjunction with* *in combination with* *in the company of* *in concert with* *in association with* *in company with* *in combinations with*
	ADJACENCY	*by* *about* *around* *near* *beside* *round* *nearest* *nearer*	*close to* *near to* *nearer to* *round about*	*on the edge of* *on the brink of* *in the vicinity of* *in the neighborhood of* *on the point of* *within reach of* *within sight of* *on the trail of* *within an inch of* *in proximity to* *within a mile of* *on course for*

AXIAL				
				on the verge of
				to the verge of
				at the doorstep of
				under the nose of
				within a stone's throw of
				on the very point of
				within a stone's throw from
				within the verge of
				within a small area of
	CONTIGUITY		next to	in touch with
				in contact with
	SEPARATION	off	far from	with the exception of
		past	off of	to the exclusion of
		besides	apart from	beyond the shadow of
		aside	aside from	
	OPPOSITE	against	up against	in opposition to
		across	across from	
		opposite	opposite of	
	OTHERS	abroad		in the face of
		aboard		in the hands of
		touching		in the shadow of
				in parallel with
				in face of
				at a height of
				under the eyes of
				on board of
				as far as
	INTERIOR	in	inside of	in the area of
		within		in the region of
		inside		in the space of
				in the sphere of
				on the premises of
				within the scope of
				within the realm of
				within the limits of
				within the boundaries of
				within the range of
				within the bounds of
				within the field of
				within the space of
				within the span of
				within the orbit of
				within the realms of
				within an area of
				within the radius of
				within a circumference of
				within a distance of
	EXTERIOR	outside	outside of	beyond the limits of
		out		beyond the field of
				beyond the range of
				outside the boundaries of
				outside the range of
				outside the reach of
				outside the limits of
	SUPERIOR	on		on top of

	Primary	Composite	Complex
	up upon above atop		at the top of at the head of
INFERIOR	under down below beneath underneath		at the bottom of at the base of at the foot of at the feet of on the underside of under the heel of
ANTERIOR	before afore	ahead of	in front of at the forefront of in the forefront of in the foreground of
POSTERIOR	after behind following	subsequent to	in back of in the back of in the wake of on the back of at the back of on the heels of on the track of at the heels of on a background of
LATERAL	beside	right to left to	on the side of on the right of to the left of on the right side of by the side of on the left side of along the side of to the right of on the left of on the flank of

Table 5.4 Spatial prepositions in Modern English

The distribution of spatial prepositions in Table 5.4 indicates a number of interesting aspects. First of all, there is only one preposition that denotes a regional location, i.e., the primary preposition *at*. Since this is a very general spatial relation, there are no composite or complex prepositions, which tend to be more specific in designating spatial relations.

Association and Adjacency are closely related, and there are a large number of prepositions across primary, composite and complex categories. Complex prepositions in these categories tend to carry more than spatial meaning. For instance, a number of 'edge'-related prepositions, e.g., *on the edge of, on the brink of, on the point of, on the verge of, to the verge of, within the verge of*, etc., tend to encode imminence of an event, a clear instance of space-to-time metaphor as well as of subjectification.

Also notable is the multiplicity of complex prepositions in the Interior category. They tend to be headed by the preposition *in* or *within*, the latter being far more common, which denotes the outer boundary within which an entity is located. And the nature of the region is indicated by the noun following, e.g., *realm, scope, sphere, area*, etc. The opposite axial notion Exterior does not have as many member prepositions as Interior, but there are identical nouns in both categories, thus, the only difference being Prep₁ *within* vs. *outside*, e.g., *limits, range, reach, field, boundaries*, etc. Similarly, the same nouns when combined with the Prep₁ *beyond* form Ulterior prepositions.

Another interesting point is that there are Interior prepositions that are similar to Adjacency, when they involve *within* as their Prep1. When the noun denotes some general spatial notions, e.g., *range, field, boundaries*, etc., the complex preposition involving it marks Inferior, whereas when the noun denotes a minimal unit, e.g., *a mile, an inch*, etc., or the noun implies limited distance, e.g., *reach, sight, a stone's throw*, etc., or the noun denotes inherently small extent, e.g., *verge*, etc., the preposition involving it marks Adjacency.

5.3.2 Frequencies of Spatial Prepositions

As noted above, there is an inventory of 61 primary, 32 composite and 120 complex prepositions denoting spatial relationships, totaling 213. Not only their morphosyntactic makeup but also their individual strength varies to a great extent. Table 5.5 shows the frequency of the spatial prepositions in four different frequency ranges, along with their lexical sources.

Frequency Range	Spatial Preposition	(Lexical) Source	PMW
HIGH (1,000~ pmw) (n=10)	*of*	*of* (prep.) 'away from'	23,159
	in	*in* (prep.) 'in'	15,670
	to	*to* (prep.) 'in the direction of'	9,232
	with	*wið* (prep.) 'against'	6,443

	on	*an* (prep.) 'on'	6,080
	at	*æt* (prep.) 'at'	4,024
	from	*fram* (prep.) 'forward from'	3,711
	by	*bí* (prep.) 'by, near'	3,372
	about	*on-but* (pref.adv) 'on outside'	2,428
	into	*in-to* (prep.prep.) 'into'	1,462
	through	*dorh* (prep.) 'through'	752
	after	*æfter* (prep.) 'behind, later in time'	745
	over	*over* (prep.) 'beyond'	680
	out of	*utt* (adv.) 'out(side)'	621
	between	*bi-tweonum* (pref.n.) 'by two'	559
	against	*again-s* (prep.suf.) 'in hostility'	468
	before	*be-forne* (pref.adv.) 'in front of'	403
	under	*under* (prep.) 'beneath, among'	374
	around	*a-round* (pref.n.) 'on ring'	319
	among	*on-ymong* (prep.n.) 'on company'	268
Medium	off	*of* (prep.) 'away from'	259
(100~999 pmw)	within	*with-inne* (prep.prep.) 'with in'	244
(n=23)	back to	*bæc* (n.) 'back of body'	228
	across	*a-cross* (prep.n.) 'on cross'	226
	up	*uppan* (prep.) 'upon'	209
	behind	*bi-hindan* (pref.n.) 'by behind'	203
	toward	*to-weard* (prep.suf.) 'toward direction'	181
	upon	*up-on* (adv.prep.) 'toward above'	141
	up to	*up to* (prep.prep.) 'up to'	141
	away from	*on-way* (prep.n.) on-way 'above a track'	128
	near	*neah-r* (adv.suf.) 'closer, nearer'	112
	beyond	*be-geond* (pref.adj.) 'around across'	111
	outside	*out-sídan* (pref.n.) 'outside'	107
	along	*and-long* (pref.adj.) 'against line'	94
	above	*a-bove* (pref.adv.) 'on high'	90
Low	along with	*and-long* (pref.adj.) 'against line'	88
(10~99 pmw)	onto	*on-to* (prep.prep.) 'toward and upon'	87
(n=40)	throughout	*through-out* (prep.adv.) 'through out'	86
	in front of	*front* (n.) 'forehead, face'	84

inside	*in-sídan* (adj.n.) 'inside'	78
down	*down* (adv.) 'in a descending direction'	70
close to	*close* (adj.) 'closed, shut'	70
towards	*to-weard* (prep.suf.) 'toward direction'	58
past	*pass* (pp.v.) 'exceed, surpass'	58
next to	*next* (super.adv.) 'nearest'	55
via	*via* (Lat.n.) 'way'	51
in the middle of	*middle* (n.) 'middle part'	41
below	*be-low* (pref.adj.) 'around low'	38
beneath	*be-niðan* (pref.adv.) 'around below'	34
beside	*be sídan* (prep.n.) 'by side'	34
ahead of	*a-head* (prep.n.) 'on head'	31
outside of	*out-sídan* (adj.n.) 'outside'	30
on top of	*top* (n.) 'tuft, crest, head hair'	29
far from	*far* (adj.) 'remote'	23
right to	*reoht* (adj.) 'just, correct'	20
out from	*utt* (adv.) 'out(side)'	18
off of	*of* (prep.) 'away from'	18
abroad	*a-broad* (prep.n.) 'on a body of water'	18
besides	*be sídan* (prep.n.) 'by side'	16
together with	*together* (prep.adv.) 'to together'	16
alongside	*and-long-sídan* (pref.adj.n.) 'against line of the side'	15
down from	*down* (adv.) 'in a descending direction'	15
amid	*on-mid* (prep.n.) 'on middle'	15
at the top of	*top* (n.) 'tuft, crest, head hair'	14
up against	*again-s* (prep.suf.) 'in hostility'	13
in the face of	*face* (Fr.n.) 'countenance'	13
apart from	*a-part* (Fr.prep.n.) 'to side'	13
unto	*un(till)-to* (prep.prep.) 'onward to'	12
inside of	*in-sídan* (adj.n.) 'in side'	11
aside from	*a-sídan* (prep.n.) 'on side'	10
in the midst of	*midst* (super.adj.) 'most central'	10
atop	*a-top* (prep.n.) 'on the highest point'	10
amongst	*amongst* (prep.suf.super.) 'among'	10

---

	in the back of	*bæc* (n.) 'back of body'	9
	aboard	*a-bord* (prep.n.) 'on board'	9
	underneath	*under-nethen* (prep.adv.) 'under below'	9
	in the wake of	*wake* (SC.n.) 'track of a vessel'	9
	round	*round* (n.) 'ring'	9
	at the bottom of	*botm* (n.) 'lowest part of object'	9
	on the side of	*sídan* (n.) 'flank of person'	8
	in touch with	*tocher* (Fr.n.) 'touch'	8
	on the edge of	*ecg* (n.) 'corner, edge'	7
	left to	*leoft* (adj.) 'left'	7
	in the hands of	*hanða* (n.) 'hand'	7
	on the back of	*bæc* (n.) 'back of body'	6
	in the course of	*cours* (Fr.n.) 'course, running'	6
	across from	*a-cross* (prep.n.) 'on cross'	6
	opposite of	*opposite* (Fr.Lat.n.) 'opposite side'	6
	with the exception of	*exception* (Fr.Lat.n) 'excepting'	6
Very Low	*from under*	*under* (prep.) 'beneath, among'	6
(~9 pmw)	*on the way to*	*uuaeg* (n.) 'way, path'	6
	following	*follow-ing* (prp.v.) 'following'	5
(n=140)	*on the verge of*	*verge* (Fr.n.) 'edge, rod, twig'	5
	in connection with	*conneccion* (Fr.n.) 'connection'	5
	in conjunction with	*conjunction* (Fr.n.) 'joining together'	5
	in the direction of	*direction* (Lat.n.) 'directing'	5
	aside	*a-sídan* (prep.n.) 'on side'	5
	in the area of	*area* (Lat.n.) 'space'	4
	in the heart of	*heorte* (n.) 'heart'	4
	out	*ūt(e)* (n.) 'out(side)'	4
	in contact with	*contact* (Lat.n.) 'touching'	4
	at the back of	*bæc* (n.) 'back of person'	4
	amidst	*amid-s-t* (adv.suf.super.) 'most central'	3
	at the base of	*base* (Fr.n.) 'bottom'	3
	opposite	*opposite* (Fr.Lat.n.) 'opposite side'	3
	at the foot of	*foet* (n.) 'foot'	3
	en route to	*route* (Fr.n.) 'way, route'	3

on the road to	*road* (n.) 'journey'	2
at the head of	*heafod* (n.) 'head'	2
in the shadow of	*scead(u)we* (n.) 'shadow, shade'	2
on the brink of	*brink* (Sc.n.) 'brink, edge'	2
in opposition to	*opposition* (Fr.Lat.n.) 'contrary argument, objection'	2
on the right of	*reoht* (adj.) 'just, correct'	2
in combination with	*combination* (Fr.n.) 'combination'	2
on the heels of	*hæla* (n.) 'heel'	2
to the front of	*front* (n.) 'forehead, face'	2
in between	*bi-tweonum* (pref.n.) 'by two'	2
in the company of	*compagnie* (Fr.n.) 'society, friendship'	2
to the left of	*leoft* (adj.) 'left'	2
near to	*neah-r* (adv.suf.) 'closer, nearer'	2
from among	*on-ymong* (prep.n.) 'on company'	2
at the forefront of	*fore-front* (pref.n.) 'before forehead, before face'	1
on the right side of	*reoht* (adj.) 'just, correct'; *sídan* (n.) 'flank of person'	1
nearest	*nior-est* (adj.super.) 'closest'	1
in the vicinity of	*vicinity* (Fr.Lat.n.) 'proximity'	1
beyond the scope of	*scope* (It.n.) 'extent'	1
by the side of	*sídan* (n.) 'flank of person'	1
in concert with	*concert* (Fr.n.) 'concert, harmony'	1
abreast	*a-breast* (prep.n.) 'on breast'	1
on the left side of	*leoft sídan* (adj.n.) 'left side, left flank'	1
nearer	*neah-r-er* (adv.suf.comp.) 'more closer, more nearer'	1
in association with	*association* (Fr.Lat.n.) 'association'	1
from between	*bi-tweonum* (pref.n.) 'by two'	1
beyond the reach of	*reach* (n.) 'continuous stretch/course'	1
in the space of	*space* (Fr.n.) 'extent, room'	1
at the feet of	*fēt* (n.pl.) 'feet'	1
to the exclusion of	*exclusion* (Lat.n.) 'shutting out'	1

in the neighbourhood of	neighbour-hood (n.suf.) 'neighborhood'	1
subsequent to	subsequent (Fr.adj.) 'subsequent'	1
nearer to	nior-er (adj.comp.) 'closer'	1
in back of	bæc (n.) 'back of body'	1
within the scope of	scope (It.n.) 'extent'	1
in the forefront of	fore-front (pref.n.) 'before forehead'	0
along the side of	sídan (n.) 'flank of person'	0
in the region of	regeoun (Fr.Lat.n.) 'region'	0
within the realm of	raume (Fr.n.) 'kingdom'	0
on the point of	puint (Fr.n.) 'point'	0
within reach of	reach (n.) 'continuous stretch/course'	0
from a position of	pocicioun (Fr.Lat.n.) 'position'	0
within sight of	sihð (n.) 'vision'	0
within the limits of	lemet (Fr.Lat.n.) 'boundary'	0
on the trail of	trail (n.) 'trailing part of robe, gown, etc.'	0
within the boundaries of	bound-ary (n.suf.) 'limit'	0
within the range of	rangh (Fr.n.) 'line of persons'	0
within the bounds of	bound (n.) 'limit'	0
round about	round (n.) 'ring'	0
in parallel with	paralel (Fr.Lat.n.) 'parallel'	0
to the right of	reoht (n.) 'proper, just action'	0
beyond the limits of	lemet (Fr.Lat.n.) 'boundary'	0
on the underside of	under-side (pref.adj.) 'lower side'	0
within an inch of	ynce (n.) 'inch'	0
in the sphere of	sper (Fr.Lat.n.) 'sphere'	0
alongside of	and-long-side (pref.adj.n.) 'against line of the side'	0
in proximity to	proxymyte (Fr.n.) 'proximity'	0
en route from	route (Fr.n.) 'way, route'	0
within the field of	felth (n.) 'field'	0
within a mile of	mil (n.) 'a Roman unit mile'	0
beyond the bounds of	bound (n.) 'limit'	0
on the left of	leoft (adj.) 'left'	0
in face of	face (Fr.n.) 'countenance'	0
in company with	compagnie (Fr.n.) 'society, friendship'	0

within the space of	*space* (Fr.n.) 'extent, room'	0
from the position of	*pocicioun* (Fr.Lat.n.) 'position'	0
beyond the range of	*rangh* (Fr.n.) 'line of persons'	0
outside the boundaries of	*bound-ary* (n.suf.) 'limit'	0
on course for	*cours* (Fr.n.) 'course, running'	0
outside the range of	*rangh* (Fr.n.) 'line of persons'	0
at a height of	*híehþo* (n.) 'height'	0
to the verge of	*verge* (Fr.n.) 'edge, rod, twig'	0
at the doorstep of	*door-step* (n.n.) 'doorstep'	0
in the foreground of	*fore-ground* (pref.n.) 'foreground'	0
under the eyes of	*æge* (n.) 'eye'	0
within the span of	*span* (n.) 'span'	0
under the nose of	*nosu* (n.) 'nose'	0
beyond the shadow of	*scead(u)we* (n.) 'shadow, shade'	0
outside the reach of	*reach* (n.) 'continuous stretch/course'	0
on the track of	*trak* (Fr.n.) 'track'	0
touching	*tocher* (Fr.v.) 'touch'	0
at the heels of	*hæla* (n.) 'heel'	0
on the premises of	*premis* (Fr.n.) 'premise'	0
under the heel of	*hæla* (n.) 'heel'	0
on board of	*bord* (n.) 'board'	0
on route to	*route* (Fr.n.) 'way, route'	0
within a stone's throw of	*stan* (n.) 'stone'; *throw* (n.) 'throw'	0
outside the limits of	*lemet* (Fr.Lat.n.) 'boundary'	0
on a background of	*back-ground* (adj.n.) 'background'	0
within the orbit of	*orbite* (Fr.n.) 'orbit'	0
on the flank of	*flanc* (Fr.n.) 'flank'	0
as far as	*feor* (adj.) 'far, remote'	0
within the realms of	*raume* (Fr.n.) 'kingdom'	0
afore	*on-forne* (pref.adv.) 'on before'	0
within an area of	*area* (Lat.n.) 'space'	0
in combinations with	*combination* (Fr.n.) 'combination'	0
within a distance of	*destance* (Fr.n.) 'distance'	0
beyond the field of	*felth* (n.) 'field'	0

within the radius of	*radius* (Lat.n.) 'radius'	0
on route from	*route* (Fr.n.) 'way, route'	0
on the very point of	*puint* (Fr.n.) 'point'	0
within a stone's throw from	*stan* (n.) 'stone'; throw (n.) 'throw'	0
within the verge of	*verge* (Fr.n.) 'edge, rod, twig'	0
upwards of	*upweard-es* (adv.adv.gen.suf.) 'upward'	0
within a circumference of	*circumsaunce* (Fr.n.) 'circumstance'	0
within a small area of	*area* (Lat.n.) 'space'	0

Table 5.5 Frequency and lexical sources of spatial prepositions in Modern English

The frequency table shows a few interesting aspects about English spatial prepositions. Even though there are items that show a noticeably lower frequency than the one immediately preceding them, the frequency drop is particularly noticeable at the boundary of High and Medium frequency ranges. The last item in High, i.e., *into* occurring at 1,462 tokens pmw, makes a sharp contrast with the first item in Medium, i.e., *through,* occurring at 752 tokens pmw, accounting for a 48.5% drop.

The table also shows that there are a small number of High frequency prepositions, i.e., 10 of them, accounting for less than 5 percent of all spatial prepositions. These highly specialized spatial prepositions are all primary prepositions. In fact, the prepositions in High and Medium frequency categories are predominantly primary prepositions, i.e., out of 33, only 4 (*out of, back to, up to,* and *away from*) are composite prepositions and there is no complex preposition in the High and Medium frequency categories. Complex prepositions are predominantly located in the Very Low category. Note that out of 140 Very Low Frequency range prepositions, only 13 (9.3%) are primary prepositions.[4]

Therefore, the overall distribution is such that English spatial prepositions

---

4) It is worth noting, however, that participle-derived forms (e.g., *following* and *touching*) and comparative/superlative-inflected forms (e.g., *nearer* and *nearest*) may be technically primary (by virtue of consisting of one word) but are morphologically complex.

comprise a small number of highly frequent primary prepositions and a large number of complex prepositions that are very infrequently used (note that there are as many as 71 prepositions that are attested for 0 pwm in the corpus, which means that they are attested for fewer than 500 raw tokens). This is clearly suggestive of the coextensive development of grammaticalizing forms with respect to their morphosyntactic composition (length), functional generality (specificity), and circulation (frequency).

From the (lexical) source information in the list, a number of forms that are single words in form in contemporary English are in fact historically polymorphemic. They include the *a*-derived and *be*-derived forms noted above, but there are other cases as well, with variable degrees of transparency. Some of such forms are shown in (6):

(6) a. *into*   ⟨ *in + to*
     b. *within*   ⟨ *with + in*
     c. *upon*   ⟨ *up + on*
     d. *outside*   ⟨ *out + side*
     e. *inside*   ⟨ *in + side*
     f. *toward*   ⟨ *to-weard*
     g. *together* ⟨ *to-gether*
     h. *near*   ⟨ *neah-r*

In examples in (6), the internal composition of (6f-h) is opaque largely because such components as *weard, gether,* and *neah* do not exist in Modern English. It is particularly notable that *near* is in fact a comparative of *neah* 'close' (related to MoE *nigh*), thus, meaning 'closer'. When the comparative morpheme becomes not salient any more, it comes to be regarded as the base form, prompting the derivation of *nearer* and *nearest* (for more discussion see I Choi 2021).

It is apparent from the list that spatial prepositions include a number of closely related forms, e.g., *toward/towards, beside/besides, among/amongst, amid/amidst, of/off*, etc., largely due to fossilization of the participating morphemes. According to *Oxford English Dictionary*, *-(e)s* is the adverbial genitive, and *-t* is excrescent, which probably was reinforced by association with superlatives in *-st*, as in *alongst, amidst, betwixt,* etc. The two prepositions *of* and *off* are of the same origin but *off,* according to *Oxford English Dictionary,* was more often used for the stressed form, and with different pronunciations, and the two came to develop into different prepositions in form and function in Modern English.

One of the most prominent aspects of the prepositions in the list is the fact that there are numerous forms that originated from French and/or Latin lexemes, e.g., *face, apart, close, course, opposite,* etc. This is particularly prominent with the complex prepositions. Since grammatical forms, as compared with lexical items, are borrowed from a different language at a much lower frequency, this is an interesting issue, which we will discuss in 5.3.3.3.

5.3.3. Grammaticalization Sources

English prepositions originated from diverse sources but mostly from nouns, a characteristic shared by most languages (see other chapters for other languages) (see Table 5.5 above). Also as noted above, English has a number of prepositions that involve words or phrases of French and/or Latin origin. In addition, an important note on sources concerns adverbs. As noted, prepositions may be used intransitively, in which case preposition shifts its function (as well as grammatical category for some frameworks). Since this is an important issue, we return to this in 5.4.4.2.

5.3.3.1 Nominal Sources

Granting that part of speech for particular word as a source lexeme can vary (cf. *round* n. 'ring', *round* adj. 'ring-shaped', etc.), and thus that the exact number can be inconclusive, there are about 88 nouns that serve as the source of prepositions, some of which are listed in (7) through (9):

(7) Body-part terms

heafod	(n.) 'head'	*face*	(Fr.n.) 'face, countenance'
æge	(n.) 'eye'	*front*	(n.) 'forehead, face'

nosu	(n.) 'nose'	*bæc*	(n.) 'back of body'
top	(n.) 'tuft, crest, head hair'	*handa*	(n.) 'hand'
breast	(n.) 'breast'	*fēt*	(n:pl.) 'feet'
flanc	(Fr.n.) 'flank'	*foet*	(n.) 'foot'
sídan	(n.) 'flank of person'	*hæla*	(n.) 'heel'
heorte	(n.) 'heart'		

(8) Spatial extent terms

area	(Lat.n.) 'space'	*premis*	(Fr.n.) 'premise'
background	(adj.n.) 'background'	*proxymyte*	(Fr.n.) 'proximity'
bound	(n.) 'limit'	*raume*	(Fr.n.) 'kingdom'
bound-ary	(n.suf.) 'limit'	*reach*	(n.) 'continuous stretch'
circumsaunce	(Fr.n.) 'outskirts'	*regeoun*	(Fr.Lat.n.) 'region'
destance	(Fr.n.) 'distance'	*scope*	(It.n.) 'extent'
felth	(n.) 'field'	*space*	(Fr.n.) 'extent, room'
fore-ground	(pref.n.) 'foreground'	*span*	(n.) 'span'
hiehþo	(n.) 'height'	*sper*	(Fr.Lat.n.) 'sphere'
lemet	(Fr.Lat.n.) 'boundary'	*vicinity*	(Fr.Lat.n.) 'proximity'
neighbour-hood	(n.suf.) 'neighborhood'		

(9) Geometric configuration terms

part	(Fr.n.) 'side'	*hindan*	(n.) 'behind'
middle	(n.) 'middle part'	*ūt(e)*	(n.) 'out(side)'
mid	(n.) 'middle'	*orbite*	(Fr.n.) 'orbit'
base	(Fr.n.) 'bottom'	*radius*	(Lat.n.) 'radius'
botm	(n.) 'lowest part of object'	*round*	(n.) 'ring'
brink	(Sc.n.) 'brink, edge'	*cross*	(n.) 'cross'
ecg	(n.) 'corner, edge'	*opposite*	(Fr.Lat.n.) 'opposite side'
puint	(Fr.n.) 'point'	*paralel*	(Fr.Lat.n.) 'parallel'
verge	(Fr.n.) 'edge, rod, twig'		

The nouns listed in (7) are of body-parts.[5] These 15 nouns are mostly native words, involving only two words of French origin, i.e., *face* and *flank,* which are very infrequent in use. The predominance of native terms suggests that body-part terms belong to the basic-level vocabulary. Multiplicity of body-part-based prepositions suggests that English productively uses the body-part model in grammaticalization of spatial grams (Heine, et al. 1991, Heine 1997). Also notable in the list is that there are more top/front-related terms than bottom/back-related terms, which is consonant with the observation that top and front are the areas suitable for optimal perception and thus are considered 'positive' directions (Andersen 1978: 343, Heine 1997, see 10.1.2 for further discussion).

The nouns listed in (8) are those that denote spatial extent. The major function of these terms is to delimit the range of the presence of an entity, physical or abstract, being predicated of. It is notable, in relation to body-part terms, that the proportion of borrowings in this group increases considerably, i.e., 12 out of 21, accounting for 57.1%. These spatial extent nouns are used in complex prepositions, and thus are used at a relatively lower frequency. Multiplicity of the terms of spatial extent is a noteworthy phenomenon as compared to other languages, because languages do not seem to involve this many words of spatial extent in grammaticalization of adpositions (see 5.3.3.3 for further discussion).

The nouns listed in (9) are those that denote geometric configuration. It is natural that such configurational terms are recruited for creating spatial prepositions for their immediate relevance to the target functions. Relational terms are among the primary categories of spatial gram sources (Heine 1997, Svorou 1994). There are many borrowings included in this group as well, 9 out of 17, accounting for 52.9%. Just as is the case with the nouns of spatial extent, prepositions involving geometric configurational nouns are used as a relatively lower frequency. Talmy (1983, 2000) argues that when spatial language references topological relations, shape and magnitude are irrelevant to the appropriateness of the expression.

---

[5] According to Bowden (1992: 35), body part nouns constitute the most highly exploited source category for locatives in Oceanic languages. Esseesy (2010: 40-42) also reports that body-part terms are the common source of prepositions in Arabic.

However, the presence of such lexemes as *edge, point, corner, orbit,* and *radius* runs counter the claim.

5.3.3.2 Verbal Sources

There are a number verbs that participate in the formation of prepositions, but the number of such source verbs is much smaller than the number of source nouns. These verbs are shown in (10) (PP denotes past participle; PRP denotes present participle):

(10) Participial sources

a. *past:*	(PP) *pass* 'exceed' 'surpass'
b. *during:*	(PRP) *dure,* Fr. *dure-r* 'persist, continue'
c. *pending:*	(PRP) *pend,* Fr. *pendre* 'depend'
d. *notwithstanding:* (PRP) *withstand* 'resist, oppose'	
e. *according to:*	(PRP) *accord,* Fr. *acorder* 'agree'
f. *pertaining to:*	(PRP) *pertain* 'belong' (partly from Fr.)
g. *touching:*	(PRP) *touch,* Fr. *tocher* 'touch'
h. *following:*	(PRP) *folgian/fylgan* 'follow'
i. *considering:*	(PRP) *consider,* Fr. *considérer* 'examine'
j. *barring:*	(PRP) *bar* 'exclude, set aside'
k. *concerning:*	(PRP) *concern* 'refer/relate to' (partly from Fr.)
l. *excepting:*	(PRP) *except,* Fr. *excepte-r* 'take out'
m. *excluding:*	(PRP) *exclude,* Lat. excludere 'shut out'
n. *including :*	(PRP) *include* 'confine, enclose' (partly from Fr.)
o. *regarding:*	(PRP) *regard,* Fr. *regarder* 'consider, look after'
p. *respecting:*	(PRP) *respect,* Lat. *respect-* 'look around/back'

As is common with some Germanic as well as Romance languages, verbs tend to be in the participial forms when they develop into prepositions. *Past* in (10a) is the only form developed from a past participial form, and *during* (10b) and *pending* (10c) are also unique in that their verb forms have not survived in contemporary English. *Notwithstanding* (10d) is a good example of 'univerbation' (Lehmann 2015[1982]), whereby multiple morphemes that were formerly independent words coalesced into a word. *According to* (10e) and *pertaining to* (10f) are the only composite prepositions in the group.

Since transitive verbs can take a noun phrase complement and participial verbs can be syntactically detached from the clausal subject (note that in this case the form is no longer limited to the function of complement to a preceding noun phrase and can acquire relative syntactic independence), participial forms of transitive verbs can be a good candidate for prepositions and conjunctions (see Hopper and Traugott 2003[1993], H Lee 2011, H Yi 2009, 2018). *Touch* is peculiar in that it was borrowed from French and serves as the source of two prepositions *touching* and *in touch with*. *Touching* is based on the verb *touch,* a borrowed word from French verb *tocher* 'touch', but *touch* in *in touch with* is from the noun *tocher* 'touch', formally identical with the verb. *Oxford English Dictionary* further suggests a possibility that *touching* is from Middle French *touchant*. In fact, *touchant* itself was a preposition in English from the 14th to 17th centuries, a borrowing of French preposition *touchant*. This suggests that French influence on English goes beyond lexical borrowing (see 5.3.3.3 below).

5.3.3.3 Borrowings

As noted above, a good proportion of English prepositions are borrowings from French, many of which can be traced back to Latin. This is evident from (10) above, that many verb-based prepositions are of French (and Latin) origin. Furthermore, a fairly large proportion of the nouns in complex prepositions is of French (and Latin) origin (see Table 5.4 and examples in (8) above).

There are a handful of prepositions from Italian and Scandinavian languages as well, e.g., *scope* (It.) 'extent', *brink* (Sc.) 'brink, edge'. There are as many as 52 prepositions that are built on French borrowings, 22 prepositions that are related to Latin words or borrowings. Considering that borrowing of grammatical forms is not as frequent as lexical borrowing, this state of affairs poses an intriguing question.

Hoffmann (2005), drawing upon historical data from such corpora as Gutenberg, Helsinki, ARCHER, CEEC, ICAMET, Lampeter, and ZEN, extensively studies this topic, and notes that a large number of French words are borrowed into English in the form of complex prepositions. In many cases, the borrowing of the head noun from French and its use in complex prepositions are not separated by a long period of time. In such cases the emergence of complex prepositions does not occur with the head noun attaining a high frequency of use (and substantial level of semantic generalization). This goes against the widely held view that generalization is closely tied to, or even is a precondition of, grammaticalization, and thus poses an important question as to the motivation and mechanism of grammaticalization. Hoffmann (2005) argues for analogy-based grammaticalization. In other words, when the template P–N–P is firmly entrenched, language users simply insert a novel form in the N slot, regardless of whether the form is new or old. In such cases the noun recruited does not have to attain the high frequency to participate in the grammaticalization process, and the complex preposition does not have to attain the high frequency to become an established member of the prepositional category.

The concept of analogy as a mechanism has been largely dismissed, because it has been commonly assumed that reanalysis actualizes rule change (thus grammaticalization) whereas analogy promotes spread or leveling. K Ahn (2015) analyzes English complex prepositions on a large scale, focusing on the forms that experience non-gradual grammaticalization, and argues that formal template and semantic affinity trigger analogy-driven grammaticalization. Ahn (2009a,b) also argues for analogy-driven grammaticalization of causal complex prepositions prompted by semantic attraction. Similarly, S Rhee (2012a, 2014), Rhee and Koo (2015) argue for analogy-driven grammaticalization of complementizers and connectives in Korean.

5.3.3.4 Multiple Sources and Layered Prepositions

As has been noted, there are multiple sources of grammaticalizing prepositions. Since different grammaticalization scenarios from multiple sources often lead to the development of grammatical forms of an identical function, the layering phenomenon is commonly observed.

In Table 5.4, there are multiple forms listed for the same/similar function. For instance, there are as many as nine different prepositions that signal Path (Perlative), as exemplified with constructed examples, in (11):

(11) Path

a.	*through*	They walked through the woods.
b.	*throughout*	People applauded throughout the performance.
c.	*via*	Reports from the scene are coming in via satellite.
d.	*on the way to*	I heard the news on the way to work.
e.	*on the road to*	She is on the road to recovery.
f.	*en route to*	The ambulance is en route to the hospital.
g.	*on route to*	The victim died on route to hospital.
h.	*en route from*	The plane was hijacked en route from Greece to Lithuania.
i.	*on route from*	The plane was on route from Afghanistan when the accident occurred.

As is obvious, many of the listed prepositions can be interchangeably used. It is also true that they are not completely synonymous, even though they all signal the path in one or another. In other words, these prepositions have slightly variable focus, in addition to Path-marking, e.g., profiling the source and the goal for *through*, *throughout* for sustenance, *via* for means, etc. Also, *way-*, *road-*, and *route-*forms are similar for their head noun semantics and are synonymous, but the final *to* and *from* differently highlight the goal and source, respectively. However, *en route* and *on route* are indistinguishable, even though their genre or register specialization may differ.

A particularly noteworthy case is Interior, in which as many as 20 prepositions are layered. The highest frequency *in* designates a general internal location and the three primary and composite prepositions, *within, inside* and *inside of* may be regarded as emphatic variants and further, the last two formal variants with differential degrees of structural erosion. However, the most spectacular layering is in the complex preposition group, in which diverse spatial extent nouns occur mostly in the template of *(with)in the N of.* Since there are multiple forms that do not exhibit any functional differences, the occurrence rate of individual forms is rather low, even though their aggregate occurrence rate may not be. In other words, prepositions in this category (and most other categories as well) are diffuse and do not exhibit extensive specialization.

5.4 Ongoing Grammaticalization of Spatial Prepositions

5.4.1 Selection Criteria

As is the case with Korean, in which a small number of primary postpositions occur at a very high frequency whereas a large number of complex postpositions occur at a considerably low frequency (see Chapter 3), a similar state of affairs is observed with English prepositions. In this section we will address ongoing grammaticalization in English prepositional system.

In order to investigate ongoing grammaticalization among spatial prepositions in English, we first need to select optimal prepositions that are currently undergoing grammaticalization. The entire inventory consists of 684 prepositions, i.e., 97 primary, 64 composite, and 523 complex prepositions. Out of these, we select the items that qualify all of the following conditions, with arguably arbitrary cut-off points, as in (12):

(12) (i)   It is not in the primary prepositional category in contemporary English (587 items);
    (ii)   It encodes spatial relationship (152 of them);
    (iii)   It is attested for more than 10,000 times in the corpus (25 of them).

Condition (i) is to ensure that the target preposition is not yet established as a fully grammaticalized preposition. Condition (ii) is to restrict the target items within our research focus, i.e., spatial preposition. Condition (iii) is to ensure that the item is a viable one, not a chance occurrence attributable to idiolectic styles or that the form is not at a very incipient stage where the form's viability is yet uncertain. The frequency of 10,000 in the one-billion word corpus is about 10 occurrences per million words, which coincides with the cut-off point for Medium Frequency range in Table 5.5 above. The 25 target forms, supposedly actively undergoing grammaticalization, are listed in Table 5.6.

Frequency Range	Spatial Preposition	(Lexical) Source	PMW
Medium (100~999 pmw) (n=4)	*out of*	*utt* (adv.) 'out(side)'	621
	back to	*bæc* (n.) 'back of body'	228
	up to	*up to* (prep.prep.) 'up to'	141
	away from	*on-way* (prep.n.) on-way 'above a track'	128
Low (10~99 pmw) (n=21)	*along with*	*and-long* (pref.adj.) 'against line'	88
	in front of	*front* (n.) 'forehead, face'	84
	close to	*close* (adj.) 'closed, shut'	70
	next to	*next* (super:adv.) 'nearest'	55
	in the middle of	*middle* (n.) 'middle part'	41
	ahead of	*a-head* (prep.n.) 'on head'	31
	outside of	*out-sídan* (adj.n.) 'outside'	30
	on top of	*top* (n.) 'tuft, crest, head hair'	29
	far from	*far* (adj.) 'remote'	23
	right to	*reoht* (adj.) 'just, correct'	20
	out from	*utt* (adv.) 'out(side)'	18
	off of	*of* (prep.) 'away from'	18
	together with	*together* (prep.adv.) 'to together'	16
	down from	*down* (adv.) 'in a descending direction'	15
	at the top of	*top* (n.) 'tuft, crest, head hair'	14
	up against	*again-s* (prep.suf.) 'in hostility'	13
	in the face of	*face* (Fr.n.) 'countenance'	13
	apart from	*a-part* (Fr.prep.n.) 'to side'	13
	inside of	*in-sídan* (adj.n.) 'in side'	11
	aside from	*a-sídan* (prep.n.) 'on side'	10
	in the midst of	*midst* (super.adj.) 'most central'	10

Table 5.6 Grammaticalizing spatial prepositions in Modern English

5.4.2 General Characteristics

The 25 target items bear special significance in grammaticalization of English prepositions and further in the studies of grammaticalization in languages typologically similar to English. We will discuss their characteristics more in detail.

The overall distribution of grammaticalizing prepositions is such that they are predominantly composite prepositions (19 out of 25), whereas complex prepositions constitute a smaller portion (6 out of 25). These figures show that a large proportion of spatial composite prepositions (19 out of 32; 59.4%) are actively undergoing grammaticalization in PDE, whereas a much smaller proportion of spatial complex prepositions (6 out of 120; 5%) are doing so. This asymmetry clearly indicates that composite prepositions are not only structurally simpler but also functionally stronger than complex prepositions. This may even suggest a general directionality of grammaticalization paths, i.e., [complex preposition 〉 composite preposition 〉 primary preposition].

In the following, we will discuss some of the grammaticalizing prepositions in such categories as Source, Separation, Interior, and Exterior.

[Sources (Ablatives)]
Prepositions marking the Source, most often termed as ablatives, are commonly found across languages. Grammaticalization of such source-marking prepositions in English is noteworthy in that there are multiple forms in the category, and yet they are robustly represented in terms of use frequency. In other words, the common phenomenon of 'spreading thin' with multiple forms is not observable in this case. The source-marking prepositions are as listed in (13):

(13) Ablatives
    a. *of*   23,159
    b. *from*   3,711
    c. *out of*   621
    d. *away from*   128
    e. *out from*   18

f.	*down from*	15
g.	*across from*	6
h.	*from under*	6
i.	*from among*	2
j.	*from between*	1
k.	*from a position of*	0
l.	*from the position of*	0

As seen in the list, there are as many as four actively grammaticalizing prepositions, i.e., *out of, away from, out from,* and *down from* (13c-f), which are in competition with other source-marking prepositions, some primary, some composite and complex. Among these four, the competition seems to be not functionally conflicting because they have slightly different specialization, i.e., *out of* is profiling the trajector coming out of an enclosed space, whereas *away from* is simply profiling detachment from an entity. *Out from* carries more emphatic overtone than *out of,* and *down from* contains the semantic component that the trajector is in the descending motion.

As compared to *down from, across from* is semantically more marked in that the movement involves a particular kind of trajectory (i.e., crossing a plane from one side to another), whereas *down from* is slightly more general and unmarked in the real world, because descent is a common trajectory in the world where gravity is omnipresent. Likewise, all the composite and complex prepositions that are of a lower frequency are semantically more specific, which could have contributed to a lower level of productivity in use.

When the four grammaticalizing prepositions are compared with the higher frequency items, i.e., *of* and *from,* the immediately noticeable difference is that *of* and *from* are semantically much more general than the four. The preposition *of* has been semantically bleached to such an extent that its use is not restricted to encoding spatial sources, e.g., *loads of food, a bottle of beer, the face of a con artist, dresses of silk, fond of swimming,* etc. This is not surprising considering that it is the most frequently used preposition in English, thus, one that supposedly has undergone semantic generalization to the greatest extent. The preposition *from* is often in direct competition with *out of,* but *from* is also semantically lighter as compared to *out of,* since the latter, having two words *out* and *of*, profiles different aspects, such as association, privation, dissociation, etc. (for detailed discussion, see S Rhee 2012b).

All these point to the fact that semantic generality/specificity is among the most important determinants of grammaticalization, because that directly affects the use frequency. This is in line with the generally received idea of the crucial role of frequency in grammaticalization noted in Bybee (1985, 2011), Bybee et al. (1994), and many others.

[Separatives]

There are a number of prepositions marking separation and distance (Separative, Ablative, Distantive, depending on the focus). Separative is related to but not identical with ablative, in that ablative signals that the departure point is part of the trajectory whereas separative does not necessarily do so but emphasizes the gap between the focused and the referenced entity/location. There are half a dozen prepositions that carry the separative function, as listed in (14):

(14) Separatives

a.	*from*	3,711
b.	*off*	259
c.	**far from**	23
d.	**apart from**	13
e.	**aside from**	10
f.	*aside*	5
g.	*beyond the shadow of*	0

Three prepositions, *far from, apart from,* and *aside from* mark separation and distance from the referenced entity. *Far from,* by virtue of the presence of the adjective *far,* stresses the distantness between two locations, thus is more efficient for emphasis than *apart from* and *aside from,* which only denote separation without degree specification. Since semantic generality is closely related to the level of productivity, the lower frequency level of *apart from* and *aside from* as compared to the emphatic *far from* is somewhat puzzling. One possibility is that since *apart from* and *aside from* are very similar in meaning, the two forms are being divided in use for encoding an identical concept and consequently occur at a lower frequency individually.

From, as noted above, is semantically general and thus marks a wide range of concepts directly or indirectly related to departure, e.g., departure point, source, cause, material, deterrence, separation, etc. (cf. *come from work, hear from a friend, die from the injuries, brewed from millet, shelter from the storm, keep from the public*, etc.). *Far from, apart from* and *aside from* do not share this semantic versatility; they simply highlight the presence of distance. *Off*, fully grammaticalized as a primary preposition, is in some respect in competition with the three grammaticalizing prepositions. Just as is the case with *from, off* is semantically general and thus occurs at a very high frequency. For instance, in addition to separation (e.g., *take a book off my desk*), *off* marks apartness (e.g., *keep off the grass*), disconnection (e.g., *be off the medicine*), nearness (*off the west coast*), etc. Thus, *off* has become a fully grammaticalized, and semantically generalized, primary preposition.

At the lower end, *aside* and *beyond the shadow of* are also marking separation. The latter's being infrequent is easily explained as it is highly specific in meaning, potentially metaphorical in origin, and highly compositional in form. However, *aside* is peculiar in that it is a fully developed primary preposition but is far less frequently used than the three composite prepositions currently undergoing active grammaticalization. The reason is unclear, but it is possibly because it is primarily used as an adverb. For instance, a COCA search returns 40,139 hits for *aside*'s adverbial usage (note that it is about 4 times as frequent as the prepositional use). In other words, *aside* is being specialized as an adverb rather than a preposition, allowing its reinforced relative, *aside from*, to carry the prepositional function.

(15) Interiors

in	15,670	*in the area of*	4
within	244	*in the space of*	1
inside	78	*within the scope of*	1
inside of	11	*in the region of*	0

within the realm of	0	*within the span of*	0
within the limits of	0	*on the premises of*	0
within the boundaries of	0	*within the orbit of*	0
within the range of	0	*within the realms of*	0
within the bounds of	0	*within an area of*	0
in the sphere of	0	*within a distance of*	0
within the field of	0	*within the radius of*	0
within the space of	0	*within a circumference of*	0

Interior prepositions are impressively numerous, i.e., 24 in total, but only one of them, i.e., *inside of,* is undergoing grammaticalization with a reasonable degree of viability. It has three powerful competitors, *in, within,* and its own relative *inside.* Just as is the case with other categories we have reviewed, semantic generality seems to be the primary factor of this distributional disparity, along with formal simplicity. The prepositions *in* and *within* are semantically general and can be used in a wide range of contexts, often extending to non-spatial domains. *Inside* is evidently in direct competition with *inside of,* but the former has primacy over the latter. *Inside* is interesting that it is divided nearly equally between the prepositional and adverbial functions. For instance, COCA searches return 78 tokens pmw (78,021 hits) for prepositional use and 72 tokens pmw (72,434 hits) for adverbial use. Thus, it can be said that *inside,* originating from *in side,* historically a construction of an adjective and a noun (*Oxford English Dictionary*), becomes a noun, adjective, adverb, and preposition across time, and the periphrastic, and relatively compositional, *inside of* cannot gain ground in the competition with the simpler *inside.* The exact reason for this peculiarity needs further research.

At the lower end, there are as many as 20 competitors, all of which are complex prepositions. Though numerous, these do not create any meaningful level of competition, considering their extremely low use frequency (note that 0 pmw denotes lower than 500 token frequencies in the corpus). These are all highly specific in meaning and also highly compositional in construction (note that all of them are of the PDNP structure, still containing an article, the disappearance of which is among the first indications of grammaticalization in earnest).

(16) Exteriors

outside	107	*outside the boundaries of*	0
outside of	31	*outside the range of*	0
out	4	*outside the reach of*	0
beyond the limits of	0	*outside the limits of*	0
beyond the bounds of	0	*beyond the field of*	0
beyond the range of	0		

The last category of our discussion concerns the Exteriors. They are not as numerous as their polar opposite Interiors (i.e., 11 vs. 24), and the aggregate tokens are also far below those of Interiors, accounting for less than 1 percent (i.e., 142 pmw vs. 16,012 pmw), suggesting human propensity for the inclusion-oriented construal over the exclusion-oriented construal of spatial configuration.

It is interesting to note that nearly identical pattern is found between these Exteriors and the Interiors that we addressed above. For instance, the primary preposition *outside* outnumbers the composite preposition *outside of* (note that *inside* outnumber *inside of*), and most competitors at the lower end are not of comparable strength. Nearly all of them are complex prepositions with the PDNP structure (note the similar pattern with the Interiors). One primary preposition *out* is outnumbered by *outside of,* but the relatively weaker strength of *out* as a preposition may have to do with its specialization as an adverb. A COCA search returns 1,828 tokens pmw (1,828,247 hits) of adverbial usage, more than 450 times of the prepositional usage.

From the foregoing discussion, the correlation among formal shape (i.e., primary vs. composite vs. complex), semantic generality, and use frequency proves to be robust. Sometimes, part-of-speech specialization plays a role in that formally identical expression may carry one function in the main and another as an ancillary function, allowing other expressions to specialize in the latter function. A defining characteristic of grammaticalization is the directionality in a number of domains, but it is evident from the above that the changes in form, meaning, and function occur in tandem.

5.4.3 Grammaticalization Mechanisms

As we have done with the languages addressed in previous chapters, we examine grammaticalization scenarios of English prepositions with respect to the grammaticalization mechanisms proposed by Kuteva et al. (2019), i.e., extension, desemanticization, decategorialization, and erosion.

5.4.3.1 Extension

Extension of usage context is well attested in grammaticalization processes of English prepositions. The extension is enabled by desemanticization (see 5.4.3.2 below), whereby a gram changes its meaning by becoming more general. A good example is the body-part terms. In 5.3.3.1, we noted that there are a number of body-part terms that developed into prepositions. For instance, *aside, inside, outside, by the side of,* etc. originated from the body-part noun *sídan* 'flank of person'; *atop, on top of, at the top of,* etc. originated from the body-part term *top* (n.) 'hair on head, tuft, crest'; *back to, in the back of, on the back of, at the back of,* etc. originated from the body-part term *bæc* (n.) 'back of body'; *in front of* originated from the body-part term *front* (n.) 'forehead, face', among many others. Needless to say, these prepositions can be used in context when the spatial location being referred to is not involving body-part. A good example of *front* 'forehead' is exemplified in (17), taken from *Oxford English Dictionary*, with modern translations added:

(17) a. [forehead] c1290 *Bote fram þe riȝt half of is frount.* 'but from the right half of his forehead' (S. Eng. Leg. I. 169/2176)

b. [the whole face] 1398 *Januarius is paynted wyth two frontes to shewe and to teche the begynnynge and ende of the yere.* 'Januarius is painted with two faces to show and to preach the beginning and end of the year.' (J. Trevisa tr. Bartholomew de Glanville De Proprietatibus Rerum (1495) ix. ix. 354)

c. [object's front side] c1540 (▸ ?a1400) *In þat frunt of þat faire yle Was a prouynse of prise.* 'In that front of the isle was a province of wealth.' (Gest

Historiale Destr. Troy (2002) f. 164v)

d. [first period of time] 1609 *Philomell in summers front doth singe* 'Philomel in summer's front does sing.' (W. Shakespeare Sonnets cii. sig. G2)

e. [at a position before] 1698 *I saw..a pragmatical Portugal..in the front of 40 men marching to the Governor's.* (J. Fryer New Acct. E.-India & Persia 144)

f. [priority] 1878 *Placing social aims at the head and front of his life.* (J. Morley Condorcet 37)

The examples in (17), only selectively taken from *Oxford English Dictionary*, show the semantic change that can be summarized as [forehead ⟩ whole face ⟩ object's front side ⟩ first period of time ⟩ at a position before ⟩ priority]. This line of change is in consonance with the ontological shift in metaphorization proposed by Heine et al. (1991a): [person ⟩ object ⟩ process ⟩ space ⟩ time ⟩ quality]. What is important is that (17e) could have been only literally interpretable as "in the forehead of 40 men" around the 13th century, i.e., before *in (the) front of* grammaticalizes into a preposition. As the meaning of involved words changes, typically via generalization through metonymization (e.g., forehead ⟩ face) and metaphorization (e.g., human forehead to object's or time's or priority's front), the expressions involving them can be used in wider contexts.

The cases like front described above concern semantics of the lexemes and thus interpretive inadequacy is normal and thus of little theoretical importance. More interesting instances concern verb-based grammaticalization, e.g., *following, touching, past,* etc., for involvement of loosening syntactic constraints. For instance, *following* is originally a present participle of the verb *follow.* Its first prepositional use, as recorded in *Oxford English Dictionary,* dates from 1841, with the meaning of 'subsequent to, in consequence of, after, etc.', exemplified in (18b):

(18) a. 1683 *She plunges her self again in the pit seeing a cure, not following the star of the Scripture.* (W. Houschone Scotl. pulling down Gates of Rome 12)

b. 1841 *In the month of June, following this council, Tecumseh made a visit to fort Wayne.* (B. Drake Life of Tecumseh x. 158) c.	1968 *Used car prices are going up, <u>following</u> the Budget.* (Observer 24 Mar. 6/4)

In (18a), *following* is a present participle, and thus its syntactic and semantic subject is the main clause subject, i.e., *she.* When it becomes grammaticalized into a preposition, its syntactic and semantic subject may or may not be identical with the main clause subject. For instance, the syntactic-semantic subject of *following* in (18b) can be the main clause subject *Tecumseh* (i.e., Tecumseh followed the council which also went to Fort Wayne, or he followed the resolutions made by the council, etc.), or its subject may be *the month of June* (i.e., this council met before June), or its subject may be exophoric and not present in the sentence (i.e., the source of information is this council, thus equivalent to "according to this council"). Likewise, *following* in (18c) does not have *used car prices* as its syntactic-semantic subject. Its subject, if to be identified, is the information being reported, thus equivalent to "according to", as an indicator of the source of information. *Following* in (18b) and (18c) is an unambiguous example of prepositional usage. In prepositional usage, the syntactic-semantic subject may be variable, as seen above, and thus, *Oxford English Dictionary* comments on its prepositional use: "The use of *following* as a preposition has in the past been considered by some to be incorrect, particularly since it can sometimes create ambiguity." (see entry for *following*, prep.).

5.4.3.2 Desemanticization

Desemanticization is a robust parameter of grammaticalization. Since lexical meanings tend to be specific whereas grammatical meanings are necessarily general (note that grammatical notions are relational and abstract), grammaticalization involves a level of abstraction in the meaning of lexical items involved. For instance, the English verb of locomotion *go* and the future marker developed from it, i.e., *be going to,* clearly show a different level of abstraction. The same is applicable to the grammaticalization of prepositions.

Among the most frequently cited examples in grammaticalization studies across languages is the body-part term *back.* In English, as noted above, the historical form of the lexeme is *bæc* (n.) 'back of body', attested in Old English, referring to the body-part back of humans or vertebrated animals (*Oxford English Dictionary*). The information about back in *Oxford English Dictionary* is presented in (18), with modern translations added:

(18) a. [back of body] c1400 (?c1390) *Of bak & of brest al were his bodi sturne.* 'Of back and of breast, all were his strong body.' (Sir Gawain & Green Knight (1940) l.143)

b. [whole body to be clothed] 1549 *Borrow of thy two next neighbours, that is to say, of thy backe and thi belly.* 'Borrow from two of your neighbors, that is to say, for your body [clothing] and your belly [food].' (T. Solme in H. Latimer 2nd Serm. before Kynges Maiestie To Rdr. sig. Avi)

c. [hinder side of things] 1626 *Trees, set vpon the Backes of Chimneys, doe ripen Fruit sooner.* 'Trees set upon the back of chimneys do ripen fruit sooner.' (F. Bacon Sylua Syluarum §856)

d. [the time after; obsolete] 1673 *I must be..your debtor till the back of Whitsontide.* (J. Flamsteed Let. 5 May in Corr. (1995) I. 208)

e. [behind (preposition)] 1895 Trilby, *as a name, must have been lying* perdu *somewhere, as they say, 'at the back of my head', as important things so often do.* (G. Du Maurier in Idler Dec. 420/2)

The examples in (19) show the gradual semantic change of *back* from the body-part term to a posterior preposition *at the back of*, through a series of desemanticization per metonymy and metaphor, i.e., [body-part back 〉 whole body 〉 object's backside 〉 temporal posterity] and then further to preposition. The phrasal use, the prepositional use being part of it, is first attested in c1430, according to *Oxford English Dictionary*, mostly in the form of *at one's back*. In the citations, the first occurrence of *at the back of* is 1895, as shown in (18e).

5.4.3.3 Decategorialization

Decategorialization occurs in the course of grammaticalization typically involving nouns and verbs, because these nuclear lexemes lose the syntactic and semantic focus in the grammaticalizing construction. Even though decategorialization occurs gradually, its manifestation is visible only after the change occurred. For instance, we have seen the example of the preposition *following* in (18) above, repeated here for convenience as (19) along with their modified counterparts:

(19) a. 1683 *She plunges her self again in the pit seeing a cure, not <u>following</u> the star of the Scripture.* (W. Houschone Scotl. pulling down Gates of Rome 12)

  a' *She plunges her self again in the pit seeing a cure, not <u>carefully</u> <u>following</u> the star of the Scripture.* ((20a) modified)

  b. 1968 *Used car prices are going up, <u>following</u> the Budget.* (Observer 24 Mar. 6/4)

  b' **Used car prices are going up, <u>carefully</u> <u>following</u> the Budget.* ((20b) modified)

As shown in (19), when *following* is a present participle of the verb *follow,* i.e., a member of the primary category, it can be modified by a manner adverb such as *carefully* (cf. (19a) and (19a')), whereas when it is a preposition, i.e., not a member of the verb category, it cannot be modified by a manner adverb (cf. (19b) and (19b')). This is a clear indication of the loss of a verbal characteristic.

   Nouns also experience decategorialization in the course of grammaticalization. We noted above that the noun *top* started its life as a noun denoting 'hair on head, crest, or tuft', thus referring to the top-most part or the hair thereof. The word has undergone semantic and functional change developing into a preposition in the form of *on the top of* and its more reduced counterpart *on top of* with the meaning 'above, upon, close upon, following upon; in addition to' (*Oxford English Dictionary,* see entry for 'top'), as illustrated below with the examples taken from *Oxford English Dictionary* and modified counterparts:

(20) a. [head, head-hair] 1535 *Then the angel..toke him by the <u>toppe</u>, and bare him by the hayre of the heade.* (Bible (Coverdale) Bel & Dragon i. F)

  b. 1650 *We deck ourselves with birds feathers, the <u>tops</u> of herons.* (Earl of

Monmouth tr. J. F. Senault Man become Guilty 353

c.   a1643 *This white top writeth my much years.* (W. Cartwright Ordinary (1651) ii. ii. 25)

d.   1977 *He really felt he was getting on top of the situation.* ('A. York' Tallant for Trouble vi. 87)

d'.   **They really felt they were getting on tops of the situation.* ((21d) modified)

d".   **He really felt he was getting on the very top of the situation.* ((21d) modified)

As shown in (20a), (20b) and (20c), the noun *top* can be modulated with pluralization or can be modified by an adjective. On the other hand, the preposition *on top of* is structurally frozen, i.e., has lost the nominal characteristic of *top* in it and cannot be pluralized (cf. (20d')) nor can it be modified (cf. (20d")). All these clearly indicate the loss of the major category characteristics of the participating core lexeme.

5.4.3.4 Erosion

Erosion, or reduction in phonetic volume, is also common even though it is not a prerequisite to grammaticalization. In the case of grammaticalization of complex and composite prepositions in English, the most prominent erosion occurs with the article. This is a common characteristic in article languages, such as Spanish, as well (see 6.4.3.4). Incidentally, articles in German tend to be contracted, thus become reduced in phonetic volume, in the environment of two function words occurring next to each other (e.g., [am] ⟨ an dem, [anə] ⟨ an die, etc.) (see Schiering 2010: 92, Kohler 1995: 205ff; see also Lehmann 2015[1982]).

English prepositions show erosion in gradience according to their level of grammaticalization. We observed that there are about 213 spatial prepositions across four different frequency ranges. The prepositions in the four ranges have different proportion of retaining the article in the preposition, as shown in Table 5.7.

Frequency Range (no. of preps)	Primary (% in range)	Composite (% in range)	Complex (% in range)	
			(w/o article)(%)	(w/article)(%)
High (10)	10 (100%)	0	0	0
Medium (23)	19 (82.6%)	4 (17.4%)	0	0
Low (40)	19 (47.5%)	15 (37.5%)	6 (15.0%)	
			2 (33.3%)	4 (66.7%)
Very Low (140)	13 (9.3%)	13 (9.3%)	114 (81.4%)	
			23 (20.2%)	91 (79.8%)

Table 5.7 Frequency and erosion in English spatial preposition

Table 5.7 shows that article is found only in the Low and Very Low frequency range groups, since complex prepositions by our working definition are those that can accommodate an article, i.e., PDNP structures. It also shows that there are no prepositions containing an article in the High and Medium frequency groups. Complex prepositions are predominantly located in the Very Low frequency group (i.e., 114 out of 120, accounting for as high as 95%). When we compare the proportions of the prepositions retaining articles across the Low and Very Low frequency ranges, we see that 2 out of 6 (33.3%) in the Low frequency range have lost the article, whereas in the Very Low frequency range, only 23 out of 114 (20.2%) have lost the article. This is an indication of correlation between frequency and formal erosion (i.e., omission of the article). The lower the frequency, the more likely the preposition retains the article, and vice versa.

5.4.4 Grammatical Functions

5.4.4.1 Beyond Space

As has been observed across languages, spatial grams designate more than spaces: their meanings are extended to more abstract domains along the ontological continuum as proposed by Heine et al. (1991a). Semantic extension patterns of spatial adpositions have been addressed in the literature (e.g. S Rhee 2002a,b,c, Tyler and Evans 2003, J Baik 2004, 2005). Some of the semantic extension patterns are as shown in the following examples taken from S Rhee (2006a):

(21) *at*: Spatial 〉 Temporal 〉 Abstract Point
    a. *I waited for him at the door.*   [Location]
    b. *He arrived at noon.*   [Temporal]
    c. *I got a loan at a low rate.*   [Abstract Point]

(22) *in*: Location 〉 Direction/Motion 〉 Temporal/Abstract State...
    a. *He is in the building.*   [Location]
    b. *He will be back in five minutes.*   [Temporal]
    c. *He got in the car.*   [Direction/Motion]
    d. *He is in tears / good health.*   [State]

(23) *out, up, down*: Direction/Motion 〉 Location 〉 ...
    a. *He jumped out the window.*   [Motion]
    b. *He looked out the window.*   [Direction]
    c. *He lives out West.*   [Location]

As shown in the examples above, the most essential semantic notion of spatial prepositions, i.e. Location, typically undergoes the directional change from [Space 〉 Time], one of the most widely attested metaphorization processes. However, S Rhee (2006a) notes that most composite and complex prepositions tend to have more conservative semantics, suggesting that they have not undergone extensive semantic change, thus in harmony with the Parallel Reduction Principle (Bybee et al. 1994).

It is also notable that many English prepositions have their specialization in emotion constructions as instances of extension from spatial function. Radden (1981, 1985), Dirven (1995, 1997), Rudanko (1996), and E Kim (2015, 2018), among others, show that English prepositions mark emotion causality, often retaining the original image schemas associated with the locative prepositions.

Even though semantic generalization of the core lexemes extends the function of prepositions, there are more serious issues involving grammatical categories, to a discussion of which we now turn.

5.4.4.2 Beyond Preposition

When prepositions in English are used for grammatical functions other than prepositions, the immediately relevant category is adverbs (see 5.2 above, and S Rhee 2002b). Since English prepositions having dual preposition-adverb category membership is so common and are functionally related that some researchers regard the adverbial use as intransitive prepositional use (Burton-Roberts 1991, Huddleston and Pullum 2002, among others) or prepositional adverbs (Quirk et al. 1985: 713-716). From such a view, a regular preposition is a transitive preposition in contrast with complement-less counterpart is an intransitive preposition, as contrasted in the following constructed examples (also see example (2) above):

(24) a. *The key is <u>by</u> the door.*
      b. *My friend stopped <u>by</u>.*

(25) a. *I will take you <u>across</u> the border.*
      b. *It was difficult to get our message <u>across</u>.*

Another common category to which prepositions develop into is conjunctions, as exemplified in the following:

(26) a. *He stood up <u>before</u> a whole roomful of people.*
      b. *Wash your hands <u>before</u> you come to the table.*

(27) a. *We have been in business <u>since</u> 1958.*
      b. *I had to go alone <u>since</u> she refused to go with me.*

A more intriguing category in functional extension of prepositions is postposition, i.e., when it occurs after the complement, as shown in the following:[6]

(28) a. *Notwithstanding some objections, we decided to move forward.*

  b. *Serious injuries notwithstanding, he won the match.*

(29) a. *His name was printed below the title.*

  b. *It has been buried 20 feet below.*

Some instances of functional extension to other grammatical categories are common as from preposition to adverb or conjunction, but there are other, more local and idiosyncratic, cases as well. For instance, Hoffmann (2005, chapter 7) investigates the use of the complex preposition *in terms of,* and notes that it carries the hedging function, especially in such registers as public debates, discussions, meetings, business or committee meetings. Based on the collocation patterns, syntactic behavior, and discursive functions, he characterizes its function as that of a discourse marker, typically used for filling pauses to buy time in searching for a suitable expression, indicating hesitation, etc.

Another notable study of functional extension is Givón (2021), who extensively discusses the development of case-marking adposition to verbal affix, through the 'zeroing out' (p. 31) of the nominal object due to predictability in appropriate discourse context. This study, however, does not pursue an investigation into this intriguing topic.

---

6) Lehmann (2015[1982]: 176) notes that in German, a language genealogically closely related language to English, some secondary adpositions, including *wegen* 'because of', *gemäß* 'in conformity with', *entsprechend* 'corresponding to', *zufolge* 'acccording to', *entlang* 'along', may be used either as prepositions or as postpositions, even though all the primary adpositions in German are exclusively prepositions. Smessaert et al. (2014) discuss prepositions, postpositions, circumpositions in Dutch, a language genealogically close to English. Thus, the directionality of functional extension needs more research. For discussion of the English temporal postposition *ago*, see Kurzon 2008).

5.5 Summary

In this chapter we have looked at the prepositional system in English from a grammaticalization perspective. We classified prepositions according to their formal make-up, i.e., primary for single-word prepositions, composite for two-word prepositions, and complex for prepositions with three or more words. English has a large number of prepositions that belong to primary, composite, and complex prepositional categories. English has a large number of primary prepositions, numbering 97, which sharply contrasts with Spanish (see chapter 6), which has only 25 of them. English also has a large number of composite and complex prepositions, numbering about 64 and 523, respectively. The total number of prepositions in English is 684. These numbers are inconclusive due to the fuzzy boundary between complex prepositions and syntactic constructions (for similar states affairs in Spanish, see chapter 6).

The prepositions widely vary in their use frequency. For instance, from a statistical survey based on the one-billion word corpus COCA, the preposition of the highest frequency, i.e., *of,* records higher than 23,000 pmw, whereas there are as many as 71 prepositions that are attested for 0 pwm in the corpus, which means that they are attested for fewer than 500 raw tokens. All prepositions in the High frequency range, and nearly all prepositions in the Medium frequency range are primary prepositions. On the other hand, a vast majority of complex prepositions are in the Very Low frequency range.

An important sources of prepositions are nouns, whereas verbs are very few. An idiosyncrasy is the large number of borrowings from French, many of which are also related to Latin. When the French or Latin words are borrowed, they are put into the noun slot of the well-established PDNP structural template.

In the inventory of 684 prepositions, 213 of them are spatial prepositions. The proportion across the formal types exhibits asymmetry, i.e., about 63% of the primary prepositions, 50% of the composite prepositions, and about 23% of the complex prepositions are spatial prepositions, showing a decreasing proportion across the formal types along the increasing structural complexity.

Out of these 213 spatial prepositions, we selected 25 of them, which are regarded as actively undergoing grammaticalization with a degree of viability. After comparing some of them with other prepositions that are thought to be their competitors, we came to a conclusion that semantic generality/specificity is among the most important determinants of grammaticalization, confirming the hypothesis that frequency plays a critical role in grammaticalization, because the frequency crucially depends on the level of semantic generality. We also noted that some forms have multiple memberships in grammatical categories, and have differential degrees of specialization in these multiple categories. Further, we noted that a defining characteristic of grammaticalization is the directionality in a number of domains, and that the changes in form, meaning, and function occur in tandem.

We reviewed grammaticalization mechanisms, such as extension, desemanticization, decategorialization, and erosion, and noted that grammaticalization of English prepositions is consonant with these mechanisms.

With respect to grammatical functions, we observed that spatial prepositions often develop into prepositions for more abstract notions, such as time, quality, etc. More importantly, many prepositions also function as adverbs, or 'intransitive prepositions' by some researchers, as conjunctions, and some as discourse markers. The discourse marker function has been briefly noted with respect to *in terms of* addressed in Hoffmann (2005), but there are other prepositions functioning similarly, which merit future research.

Grammaticalization of Prepositions in Spanish

6.1 Introduction

As is the case with other languages, Spanish has a well-developed system of adpositions with a large number of members in the functional paradigm. As we shall see, Spanish shares many features with other languages but at the same time displays unique features due to historical reasons. From a grammaticalization perspective, some of the features are noteworthy since they carry a number of theoretical implications. We discuss them from the system-internal as well as typological and crosslinguistic perspectives.[1]

6.2 Prepositions in Spanish

Spanish prepositions, like those in English, are generally considered to constitute a grammatical, thus closed, category with a relatively limited number of members (K Kim

---

[1] The author is deeply indebted to Spanish linguists, Kyunghee Kim and Heeran Lee, in writing this chapter. All errors, however, are mine.

and Rhee 2018). However, this category of 'prepositions', also like the one in English, shows a level of categorial fluidity in that it borders on other grammatical categories. For instance, one of the most prestigious reference grammars in the Spanish-speaking world, *Nueva Gramática de la Lengua Española* (2009; *NGLE*) by Asociación de las Academias, notes that the members in the preposition category are not of equal status because some of them are of little use, others have entered the category not long ago, and still others have only partial properties of the category (p. 2228). It further presents, without argument, that it is 'usually understood' ("suele entenderse") that the following 23 formants are prepositions in Spanish (pp. 2228) (English translations added):

(1) *a* 'to, at'[2]   *ante* 'before'   *bajo* 'under'
     cabe 'next to'   *con* 'with'   *contra* 'against, opposite'
     de 'of'   *desde* 'since'   *durante* 'during'
     en 'in'   *entre* 'between, among'   *hacia* 'toward'
     hasta 'until'   *mediante* 'through'   *para* 'for'
     por 'for, by'   *según* 'following'   *sin* 'without'
     so 'under'   *sobre* 'on'   *tras* 'after'
     versus 'against'   *vía* 'through'

However, *NGLE* further notes that the following prepositions have peculiarities as compared to the other members of the category, as summarized in (2) (pp. 2228-2233):[3]

(2) a. *cabe* [= *junto a*] 'next to'; *so* [= *bajo*] 'under'
     b. *hasta* 'until'
     c. *según* [= *conforme a*; *de acuerdo con*] 'following, according to', [= *en función de*; *dependiendo de*] 'in function of, according to, depending on'

---

[2] The function of the Spanish preposition *a* is numerous, and according to Kyunghee Kim (p.c.), it often corresponds to English *at*.

[3] Certain functions, e.g. *versus* 'toward' and *vía* 'for', are obsolete in Modern Spanish (Kyunghee Kim, p.c.).

d. *durante* 'during'; *mediante* 'through'

e. *pro* [= *en favor de*] 'in favor of'

f. *versus* [= *hacia*] 'toward', [= *contra*] 'against', [= *frente a*] 'versus'

g. *vía* 'via', [= *por*] 'for, through'

According to *NGLE*, *cabe* 'next to' (< *cabde* < *a cabo de*) and *so* 'under' in (2a) are old forms that were used productively in medieval times but are no longer so in contemporary Spanish. *Hasta* in (2b) is homonymous with the adverb *hasta* 'even', but unlike the latter, it has prepositional properties, such as taking an oblique-case marked pronoun (e.g., *hasta mí*). The preposition *según* in (2c), developed from the Latin *secundum* (< *sequi* 'follow'), is the only tonic preposition and has various unique uses. *Durante* and *mediante* in (2d) stand out as they originated from participial forms of the verbs *durar* 'last' and *mediar* 'mediate'. The former is etymologically related to and is developmentally paralleled by the English preposition *during* (see S Kim 2015 for the grammaticalization of *during*). *Por* in (2e) is undoubtedly a preposition but it is often thought to be closer to the 'separable prefixes' ("prefijos separables"). *Versus* in (2f), a Latin preposition reintroduced from English, has two distinctive functions of marking 'toward' and 'against' depending on the context and its use is genre-sensitive, largely restricted to scientific, sports, and legal texts.[4] The preposition *vía* is used strictly for physical sense to indicate the place which one passes or where one stops on a journey.

The primary prepositions have developed from diverse sources, as is the case in most languages. The origins of the prepositions have been investigated in a body of research (Corominas and Pascual 1981, De Silva 1985, Portilla 2011, K Kim 2018, Kim and Rhee 2018, K Kim 2019). The sources include not only nouns, verbs, etc. but also inherited and borrowed forms (see 6.3.3 for more discussion).

For Spanish prepositions, not only the properties of individual forms but also their productivity is variable. For instance, in a quantitative investigation based on the 170-million word corpus CREA (Corpus de Referencia de Español Actual)

---

[4] The 'toward' function is now obsolete in Modern Spanish (Kyunghee Kim, p.c.).

developed by Real Academia Española, their token frequencies as prepositions show a large variation, as shown in Table 6.1, in which two primary prepositions *excepto* and *salvo* are included in addition to the *NGLE* inventory (see *NGLE* 2233, 2464-2465 for discussion on these extra items). As the Table 6.1 shows, even within the same frequency range, individual forms show a great variability. For instance, the preposition with the highest frequency, *de*, occurring over 61,000 pmw (over 10 million raw tokens in the corpus) is over 40 times as frequent as *entre*, recording about 1,481 pmw (252,000 raw tokens) within the same High frequency range. Also notable is that the two members *cabe* 'next to' and *so* 'under', as *NGLE* noted (see above), do not record any occurrences.

Frequency Range	Primary Preposition	Meaning	PMW
High (1,000~ wpm) (n=9)	*de*	'of'	61,012
	en	'in'	23,944
	a	'to, at'	19,380
	con	'with'	8,755
	por	'by, through'	8,627
	para	'for'	6,084
	sobre	'on'	1,699
	sin	'without'	1,486
	entre	'between, among'	1,481
Medium (100~999 wpm) (n=10)	*desde*	'since'	982
	contra	'against, opposite'	610
	hasta	'until'	580
	durante	'during'	576
	hacia	'toward'	501
	ante	'before'	491
	tras	'after'	288
	según	'following, according to'	287
	bajo	'under'	188
	mediante	'through'	162

Low (10~99 pwm) (n=2)	*excepto*	'except'	20
	vía	'through'	15
Very Low (~9 pwm) (n=4)	*versus*	'against'	3
	salvo	'except'	1
	cabe	'next to'	0
	so	'under'	0

Table 6.1 Frequency of primary prepositions in Modern Spanish

The categorial fluidity with Spanish prepositions is such that *NGLE* comments on two more relevant categories in its discussion of prepositions, as in (3), even though they are not given the prepositional status officially (cf. (1) above).

(3) a. *donde* 'in the house of', *cuando* 'at the time of', *como* 'of, like, as'
     b. *excepto* 'except', *menos* 'less', *salvo* 'except'

NGLE states that the relative adverb *donde* 'where' in (3a) can sometimes function like a preposition as in *Pirulo bebía un pisco donde María* 'Pirulo drank a pisco in the house of Maria', in which *donde* designates the location with the meaning 'at the house of' 'at the establishment of' (pp. 2232-2233). Similarly, *cuando* 'while' carries the function similar to that of a preposition as in *cuando la guerra* 'at the time of war' (p. 2233). *Como* is sometimes used as an alternative of *de* 'of' to designate 'like, of' as in *Este cuarto se usa como/de almacén* 'This room is used as a warehouse', in which *como* "can be assimilated to the group of prepositions" (p. 2233, trans. SR). But *NGLE* states that despite their resemblance to prepositions, they have never been accepted to the language of the educated. As for the last category (3b), *NGLE* notes that *excepto, menos,* and *salvo,* even though they are sometimes considered prepositions, are not usually classified as such in contemporary Spanish and are rather assimilated to conjunctions (*NGLE* pp. 2233, 2464-2465).

All the foregoing description of the primary prepositions in Spanish points to the facts that the overall system is well-established, and that despite the apparent stability, delimitation of the prepositional category is still a moot point in contemporary Spanish linguistics.

In the above, we noted that Spanish primary prepositions, numbering around two dozen, have come from various sources through diverse channels. They also exhibit a great level of variation in terms of use frequency, as shown in Table 6.1. Their variable strengths notwithstanding, it appears that the members in the inventory form a reasonably stable paradigm, as shown by the fact that an absolute majority (19 out of 25) belong to the High and Medium frequency ranges.

However, this impression of apparent stability disappears when we consider composite and complex prepositions. If we use the working definition for distinguishing prepositional constructions by the number of words involved, i.e., composite prepositions for two-word forms and complex prepositions for those involving three or more words, the prepositions border on syntactic constructions. Such non-primary prepositions form a large continuum upon which forms can be mapped depending on their levels of conceptual consolidation. In other words, many are unambiguously highly univerbated as a conceptually unified entity carrying prepositional functions, and thus are placed on one end of the continuum, whereas others are unclear as to whether they are simply syntactic constructions or have gained the properties of the prepositional category and thus are placed on the other end of the continuum. Because of their structural complexity, many reference grammars or pedagogical grammars tend to restrict the membership of the prepositional category to the primary prepositions (i.e., one-word forms) only (cf. Bello 1847: 697-703), whereas others are classified as 'prepositional idiomatic phrases' (Kim and Rhee 2018).

This conservative attitude toward the prepositional category makes a sharp contrast with some grammarians who held a more lenient view about categories even centuries ago. For instance, Nebrija (1989[1492]: 207-208) presents a large number of prepositions depending on their morphosyntactic properties, i.e., those used with the nouns with accusative case, those with the genitive case (thus, accompanying *de* 'of'), and those that take both. From this viewpoint, those that accompany accusative-marked noun phrases (e.g., *para mí* 'for me') are primary prepositions, and those that accompany genitive-marked noun phrases (e.g., *dentro de casa* 'inside the house') are composite/complex prepositions. In mainstream modern linguistics, notably those that subscribe to the framework laid by *NGLE*, the category of preposition is thought to include primary as well as non-primary forms since the latter carry the comparable function as shown in (4) and (5):

(4) a. *Se enfadaron por una tontería.*
    b. *Se enfadaron a causa de una tontería.*
       'They got angry for a foolish thing.'
                                   (Alarcos Llorach 1994: 217; translation added)

(5) a. *Desde el lunes, cierran por las tardes.*
    b. *A partir del lunes, cierran por las tardes.*
       'From Monday, they close in the afternoons.'
                                   (adapted from K Kim 2019: 20; translation added)

In (4) above, the primary preposition *por* 'for, by, over, at, because of' and the complex preposition *a causa de* 'because of, on account of' are functional equivalents. Similarly, in (5), the primary preposition *desde* 'from' is functionally equivalent to the complex preposition *a partir de* 'from'.

Composite prepositions are sometimes called as LP, i.e., from their structure [léxico + preposición], and Cifuentes (2003) lists as many as 136 LPs, consisting of the lexical categories from adverbs (e.g., *abajo de, debajo de*, etc.) nouns (e.g., *cara a, caso de*, etc.), adjectives (e.g., *acorde con, distante de*, etc.), and verbs (e.g., *aparte de, pese a*, etc.). These composite forms, numbering around 136, are listed in Table 6.2 (N.B.: LPs are not separately listed in Cifuentes 2003 but are sorted from the list of combinatorial forms of prepositions).

abajo de	'under'	*además de*	'in addition to'
acerca de	'concerning'	*adentro de*	'inside'
acorde con	'according to'	*afuera de*	'outside of'
adecuadamente a	'appropriately to'	*aisladamente a*	'in isolation to'
adecuadamente con	'appropriately with'	*allende de*	'beyond'
adelante de	'ahead of'	*alrededor de*	'about'

alternativamente a	'alternatively to'	cuanto a	'as for'
análogamente a	'analogously to'	cuestión de	'in the matter of'
análogo a	'analogous to'	cuidadosamente de	'carefully of'
angularmente a	'angularly to'	debajo de	'under'
anteriormente a	'prior to'	debido a	'because of'
antes de	'prior to'	delante de	'in front of'
apartadamente de	'apart from'	dentro de	'within'
aparte de	'apart from'	desagradablemente a	'unpleasantly to'
apegadamente a	'attached to'	desconfiadamente de	'distrustfully of'
arriba de	'above'	después de	'after'
atentamente a	'attentively to'	detrás de	'in back of'
atrás de	'behind of'	diagonalmente a	'diagonally to'
ávidamente de	'eagerly of'	diferentemente de	'differently from'
bajo de	'under'	distante de	'distant from'
cabe a	'fitting'	distintamente de	'distinctly from'
camino a	'on the way to'	encima de	'above'
camino de	'on the way of'	enfrente de	'in front of'
cara a	'facing'	entremedias de	'in between'
casi a	'almost to'	esquina a	'at the corner of'
caso de	'in case of'	excepto en	'except in'
cerca de	'near'	exteriormente a	'outwardly to'
cercanamente a	'closely to'	favorablemente a	'favorably to'
cercano a	'close to'	frente a	'versus'
cercano de	'close to'	frente de	'in front of'
circularmente a	'circularly to'	frontero a	'frontier to'
como a	'like'	fuera de	'outside'
como de	'like'	gracias a	'thanks to'
como en	'like in'	gratamente a	'pleasantly to'
confiadamente con	'confidently with'	hostilmente a	'hostilely to'
conforme a	'according to'	hostilmente con	'hostilely with'
conforme con	'agreeing with'	hostilmente contra	'hostilely against'
conjuntamente a	'jointly to'	idénticamente a	'identically to'
conjuntamente con	'jointly with'	incluso en	'even in'
conscientemente de	'consciously of'	incongruentemente con	'incongruously with'
consecuentemente a	'consequently to'	independientemente de	'independently of'
consecuentemente con	'consequently with'	indiferentemente a	'indifferently to'
consecutivamente a	'consecutively to'	indistintamente de	'indistinctly from'
contradictoriamente a	contradictorily to'	inferiormente a	'inferior to'
contradictoriamente con	'contradictorily with'	indistintamente de	'inversely to'
contrariamente a	'contrary to'	junto a	'next to'
correlativamente a	'correlatively to'	junto con	'with'

junto de	'together with'	*preferiblemente a*	'preferably to'
lateralmente a	'laterally to'	*previamente a*	'prior to'
lejos de	'far from'	*proporcionalmente a*	'proportionally to'
longitudinalmente a	'longitudinally to'	*próximamente a*	'close to'
luego de	'after'	*próximo a*	'next to'
menos en	'less in'	*referente a*	'relating to'
merced a	'thanks to'	*relativo a*	'relative to'
motivado a	'motivated to'	*respecto a*	'about'
no obstante	'notwithstanding'	*respecto de*	'in respect of'
oblicuo a	'oblique to'	*rumbo a*	'toward'
orilla a	'at the shore to'	*salvo en*	'except in'
orilla de	'at the shore of'	*semejante a*	'similar to'
orillas de	'at the shores of'	*semejantemente a*	'similarly to'
paralelamente a	'in parallel to'	*separadamente de*	'separately from'
paralelo a	'in parallel to'	*simétricamente a*	'symmetrically to'
pendiente de	'pending'	*simultáneamente a*	'simultaneously to'
perpendicular a	'in perpendicular to'	*subordinadamente a*	'subordinate to'
perpendicularmente a	'in perpendicular to'	*sumisamente a*	'submissively to'
pese a	'although'	*tocante a*	'regarding'
posteriormente a	'later to'	*tras de*	'behind'
preferentemente a	'preferably to'	*ulteriormente a*	'subsequently to'

Table 6.2 Composite prepositions in Modern Spanish

In addition to the composite prepositions listed in Table 6.2, there are a large number of complex prepositions in contemporary Spanish, such as *al lado de* 'on the side of', *a mediados de* 'around', *al través de* 'across from', etc. These complex prepositions have the structural composition of Preposition + (Determiner) + Noun + Preposition, thus, often referred to as P(D)NP structures. There are two noteworthy aspects in this context. First, successive occurrence of a preposition and a determiner often leads to the fusion of the two, as in the change from [a el norte de] to [al norte de] 'to the north of' and from [a el lado de] to [al lado de] 'on the side of', in which *a* 'to' and *el* 'the' are fused (N.B.: this is not a preposition-specific but general rule in Spanish). Since the preposition *a* and the eroded determiner *el* are still relatively visible (by virtue of it being a general rule), the mere number of words in the construction does not mean much. Incidentally, this phonological process seems to be due to the succession of two vowels, because the feminine definite article *la* is not subject to the phonological process (which is also a general rule). Similarly, when the Preposition₁ is *de* 'of', it may be fused with the following element as in [de bajo de] to [debajo de] (*de* 'of', *bajo* 'low, under') (De Silva 1985: 155) or [de trás de] to [detrás de] (*de* 'of', *trás* 'after') (De Silva 1985: 164).

Another important point is the coexistence of forms that are diachronically related having the identical etymon, a point discussed in Kim (2018, 2019). The following are the list of such related forms.

(6) a. *camino a/de*   *en camino de*   'on the way to'
     b. *cara a*   *de cara a*   'facing'
     c. *caso de*   *en (el) caso de*   'in the case of'
     d. *cuestión de*   *en cuestión de*   'in the matter of'
     e. *gracias a*   *en gracias a/de*   'thanks to'
     f. *merced a*   *a (la) merced de*   'thanks to'
     g. *orilla(s) a/de*   *a orillas de*   'at the shore of'
     h. *respecto a/de*   *con respecto a*   'about'
     i. *rumbo a*   *con rumbo a*   'heading for'

It is true that the paired prepositions originated from the identical source, suggesting that the first of the pair is the eroded form of the second. However, Kim (2018: 27-28) notes that even though they are etymologically related, they do have different functions depending on the use contexts. This can be illustrated by the examples in (7) and (8), modified from Kim (2019: 12, 15-16) with translation added:

(7) a. *Ponte <u>hacia</u> la pared.*
     b. *Ponte <u>de cara a</u> la pared.*
        'Face the wall. (Stand up to the wall.)'

(8) a. *También es una base muy buena <u>de cara a</u> entender como funciona un ordenador.*
        'It is also a very good basis for understanding how a computer works.'
     b. *<u>De cara a que</u> la primavera sea lo más llevadera posible, el Ministerio de*

Sanidad y Consumo ofrece una serie de consejos a los pacientes.

'In order to make spring as bearable as possible, the Ministry of Health and Consumption offers a series of advice to patients.'

K Kim (2018, 2019) argues that the composite preposition *cara a* and the complex preposition *de cara a* are compatible in the context of (7), whereas in purpose-marking contexts like (8), only *de cara a* is acceptable, thus clearly showing functional divergence. Despite the presence of interchangeability in certain contexts, their functional split has led to regarding these related forms as distinct prepositions (K Kim 2019: 15).

The inventory of the complex prepositions in Spanish is among the most controversial issues, largely because P(D)NP constructions, especially the non-eroded PDNP constructions, blend into syntactic constructions. For instance, K Kim (2019: 18) notes that Ueda (1990) lists 428 items, Koike (1997) 425 items, and Cifuentes (2003) 459 items. Since there are variations, the collapsed list contains 568 items (Kim 2019: 18), and the number, of course, remains inconclusive (see Appendix 3 for a list of 690 composite and complex prepositions, based on Cifuentes 2003).[5]

It is notable that the inventory of composite and complex prepositions bears diverse characteristics of on-going grammaticalization. For instance, in the typical $P_1(D)NP_2$ structure, there are a number of different kinds of structural variation as shown in (9):

(9) a. Omission of P_1: *(a) orillas de* 'on the shores of, at the verge of', *(en) (el) caso de* 'in the case of', *(en) cuanto a* 'as to, regarding'...

   b. Replacement of P_1: *a/en favor de* 'in favor of', *a/con diferencia de* 'with difference of', *a/en fuerza de* 'in force of'...

   c. Omission of D: *a(l/la) par de* 'on par with', *a (la) ley de* 'to law of', *a (la) manera de* 'in the way of, by way of'...

   d. Pluralization of N: *a golpe(s) de* 'at the stroke of', *a fin(es) de* 'at the end of', *a*

---

[5] Parenthetically indicated variants in Cifuentes (2003) are individually counted.

mano(s) de 'at the hand of'...

    e. Variation of N: *a la busca/búsqueda de* 'in search of', *por encima/cima de* 'above, on top of', *por mandado/mandato de* 'by command of'...

    f. Modification of N: *al (otro) lado de* 'at the (other) side of', *en (íntimo) contacto con* 'in (close) contact with'...

    g. Replacement of P₂: *a punto de/a* 'at the point of', *al contacto de/con* 'to the contact of', *cercano a/de* 'close to'...

The types of variability in (9) indicates that these non-primary forms have not yet been fully entrenched in form and function (see 6.4 for more discussion).

6.3 Spatial Prepositions

6.3.1 Characteristics of Spatial Prepositions

Many, if not most, prepositions in Spanish encode diverse spatial relationships. It is also to be noted that the classification is not mutually exclusive. For example, Directional is closely related to Goal, the difference being static vs dynamic, i.e., the focus on the designation of simple orientation (Directional) or on the arrival at the destination (Goal). Similarly, Path and Medial are closely related to the point of being indistinguishable in many cases. Their difference is whether the focus is on the overall trajectory (Path) or on the state of being around the middle of the whole trajectory (Medial). Association, Adjacency and Contiguity are also in a close relationship. The differences, again, come from the differential focus, i.e., on togetherness (Association), on being in the vicinity (Adjacency), or on being next to each other without a gap (Contiguity).

    Another important aspect is that the distinction between spatial and non-spatial prepositions is often unclear. For instance, Association, typically marked by *con* 'with' often takes a human noun, e.g., *con mis amigos* 'with my friends', or an object noun, e.g., *con leche* 'with milk', in which case, *con* is intuitively not associated with a space but with an entity. However, when the preposition takes a place noun, e.g., *con mi compañía* 'with my company', the spatial meaning becomes more evident.

As has been noted above, many prepositions in Spanish encode spatial relationship. There are a total of 169 prepositions, inclusive of primary, composite, and complex groups, that mark spatiality (note that some complex prepositions are listed in multiple categories, e.g., *a medio a, en mitad de,* etc.). The spatial prepositions are listed in Table 6.3.

AXIS		PRIMARY (n=19)	COMPOSITE (n=51)	COMPLEX (n=99)
	REGIONAL			
	DIRECTIONAL	*a* 'to' *para* 'to, for, bound for' *hacia* 'toward'	*cara a* 'facing' *rumbo a* 'heading for'	*de cara a* 'towards' *en dirección a* 'towards' *con dirección a* 'towards' *de frente a* 'facing' *con rumbo a* 'heading for' *de paso hacia* 'towards'
	SOURCE	*de* 'of, from' *desde* 'from'		*a partir de* 'from'
	GOAL	*a* 'to' *hasta* 'up to'		*con destino a* 'bound for' *con destino en* 'bound for'
NON-AXIAL	PATH	*mediante* 'through' *vía* 'through'		*a través de* 'through' *al través de* 'through' *de través a* 'through to' *a mitad de* 'halfway through' *en mitad de* 'on the way of' *por mitad de* 'halfway through' *de paso a* 'from the way to' *de paso para* 'through' *por medio a* 'through' *a medio a* 'halfway through' *por intermedio de* 'through' *por vía de* 'through' *en camino de* 'on the way to' *por conducto de* 'through'
	MEDIAL	*entre* 'between, among'	*entremedias de* 'in between'	*a medio a* 'halfway through' *a medio de* 'amid' *en medio a* 'in the middle of' *en medio de* 'in the middle of' *por medio de* 'in the middle of' *a mediados de* 'in the middle of' *por entremedias de* 'in between' *a mitad de* 'halfway through' *en mitad de* 'on the way of' *por mitad de* 'halfway through' *en el centro de* 'in the center of' *en vías de* 'in the middle of' *en el corazón de* 'in the middle of'

ULTERIOR		*allende de* 'beyond'	
ASSOCIATION	*con* 'with'	*junto a* 'alongside, next to' *junto de* 'together with' *junto con* 'together with'	*en compañía de* 'with' *en unión de* 'with'
ADJACENCY		*cerca de* 'near' *cercano a* 'close to' *cercano de* 'close to' *cercamente a* 'close to' *próximo a* 'close to' *próximamente a* 'close to' *alrededor de* 'around'	*en los alrededores de* 'around' *en derredor de* 'around' *en torno a* 'around, about' *en torno de* 'around' *al lado de* 'near, at the side of' *a flor de* 'on surface of' *al amor de* 'near' *a tiro de* 'within range of' *al arrimo de* 'around'
CONTIGUITY	*cabe* 'next to'	*junto a* 'next to'	*a continuación de* 'next to' *a raíz de* 'next to, following'
SEPARATION		*lejos de* 'away from' *aparte de* 'away from' *apartamente de* 'away from' *distante de* 'distant from' *aisladamente a* 'in isolation to'	*al margen de* 'apart from'
OPPOSITE	*contra* 'opposite, against'		*en contra de* 'opposite, against' *por contra de* 'opposite, against' *a contra de* 'opposite, against' *al otro lado de* 'on the other side of' *del otro lado de* 'on the other side of' *en oposición a* 'opposite to'
OTHERS		*orilla de* 'at the shore of' *orilla a* 'at the shore of' *paralelo a* 'in parallel to' *paralelamente a* 'in parallel to' *perpendicular a* 'perpendicular to' *perpendicularmente a* 'perpendicular to' *esquina a* 'at a corner to' *oblicuo a* 'oblique to' *oblicuamente a* 'obliquely to' *longitudinalmente a* 'longitudinally to' *diagonalmente a* 'diagonally to'	*a final de* 'at the end of' *a finales de* 'at the end of' *al final de* 'at the end of' *a los finales de* 'at the end of' *al fin de* 'at the end of' *a fines de* 'at the end of' *al extremo de* 'at the end of' *al término de* 'at the end of' *en pie de* 'at the end of' *al borde de* 'on the verge of' *a filo de* 'on the edge of' *al filo de* 'on the edge of' *a la vera de* 'at the edge of' *al principio de* 'at the beginning of' *al comienzo de* 'at the beginning of' *de vuelta a* 'back to' *de vuelta de* 'back from' *de regreso a* 'back to' *de regreso de* 'back from' *a orillas de* 'at the shore of' *en paralelo con* 'parallel to' *en paralelo a* 'parallel to'

AXIAL	**INTERIOR**	*en* 'in'	*dentro de* 'within' *adentro de* 'inside'	*en el interior de* 'inside' *al interior de* 'inside' *por dentro de* 'inside'
	EXTERIOR		*afuera de* 'outside of' *fuera de* 'out of' *exteriormente a* 'externally to'	*al exterior de* 'outside of' *en el exterior de* 'outside of'
	SUPERIOR	*sobre* 'on'	*encima de* 'on top of' *arriba de* 'above'	*por encima de* 'above' *por cima de* 'over top of' *en lo alto de* 'at the top of' *en cabeza de* 'at the head/top of'
	INFERIOR	*bajo* 'under' *so* 'under'	*bajo de* 'below' *debajo de* 'below' *abajo de* 'below' *inferiormente a* 'below'	*por bajo de* 'below, under' *por debajo de* 'below' *a pie de* 'at the bottom of' *al pie de* 'at the bottom of' *al fondo de* 'to the bottom of' *en el fondo de* 'at the bottom of'
	ANTERIOR	*ante* 'before'	*delante de* 'in front of' *enfrente de* 'in front of' *frente a* 'in front of' *frente de* 'in front of' *adelante de* 'ahead of' *frontero a* 'in front of'	*por delante de* 'ahead of' *al frente de* 'at the front of' *en frente de* 'in front of'
	POSTERIOR	*tras* 'behind, after'	*detrás de* 'behind' *tras de* 'after' *atras de* 'at the back of'	*por detrás de* 'behind' *posteriormente a* 'subsequently to' *a espaldas de* 'behind' *a raíz de* 'next to, following'
	LATERAL		*lateralmente a* 'laterally to'	*a la derecha de* 'to the right of' *por derecho de* 'by right to' *a la izquierda de* 'to the left of' *al lado de* 'on the side of' *a ambos lados de* 'on both sides of'

Table 6.3. Spatial prepositions in Modern Spanish

Table 6.3 exhibits a number of interesting aspects of the spatial prepositions in Spanish, some applicable to Spanish prepositions in general. First of all, Spanish does not have a preposition that specializes in designating a Regional, roughly equivalent to the English *at* or Korean *-ey*. Instead, it uses more fine-grained distinctions of the relationship, such as *en* 'in' *a* 'to', *de* 'from' *por* 'by', etc., e.g., *en casa* 'at home', *a las tres* 'at 3 o'clock', *por las noticias* 'at the news', etc.

Secondly, as compared to the primary prepositions, composite and complex prepositions are far greater in number. In other words, there are 19 primary prepositions, but as many as 150 composite and complex prepositions that encode spatial relationships. Furthermore, there are a large number of composite and complex prepositions in the "Others" category, i.e., those that do not fit in the general classification of specific spatial relationship, e.g., those referring to the 'end' or 'beginning' (sequentiality), returning (regression), diverse angular concepts (parallel, oblique, perpendicular, etc.), among others.

Finally, yet most importantly, the main factor for multiplicity of complex prepositions is that they occur in structural variations. For instance, there are as many as 14 complex prepositions for Path, but only 8 lexical forms are involved, i.e., *través* 'traverse', *mitad* 'half', *paso* 'passage', *medio* 'means, medium', *intermedio* 'halfway', *vía* 'way', *camino* 'way' and *conducto* 'conduit, channel'. Furthermore, certain cases involve simply spelling variation. For instance, *enfrente de* 'in front of' and *en frente de* 'in front of' are identical not only in their source but also in their function, the former being more reduced in orthography, presumably reflecting the increase of internal cohesion in the mind of language users. Structural variation is indicative of the form not having fully grammaticalized (see 6.4.3.4 for more discussion).

6.3.2 Frequencies of Spatial Prepositions

Spatial prepositions exhibit wide variation in terms of use frequency. The highest frequency of over 61,000 pmw is recorded by *de* 'of, from', with no attested use tokens with *apartadamente de* 'away from, apart from', *entremedias de* 'in between', *por entremedias de* 'in between', *cabe* 'next to' and *so* 'under'. A caveat in this context is that not all uses of *de* are of purely spatial relationship (i.e., 'from') since its other dominant uses include marking possession (i.e., 'of').

The spatial prepositions can be grouped according to their frequency following the general scheme, i.e., High for 1,000 pmw tokens (250,000 raw tokens) or above, Medium for 100~999 pmw tokens (25,000~249,999 raw tokens), Low for 10~99 pmw tokens (2,500~24,999 raw tokens), and Very Low for 9 pmw (2,499 raw tokens) or below, based on CREA token frequency, admitting arbitrariness in deciding the cut-off points. The frequency-based list of 169 prepositions with their lexical sources is in Table 6.4.

Frequency Range	Spatial PREP	Source (L: Latin)	PREP Meaning	PMW
High (1,000~ pmw)	de	L. de 'of, from'	of	61,012
	en	L. in 'in'	in	23,944
	a	L. ad 'to'	to	19,379
	con	L. cum 'with'	with	8,755
	para	L. por ad 'through to'	for	6,084
	sobre	L. super 'on'	on	1,699
	entre	L. inter 'between'	between	1,480
Medium (100~999 pmw)	desde	L. de ex de 'from from from'	from	982
	contra	L. contra 'against'	against, opposite	610
	hasta	Arb. háttà 'until, up to'	until, up to	580
	hacia	faz 'face'	toward	501
	ante	L. ante 'before'	before	491
	tras	L. trans 'after'	after	288
	a través de	través 'deviation'	via, through	206
	dentro de	dentro 'inside'	within	194
	bajo	bajo 'base'	below, under	179
	mediante	mediar 'mediate'	through, by means of	162
	a partir de	partir 'part, divide'	from, apart from	129
	junto a	junto 'near, together'	next to	119
Low (10~99 pmw)	cerca de	cerca 'near, nearly'	near	91
	fuera de	fuera 'outside'	outside	85
	alrededor de	alrededor 'around'	around, about	60
	encima de	cima 'top'	above	59
	junto con	junto 'near, together'	together with	56
	en torno a	torno 'turn, wheel'	around	51
	a fin de	fin 'end'	at the end of	47
	detrás de	L. trans 'after'	in back of	45
	por encima de	cima 'top'	above	42
	en medio de	medio 'half'	between	40
	por medio de	medio 'half'	through	39
	en contra de	L. contra 'against'	against, opposite	39
	lejos de	lejos 'far'	far from	36
	debajo de	bajo 'base'	under	35
	delante de	L. ante 'before'	in front of	28
	al lado de	lado 'side'	next to	21
	al final de	final 'end'	at the end of	20
	a finales de	final 'end'	at the end of	19
	cara a	cara 'face'	facing	19
	al margen de	margen 'margin'	outside of, apart from	19
	en el centro de	centro 'center'	in the center of	18
	por debajo de	bajo 'base'	below	17
	en el interior de	interior 'interior'	inside of	16

al frente de	frente 'front'	in front of	16
a raíz de	raíz 'base, root'	next to, following	15
vía	vía 'way'	via, through	14
a mediados de	mediados 'middle'	in the middle of	11
en compañía de	compañía 'company'	in company of	10
rumbo a	rumbo 'course'	toward	10
al pie de	pie 'foot'	at the foot of	10
al borde de	borde 'edge'	at the edge of	9
de cara a	cara 'face'	facing	9
en el fondo de	fondo 'bottom'	at the bottom of	8
cercano a	cerca 'near'	close to	8
a fines de	fin 'end'	at the end of	8
en dirección a	dirección 'direction'	in direction to	7
al término de	término 'end'	at the end of	7
próximo a	próximo 'next'	next to	7
en vías de	vías 'ways'	in the middle of	6
al otro lado de	lado 'side'	at the other side of	6
al principio de	principio 'beginning'	at the beginning of	6
al interior de	interior 'interior'	inside	6
arriba de	arriba 'up, overhead'	above	5
tras de	L. trans 'after'	after	5
con destino a	destino 'destination'	bound for	5
por delante de	L. ante 'before'	in front of	5
al fondo de	fondo 'bottom'	at the bottom of	5
al comienzo de	comienzo 'beginning'	at the beginning of	5
en mitad de	mitad 'half'	in the middle of	4
en el corazón de	corazón 'heart'	in the heart of	4
a mitad de	mitad 'half'	in the middle of	4
bajo de	bajo 'base'	under	4
de regreso a	regreso 'return'	back to	4
abajo de	bajo 'base'	under	4
en torno de	torno 'turn, wheel'	around	3
en lo alto de	alto 'high'	on top of	3
en los alrededores de	alrededor 'around'	around	3
al fin de	fin 'end'	at the end of	3
al extremo de	extremo 'end'	at the end of	3
por detrás de	L. trans 'after'	behind	3
enfrente de	frente 'front'	in front of	3
frente de	frente 'front'	in front of	3
orilla de	orilla 'shore'	at the shore of	3
de vuelta a	vuelta 'return'	back to	3
posteriormente a	posterior 'posterior'	later to	2
en pie de	pie 'foot'	at the end of	2
adentro de	dentro 'inside'	inside	2

Very Low
(~ 9 pmw)

por vía de	*vía* 'way'	through	2
a final de	*final* 'end'	at the end of	2
por intermedio de	*intermedio* 'middle'	through	2
paralelo a	*paralelo* 'parallel'	parallel to	2
a espaldas de	*espalda* 'back'	behind	2
a flor de	*flor* 'flower'	around, at the surface of	2
afuera de	*fuera* 'outside'	outside	2
a la derecha de	*derecha* 'right'	to the right of	2
a ambos lados de	*lado* 'side'	on both sides of	2
a pie de	*pie* 'foot'	at the foot of	2
del otro lado de	*lado* 'side'	on the other side of	2
al filo de	*filo* 'edge'	on the edge of	2
paralelamente a	*paralel* 'parallel'	parallel to	2
a la izquierda de	*izquierda* 'left'	to the left of	1
aparte de	*aparte* 'apart'	apart from	1
de vuelta de	*vuelta* 'return'	back from	1
adelante de	L. *ante* 'before'	ahead of	1
distante de	*distante* 'distant'	distant from	1
perpendicular a	*perpendicular* 'perpendicular'	perpendicular to	1
a continuación de	*continuación* 'continuation'	in continuation of	1
en unión de	*unión* 'union'	in union of	1
frente a	*frente* 'front'	in front of	1
de frente a	*frente* 'front'	facing	1
esquina a	*esquina* 'corner'	corner to	1
en oposición a	*oposición* 'opposition'	in opposition to	1
al través de	*través* 'traverse'	through	1
cercano de	*cerca* 'near'	near	1
por conducto de	*conducto* 'conduit'	through	1
en el exterior de	*exterior* 'exterior'	on the outside of	1
a orillas de	*orilla* 'shore'	at the shore of	1
de paso a	*paso* 'passage'	from the way to	1
en camino de	*camino* 'way'	on the way to	1
por dentro de	*dentro* 'inside'	inside	1
en cabeza de	*cabeza* 'head'	at the head of	1
a la vera de	*vera* 'edge'	at the edge of	1
de regreso de	*regreso* 'return'	back from	1
al exterior de	*exterior* 'exterior'	outside of	1
al amor de	*amor* 'love'	near	1
en paralelo con	*paralel* 'parallel'	in parallel with	1
con rumbo a	*rumbo* 'course'	heading for	1
a tiro de	*tiro* 'throw'	within range of	1
en paralelo a	*paralelo* 'parallel'	parallel to	1
en frente de	*frente* 'front'	in front of	0

por mitad de	*mitad* 'half'	halfway through	0
con dirección a	*dirección* 'direction'	with direction to	0
próximamente a	*próximo* 'near'	near	0
de paso para	*paso* 'passage'	on the way to	0
orilla a	*orilla* 'shore'	at the shore of	0
por derecho de	*derecho* 'right'	by right to	0
de paso hacia	*paso* 'passage'	on the way to	0
en medio a	*medio* 'half'	in the middle of	0
en derredor de	*derredor* 'around'	around	0
perpendicularmente a	*perpendicular* 'perpendicular'	perpendicular to	0
por bajo de	*bajo* 'base'	below, under	0
con destino en	*destino* 'destination'	bound for	0
por medio a	*medio* 'half'	through	0
lateralmente a	*lateral* 'lateral'	laterally to	0
al arrimo de	*arrimo* 'bringing close'	near	0
junto de	*junto* 'together'	alongside	0
oblicuamente a	*oblicuo* 'oblique'	obliquely to	0
allende de	*allende* 'beyond'	beyond	0
por cima de	*cima* 'top'	over top of	0
exteriormente a	*exterior* 'exterior'	externally to	0
a medio de	*medio* 'half'	amid	0
longitudinalmente a	*longitudinal* 'longitudinal'	longitudinally to	0
frontero a	*frontero* 'front'	in front of	0
por contra de	*contra* 'against'	against, opposite	0
aisladamente a	*aislado* 'isolated'	in isolation to	0
oblicuo a	*oblicuo* 'oblique'	oblique to	0
a filo de	*filo* 'edge'	on the edge of	0
cercanamente a	*cerca* 'near'	close to	0
a los finales de	*final* 'end'	at the end of	0
a medio a	*medio* 'half'	halfway through	0
atras de	L. *trans* 'after'	at the back of	0
inferiormente a	*inferior* 'inferior'	below	0
de través a	*través* 'traverse'	through to	0
diagonalmente a	*diagonal* 'diagonal'	diagonally to	0
a contra de	*contra* 'against'	against, opposite	0
apartadamente de	*aparte* 'apart'	away from	0
entremedias de	*media* 'half'	in between	0
por entremedias de	*media* 'half'	in between	0
cabe	*cabo* 'end, tip'	next to	0
so	L. *sub* 'under'	under	0

Table 6.4. Frequency and lexical sources of spatial prepositions in Modern Spanish

The frequency table shows a few interesting aspects about Spanish spatial prepositions. Even though there are items that show a noticeably lower frequency than the one immediately preceding them, the extent of the frequency drop is particularly big between the 5th *para* (6,084 pmw) and the 6th *sobre* (1,699 pmw). The frequency of *para* may contain noise, i.e., the verb *parar* inflected for 3rd person singular present, but at the same time, data for *sobre* may also contain noise, i.e., the noun *sobre* 'envelop'. Still the frequency drop of 72.1% is remarkable. It is to be noted that this gap cannot be fully accounted for just with reference to the functional generality, i.e., *para* 'for' is not only used for direction 'to, toward' but also for benefactive 'for the benefit of', etc. It is because *sobre* is also functionally generalized from the locational superiority (i.e., 'on') to more abstract thematicity (i.e., 'about'), etc. Another instance of noticeable frequency change is at the boundary of High and Medium frequency ranges, i.e., 1,480 pmw tokens of *entre* and 982 pmw tokens of *desde*. It can be said that, in Hopper's (1987) and Hook's (1991) terms, the top seven items have gained a high level of 'specialization'.

Another important aspect is that despite the vast multiplicity in number there are a large number of prepositions that are rarely used or not at all used on a regular basis. For instance, out of a total of 169 prepositions, as many as 120 of them, accounting for 71.0%, are low in actual use frequency, i.e., below 10 pmw. These include those that were productive in the history of Spanish, e.g., *cabe* 'next to', *so* 'under', as well as those that may be at the incipient stages of grammaticalization (see 6.3.3.4 and 6.4.2 for more discussion).

6.3.3 Grammaticalization Sources

6.3.3.1 Inherited Prepositions

In terms of grammaticalization sources, Spanish prepositions developed from a few notable sources, some universally shared, some language-specific. Since Spanish is a Romance language, it retains the features of Latin to a great extent, including not only lexical forms but also grammatical forms (see Hoelbeek 2017 for discussion on grammaticalization in Romance languages). Inheritance from Latin is one such category, as listed in (10), in which Modern Spanish prepositions are either identical with or minimally different from Latin prepositions in form:

(10) Inherited from Latin prepositions

    a. *ad* > *a* 'to'   b. *ante* > *ante* 'before'

    c. *cum* > *con* 'with'   d. *de* > *de* 'of'

    e. *in* > *en* 'in'   f. *inter* > *entre* 'between'

    g. *per* > *por* 'by'   h. *sine* > *sin* 'without'

    i. *sub* > *so* 'under'   j. *secundum* > *según* 'following, according to'

    k. *super* > *sobre* 'on'   l. *trans* > *tras* 'after'

Furthermore, many prepositions in Spanish can be traced back to Latin lexical forms, from which grammatical functions arose. These are the cases that involved 'evolutive' grammaticalization, i.e., one not from external forces but by language-internal change processes, as listed in (11), based on De Silva (1985) and elsewhere:

(11) a. *bajo*: (< L. *bassus* n. 'fat, low') > *baxo* > Sp. *bajo* p. 'below, under'

    b. *hacia*: (< L. *faz* 'face' + a 'to') > *fazia* > *hazia* > Sp. *hacia* p. 'toward'

    c. *via*: (L. *via* n. 'way') > Sp. *vía* p. 'via, through'

    d. *cabe*: (< L. *caput* n. 'head') > Sp. *cabo* n. 'end, tip' > *a cabo de* > *cabde* > *cabe* p. 'next to'

    e. *durante*: (< L. *durare* v. 'endure, last') > Sp. prp. *durante* 'continuing' > p. 'during'

    f. *mediante*: (< L. *mediare* v. 'to be in the middle') > Sp. prp. *mediante* 'being in the middle' > p. 'through, by means of'

    g. *excepto*: (< L. *excipiere* v. 'except, take out'; *exceptus* pp. 'excepted, taken out') > Sp. *excepto* p. 'except'

    h. *salvo*: (< L. *salvāre* v. 'save, reserve'; *salvus* pp. 'saved, reserved') > Sp. *salvo* p. 'except'

    i. *contra*: (L. *contra* ad. 'contrarily') > Sp. *contra* p. 'contra, against'

    j. *desde*: (< L. *de* p. 'from' + *ex* p. 'out of') > *des* >> + *de* > Sp. *desde* p. 'from'

    k. *para*: (< L. *por* p. 'through' + *ad* 'to') > Sp. *para* p. 'for'

As (11) shows, primary prepositions are predominantly from nominal (5a–d) and verbal sources (11e–h). Evidently, it is likely that the nominal-source prepositions emerged through the PDNP constructions, even though it is not clear in some cases (see 6.3.3.2). Verbal-source prepositions are invariably through the participial forms, either present participle as in *durante* 'during' and *mediante* 'mediating', or past participle as in *excepto* 'excepted' and *salvo* 'saved' (see 6.3.3.3). These scenarios resemble the patterns observed in the grammaticalization of English prepositions (see Ch. 5).

The preposition *contra* 'contra, against' originates from Latin adverb *contra* 'contrarily, against'. *NGLE* (p. 2246), however, notes that based on the presence of *en contra de, contra* may be a noun (substantive). The prepositions *desde* and *para* (5j–k) are peculiar in that they have multiply-stacked prepositions. The Spanish preposition *desde* is "doubly pleonastic as its Latin components (*de ex de*) can be translated as 'from from from'" (De Silva 1985: 161). This kind of redundancy, though not common, is observed in the course of grammaticalization and lexicalization (typically in phraseology), largely due to the fact that language users are either unaware of the function of the forms that have been semantically bleached (e.g., English *off of*, French *Qu'est-ce que c'est?* 'What's that?' (lit. 'What is it that it is?'), Korean *na-y-ka* 'I-NOM-NOM', double negation in many languages, among many others) or are inclined to reinforce the weakened meaning of the forms (e.g., English *collaborate together, circle around, new innovations, past history, a variety of different ideas*, etc., sometimes labeled as tautology).

There is still another source, i.e., borrowing from other languages, as shown in (12):

(12) Borrowing from other languages
    a. Arb. *háttà* p. 'until, up to' ⟩ *adta, ata, fasta, fata* ⟩ Sp. *hasta* p. 'until'
    b. L. *versus* ad. 'toward' ⟩ E. *versus/vs.* p. 'against' ⟩ Sp. *versus* p. 'against'

Kim and Rhee (2018) note that *hasta* is the only preposition borrowed from Arabic, and comment that the paucity of Arabic-based prepositions is somewhat extraordinary considering the 8-century long colonization by Arabs (711~1492).

Unlike many colonization situations (e.g., by Romans), according to Kim and Rhee (2018), Arabs did not force their subjects to use Arabic, and thus Spanish was spared from extensive influence of the language of the conquerors. Even though some influence was inevitable in the lexicon (e.g., *aceituna* 'olive' ⟨ *az-zaytūna* 'the olive'; *guitarra* 'guitar' ⟨ *qīṭārah* 'guitar'; *limón* 'lemon' ⟨ *laymūn, naranja* 'orange' ⟨ *nāranǧ* 'orange', etc.), grammatical borrowing, which is usually more difficult than lexical borrowing, remained limited.

The journey of *versus* is more complicated. The lexeme *versus* was an adverb in Latin with the meaning of 'toward'. The preposition was borrowed by English, first attested in 1447-1448, with the meaning of 'against' to denote a legal action (*OED*, entry for *versus*). According to Corominas and Pascual (1981) and Portilla (2011), the English *versus* was borrowed by Spanish for an oppositional meaning, thus constituting an instance of 'indirect borrowing'.

6.3.3.2 Nominal Sources

Just as is common in other languages, Spanish has prepositions originated from nominal sources. However, very few primary prepositions are products of noun grammaticalization. For instance, out of the 25 primary prepositions, only four, i.e., *bajo* 'under' (⟨ n. 'base'), *hacia* 'until' (⟨ n. *faz* 'face'), *vía* 'via, through' (⟨ n. 'way'), and *cabe* 'next to' (⟨ n. 'end, tip'), are such instances of grammaticalization from nouns.

Noun-derived composite prepositions (i.e., a subtype of LP, see 6.2) are relatively fewer as well (see K Kim 2019). There are 136 composite prepositions but noun-derived prepositions constitute a minority. Such instances are *camino a/de* (⟨ *camino* 'way'), *cara a* (⟨ *cara* 'face'), *caso de* (⟨ *caso* 'case, occurrence'), *cuestion de* (⟨ *cuestion* 'question'), *esquina a* (⟨ *esquina* 'corner'), *gracias a* (*gracia* 'grace'), *merced a* (*merced* 'mercy'), *orilla(s) a/de* (⟨ *orilla* 'shore'), *respecto a/de* (⟨ *respecto* 'respect'), and *rumbo a* (⟨ *rumbo* 'course, direction'). Since nouns do not have a linking function by themselves, they can be functional only in combination with a preposition that follows them (see 6.4.3.1 for more discussion). This is well illustrated in the following example, which involves the noun-based composite preposition *camino de* 'on the way to':

(13) *Iban camino de la estación cuando los encontramos.*

'They were on the way to the station when we met them.'

(RAE 2008, 249; as cited in K Kim 2019: 15, translation added)

When complex prepositions are considered, the situation changes dramatically. It is simply because complex prepositions, numbering around 690 and with a fuzzy category boundary, are nearly always of the P(D)NP structure, thus involving a noun as its central component. In other words, a vast majority of the complex prepositions in Spanish are all noun-derived prepositions. It is also notable in this context that the noun-based composite prepositions have their counterparts in the complex preposition group. For instance, both the composite preposition *camino a/de* and the complex preposition *en camino de* involve the noun *camino* 'way', and thus strongly suggest that the composite form is the eroded counterpart of the more conservative complex form. The same is applicable to *cara* 'face', *frente* 'forehead, front', *gracia* 'grace', etc. (see 6.2 above). At the same time, it is notable that some instances of composite-complex pairs are not interchangeable, and thus both of them are given a separate prepositional status, a point discussed in K Kim (2019) (see 6.2, above).

Some studies address the nature of the nouns that are typically involved in the grammaticalization of composite/complex prepositions. Eom (2018), in her discussion on English complex prepositions, asserts that for a syntactic construction to grammaticalize into a complex preposition, the noun must encode relationality and be of low conceptual centrality, and, thus, further challenges the widely-held notion that high frequency is a precondition of grammaticalization (see also K Ahn 2015 for detailed semantic characterization of nouns in complex prepositions). Similarly, Y Matsumoto (1998) notes that semantic change into adpositions involves gaining relationality, because adpositions are two-place predicates. With this regard, certain complex prepositions as listed in some studies (e.g. Cifuentes 2003) are somewhat dubious as to their qualification as prepositions. For instance, *por boca de* 'in wide circulation by, being widely talked about among' (lit. 'through mouth of'), *con emisión de* 'with issuance of', *con la disculpa de* 'with the apology of', among many others, do not seem to encode relationality.

Still another intriguing aspect of noun-based prepositions is that there are formal and semantic twins among complex prepositions, as shown in (14):

(14) a. *a la busca/búsqueda de*   'in search of'
      b. *en busca/búsqueda de*   'in search of'
      c. *por encima/cima de*   'on top of'
      d. *por mandado/mandato de* 'by command of'
      e. *en (h)armonía con*   'in harmony with'

(14a) and (14b) involve the noun *busca* 'search' and *búsqueda* 'search', the former less frequent as a noun in Modern Spanish, and the four complex prepositions carry the same meaning.[6] (14c) shows *cima* 'top' and the grammaticalized (and univerbated) preposition *encima* 'above, over' or an adverb 'on top'. Thus, when *encima* occurs between two prepositions (i.e., *por and de*), it needs to be interpreted as a case of preposition stacking, i.e., *por en cima*, from which the last two words become coalesced into *encima*. (14d) shows a variation between *mandado* 'order, errand, job' and *mandato* 'mandate, term', both etymologically derived from the past participle of *mandar* 'send' (*Diccionario Etimológico Castellano En Línea*). The lexeme *(h)armonía* in (14e), originating from Greek *harmonia* 'harmony, agreement, concord' (De Silva 1985: 51), shows a spelling variation. Despite the differences in detail, it can be assumed from the variation that these complex prepositions have not (yet) fully grammaticalized, since grammaticalization normally accompanies formal fixation.

6.3.3.3 Verbal Sources

As has been noted in 6.2, some prepositions have originated from verbs. Some primary prepositions, *durante* 'during' (< *durar* 'to last'), *mediante* 'through' (< *mediar* 'to mediate', *excepto* 'except' (< *exceptuar* 'to exempt') and *salvo* 'except' (< *salvar* 'to

---

[6] A corpus example search provided by online searchable *SpanishDict* (spanishdict.com) returns about 1,500 instances of *busca* as a noun, whereas the search returns about 13,000 instances of the noun *búsqueda* (accessed May~September 2021).

save, reserve'), are instances of grammaticalization of verbs from present participles or past participles of the verbs. Participial forms of verbs are particularly efficient to encode relationality because they change the verbal valence and temporality. In other words, they reduce the number of arguments, change a finite clause (i.e., temporal) into an atemporal expression, and encode particular thematic roles. This is well illustrated with the development of English prepositions and conjunctions from verbal sources. For instance, the present participle tends to semantically encode agentivity (e.g., from [when we exclude the case] to [excluding the case]), whereas the past participle tends to semantically encode thematicity (e.g. from [when we grant that the story is true] to [granted that the story is true]) (see H Lee 2011). In essentially the same manner, the Spanish participial forms *durante, mediante, excepto* and *salvo* develop into prepositions.

Among the composite prepositions, a few of them are also instances of verbal grammaticalization. For instance, prepositions *pese a* 'despite' (< *pesar* 'to weigh'), *aparte de* 'apart from' (< *apartar* 'to set aside'), *acorde con* 'according to' (< *acordar* 'to agree'), *tocante a* 'regarding' (< *tocar* 'to touch'), etc. are clear instances of grammaticalization of verbs. A caveat is that the nuclear element of these composite prepositions are not pure verbs but are those derived from them, and thus, some of them can be also analyzed as instances of development from adverbs or adjectives (see K Kim 2019: 16-17).

In the case of complex prepositions, on the other hand, instances of verbal grammaticalization are (nearly) non-existent, largely because the structural frame P(D)NP does not allow a verb to participate in it. There are complex prepositions that do derive from verbs, e.g., *por lo que respecta a* 'with respect to', *por lo que se refiere a* 'as regards', *en lo que afecta a* 'in what affects', *en lo que concierne a* 'with respect to', *en lo que tiene que ver con* 'in what has to do with', *en lo que toca a* 'regarding', etc., in which the finite verbs (i.e., inflected for third-person singular present) occur, i.e., *respecta* 'respects, regards', *refiere* 'refers', *afecta* 'affects', *concierne* 'concerns', *tiene* 'has', and *toca* 'touches'. However, these are structurally complex and can easily be subject to dispute as to their status as complex prepositions.

6.3.3.4 Adverbial Sources

There are a large number of complex prepositions that develop from adverbs. As indicated above, adverbs tend to be derived forms and thus they are open to controversy as to whether they are the ultimate sources. K Kim (2019: 16-17) lists a number of adverb-derived composite prepositions that do not belong to the largest source category, i.e., those derived from suffixation of *-mente*. The list is as shown in (15):

(15)

abajo de 'under'	*acerca de* 'about'	*adelante de* 'ahead of'
además de 'in addition to'	*adentro de* 'inside (of)'	*afuera de* 'outside of'
allende de 'beyond'	*alrededor de* 'about, around'	*antes de* 'prior to'
aparte de 'apart from'	*arriba de* 'above'	*atrás de* 'behind of'
bajo de 'under'	*cerca de* 'near'	*como a/de/en* 'like'
debajo de 'under'	*delante de* 'in front of'	*dentro de* 'within'
después de 'after'	*detrás de* 'in back of'	*encima de* 'above'
enfrente de 'in front of'	*entremedias de* 'in between'	*frente a* 'versus'
frante de 'in front of'	*fuera de* 'outside'	*incluso en* 'even in'
junto a 'next to'	*junto de* 'together with'	*junto con* 'with'
lejos de 'far from'	*luego de* 'after'	*menos en* 'less in'
tras de 'behind'		

Of particular importance in grammaticalization of adverbs into composite prepositions in Spanish is the use of adverbialized forms through suffixation of *-mente,* itself a grammaticalized suffix from the Latin noun *mente* 'mind + ablative case', i.e., 'with the mind' (see Hopper and Traugott (2003[1993]: 140-141). The suffix *-mente* transforms an adjective into an adverb, e.g., *consecutivo* 'consecutive' to *consecutivamente* 'consecutively', *análogo* 'analogous' to *análogamente* 'analogously', etc. An adverb by itself lacks the relationality, and thus cannot be used as a preposition. However, when it accompanies a linker it can be used as a preposition, as in *consecutivamente a* 'consecutively to', *análogamente a* 'analogously to', etc. This type of grammaticalization represents the largest subgroup of adverb-based composite prepositions in Spanish (note that Cifuentes' 2003 list contains 58 such cases).

6.3.3.5 Multiple Sources and Layered Prepositions

Multiplicity of prepositional sources is directly related to the layering phenomena in grammaticalization. In fact, the layering is doubly multi-planed through multiple sources and multiple formal variants. First of all, many Spanish prepositions encode the Prolative/Perlative (traversal) relationship, as shown in (16):

(16) a. *mediante*   'through'
   b. *vía*   'through, via'
   c. *de través a*   'through'
   d. *por conducto de*   'through'
   e. *por intermedio a* 'through'
   f. *por medio de*   'through'
   g. *a lo ancho de*   'across'

(16) lists seven prepositions designating the traversal ('through') relationship. However, they come from all different lexical sources and presumably with differential temporal depth. It is well-known that language users are somewhat 'irresponsible' and make new linguistic forms, the function of which is already carried by one or more well-established grammatical markers (Koo and Rhee 2013). It may also have to do with the desire to be more specific in encoding spatial relationship (cf. Rohdenburg's 'complexity principle'; 1996: 152; see 11.1 for more discussion). These Perlative/Prolative prepositions belong to the primary and complex prepositional categories.

As is noted above, the layering may involve formal variation. This state of affairs is well illustrated in the following set of examples:

(17) a. *contra*   'against, opposite to'
   b. *a contra de*   'against, opposite to'
   c. *en contra de*   'against, opposite to'
   d. *por contra de* 'against, opposite to'

As shown in (17), *contra* is a primary preposition showing locational or other conceptual contrasts. However, in contemporary Spanish there exist structural variants, with the same meaning. It is not only possible but also reasonable from the crosslinguistic perspective to hypothesize that the longer variants (17b~d) are earlier forms and the simpler variant (17a) is the innovation, i.e., the product of further grammaticalization.

Multiple layers are even more pronounced with other cases, in which both formal variants and multiple sources are involved. For instance, there are numerous forms designating the causal (cause/reason) relationship, as shown in (18):

(18) a.   *debido a*   'because of'
    b.   *con razón a*   'for the reason of'
    c.   *con razón de*   'for the reason of'
    d.   *en razón a*   'for the reason of'
    e.   *en razón de*   'for the reason of'
    f.   *por razón a*   'for the reason of'
    g.   *por razón de*   'for the reason of'
    h.   *a causa de*   'because of'
    i.   *por causa de*   'because of'
    j.   *por culpa de*   'because of'
    k.   *por motivo de*   'because of, by reason of'
    l.   *a raíz de*   'because of, in the wake of'
    m.   *gracias a*   'thanks to, due to'
    n.   *merced a*   'thanks to, due to'

The items listed in (18) all designate causality with some minor differences in their shade of meaning. They belong to different formal categories of composite and complex prepositions. The fourteen forms (N.B.: this, however, is not exhaustive) come from only 8 different source lexemes, because *razón* 'reason' and *causa* 'cause' are involved in multiple forms.

6.4 Ongoing Grammaticalization of Spatial Prepositions

We noted earlier that the Korean postpositional system is peculiar in that there are a small number of primary postpositions that occur at a very high frequency and a large number of complex postpositions that are of relatively lower frequency (see Chapter 3, for similar situations in English, see Chapter 5). A similar state of affairs is observed in the Spanish prepositional system, in which only about two dozen primary prepositions are used at a very high frequency and complex prepositions numbering in the hundreds are in the process of active grammaticalization. Since most of these fall under our focused interest, we will discuss their grammaticalization in the following.

6.4.1 Selection Criteria

In order to investigate the ongoing grammaticalization among spatial prepositions in Spanish, we first need to select optimal prepositions that are currently undergoing grammaticalization. The entire inventory of prepositions, inclusive of primary, composite, and complex forms, the latter two based on Cifuentes (2003) (albeit the category membership for certain items is disputable), consists of 851 prepositions, i.e., 25 primary, 136 composite, and 690 complex prepositions. Out of these 851, we select the items that satisfy all of the following qualifying conditions, with arguably arbitrary cut-off points, as in (19):

(19) (i)   It is not in the primary prepositional category in contemporary Spanish (826 items);
   (ii) It encodes spatial relationship (150 of them);
   (iii) It is attested for more than 10 pmw in the corpus (33 of them).

Condition (i) is to ensure that the preposition is not yet established as a fully grammaticalized preposition. Condition (ii) is to restrict the target items within our research focus, i.e., spatial preposition. Condition (iii) is to ensure that the item is a viable one, not a chance occurrence attributable to idiolectic styles or that the form is not at a very incipient stage where the form's viability is yet uncertain. The frequency of 10 pmw in the 170-million word corpus is about 1,700 raw tokens. The 33 target forms, supposedly actively undergoing grammaticalization, are listed in Table 6.5.

Frequency Range	Spatial PREP	Source (L: Latin)	PREP Meaning	Frequency	PMW
Medium (100~999 pmw)	a través de	través 'deviation'	via, through	34,989	206
	dentro de	dentro 'inside'	within	32,915	194
	a partir de	partir 'part, divide'	from, apart from	21,971	129
	junto a	junto 'near, together'	next to	20,200	119
Low (10~99 pmw)	cerca de	cerca 'near, nearly'	near	15,396	91
	fuera de	fuera 'outside'	outside	14,474	85
	alrededor de	alrededor 'around'	around, about	10,154	60
	encima de	cima 'top'	above	10,094	59
	junto con	junto 'near, together'	together with	9,576	56
	en torno a	torno 'turn, wheel'	around	8,688	51
	a fin de	fin 'end'	at the end of	8,010	47
	detrás de	L. trans 'after'	in back of	7,634	45
	por encima de	cima 'top'	above	7,136	42
	en medio de	medio 'half'	between	6,813	40
	por medio de	medio 'half'	through	6,688	39
	en contra de	L. contra 'against'	against, opposite	6,629	39
	lejos de	lejos 'far'	far from	6,103	36
	debajo de	bajo 'base'	under	5,987	35
	delante de	L. ante 'before'	in front of	4,832	28
	al lado de	lado 'side'	next to	3,654	21
	al final de	final 'end'	at the end of	3,410	20
	a finales de	final 'end'	at the end of	3,262	19
	cara a	cara 'face'	facing	3,197	19
	al margen de	margen 'margin'	outside of, apart from	3,185	19
	en el centro de	centro 'center'	in the center of	3,074	18
	por debajo de	bajo 'base'	below	2,870	17
	en el interior de	interior 'interior'	inside of	2,773	16
	al frente de	frente 'front'	in front of	2,770	16
	a raíz de	raíz 'base, root'	next to, following	2,605	15
	a mediados de	mediados 'middle'	in the middle of	1,829	11
	en compañía de	compañía 'company'	in company of	1,664	10
	rumbo a	rumbo 'course'	toward	1,634	10
	al pie de	pie 'foot'	at the foot of	1,620	10

Table 6.5 Grammaticalizing spatial prepositions in Modern Spanish

6.4.2 General Characteristics

The 33 target items listed in Table 6.5 bear special significance in grammaticalization studies in a number of ways. We will discuss them as a whole and then in groups in the following.

It is apparent from the items listed in Table 6.5 that none of them are in the High frequency range (cf. Table 6.4), with the highest frequency only at 206 pmw of *a través de* 'via, through'. Nearly all of them are in the Low frequency group, indicating that most grammaticalizing prepositions in Spanish are weak in terms of their functional strength. It is also noteworthy that only three primary prepositions fall within the frequency range, which are *bajo* 'below, under' (179 pmw), *mediante* 'through, by means of' (162 pmw), and vía 'via' toward the lower end. Also notable is the fact that composite prepositions, numbering 13, are located toward the upper end as compared to the complex forms, numbering 20, which are clustered toward the lower end of the frequency ranking.

In the 33 target items, there are only two complex prepositions with the PDNP structure, i.e., one containing the determiner: *en el centro de* 'in the middle of, at the center of' and *en el interior de* 'inside of', which, however, are located toward the lower end of the frequency ranking. This shows that structurally complex forms tend to be less grammaticalized and accordingly are less frequently used as compared to more eroded forms. In other words, currently grammaticalizing prepositions are either composite forms (LPs) or PNP complex forms, effectively excluding PDNP complex forms.

[*Contra, Tras* and *bajo*] Three primary prepositions *contra* 'against, opposite', *tras* 'behind, after' and *bajo* 'under' belong to the Medium frequency group, and they have functional and formal relatives in the target list, as shown in (20) through (22), along with the token frequencies from CREA, with the target items marked in bold:

(20) *contra*

a.	*contra*	'against, opposite'	610
b.	**en contra de**	**'against, opposite'**	**39**
c.	*por contra de*	'against, opposite'	0
d.	*a contra de*	'against, opposite'	0

(21) *tras*

a.	*tras*	'after, behind'	288
b.	**detrás de**	**'after, behind'**	**45**
c.	*por detrás de*	'after, behind'	3

(22) *bajo*

a.	*bajo*	'below, under'	179
b.	debajo de	**'under'**	**35**
c.	**por debajo de**	'below'	17
d.	*bajo de*	'under'	4
e.	*abajo de*	'under'	4
f.	*por bajo de*	'below, under'	0

The prepositions based on *contra, tras* and *bajo* are interesting in that the base forms are primary prepositions and are used at a considerably higher frequency, and at the same time, one each of their relatives is in the actively grammaticalizing group, which is used at a considerably lower frequency. At the same time other relatives, except for *por debajo de,* are used at nearly negligible frequencies. As for *contra,* its meaning is both of spatial ('opposite') and of abstract opposition ('against'), the latter being far more frequent. The complex preposition *en contra de* is similarly specializing in abstract opposition. The primacy of *contra* as opposed to *en contra de* is then primarily due to the formal simplicity (note that, in general, highly grammaticalized forms tend to be shorter and occur at a high frequency).

Similarly, the primary preposition *tras* has temporal as well as spatial meanings ('after' and 'behind'), whereas *detrás de* is primarily a spatial preposition. The functional versatility of *tras* may be partly responsible for its higher frequency along with the formal simplicity, a point recurrently corroborated.

Bajo is the simplest in form among its relatives and belongs to the primary preposition group. Among the other five *bajo*-derived prepositions, *debajo de* and *por debajo de* are the only two belonging to the ongoing grammaticalization group. Once again, formal simplicity is of issue here. The more complex *por debajo de* is further analyzable as *por de bajo de* [by of base of] and is of lower frequency than its simpler relatives *bajo* and *debajo de* (for similar state of affairs, see *por encima de*, below).

Furthermore, the three prepositions, *contra, tras,* and *bajo* are classified in multiple grammatical categories, i.e., preposition and noun for *contra* and *tras*; preposition, noun, adjective, and adverb for *bajo. Contra* is primarily a preposition in the forms of either *contra* (47.5%) or *en contra de* (31.6%) and its nominal use is marginal (2.5%); *tras* can be a preposition 'after, behind' or a noun 'backside', but the nominal use is not attested at all; and *bajo* is predominantly a preposition (60%), but it also functions as an adjective (28%), adverb (6%) and noun (1%) in a random sample investigation (Heeran Lee p.c.).[7] All these are indicative of the fact that *contra, tras* and *bajo* are highly specialized in the prepositional function.

[*Junto* and *cima*] The prepositions based on *junto* 'together' and *cima* 'top' are notable in that they do not have functional competitors in the High or Medium frequency groups but have two functionally and formally close relatives each in the actively grammaticalizing group. Their relatives and token frequencies are shown in (23) and (24):

(23) *junto*

a.	*junto a*	'next to, beside, close to'	119
b.	*junto con*	'together with, along with'	56
c.	*junto de*	'together with'	0

(24) *encima*

a.	*encima de*	'above, over, up'	59
b.	*por encima de*	'above'	42
c.	*por cima de*	'above'	0

---

7) Incidentally, *bajo* can be an inflected finite verb for 1st person present tense, which accounts for 3 percent of corpus tokens.

As seen in the frequency data in (23), composite prepositions *junto a* and *junto con* are both in the ongoing grammaticalization group, the former twice as strong as the latter. Their semantic functions are similar but slightly different in detail. As the glosses show, *junto a* indicates spatial closeness (vicinity or proximity) whereas *junto con* is more closely related to togetherness (accompaniment or association). Since closeness is intuitively more general than togetherness (note that closeness involves only one focused entity whereas togetherness involves two focused entities), the former seems to occur more frequently in language use. For this reason, therefore, even though the two share the same lexical source, they are differently specialized in function and thus are of different usage frequency levels.

With respect to *encima* in (24), which can be further analyzed as *en* 'on' + *cima* 'top', the situation is slightly different. In form, the stronger *encima de* is a composite preposition whereas *por encima de* is a complex preposition, but for reason of analyzability of *encima* as *en+cima*, *encima de* is tantamount to a complex preposition with the structure of *en cima de* [on top of]. This is particularly true because in Modern Spanish the lexeme *cima* 'top' is still in use (also note the complex preposition *por cima de*), even though its frequency is not as high as the more grammaticalized *encima* (cf. *cima* occurs only 9 times pmw in CREA, sharply contrasting with *encima de* occurring 60 times pmw). From this perspective, *por encima de* involves multiply stacked prepositions either holistically 'by above of' or analytically 'by on top of'. The relatively lower frequency of *por encima de* vis-à-vis *encima de* may have to do with its formal complexity.

In this respect, *por cima de* is peculiar. It records 0 pmw frequency (actual token frequency of only 8 times in the corpus). Considering that the structural complexity of *por cima de* is not much higher than *encima de* (note that this can be decomposed as *en+cima de*), and even lower than its upper-hand *por encima de*, its low token frequency is unexpected. The fact that the P_1 in composite/complex preposition favors *en* over *por* may be partially responsible for the relatively lower frequency of *por cima de*, but that alone cannot account for its lower frequency as compared to *por encima de*, which also involves *por*. Another possibility, or at least one of the multiple contributing factors, is that *cima* as an autonomous noun does not have a strong representation in the mental lexicon whereas *encima*, though decomposable, has a strong representation, which may have led to a situation where the strong form is recruited in the complex preposition formation. This is indeed a good possibility, if we consider the fact that *cima* occurs only 1,520 times (9 pmw), whereas *encima* occurs as many as 21,065 times (124 pmw) in the CREA corpus. This strongly suggests that grammaticalization is a result of an interplay of intricately-related multiple factors.

[*Fin* and *medio*] The complex prepositions built around *fin* and *medio* also present interesting aspects of grammaticalization of prepositions in Spanish. They have multiple complex prepositions that belong to the actively grammaticalizing group. Their relatives are listed in (25) and (26):

(25) fin

a.	*a fin de*	'at the end of, for the purpose of'	47
b.	*al fin de*	'at the end of'	20
c.	*a finales de*	'at the end of'	19
d.	*a fines de*	'at the end of'	8
e.	*a final de*	'at the end of'	2
f.	*a los finales de*	'at the end of'	0

(26) medio

a.	*en medio de*	'between, among, amid, amidst'	40
b.	*por medio de*	'through, by means of'	39
c.	*por intermedio de*	'through'	2
d.	*en medio a*	'in the middle of'	0
e.	*por medio a*	'by means of'	0
f.	*a medio de*	'in the middle of'	0
g.	*a medio a*	'to medium to'	0

As shown in (25), *fin* has as many as six complex prepositions that are formally and functionally related. *A fin de,* the simplest one of them all, is of the highest frequency. From its composition, it evidently started its life as a spatial preposition, but in

Modern Spanish it primarily encodes temporal and purposive meaning, unlike its relative *al fin de,* involving the article, which carries more concrete meaning (Kyunghee Kim, p.c.). A noteworthy aspect with them is that the head noun in the preposition has variations, i.e., *fin* 'end', *fines* 'ends', *final* 'final', *finales* 'finals', all descended from the Latin lexeme *finis* 'limit, end' (De Silva 1985: 230). Of these, *a fin de* has, in addition to the spatial terminus meaning 'end', other subjectified meanings such as purposive or intentional 'to, in order to, for the purpose of'. This semantic multiplicity seems, at least in part, to be responsible for its relative high frequency as compared to its relatives. Those with the plural forms in the prepositional composition are relatively of low frequency.

The *medio*-based prepositions in (26) are also variegated, even though the five lower frequency forms are very weak in usage. Developed from the same source lexeme *medio* 'half', *en medio de* and *por medio de* are of comparable strength but their meanings carry subtle differences. *En medio de* encodes typical concept of medial location, whereas *por medio de* encodes more abstract meaning of medium, instrumentality, and passage. For this notional divergence, the two cannot have been in functional competition. Instead, *en medio de* must have competed and be competing with *entre* 'between, among', which is more grammaticalized and stronger, whereas *por medio de* must have competed with *a través de* 'through', *por* 'by', *mediante* 'by means of', among others.

[*Partir, lejos, margen* and *centro*] The final group for discussion includes the composite/complex prepositions *a partir de* 'apart from', *lejos de* 'far from', *al margen de* 'outside of', and *en el centro de* 'in the center of', all of which do not have direct formal relatives in the system of prepositions in Spanish. In terms of their function, there may be somewhat indirect competitors such as *a partir a, al margen de, fuera de, afuera de* 'outside', etc. for the meaning of exclusion 'apart from'. However, the prepositions from these source lexemes are relatively specific in meaning, i.e., *partir* 'depart', *lejos* 'far', *margen* 'margin', and *centro* 'center'. This suggests that these concepts are general enough to motivate a construction involving them to grammaticalize, but at the same time specific enough not to have direct competitors and not to advance to the higher level of grammaticalization into primary prepositions.

From the foregoing discussion, we can see that there is a strong correspondence between the use frequency and formal reduction as indicated by the phonetic volume and structural complexity. There also seems to be a correspondence between the use frequency and the degree of semantic generality, which, however, needs more fine-grained research.

6.4.3 Grammaticalization Mechanisms

As we have done with the languages addressed in previous chapters, we examine grammaticalization scenarios of Spanish prepositions with respect to the grammaticalization mechanisms proposed by Kuteva et al. (2019), i.e., extension, desemanticization, decategorialization and erosion.

6.4.3.1 Extension

Extension, the increase of the context in which a grammatical form can occur, is well attested in grammaticalization processes of Spanish prepositions. A very good example is found with noun-based composite prepositions, such as *camino a/de* (< *camino* 'way') 'towards', *cara a* (< *cara* 'face') 'towards', *caso de* (< *caso* 'case, occurrence') 'in case of', *cuestion de* (< *cuestion* 'question') 'in the matter of', *esquina a* (< *esquina* 'corner') 'at the corner of', *gracias a* (< *gracia* 'grace') 'thanks to', *merced a* (< *merced* 'mercy') 'thanks to', *orilla(s) a/de* (< *orilla* 'shore') 'at the shore of, at the verge of', *respecto a/de* (< *respecto* 'respect') 'about', and *rumbo a* (< *rumbo* 'course, direction') 'toward' (see 6.3.3.2 above). The use context extension of *cara* is exemplified in (27) and (28):

(27) a. *Garantizamos la total transparencia de nuestra actividad <u>cara a</u> nuestros clientes.*
          'We guarantee total transparency of our activity <u>to</u> our clients.'

                                                                      (*SpanishDict*)
      b. *Garantizamos la total transparencia de nuestra actividad.*

'We guarantee total transparency of our activity.'

    c.   *cara a nuestros clinentes*
        '(a) face to our clients'

(28) a.   *Que el Señor lo conserve en su paz y que evolucione cada vez más, <u>rumbo</u> <u>a</u> la perfección.*
        'May the Lord keep him in His peace and may he increasingly evolve towards perfection.'   (*SpanishDict*)

    b.   *Que el Señor lo conserve en su paz y que evolucione cada vez más.*
        'May the Lord keep him in His peace and may he increasingly evolve.'

    c.   *<u>rumbo a</u> la perfección*
        '(a) course to perfection'

Examples (27a) involves the preposition *cara a* 'towards'. As indicated, *cara* is a noun denoting 'face' and *rumbo* is also a noun denoting 'course, direction, route'. Example (27a) includes (27b) as its part, i.e., the main clause, which in itself is a complete sentence, and (27c). Therefore, in its non-grammaticalized interpretation, (27c), headed by a noun, should simply mean '(a) face to our clients'. Syntactically, the noun phrase (27c) does not have the linking function and thus cannot be conjoined with (27b), a complete sentence. When *cara a* changes its meaning from '(a) face to' to 'to, towards', it can function as a linker to produce the meaning of (27a).

Examples (28a) involves the preposition *rumbo a* 'towards'. In exactly the same manner as *cara* in (27), (28a) contains (28b) as a complete sentence (note that *evolucinonar* 'evolve' is an intransitive verb, not requiring a theme argument). (28c) is a segment (i.e., a noun phrase), which, in its original function, cannot be adjoined to (28b), for the lack of linking function. As *rumbo a* changes from its source nominal meaning '(a) course to' to 'toward', it can now function as a linker, i.e., a preposition.

As shown with examples above, usage contexts get extended as a construction [noun + prep] develops into a composite preposition. Even though extension occurs universally across grammaticalization scenarios, the development from the [noun + prep] into a preposition constitutes an excellent example of extension.

6.4.3.2 Desemanticization

Desemanticization, the loss of meaning content, is also frequently observed in the course of grammaticalization of Spanish prepositions. Many prepositions in Spanish develop from nouns denoting space. As the space-specific meaning becomes generalized, the form can encode diverse non-spatial meanings as well.

Among the most frequently observed desemanticization patterns is the loss of semantic restriction. In other words, at an earlier stage, a form is restricted to the function of spatial designation, and then the domain-specific restriction is lifted, whereby non-spatial meanings arise due to the image-schematic meaning transferred to other conceptual domains. In such cases, the metaphorical transfer from [space] to [time] and/or to [quality] is nearly universal in languages. For instance, the following examples show the [space 〉 time] transfer due to desemanticization, i.e., (29a) for spatial meaning and (29b) and (29c) for temporal meaning:

(29) *tras* 'behind' 'after'

    a. *La biblioteca de nuestro pueblo está <u>tras</u> el banco.*
        'The library in our town is <u>behind</u> the bank.'   (*SpanishDict*)

    b. *Con la protesta de ciertos catalanistas, que consideraban aquello un espectáculo del sur, su música retumbó en Barcelona <u>tras</u> muchos años de silencio.*
        'With the protest of certain Catalanists, who considered this a spectacle of the South, their music reverberated in Barcelona <u>after</u> many years of silence.'   (1996 La vida según... Peret, CREA)

    c. *... los presos cuando salen <u>tras</u> cumplir su condena, pequeña o grande, están más predispuestos a delinquir de nuevo.*

'...prisoners, when they leave <u>after</u> serving their sentence, small or large, are more predisposed to commit crimes again'

(1987, Vida y muerte en las cárceles, CREA)

Similarly, the preposition *contra* 'against' (and *en contra de* 'against') also exhibits desemanticization from its original meaning of spatial directionality (30a) to the non-spatial meaning, e.g., an abstract entity such as terrorism and wedding (30b-c), as shown in the following examples, taken from *SpanishDict*.

(30)   *contra* 'against'

    a. *Sí, estornudó y se golpeó la cabeza <u>contra</u> la pared.*
        'Yeah, he sneezed and smacked his head <u>against</u> the wall.'

    b. *Nuestra primera tarea es reforzar la coalición <u>contra</u> el terrorismo.*
        'Our first task is to strengthen the coalition <u>against</u> terrorism.'

    c. *Has estado <u>en contra de</u> esta boda desde el principio.*
        'You have been <u>against</u> this wedding from the beginning.'

This process is quite frequent as shown in Table 6.6, which shows some prepositions with their lexical meaning along with desemanticized prepositional meaning (note, however, that neither the listing in Table 6.6 nor the semantic domains specified are meant to be exhaustive).

PREP	Lexical Source	Lexical Source Meaning	Desemanticized PREP Meaning	Semantic Domains
dentro de	*dentro*	'inside'	'within' 'inside of' 'into'	Space, Time, Abstract entity,
bajo	*bajo*	'base'	'below', 'under'	Space, Abstract entity
alrededor de	*alrededor*	'around'	'around', 'about'	Space, Time, Number
encima de	*cima*	'top'	'above', 'over', 'on top of'	Space, Abstract entity
en torno a	*torno*	'turn, wheel'	'around'	Space, Abstract entity
en torno de	*torno*	'turn, wheel'	'around'	Space, Abstract entity
por encima de	*cima*	'top'	'above'	Space, Abstract entity
en medio de	*medio*	'half'	'between', 'amid(st)', 'among'	Space, Time, Abstract entity
por medio de	*medio*	'half'	'through' 'by means of'	Space, Means, Abstract entity

cara a	cara	'face'	'facing'	Space, Abstract entity
al margen de	margen	'margin'	'outside of', 'apart from'	Space, Abstract entity
al frente de	frente	'front'	'in front of', 'at the head of', 'at the forefront of', 'in charge of'	Space, Abstract entity
vía	vía	'way'	'via, through'	Space, Means, Abstract entity
rumbo a	rumbo	'course'	'toward'	Space, Abstract entity
al pie de	pie	'foot'	'at the foot of', 'at the bottom of', 'outside'	Space
al borde de	borde	'edge'	'at the edge of', 'on the brink of', 'on the verge of'	Space, Abstract entity
en lo alto de	alto	'high'	'on top of'	Space, Abstract entity

Table 6.6 Desemanticization of Spanish prepositions

6.4.3.3 Decategorialization

Operation of the mechanism decategorialization is also well observed in the grammaticalization of Spanish prepositions. As has been illustrated with reference to other languages, like English, in particular, for the typological affinity between them, nominal category characteristics are susceptible to loss when a noun is involved in the grammaticalizing construction. Since Spanish prepositions, especially composite and complex prepositions, involve nouns in the majority, we can review their nominal category behavior. In Spanish, nominal characters include pluralizability, nominal modifiability, and article omissibility.

As a general rule, primary and composite prepositions that developed from nouns cannot be modulated with respect to number. For instance, in Modern Spanish, the word *vía* can be used as a noun *vía* 'way' or a primary preposition *vía* 'via, through' as in (31) and (32), taken from CREA:

(31) a.   *Esto era una vía de alta velocidad entonces.*
       'This was a high speed road then.'
       (1991 Escuela de Ingenieros de Caminos, Canales y Puertos, conferencia, Madrid, CREA, translation added)

   b.   *Eran las vías de alta velocidad entonces.*
       'They were the high speed roads then.'
       ((a) modified)

(32) a.   *...si creen en esa fórmula, incluyan en su dictamen la fórmula del voto de los mexicanos en el extranjero <u>vía</u> correo.*

'...if they believe in that formula, include in their opinion the formula for the vote of Mexicans abroad <u>via</u> mail.' (modified from 1999, Sesión pública extraordinaria de la Honorable Cámara de Senadores, celebrada el jueves 8 de julio de 1999, Mexico, CREA, translation added)

b.   **...si creen en esa fórmula, incluyan en su dictamen la fórmula del voto de los mexicanos en el extranjero <u>vías mensajeros</u>.*

((a) modified; intended: ... the vote of Mexicans abroad <u>via couriers</u>)

Doubtlessly, *vía* in (31a) is a noun denoting 'road, way', properly marked with the feminine indefinite article *una,* thus, 'a road', whereas *vías* in (31b) is the pluralized counterpart (with feminine plural definite article *las*). On the other hand, *vía* in (32a) is a preposition, thus lacking an article, and the segment of the excerpt means 'vote via mail' or 'vote through mail', in which *vía* denotes the means. However, (32b), modified for plural marking with the intended meaning 'the vote via mail and couriers' or 'the vote through mail and couriers', is not acceptable, which indicates that the preposition *vía* is fully grammaticalized and is formally frozen. This general pattern is applicable to other noun-based primary prepositions such as *bajo* 'under' (《 n. 'base'), *cabe* 'next to' (《 n. 'end, tip'), etc. (note that *hacia* 'until' is opaque as to its origin since the base noun *faz* 'face' is now obsolete).

The situation is similar with the noun-derived composite prepositions. Thus, the prepositions, *camino a/de* (《 *camino* 'way'), *cara a* (《 *cara* 'face'), *caso de* (《 *caso* 'case, occurrence'), *cuestion de* (《 *cuestion* 'question'), *esquina a* (《 *esquina* 'corner'), *merced a* (《 *merced* 'mercy'), *respecto a/de* (《 *respecto* 'respect'), and *rumbo a* (《 *rumbo* 'course, direction'), cannot be modulated by pluralization. Conversely, plural-based *gracias a* (《 *gracia* 'grace') cannot be modulated as **gracia a,* a singular-noun counterpart. It appears that *orilla(s) a/de* (《 *orilla* 'shore') 'at the shore(s) of, at the brink(s) of' is the only exceptional composite preposition in this regard, which suggests that *orilla(s) a/de* has not been grammaticalized to the extent of other composite prepositions.

The situation is a little more inconsistent with complex prepositions. In most cases, formal fossilization in the form of singular noun is complete and thus plural modification is not allowed, as shown in (33):

(33) a. *Consiguió su éxito <u>a base de</u> su esfuerzo.*
          'He achieved his success <u>based on</u> his efforts.'
     b. **Consiguio su exito <u>a bases de</u> su esfuerzo.* (*bases*: pl. of *base*)
                                              (K Kim 2019: 12, translation added)

However, there are a few cases that still retain flexibility with respect to number, as listed in (34):

(34) a. *a golpe(s) de*   'at the stroke(s) of'
     b. *a fin(es) de*   'for the purpose of, at the end of'
     c. *a mano(s) de*   'by the hand(s) of, at the hand(s) of'
     d. *a(l) final/finales de*   'at the end(s) of'
     e. *en la(s) víspera(s) de* 'on the eve(s) of'

Noun modifiability decreases as grammaticalization advances. Therefore, the composite preposition *gracias a* 'thanks to' cannot be modified with a quantifying adjective *muchas* 'many', even though it is possible when *gracias* is a regular plural noun (e.g., *¡Muchas gracias!*). This is seen in the following constructed examples.

(35) a. *<u>Gracias a</u> su ayuda pude terminar mi tarea.*
          '<u>Thanks to</u> your help I could finish my homework.'
     b. **<u>Muchas gracias a</u> su ayuda pude terminar mi tarea.*
          ((a) modified, intended: <u>Many thanks to</u> your help...)

However, there are prepositions that allow a modifier, as is seen in (36), in which a modifier qualifies the meaning of the head noun:

(36) a.   *al lado de*   'next to, beside'
     a'. *al <u>otro</u> lado de* 'on the <u>other</u> side of'

b.	*del lado de*	'on the side of'
b'.	*del <u>otro</u> lado de*	'on the <u>other</u> side of, from across'
c.	*en contacto con*	'in contact with/of, ahold of'
c'.	*en <u>íntimo</u> contacto con*	'in <u>close</u> contact with'

An interesting fact about the modified versions of complex prepositions is that they are also regarded by some researchers as complex prepositions (e.g., Cifuentes 2003) (note the distinctively different functions between the modified and non-modified forms involving *lado*). The possibility of noun modification strongly suggests the relative lower degrees of grammaticalization of complex prepositions.

As for article uses, a general tendency in grammaticalization is to lose the article, e.g., from PDNP to PNP, and once grammaticalization reaches a certain point, modulation with an article becomes unacceptable. One caveat in this context is that the use of an article is not as strict as in English and the rules governing their use are different from English (Givón 1981, Heine 1997, Lyons 1999, Herslund 2012, Khokhlova 2014, Sommerer 2018, Navarro Melara 2021, among others). Therefore, the absence or presence of an article cannot be a solid diagnostic of grammaticalization in Spanish; it can be regarded only as an indirect sign of degrees of grammaticalization. The complex prepositions exhibiting variation with respect to article use are listed in part in (37):

(37)	*a(l/la) par de*	'on a par with'
	a (la) ley de	'to law of'
	a (la) manera de	'by way of'
	a (la) medida de	'to the measure of'
	a (la) merced de	'at the mercy of'
	a (la) vista de	'in view of'
	a(l) filo de	'on the edge of'
	a(l) final/finales de	'at the end of'
	a(l) modo de	'by way of'
	a(l) servicio de	'at the service of'
	a(l) son de	'at the sound of'

con (la) esperanza de	'with hope of'	
con (la) intención de	'with the intention of'	
en (la) obligación de	'in obligation of'	
en (lo) tocante a	'regarding'	

6.4.3.4 Erosion

The last mechanism is erosion, whereby the phonetic substance of the grammaticalizing construction is gradually lost. When grammaticalization leads a syntactically complex construction to a preposition, the most remarkable processes in erosion involve the deletion of an article, thus PDNP developing into PNP (see also 3.4.3.3 above). For instance, a large majority of composite and complex prepositions do not contain an article, i.e., 571 out of 690 (accounting for 82.8%).

The variable levels of erosion is well illustrated in the comparison of complex prepositions, shown in Table 6.7.

Complex preposition (w/o article)	Token frequency Raw (PMW)	with article	Token frequency Raw (PMW)	% w/o article
en torno a	8,688 (51)	en el torno a	0 (0)	100%
en favor de	3,738 (22)	en el favor de	5 (0)	99.9%
a raíz de	2,605 (15)	a la raíz de	28 (0)	98.9%
en dirección a	1,262 (7)	en la dirección a	15 (0)	98.8%
en vías de	1,055 (6)	en las vías de	39 (0)	96.4%
a manera de	851 (5)	a la manera de	685 (4)	55.4%

Table 6.7 Article deletion in complex prepositions in Spanish

Table 6.7 shows the general tendency that the more frequently used a complex preposition (largely corresponding to higher degree of grammaticalization), the more likely the preposition occurs without a definite article in it. However, it must be noted that this is only a general tendency and that there are many cases that do not fit in the pattern in a statistically streamlined fashion. For instance, *con destino a* occurs only 848 times but it is nearly entirely used without the article as is shown by the fact that *con el destino a* occurs only once in CREA. Even a more extreme and converse case is *en el centro de* 'in the center of' (with the article *el*), which occurs for 3,074 times, whereas its article-less *en centro de* occurs only for 400 times.

Another type of erosion involves the omission of the first preposition (P_1) in the source structure (P_1NP_2.). There are a few such cases among the complex prepositions. This is shown in (38):

(38) a.   *a orillas de*   *orillas de*   'on the shores of, at the edge of'
      b.   *en el caso de*   *el caso de*   'in the case of, in case of'
      c.   *en cuanto a*   *cuanto a*   'in terms of, with regard to, as to'

From a structural point of view, the erosion of P_1 is peculiar because P_1 is the linker between the forgoing expression and the following noun. Since the noun by itself does not have the capability to link itself with others, the disappearance of P_1 leaves the noun structurally stranded. When the structural incompatibility occurs, there also occurs structural reanalysis, whereby language users give the stranded noun (and the forms accompanied by it) a linker status, i.e., a preposition. This particular type of erosion is not very common in the development of prepositions, but the presence of purely noun-based primary prepositions, e.g., *vía, bajo,* strongly suggests that this procedure has occurred to them, e.g., [por vía de] > [vía], [de bajo de] > [bajo], etc. This is a theoretically significant issue, because attribution of a linking function to a noun can be interpreted as an instance of 'absorption' (see 10.4 for more discussion).

Still another type of erosion involves P_2. This process is analogous to the omission of P_1 and the effect is the same, i.e., stranding of the noun, the only difference being the loss of connection between the noun and the following noun phrase instead of the preceding forms. Such an example is *no obstante (a/de)* 'notwithstanding'. This type of erosion, however, is not common in the grammaticalization of prepositions in Spanish.

6.4.4 Grammatical Functions

Spanish prepositions, inclusive of primary, composite and complex prepositions, are vast in number, i.e., around 715 in total, and, accordingly, carry diverse functions. Of these, around 169 of them mark spatial relationship. We also noted that these spatial prepositions also often encode temporal relationship, which is crosslinguistically a common phenomenon. Furthermore, their functions often extend to other abstract domains via desemanticization (see 6.4.3.2 above). This is exemplified in the following examples of *dentro de* 'within, inside', modified from *SpanishDict*.

(39) a. [space]

Vivimos dentro de un universo que se expande y evoluciona.

'We live <u>within</u> a universe that is expanding and evolving.'

b. [time]

Tenemos que estar en la fiesta dentro de una hora.

'We've got to be at the party <u>in</u> an hour.'

c. [abstract entity]

La Unión debe desarrollar su política dentro de este contexto.

'The Union should develop its policy <u>within</u> this context.'

An intriguing aspect of functional extension is the development of prepositions into postpositions. Even though these cases are small in number, it is noteworthy from the theoretical perspective. This has been noted as early as 1847 by Bello (1847), who noted that *afuera, adentro, arriba, abajo, adelante, atrás, antes,* and *después* are clearly prepositions in function but can occur after a noun phrase. Bello (1847: 299, as cited in Kim and Rhee 2018: 25) provides the following instances (translations added):

(40) a. *cuesta <u>arriba</u>*　　'up the hill, upward the slope'

　　 b. *río <u>abajo</u>*　　　'down the river, downstream'

　　 c. *tierra <u>adentro</u>*　　'into the inland, inland'

　　 d. *mar <u>afuera</u>*　　　'out at see, far offshore'

e. *meses antes*   'months before, months earlier'
f. *días después*   'days after, days afterwards'
g. *años atrás*   'years ago, years back'
h. *camino adelante* 'way forward, way ahead'

These expressions are still in use in Modern Spanish, all attested in CREA. Considering the typological fact that Spanish is a prepositional language, the existence of postpositions presents a fresh insight in the study of adpositions (see Chapter 5 for English). When a form can be used either as a preposition or a postposition, the form is sometimes called an 'ambiposition' (Reindl 2001, Libert 2006). Prepositional languages having postpositions or ambipositions often present quandary for grammarians, who, then, are inclined to classify the postpositions and ambipositions as adverbs.

6.5 Summary

In this chapter we have looked at the prepositional system in Spanish from a grammaticalization perspective. Spanish has a large number of prepositions that belong to primary, composite, and complex prepositional categories. Even though primary prepositions are relatively not numerous, numbering about 25, composite prepositions and complex prepositions are great in number, with 136 and 690, respectively, thus 851 as all combined. These numbers are inconclusive of items at the fuzzy boundary between complex prepositions and syntactic constructions.

These prepositions widely vary in terms of their strength of representation, as evidenced by the use frequency in corpora, from as high as 61,000 pmw (for *de*) to no attestation (for *cabe, so, apartadamente de, entremedias de,* and *por entremedias de*) in CREA. These prepositions have developed through a few common paths, such as inheritance from Latin, borrowing, and language-internal evolution, the last constituting the vast majority. In the last category, we noted that there are many complex prepositions that show structural variations through such processes as omission of P_1, replacement of P_1, omission of the article, pluralization of the noun, synonymous variation of the noun, modification of the noun, and replacement of P_2. Primary and composite prepositions derived from nouns are relatively fewer in number, but complex prepositions develop predominantly from the nominal sources, by virtue of having the P(D)NP structure. Prepositions from verbal sources typically develop from participial forms, and such prepositions are nearly non-existent in the complex preposition group. Another common source is adverbs, of which the *-mente*-suffixed forms constitute a large group with 58 members.

An important aspect of prepositions in Spanish is that a single function may be carried by multiple forms, thus, creating multiple layers, which also come from diverse sources. Some of the multiple layers are in fact those that developed from the same source but with variable degrees of erosion.

When the spatial prepositions are classified, 169 of them are found, which, as in other languages, encode diverse non-axial and axial relationship. When certain criteria are applied, about 33 of them are thought to be actively undergoing grammaticalization. None of these selected prepositions are in the High frequency group, and most of them are at around the border of Medium and Low frequency groups, with a nearly equal number of composite and complex prepositions. We further grouped these 33 grammaticalizing spatial prepositions by their characteristic features, and noted that there is always an effect of formal complexity, i.e., a tendency that the simpler a form is, the higher its frequency.

We reviewed the grammaticalization scenarios with respect to mechanisms. It was found that the four mechanisms, extension, desemanticization, decategorialization, and erosion well capture the gradual nature of grammaticalization of prepositions in Spanish. Further, differential degrees of structural variability is largely coextensive with the use frequency and degrees of grammaticalization.

Spatial prepositions typically carry extended functions in other semantic domains, such as temporal and other abstract domains. And we also noted that there are ambipositions in Spanish that can function as both a preposition and a postposition.

Grammaticalization of Adpositions in Chinese

7.1 Introduction

Blessed with an unbroken history of over 3,000 years of written tradition, Chinese presents a unique and interesting state of affairs from a linguistic point of view.[1] It does so especially with respect to the adpositional system in contemporary Chinese. Even though most languages exhibit a strong preference for either a prepositional or postpositional system over the other (Greenberg 1963), Chinese has a well-developed prepositional system as well as an equally strong postpositional system.[2] Furthermore, there is an intricate interplay of word-order change that occurred in the history of Chinese (cf. Li and Thompson 1974b, 1976, Sun 1996 for Chinese; see also Fischer 2010 for Germanic and Romance languages). This chapter describes the

---

[1] This chapter is greatly aided by Chinese linguists, Xiao He, Lin Zhang, Yeon Jin Ahn, Seon-A Kwun, and other colleagues, for data collection and occasional consultation. All errors in interpretation and argumentation are, however, solely the author's.

[2] Shin (2009: 186), based on the early versions of *Laoqida*, hypothizes the presence of postpositions in Chinese spoken in the northern areas of China (*Han'eryanyu*) as attributable to language contact with Altaic languages (see also F Wu 2005 and references therein, for discussion on contact-induced grammaticalization).

dual system of adpositions in Chinese, focusing on the spatial adpositions that are actively undergoing grammaticalization. Further, it will discuss some noteworthy aspects of grammaticalization scenarios from typological and comparative linguistic perspectives.

7.2 Adpositions in Chinese

As briefly alluded to above, Chinese has a dual system of adposition, consisting of prepositions and postpositions.[3] In the research tradition in Chinese linguistics, prepositions are largely discussed under the label of *jiècí* (介詞/介词), even though the term 'adposition', encompassing preposition (*qiánzhící*, 前置詞/前置词) and postposition (*hòuzhící*, 後置詞/后置词), is sometimes referred to as *fùzhící* (附置詞/附置词) (cf. J Shen 1989 uses *fùzhící* (附置詞/附置词) in his translation of Comrie's (1981) 'adposition', as cited in D Liu 2004).[4] J Ma (2003[1898]), a pioneering study of ancient Chinese adpositions, used the term *jièzì* (介字) 'lit. inducting word, in-between word', to refer to the group of forms functioning as prepositions and/or postpositions (e.g., *zhī* (之), *yú* (于), *yǐ* (以), *yǔ* (與/与), *wèi* (爲/为)), but J Li (1933[1924]), largely following J Ma (2003[1898]) otherwise, named it *jiècí* (介詞, 介词) in describing Modern Chinese adpositions.[5] In addition to the most widely used *jiècí* (介词), other terms known to refer to Chinese adpositions include *guānxìcí* (關係詞/关系词; S Lu 1980, 1984) 'relation word'; *liánjiécí* (連結詞/连结词; L Wang 1985) 'connecting word'; *bèiyǐndǎocí* (被引导词; M Gao 1948) 'guided word'; *fùdòngcí* (副動詞/副动词; S Ding 1952) 'adverb, adverbialized verb'; *cìdòngcí* (次動詞/次动词; S Ding 1961) 'secondary verb'; *zhùdòngcí*

---

3) See 7.4.4.2 for a brief discussion on circumpositions.

4) One caveat with respect to the notation of Chinese prepositions, more generally of Chinese, is that Chinese makes use of simplified characters to increase convenience but there occur many classical characters in research due to the fact that the written records prior to the writing reform in 1956 are written in classical characters. In this chapter we use both characters if both are prominent but only one of the two, otherwise.

5) Incidentally, *yú* (于) was also formerly written as '於', which was removed and replaced by '于'.

(助動詞/助动词; L Wang 1985) 'auxiliary verb', among others (D Liu 2004).[6] Furthermore, since Chinese prepositions are homophonous with verbs in form and similar to serialized verbs in structure, the term 'co-verb' has also been used for them (Li and Thompson 1974a).[7]

It has long been acknowledged by Chinese linguists and grammarians that all grammatical items (*xūcí*; 虛詞/虚词; 'empty words', grammatical words) originated from lexical items (*shící*; 實詞/实词; 'substantive words', content words), a remark recorded as early as the 14th century by Zhou Bo-qi (1298-1369). In the contemporary linguistic tradition, however, attention has been paid mostly to prepositions, which have mostly developed from verbs, whereas postpositions, typically developing from nouns, have been largely ignored (D Liu 2004). These postpositions comprise a number of relational nouns, which have been discussed under the label of *fāngwèicí* (方位詞/方位词) 'position words' 'localizers', a category never acknowledged to be comparable to prepositions. They were addressed in earnest by Z Yu (1986, as cited in D Liu 2004, Peyraube 1994, 2003, and Chappell and Peyraube 2008, Peyraube 1994, 2003, among others).

The data for analysis has been obtained from the modern Chinese section of the CCL (The Center for Chinese Linguistics at Peking University) online corpus, consisting of 581,794,456 characters. For its logographic nature of the Chinese characters, each character or letter has a meaning (thus a word) as well as a sound (thus a grapheme) (e.g., 点 *diǎn* 'dot', 油 *yóu* 'oil'). However, Chinese words are predominantly bigrams, consisting of two characters (e.g., 工作 *gōngzuò* 'work', 成功 *chénggōng* 'success, succeed'), even though each letter in these words does have a meaning (e.g., *gōng* 工 'work' *zuò* 作 'do', 成 *chéng* 'complete', 功 *gōng* 'achievement'), a combination of which differs semantically from the two-character words. For this reason, there have been attempts to calculate the number of words from the

---

[6] Some authors, e.g., Yip and Rimmington (1997: 114-119), distinguish coverbs and prepositions. For discussion on difficulties involving coverbs, prepositions, and postpositions in categorization, see Paul (2015: 55-60, 93-99).

[7] Li and Thompson (1974a: 272), however, suggest the use of the term 'preposition' instead of the language-particular word class 'co-verbs'.

character counts.8) Based on an empirical study of word vs. character ratio, i.e., 1: 1.3, the frequency is calculated based on this ratio, and the 581,794,456-character corpus size is recalculated as consisting of about 447,534,196 words.

In this chapter we will address adpositions in Chinese as a whole, but for convenience we will divide them in subgroups. Chinese prepositions have been classified by Chinese linguists in a number of ways, e.g., J Ma (2003[1898]), C Jin (1996), Y Fu and X Zhou (1997), D Liu (2004), C Chen (2004), B Ma (2002), S Heo (2005), B Zhang (2010: 215), N Lu (2015), Choi and Kwun (2012, 2017), among many others.

Even though there are many different ways of classifying them, we will arrange them in a way similar to how we classified adpositions in the other languages addressed here to facilitate comparison. First of all, the adpositions are divided into prepositions and postpositions in a straightforward way, i.e., preposition, if it is affixed at the front of the host noun; postposition, if affixed at the end of it. If the adposition is a unigram, it is further classified as a primary adposition; if the adposition is a bigram, and thus has two meaningful characters, it is classified as a composite adposition; and if the adposition has the residue of syntactic construction, e.g., involving the linkers *zhī* (之) 'of' or *de* (的) 'of', it is classified as complex adposition, instead of composite adposition. As shall be clear in the following exposition, complex adpositions occur only as postpositions. There are also 'circumpositions', i.e., those that occur in split form (Koopman 2000, Huddleston and Pullum 2002, Haspelmath 2003), but we will only mention them briefly in 7.4.4.2.

Grammatical category is a particularly cumbersome issue for isolating languages like Chinese and Thai because of their categorial fluidity associated with their formal conservative nature and functional relatedness among items in the 'heterosemy'

---

8) According to the *Frequency Dictionary of Modern Chinese (FDMC* 1986, as cited in Zhang et al. 2001), 26.7% of the top 9,000 most frequent words are unigrams; 69.8%, bigrams; 2.7%, trigrams; 0.007%, quadrigrams; and 0.0002%, pentagrams, and in Y Liu (1987), 75% bigrams and 14% trigrams, among others (as cited in Fung and Wu 1994: 2). The word vs. character ratio in a running text is variable by the text type. In a hand-counted cursory survey of a Biblical text by the author, the ratio is about 1:1.2. According to an online source (www.chinaministry.org/archives/9697), the ratio from the entire text of the Chinese Union Version of the Bible is 1:1.3 (929,990 characters, 715,662 words), the ratio we adopt in this study.

relations (Lichtenberk 1991).[9] Thus, some researchers, e.g., D Liu (2008), B Zhang (2010), among others, use non-discrete categorization by subscribing to 'prototype theory' (Rosch 1973, 1975, 1978, Taylor 1988), whereby differentiating prototypical and peripheral members in different groups. Furthermore, adpositions, being a functional category, are susceptible to rise and fall in the course of functional competition, and as a result there are forms whose functions are weak to the point of being ignored by researchers. For this reason, researchers have different criteria and different inventories of adpositions. From existing literature, D Liu (2004), S Heo (2005), W Park (2012), H Lin (2014), X He (2016), J Xing (2013), and elsewhere, we present 42 primary prepositions in Chinese in Table 7.1.

	Preposition		Meaning
a.	*àn*	按	'according to, following'
b.	*bǎ*	把	ACC
c.	*bèi*	被	'by'
d.	*bǐ*	比	'than'
e.	*cháo*	朝	'to, towards'
f.	*chèn*	趁	'at the time of, utilizing, taking the advantage of'
g.	*chòng*	冲/衝	'on the strength of, on the basis of, because'
h.	*chú*	除	'except, in addition to'
i.	*cóng*	从/從	'from'
j.	*dǎ*	打	'from'
k.	*dāng*	当/當	'towards, at the time of'
l.	*dào*	到	'to, up to, till'
m.	*duì*	对/對	'in, for, to'
n.	*gěi*	给/給	DAT 'to, for'
o.	*gēn*	跟	'with'
p.	*guǎn*	管	ACC/TOP 'as for, with regard to'
q.	*hé*	和	'with'
r.	*jiāng*	将/將	ACC/THM 'to'
s.	*jiào*	叫	'by'

---

[9] The categorial fluidity and non-discrete categorial boundary are also shared by Cantonese Chinese, a language closely related to Mandarin Chinese (see Matthews and Yip 2011[1994]: 130-143).

t.	*jù*	据/據	'according to'
u.	*lián*	连/連	'even'
v.	*lùn*	论/論	'by, regarding, in terms of, by the unit of'
w.	*píng*	凭/憑	'relying on, based on, depending on'
x.	*ràng*	让/讓	'by'
y.	*rú*	如	'like, similar to'
z.	*tì*	替	'for'
aa.	*tóng*	同	'with'
ab.	*wǎng*	往	'to, towards'
ac.	*wèi*	为/為	'for, for the purpose of'
ad.	*xiàng*	像	'like, similar to'
ae.	*xiàng*	向	'towards, to'
af.	*yán*	沿	'along, following'
ag.	*yǐ*	以	'with, by, according to, because of, from'
ah.	*yī*	依	'according to'
ai.	*yòng*	用	'by means of, in a way of'
aj.	*yóu*	由	'by, through, from'
ak.	*yú*	于/於	'in, to, towards, from, than, by, regarding'
al.	*yǔ*	与/與	'with'
am.	*zài*	在	'at'
an.	*zhào*	照	'to, towards'
ao.	*zhe/ zháo/ zhuó*	着/著	EMPH
ap.	*zì*	自	'from'

Table 7.1 Primary prepositions in Modern Chinese

As shown in the list, there are case markers, e.g., *bǎ* 把 (b), a marker of an object, similar to the Accusative case marker (see Li and Thompson 1976 for its grammaticalization, and 7.4.3.2 for more discussion); *gěi* 给/給 (n), a marker of goal or Dative; *guǎn* (管) (p), similar to the Dative case marker but also marking Topic; *jiāng* (将/將) (r), similar to the Accusative case marker indicating theme affected by an action, etc.[10] In Archaic Chinese *yǐ* 以 (ag) and *yú* 于/於 (ak) were common Dative

---

markers as well (Peyraube 1986a: 27, as cited in Bailblé 2015: 120). However, most prepositions signal non-syntactic roles.

Chinese has composite prepositions, i.e., consisting of two or more characters, as listed in Table 7.2, numbering 14, even though the list can be expanded when different criteria are adopted.

	Preposition		Meaning
a.	*ànzhào*	按照	'in the light of, according to'
b.	*chènzhe*	趁着/趁著	'taking advantage of'
c.	*duìyú*	对于/對於	'about, regarding'
d.	*gēnjù*	根据/根據	'according to'
e.	*guānyú*	关于/關於	'regarding'
f.	*shùnzhe*	顺着/順著	'along, following'
g.	*tōngguò*	通过/通過	'through, by way of'
h.	*wèile*	为了/為了	'for, for the benefit of'
i.	*wèizhe*	为着	'for, for the benefit of'
j.	*yánzhe*	沿着/沿著	'along, following'
k.	*yīzhào*	依照	'following, according to'
l.	*yóuyú*	由于/由於	'for, for the purpose of, because of'
m.	*zhìyú*	至于/至於	'as for, regarding'
n.	*zìcóng*	自从/自從	'from, since'

Table 7.2 Composite prepositions in Modern Chinese

As shown in the list, composite prepositions are much smaller than primary prepositions, but their semantics greatly varies as is the case with the primary prepositions.

One notable formal aspect is that there are a number of forms involving the preposition *zhe* (着/著) as in (b), (f), (i), and (j), which are mostly combinations of prepositions. The meaning of preposition *zhe* (着/著) is largely vague, but since its verbal meaning 'touch', denoting contact, carries the function of adding emphatic meaning, as shown in the following examples, taken from the *Eduworld SCCK*

Dictionary and *Hongloumeng*, with added glossing and translation:[11]

(1) a. 趁 年轻 , 多 学习。

    __Chèn__   *niánqīng,*   *duō*   *xuéxí.*

    utilizing   youth   much   study

    'One must study hard utilizing their youth.'

(Eduworld SCCK Dictionary)

    b. 看 至此, 意趣 洋洋, 趁着 酒兴, 不禁 提 笔 续 曰。

    Kàn *zhìcǐ,* *yìqù* *yángyáng,* *__chènzhe__*   *jiǔxìng,*

    see this spirit full   **taking.advantage.of** intoxication

    bùjīn   *tí*   *bǐ*   *xù*   *yuē.*

    cannot.help lift brush continue speak

    'Seeing this and taking advantage of intoxication, (he) couldn't help but lift the brush and continued to talk.'

(Hónglóumèng, as modified from Choi & Kwun 2012: 488)

Such emphasis effect by the addition of the preposition *zhe* (着/著) is also seen in its function as a passive marker (cf. I Kim 2010, J Wang 2013, 2014), i.e., affectedness from the notion of contact, and in its aspectual meaning of persistence of state (cf. Choi and Kwun 2012), i.e., persistence from the notion of non-detachedness. Even though the list includes only four such cases, the process seems to be a productive means of formation of composite prepositions. For instance, Choi and Kwun (2014, 2017), making reference to C Chen (2004: 89), note that many prepositions do form composite forms in combination with *zhe* (着), e.g., *āizhe* (挨着) 'next to', *jiùzhe* (就着) 'with, with regard to, about', *běnzhe* (本着) 'in, based on', *bènzhe* (奔着) 'for, toward the goal of', *cháozhe* (朝着) 'toward', *chènzhe* (趁着) 'taking advantage of', *chéngzhe* (乘着) 'taking the advantage of, by, making the most of', *chòngzhe* (冲着) 'toward', *dāngzhe*

---

11) Chinese sentences do not contain inter-lexical spaces, but for the sake of visual clarity words are written with spaces in examples. Also note, however, that word boundaries are often not straightforward.

(当着) 'in front of', *jièzhe* (借着) 'by', *jǐnzhe* (尽着) 'to the best of', *màozhe* (冒着) 'risking, persevering', *píngzhe* (凭着) 'according to, relying on', *rènzhe* (任着) 'let...continuing', *shùnzhe* (顺着) 'following, along', *suízhe* (随着) 'following', *xúnzhe* (循着) 'following', *xiàngzhe* (向着) 'toward', *yánzhe* (沿着) 'along', *yīzhàngzhe* (依仗着) 'depending on', *yīzhe* (依着) 'following', *zhàozhe* (照着) 'according to', *zhēnduìzhe* (针对着) 'aiming at', *wèizhe* (为着) 'for attaining', *duìzhe* (对着) 'towards', etc. (see also S Park 2015). Incidentally, J Choi and S Kwun (2012) also note that *le* (了), albeit much smaller in extent, participates in a similar process, e.g., *chúle* (除了) 'except', *wèile* (为了) 'for, in order to', *duìle* (对了) 'about', among others.[12] Starting its life as a verb denoting 'complete, finish', the lexeme *le* (了) has become a marker of perfect in Modern Chinese. The relation between emphasis and 'complete' is intuitively clear.

Primary and composite prepositions, numbering 56 altogether, vary to a great extent not only in meaning but also in their strengths in contemporary Chinese. A quantitative analysis based on the CCL Corpus shows the frequency ranking, as in Table 7.3.[13] The list shows that many of them (i.e., 32 out of 56) occur in the High and Medium frequency ranges, reflecting that they have been well established as prepositions in Modern Chinese.

Frequency Range	Preposition		Meaning	PMW
High (1,000~ pmw) (n=6)	*zài*	在	'at'	3,955
	yǐ	以	'with, by, according to, because of, from'	1,933
	duì	对/對	'in, for, to'	1,821
	yú	于/於	'in, to, towards, from, than, by, regarding'	1,801
	wèi	为/為	'for, for the purpose of'	1,233
	cóng	从/從	'from'	1,072

---

[12] Choi and Kwun (2014, 2017) list the forms only and the meanings of each form are added by the author. Any infelicitous semantic labeling is the author's responsibility. Lin Zhang (p.c.) notes that *duìle* (对了) is not a preposition but a discourse marker of sudden remembrance ('Oh, I almost forgot!') in Present-Day Chinese.

[13] Since Chinese morphemes are versatile, in general, the number of prepositional usage is projected based on a random sample of the hit-record of the lexeme. Thanks go to Xiao He and Lin Zhang for their assistance.

	bǎ	把	ACC	855
	zì	自	'from'	827
	yǔ	与/與	'with'	696
	yòng	用	'by means of, in a way of'	647
	yóu	由	'by, through, from'	618
	xiàng	向	'towards, to'	592
	jù	据/據	'according to'	522
	jiāng	将/將	ACC/THEME 'to'	520
	hé	和	'with'	519
	bǐ	比	'than'	416
	dào	到	'to, up to, till'	375
	gěi	给/給	DAT 'to, for'	312
Medium	*bèi*	被	'by'	307
(100~999 pmw)	*zhào*	照	'to, towards'	251
(n=26)	*chú*	除	'except, in addition to'	248
	tōngguò	通过/通過	'through, by way of'	229
	àn	按	'according to, following'	208
	wǎng	往	'to, towards'	197
	dāng	当/當	'towards, at the time of'	177
	gēnjù	根据/根據	'according to'	174
	xiàng	像	'like, similar to'	167
	guānyú	关于/關於	'regarding'	155
	gēn	跟	'with'	145
	tóng	同	'with'	138
	ànzhào	按照	'in the light of, according to'	109
	yī	依	'with, by, according to, because of, from'	109
	rú	如	'like, similar to'	76
	cháo	朝	'to, towards'	68
	tì	替	'for'	67
	wèile	为了/為了	'for, for the benefit of'	55
	duìyú	对于/對於	'about, regarding'	34
	yán	沿	'along, following'	34
	yóuyú	由于/由於	'for, for the purpose of, because of'	33
Low	*píng*	凭/憑	'relying on, based on, depending on'	33
(10~99 pmw)	*zhìyú*	至于/至於	'as for, regarding'	33
(n=15)	*chōng/* *chòng*	冲/衝	'on the strength of, on the basis of, because'	22
	yīzhào	依照	'following, according to'	19
	yán zhe	沿着/沿著	'along, following'	15
	jiào	叫	'by'	15

lián	连/連	'even'		15
chèn	趁	'at the time of, utilizing, taking the advantage of'		13
ràng	让/讓	'by'		8
shùnzhe	顺着/順著	'along, following'		6
dǎ	打	'from'		6
guǎn	管	ACC/TOP 'as for, with regard to'		6
wèi zhe	为着/為著	'for, for the benefit of'		2
chènzhe	趁着	'taking the advantage of'		1
zìcóng	自从/自從	'from, since'		0
zhe/ zháo/ zhuó	着/著	EMPH		0
lùn	论/論	'by, regarding, in terms of, by the unit of'		0

Very Low (~9 pmw) (n=9)

Table 7.3 Frequency of primary and composite prepositions in Modern Chinese

As indicated briefly above, Chinese also has a number of primary and composite postpositions, numbering 25 altogether (18 primary and 7 composite postpositions). They are listed in Table 7.4, arranged according to their meaning.

	Postposition		Meaning
a.	*shàng*	上	'on, above, upon, on top of'
b.	*shàngmiàn*	上面	'above, on top of, on'
c.	*xià*	下	'under, below, underneath'
d.	*qián*	前	'before, ago, in front of'
e.	*shàngxià*	上下	'beside, close to, about'
f.	*hòu*	后/後	'after, behind'
g.	*bèi/ bēi*	背	'in back of, in the rear of'
h.	*zhōng*	中	'in, during, among, within'
i.	*lǐ*	里/裏	'inside'
j.	*wài*	外	'outside, beyond, besides'
k.	*wàimiàn*	外面	'outside'
l.	*jiān*	间/間	'between, within, among'
m.	*dǐng*	顶/頂	'on top of, in stead of, despite'
n.	*biān*	边/邊	'at the side of, beside, next to'
o.	*páng*	旁	'beside, next to'
p.	*zuǒyòu*	左右	'beside, close to, about'
q.	*qǐ*	起	'from' (time)
r.	*lái*	来/來	'by agency of, causing, from' (time)
s.	*wéizhǐ*	为止/爲止	'until, till'

t.	*chù*	处/處	'at the place of'
u.	*bān*	般	'like, similar to'
v.	*yíyàng*	一样/一樣	'like, just like, alike, equal to'
w.	*shìde*	似的	'like'
x.	*zhī*	之	'of'
y.	*de*	的	'of'

Table 7.4 Primary and composite postpositions in Modern Chinese

Postpositions *zhī* (之) (x) and *de* (的) (y) are highly polyfunctional but are primarily Genitive markers. The former has a long history through which it developed many functions (H Liu 2016), but has declined in productivity and is used in literary styles in contemporary Chinese (K Lee 2011). The latter is also polyfunctional and has taken over the Genitive marking function of *zhī* (之). The prolificity of *de* (的) is possibly part of Europeanization as argued in L Wang (1985, see Cordes 2014).

It is evident from the list that there are multiple forms that are related not only semantically but also formally. For instance, the postpositions denoting Superior spatial concept 'top' (i.e., *shàng* (上) in (a) and *shàngmiàn* (上面) in (b)) are both based on the lexeme *shàng* (上)) and, similarly, the postpositions denoting Exterior spatial concept 'outside' (i.e., *wài* (外) in (i) and *wàimiàn* (外面) in (j)) are both based on the lexeme *wài* (外), the only difference being the latter further including the noun *miàn* (面) 'side, face'.

Most postpositions in Table 7.4 involve relational nouns, e.g., (a) through (p), a common aspect of adpositions across languages. When relational nouns are directly attached to a host noun, they function as postpositions, but in terms of word formation, the process is similar to compounding (which, incidentally, is a common process in Korean, cf. 3.4.3.4 and 3.4.4.1). However, D Liu (2004) notes that relational nouns, e.g., *shàng* (上), are no longer full-fledged nouns as is evident in the fact that *shàng* (上), for example, cannot occur with the Genitive *de* (的) 'of' as in **zhàn zài zhuō de shàng* (站在桌的上) [stand exist desk of top] '(intended): (He) is standing on top of the desk.' Furthermore, since Chinese relational nouns also participate in compounding with a function similar to derivational prefixes, e.g., *shàngyī* (上衣) 'jacket' (< 'top clothes'), *shàngjí* (上級) 'upper grade, higher level' (< 'top grade'), etc., the positionality of these relational nouns is important in their functional differentiation. The development of postpositions from a process similar to compounding, e.g., *shù-xià* (树下) ['tree-bottom' > '(at/to a location) under the tree'], is motivated by interpreting an inherently static entity, such as a tree, as being in relation to other entities, events or activities, which are potentially dynamic, e.g., one sleeping under its shade, taking cover from rain shower, etc.

There are instances, however, in which a more explicit marker of relation is involved, i.e., complex postpositions. There are 10 such instances, as listed in Table 7.5.

	Postposition		Meaning
a.	*zhījiān*	之间/之間	'between, among'
b.	*zhīshàng*	之上	'above'
c.	*zhīxià*	之下	'under'
d.	*zhīqián*	之前	'before'
e.	*zhīhòu*	之后/之後	'after, following'
f.	*yǐqián*	以前	'before'
g.	*yǐhòu*	以后/以後	'after'
h.	*yǐnèi*	以内	'within'
i.	*yǐwài*	以外	'outside, beyond, except for, over'
j.	*yǐlái*	以来/以來	'since'

Table 7.5 Complex postpositions in Modern Chinese

As shown in the list, complex postpositions involve linkers such as Genitive *zhī* (之) 'of' and Ablative *yǐ* (以) 'from', both prepositions themselves ((x) and (y) in Table 7.4). The presence of these linkers indicates that the source structure of the phrases involving them is periphrastic (and thus syntactic) rather than morphological, thus, given the label 'complex' postpositions. As D Liu (2004) notes, *yǐ* (以), a marker of Instrumental (i.e., means or manner) and Ablative (i.e., starting point, reference point), is archaic in Modern Chinese, and the Genitive *zhī* (之) has largely been replaced by its modern-day counterpart *de* (的). It is interesting to note that in the structure of [N$_1$-*zhī*-N$_2$] 'N$_2$ of N$_1$', *zhī* occurs after N$_1$ and before N$_2$, i.e., a structure in which the cohesion of the linker *zhī* 'of' may exist between N$_1$ and *zhī* or between *zhī* and N$_2$. With respect to the bonding between *zhī* and N$_2$ we can recall J Ma (2003[1898]), who states that the *jièzi* (介字), including *zhī*, precedes a noun (note, however, that this position is criticized by D Liu 2004). If the function of *zhī* (之) was reinterpreted as a postposition, the structural reanalysis must have gone from [N$_1$-[*zhī*-N$_2$]] to [[N$_1$-*zhī*]-N$_2$]]. Then, an interesting picture emerges from this context. The development of such complex postpositions as *zhījiān* (之间/之間) 'between, among', *zhīshàng* (之上) 'above', etc. (i.e., (a) through (e) in Table 7.5), must have undergone increasing bonding in the prepositional use in [*zhī*-N$_2$], in which N$_2$ is a relational noun, and afterwards, [*zhī*-N$_2$] as a whole has also undergone increasing bonding in the postpositional use as in [N$_1$-[*zhī*-N$_2$]]. To illustrate with the relational noun 'interval', the construction [*zhī*-'interval'] first develops to mean 'between', in which *zhī*- functions like a preposition, and then [N$_1$-[*zhī*-'interval']] develops into 'between N$_1$', in which [*zhī*-'interval'] 'between' functions like a postposition.

Postpositions, as is the case with prepositions, have variable functional strengths, as reflected in the token frequency in the corpus. The figures are based on pmw, and the range division is based on the general scheme. The frequency information of 35 postpositions (18 primary, 7 composite, and 10 complex) is given in Table 7.6.

Frequency Range	Postposition		Meaning	PMW
High (1,000~ pmw) (n=4)	*de*	的	'of'	4,895
	zhōng	中	'in, during, among, within'	2,026
	shàng	上	'on, above, upon, on top of'	1,352
	lǐ	里/裏	'inside'	1,221
Medium (100~999 pmw) (n=7)	*zhī*	之	'of'	575
	qián	前	'before, ago, in front of'	515
	wài	外	'outside, beyond, besides'	340
	jiàn/jiān	间/間	'between, within, among'	298
	xià	下	'under, below, underneath'	215
	zhījiān	之间/之間	'between, among'	164
	hòu	后/後	'after, behind'	103
Low (10~99 pmw) (n=15)	*yíyàng*	一样/一樣	'like, just like, alike, equal to'	92
	biān	边/邊	'at the side of, beside'	85
	yǐlái	以来/以來	'since'	83
	qǐ	起	'from'	52

lái	来/來	'by agency of, causing, from'	45
páng	旁	'beside'	40
zuǒyòu	左右	'beside, close to, about'	33
yǐwài	以外	'outside, beyond, except for, over'	32
bān	般	'like, similar to'	31
zhīxià	之下	'under'	26
zhīhòu	之后/之後	'after, following'	26
dǐng	顶/頂	'on top of, in stead of, despite'	18
yǐhòu	以后/以後	'after'	15
zhīshàng	之上	'above'	14
chù	处/處	'at the place of'	11
Very Low (~9 pmw) (n=9)	*yǐnèi*	以内	'within'	8
	yǐqián	以前	'before'	7
	zhīqián	之前	'before'	5
	shìde	似的	'like'	4
	wàimiàn	外面	'outside'	3
	shàngxià	上下	'beside, close to, about'	3
	shàngmiàn	上面	'above, on top of, on'	2
	bèi/ bēi	背	'in back of, in the rear of'	0
	wéizhǐ	为止/爲止	'until, till'	0

Table 7.6 Frequency of postpositions in Modern Chinese

The list shows that, as compared with prepositions, even though a handful of them are highly productive, overall a much smaller proportion of postpositions are in the stable frequency range, i.e., only 11 out of 35 are in the High and Medium frequency ranges.

The frequency ranking of postpositions in Modern Chinese shown in Table 7.6 also shows that *de* (的) 'of' and *zhōng* (中) 'in, during, among, within' are by far the most frequent postpositions. This observation runs counter the claim advanced by S Lu (1965, as cited in D Liu 2004) that *shàng* (上) 'on, above, upon, on top of' and *lǐ* (里/裏) 'inside' are of the highest frequency and *zhōng* (中) 'in, during, among, within' follows them. As shown in the list, *shàng* (上) and *lǐ* (里/裏) are frequent but not as frequent as *zhōng* (中). Eleven postpositions are frequently used (in the High and Medium frequency ranges), all of which but one (i.e., *de* (的) 'of') originated from relational nouns. It is also notable that among those eleven productive postpositions there are as many as four postpositions that denote notions related to Interiority, e.g., interior or inclusion, i.e., *zhōng* (中) (2nd), *lĭ* (里/裏) (4th), *jiàn/jiān* (间/間) (8th), and *zhījiān* (之间/之間) (10th).

Another point to note is that the postpositions denoting top/front are generally more frequent than those related to bottom/back. The first group includes *shàng* (上) (1,352 pmw), *zhīshàng* (之上) (14 pmw), *qián* (前) (515 pmw), *yĭqián* (以前) (7 pmw), *zhīqián* (之前) (5 pmw) and *shàngmiàn* (上面) (2 pmw), whereas the second group includes *xià* (下) (215 pmw), *hòu* (後/后) (103 pmw), *zhīxià* (之下) (26 pmw), *zhīhòu* (之後 /之后) (26 pmw), *yĭhòu* (以後/以后) (15 pmw), and *bèi/bēi* (背) (not attested); thus, collectively, 1,895 attestations for the top/front-group vis-à-vis 385 attestations for the bottom/back-group. As is the case in other languages, this is consonant with the observation that top and front are the areas suitable for optimal perception and thus are considered 'positive' directions (Andersen 1978: 343; Heine 1997).

7.3 Spatial Adpositions

7.3.1 Characteristics of Spatial Adpositions

Many adpositions in Chinese encode diverse spatial relationships, a characteristic shared by adpositions in many other languages. Encoding spatial relationship is a lot more prevalent with postpositions, simply due to the fact that postpositions are mostly based on relational nouns. The types of spatial relationships are variable and each adposition's level of specialization is widely variable. Those that are deemed to encode spatial relationship, however, numbering 45 altogether, are listed in Table 7.7 for prepositions and Table 7.8 for postpositions. In addition, their distribution across diverse spatial functions, glossing over minute details, is shown in Table 7.9.

	Preposition		Meaning
a.	*zài*	在	'at'
b.	*yĭ*	以	'with, by, according to, because of, from'
c.	*yú*	于/於	'in, to, towards, from, than, by, regarding'
d.	*cóng*	从/從	'from'

e.	*zì*	自	'from'
f.	*yǔ*	与/與	'with'
g.	*yóu*	由	'by, through, from'
h.	*xiàng*	向	'towards, to'
i.	*hé*	和	'with'
j.	*dào*	到	'to, up to, till'
k.	*gěi*	给/給	DAT 'to, for'
l.	*zhào*	照	'to, towards'
m.	*tōngguò*	通过/通過	'through, by way of'
n.	*wǎng*	往	'to, towards'
o.	*dāng*	当/當	'towards, at the time of'
p.	*gēn*	跟	'with'
q.	*tóng*	同	'with'
r.	*cháo*	朝	'to, towards'
s.	*yán*	沿	'along, following'
t.	*yánzhe*	沿着/沿著	'along, following'
u.	*dǎ*	打	'from'

Table 7.7 Spatial prepositions in Modern Chinese

	Postposition		**Meaning**
a.	*shàng*	上	'on, above, upon, on top of'
b.	*shàngmiàn*	上面	'above, on top of, on'
c.	*xià*	下	'under, below, underneath'
d.	*shàngxià*	上下	'beside, close to, about'
e.	*qián*	前	'before, ago, in front of'
f.	*hòu*	后/後	'after, behind'
g.	*bèi/ bēi*	背	'in back of, in the rear of'
h.	*zhōng*	中	'in, during, among, within'
i.	*lǐ*	里/裏	'inside'
j.	*wài*	外	'outside, beyond, besides'
k.	*wàimiàn*	外面	'outside'
l.	*jiān*	间/間	'between, within, among'
m.	*dǐng*	顶/頂	'on top of, in stead of, despite'
n.	*biān*	边/邊	'at the side of, beside, next to'
o.	*páng*	旁	'beside, next to'
p.	*zuǒyòu*	左右	'beside, close to'
q.	*wéizhǐ*	为止/爲止	'until, till'
r.	*chù*	处/處	'at the place of'
s.	*zhījiān*	之间/之間	'between, among'

		之上	'above'
t.	*zhīshàng*	之上	'above'
u.	*zhīxià*	之下	'under'
v.	*yǐnèi*	以内	'within'
w.	*yǐwài*	以外	'outside, beyond, except for, over'

Table 7.8 Spatial postpositions in Modern Chinese

		PREPOSITION		POSTPOSITION		
	AXIS	Primary (n=19)	Composite (n=3)	Primary (n=14)	Composite (n=5)	Complex (n=9)
Non-axial	REGIONAL	*zài* 'at'		*chù* 'at'		
	DIRECTIONAL	*yú* 'towards, from' *xiàng* 'towards, to' *zhào* 'towards, to' *wǎng* 'towards, to' *dāng* 'towards' *cháo* 'towards, to'				
	SOURCE	*yǐ* 'from, with' *yú* 'from, to, towards' *cóng* 'from' *zì* 'from' *yóu* 'from, through' *dǎ* 'from'				
	GOAL	*yú* 'to, towards, from' *dào* 'to, up to' *gěi* 'to'			*wéizhǐ* 'until, till'	
	PATH	*yóu* 'through, from'	*tōngguò* 'through, by way of'			
	MEDIAL			*zhōng* 'in, within, among' *jiān* 'between, among'		*zhījiān* 'between, among'
	ULTERIOR			*wài* 'beyond, outside'		*yǐwài* 'outside, beyond'
	ASSOCIATION	*yǔ* 'with' *hé* 'with' *gēn* 'with' *tóng* 'with' *yán* 'along'	*yánzhe* 'along' *shùnzhe* 'along'	*de* 'of' *zhī* 'of'		

	ADJACENCY			zuǒyòu 'close to, beside' shàngxià 'close to, beside'
	CONTIGUITY	páng 'beside, next to' biān 'beside, next to'			
	SEPARATION				
	OPPOSITE				
	INTERIOR	zhōng 'in, within, among' lǐ 'inside'			yǐnèi 'within'
	EXTERIOR	wài 'outside, beyond'	wàimiàn 'outside'	yǐwài 'outside, beyond'	
	SUPERIOR	shàng 'on, above' dǐng 'on top of'	shàngmiàn 'on, above'	zhīshàng 'above'	
Axial	INFERIOR	xià 'under, below'		zhīxià 'under'	
	ANTERIOR	qián 'before, in front of'		zhīqián 'before' yǐqián 'before'	
	POSTERIOR	hòu 'behind, after' bèi/bēi 'in back of'		zhīhòu 'after, following' yǐhòu 'after'	
	LATERAL	biān 'at the side of' páng 'beside'	zuǒyòu 'beside, close to'		

Table 7.9 Spatial adpositions in Modern Chinese

As shown in Tables 7.7 through 7.9, there are a few noteworthy aspects on Chinese spatial adpositions. It is apparent that adpositions are diverse in their grammatical meanings, but postpositions tend to specialize in encoding spatial (and space-based abstract) relationships because most of them involve relational nouns. Spatial prepositions encoding non-axial notions tend to be largely primary prepositions and there are many categories in which multiple forms are layered, especially in

Directionals, Ablatives (Sources), and Associatives. In our broad generalization, the domain of axial spatial notions is occupied entirely by postpositions; no prepositions are found in it.

7.3.2 Frequencies of Spatial Adpositions

The spatial adpositions discussed above are variable in semantics but they also have a great level of variability in their functional strength, as reflected in token frequency. The frequency information of the spatial prepositions is shown in Table 7.10.

Frequency Range	Preposition		Meaning	PMW
High (1,000~ pmw) (n=4)	*zài*	在	'at'	3,955
	yǐ	以	'with, by, according to, because of, from'	1,933
	yú	于/於	'in, to, towards, from, than, by, regarding'	1,801
	cóng	从/從	'from'	1,072
Medium (100~999 pmw) (n=13)	*zì*	自	'from'	827
	yǔ	与/與	'with'	696
	yóu	由	'by, through, from'	618
	xiàng	向	'towards, to'	592
	hé	和	'with'	519
	dào	到	'to, up to, till'	375
	gěi	给	DAT 'to, for'	312
	zhào	照	'to, towards'	251
	tōngguò	通过/通過	'through, by way of'	229
	wǎng	往	'to, towards'	197
	dāng	当	'towards, at the time of'	177
	gēn	跟	'with'	145
	tóng	同	'with'	138
Low (10~99 pmw) (n=3)	*cháo*	朝	'to, towards'	68
	yán	沿	'along, following'	34
	yánzhe	沿着/沿著	'along, following'	15

			Very Low (~9 pmw) (n=1)			

Very Low (~9 pmw) (n=1)	*dǎ*	打	'from'	6

Table 7.10 Frequency of spatial prepositions in Modern Chinese

As shown in Table 7.10, the most frequently used spatial preposition in Modern Chinese is *zài* (在), one that marks a general location (Regional). Even though there are a few that belong to the Low and Very Low frequency ranges, most of them (17 out of 21) are robustly attested, i.e., higher than 100 pmw, suggesting that Chinese prepositions are well entrenched in the system (see 7.4 for more discussion). The frequency information of the spatial postpositions is given in Table 7.11.

	Postposition		Meaning	PMW
High (1,000 pmw) (n=4)	*de*	的	'of'	4,895
	zhōng	中	'in, during, among, within'	2,026
	shàng	上	'on, above, upon, on top of'	1,352
	lǐ	里/裏	'inside'	1,221
Medium (100~999 pmw) (n=7)	*zhī*	之	'of'	575
	qián	前	'before, ago, in front of'	515
	wài	外	'outside, beyond, besides'	340
	jiàn/jiān	间/間	'between, within, among'	298
	xià	下	'under, below, underneath'	215
	zhījiān	之间/之間	'between, among'	164
	hòu	后/後	'after, behind'	103
Low (10~99 pmw) (n=8)	*biān*	边/邊	'at the side of, beside'	85
	páng	旁	'beside'	40
	zuǒyòu	左右	'beside, close to, about'	33
	yǐwài	以外	'outside, beyond, except for, over'	32
	zhīxià	之下	'under'	26
	dǐng	顶/頂	'on top of, in stead of, despite'	18
	zhīshàng	之上	'above'	14
	chù	处/處	'at the place of'	11

	yǐnèi	以内	'within'	8
	shàngxià	上下	'beside, close to, about'	3
Very Low (~9 pmw) (n=6)	*wàimiàn*	外面	'outside'	3
	shàngmiàn	上面	'above, on top of, on'	2
	wéizhǐ	为止/爲止	'until, till'	0
	bèi/ bēi	背	'in back of, in the rear of'	0

Table 7.11 Frequency of spatial postpositions in Modern Chinese

Table 7.11 shows that the most frequently used postposition in Modern Chinese is *de* (的) 'of', the innovated Genitive replacing *zhī* (之), exceeding the frequency recorded by the most frequently used preposition *zài* (在) (see above). Even though there are many postpositions that occur at relatively high frequencies (11 in High and Medium frequency ranges), there are many more postpositions that occur at a lower frequency (14 in Low and Very Low frequency ranges). It is also notable that there are closely related primary and complex postpositions in terms of their origin, i.e., those that involve relational nouns and those that involve, in addition to the identical relational nouns, the syntactic linker *zhī* (之) that has been fossilized in the complex postposition.

7.3.3. Grammaticalization Sources

Chinese adpositions originated from diverse sources. As is the case with isolating languages in general, identifying the grammatical categories of source lexemes is often difficult. There are two main sources of such difficulties.

First of all, as is widely known, grammatical categories in isolating languages are much more fluid than languages of other types. Thus, most words that are used as adpositions also belong to other grammatical categories. For instance, *zài* (在), the most frequent spatial preposition to mean 'at', also belongs to the verb category to mean 'exist, be at', and a sentence involving the word is often compatible with two interpretations as shown in (2):

(2) 我 在 图书馆 学习。

	Wǒ	***zài***	*túshūguǎn*	*xuéxí.*
(i)	I	**at**	library	study
(ii)	I	**be.at**	library	study

(i) 'I study in the library.'
(ii) 'I am at the library and study.'

Another difficulty comes from the gradual nature of semantic change. When a word grammaticalizes to assume a grammatical function, the lexical meaning is likely to have undergone much semantic change by then, often retaining the older meanings. Therefore, we cannot assume that the identified "oldest" meaning is the one from which the grammatical meaning emerged. For instance, *guǎn* (管) is a preposition denoting 'as for, with regard to' and as an Accusative to mark a topic in Modern Chinese. The original meaning of the word *guǎn* (管) was 'pipe, tube', likely to be made of bamboo, as is evident from the letter containing the top radical (⺮ = 竹) denoting 'bamboo'. This nominal 'tube' meaning still survives in Modern Chinese (accounting for 2% of occurrences in the CCL Corpus). However, the word *guǎn* (管) also has the verbal meaning 'control, manage' (obviously from the 'connection' meaning from a 'tube, pipe', presumably developed at a later time).[14] The development may also have been influenced by the homophonic *guān* (官) 'control, administer, etc.' As a matter of fact, this verbal usage is the predominant one, accounting for 89% of the total occurrences (see Table 7.13 below). Since this is a transitive verb taking a nominal complement and carries the 'control, manage' meaning, it is obvious that the grammaticalization occurred based on this verbal use, as [control X 〉 about X], i.e., from a phrasal structure, is conceptually better motivated than [tube X 〉 about X], i.e., from nominal compounding. For this reason, what is important is not merely finding the original meaning of a source lexeme but identifying the point in time when grammaticalization occurred and what meanings were available at the time to motivate the functional shift. Such information,

---

14) The verbal usage with the 'control' meaning is also old, occurring as early as in 1st and 2nd century texts such as *Shǐjì* (史记), as indicated in *Handian* (汉典; www.zdic.net).

however, is only possible from a microscopic investigation, which is beyond the scope of this macroscopic investigation.

Notwithstanding such difficulties, classification can also be relatively straightforward, if the grammatical category of the lexeme's other productive usage as well as the available meanings is carefully considered. We discuss primarily nouns and verbs, even though there are other sources as well.

7.3.3.1 Nominal Sources

Many adpositions in Chinese developed from nominal sources. A partial list of such adpositions is shown in Table 7.12, based on some historical research and etymological resources.[15]

		Adposition		Meaning	Etymology
Preposition	a.	*gēnjù*	根据/根據	'according to'	n. basis, ground
	b.	*hé*	和	'with'	n. harmony, peace
	c.	*jiāng*	将/將	ACC/THEME 'to'	n. future, general
	d.	*xiàng*	像	'like, similar to'	n. picture
	e.	*xiàng*	向	'towards, to'	n. direction ‹ house with a window
	f.	*yóu*	由	'by, through, from'	n. cause, reason
	g.	*zì*	自	'from'	n. self, a. private
Postposition	a.	*shàng*	上	'on, above, upon, on top of'	n. top, a? up(per)
	b.	*shàngmiàn*	上面	'above, on top of, on'	n.n. top face
	c.	*dǐng*	顶/頂	'on top of, in stead of, despite'	n. top, summit (v. carry on the head)
	d.	*shàngxià*	上下	'beside, close to, about'	n.n. top down
	e.	*xià*	下	'under, below, underneath'	n/a?. down

---

15) Etymological dictionaries consulted include *Handian* (汉典), available online (www.zdic.net), accessed in August–September, 2021; Chinese Etymology available online (hanziyuan.net), accessed in June–September 2021; and *A Chinese Etymological Dictionary* by Y Ha (2021[2014]), among others.

f.	*qián*	前	'before, ago, in front of'	n. front, n/a?. forward
g.	*hòu*	后/後	'after, behind'	n/a?. afterward
h.	*bèi/ bēi*	背	'in back of, in the rear of'	n. back, v. betray
i.	*páng*	旁	'beside, next to'	n. side
j.	*biān*	边/邊	'at the side of, beside, next to'	n. side, edge, margin
k.	*zhōng*	中	'in, during, among, within'	n. center
l.	*jiān*	间/間	'between, within, among'	n. midpoint
m.	*lǐ*	里/裏	'inside'	n. inside
n.	*wài*	外	'outside, beyond, besides'	n. outside
o.	*wàimiàn*	外面	'outside'	n.n. outside face
p.	*zuǒyòu*	左右	'beside, close to, about'	n. left hand + n. right hand, circumstance?
q.	*chù*	处/處	'at the place of'	n. place, locale
r.	*bān*	般	'like, similar to'	n. large boat, sort, category, (v. control)
s.	*yíyàng*	一样/一樣	'like, just like, alike, equal to'	n.n. one pattern
t.	*de*	的	'of'	n. center of archery target

Table 7.12 Chinese adpositions from nominal sources

Table 7.12 presents a few noteworthy aspects with the nominal sources of grammaticalization. First of all, nominal sources are more strongly associated with the postpositions than with the prepositions.[16] This tendency of noun-postposition association is even more prominent if the postpositions developing from complex structures, shown in Table 7.14 below, are considered, because they are largely formed by a noun accompanying a preposition.

Among the noun-derived prepositions, conceptual motivation is rather straightforward, e.g., (a) 'basis' ⟩ 'according to' (from foundation), (b) 'harmony' ⟩

---

[16] F Wu (2008) asserts that *hòu* (背) 'back' originated in the conception of 'motional' process, thus, suggesting a source-model not precisely corresponding to that for the mainstream BACK-REGION grams.

'with' (from compatibility), (c) 'future' 〉 'to' (from directedness), (d) 'picture' 〉 'like' (from similarity), (e) 'direction' 〉 'to' (from directedness), and (f) 'cause' 〉 'by, through' (from enabling instrumentality). The development of the preposition *zi* 'from' from 'self' (g) is less straightforward. Since 'self' or 'self's body' is typically associated with the grammaticalization of an intensifier (Kuteva et al. 2019), designating a reference point with emphasis may have developed into the 'starting point' meaning through subjective reinterpretation. In fact, *Handian* (汉典), an online Chinese etymology source, indicates that the character *zi* (自) had the 'self'-related meanings directly relevant to Ablative, such as 'beginning' and 'origin', as well.

On the other hand, there are a large number of postpositions that developed from nominal sources. The major reason of the predominance of the pattern is that the nouns in the source constructions are mostly relational nouns, such as 'top' and 'down' in the vertical axis ((a) through (e)); 'front' and 'back' in the horizontal axis ((f) through (h)); 'center' and 'edge' in the central-peripheral axis ((i) through (k)); and 'inside' and 'outside' in the interior-exterior axis ((l) through (o)). The postposition *zuǒyòu* (p) is from a compound of 'left hand (*zuǒ*) and right hand (*yòu*)', from which the 'circumstance, good or bad options, etc.' meaning developed (note that the 'left' and 'right' meanings are still strong in Sino-Korean and Sino-Japanese). In Modern Chinese it specializes in indicating a round figure (Paris and Vinet 2010).

The use of relational nouns in designating a particular location of an entity denoted by the host noun, thus forming a nominal compound, is likely to be the strategically favored word-formation patterns in Chinese, as briefly noted above. For instance, when the relational noun occurs following another noun, it tends to mean the part denoted by the relational noun, of the referenced host noun, as in (3a), whereas when the relational noun occurs before another noun, it tends to mean the kind of the host noun, designated by the relational noun, as in (3b). This contrast is well illustrated in the following:

(3)   a.   N-RN

        *qígān-**shàng*** (旗杆上) 'flagpole-top'

           〉 '(lit) the top part of the flagpole' 〉 'on the flagpole'

b. RN-N

shàng-_jí_ (上級) 'top-class'

〉 '(lit) the top kind of class' 〉 'upper grade, top grade'

The other cases in the table do not involve relational nouns, but indicates the 'place' (q), 'category' (r), or 'identical pattern' (s), from which the grammatical markers signaling a general location (_chù_) and similarity (_bān_ and _yíyàng_) developed, respectively.

7.3.3.2 Verbal Sources

As is the case in many languages, a large number of Chinese grammatical markers develop from verbs (J Xing 2003), and adpositions are among them (see Paul 2015: 55-92, Bisang 2020). We have seen in the above exposition that many postpositions develop from nouns. When the verbal sources of adpositions are considered, however, the situation is reversed, i.e., prepositions predominantly develop from verbal sources, whereas there are very few prepositions that develop from nominal sources. The adpositions that developed from verbal sources are listed in Table 7.13.

		Adposition		Meaning	Etymology
	a.	_àn_	按	'according to, following'	v. press (w/ hand)
	b.	_bǎ_	把	ACC	v. hold, take
	c.	_bèi_	被	'by'	v. cover (n. bedding)
	d.	_bǐ_	比	'than'	v. compare
	e.	_cháo_	朝	'to, towards'	v. face, visit (n. morning, dynasty)
Preposition	f.	_guǎn_	管	ACC/TOP 'as for, with regard to'	v. manage (n. tube)
	g.	_chèn_	趁	'at the time of, utilizing, taking the advantage of'	v. chase, take advantage of
	h.	_chènzhe_	趁着	'taking the advantage of'	v. take advantage
	i.	_chòng_	冲/衝	'on the strength of, on the basis of, because'	v. soar, pour boiling water over
	j.	_chú_	除	'except, in addition to'	v. remove (palace steps)

k.	*cóng*	从/從	'from'	v. follow
l.	*dǎ*	打	'from'	v. strike
m.	*dāng*	当/當	'towards, at the time of'	v. face, do
n.	*dào*	到	'to, up to, till'	v. arrive at
o.	*duì*	对/對	'in, for, to'	v. be correct, be right, face, oppose
p.	*gěi*	给/給	DAT 'to, for'	v. give
q.	*gēn*	跟	'with'	v. follow (n. heel)
r.	*jiào*	叫	'by'	v. call, shout
s.	*jù*	据/據	'according to'	v. occupy, take possession of
t.	*lián*	连/連	'even'	v. join, connect, adv. even
u.	*lùn*	论/論	'by, regarding, in terms of, by the unit of'	v. debate, n. discourse
v.	*píng*	凭/憑	'relying on, based on, depending on'	v. lean on
w.	*ràng*	让/讓	'by'	v. allow, yield
x.	*rú*	如	'like, similar to'	v. like (now if)
y.	*tì*	替	'for'	v. replace, change
z.	*tōng guò*	通过/通過	'through, by way of'	v. pass
aa.	*wǎng*	往	'to, towards'	v. go, depart
ab.	*wéi*	为/為	'for, for the purpose of'	v. do ⟨ feed an elephant
ac.	*yán*	沿	'along, following'	v. follow a course
ad.	*yǐ*	以	'with, by, according to, because of, from'	v. take, use, consider as (p. by means of)
ae.	*yī*	依	'with, by, according to, because of, from'	v. depend on, consent
af.	*yòng*	用	'by means of, in a way of'	v. use
ag.	*yú*	于/於	'in, to, towards, from, than, by, regarding'	v. go to, take (compared to)
ah.	*yǔ*	与/與	'with'	v. give; and, with
ai.	*zài*	在	'at'	v. be at
aj.	*zhào*	照	'to, towards'	v. shine, illuminate
ak.	*zhe/ zháo/ zhuó*	着/著	EMPH	v. make move, take; (n. chopsticks)

Postposition				
	a.	*zhī*	之	'of'	v. go forward
	b.	*lái*	来/來	'by agency of, causing, from' (time)	v. come

c.	*qǐ*	起	'from' (time)	v. rise, stand up
d.	*shide*	似的	'like'	v/a. resemble, similar + v. have clear, target
e.	*wéizhǐ*	为止/爲止	'until, till'	v. do, feed an elephant + n. foot / v. stop

Table 7.13 Chinese postpositions from verbal sources

D. Liu (2004) notes that prepositions tend to develop from verbs, and further that only a few prepositions have the sole prepositional function while most others have the dual functions of preposition and verb. The gradience with respect to semantic bleaching and, consequently, the overlap of initial and innovative, as well as intermediate functions is pervasive in Chinese grammar (cf. *KU-CKD* 1995, M Hu 1996, A Choi 2001, Ahn and Song 2008, S Kim 2004, among numerous others). Thus, the adpositions in the list may display variable degrees of the characteristics of verbs (see 7.4.3.3 below for more discussion).

The preposition *bèi* (被), in preposition (a), is semantically peculiar in that the word originally meant 'bedding, quilt, etc.', and developed into the primary marker of Passive, attributing 'affectedness' to the theme in Modern Chinese, as is widely discussed in the literature (Peyraube 1989, H Zhang 1991. C Sun 1996. J Ting 1998, J Choi 2003, Choonharuangdej 2003, H Yin 2004, Y Kim 2008, Choi and Ahn 2013, among many others, see also Libert 2013 for an overview of the debate on its grammatical status). Even though 'bedding, quilt' is the oldest meaning of the source lexeme, it seems that the prepositional meaning 'by' developed not from the nominal meaning but from the verbal meaning 'cover', because covering often results in restriction of the covered entity (also note that it is heterosemous with the Passive marker *bèi*).

The verbs involved in the grammaticalization of prepositions present a sharp contrast with those of postpositions, in that the former are invariably transitive and thus take a noun as their complement (note, however, that English translations may not provide straightforward clues to transitivity, e.g., (i) 'soar', (n) 'arrive at', (aa) 'go', etc.). Needlessly, this is the syntactic environment in which prepositions may emerge (cf. English verbal prepositions *following* as in *Following the band, there came a parade*; or *considering* as in *Considering his age, his skills are remarkable*, etc.; see 5.3.3.2 for more English examples).

There are a few groups of meaning-based source lexemes listed in Table 7.13 that bear significance. First of all, there is a group of verbs that denote goal-centered directionality as in (4):

(4) a. (e) *cháo*   v. 'face, visit'   〉 'to, towards'
     b. (m) *dāng*   v. 'face'   〉 'towards, at the time of'
     c. (n) *dào*   v. 'arrive at'   〉 'to, up to, till'
     d. (o) *dui*   v. 'face'   〉 'to, in, for'
     e. (p) *gěi*   v. 'give'   〉 'to, for'
     f. (aa) *wǎng*   v. 'go, depart'   〉 'to, towards'
     g. (ag) *yú*   v. 'go to'   〉 'to, towards, in, from, than...'

The lexical source meaning of the Directionals shown in (4) makes reference to locomotion (e.g., 'go') or movement potential (e.g., 'face'). These meanings are simplified by losing concrete lexical content in grammaticalization (cf. *Verbleichung* 'fading' Gabelentz 1901[1891]; *Affaiblissement* 'weakening' Meillet 1912) and the schematic meaning of towardness, i.e., directionality, is transferred to their grammatical functions.

Another group concerns either contact or following as shown in (5):

(5) a. (a) *àn*   v. 'press'   〉 'according to, following'
     b. (l) *dǎ*   v. 'strike'   〉 'from'
     c. (s) *jù*   v. 'occupy, take' 〉 'according to'
     d. (ad) *yǐ*   v. 'take, use'   〉 'according to, with, by, from'
     e. (k) *cóng*   v. 'follow'   〉 'from'
     f. (q) *gēn*   v. 'follow'   〉 'with'
     g. (v) *píng*   v. 'lean on'   〉 'based on, depending on'
     h. (ae) *yī*   v. 'depend on'   〉 'according to, with, by, from'

The verbs listed in (5) are the lexemes from which Ablative (source) and its conceptually-related markers emerged. As shown, the source semantics of the verbs in (5a) through (5d) makes reference to contact and manipulation, whereas that of (5e) through (5h) concerns following and its subjectively extended meaning of obeisance and compliance. These 'touch' and 'follow' meanings also give rise to the grammatical meaning of basis or ground, by virtue of making a firm contact with the referenced entity or not losing track of the entity. The grammaticalization of the first category seems diffuse, but the latter pattern is well attested across languages (Kuteva et al. 2019).

The verbs that may belong to the group illustrated in (5) above but display a slight difference are (b) *bǎ* and (ak) *zhe/zháo/zhuó*. The verb *bǎ* originally meant 'hold, take' (and, in fact, it still does as a lexical verb), and it developed into a marker of theme or object of an action, similar to Accusative (see 7.2 above). Even though the link between 'take' and Accusative may not be apparent, the development seems to be straightforward if we consider the fact that direct object marking began in the context where the object was 'affected' by an action, a state of affairs due to the semantic vestige of 'holding' (see Li and Thompson 1976; see 7.4.3.2 for more illustration).

The developmental path of the preposition *zhe/zháo/zhuó* (着/著, also occurring as 箸 in historical texts) is peculiar. The preposition, written interchangeably, is among the primary markers of aspect in Modern Chinese (Sun 1998), and as a preposition it carries the function of marking emphasis. The character 着 (*zháo/zhāo/zhe*) is a verb form to mean 'wear (clothes), equip, put on, make contact, take action, etc.', whereas 著 (*zhù/zhuó/zhe*), as a verb, means 'manifest, write, show', thus, often linked to books of noteworthy value or a person of distinguished caliber. On the other hand, 箸 (*zhù*), is a noun denoting chopsticks (evidently made of bamboo, as shown by the top radical ⺮ (= 竹) 'bamboo'). Due to the similarity in form and meaning, their developmental paths converged over time.[17] All these show that

---

17) According to Y Ha (2021[2014]: 677), 箸 (*zhù*) denoted n. 'chopsticks'; later v. 'put aside cooked food with chopsticks', 'set aside', 'set down' (thus, converging with 着 v. 'put down/on, equip'); and further adj. 'distinct, manifest, etc.' (thus, converging with 著 v./adj. 'manifest, write, show').

language change is a multi-faceted phenomenon.

A final short note relates to (p) *gěi* (給) 'give' that grammaticalized to Dative 'to, for'. The grammaticalization of this lexeme is among the most widely researched topics (Ohta 1958, C Sun 1996, H Yin 2004, F Qun 2005, O Her 2006, J Choi 2007, M Wong 2009, H Park 2012, S Ahn 2012, Sanders and Uehara 2012). In addition to Dative, there are multiple functions carried by *gěi*, e.g., Beneficiary, Purposive, Passive, among others. The development concerned here, i.e., ['give' > 'to'] is among the most frequently attested grammaticalization scenarios (cf. Kuteva et al. 2019).

7.3.3.3 Other Sources

There is still another group of postpositions which involve multiple forms in syntactic construction including an adposition, thus, all belonging to the complex postposition group. There are 10 such forms, listed in Table 7.14.

	Postposition		Meaning	Source
a.	*yǐhòu*	以后/以後	'after' (time)	p. by means of + n/a?. afterward
b.	*yǐlái*	以来/以來	'since' (time)	p. by means of + v. come
c.	*yǐnèi*	以内	'within'	p. by means of + n. inside
d.	*yǐqián*	以前	'before' (time)	p. by means of + n. front, n/a?. forward
e.	*yǐwài*	以外	'outside, beyond, except for, over'	p. by means of + n. outside
f.	*zhīhòu*	之后/之後	'after, following' (time)	p. of (v. go forward) + n/a?. afterward
g.	*zhījiān*	之间/之間	'between, among'	p. of (v. go forward) + n. midpoint
h.	*zhīqián*	之前	'before' (time)	p. of (v. go forward) + n. front, n/a?. forward
i.	*zhīshàng*	之上	'above'	p. of (v. go forward) + n. top, a? up
j.	*zhīxià*	之下	'under'	p. of (v. go forward) + n/a?. down

Table 7.14 Chinese adpositions from complex sources

All the forms listed in Table 7.14 involve either *yǐ* 'by means of, with, by, according to, because of, from' or *zhī* 'of', which are adpositions developed from verbs, i.e., *yǐ* 'take, use, consider as' and *zhī* 'go forward'. The verb *yǐ* developed into a preposition whereas *zhī* developed into a postposition. The latter, however, has (nearly completely) been replaced by *de* (的) as a Genitive postposition in Modern Chinese. Therefore, the adpositional function of *zhī* largely survives in these complex postpositions, even though it has other functions of indicating a pronoun 'this, that, she, he, etc.'.

7.3.3.4 Multiple Sources and Layered Adpositions

As has been noted in the preceding exposition, there are multiple sources of grammaticalizing adpositions in Chinese. Since different grammaticalization scenarios from multiple sources often lead to the development of grammatical forms of an identical function, 'layering' phenomenon (Hopper 1991) is commonly observed, a state of affairs frequently observed across languages.

In Table 7.9 above, 7.3.1, there are multiple forms listed for the same/similar functions among the spatial adpositions. Multiplicity of forms is particularly prominent in the Directionals (6 forms), Ablatives (6 forms), and Associatives (7 forms). The multiple forms layered in the grammatical domain of Directionals are exemplified in (6):

(6) Directionals 'towards, to', Primary prepositions

     a. *yú* (于/於)

       问 道 于 盲

       *wèn   dào   **yú**   máng*

       ask   way   **DIR**   blind

       'ask a blind person for directions' (idiom for folly)

     b. *xiàng* (向)

       飞 向 东南

       *fēi **xiàng** dōngnán*

       fly **DIR**   southeast

       'fly southeast'

c. *zhào* (照)

照 敌人 开枪

zhào *dírén* *kāi* *qiāng*

DIR enemy open gun

'shoot at the enemy'

d. *wǎng* (往)

往 前 看

wǎng *qián* *kàn*

DIR front look

'look ahead'

e. *dāng* (当/當)

当 众 出丑

dāng *zhòng* *chūchǒu*

DIR crowd make.fool.of

'make a fool of oneself in public' (lit. toward the crowd)

f. *cháo* (朝)

大步 朝 前 走

dà *bù* **_cháo_** *qián* *zǒu*

big step **DIR** front go

'stride forward' (lit. big step going toward the front)

A fine-grained analysis for individual prepositions is beyond the scope of the present research, but in a broad characterization, the six prepositions share the function of marking Directional. The functions of certain prepositions cannot easily be differentiated, e.g., (b) *xiàng* (向), (d) *wǎng* (往), and (f) *cháo* (朝).[18] However, it would

---

18) For instance, Lin Zhang (p.c.) states that *xiàng* (向), *wǎng* (往), and *cháo* (朝) are largely interchangeable and have similar collocational patterns, e.g., preceding nouns of cardinal directions and pronouns.

be incorrect to assume that they are all interchangeable, because they carry subtle differences, which make them not always interchangeable. For instance, (a) *yú* (于/於) is found only in literary or archaic styles, whereas all others are commonly used in colloquial styles. Even in the colloquial style, the prepositions exhibit functional differences, though often very subtle. The directional (b) *xiàng* (向) typically takes a nominal for cardinal directions (e.g., east, west, south, north) or for relations (e.g., front, back, etc.) (Lin Zhang, p.c.). The preposition (e) *dāng* (当) is least prototypical of Directional, because its directionality has been demoted almost to a point of bordering on Locative. For instance, the example 'make a fool of oneself toward the crowd' (10e) is nearly the same as 'make a fool of oneself in public', due to the fact that the person concerned may be conceptualized as "being a part of the public" instead of "facing the public".[19]

A similar observation can be made with Ablatives. The usage of Ablative prepositions is exemplified in (7):

(7) Ablatives, Primary prepositions 'from'
    a.   *yǐ* (以)

        上 以 天子, 下 至 庶人

shàng	**_yǐ_**	*tiānzǐ,*	*xià*	*zhì*	*shùrén*
top	**ABL**	emperor	bottom	ALL	common.person

        'from the Emperor above to the common people below'

    b.   *yú* (于/於)

        青 出 于 蓝。

qīng	*chū*	**_yú_**	*lán*
blue	come	**ABL**	indigo.plant

---

[19] However, the directionality sense, though bleached, still survives in other usages as well, such as conjunction. For instance, in *dāng-wǒ-dàojiā-shí* (当我到家时) [DIR-I-arrive.home-time] 'when I arrived at home', the construal of the event is such that the progression of time is moving in the direction of a series of events, and the conjunction *dāng* designates the directionality of the time at which I arrive at home and makes it a background of the main clause event.

'Blue pigment is obtained from the indigo plant.'[20]

c. *cóng* (从/從)

从 南 到 北

cóng *nán* *dào* *běi*

ABL south ALL north

'from south to north'

d. *zì* (自)

来 自 各 国 的 朋友

lái **_zì_** *gè* *guó* *de* *péngyou*

come **ABL** each country of friends

'friends coming from all over the world'

e. *yóu* (由)

由 此 可知。

yóu *cǐ* *kězhī*

ABL this possible .know

'From this we can see.'

f. *dǎ* (打)

你 打 哪儿 来?

Nǐ **_dǎ_** *nǎr* *lái?*

you **ABL** where come

'Where are you coming from?'

---

20) The idiomatic expression *qīng-chū-yú-lán* (青出于蓝) in (7b) originated from an idiom *qīng-chū-yú-lán, qīng-yú-lán* (青出于蓝 青於蓝) 'The blue dye derives from the indigo plant, but it is bluer than the indigo plant', used with reference to a disciple who excels their master. This idiom is attributed to Xunzi, 3rd c. BCE.

The six Ablatives in (7) above all mark the starting point, and many of these, (c) *cóng* (从), (d) *zì* (自), (e) *yóu* (由), and (f) *dǎ* (打), are largely interchangeable. However, (a) *yǐ* (以), (b) *yú* (于), (d) *zì* (自), and (e) *yóu* (由) are found in literary genre and carry an archaic flavor, and thus, are rarely used in the colloquial genre. Furthermore, (f) *dǎ* (打) is dialectal, usually found in the northern dialects. It is nearly identical to (c) *cóng* (从), otherwise (Lin Zhang, p.c.).

There is an interesting aspect associated with (b) *yú* (于); it is indicated as the Ablative 'from' here but it also functions as the Directional 'to'. This is somewhat peculiar in that they are nearly opposites in terms of directionality (cf. 'autoantonymy' Murphy 2003; 'contronymy' Karaman 2008; see also J Kim 2020). This is largely due to the bleaching of meaning, which then enables different pragmatic interpretations of functions in the use context. Incidentally, a similar state of affairs is attested in Korean and Japanese, e.g., KOR *hanthey* 'to' also functioning as 'from'; and JPN *-ni* 'to' also functioning as 'from' (S Rhee 2010: 587, JPN attributed to Peter Sells p.c.).

What is significant in this context is that many different sources develop into the markers of a same or similar function, thus forming multiple layers. This is in line with the observation in grammaticalization studies that source lexemes that may be different, sometimes to a great extent, in semantics or even in grammatical categories, may gradually become similar en route in terms of meaning and morphosyntactic behavior, and eventually become indistinguishable (cf. 'grammaticalization channels' Givón 1979, Heine 1981, Lehmann 2015[1982], Heine and Reh 1984; 'universal paths' Bybee et al. 1994).

Another point worth mentioning is that despite the presence of multiple forms layered in a single conceptual category, it is usually the case that no two of them are completely synonymous but display different degrees of strength in more detailed subdivision of functions (cf. 'specialization' Hopper 1991, Hopper and Traugott 2003[1993]). This state of affairs strongly points to the fact that the lines dividing the notions of grammatical categories are largely arbitrarily drawn for methodological convenience and, thus, that setting up the categories strongly depends on the granularity of their categorization by the researchers.

7.4 Ongoing Grammaticalization of Spatial Adpositions

7.4.1 Selection Criteria

We have discussed various aspects of Chinese adpositions in the preceding exposition. Now we move on to a discussion of spatial adpositions that are deemed to be actively grammaticalizing at the moment. In order to investigate ongoing grammaticalization among Chinese adpositions, we first need to select the optimal adpositions that are currently undergoing grammaticalization. The entire inventory consists of 91 adpositions, i.e., 56 prepositions (42 primary and 14 composite) and 35 postpositions (18 primary, 7 composite, and 10 complex). Out of these, we select the items that satisfy all of the following conditions, as used in our investigations of other languages, with arguably arbitrary cut-off points:

(8) (i)   It is not in the primary adpositional category in contemporary Chinese (31 adpositions out of 91);

(ii) It encodes spatial relationship (12 of them; 2 prepositions and 10 postpositions);

(iii) It is attested at least 10 wpm (7 of them; 2 prepositions and 5 postpositions).

As is the case with other languages addressed here, condition (i) is to ensure that the target preposition is not yet established as a fully grammaticalized adposition. Condition (ii) is to restrict the target items to our research focus, i.e., spatial adpositions. Condition (iii) is to ensure that the item is a viable one, not a chance occurrence attributable to idiolectic styles or that the form is not at a very incipient stage where the form's viability is yet uncertain. The frequency of 10 occurrences per million words is equivalent to 5,817 raw occurrences of character (equivalent to 4,475 words) in the CCL Corpus, which coincides with the cut-off point for Low Frequency range in Tables 7.3 and 7.6 above. Thus, this cut-off point is to eliminate the Very Low frequency items from the inventory. The 7 target forms, supposedly actively undergoing grammaticalization, are listed in Table 7.15.

Frequency Range	Preposition		Meaning	PMW
High (1,000~ pmw)	(none)			
Medium (100~999 pmw)	*tōngguò*	通过/通過	'through, by way of'	229
Low (10~99 pmw)	*yánzhe*	沿着/沿著	'along, following'	34

Frequency Range	Postposition		Meaning	PMW
High (1,000 pmw)	(none)			
Medium (100~999 pmw)	*zhījiān*	之间/之間	'between, among'	164
Low (10~99 pmw)	*zuǒyòu*	左右	'beside, close to, about'	33
	yǐwài	以外	'outside, beyond, except for, over'	32
	zhīxià	之下	'under'	26
	zhīshàng	之上	'above'	14

Table 7.15 Grammaticalizing spatial adpositions in Modern Chinese

7.4.2 General Characteristics

The 7 target items in Table 7.15 bear special significance in the grammaticalization of Chinese adpositions and further in the studies of grammaticalization in languages typologically similar to Chinese, such as Thai. We will discuss their characteristics more in detail.

First of all, there are only two prepositions that are classifiable as actively grammaticalizing, which, as compared to other languages, is a unique situation, requiring an explanation. First of all, we find at first sight that composite prepositions are much fewer than primary prepositions, i.e., 14 vs. 42, and further that among the spatial prepositions the disparity is greater, i.e., 2 vs. 19. This clearly indicates that spatial prepositions are nearly always primary prepositions (i.e., 90.5%). Furthermore, since most spatial prepositions are in the High and Medium frequency ranges (17 out of 21), leaving three in the Low and only one in the Very Low frequency ranges, it is a reasonable generalization to say that spatial prepositions in Chinese are relatively well established, i.e., they are used at a reasonably high frequency. However, in order to see the dynamics of grammaticalization, we will look into these two grammaticalizing spatial prepositions in more detail.

The preposition *tōngguò* (通过/通過) is one of the two Perlatives (i.e., marking Path). As compared to other functions for which multiple forms are layered in contemporary Chinese, the Path markers are of a small number. The more frequent competitor of *tōngguò* (通过/通過) is *yóu* (由), which, incidentally is also a marker of source (Ablative). The functional diversity of *yóu* (由) naturally overpowers *tōngguò* (通过/通過) in text frequency. In fact, the usage of *yóu* (由) as a grammatical marker of Path is attested as early as in the classical literature, Confucius's *Lúnyǔ* (论语) [The Analects] dated from around the 6th c. BCE (*Handian* (汉典), entry of 由). Since the emergence of the preposition *tōngguò* (通过/通過), as is evident from its compound structure, is clearly a modern innovation, its weaker functional strength in relation to *yóu* (由), i.e., 229 vs. 618 pmw, is in complete conformity with the general prediction. In other words, *tōngguò* (通过/通過) is chronologically newer and functionally more restrictive than its competitor *yóu* (由), and consequently it is grammaticalized to a smaller extent and is used less frequently than *yóu* (由).

The other preposition, *yánzhe* (沿着/沿著), presents a different situation. It is a member of a densely populated functional category, i.e., Associatives, in which five primary prepositions *yǔ* (与), *hé* (和), *gēn* (跟), *tóng* (同), and *yán* (沿), and a composite preposition *shùnzhe* (顺着/順著), all denoting the notion of association, 'with, along with'. Incidentally, this is the conceptual space, to which *yǔ* (与), one of the oldest and most polyfunctional grammatical forms, belongs. The overall picture of functional strengths of these competitors is as shown in (9), in descending order of use frequency, in which *yánzhe* (沿着/沿著) is highlighted in bold:

(9) Associatives

a.	*yǔ* (与)	'with, and, to, for'	696 pmw
b.	*hé* (和)	'with, to, as, and'	519 pmw
c.	*gēn* (跟)	'with, to, from, as'	145 pmw
d.	*tóng* (同)	'with, for'	138 pmw
e.	**yánzhe (沿着/沿著)**	'along, following'	**34 pmw**

f.	*yán* (沿)	'along, following'	15 pmw
g.	*shùnzhe* (顺着/順著)	'along, following'	6 pmw

The frequency ordering in (9) clearly shows the disadvantageous situation for *yánzhe* (沿着/沿著); in terms of frequency as many as four competitors outnumber *yánzhe* (沿着/沿著), with the oldest form *yǔ* (与) at the lead. These competitors are all primary prepositions and are highly polyfunctional, accounting for their relative primacy over the more recent and composite preposition *yánzhe* (沿着/沿著).

The preposition *yán* (沿) (9f) is the only primary preposition displaying a weaker force as compared to *yánzhe* (沿着/沿著). The reason is not clear but its lexical semantics may be a contributing factor, i.e., *yán* (沿), as a noun, denotes the edge or border, originally referring to the coast (as indicated by the radical '氵' (= 水) denoting 'water'), and, as a verb, denotes 'float downstream', again reflecting its nominal meaning. As a matter of fact, in Modern Chinese, *yán* (沿) is still productively used as a verb (32%, 13 pmw) and noun (30%, 12 pmw) (cf. its prepositional usage 38%, 15 pmw). Furthermore, the innovation of the word as a preposition seems to be very recent or weak.[21] All these can be regarded as the cause for the relatively weak strength of *yán* (沿). Since *yánzhe* (沿着/沿著) and *yán* (沿) both involve the lexeme *yán* (沿), it can be further deduced that *yánzhe* (沿着/沿著) has diverged from *yán* (沿) (cf. 'divergence' Hopper 1991) by means of compounding with the extremely versatile *zhe* (着/著), is actively specializing as an Associative preposition, leaving behind *zhe* (着/著), its origin, for the mixed functions of nominal, verbal, and prepositional usages.

As for *shùnzhe* (顺着/順著) (9g), its functional weakness seems to be directly associated with its being a composite form. Its strength is so weak that it still belongs to the Very Low frequency range, recording only 6 pmw.

We now turn to a discussion of the postpositions that are regarded as actively grammaticalizing. As shown in Table 7.15, above, there are five such postpositions, i.e., *zhījiān* (之间/之間) 'between, among', *zuǒyòu* (左右) 'beside, close to, about', *yǐwài*

---

[21] For instance, as of August 2021, *Handian* (汉典) does not (yet) list its prepositional usage.

(以外) 'outside, beyond, except for, over', *zhīxià* (之下) 'under', and *zhīshàng* (之上) 'above'. The first point is that *zhījiān* (之间/之間) 'between, among' is the only postposition in the Medium frequency range and all others are in the Low frequency range. There is no grammaticalizing postposition in the High frequency range, and, in fact, all postpositions, except for *zhījiān* (之间/之間), in the High and Medium frequency range are primary postpositions, pointing to the frequently observed correlation between formal simplicity and use frequency (and greater grammaticalization).

Another important aspect is that most postpositions in this group are complex postpositions and have their functional competitors in the primary postposition group that are etymologically related. The composite postposition *zuǒyòu* (左右) 'beside, close to, about' is the only exception in this regard. The relation between those pairs is shown in Table 7.16:

Core Lexeme	Primary POST	PMW	Complex POST	PMW
jiān (间/間)	*jiān* (间/間) 'before, ago, in front of'	298	*zhījiān* (之间/之間) 'between, among'	164
wài (外)	*wài* (外) 'outside, beyond, besides'	340	*yǐwài* (以外) 'outside, beyond, except for, over'	32
xià (下)	*xià* (下) 'under, below, underneath'	215	*zhīxià* (之下) 'under'	26
shàng (上)	*shàng* (上) 'on, above, upon, on top of'	1,352	*zhīshàng* (之上) 'above'	14

Table 7.16 Primary vs. complex postpositions in Modern Chinese

Functional competition between the etymologically related forms is obvious, considering their semantic relatedness. Also obvious is that the primary postpositional counterparts far exceed their complex postpositional counterparts, most strikingly with *shàng* (上) vs. *zhīshàng* (之上), i.e., 1,352 pmw vs. 14 pmw. Comparing their formal composition, the relative weakness of the complex postpositions seems to be due to their morphosyntactic complexity, i.e., of their phrasal nature.

Also important aspect of these postpositions is that since it is a historical fact that the use of Genitive *zhī* (之) has largely been replaced by its successor *de* (的), it is possible that the complex forms involving *zhī* are of an older origin than those that do not. If this is so, the primary forms may be the simplified versions of the complex forms through phonetic reduction, in the process of their grammaticalization. However, since the development of the primary forms, in principle, could have emerged from the direct combination of the relational nouns, as well, the question as to which of the two hypotheses reflects the historical reality requires a more fine-grained token-based diachronic analysis.

7.4.3 Grammaticalization Mechanisms

We have seen in the preceding exposition an overall portrayal of adpositions in Modern Chinese. We now turn to a discussion of Chinese adpositions in view of the grammaticalization mechanisms proposed by Kuteva et al. (2019), i.e., extension, desemanticization, decategorialization and erosion.

7.4.3.1 Extension

Extension or usage context expansion is prominent in grammaticalization of Chinese adpositions. The extension is largely due to their semantic change, from concrete to abstract meanings, while retaining the older meanings. Since semantic generalization, rather than semantic narrowing, is a general tendency, extension of usage context of a grammaticalizing form is a robust phenomenon.

As extension occurs across time, a more fruitful discussion should involve a diachronic investigation, but in this macroscopically-oriented research, a discussion of gradual progression of extension for individual adpositions is not attempted here. There are numerous instances of extension since the process is associated with all grammaticalizing forms, and thus, we will restrict our illustration to one exemplary case, *xiàng* (向).

The history of *xiàng* (向) 'toward, to' presents an interesting change in meaning, and accordingly extension of usage. According to *Handian* (汉典) and Y Ha

(2021[2014]: 906), it started its life as a pictogram in the oracle bone inscriptions (ca. 1200 BCE) depicting a house with a window or a window facing the north. From this the nominal meaning of 'direction' (disregarding its earlier restriction to the north) emerged. The directional meaning gave rise to the verbal usage of 'to face, go, side with, revere, etc.' (*Handian*; 汉典, entry for 向). Since all these meanings involve directionality, a prepositional meaning 'to, toward' emerged, e.g., *xiàng-rì* (向日) [toward-day] denoting 'tomorrow' 'the next day', etc.[22] An interesting direction of the change is also observed in the fact that it also came to denote 'from', attested in an early Ming Dynasty novel, *Shuǐhǔzhuàn* (水浒传) (*Handian* (汉典), entry for 向) (note the reversal of meaning similar to the contronymous *yú* (于) in 7.3.3.4). Furthermore, it also developed into 'always, all along, past, before, just now, etc.', suggesting an extension to adverbial functions, e.g., *Chén-xiàng-méng-guóēn* (臣向蒙国恩) [minister-always-receive-imperial.favor] 'Ministers always receive the Emperor's grace; Ministers have received the Emperor's grace all along', also attested in an early Ming Dynasty novel, *Sānguóyǎnyì* (三国演义; 1522) (*Handian* (汉典), entry for 向).

All along the progression of semantic and categorial change, though not all can be characterized as grammaticalization, the usage of *xiàng* (向) also expanded. Undoubtedly, the original meaning of 'a house with a window' or 'a window facing the north' should have constrained the word's usage to a great extent, and the restriction should have eased as the meaning was generalized, resulting in extension of usage context, not only in terms of autonomous lexical use but also interaction with neighboring lexemes such as compounding. Extension of use enabled by the lexeme's change of word class, i.e., to verb, should be greater not only in terms of syntax but also semantics because in the verbal category diverse meanings associated with directionality also emerged as indicated above (note that this change is still not subsumable under grammaticalization). Similarly, the extension into the adverbial function must have contributed to the extension of the usage context of *xiàng* (向) (note that adverbial formation carries the potential of being regarded as an instance of grammaticalization, see Heine et al. 1991a; cf. Jespersen 1924). Even though the

---

[22] This expression, however, according to Lin Zhang (p.c.), is not in use in Present-Day Chinese.

categorial and semantic change cannot be presented in a streamlined way, the context extension can be as in (10), with its syntactic constituent scope and complements:

(10) a. noun 'a house/northern window'   NP (no complement)
　　b. noun 'direction'   NP (directional noun for compounding)
　　c. verb 'face, go, revere, side with.' VP (NP complement)
　　d. adverb 'always, etc.'   IP (Clausal complement)
　　e. preposition 'to, toward'   PP (NP complement)

In Modern Chinese, the 'house, window' meaning in (10a) does not survive any longer and some other meanings such as 'go' are also no longer available (Lin Zhang, p.c.), but nominal, verbal, adverbial, and prepositional usages all survived, and, thus, the word's use context remains wider than the earlier nominal uses.

7.4.3.2 Desemanticization

Desemanticization is clearly observable in the development of Chinese adpositions. It is particularly true with the prepositions developed from verbal sources. Li and Thompson (1974a: 260) state that grammaticalization of verbs into prepositions ('co-verbs' in their terminology) involves the losing of the semantic property 'action' (even though non-action verbs like *zài* 'be at' is an exception). Desemanticization can be illustrated with *bǎ* 把, a marker of an object, similar to the Accusative case marker. The preposition originated from the verb *bǎ* 把 'take, grab, hold'. Li and Thompson (1976: 485) present 8th century data, taken from one of the poems by Dù-fǔ (杜甫; 712-770), shown in (11) with some modification:

(11)　醉 把 茱萸仔 细 看。
　　　Zuì　**bǎ**　　　*zhūgēnzǐ*　　*xì*　　*kàn.*
　　　drunk　**take/ACC**　dogwood-tree　careful　look
　　　(i)　'While drunk, I took the dogwood tree and carefully looked at it.'
　　　(ii)　'While drunk, I carefully looked at the dogwood tree.'
　　　　　　　　　　　　　　　　(Dù-fǔ 8th c., Li & Thompson 1976: 485)

Example (11) above can be interpreted in two ways, i.e., (i) *bǎ* as a verb denoting 'take' and (ii) *bǎ* as an Accusative case marker, and constitutes an excellent example of the incipient stage of grammaticalization (cf. 'bridging context' Heine 2002), illustrating a syntactic change from bi-clausal to mono-clausal structure (Hopper and Traugott 2003[1993]: 28). Since the Accusative *bǎ* developed from the verb of grasping, *bǎ* could be used only in the context involving an action toward a tangible entity, i.e., the object noun is 'grabbed'. In Modern Chinese we have diverse uses of the preposition *bǎ*, as is partially illustrated in the following ((12a) is from Lin Zhang (p.c.), and (12b-e) are taken from *KU-CKD*, with glosses and translations added):

(12)   a.   我 把 面包 吃 了。

         Wǒ ***bǎ***   *miànbāo*   *chī*   *le.*
         I   **ACC**   bread   eat   PERF
         'I ate the bread.'

   b.   把 头 一 扭

         bǎ   *tóu*   *yì*   *niǔ*
         ACC   head   one   twist
         'twist one's head'

   c.   把 他 乐坏 了。

         Bǎ   *tā*   *lè*   *huài-le.*
         ACC   3sg   happy   very-PERF
         '(I) made him very happy.'

   d.   把 东城 西城 都 跑 遍 了。

         Bǎ   *dōngchéng*   *xīchéng*   *dōu*   *pǎo*   *biàn*   *le.*
         ACC   east.castle   west.castle   all   run   around   PERF
         'I ran all around the East Castle and West Castle.'

e. 他能把你怎么样?

   *Tā néng **bǎ** nǐ zěnmeyàng?*

   3sg can **ACC** you how

   'What can he do (with/to) you?'

Examples in (12) supposedly show variable degrees of semantic bleaching in the course of development of *bǎ* (把) 'take, grab', and thus, gradual desemanticization of the physical manipulation meaning. In Present-Day Chinese, according to Lin Zhang (p.c.), the 'prehension' meaning (i.e., of physical holding) from *bǎ* (把) is no longer felt by the speakers. Since *bǎ* (把) was the verb of holding in origin, it can be hypothesized that the type of example (12a), in which holding an object is involved (note that eating bread typically involves holding it) is of the oldest use. Example (12b) has the 'head' as the prepositional complement of *bǎ*, which, however, cannot be held; it is simply affected by the twisting action. In example (12c), the prepositional complement 'him' is not involved in a physical 'taking' or 'grabbing' action, but is affected by the entertaining action. In example (12d), the complement 'East Castle and West Castle' does not denote an entity physically held nor is it meaningfully affected by 'my' strolling. In example (12e), the complement 'you' is not physically held by 'him' and may only be a potentially affected entity. Presumably, this type of desemanticization is present in all or most instances of grammaticalization of Chinese adpositions. Desemanticization is often hypothesized as a necessary condition of grammaticalization. This is a reasonable hypothesis, considering that grammatical meanings are, in general, more abstract than lexical meanings.

Despite such a predominant tendency, however, there is a group of cases that exhibit only a limited extent of desemanticization in grammaticalization. The group is that of common relational nouns, which often develop into axial spatial adpositions. Thus, when the source and the target meanings of those that involve relational nouns are compared, there is no noticeable degree of desemanticization, as shown, in part, in (13):

(13) a. *shàng* (上) top ⟩ 'on, above, upon, on top of'

   b. *xià* (下) down ⟩ 'under, below, underneath'

c.	*qián*	(前)	front, forward	〉'before, ago, in front of'
d.	*hòu*	(后/後)	behind, rear, after	〉'after, behind'
e.	*lǐ*	(里/裏)	inside	〉'inside, in'
f.	*wài*	(外)	outside	〉'outside, beyond, besides'

The relational nouns serving as the sources of the postpositions already had many meanings in spatial and temporal domains and thus the postpositional meanings do not exhibit extensive desemanticization.

However, it would be incorrect to assume that postpositions that developed from relational nouns have not undergone semantic bleaching at all. D Liu (2004) and R Yao (2013) note that semantic bleaching did occur to the relational nouns, e.g., *lǐ* (里/裏) 'inside', *zhōng* (中) 'in, during, among, within', *shàng* (上) 'on, above, upon, on top of', *xià* (下) 'under, below, underneath', etc. to such a great extent that these postpositions are sometimes interchangeable for both concrete and metaphorical meanings. Similarly, Chappell and Peyraube (2008) state that Chinese adpositions based on relational nouns ('localizers' in their term) have undergone desemanticization from specific and prototypical reference to general reference, through reinterpretation.[23] This state of affairs underscores the facts that desemanticization is not dichotomous but gradient and that even in cases in which the target meanings of a form do not appear to be very different from their source meanings, desemanticization is likely to be observable from a deeper analysis.

7.4.3.3 Decategorialization

As a grammaticalizing lexeme moves from a primary category (e.g., nouns and verbs) to a grammatical category (e.g., prepositions and postpositions), the form is likely to lose the categorial characteristics associated with the primary category. Such decategorialization phenomena occur gradually at variable speed depending on individual forms, and thus some adpositions may be grouped together according to

---

[23] Also note that Old Chinese, unlike Modern Chinese, did not have overt localizers (Roberts 2017: 333, cf. Peyraube 2003, Huang 2009).

the degree of decategorialization. For instance, A Choi (2001: 21-22), based on a number of sources, e.g., *KU-CKD,* M Hu (1996), Y Li (1995), presents the following list:

(14) a. Group A [Still retaining source meanings and functions to a great extent (29 adpositions)]: *cháo* (朝), *dào* (到), *duì* (对/對), *chú* (除), *zài* (在), *xiàng* (向), etc.
    b. Group B [Still retaining source meanings but have nearly lost the verbal functions (21 adpositions)]: *chèn* (趁), *chènzhe* (趁着), *chòng* (冲/衝), *gēnjù* (根据/根據), etc.
    c. Group C [Having lost the source meanings and functions nearly entirely (43 adpositions)]: *àn* (按), *bǎ* (把), *bèi* (被), *dǎ* (打), *dāng* (当/當), etc.
    d. Group D [Having the adpositional usage only (11 adpositions)]: *ànzhào* (按照), *duìyú* (对于/對於) *guānyú* (关于/關於), *wèile* (为了/為了), etc.

Since Chinese tends to be generally resistant to change in terms of morphosyntax, identifying changes constituting decategorialization is relatively more difficult than in other languages. For instance, the adpositions in Groups A and B may still retain the verbal characteristics, though to variable degrees, and thus grammaticalizing grams tend to have 'Janusian' characteristics (Heine 1992a,b) between verbs and adpositions, analogous to 'mermaid constructions' (Tsunoda 2020). Therefore, when a morphosyntactic manipulation presumably impossible for an adposition is applied to an example of adpositional usage, the adposition may immediately render itself for a verbal interpretation since the adpositional meanings tend to retain verbal meanings and its structural slot tends to be identical with the verbal slot as well.

    Since the grammaticalization of verbs into prepositions does involve syntactic reanalysis but not noticeable syntagmatic change, the surface structure often remains unchanged. Therefore, even when an adverbial modifier is inserted in two sentences, involving a word that functions as a verb in one and a preposition in another, acceptable syntactic conditions often remain the same.

    Since grammaticalization of verbs into prepositions involves the structural change from bi-clausal to mono-clausal sentence type, the development of verb-based preposition typically occurs in serial verb constructions. As grammaticalization proceeds, the verbal nature of one of the serialized verbs is gradually lost, an instance of decategorialization. In an elaborate analysis, Li and Thompson (1974a) discuss such cases. They present a number of differences between serial verbs and prepositions ('co-verbs' in their term); serial verb sentences express two actions, whereas prepositional sentences do not (an instance of desemanticization of 'action' component in meaning); the object of the first verb in a serial verb sentence cannot become the head noun of a relative clause whereas, the object of the preposition can (an instance of decategorialization, i.e., loss of verbal characteristics), among others. This means that identifying decategorialization may require a battery of tests in fine-grained analyses.

Relational nouns, as we noted in 7.4.3.2 above, tend to carry over their relational meanings to postpositional meanings without any significant loss. Thus, decategorialization of relational nouns in the process of their development into postpositions tends to be only marginal. However, as noted in 7.2, D Liu (2004) notes that relational nouns, e.g., *shàng* (上), are no longer full-fledged nouns as is evidenced by the fact that *shàng* (上), for example, cannot occur with the Genitive *de* (的) 'of' as in **zhàn zài zhuō de shàng* (站在桌的上) [stand exist desk of top] '(intended): (He) is standing on top of the desk.' It is acceptable to say *zhàn zài zhuōzi shàng* (站在桌子上) '(He) is standing on top of the desk', i.e., without the Genitive *de* (的) 'of', a clear case of decategorialization.

7.4.3.4 Erosion

As we have seen above, some changes involved in the grammaticalization of Chinese adpositions, e.g., desemanticization and decategorialization, seem to be relatively limited in extent, as compared to other languages whose grammaticalization scenarios have been reported. A similar observation can be made with respect to erosion, or reduction in phonetic substance. The limited extent of erosion is largely due to the restrictiveness of morphosyntactic change, one of the features characteristic of an isolating language (see also Bisang 2020). Erosion in general tends to involve structural reduction or reductive pronunciation of individual phonemes for the sake of economy in articulatory gesture.[24]

The conservative nature of Chinese morphosyntax makes the first type of reduction relatively rare. However, there is a case that may fall in this category. For instance, as we observed in 7.4.2, above, with respect to primary and complex postpositions involving the Genitive *zhī* (之) and its counterpart without it, e.g., *zhīshàng* (之上) vs. *shàng* (上), the complex postpositions involving the Genitive are presumably older, as is plainly seen by the fact that the Genitive *zhī* is an old gram no longer used in this type of structure but the more recent Genitive *de* (的) is used instead. Therefore, it is reasonable to assume that the primary forms may be the simplified versions of the complex forms through phonetic reduction, in the process of their grammaticalization, which, if indeed true. is a good instance of erosion.[25]

Erosion in terms of phonological change is similarly subtle. Chinese is a tone language, i.e., tones are lexically specified. When two or more syllables occur side by side, their tones may undergo change, a phenomenon known as 'tone sandhi', which often depends on the syntactic structure (Duanmu 2005). In his discussion of tone sandhi in Chinese (and some Chinese dialects), Duanmu (2005), noting that verbs carry higher information load and thus are often stressed, whereas prepositions carry lighter information load and thus are often unstressed ('the information-stress principle'), presents the differences in stress, which, for our purposes, can be interpreted as an instance of phonological reduction. For instance, Duanmu (2005: 19) notes that heavy vs. light stress can form a minimal pair, i.e., a lexical word is stressed and its functional counterpart is unstressed. He uses the verb *zhāo* (着) 'contact, touch' (heavy) and the aspectual marker *zhe* (着) 'be doing' (light), but this situation is also applicable to the EMPH preposition *zhe* (着).

A caveat in this context is that such tonal reduction seems to be reversed in certain cases. For instance, in the change from the verb *chōng* (冲/衝) 'pour, wash out,

---

[24] Despite its resistant tendency to reduction, Chinese does have instances of reduction. For instance, Peyraube (2015: 114) reports many examples of fusions or bonding in the history of Chinese, as exemplified in the contractions of juxtaposed grammatical forms in Classical Chinese (Late Archaic, 5th - 2nd c. BCE): [*zhī* '3rd pronoun' + *yú* 'to, at' 〉 *zhū*] and [*bù* 'not' + *zhī* '3.pronoun' 〉 *fú*], etc. (see also Peyraube 1986a,b, 1999, 2015).

[25] We also noted in 7.4.2, however, that the development of the primary forms, in principle, could have emerged from the direct combination of the relational nouns, as well.

impact' to the preposition *chòng* (冲/衝) 'on the strength of, on the basis of, because', the change from the 1st level-tone in the verb to the 4th falling-tone can be regarded, from certain viewpoints, as an instance of increase in tonal quality, or, at least, it is not clear as to increase or decrease of phonetic substance. Furthermore, there seem to be very few instances of diverging tones that can be presumed to be a consequence of grammaticalization (Lin Zhang, p.c.).

In sum, erosion is not prominent in the grammaticalization of adpositions in Chinese largely due to its conservative morphosyntax. However, it is possible that phonetic reduction at a micro-level, e.g., stress reduction, etc., may sometimes be observable.

7.4.4 Grammatical Functions

7.4.4.1 Beyond Space

We have seen, though in a cursory manner, the adpositional system in Modern Chinese and its development largely from nominal and verbal sources, focusing on spatial adpositions, especially those that seem to be in active grammaticalization processes at the moment. There are many functions in addition to marking spatial relationships. Such extension across functional domains can be exemplified in the following constructed examples, in which prepositions marking spatial relationships extend their function to temporal marking:

(15) *zài* 在 'at'
    a.   我 住 在 北京。
            Wǒ zhù   *zài Běijīng.*
            I   reside   **at** Beijing
            'I live in Beijing.'

    b.   那 件事 发生 在 去年 冬天。
            Nà   *jiànshì*   *fāshēng*   *zài*   *qùnián*   *dōngtiān.*
            that   incident   occur   **at** last.year   winter
            'The incident occurred last winter.'

(16) *cóng* 从/從 'from'

    a. 我 从 北京 飞 到 南京。

        Wǒ **_cóng_** *Běijīng*   *fēi dào*   *Nánjīng.*

        I   **from** Beijing   fly till   Nanjing

        'I flew from Beijing to Nanjing.'

    b. 我 从 早上 工作 到 晚上。

        Wǒ **_cóng_** *zǎoshang gōngzuò* *dào*   *wǎnshang.*

        I   **from** morning work   till   night

        'I work from morning till night.'

(17) *zì* 自 'from'

    a. 他 来 自 美国。

        Tā *lái*   **_zì_**   *Měiguó.*

        he   come **from** America

        'He is from America.'

    b. 他 自 小 在 这儿 长大。

        Tā **_zì_**   *xiǎo zài*   *zhèr*   *zhǎngdà.*

        he **from** small at   here   grow.up

        'He grew up here from childhood.'

(18) *dào* 到 'to'

    a. 退休 后, 他 到 农村 去 了。

        Tuìxiū   *hòu, tā* **_dào_** *nóngcūn*   *qù-le.*

        retirement after he **to**   farming.village go-PERF

        'After retirement, he went to the countryside.'

    b. 我 努力 工作 到 今天。

        Wǒ nǔlì *gōngzuò* **_dào_** *jīntiān.*

        I   hard work   **till**   today

        'I have worked hard till today.'

In examples (15) through (18) above, all (a) examples mark spatial relationships whereas all (b) examples mark temporal relationships. As has been pointed out repeatedly in the discussion of other languages, this type of metaphorical extension is common across languages.

Cross-domain extension from spatial marking is not limited to temporal marking, but may involve other abstract domains, which is also very common. This is exemplified in the following:

(19) a. *qiáo-xià* (桥下)   [bridge-under]   'under the bridge'
      b. *míng-xià* (名下)   [name-under]   'under the name'
      c. *qíngkuàng-xià* (情况下) [situation-under]   'under the circumstances'
      d. *bāngzhù-xià* (帮助下) [help-under]   'under/with the help'

The examples in (19) show various kinds of situations humans conceptualize as the "under" relationship with respect to another entity, concrete or abstract. This type of extension, as shown by nearly the same translation in English, is also common across languages.

7.4.4.2 Beyond Prepositions and Postpositions

Since Chinese lexemes are versatile in terms of grammatical categories, a word can often be used across multiple word classes. Therefore, it is common for words in the primary word classes, e.g., nouns and verbs, to be used as adjectives, adverbs, etc. As most prepositions and postpositions developed from verbs and nouns, and these heterosemous source lexemes are mostly still in use, most adpositions have heterosemous words in many word classes, e.g., adjectives and adverbs, in addition to verbs and nouns. For our purposes, adjectives and adverbs do not concern us since they are primary or semi-primary classes. However, there are meaningful functional extensions of adpositions, such as affixes, modal markers, aspectual markers, conjunctions, etc. We will briefly look at conjunctions, exemplified in the following, modified from *KU-CKD*:

(20) a. 自非亭午夜分, 不见曦月。

    Zì fēi tíngwǔ   yèfēn,   bù   jiàn   xī   yuè.

    if not midday midnight not see daylight moon

    'If there were no days or nights, one cannot see the sun or the moon.'

  b. 如果 你 不来, 那么 谁 来?

    Rúguǒ nǐ   bù lái,   nàme   shéi   lái?

    if   you   not come then   who   come

    'If you don't come, who will come?'

In (20), the words *zì* (自) and *rú* (如), which can function as prepositions for 'from' and 'like', are used as conditional conjunctions. The conceptual motivation behind this development is clear: 'from', as a source marker, is extended to mark a hypothetical basis of an assertion, and 'like', as a similative marker, is extended to mark equality of the situations being compared.

    One final note is that, in addition to prepositions and postpositions, Chinese has circumpositions, i.e., those that consist of multiple forms occurring with a constituent between them. Some notable analyses include D Liu (2002), C Chen (2004), among others. There are many such forms, some of which are listed below:

(21)   a. *zài... shàng*   (在...上)   'at the top of'

        b. *cóng... lǐ*   (从...里/從...裏)   'from inside'

        c. *cóng... qǐ*   (从...起/從...起)   'since'

(22)   a. *bǐ... láide*   (比...来得/比...來得)   'better than'

        b. *tōngguò... lái*   (通过...来/通過...來)   'through'

        c. *duì... láishuō*   (对...来说/對...來說)   'about'

The circumpositions listed in (21) consist of a preposition and a postposition and those in (22), a preposition and a word that is not a postposition. Since there are numerous forms (cf. D Liu 2002 lists 8 forms for the type in (21), and 24 for the type in (22)), there should be numerous grammaticalization scenarios, the discussion of which is beyond our immediate interest.

7.5 Summary

In this chapter we have looked at the adpositional system in Chinese from a grammaticalization perspective. We classified the adpositions into prepositions and postpositions, and further divided the two groups into primary, composite, and complex adpositions, according to their formal composition, i.e., one-word forms as primary, two-word forms as composite, and those that contain a syntactic linker as complex adpositions. Whether a particular word is an adposition or not is often debatable due to the conservative nature of Chinese morphosyntax and the gradient nature of grammaticalization, and consequently, the adposition inventory is controversial. In the present study, the inventory of prepositions includes 42 primary and 14 composite prepositions, and that of postpositions includes 18 primary, 7 composite and 10 complex postpositions, thus all taken together, 91 adpositions. Adpositions are diverse in their grammatical meanings, but postpositions tend to encode spatial (and more abstract) relationships because most of them involve relational nouns.

Spatial prepositions encoding non-axial notions tend to be largely primary prepositions and there are many conceptual categories in which multiple forms are layered, especially in Directionals, Ablatives (Sources), and Associatives. The domain of axial spatial notions is occupied entirely by postpositions; no prepositions are found in it.

In terms of grammaticalization sources, nominal sources are more strongly associated with the postpositions than with the prepositions, and conversely, prepositions are predominantly associated with verbal sources. As is usually the case, many adpositions, each from different sources, develop into identical or nearly identical functions, thus creating multiple layers.

Applying a similar set of criteria to 91 adpositions, we separated those that are presumably actively undergoing grammaticalization, only two prepositions and five postpositions. When the proportion is considered, the overall picture indicates that spatial prepositions in Chinese are relatively well established, despite much intercategorial fluidity. From a closer look, we argued that an individual form's strengths (as reflected in token frequency) are directly related to the level of their formal complexity.

When the grammaticalization scenarios are reviewed with respect to mechanisms, i.e., extension, desemanticization, decategorialization, and erosion, extension is well attested, as manifested in the change from nominal or verbal sources to adpositions. Desemanticization is often deemed to be robust, but in the cases of Chinese postpositions, desemanticization is not prominent because they mostly developed from relational nouns and still retain such relational meanings. Decategorialization is only weakly manifested, largely due to the fact that adpositions often retain verbal characteristics in terms of morphosyntax. Similarly, erosion is not prominent, also due to the language's conservative morphosyntactic behavior.

We also discussed that many (or most) adpositions extended their functions from space to time or other abstract domains, as is commonly attested across languages. In addition, we noted in passing that there are many circumpositions, though not yet actively researched to date by grammaticalizationists.

From the exposition in this chapter, we can see that Chinese adpositions display a number of shared features with those in other languages, but they also carry quite distinct characteristics not found in other languages.

Grammaticalization of Prepositions in Thai

8.1 Introduction

Thai has a set of well-developed prepositions.[1] However, the term 'preposition' had not been in use by Thai linguists and grammarians until Uppakitsinlapasan (1953: 58-70) wrote his *Siamese Grammar: Morphology* (as cited in Warotamasikkhadit 1988: 70). Owing to the typological characteristics of an isolating language, these prepositions occur without change in form, and thus the usage of the source category items or the usage of grammaticalized prepositions is often indistinguishable. The level of functional ambiguity varies a great deal by the individual forms and by researchers, a situation similar to Chinese (see 7.2). With this regard, Schiller (1992) is right in stating that the southeastern languages of Asia pose a great difficulty if one adopts an ethnocentric perspective, and further even greater difficulties if one attempts to fit the forms in those languages in the putative universal categories.

In this chapter, we will briefly address the issues in and positions toward the grammatical category of preposition in Thai first, argue for the presence of

---

[1] This chapter is greatly indebted to Thai linguists, Kyungeun Park, Kultida Khammee, Kewalin Simuang, Supakit Buakhao, Bo-Eun Kim and Ji-Eun Park. All errors, however, are the author's.

prepositions in Thai, and then discuss diverse aspects of grammaticalization of prepositions, with special focus on those that signal spatial relationship. We will also look into the grammaticalization scenarios exhibited by those that are supposedly undergoing active grammaticalization in Modern Thai according to the set criteria applied to other languages. Further, we will discuss some noteworthy aspects from a typological and comparative linguistic perspective. Frequency data has been taken from the online searchable corpus, Thai National Corpus, developed by Chulalongkorn University (http://www.arts.chula.ac.th/~ling/ThaiConc/), consisting of 33,394,574 words.

8.2 Prepositions in Thai

As noted above, due to the typological characteristics of an isolating language, whether a particular word has grammaticalized or not has often been a topic of scholarly debate in Thai linguistic circles. Prepositions are one such controversial grammatical categories. Radical positions on the issue deny the existence of the category 'preposition' altogether in Thai, for the members still retain their source category traits.[2] For instance, Warotamasikkhadit (1988, 1994) argues that the so-called prepositions in Thai do not form a uniform category as English prepositions do (cf. Curme 1947: 27-29, Fries 1952: 95-96) and that those that are thus called are in fact verbs (e.g., *taam* (ตาม) 'follow', *càak* (จาก) 'leave, depart', etc.), nouns (e.g., *khɔ̌ɔŋ* (ของ) 'thing', *thîi* (ที่) 'place', etc.), conjunctions (e.g., *phûa* (เพื่อ) 'for', *tæ̀æ* (แต่) 'but', etc.), or are forms derived from the deep structure (*dûay* (ด้วย) 'with' from *chay* (ใช้) 'use', and *kæ̀æ* (แก่) 'to' from *hay* (ให้) 'give'), even though the process involved in the last category has not been made clear by the author.[3] On the other hand, many more scholars acknowledge the existence of prepositions in Thai

---

2) As is pointed out by Slater (2000), sometimes a more vague label such as 'particle' is used to include prepositions by some linguists (Bussmann 1996, Jespersen 1924, among others).

3) Note that there are multiple ways of transcribing Thai script, and forms may occur in variable forms (e.g. *haj, hay, hây,* etc. for 'give/for/to'), when they are cited from different sources.

(e.g., Noss 1964, Kölver 1984, Savetamalya 1989, Witayasakpan 1992, Indrambarya 1995, 2008, Clark and Prasithrathsint 1985, Bisang 1996, Intratat 1998, Iwasaki and Yap 1998, J Lee 2000, Prasithrathsint 2000, Smyth 2002, Chamniyom 2003, Zlatev 2003, Iwasaki 2004, K Takahashi 2008, 2012, Iwasaki and Ingkaphirom 2005, H Jung 2006, Prasithrathsint 2010a,b, Natthawan 2011, Loss 2017, K Park 2017a,b, Park and Rhee 2018, Rutherford and Thanyawong 2019, among many others).

In order to avoid terminological issues, some researchers adopt the term 'coverbs', originally coined for Chinese linguistics (Li and Thompson 1981) to refer to the words that are lexically verbs but function as prepositions, retaining both the verbal and prepositional traits (Thepkanjana and Uehara 2008). Similarly, in his analysis of the Thai verb *haj* (ให้) 'give', often analyzed as a preposition or an auxiliary, H Jung (2004) claims that it is, in fact, a coverb. He extends the claim to other verbs such as *paj* (ไป) 'go' and *maa* (มา) 'come'. Diller (2008), in his overview of research on Thai grammar, correctly notes that classification of items undergoing progressive grammaticalization is bound to vary according to the researchers' perspectives.

Notwithstanding the persisting controversy over word classes, however, decades-old reference grammars, e.g., *Thai Reference Grammar* by Noss (1964), and more recent *Thai: An Essential Grammar* by Smyth (2002) and *A Reference Grammar of Thai* by Iwasaki and Ingkaphirom (2005), among others, recognize the presence of the prepositional category with a large number of members and provide excellent descriptions of the members. In particular, Kölver (1984) addresses prepositions (and serial verb constructions) to a great extent from a more fluid and typological perspective of grammar in her AKUP monograph.

These authors do recognize the fluidity within and across grammatical categories. For instance, among the early studies, Noss (1964: 146) notes that the class of prepositions, which, by definition, introduce exocentric complement phrases, is not very large, but must be considered open. It is largely because, according to Noss (1964), its members include homonyms of both substantive and predicative lexemes, which, when stressed, are heads of endocentric expressions.[4]

If we regard grammar not as a self-contained *a priori* system but one that is fluid and ever 'emergent' (Hopper 1987; see also H Koo 2020), and if we further consider that a word's acquisition of grammatical nature, however minimal, is an instance of grammaticalization (Kuryłowicz 1975[1965]), we come to the conclusion that Thai indeed has a large number of prepositions, each with variable degrees of grammaticalization, some already well-established, others being actively grammaticalized, and still others at the incipient stage of grammaticalization.

Adopting such fluid perspectives on grammar, we can recognize a large number of prepositions that carry diverse grammatical and semantic functions in Thai. It has a number of markers across such categories as, following the classification of Lehmann (2004: 1845-1851), Sylak-Glassman et al. (2015: 83), Blake (2004[1994]), among others, 'grammatical', 'local', and '(non-local) case' markers. Grammatical cases, marking the grammatical relationship among arguments with respect to the state or event denoted by the predicate, are developed to a relatively lesser degree as compared to Korean and Japanese, in that sentential subjects and the objects occur without a marker (e.g., Nominative case marker or Accusative case marker) but are determined by way of the word order, or structural configuration, as shown in (1a). Grammatical case markers that occur in Thai are Dative *kɛ̀ɛ* (แก่) 'to' and Genitive *khong* (ของ) 'of', as exemplified in (1b) and (1c):[5]

(1) a.　ฉัน มี ปากกา
　　　 chan　mi　　bakka
　　　 I　　 have　pen
　　　 'I　　 have a pen.'

---

4) Noss (1964), however, lists a large number of prepositions in six categories based on the construction types and meanings: 10 forms in the /*naj*/ class ('locative reference'), 14 forms in the /*caak*/ class ('direction and limits of motion'), 32 forms in the /*dooj*/ class ('temporal, spatial or logical condition'), 17 forms in the /*rɔɔp*/ class ('route or timing of motion or distribution'), 14 forms in the /*sǎg*/ class ('attitude toward the accuracy, size, distribution, or inclusiveness of a numeral expression', and 2 forms in the miscellaneous class (for *hây* and *aw,* 'transfer of possession or instrumentality'). Note that his notation is different from the one adopted here.

5) Thai orthography does not use inter-lexical spacing, but for expositional clarity Thai script in our examples is provided with word boundaries marked by a space.

b. พิชัย ให้ หนังสือ แก่ สุมาลี

    Phíchay   hây   náŋsǔu   __kɛ̀ɛ__   Sùmaalii

    [name]   give   book   **to**   [name]

    'Pichay gives a book to Sumalee.'   (Iwasaki & Ingkaphirom 2005: 114)

c. นี่ หนังสือ ของ ฉัน

    ni   náŋsǔu   __khong__   chan

    this   book   **of**   I

    'This is my book.'

In addition to grammatical case markers, there are other prepositions that mark a spatial location, i.e., 'local case', such as *thii* (ที่) 'at' in (2a), and *caak* (จาก) 'from' and *thung* (ถึง) 'till' in (2b):

(2) a. พบ กัน ที่ บ้าน เพื่อน

    phop kan   __thii__   baan   phuan

    meet together   **at**   house   friend

    'We met at a friend's house'   (modified from Noss 1964: 149)

b. แม่ ขาย ของ จาก เช้า ถึง ค่ำ

    mae   khai khong __caak__ chaw   __thung__ kham

    mother   sell thing **from** morning **till** evening

    'Mother sold things from morning till evening.'

                                     (modified from H Jung 2006: 128)

In addition, Thai has a large number of 'non-local case' markers, which signal diverse concepts other than space, e.g., the Benefactive *hay* (ให้) 'for' in (3a), referential *suan* (ส่วน) 'as for' in (3b), means of transportation *khap* (ขับ) 'by' in (3c), and Comitative *kap* (กับ) 'with' in (3d):

(3) a. ผม ซื้อ หนังสือ ให้ คุณ

   phom   *suu*   *náŋsʉ̌u*   ***hay***   *khun*

   I   buy   book   **for**   you

   'I bought a book for you.'   (modified from Smyth 2002: 111)

   b. ส่วน ผม คิด ว่า ไม่ ดี เลย

   suan   *phom*   *khit*   *waa*   *may*   *dii*   *ləəy*

   as.for   I   think   COMP   not   good   at.all

   'As for me, I don't think it is good at all.' (modified from Smyth 2002: 112)

   c. ผม ขับ รถ มา

   phom   ***khap***   *rot*   *maa*

   I   **by**   car   come

   'I came by car (as the driver)/I drove here.' (modified from Smyth 2002: 114)

   d. ฉัน ไป กับ เพื่อน

   chan   *pay*   ***kap***   *phuan*

   I   go   **with**   friend

   'I went with a friend.'   (modified from Smyth 2002: 114)

What is important in this context is that in an isolating language like Thai, the syntactic configuration is the most important factor in determining the part of speech of a particular form, even though that does not always provide an unambiguous clue for the decision. For instance, Indrambarya (2008), in a counterargument of Warotamasikkhadit (1992), who asserts that there are no prepositions in Thai, notes that in the syntactic configuration of [NP V NP __ NP], the items that may fill the slot may be thought to be of various parts of speech. She analyzes that the slot can be occupied by a preposition as in her earlier analysis (1995) and Prasithrathsint (2000), but may also be filled in by a verb (Indrambarya 1995), a noun (Savetamalya 1989, Indrambarya 1995, Prasithrathsint 2000), an adverb (Indrambarya 1995), and even a conjunction (Warotamasikkhadit 1992).

   Similarly, Schiller (1992), in his discussion on Southeast Asian languages, asserts that the characteristics of the grammatical categories in the languages in this area cannot be placed in a straight-jacket but can be better explained when we adopt the notions of 'syntactic polysemy' and 'syntactic flexibility' (Ratliff 1991). Also, on the inherent versatility of Thai lexemes in terms of their syntactic function, Sak-Humphry et al. (1997), noting that identifying forms as words in isolating languages which do not have inflectional morphology is not an easy task, assert that distribution is the most important determinant in case of homophones. To illustrate variable interpretations of the functions of *khaw* (เข้า) 'enter' and *pɔɔk* (ออก) 'leave', they present the following examples (4) and (5), presented with modification:

(4) *khaw* 'enter'

    นก บิน เข้า ไป ใน กรง

    *nok bin **khaw** pay nay krong.*

   (i)   The bird flew to the inside of the cage.

   (ii) The bird flew in to the inside of the cage.

   (iii) The bird flew to enter the inside of the cage.

(5) *pɔɔk* 'leave'

    นก บิน ออก จาก กรง

    *nok bin **pɔɔk** caak krong*

   (i)   The bird flew from the cage.

   (ii) The bird flew out from the cage.

   (iii) The bird flew to leave the cage.

As is evident in the examples, the two lexemes *khaw* (เข้า) and *pɔɔk* (ออก) may be interpreted as a preposition, adverb, or even a verb. The authors, through application of a number of tests, analyze them as deverbal adverbs, but this phenomenon straightforwardly shows the multifunctionality of Thai lexemes, which is the source of the controversy.

From currently available literature (Noss 1964, Indrambarya 1992, 1995, Intratat 1996, J Song 1997, J Lee 2000, Smyth 2002, Kullavanijaya 2003, Iwasaki and Ingkaphirom 2005, K Takahashi 2005, H Jung 2006, Rangkupan 2007, Post 2007,

Prasithrathsint 2010a,b, Natthawan 2011, K Park 2017a,b, Park and Rhee 2018, among others) a total of 181 prepositions are collected. Thai prepositions can be classified along a number of formal and functional variables. The most straightforward way is by means of their formal shape, i.e., the formal complexity depending on the number of lexemes they involve. Even though lexemes in isolating languages tend to resist formal change, typically reduction in phonetic substance, there occur a number of words and phrases that have undergone conceptual integration to a great extent resulting in idioms and even phonologically reduced forms.[6] Even though the degree of grammaticalization cannot be measured simply based on the formal characteristics, if we assume that the prepositions consisting of a single lexeme, other things being equal, is relatively more grammaticalized than the bi- or poly-lexemic forms, they may be treated as primary prepositions, as we have treated other languages. In the same line of reasoning, two-lexemic prepositions are regarded as composite prepositions and those of three or more lexemes are complex prepositions, for convenience. there are 101 primary prepositions, as listed in Table 8.1, shown in functional clusters.

Primary Preposition		Meaning
nay	ใน	in
ʔùu	อยู่	at
thîi	ที่	at
tɔɔn	ตอน	at (time of day) (colloq.); during, when (colloq.)
mûa	เมื่อ	at the time of
weelaa	เวลา	during the time of, at or in
pràcam	ประจำ	at, over
khɔ̌ɔŋ	ของ	of
hæ̀æŋ	แห่ง	of
hây	ให้	for

---

[6] For instance, the Thai sentence-final particle *khráp* used in polite male speech is historically a fusion of a two-verb sequence, part of the humilific expression *khɔ̌ɔráp thôot* 'beg to receive punishment' (*khɔ̌ɔ* (V) 'beg', *ráp* (V) 'receive') (Matisoff 1991a: 443).

phûa	เพื่อ	for, for the purpose of
sămràp	สำหรับ	for, as for, as far as x is concerned
sùan	ส่วน	for, as for
rûaŋ	เรื่อง	on the subject of
tɔ̀ɔ	ต่อ	against, per, to (affect)
yɔ́ɔn	ย้อน	against
mǽæ	แม้	in spite of, despite
bon	บน	on, above
nŭa	เหนือ	above, north of
lâaŋ	ล่าง	under
tây	ใต้	under, south of
nâa	หน้า	in front of
kàp	กับ	with
kà	กะ	with
ʔaw	เอา	with
dûay	ด้วย	with
phrɔ́ɔm	พร้อม	with, together with
taam	ตาม	along, according to, by, along
troŋ	ตรง	according to, at, from
khâam	ข้าม	across
thálú	ทะลุ	across
tàaŋ	ต่าง	in place of
lɔ̂ɔt	ลอด	through, via
phàan	ผ่าน	through, via, by means of
thûa	ทั่ว	throughout, pervading, all over
talɔ̀ɔt	ตลอด	throughout, all over
klaaŋ	กลาง	in the middle of
rawàaŋ	ระหว่าง	between, among
dooy	โดย	by, via, with
khâaŋ	ข้าง	by, by the side of, near
klây	ใกล้	near
tìt	ติด	next to
rim	ริม	by the side of, near, close by, on the edge of

fàay	ฝ่าย	on the part of, from the side of
khwǎa	ขวา	right to
sáay	ซ้าย	left to
cuan	จวน	almost
kùap	เกือบ	almost
raaw	ราว	approximately
rɔ̂ɔp	รอบ	around, round
thǎæw	แถว	around
ʔɔ̂ɔm	อ้อม	around, detouring, half-circling
klay	ไกล	far
tæ̀æ	แต่	but, without
ráy	ไร้	without
pràatsacàak	ปราศจาก	without
wéen	เว้น	except for
nɔ̂ɔk	นอก	outside of
ʔɔ̀ɔk	ออก	out
càak	จาก	from
chàphɔ́	เฉพาะ	restricted to
kràthâŋ	กระทั่ง	only, solely, even
phɔ̂ŋ	เพิ่ง	only, just (time)
phûŋ	พึ่ง	only, just (time)
phiaŋ	เพียง	only
khûn	ขึ้น	to
kæ̀æ	แก่	to, for
thǔŋ	ถึง	to, till
yaŋ	ยัง	to
khâw	เข้า	into
sày	ใส่	into, at so as to hit
loŋ	ลง	into, down
pen	เป็น	into (transform)
sùu	สู่	toward
con	จน	until
kɔ̀ɔn	ก่อน	before (time limit)

chǎn	ฉัน	similar to, in a manner characteristic of
chêen	เช่น	as, like
khláay	คล้าย	like
mǔan	เหมือน	like
thâw	เท่า	like
kəən	เกิน	over
phón	พ้น	beyond, past, clear of, free of
lǎŋ	หลัง	behind
kwàa	กว่า	than
bùak	บวก	plus
ʔìik	อีก	another, an additional number of
ləəy	เลย	past (space), over (space-time), beyond (time)
khɛ̂ɛ	แค่	stopping at, going no further than
khróp	ครบ	completing a set, the full amount of
mòt	หมด	depleting a set, the last bit of
phɔɔ	พอ	as soon as the time of
phrɔ́	เพราะ	because of
sàk	สัก	the exact number of, the unreal quantity of
than	ทัน	in time for, catching up with
tháŋ	ทั้ง	a complete set of
tem	เต็ม	full of, filling up
pràmaan	ประมาณ	approximately
tâŋ	ตั้ง	all of, as much as, the surprisingly high number of
thaaŋ	ทาง	in the direction of, by way of, via
thɛɛn	แทน	instead of, so as to replace

Table 8.1 Primary prepositions in Modern Thai

The 101 primary prepositions in Thai is the largest number among the languages addressed here, closely followed by English, which has 97 primary prepositions. When compared to other languages, especially for example, Korean with 24 postpositions and Spanish with 25 prepositions, the number is extraordinarily high.

From the list, it is observable that there are multiple forms seemingly carrying a similar function. For instance, there are about six different forms marking a general location (Locative or Regional), either strictly spatial and/or for temporal, i.e., *thîi* (ที่), *ʔùu* (อยู่), *pràcam* (ประจำ), *tɔɔn* (ตอน), *mûa* (เมื่อ), and *weelaa* (เวลา), and similarly, there are five different forms marking togetherness, such as accompaniment (Comitative) or instrumentality (Instrumental), i.e., *kàp* (กับ), *dûay* (ด้วย), *ʔaw* (เอา), *kà* (กะ). and *phrɔ́ɔm* (พร้อม). There are also multiple prepositions marking similarity (Similative), i.e., *mǔan* (เหมือน), *khláay* (คล้าย), *thâw* (เท่า), *chêen* (เช่น), and *chǎn* (ฉัน). Needless to say, these multiple forms occupying the same conceptual space do not have comparable strengths, as shall be discussed below.

It is also notable that many Thai prepositions occur in a structurally more complex form, thus creating bi-morphemic composite prepositions or poly-morphemic complex prepositions. For instance, Smyth (2002; Chapter 8) lists the prepositions according to their combination patterns, as in (6), shown with modification:

(6) a. *khang* ('side') + Prep: *nay* ('in'), *nook* ('outside'), *bon* ('on'), *laang* ('under'), *naa* ('in front of'), *lang* ('behind'), *khaang* ('by, beside, near')

    b. *phaay* ('side, part') + Prep: *nay* ('in'), *nook* ('outside'), *taay* ('under'), *naa* ('in front of'), *lang* ('behind')

    c. *thaang* ('way') + 'right/left':   *khwaa* ('right'), *saay (muu)* ('left (hand)'

    d. non-prefixed: *rawaang* ('between'), *klay* ('far'), *klây* ('near'), *trong khaam* ('opposite'), *rim* ('on the edge of'), *taam* ('along')

A quantitative analysis shows that not all the patterns shown in (6) are productive, but Thai has composite and complex prepositions, created by following some of the patterns shown above or otherwise.[7] There are 71 composite prepositions in Modern

---

[7] For instance, *thaaŋ sáay muu* (ทางซ้ายมือ) 'on the left hand side of' is structurally possible but it records 0 pmw in the corpus (only 6 tokens), and the even less frequent *thaaŋ khwǎa muu* (ทางขวามือ) 'on the right hand side of', also records 0 pmw (only 2 tokens).

Thai, as listed in Table 8.2, also arranged according to their functions.

Composite Preposition		Meaning
hây kæ̀æ	ให้แก่	for
hây kàp	ให้กับ	with
phrɔ́ɔm dûay	พร้อมด้วย	with, together with
phrɔ́ɔm kàp	พร้อมกับ	with
rûam kàp	ร่วมกับ	together with, along with
mây kìaw	ไม่เกี่ยว	without
kìaw kàp	เกี่ยวกับ	about, on
khâaŋ bon	ข้างบน	on
khâaŋ khâaŋ	ข้าง ๆ	next to, beside (location)
tìt kàp	ติดกับ	next to
thæ̆æw thæ̆æw	แถว ๆ	near (location)
klây kàp	ใกล้กับ	close to, near to
klây klây	ใกล้ ๆ	near (location)
raaw raaw	ราว ๆ	approximately
rɔ̂ɔp rɔ̂ɔp	รอบ ๆ	around, round
ʔɔ̂ɔm ʔɔ̂ɔm	อ้อม ๆ	around, detouring, half-circling
khâaŋ lâaŋ	ข้างล่าง	underneath, downstairs
khâaŋ tây	ข้างใต้	under
phaay tây	ภายใต้	under, inferior position
khâaŋ lăŋ	ข้างหลัง	behind
lăŋ càak	หลังจาก	behind
khâaŋ nâa	ข้างหน้า	in front of
tɔ̀ɔ nâa	ต่อหน้า	in front of
phaay nâa	ภายหน้า	ahead, in the future
khâaŋ nay	ข้าง ใน	in
phaay nay	ภายใน	within, internal, within (time limit)
phaay nɔ̂ɔk	ภายนอก	outside, external
ʔɔ̀ɔk càak	ออกจาก	out of
khaâŋ nɔ̂ɔk	ข้างนอก	outside
con kràthâŋ	จนกระทั่ง	until

con thŭŋ	จนถึง	till
cuan cà	จวนจะ	almost
kùap cà	เกือบจะ	almost
wéen tææ	เว้นแต่	except for
yók wén	ยกเว้น	except
hàaŋ càak	ห่างจาก	far from
dooy chàphɔ́	โดยเฉพาะ	restricted to
chàphɔ́ tææ	เฉพาะแต่	only, just
phiaŋ tææ	เพียงแต่	only, just
mǽæ kràthâŋ	แม้กระทั่ง	only, solely, even
dooy phàan	โดยผ่าน	across
kɔɔránii khɔ̌ɔŋ	กรณีของ	in case of
khon lá	คนละ	each, different, ···at a time
mǽæ tææ	แม้แต่	despite, in spite of
mǽæ wâa	แม้ว่า	despite, in spite of
mŭan kàp	เหมือนกับ	like
mây mŭan	ไม่เหมือน	unlike
mûa weelaa	เมื่อเวลา	during the time of, at or in
nay ráwàaŋ	ในระหว่าง	during
nay naam	ในนาม	on behalf of
nɔ̂ɔk càak	นอกจาก	in addition to
bùak kàp	บวกกับ	plus, in addition to
nûaŋ càak	เนื่องจาก	because of
pay yaŋ	ไปยัง	to
phàan thaaŋ	ผ่านทาง	via
phaay lăŋ	ภายหลัง	afterwards, later on
pràkɔ̀ɔp dûay	ประกอบด้วย	consist of, include
ruam thŭŋ	รวมถึง	including
taam lăŋ	ตามหลัง	along, after, following
taam thîi	ตามที่	according to
thâw kàp	เท่ากับ	like
tàaŋ càak	ต่างจาก	unlike
tàaŋ kàp	ต่างกับ	different from

talɔ̀ɔt con	ตลอดจน	as well as, plus, in addition to
tâŋ tὲæ	ตั้งแต่	since
tὲæ chàphɔ́	แต่เฉพาะ	only, just
thŭŋ khêæ	ถึงแค่	only to the point of
tὲæ phiaŋ	แต่เพียง	only, just
tὲæ lá	แต่ละ	each, different, ⋯at a time
thæɛn thîi	แทนที่	instead of
troŋ khâam	ตรงข้าม	opposite, on the other side of

Table 8.2 Composite prepositions in Modern Thai

The list in Table 8.2 shows again that there are certain conceptual domains to which multiple forms belong. For instance, there are multiple forms in the domain of marking togetherness, such as accompaniment (Comitative) and instrumentality (Instrumental), i.e., *hây kàp* (ให้กับ), *phrɔ́ɔm dûay* (พร้อมด้วย), *phrɔ́ɔm kàp* (พร้อมกับ), and *rûam kàp* (ร่วมกับ). Note that this conceptual domain has multiple primary prepositions as well (see Table 8.1 above). There are also multiple forms in the domain of marking closeness such as Proximative and Contiguitive, i.e., *khâaŋ khâaŋ* (ข้าง ๆ), *tìt kàp* (ติดกับ), *thὲæw thὲæw* (แถว ๆ), *klây kàp* (ใกล้กับ), *klây klây* (ใกล้ ๆ). Also noteworthy is that there are composite forms created by reduplication of the primary prepositions, i.e., repeating the mono-morphemic preposition, e.g., *khâaŋ khâaŋ* (ข้าง ๆ) 'next to, beside', *thὲæw thὲæw* (แถว ๆ) 'near', *klây klây* (ใกล้ ๆ) 'near', *raaw raaw* (ราว ๆ) 'approximate', *rɔ̂ɔp rɔ̂ɔp* (รอบ ๆ) 'around', *ʔɔ̂ɔm ʔɔ̂ɔm* (อ้อม ๆ) 'around, detouring', etc., which are marked by the Thai *máyyamók* symbol (ๆ). The effect of reduplication is not noticeably strong but it tends to add some emphasis to the prepositional meaning.

Thai also has complex prepositions. However, unlike most other languages, in which complex adpositions exist in a large number, Thai has only a small number of complex prepositions. This is an interesting aspect, and will be discussed more in 10.3. Complex prepositions are listed in Table 8.3.

Complex Preposition		Meaning
ʔan nûaŋ càak	อันเนื่องจาก	because of
ʔan nûaŋ maa càak	อันเนื่องมาจาก	because of
nûaŋ maa càak	เนื่องมาจาก	because of, due to
chêen diaw kàp	เช่นเดียวกับ	as, like
hàaŋ klay càak	ห่างไกลจาก	far from
nay naam khɔ̌ɔŋ	ในนามของ	on behalf of
nɔ̀ɔk nŭa càak	นอกเหนือจาก	in addition to
phaay nay khɔ̌ɔŋ	ภายในของ	inside of
phaay nɔ̀ɔk khɔ̌ɔŋ	ภายนอกของ	outside of

Table 8.3 Complex prepositions in Modern Thai

From a small inventory of complex prepositions it is apparent that the last component in the string is invariably a primary preposition. The linking function of these complex prepositions is performed by these primary prepositions, i.e., notably *khɔ̌ɔŋ* (ของ) 'of' and *càak* (จาก) 'from', and less frequently *kàp* (กับ) 'with', a crosslinguistically common pattern. This tendency is so strong that some authors include in the inventory of composite prepositions such forms as *khâw pay* (เข้าไป) [into-go], *khûn pay* (ขึ้นไป) [up-go], *thàt pay* (ถัดไป) [next-go], etc. in which *pay* (ไป) 'go' is reinterpreted as a preposition and the participating forms are presumed to have internal cohesion.[8] This shows the language users' analogical tendency of innovating new forms based on existing structural templates.

As is the case with other languages discussed thus far, the prepositions listed in the above are of great variation in terms of frequency. Since prepositions have

---

[8] These are not included since most Thai consultants intuitively feel that they are syntactic constructions that have not yet acquired a sufficient level of structural cohesion. This is an instance of variable intuition on grammatical status of linguistic forms, particularly prominent in the study of isolating languages. A wide range of semantic polysemy of the verb *pay* 'go' also contributes to the variability of interpretation (see K Park 2011 for the polysemy analysis of *pay*).

variable strengths in use, the mere number of forms does not matter much. For example, in the corpus some of them occur at a high frequency with over 15,000 tokens pmw, e.g., *nay* (ใน) 'in' and *khɔ̌ɔŋ* (ของ) 'of', whereas a large number of them either occur at 0 pmw (fewer than 16 occurrences in the corpus) or do not occur at all. The frequency ranking of the prepositions, primary, composite and complex, all combined, is shown in Table 8.4.

Frequency Range	Preposition		Meaning	PMW
High (1,000~ pmw) (n=12)	*nay*	ใน	in	16,036
	khɔ̌ɔŋ	ของ	of	15,047
	kàp	กับ	with	4,978
	càak	จาก	from	4,938
	taam	ตาม	along, according to, by, along	3,092
	thaaŋ	ทาง	in the direction of, by way of, via	2,877
	dûay	ด้วย	with	2,649
	thɯ̌ŋ	ถึง	to, till	1,992
	tɔ̀ɔ	ต่อ	against, per	1,700
	kwàa	กว่า	than	1,394
	tháŋ	ทั้ง	a complete set of	1,213
	dooy	โดย	by, via, with	1,066
Medium (100~999 pmw) (n=54)	*hæ̀æŋ*	แห่ง	of	999
	thîi	ที่	at	993
	sǎmràp	สำหรับ	for, as for, as far as x is concerned	953
	kæ̀æ	แก่	to, for	868
	hây	ให้	for	857
	rawàaŋ	ระหว่าง	between, among	833
	bon	บน	on, above	804
	kìaw kàp	เกี่ยวกับ	about, on	720
	kɔ̀ɔn	ก่อน	before (time limit)	698
	phiaŋ	เพียง	only, just	626
	ʔìik	อีก	another, an additional number of	624
	phɯ̂a	เพื่อ	for, for the purpose of	557

pen	เป็น	into (transform)	516
sùu	สู่	toward	488
rûaŋ	เรื่อง	on the subject of	459
tàæ	แต่	but, without	449
phaay nay	ภายใน	within, internal, within (time limit)	434
pràcam	ประจำ	at, over	348
sàk	สัก	the exact number of, the unreal quantity of, approximately	340
khâæ	แค่	stopping at, going no further than	335
yaŋ	ยัง	to	333
pràmaan	ประมาณ	approximately	332
tâŋ tàæ	ตั้งแต่	since	324
talɔ̀ɔt	ตลอด	throughout, all over	268
mûa	เมื่อ	at the time of	264
phàan	ผ่าน	through, via, by means of	257
tàæ lá	แต่ละ	each, different, ···at a time	253
nɔ̂ɔk	นอก	outside of	245
hây kàp	ให้กับ	with	244
lăŋ	หลัง	behind	243
kəən	เกิน	over	239
troŋ	ตรง	according to, at, from	236
pay yaŋ	ไปยัง	to	234
con thŭŋ	จนถึง	till	230
hây kàæ	ให้แก่	for	214
thææn	แทน	instead of, so as to replace	196
thûa	ทั่ว	throughout, pervading, all over	192
klây	ใกล้	near	185
ʔaw	เอา	with	179
chàphɔ́	เฉพาะ	restricted to	178
khâaŋ	ข้าง	by, by the side of, near	172
phrɔ́	เพราะ	because of	166
phaay tây	ภายใต้	under, inferior position	160
ʔɔ̀ɔk càak	ออกจาก	out of	146

	tây	ใต้	under, south of	142
	rɔ́ɔp	รอบ	around, round	140
	thâw kàp	เท่ากับ	like	138
	nâa	หน้า	in front of	132
	kùap	เกือบ	almost	126
	nǔa	เหนือ	above, north of	123
	phrɔ́ɔm	พร้อม	with, together with	121
	rim	ริม	by the side of, near, close by, on the edge of	109
	loŋ	ลง	into, down	103
	rûam kàp	ร่วมกับ	together with, along with	103
	raaw	ราว	approximately	95
	ruam thǔŋ	รวมถึง	including	95
	tàaŋ	ต่าง	in place of	90
	khâw	เข้า	into	85
	klaaŋ	กลาง	in the middle of	81
	sùan	ส่วน	for, as for	78
	phrɔ́ɔm kàp	พร้อมกับ	with, together with	77
	talɔ̀ɔt con	ตลอดจน	as well as, plus, in addition to	72
	khon lá	คนละ	each, different, ···at a time	66
	mǽæ tæ̀æ	แม้แต่	despite, in spite of	64
Low	*mǔan*	เหมือน	like	64
(100~99 pmw)	*chêen diaw kàp*	เช่นเดียวกับ	as, like	61
(n=54)	*tem*	เต็ม	full of, filling up	57
	weelaa	เวลา	during the time of, at or in	56
	fàay	ฝ่าย	on the part of, from the side of	55
	con	จน	until	53
	khûn	ขึ้น	to	51
	lǎŋ càak	หลังจาก	behind	51
	tâŋ	ตั้ง	all of, as much as, the surprisingly high number of	47
	khâam	ข้าม	across	45
	khróp	ครบ	completing a set, the full amount of	42

khláay	คล้าย	like	42
phróɔm dûay	พร้อมด้วย	with, together with	40
thâw	เท่า	like	39
sày	ใส่	into, at so as to hit	36
tὲɛ phiaŋ	แต่เพียง	only, just	36
nay ráwàaŋ	ในระหว่าง	during	35
nûaŋ càak	เนื่องจาก	because of	34
ʔùu	อยู่	at	33
thǎɛw	แถว	around	32
tɔ̀ɔ nâa	ต่อหน้า	in front of	32
hàaŋ càak	ห่างจาก	far from	31
tɔɔn	ตอน	at (time of day) (colloq); during, when (colloq)	30
ʔan nûaŋ maa càak	อันเนื่องมาจาก	because of	27
kà	กะ	with	27
rɔ̂ɔp rɔ̂ɔp	รอบ ๆ	around, round	25
mûa weelaa	เมื่อเวลา	during the time of, at or in	24
mǔan kàp	เหมือนกับ	like	24
nɔ̂ɔk càak	นอกจาก	in addition to	23
chêen	เช่น	as, like	22
dooy chàphɔ́	โดยเฉพาะ	restricted to	20
nay naam	ในนาม	on behalf of	19
phaay lǎŋ	ภายหลัง	afterwards, later on	18
klay	ไกล	far	17
khâaŋ khâaŋ	ข้าง ๆ	next to, beside (location)	16
dooy phàan	โดยผ่าน	across, via, through	16
yók wén	ยกเว้น	except	16
than	ทัน	in time for, catching up with	16
ʔɔ̀ɔk	ออก	out	16
klây klây	ใกล้ ๆ	near (location)	13
con kràthâŋ	จนกระทั่ง	until	11
mɛ́ɛ kràthâŋ	แม้กระทั่ง	only, solely, even	11
thɛɛn thîi	แทนที่	instead of	10
mɛ́ɛ	แม้	in spite of, despite	10

phaay nɔ̂ɔk	ภายนอก	outside, external	8
phón	พ้น	beyond, past, clear of, free of	8
mòt	หมด	depleting a set, the last bit of	8
raaw raaw	ราว ๆ	approximately	7
nɔ̂ɔk nʉ̌a càak	นอกเหนือจาก	in addition to	7
pràkɔ̀ɔp dûay	ประกอบด้วย	consist of, include	7
phiaŋ tὲæ	เพียงแต่	only, just	7
phɔɔ	พอ	as soon as the time of	7
tàaŋ càak	ต่างจาก	unlike	7
khâaŋ lǎŋ	ข้างหลัง	behind	7
taam lǎŋ	ตามหลัง	along, after, following	6
tìt	ติด	next to	6
thálú	ทะลุ	across	5
tὲæ chàphɔ́	แต่เฉพาะ	only, just	5
bùak kàp	บวกกับ	plus, in addition to	4
troŋ khâam	ตรงข้าม	opposite, on the other side of	4
kràthâŋ	กระทั่ง	only, solely, even	4
thὲæw thὲæw	แถว ๆ	near (location)	4
pràatsacàak	ปราศจาก	without	4
lɔ̂ɔt	ลอด	through, via	4
tàaŋ kàp	ต่างกับ	different from	3
khaâŋ nɔ̂ɔk	ข้างนอก	outside	3
khâaŋ nay	ข้างใน	in	3
khâaŋ nâa	ข้างหน้า	in front of	3
ʔan nʉ̂aŋ càak	อันเนื่องจาก	because of	3
hàaŋ klay càak	ห่างไกลจาก	far from	3
chàphɔ́ tὲæ	เฉพาะแต่	only, just	3
wéen tὲæ	เว้นแต่	except for	3
khâaŋ bon	ข้างบน	on	2
phɔ̂ŋ	เพิ่ง	only, just	2
kùap cà	เกือบจะ	almost	2
mây mʉ̌an	ไม่เหมือน	unlike	1
nay naam khɔ̌ɔŋ	ในนามของ	on behalf of	1

Very Low
(~9 pmw)
(n=61)

khâaŋ lâaŋ	ข้างล่าง	underneath, downstairs	1
phaay nay khɔ̌ɔŋ	ภายในของ	inside of	1
khâaŋ tây	ข้างใต้	under	1
phàan thaaŋ	ผ่านทาง	via	1
lâaŋ	ล่าง	under	1
kɔɔránii khɔ̌ɔŋ	กรณีของ	in case of	0
mɛ́ɛ wâa	แม้ว่า	despite, in spite of	0
taam thîi	ตามที่	according to	0
ráy	ไร้	without	0
mây kìaw	ไม่เกี่ยว	without	0
ləəy	เลย	past (space), over (space-time), beyond (time)	0
phaay nɔ̂ɔk khɔ̌ɔŋ	ภายนอกของ	outside of	0
nûaŋ maa càak	เนื่องมาจาก	because of, due to	0
chǎn	ฉัน	similar to, in a manner characteristic of	0
thǔŋ khɛ̂ɛ	ถึงแค่	only to the point of	0
cuan cà	จวนจะ	almost	0
tìt kàp	ติดกับ	next to	0
ʔɔ̂ɔm ʔɔ̂ɔm	อ้อม ๆ	around, detouring, half-circling	0
klây kàp	ใกล้กับ	close to, near to	0
ʔɔ̂ɔm	อ้อม	around, detouring, half-circling	0
wéen	เว้น	except for	0
sáay	ซ้าย	left to	0
khwǎa	ขวา	right to	0
yɔ́ɔn	ย้อน	against	0
cuan	จวน	almost	0
bùak	บวก	plus	0
phaay nâa	ภายหน้า	ahead, in the future	0
phûŋ	พึ่ง	only, just (temporal)	0

Table 8.4 Frequency of Thai prepositions

The frequency list in Table 8.4 shows a number of interesting aspects of Thai prepositions. First of all, a large portion of prepositions in Thai, 61 out of 181 (33.7%), belong to the Very Low frequency range, suggesting that they do not have much viability as grammatical forms. This proportion may not be directly compared to other languages because Table 8.4 includes complex forms, but since Thai has only nine complex prepositions (and seven belong to this range), the data is not skewed to a meaningful degree. Multiplicity of forms in the Very Low frequency range is particularly notable (see Chapter 10 for further discussion).

As is usually the case in other languages, all 12 prepositions in the High frequency range are primary forms. Among 54 Medium frequency range prepositions 42 of them (78%) are primary prepositions, and no complex preposition is found in the range, again suggesting the correlation among form, frequency, and grammaticalization. The proportion changes in the Low frequency range; about half (26; 48%) of them are primary prepositions and so are composite prepositions (26; 48%), whereas only two complex prepositions belong to the range. Since Thai has a very small number of complex prepositions, even in the Very Low frequency range, only seven of them (12%) are found (which, incidentally, is the absolute majority of nine complex prepositions), whereas as many as 21 primary prepositions (34%) belong to it, a considerably high ratio considering a general pattern that no or very few primary adpositions are found in the Very Low frequency range in other languages.

8.3 Spatial Prepositions

8.3.1 Characteristics of Spatial prepositions

Among the 181 prepositions, inclusive of primary, composite, and complex in form, a large proportion of them designate the spatial location of an entity with reference to a landmark. The landmark is not necessarily a space since an entity occupying a space can serve as the reference point of the trajector or as the background of the figure. For instance, in (7a) the preposition *rim* (ริม) 'by' (grammaticalized from the noun *rim* (ริม) 'rim, edge') marks a spatial location (i.e., margin) with reference to a river, thus 'at riverside', a typical instance of spatial preposition. In (7b) the preposition *nâa* (หน้า) 'in front of' (grammaticalized from the noun *nâa* (หน้า) 'face') designates a spatial (i.e., frontal) location with reference to the temple. And in (7c), the preposition *lǎŋ* (หลัง) 'behind' (grammaticalized from the noun *lǎŋ* (หลัง) 'back (body-part)') marks an abstract spatial (i.e., posterior) location with reference to the surface manifestation of a person's smile.

(7) a. เรา จะ จัด งาน ริม แม่น้ำ

      raw   *cà*   *càt*   *ŋaan*   **_rim_**   *mɛ̂ɛnáam*

      we   will   arrange   party   **by**   river

      'We will arrange a party by the river.'

    b. เขา มา หน้า วัด

      khǎw   *maa*   **_nâa_**   *wát*

      he   come   **front**   temple

      'He came in front of the temple.'

    c. มี บางอย่าง ซ่อน อยู่ หลัง รอยยิ้ม นั้น

      mii   *baaŋ-yàaŋ*   *sɔ̂ɔn*   *yùu*   **_lǎŋ_**   *rɔɔy-yim*   *nán*

      have   something   hide   be   **behind**   smile   that

      'There is something hidden behind that smile.'

                                  (examples (a)~(c), modified from Prasithrathsint 2010b: 70-74)

Since concepts are easily extended without discrete boundaries, the spatial vs. non-spatial distinction can always be contested (see 8.4.4). Despite such quandaries in classification, however, a list of prepositions that can be arguably deemed as spatial markers can be amassed. Such spatial prepositions, numbering 91 in total, are as shown in Table 8.5.

AXIS		PRIMARY (n=55)	COMPOSITE (n=31)	COMPLEX (n=5)
	REGIONAL (n=3)	*thîi* 'at' *ʔùu* 'at' *pràcam* 'at'		
	DIRECTIONAL (n=8)	*thaaŋ* 'toward, by way of' *khûn* 'to' *khâw* 'into' *kɛ̀ɛ* 'to, for' *loŋ* 'into, down' *sùu* 'toward' *yaŋ* 'to'	*pay yaŋ* 'to'	
	SOURCE (n=2)	*càak* 'from' *troŋ* 'according to, from'		
	GOAL (n=3)	*thǔŋ* 'to, till' *khɛ̂ɛ* 'only up to'	*thǔŋ khɛ̂ɛ* 'only up to'	
	PATH (n=7)	*dooy* 'by, via, with' *phàan* 'through, by means of' *lɔ̂ɔt* 'through, via' *talɔ̀ɔt* 'throughout, all over' *thûa* 'throughout, all over' *thaaŋ* 'toward, by way of'	*phàan thaaŋ* 'via'	
	MEDIAL (n=2)	*ráwàaŋ* 'between, among' *klaaŋ* 'in the middle of'		
NON-AXIAL	ULTERIOR (n=3)	*kəən* 'over' *ləəy* 'past' *phón* 'beyond, past'		
	ASSOCIATION (n=28)	*khɔ̌ɔŋ* 'of' *ʔɔ̂ɔm* 'around' *hɛ̀ɛŋ* 'of' *khâaŋ* 'by, near' *kàp* 'with' *taam* 'along, according to, by' *dûay* 'with' *ʔaw* 'with' *rɔ̂ɔp* 'around' *klây* 'near' *rim* 'near, beside' *thɛ̌ɛw* 'around' *kà* 'with' *phrɔ́ɔm* 'with, together with' *troŋ* 'according to, from' *dooy* 'by, via, with'	*ʔɔ̂ɔm ʔɔ̂ɔm* 'around' *khâaŋ khâaŋ* 'beside, next to' *phrɔ́ɔm kàp* 'with' *hây kàp* 'with' *phrɔ́ɔm dûay* 'with, together with' *klây klây* 'near' *klây kàp* 'close to, near to' *kìaw kàp* 'about, on' *rɔ̂ɔp rɔ̂ɔp* 'around' *rûam kàp* 'with, together with' *taam lǎŋ* 'along, after' *thɛ̌ɛw thɛ̌ɛw* 'around, near'	
	ADJACENCY (n=12)	*ʔɔ̂ɔm* 'around' *khâaŋ* 'by, near' *rɔ̂ɔp* 'around' *klây* 'near' *rim* 'near, beside' *thɛ̌ɛw* 'around'	*ʔɔ̂ɔm ʔɔ̂ɔm* 'around' *khâaŋ khâaŋ* 'beside, next to' *klây klây* 'near (location)' *klây kàp* 'close to, near to' *rɔ̂ɔp rɔ̂ɔp* 'around' *thɛ̌ɛw thɛ̌ɛw* 'around, near'	
	SEPARATION (n=3)	*klay* 'far'	*hàaŋ càak* 'far from'	*hàaŋ klay càak* 'far from'
	CONTIGUITY (n=2)	*tit* 'next to'	*tit kàp* 'next to'	

	OPPOSITE (n=6)	tɔɔ 'against, per' khâam 'across' yɔɔn 'against' thálú 'across'	dooy phàan 'across' tron khâam 'opposite'	
AXIAL	INTERIOR (n=4)	nay 'in'	phaay nay 'within' khâan nay 'in'	phaay nay khɔ̌ɔn 'inside of'
	EXTERIOR (n=6)	ʔɔ̀ɔk 'out' nɔ̂ɔk 'outside of'	ʔɔ̀ɔk càak 'out of' phaay nɔ̂ɔk 'outside, external' khâan nɔ̂ɔk 'outside'	phaay nɔ̂ɔk khɔ̌ɔn 'outside of'
	SUPERIOR (n=3)	bon 'on, above' nʉ̌a 'above, north of'	khâan bon 'on'	
	INFERIOR (n=4)	tâay 'under, south of' lâan 'underneath, under, below'	phaay tâay 'under, inferior position' khâan lâan 'underneath, downstairs'	
	ANTERIOR (n=3)	nâa 'in front of'	tɔɔ nâa 'in front of' khâan nâa 'in front of'	
	POSTERIOR (n=4)	lǎn 'behind'	lǎn càak 'behind' khâan lǎn 'behind' taam lǎn 'along, after'	
	LATERAL (n=11)	khâan 'by, by the side of, near' rim 'by the side of, near' khwǎa 'right to' sáay 'left to'	khâan khâan 'next to, beside' thaan sáay 'on the left' thaan khwǎa 'on the right' khâan sáay 'left to' khâan khwǎa 'right to'	thaan sáay mʉʉ 'left to' khâan khwǎa mʉʉ 'right to'

Table 8.5 Spatial prepositions in Modern Thai

Table 8.5 presents a few notable aspects of Thai spatial prepositions. First of all, there are a large number of prepositions that mark association (Comitative, Proximative, etc.), totaling 27, many of them (16) are primary prepositions. Considering that there are 91 spatial prepositions altogether, the conceptual domain of association is particularly crowded (accounting for 29.7% of all spatial prepositions). Multiplicity of forms in a conceptual domain is also observed in directional (eight Allative prepositions) and path (seven Perlative prepositions).

Another noteworthy aspect is that non-axial domains are largely marked by primary prepositions (note that association is an exception), and composite prepositions occur predominantly in the axial concept marking.

Across the domains, one interesting state of affairs is that Thai composite and complex prepositions are built heavily on the primary preposition. Unlike other languages, in which primary linkers, such as English *of* and *to* in *by the side of, next to,* etc., are used, Thai composite and complex prepositions "recycle" the primary prepositions in a slightly different way. This is well illustrated in the following list:

(8) a. 'in'   *nay*   *phaay nay*   *phaay nay khɔ̌ɔŋ*
                   'in'   'side in'   'side in of'

     b. 'out of' *nɔ̂ɔk*   *phaay nɔ̂ɔk*   *phaay nɔ̂ɔk khɔ̌ɔŋ*
                   'out'   'side out'   'side out of'

(9) a. 'around' *rɔ̂ɔp*   *rɔ̂ɔp rɔ̂ɔp*
                   'around'   'around around'

     b. 'around' *ʔɔ̌ɔm*   *ʔɔ̌ɔmʔɔ̌ɔm*
                   'around'   'around around'

(10) a. 'behind' *lǎŋ*   *lǎŋ càak*
                   'behind'   'behind from'

     b. 'next to' *tìt*   *tìt kàp*
                   'next to'   'next to with'

(11) a. 'with'   *phrɔ́ɔm*   *dûay*   *phrɔ́ɔm dûay*
                   'with'   'with'   'with with'

     b. 'with'   *kàp*   *phrɔ́ɔm*   *phrɔ́ɔm kàp*
                   'with'   'with'   'with with'

In (8) primary, composite, and complex prepositions marking 'in' (8a) and 'out of' (8b) are built on the preposition *nay* (ใน) and *nɔ̂ɔk* (นอก), respectively, and further recruit the noun denoting 'side', which does not affect the meaning. In (9), the primary preposition is repeated, but as we noted in 8.2, the meaning is not discernibly different (only potentially emphatic). In (10), the core meaning is provided by the primary preposition and the longer forms are only further marked by another general-use preposition, such as *càak* (จาก) 'from' and *kàp* (กับ) 'with', which do not contribute to the meaning and thus, is nearly pleonastic. The pattern shown in (11) is interesting in that composite prepositions are only combinations of the two synonymous prepositions. Since each of the two primary prepositions has the same meaning as the composite form created by combining them, this process is nearly a redundant procedure.

8.3.2 Frequencies of Spatial prepositions

Spatial prepositions have different levels of functional strength, as reflected in their use frequency. The frequency information based on the corpus is presented in Table 8.6.

Frequency Range	Spatial Preposition		Meaning	PMW
High (1,000~ pmw) (n=10)	*nay*	ใน	in	16,036
	khɔ̌ɔŋ	ของ	of	15,047
	kàp	กับ	with	4,978
	càak	จาก	from	4,938
	taam	ตาม	along, according to, by	3,092
	thaaŋ	ทาง	toward, by way of	2,877
	dûay	ด้วย	with	2,649
	thʉ̌ŋ	ถึง	to, till	1,992
	tɔ̀ɔ	ต่อ	against, per	1,700
	dooy	โดย	by, via, with	1,066
Medium (100~999 pmw) (n=34)	*hæ̀æŋ*	แห่ง	of	999
	thîi	ที่	at	993
	kæ̀æ	แก่	to, for	868
	rawàaŋ	ระหว่าง	between, among	833
	bon	บน	on, above	804
	kìaɯ kàp	เกี่ยวกับ	about, on	720
	sùu	สู่	toward	488
	phaay nay	ภายใน	within, internal	434

pràcam	ประจำ	at, over	348
khɛ̂ɛ	แค่	only up to	335
yaŋ	ยัง	to	333
talɔ̀ɔt	ตลอด	all the way through	268
phàan	ผ่าน	through, via, by means of	257
nɔ̂ɔk	นอก	outside of	245
hây kàp	ให้กับ	with	244
lǎŋ	หลัง	behind	243
kəən	เกิน	over	239
troŋ	ตรง	according to, at, from	236
pay yaŋ	ไปยัง	to	234
thûa	ทั่ว	throughout, all over	192
klây	ใกล้	near	185
ʔaw	เอา	with	179
khâaŋ	ข้าง	by, by the side of, near	172
phaay tây	ภายใต้	under, inferior position	160
ʔɔ̀ɔk càak	ออกจาก	out of	146
tây	ใต้	under, south of	142
rɔ̂ɔp	รอบ	around, round	140
nâa	หน้า	in front of	132
nǔa	เหนือ	above, north of	123
phrɔ́ɔm	พร้อม	with, together with	121
rim	ริม	by the side of, near,	109
rûam kàp	ร่วมกับ	together with, along with	103
loŋ	ลง	into, down	103

	khâw	เข้า	into	85
	klaaŋ	กลาง	in the middle of	81
	phrɔ́ɔm kàp	พร้อมกับ	with, together with	77
Low (10~99 pmw) (n=20)	*fàay*	ฝ่าย	on the part of, from the side of	55
	lǎŋ càak	หลังจาก	behind	51
	khûn	ขึ้น	to	51
	khâam	ข้าม	across	45
	phrɔ́ɔm dûay	พร้อมด้วย	with, together with	40

sày	ใส่	into, at so as to hit	36
ʔùu	อยู่	at	33
tɔ̀ɔ nâa	ต่อหน้า	in front of	32
thǎɛw	แถว	around	32
hàaŋ càak	ห่างจาก	far from	31
kà	กะ	with	27
rɔ̂ɔp rɔ̂ɔp	รอบ ๆ	around, round	25
klay	ไกล	far	17
ʔɔ̀ɔk	ออก	out	16
dooy phàan	โดยผ่าน	across, via, through	16
khâaŋ khâaŋ	ข้าง ๆ	next to, beside (location)	16
klây klây	ใกล้ ๆ	near (location)	13
phaay nɔ̂ɔk	ภายนอก	outside, external	8
phón	พ้น	beyond, past, free of	8
khâaŋ lǎŋ	ข้างหลัง	behind	7
taam lǎŋ	ตามหลัง	along, after, following	6
tìt	ติด	next to	6
thálú	ทะลุ	across	5
troŋ khâam	ตรงข้าม	opposite, on the other side of	4
lɔ̂ɔt	ลอด	through, via	4
thǎɛw thǎɛw	แถว ๆ	near (location)	4
khâaŋ nâa	ข้างหน้า	in front of	3
khaâŋ nɔ̂ɔk	ข้างนอก	outside	3
khâaŋ nay	ข้างใน	in	3
hàaŋ klay càak	ห่างไกลจาก	far from	3
khâaŋ bon	ข้างบน	on	2
khâaŋ tây	ข้างใต้	under	1
phaay nay khɔ̌ɔŋ	ภายในของ	inside of	1
khâaŋ lâaŋ	ข้างล่าง	underneath, downstairs	1
lâaŋ	ล่าง	under	1
phàan thaaŋ	ผ่านทาง	via	1
sáay	ซ้าย	left to	0
klây kàp	ใกล้กับ	close to, near to	0

Very Low
(~9 pmw)
(n=30)

thɯ̆ŋ khɛ̂ɛ	ถึงแค่	only to the point of	0
lǝǝy	เลย	past, over	0
khwǎa	ขวา	right to	0
tìt kàp	ติดกับ	next to	0
yɔ́ɔn	ย้อน	against	0
ʔɔ́ɔm ʔɔ́ɔm	อ้อม ๆ	around, half-circling	0
thaaŋ sáay mɯɯ	ทางซ้ายมือ	on the left-hand side	0
ʔɔ́ɔm	อ้อม	around	0
phaay nɔ̂ɔk khɔ̌ɔŋ	ภายนอกของ	outside of	0

Table 8.6 Frequency of Thai spatial prepositions

The frequency information in Table 8.6 shows that the highest frequency prepositions are *nay* (ใน) 'in' and *khɔ̌ɔŋ* (ของ) 'of', occurring at a frequency higher than 15,000 pmw. There is a big frequency gap between these and the one following, i.e., *kàp* (กับ) 'with', the frequency of which is only a third of the first two.

Another interesting aspect is that considering that about a half of all prepositions are spatial prepositions, the fact that there are ten spatial prepositions out of 12 prepositions in the High frequency range is quite noteworthy. In other words, we can say that nearly all High frequency prepositions in Thai are spatial markers.

Still another point with respect to frequency distribution is that there are a large number of prepositions in the Very Low frequency range, a pattern already observed from all prepositions (see Table 8.4 above). In fact, as many as 11 spatial prepositions record 0 pmw, which means that they are attested fewer than 16 times in the entire corpus. Unlike these nearly non-existing prepositions, there are many prepositions that belong to the Medium frequency range, which may be regarded as relatively stable. Generally speaking, however, well over half the spatial prepositions are only weakly represented, i.e., they belong to the Low and Very Low frequency ranges.

8.3.3 Grammaticalization Sources

8.3.3.1 Nominal Sources

Thai uses diverse nouns to encode prepositional meanings, and such prepositions are called the N-prepositions (Heine et al. 1991a: 144, Intratat 1996, Prasithrathsint 2010a,b; cf. the verb-based V-prepositions, see below). Since those nouns still bear nominal characteristics, the prepositions developed from nouns have been the subject of controversy as to their grammatical status, as has often been the case for the prepositional category in general. For instance, some scholars (Starosta 1985, 1988, 2000, Savetamalya 1989, Indrambarya 1995) regard them 'relator nouns' (a term coined by L. Thompson 1965: 200-202), whereas others (Panupong 1989, Prasithrathsint 2010a,b, Loss 2017, Rutherford and Thanyawong 2019) regard them as prepositions. In fact, this type of nouns, those that bear the nominal and adpositional characteristics, is widely attested across many languages and have been labeled in various ways. For example, in addition to 'relator nouns' (Starosta 1988, 2000, Savetamalya 1989, Indrambarya 1995), 'locative nouns' (Sinha et al. 1994, Clark and Prasithrathsint 1985), 'relational nouns' (Wiennold 1995), and 'region nouns' (Zlatev 2003) have been used to label the category.

Prasithrathsint (2010b) lists 14 prepositions derived from nouns, as shown in (12):

(12)   *naa* ('face'), *lang* ('back'), *nook* ('outer part'), *nay* ('inner part'), *bon* ('upper part'), *nua* ('north'), *taay* ('south'), *klang* ('middle'), *rim* ('edge'), *thii* ('place'), *khaang* ('side'), *daan* ('side'), *thaang* ('way'), *khoong* ('thing')

Prasithrathsint (2010b), further notes from a diachronic study that *bon* (บน) 'upper part' was used as an independent noun during the Sukhothai period (13th~14th century) but it is no longer used as such in Modern Thai. The disappearance of old nominal function is also observed with *nay* (ใน) 'inside' and *nɔ̀ɔk* (นอก) 'outside'.[9]

---

[9] Prasithrathsint (2010b), in her corpus-based study, notes that there is one occurrence of the nominal

A more fine-grained analysis reveals that even within the same paradigm of prepositions, the properties of the members can have variable degrees of fit for the category. For instance, Kölver (1984), in her research on Thai local prepositions, shows that the N-prepositions have various degrees of multifunctionality in terms of various degrees of 'nominality' (p. 5). Thus, she asserts that word classes must be conceived of in terms of prototypical manifestations (cf. 'focal instances') with a graded phenomenon, which will help understand the gradual interconnection of categories in isolating languages. Thus, the forms with a high degree of multifunctionality have a high degree of syntactic versatility. In this perspective the grammaticalization of nouns into prepositions can be seen as a process of decreasing nominality and increasing relationality which brings forth 'intrinsic' prepositions (Kullavanijaya 1974: 73). The highest level of nominality (consequently the lowest level of relationality and prepositionhood) is displayed by the body-part nouns *nâa* (หน้า) 'face' and *lǎŋ* (หลัง) 'back'. A slightly lower degree of nominality is displayed by the relational nouns *klaaŋ* (กลาง) 'middle' and *khâaŋ* (ข้าง) 'side'. Further down the continuum is *thîi* 'place' and the lowest group has *tây* (ใต้) 'south', *bon* (บน) 'top', and *nay* (ใน) 'inside'.

A more comprehensive list of N-prepositions is compiled by Park and Rhee (2018), as shown in Table 8.7.

	N-Preposition		Nominal Meaning	Prepositional Meaning
a.	*khâaŋ*	ข้าง	side	beside, next to
b.	*thǎæw*	แถว	line	near
c.	*khɔ̌ɔŋ*	ของ	thing, property	of
d.	*hæ̀æŋ*	แห่ง	place	of
e.	*rɔ̂ɔp*	รอบ	round, circle	around
f.	*thaaŋ*	ทาง	way	side of
g.	*nâa*	หน้า	face	in front of
h.	*lǎŋ*	หลัง	back (body-part)	behind
i.	*nay*	ใน	inside	in(side of)

---

usage of *nɔ̀ɔk* (นอก), i.e., *pay nɔ̀ɔk* (ไปนอก) 'go abroad'.

j.	nɔ̀ɔk	นอก	outside	out(side of)
k.	ráwaàŋ	ระหว่าง	gap	between
l.	thîi	ที่	land, place	at
m.	nɯ̌ɯa	เหนือ	top	on (top of)
n.	tâj	ใต้	bottom	below, under
o.	bon	บน	top	on (top of)
p.	lâaŋ	ล่าง	bottom	under
q.	klaaŋ	กลาง	middle	in the middle of
r.	sáaj	ซ้าย	left	left to
s.	khwǎa	ขวา	right	right to
t.	chên	เช่น	kind, type	like
u.	troŋ	ตรง	straightness	(right) at

Table 8.7 Primary N-prepositions in Modern Thai (Park and Rhee 2018: 76-77)

As shown in Table 8.7, nouns serve as an important source category for the development of prepositions in Thai. It is evident that the semantics of the source nouns involves relationality, an expected state of affairs from a crosslinguistic perspective. Furthermore, the relationship between the nominal meaning and the prepositional meaning is generally straightforward.

One interesting set of items is the superiority and inferiority markers *nɯ̌ɯa* (เหนือ) 'top' and *tâj* (ใต้). According to Park and Rhee (2018), *nɯ̌ɯa* (เหนือ) 'top' also marks the cardinal direction 'north' and *tâj* (ใต้) 'bottom', 'south'. Since inscriptions dating back to the Sukhothai period (13th~14th century) use the expression *bɯ̂aŋ tiin nɔɔn* (เบื้องตีนนอน) (lit. 'the direction in which one places the feet when sleeping') to denote 'north' in contrast with *bɯ̂aŋ hǔa nɔɔn* (เบื้องหัวนอน) (lit. 'the direction in which one places the head when sleeping'), the top-north and bottom-south associations are thought to be a recent innovation. According to Brown (1983: 135ff), crosslinguistically 'north' and 'south' are nomenclaturally associated predominantly with 'up' and 'down', respectively, and he speculates that it reflects diffusion of a Western prejudice, i.e., the ubiquitous aligning of north with the top of maps.

8.3.3.2 Verbal Sources

Prepositions that develop from verbs are called V-prepositions (cf. noun-based N-prepositions, see 8.3.3.1 above). The grammatical class of verbs constitutes another major source category for grammaticalization of Thai prepositions (Intratat 1996). For instance, Diller (1994), discussing the three major grammaticalization paths of verbs, notes that verbs tend to develop into prepositions, conjunctions, and auxiliaries. Diller (2008) further states that verbs frequently develop into auxiliaries and prepositions and that the distinction between the source function and the target function is very difficult. Needless to say, the difficulty is due to the gradual nature of grammaticalization.

Due to the gradual and gradient nature of grammaticalization processes, verbs developing into prepositions tend to retain the verbal characteristics to a variable degree. Thus, Clark (1975) and Li and Thompson (1981) recognize the simultaneous verb-like and functor-like status of certain (generally preposition-like) semantically and grammatically non-main serialized verbs, employing a unique category-label "coverbs" to refer to these (Post 2007).[10] The quandary also leads Matisoff (1969, 1991a) to coining the term "verposition" to refer to essentially the same thing (as cited in Post 2007: 160). These terms help avoid the controversy that might arise if either the source category label or the target category label is used, but also help recognize as the form being in the borderland, e.g., neither a full-fledged verb nor a full-fledged preposition. Thus, Post (2007: 121) states that "analysis of *paj* as a pure functor ... (a Preposition) without reference to verblike properties seems to evade the overall *distributional* fact..." (emphasis original). In a similar line of research, Enfield (2006) analyzes the grammaticalization of Lao verbs, which, according to Diller (2008), is directly applicable to Thai as well, as shown by the paths: [verb 〉 auxiliary] and [verb 〉 coverb 〉 preposition] (e.g., *caak* v. 'leave' 〉 'from'). In other words, full verbs develop into coverbs marking semantic case for following nominals, and undergoing further entrenchment, the verbs acquire the prepositional status through losing verbal

---

[10] According to Indrambarya (1995), Kullavanijaya (1974) and Clark (1975) analyze Thai V-prepositions as coverbs, too.

characteristics.

Similarly, Indrambarya (1992), in her study of the verb *hây* (ให้) 'give', shows the multiple functions of *hây* (ให้) as the following:

(13) a. ปุ๊ก ซื้อ ขนม ให้ แดง

    puk   *su*   *khanom*   ***hây***   *deeng*

    [name]   buy   sweets   **give**   [name]

    (i) 'Puk bought sweets for Dang.'

    (ii) 'Puk bought sweets and gave (them) to Dang.'

  b. แดง ยิ้ม ให้ ฉัน

    deeng   *yim*   ***hây***   *chan*

    [name]   smile   **give**   I

    'Dang smiled at me.'   (modified from Indrambarya 1992: 1163)

Example (13a) has two readings in which the word *hây* can be interpreted either as 'for' or 'to give'; and (13b) has only one goal meaning 'to'. According to Indrambarya (1992), *hây* (ให้) with the benefactive interpretation (13a) has been analyzed either as a preposition (Kullavanijaya 1974, Dejthamrong 1970) or as a verb (Thepkanjana 1986), whereas the goal meaning *hây* (ให้) in (13b) is interpreted as a preposition due to its occurrence position (Dejthamrong 1970). However, by employing different sets of tests, Indrambarya concludes that *hây* (ให้) in (13a-i) and (13b) does not display characteristics of a verb or a preposition. Due to her perspective toward grammatical categories, in her later study, Indrambarya (1995) states that Thai does have prepositions but the number is small.

As noted in 8.2, a more lenient view of grammatical categories, such as 'emergent grammar' (Hopper 1987) or 'intercategorial fluidity' (S Rhee 2016[1998]), allows researchers to see grammatical forms in a more dynamic frame. Intratat (1996), Iwasaki and Yap (1998), Chamniyom (2003), Iwasaki (2004), Jaratjarungkiat (2019), among many others, study verbs that have acquired prepositional functions in contemporary Thai, and consider them V-prepositions. A noteworthy diachronic study is Chamniyom (2003), in which the usages of 23 pairs of verbs are traced from the Sukhothai (13th~14th century) to Rattanakosin (18th~20th century) periods, whereby the individual grammaticalization processes of V-prepositions are identified.

A noteworthy analysis of V-preposition is Kölver (1984), in which the development of Thai V-prepositions from serial verb constructions is addressed. She notes the importance of the semantics of the source verb and cooccurring forms, which contributes to the participating serial verb's acquisition of directional prepositional meaning. For instance, the goal and source meanings are implied in the verbs *maa* (มา) 'come', *khâw* (เข้า) 'enter', and *càak* (จาก) 'leave, depart' and thus they do not have to be explicit on the surface. Typically the goal meaning is more strongly implied than the source meaning, but other relations need to be explicitly specified by the meaning of prepositions, serial verb constructions, or the combination of the two. Similarly, static prepositions without a dynamic meaning acquire a directional meaning from the cooccurring verbs (e.g., 'in the house' ⟩ 'go into the house'). This shows well that the acquisition of grammaticalized meaning involves active interaction among the neighboring forms in syntagma.

In a synchronic study, Park and Rhee (2018) list 25 V-prepositions in Thai, as shown in Table 8.8.

	V-Preposition		Verbal Meaning	Prepositional Meaning
a.	*tɔ̀ɔ*	ต่อ	link	at, for each
b.	*yók weén*	ยกเว้น	exclude	except
c.	*hây*	ให้	give	to, for
d.	*sǎm ràp*	สำหรับ	befit	for
e.	*thâw*	เท่า	be equal	as (much as)
f.	*taam*	ตาม	follow	following, according to
g.	*ʔaw*	เอา	acquire	with
h.	*càak*	จาก	leave	from
i.	*thǔŋ*	ถึง	arrive	to, about
j.	*pen*	เป็น	be	into, as
k.	*sùu*	สู่	go toward	toward
l.	*kâw*	เข้า	enter	into
m.	*ʔɔ̀ɔk*	ออก	exit	out of
n.	*khûn*	ขึ้น	ascend	toward (upward)

o.	*loŋ*	ลง	descend	toward (downward)
p.	*khâam*	ข้าม	cross	opposite to
q.	*phàan*	ผ่าน	pass	through
r.	*tálú*	ทะลุ	go through	across
s.	*kəən*	เกิน	go over	over
t.	*con*	จน	reach	to, up to
u.	*kɯàa*	กว่า	pass, exceed	than
v.	*tâŋ*	ตั้ง	stop	as much as
w.	*yaŋ*	ยัง	maintain	to
x.	*ráy*	ไร้	not exist	without
y.	*praasàcàak*	ปราศจาก	not exist	without

Table 8.8. Primary V-prepositions in Thai (Park and Rhee 2018: 77-78)

8.3.3.3 Other Sources

In addition to the common lexical categories, i.e., verbs and nouns, there are other source categories for Thai prepositions, such as adjectives and adverbs. Since adjectives and adverbs are commonly regarded as constituting open classes, thus potentially, primary lexical categories, development of grammatical forms such as prepositions from these categories is in line with the tenets of grammaticalization. However, Heine and Kuteva (2007: 111) show the layering of word classes in the development of grammar, in which noun is the primary category placed at Layer 1, verb is at Layer 2, and adjective and adverb are at Layer 3, and further hypothesize that adjectives develop from adverbs and adverbs develop from nouns and verb. Furthermore, Heine et al. (1993) list a large number of adverbs as grammaticalized target items. From these perspectives, adverbs (and potentially adjectives as well) may not be the ultimate sources of Thai prepositions but may have deeper origins in noun or adverbs.

Admitting the inconclusiveness in the face of lack of historical evidence, we can see the list of Thai prepositions that developed from adjectives and adverbs, as in Table 8.9.

	Preposition		Adjectival Meaning	Prepositional Meaning
a.	*klây*	ใกล้	near	near, close to
b.	*mǔuan*	เหมือน	same	like
c.	*khláay*	คล้าย	similar	like, similar to

	Preposition		Adverbial Meaning	Prepositional Meaning
a.	*dûay*	ด้วย	also	with
b.	*kɔ̀ɔn*	ก่อน	previously	before
c.	*chàphɔ́ʔ*	เฉพาะ	specifically	only
d.	*khɛ̂ɛ*	แค่	specifically	only

Table 8.9 Thai Prepositions from adjectives and adverbs (Park and Rhee 2018: 78)

8.3.3.4 Multiple Sources and Layered Prepositions

As is the case in other languages described in the preceding chapters, Thai prepositions also show no isomorphism between form and function. We have already seen in 8.2 that there are multiple forms that represent the same prepositional concept. For instance, there are multiple Similatives, e.g., *mǔan* (เหมือน), *khláay* (คล้าย), *thâw* (เท่า), *chêen* (เช่น), and *chǎn* (ฉัน). Multiplicity of form for the same function is also observed with spatial prepositions. The existence of multiple directional markers well illustrates the point, as in (14):

(14) a. *hây* (ให้)   v. 'give'   〉〉 *hây*   prep. 'to, for'

      b. *thǔŋ* (ถึง)   v. 'arrive'   〉〉 *thǔŋ*   prep. 'to'

      c. *sùu* (สู่)   v. 'go toward'   〉〉 *sùu*   prep. 'to, toward'

      d. *con* (จน)   v. 'reach'   〉〉 *con*   prep. 'to'

      e. *yaŋ* (ยัง)   v. 'result in, cause' 〉〉 *yaŋ*   prep. 'to, toward'

      f. *pay yaŋ* (ไปยัง) v. 'go-result in'   〉〉 *pay yaŋ* prep. 'to, toward'

As shown in (14), the directional markers develop from diverse verbs, which mostly contain the semantic features of movement and/or transfer. The motivation operating behind the development of directionality meaning from these semantic features is intuitively straightforward. The one less straightforward is (14e) *yaŋ* (ยัง)

'result in, cause, create' (Kultida Khammee, p.c.). It seems that the clue lies in (14f) *pay yaŋ* (ไปยัง) 'go-result in', which denotes a movement that culminates at the arrival of the target. This meaning seems to be responsible for the 'toward-ness' meaning. In other words, the 'go result in x' meaning is subjectively shifted to 'go to' and further to a more general 'to' meaning. However, the 'culmination' meaning linger in *pay yaŋ* (ไปยัง).[11] Similarly, (14a) *hây* (ให้) 'give; to', implying the transfer of an object, can mark not only the direction but also benefaction of the recipient. All these show that grammaticalization of a particular function may occur to multiple sources but that individual forms may still retain source characteristics (cf. 'persistence', Hopper 1991).

8.4 Ongoing grammaticalization of Spatial Prepositions

8.4.1 Selection Criteria

As we have noted in 8.3.2, Thai has a dozen spatial prepositions that are well entrenched in the prepositional system and also a large number of spatial prepositions belong to the Medium frequency range, the level thought to be relatively stable. In this section we will address ongoing grammaticalization in the Thai prepositional system.

In order to investigate ongoing grammaticalization among spatial prepositions in Thai, we will first select the prepositions that are thought to be currently undergoing grammaticalization. From the entire inventory of 181 prepositions, i.e., 101 primary, 71 composite, and 9 complex prepositions, we select those that satisfy all of the following conditions, which have been used in other languages as well.

---

[11] As shown in Table 8.8 above, Park and Rhee (2018) list the lexical source of *yaŋ* (ยัง) as the verb that denotes 'maintain'. A similar reasoning is also possible with this interpretation, i.e., 'go-maintain' giving rise to the goal marking with the implication of undisturbed directional movement.

(15) (i) It is not in the primary prepositional category in contemporary Thai (80 items);

    (ii) It encodes spatial relationship (36 of them);

    (iii) It is attested more than 10 times pmw (16 of them).

Condition (i) is to ensure that the target preposition is not yet established as a fully grammaticalized preposition. Condition (ii) is to restrict the target items within our research focus, i.e., spatial preposition. Condition (iii) is to ensure that the item is a viable one, not a chance occurrence attributable to idiolectic styles or that the form is not at a very incipient stage where the form's viability is yet uncertain. The frequency of 10 pmw coincides with the cut-off point for Low frequency range in Table 8.4 above, the actual frequency of which in the corpus is 333 tokens. The 16 target forms, supposedly actively undergoing grammaticalization, are listed in Table 8.10.

Frequency Range	Spatial Preposition		Meaning	PMW
	kìaw kàp	เกี่ยวกับ	about, on	720
	phaay nay	ภายใน	within, internal	434
Medium	*hây kàp*	ให้กับ	with	244
(100~999 pmw)	*pay yaŋ*	ไปยัง	to	234
(n=7)	*phaay tây*	ภายใต้	under, inferior position	160
	ʔɔ̀ɔk càak	ออกจาก	out of	146
	rûam kàp	ร่วมกับ	together with, along with	103
	phrɔ́ɔm kàp	พร้อมกับ	with, together with	77
	lǎŋ càak	หลังจาก	behind	51
	phrɔ́ɔm dûay	พร้อมด้วย	with, together with	40
Low	*tɔ̀ɔ nâa*	ต่อหน้า	in front of	32
(10~99 pmw)	*hàaŋ càak*	ห่างจาก	far from	31
(n=9)	*rɔ̂ɔp rɔ̂ɔp*	รอบ ๆ	around, round	25
	dooy phàan	โดยผ่าน	across, via, through	16
	khâaŋ khâaŋ	ข้าง ๆ	next to, beside (location)	16
	klây klây	ใกล้ ๆ	near (location)	13

Table 8.10 Prepositions undergoing grammaticalization in Modern Thai

8.4.2 General Characteristics

The 16 prepositions that are supposed to be actively undergoing grammaticalization in Modern Thai, i.e., those that are not yet fully settled as a primary preposition nor have acquired enough functional strength to ensure viability, present a few interesting aspects of grammaticalization.

First of all, there are no complex prepositions in the group, largely because they have not attained the frequency high enough to make them stable in the system. Furthermore, the functional domains in which the grammaticalizing prepositions are located are not evenly distributed but are rather restricted. For instance, as many as eight of them (i.e., one half of the total of 16 prepositions) are markers of association (note that we already observed that this is the most crowded conceptual domain). The other remaining half are distributed in directional, separation, opposite, interior, exterior, inferior, anterior, and posterior, one in each domain. In the following, we will discuss some grammaticalizing prepositions, i.e., Proximatives, Distantives, and Comitatives, in view of their competitors.

[Proximatives]
There are five Proximatives among Thai prepositions. Their situation in grammaticalization seems to be relatively straightforward, as their functional strengths show with use frequency in the following list, in which the grammaticalizing form is highlighted in bold:

(16) Proximatives

a.	*klây*	'near'	185
b.	*khâaŋ*	'by, near'	172
c.	*rim*	'near, beside'	109
d.	**klây klây**	**'near (location)'**	13
e.	*klây kàp*	'close to, near to'	0

As shown in (16), the grammaticalizing *klây klây* (ใกล้ ๆ) has three more frequent competitors (16a-c) and one under it. The overall picture plainly shows that primary prepositions have functional primacy over the structurally more complex composite prepositions. As noted earlier, the reduplicative *klây klây* (ใกล้ ๆ) (16d) is emphatic as compared to the plain *klây* (ใกล้) (16a), and the relatively lower frequency of the phonetically heavy and semantically loaded form is an expected state of affairs. It is not clear, however, why *klây kàp* (ใกล้กับ) (lit. 'close with') (16e) is not as successful as *klây klây* (ใกล้ ๆ), which is of a similar level of phonetic complexity (see below for more discussion).

Furthermore, an addition to the puzzle is that creating a composite preposition with the primary preposition *kàp* (กับ) 'with' is a very productive means in grammaticalization of Thai prepositions, e.g., four out of 16 grammaticalizing prepositions follow that pattern. To expand the question, there is no definitive answer why not all primary forms also gave rise to the forms involving *kàp* (กับ) 'with'. Therefore, in the absence of further evidence otherwise, it can be said that there are many robust tendencies in grammaticalization but none is determinative because grammaticalizing forms are placed among a myriad of interacting factors.

[Distantives]

A similar situation is presented by the layered Distantives. There are three competing forms, as shown in (17):

(17) Distantives

a.	*hàaŋ càak*	'far from'	31
b.	*klay*	'far'	17
c.	*hàaŋ klay càak*	'far from'	3

The grammaticalizing composite preposition *hàaŋ càak* (lit. 'far from') (17a) has two other competing forms marking distance. A puzzle is that the phonetically heavier *hàaŋ càak* (หางจาก) exceeds its simpler counterpart *klay* (ไกล) (17b) and its more complex counterpart *hàaŋ klay càak* (ห่างไกลจาก) (lit. 'far far from') (17c). The relative primacy over *hàaŋ klay càak* (ห่างไกลจาก) follows expectation, since the latter is phonetically heavier, structurally more complex, and semantically marked (note that it contains two lexemes denoting 'far').

It is not immediately clear, however, how it acquired primacy over its simpler counterpart, the primary preposition *klay* (ไกล) 'far from'. It seems that differential specialization is at play. The primary preposition *càak* (จาก) 'from' is among the most frequently used preposition, ranking 4th with 4,938 tokens pmw. The basic meaning of 'from' is twofold, one is the source and the other is the separation (see S Rhee 2012b). Distantive inherently involves separation from a referenced entity and thus the notion may be weakly marked by Ablative or emphatically marked by those specializing in distance marking. Thus, in terms of conceptual motivation, the combination of 'far' and 'from' (as *hàaŋ càak* (ห่างจาก)) seems to be the optimal way of encoding Distantive. The preposition *klay* (ไกล) (17b) occurs far more frequently than *hàaŋ càak* (ห่างจาก) in the corpus (i.e., 7,146 raw tokens vs. 1,036 raw tokens), but its specialization is on the adverbial use denoting 'far' (70.5% of the time) whereas its prepositional use accounts for only 2.9% of the time (its verbal and adjectival uses account for 16.2% and 10.5%, respectively). This suggests that linguistic forms have differential specialization across multiple linguistic domains. However, specialization is merely a characterization of states of affairs describing 'how' but it does not provide any answer to 'why'. The question of why it is as it is and what processes are involved to bring about such differential specialization requires more fine-grained diachronic research.

[Comitatives]
Comitatives in Thai constitute a truly extraordinary category with an exceptionally large number of member prepositions. Even excluding peripheral members, there are as many as ten prepositions, as shown in (18):

(18) Comitatives

a.	*kàp*	'with'	4,978
b.	*dûay*	'with'	2,649
c.	*dooy*	'by, via, with'	1,066
d.	**hây kàp**	**'with'**	244
e.	*ʔaw*	'with'	179
f.	*phrɔ́ɔm*	'with, together with'	121

g.	*rûam kàp*	'with, together with'	103
h.	*phrɔ́ɔm kàp*	'with'	77
i.	*phrɔ́ɔm dûay*	'with, together with'	40
j.	*kà*	'with'	27

With many members in the conceptual space, the grammaticalization scenarios of these Comitatives present one of the most enigmatic problems. It is beyond our capability to describe all the details about the complexities, but there are a few aspects potentially relevant to differential degrees of grammaticalization.

First of all, a look at the formal composition of the Comitatives reveals that there are multiple forms involving identical lexemes, e.g., the primary preposition *kàp* (กับ) 'with' occurs in four of them (18a,d,g,h); the primary preposition *phrɔ́ɔm* (พร้อม) 'with' occurs in three of them (18f,h,i); and the primary preposition *dûay* (ด้วย) 'with' occurs in two of them (18b,i). In these cases, the primary preposition exceeds its more complex counterparts, which is an expected state of affairs in view of the correlation among formal complexity, use frequency, and degrees of grammaticalization. With one notable exception (18j), primary prepositions occur with higher frequency, and composite prepositions occur at a considerably lower frequency as compared to the primary prepositions, with two exceptions (18e,j) (note the gap between (18c) and (18d)). These findings are generally in consonance with crosslinguistic patterns.

Another issue relates to part-of-speech specialization. The primary preposition *phrɔ́ɔm* (พร้อม) 'with' is already of low frequency and, further, it specializes in conjunction (72.5% of the time). The relatively weakly grammaticalized composite prepositions *phrɔ́ɔm kàp* (พร้อมกับ) 'with' and *phrɔ́ɔm dûay* (พร้อมด้วย) 'with', as it seems, may be due to the weak level of representative prepositional strength of their core element *phrɔ́ɔm* (พร้อม). The primary prepositions *kàp* (กับ) 'with' and *dûay* (ด้วย) 'with' are among the prepositions of high frequency, but in composite prepositions *phrɔ́ɔm kàp* (พร้อมกับ) 'with' and *phrɔ́ɔm dûay* (พร้อมด้วย) 'with', the core element in their composition is not *kàp* (กับ) or *dûay* (ด้วย), but *phrɔ́ɔm* (พร้อม).

Similarly, the composite preposition *rûam kàp* (ร่วมกับ) 'with' (18g), built on the verb *rûam* (ร่วม) 'join', probably added to reinforce the conjoining meaning of

Comitative, specializes in verbal use (92.63% of the time). Thus, it can be said that the verbal expression 'join with' is currently grammaticalizing into 'with' or 'together with'. The primary preposition *ʔaw* (เอา) 'with', originating from the verb *ʔaw* (เอา) 'take', shows a higher representational strength than most composite forms, rivaling with a slightly stronger competitor *hây kàp* (ให้กับ) (18d). Interestingly enough, *ʔaw* (เอา) 'with' (18e) does not show any specialization in terms of parts of speech, i.e., it occurs as a preposition (23.4% of the time), a verb (22.6%), an adverb (26.6%), and a conjunction (27.4%), an even distributional pattern across multiple word classes. The primary preposition *kà* (กะ) 'with' (18j), an outlier as a primary preposition, is the weakest member among Comitatives. It is used as a verb denoting 'expect, estimate, measure, etc.' about half the time (48%). The lexeme *kà* (กะ) is also used as a noun to denote 'a shift' and 'a master (of a boat)', etc., but the conceptual motivation for the development from either the verbal or nominal use is not clear and should await further studies.

All these points strongly suggest that unlike inflecting or agglutinating languages, isolating languages like Thai present a problem as they do not clearly show the patterns observed in other languages. In this regard, we are advised by Bisang (1996) for a better understanding of grammaticalization scenarios in isolating languages, who notes that the coevolution of sound and meaning often observed in grammaticalization in languages of other types is not prominent in isolating languages. Another adverse aspect is that historical data that allows tracing the history of words diachronically is relatively limited. A more detailed analysis of grammaticalization scenarios of individual Thai lexemes should await more comprehensive research from Thai historical data and insights from neighboring languages.

8.4.3 Grammaticalization Mechanisms

8.4.3.1 Extension

Extension or increase in use context is a commonly attested language change in grammaticalization. Since grammaticalization involves change in the grammatical status from a major category to a minor category by losing the properties of the major category (i.e., decategorialization), the usage context is bound to increase for the relaxed constraints of the primary category. This is well illustrated in a study by K Takahashi (2012), who studies the multifunctional *hây* diachronically. In contemporary Thai, *hây* can be used as a verb, preposition, complementizer, etc. The function under our immediate interest is preposition for marking benefactive as in (19):

(19) เขา ทำ อาหาร ให้ แม่

     kháw   *tham*   *ʔahǎn*   **_hây_**   *mɛ*

    PRON   make   dishes   **BEN**   mother

    'He cooked for his mother.'   (modified from K Takahashi 2012: 128)

Her corpus-based study elegantly shows that the benefactive prepositional function only occurred in the Rattanakosin King Rama 7-9 periods (1925-1978). In the course of grammaticalization the lexeme gradually changed its usage context from the verb of change of location and change of state (from 1292 to 1925) to the purposive marker (1925-1978). Even though it is still weak as a preposition, accounting for 0.08% only in our corpus, extension of the occurrence context and its consequent grammaticalization is notable. Further discussion is to follow in 8.4.4 below.

8.4.3.2 Desemanticization

Desemanticization or loss of lexical meaning is prominent in the grammaticalization of prepositions in Thai. Prasithrathsint (2010b), for instance, analyzes the grammaticalization processes of Thai prepositions such as *lǎŋ* (หลัง) 'back; behind; after', *nɔ̀ɔk* (นอก) 'the outer part; outside', *nay* (ใน) 'the inner part; in', *bon* (บน) 'the upper part; on', etc., and states that the change from a noun to preposition occurred through certain mechanisms, e.g., reanalysis, semantic bleaching, semantic generalization, and metaphor. Of these, reanalysis is a mechanism on morphosyntax but all others relate to semantics, especially, the loss in meaning. Metaphor is often thought to be increase in meaning content, as it involves the addition of new meaning, e.g., from spatial 'in' to temporal 'in' (both encoded by the N-preposition *nay* (ใน)). However, from another perspective, metaphorization is simply another means of semantic generalization in that metaphorical extension lifts a form's usage domain restriction (e.g., spatial) and allows it to be used in another domain (e.g., temporal). For this reason, S Rhee (1996) states that semantic enrichment via metaphorization is simply another face of semantic generalization.

We also noted Kölver's (1984) study in 8.3.3.1 who invoked the notion of 'nominality' in analyzing Thai prepositions. The study elegantly captures the fact that the prepositions displaying a high degree of nominality, e.g., *nâa* (หน้า) 'face' and *lăŋ* (หลัง) 'back', also display high degree of multifunctionality and a high degree of syntactic versatility, whereas those displaying the lowest level of nominality, e.g., *tây* (ใต้) 'south', *bon* (บน) 'top', and *nay* (ใน) 'inside', have the highest degree of relationality, the lowest level of multifunctionality, and the lowest degree of syntactic versatility. In the context of the current discussion, the prepositions in the lowest degree of nominality can be said to have undergone the greatest level of desemanticization of their purely nominal properties.

8.4.3.3 Decategorialization

Since decategorialization is closely tied to extension in morphosyntax and desemanticization in meaning, decategorialization is also commonly observed in the grammaticalization scenarios of Thai prepositions. In 8.3.3.1, we noted Prasithrathsint's (2010b) study on N-prepositions. In her diachronic study, as noted earlier, she observes that *bon* (บน) 'upper part' was used as an independent noun during the Sukhothai period but it is no longer used as such in Modern Thai. The disappearance of old nominal function is also observed with *nay* (ใน) 'inside' and *nɔ̀ɔk* (นอก) 'outside'. In terms of decategorialization, the disappearance or near-disappearance of these exponents' earlier lexical category features, i.e., the nominal properties, is the extreme case of decategorialization.

8.4.3.4 Erosion

Erosion or phonological attrition is a common concomitant of grammaticalization.

However, as noted earlier, reductive phonological change is often minimal in isolating languages (Bisang 1996). Therefore, phonological reduction is not prominent in the grammaticalization scenarios in Thai. The absence of formal contrast, e.g., full vs. reduced form as in *one* vs. *a*, and *that* vs. *the* in English, is among the contributing factors to the controversy of grammatical status of grammaticalizing and grammaticalized exponents. This characteristic is also observed in Chinese (see Ch. 7).

8.4.4 Grammatical Functions

Thai prepositions are polyfunctional between their traditional source category, i.e., largely nouns and verbs, and their innovative category, i.e., preposition. When the journey of a word involves multiple categories, the polyfunctionality may also involve the intermediate category functions. This is particularly prominent phenomenon with the isolating languages. For instance, the body-part noun *nâa* (หน้า) can function across multiple grammatical categories, e.g., as a noun, adjective, preposition, and pronoun, as shown in (20) and exemplified in part in (21) (from Kultida Khammee, p.c.; note that in (21d) *mây lûak nâa* (ไม่เลือกหน้า) [not choose anyone] is an idiom 'not selectively; indiscriminately'):

(20) *nâa* (หน้า)

    a. noun: 'face', 'page', 'topping', 'cheek', 'future', 'phase'

    b. adjective: 'front', 'next', 'anterior', 'following'

    c. preposition: 'in front of', 'next to'

    d. pronoun: 'anybody', 'somebody'

(21)   a. noun 'face'

        หน้า ของ หล่อน ซีด

        <u>*nâa*</u>   *khɔ̌ɔŋ*   *lɔ̀n* *sîit*

        face   of   her pale

        'Her face is pale.'

b. adjective: 'next'

ภาค การศึกษา หน้า เริ่ม เดือน สิงหาคม

phâak   *kaansʉ̀ksǎa*   **nâa**   *râəm dʉan*   *sǐŋhǎakhom*

sector   study   **next**   start   month   August

'Next semester begins in August.'

c. preposition 'in front of; before'

แม่น้ำ อยู่ หน้า ภูเขา

mɛ̂ɛnám   *yùu*   **nâa**   *phuukhǎw*

river   exist   **before**   mountain

'There is a river in front of the mountain.'

d. pronoun 'anybody/somebody'

เขา ค้น กระเป๋า ทุกคน ไม่ เลือก หน้า

khǎw khón   *kràpǎw thúkkhon*   *mây lûak*   **nâa**

he   search   pocket everyone   not   choose   **anybody**

'He searched everyone's pockets.'

Even though the semantic designations are given in a simplified form as in the list (20) above, the list masks a wide variety of related meanings. For instance, Ukosakul (2003) discusses the conceptual metaphors involving *nâa* (หน้า) 'face', with the meanings related to countenance, ego, self-identity, dignity, pride, honor, emotions, etc. (see also Ukosakul 1999, Komin 1990, Sanit 1975 for analysis of *nâa* (หน้า) 'face').

Even after a form is grammaticalized, typically into a spatial preposition, it tends to extend its function to temporal preposition, via metaphorization which is a very strong cognitive mechanism in language use, as we have noted repeatedly (cf. Heine et al. 1991a). In this respect, Kullavanijaya's (2003) research on Thai time markers is noteworthy. In her diachronic research, she investigates the temporal markers from the Sukhothai period up to the present and finds a pattern that temporal markers in the non-monosyllabic group increase. In other words, more and more periphrastic forms are recruited to mark time. She identifies a few patterns of the development of temporal markers, as shown in (22):

(22) a. From noun phrases :

  bat nii   ⟨ *bat* 'breath' *nii* 'this'

  mua koon ⟨ *mua* 'point of time' *koon* 'preceding period'

  phaay lang ⟨ *phaay* 'side' lang 'back'

  phaay naa ⟨ *phaay* 'side' *naa* 'front'

  lang lang ⟨ *toon lang lang* ⟨ *toon lang* ⟨ *toon* 'portion' *lang* 'back'

 b. From prepositional phrases

  tee koon ⟨ *tee* 'from' *koon* 'preceding period'

  tee koon nii ⟨ *tee* 'from' *koon* 'preceding period' *nii* 'this'

 c. Spatial noun - locative prep - demonstrative pronoun *nii/nan*

  lang caak nan [back from that] 'afterwards'

  lang caak nii (pay) [back from this go] 'from now (on)'

  koon naa nii [preceding time front this] 'before now'

  koon naa nan [preceding time front that] 'before that time'

As is evident from the list, the recruited lexemes tend to involve either spatial prepositions or spatial nouns across the three types. This again points to the general crosslinguistic trend that space is often the source of time.

 Similarly, Bisang (1996) notes that *lăŋ* (หลัง) 'back, behind, after', when followed by *càak* (จาก) 'leave', functions as a conjunction *lăŋ càak* (หลังจาก) 'after, since'. Functional extension of prepositions (or adpositions, in general) into conjunctions is a crosslinguistically common developmental path triggered by functional analogy. For instance, Genetti (1991: 227) notes that this type of grammaticalization is common in Tibeto-Burman languages, e.g., Dolakhali Newari *cotan-na* [spoon-INST] 'with a spoon' and *chê-ku yer-na* [house-LOC come-when] 'when (he) came to the house', where the instrumental *-na* and subordinator *-na* are of the same origin (see also Rhee and Koo 2015, on the development of the Korean tepidity particle *-na*).

 In a similar line of research, Prasithrathsint (2010b) shows the functional extension from spatial to temporal marking of Thai N-prepositions. In her discussion of 13 linguistic forms that are ambiguous between noun and preposition without context, many of them are shown to have both the spatial and temporal marking functions, as partially exemplified in (23)-(24):

(23) a. *lăŋ* 'behind' (spatial)

มี บางอย่าง ซ่อน อยู่ หลัง รอยยิ้ม นั้น

mii	*baaŋ-yàaŋ*	*sɔ̂ɔn*	*yùu*	***lăŋ***	*rɔɔy-yim*	*nán*
have	something	hide	be	**behind**	smile	that

'There is something hidden behind that smile.'

    b.   *lăŋ* 'after' (temporal)

เรา ดู ทีวี หลัง อาหารเย็น

raw	*duu*	*thiiwii*	***lăŋ***	*aahăn-yen*
we	watch	TV	**after**	dinner

'We watched TV after dinner.'   (modified from Prasithrathsint 2010b: 72)

(24) a.   *nɔ̂ɔk* 'outside' (spatial)

คน ไทย ถอด รองเท้า ไว้ นอก บ้าน

khon	*thay*	*thɔ̀ɔt*	*rɔɔŋ-thaaw*	*way*	***nɔ̂ɔk***	*baan*
people	Thai	take.off	shoe	keep	**outside**	house

'Thai people take off their shoes and put them outside the house.'

    b.   *nɔ̂ɔk* 'at the time other than' (temporal)

นอก เวลาเรียน นักเรียน พูด ภาษาถิ่น กับ ครู

nɔ̂ɔk	*weelaa-rian*	*nak-rian*	*phuut*	*phaasaa-thin*	*kap*	*khruu*
outside	time-study	student	speak	language-local	with	teacher

'Outside the study time, students speak local dialects with their teacher.'

    (modified from Prasithrathsint 2010b: 72)

Another important study is Kullavanijaya (2008), in which the author investigates the functions of /thîi/ (ที่) from the Sukhothai (13th~14th century) to Ayutthaya (14th~18th century), Mid-Ratanakosin (19th century), and Modern Thai (20th century~present) times.[12] The lexeme started its life as a simple noun in the

Sukhothai period, with very weak usage of a 'class noun' and a compound. The form gains more of the 'class noun' function in the Ayutthaya period, but by the Mid-Ratanakosin times, the form comes to function as a preposition as well as a relative clause marker, a complementizer, a nominalizer, and a numeral marker. In Modern Thai the form acquires the classifier function as well. This is a good example of not only grammaticalization of a spatial preposition but also of functional extension to other grammatical categories, notably of a linker function, such as a complementizer and a relative marker.

Similarly, Loss (2017) investigates the development of *thîi* (ที่) 'at' from a diachronic perspective. As with Kullavanijaya (2008), he shows that *thîi* (ที่) 'at' has extended its function from a simple noun designating a place, i.e., 'land, a piece of land, place', to a class noun, and further to preposition and other grammatical functions. The prepositional function only began in the Mid-Ratanakosin period. Loss further shows that the functional extension of *thîi* (ที่) 'at' into preposition, complementizer, and relativizer, is also observed with a similar pattern in Shan, a native language of Myanmar, and that the similarity exists in other prepositions' developmental scenarios, such as *lăŋ* (หลัง) 'back/behind', *nâa* (หน้า) 'face/front', *nɔ̀ɔk* (นอก) 'outer part/outside', *klaaŋ* (กลาง) 'middle/amidst', *rim* (ริม) 'edge/beside', and *nŭa* (เหนือ) 'north/above'.

Another study on the functional extension of Thai prepositions is also found in Diller (2008). Diller notes that the Thai word *lăŋ* (หลัง) 'back, behind, after' is among the multifunctional words carrying the nominal and prepositional function, which may be interpreted as an adverb as well, and further observes that it has an additional function of classifier for houses.

---

12) The author uses the data from the Mid-Rattanakosin period. The Rattanakosin Kingdom existed from the late 18th through the early 20th century.

8.5 Summary

In this chapter, we have seen the grammaticalization scenarios of Thai prepositions prominently from such primary categories as nouns and verbs but also from other categories such as adjectives and adverbs. Among the most notable aspects is that Thai prepositions are subject to scholarly debate as to their grammatical status partly because they do not exhibit formal departure from their source lexemes and partly because they still retain their source characteristics in terms of morphosyntax and semantics.

However, we also noted that there are cases, especially those that derived from nouns, that have undergone grammaticalization to a relatively greater extent, and are not used in the nominal function, e.g., *bon* (บน) 'upper part', or those extremely rarely used, e.g., *nay* (ใน) 'inside' and *nɔ̀ɔk* (นอก) 'outside' (Prasithrathsint 2010b).

Furthermore, if we adopt a more fluid perspective on grammar, Thai can be said to have a large inventory of prepositions that are either well grammaticalized or are currently being grammaticalized (note that we identified as many as 181 prepositions but observed in 8.2 that the inventory of prepositions, particularly composite and complex prepositions, varies by researcher due to their variable perception of the internal cohesion between/among multiple words).

When the grammaticalization processes of Thai prepositions are viewed with respect to grammaticalization mechanisms, it is noteworthy that formal erosion is not prominently observed whereas desemanticization, decategorialization, and extension are relatively more readily identified. This is a general characteristic of an isolating language as we have observed with Chinese in Chapter 7.

Grammaticalization Principles and Hypotheses Revisited

In chapters 3 through 8, we reviewed the grammaticalization scenarios of adpositions in each of six languages with respect to mechanisms, such as desemanticization, extension, decategorialization, and erosion, as suggested in Heine and Kuteva (2002) and Kuteva et al. (2019). We have confirmed that all six languages largely conform, though to varying degrees, to the patterns generally reported across languages, i.e., meanings of the forms grammaticalizing into adpositions become more generalized; their usage contexts are expanded; their lexical source characteristics (mostly those of nouns and verbs) are lost; and their formal shapes (i.e., phonetic volume and structural composition) become smaller and simpler.

There are other important issues in grammaticalization studies in general, including diverse principles and hypotheses. Some of them have been already discussed in the context of describing and analyzing grammaticalization of adpositions in individual languages, e.g., layering (Hopper 1991, Heine 1994b, Hopper and Traugott 2003[1993]), specialization (Hopper 1991, Hopper and Traugott 2003[1993], Colleman and De Clerck 2011), and parallel reduction (Bybee et al. 1994, S Rhee 2003b). In this chapter, we will discuss a few more important principles and hypothesis with respect to the grammaticalization of adpositions described in the preceding chapters. We will focus on select few, i.e., divergence, persistence, source determination, unidirectionality, universal path, reanalysis and reinterpretation.

9.1 Divergence

Divergence refers to the phenomenon in which a form undergoes grammaticalization into a marker of grammatical notions, and the original lexical form remains as an autonomous element (which usually undergoes the changes as ordinary lexical items), thus displaying coexistence of two (or more) different linguistic forms sharing the same origin (Hopper 1991: 22). As the process involves a form departing semantically and functionally from its origin, it is described as 'split' in Heine and Reh (1984: 57-59).

Among the most frequently cited examples are the English indefinite article *a/an* that diverged from its lexical origin, the numeral noun *one* (Hopper 1991, Heine 1997); and the English definite article *the* that diverged from its lexical origin, the demonstrative *that* (Heine 1997). These instances involve formal differences, thus, the connection between the two diverged forms (e.g., *one* vs. *a/an* and *that* vs. *the*) is sometimes not immediately perceivable. There are instances, however, in which the two (or more) diverged forms are identical in form but are different in function (i.e., one with a lexical function and another (or more) with a grammatical function). The two English sentences in the following exemplify such cases, taken from Heine (1997: 4):

(1)　　a.　*They keep the money.*
　　　　b.　*They keep complaining.*

The examples in (1) involve a word identical in form (i.e., *keep*) but has two different functions, i.e., lexical verb denoting 'store' and the auxiliary of marking continuative or iterative aspect (cf. Freed 1979, Brinton 1988). Since divergence occurs as a form is placed in a particular morphosyntactic environment and is subject to context-specific reanalysis of the structure and reinterpretation of function, observed instances of divergence typically involve a form occurring in different contexts. For instance, the lexical verb function of *keep* in (1a) is associated with the syntactic environment in which it is followed by a theme argument ('the money'), whereas the auxiliary function in (1b) is associated with the syntactic environment in which it is followed by a V-*ing* complement ('complaining').

The six languages discussed in this book have numerous instances of divergences. A fundamental criterion in determining divergence is the presence of two or more etymologically related forms that carry lexical and grammatical functions. Since divergence concerns only the function, formal divergence is not a necessary condition. Further, since divergence may occur multiple times and the lexical function may disappear over a course of time, divergence may be associated with an etymologically related form with two or more different functions (cf. Craig 1991 'polygrammaticalization'). Therefore, the vast majority of adpositions discussed in this book display divergence. In particular, in isolating languages like Thai and Chinese, where a form typically carries diverse functions across grammatical categories, divergence is the norm rather than an exception. To illustrate, let us look at the following examples in Thai, taken from 8.4.4 and repeated here as (2) with modification:

(2)　　a. *nâa* noun 'face'

　　　　หน้า ของ หล่อน ซีด

　　　　nâa *khɔ̌ɔŋ* *lɔ̀n* *sîit*

　　　　face of　　her　　pale

　　　　'Her face is pale.'

　　　　b. *nâa* preposition 'in front of; before'

　　　　แม่น้ำ อยู่ หน้า ภูเขา

　　　　mɛ̂ɛnám *yùu* **_nâa_** *phuukhǎw*

　　　　river　　exist　**before** mountain

　　　　'There is a river in front of the mountain.'

The examples in (2) involve the word *nâa* (หน้า), which carries two different functions, one nominal, denoting 'face' and the other prepositional, denoting 'in front of'. Even though the point in time when the prepositional use as in (2b) began to emerge cannot be identified due to the lack of historical data, the putatively older meaning 'face' coexists with its newer meaning 'in front of' in contemporary Thai. In terms of the syntagmatic environment, the word in its nominal use occurs in a place that requires a noun to host a postmodifier (e.g., 'of her') and to perform the subject function of the predicate (e.g., '(be) pale'). On the other hand, the word in its prepositional use occurs in a position in which a noun (its source function) cannot fit (cf. *'River exist face mountain') but a 'connector' is required to grammatically and conceptually link 'exist' and 'mountain' with the meaning related to 'face' (thus, inviting the locational and frontal meanings).

Similarly, agglutinating languages like Korean and Japanese also exhibit a large number of cases of divergence, though not as frequently as in isolating languages. Since postpositions in Korean and Japanese have a number of primary postpositions (24 and 33, respectively), many of which are not only reduced in form but also vastly different in function from their lexical sources, divergence is relatively more difficult to identify than in isolating languages. This is well illustrated by the following Korean examples:

(3) a. *maymi-ka*   *namwu-ey*   **pwuth**-*eiss-ta*
         cicada-NOM   tree-LOC   **attach**-RES-DEC
         'A cicada is on a tree.' (lit. A cicada attached itself to a tree and remains.)

    b. *cip-**pwuthe***   *hakkyo-kkaci*   *talli-ess-ta*
         house-**ABL**   school-ALL   run-PST-DEC
         '(I) ran from home to school.'

The example in (3) show two different uses of *pwuth-*, one as a lexical verb, the other as a primary postposition. They originated from the Middle Korean verb *puth-* 'adhere, attach'. Even though they are similar in form (note that both of them have undergone vowel quality change from [ɯ], represented as 'u' in romanization, to [u], represented as 'wu' in romanization, an instance of tongue retraction), most contemporary Korean speakers fail to recognize their connection (see 3.3.3.2).

The situation with inflectional languages similarly exhibits divergence. Many

Spanish prepositions, for example, have their heteronyms that carry earlier, often lexical, functions. The Spanish primary preposition *bajo* 'below, under' has its relative *bajo* n. 'base, bottom, lower floor' and adj. 'short, low', among others, as exemplified in (4):

(4) a. *Ellos viven   en el **bajo**.*
         theylive:3pl   on the **lower.floor**
         'They live on the first (lower) floor.'

     b. *El almacén está en los   **bajos** del   bar.*
         the storage is   in the:M.PL **base:pl** of.the   bar
         'The storage is in the basements (lower floors) of the bar.'

     c. *El niño es   un poco **bajo** para su edad.*
         the boy   be:3sga   little   **short** for   his age
         'He is a bit short for his age.'

     d. *Esta mesa es   demasiado **baja** para trabajar bien.*
         this   table be:3sg   too   **low**   for   work   well
         'This table is too low to work comfortably.'

     e. *El caballero lleva   el sombrero **bajo**   el brazo.*
         the gentleman carry:3sg the hat   **under**   the arm
         'The gentleman carries his hat under his arm.'

Examples (4a) and (4b) are where *bajo* is used as a noun denoting 'lower/first floor'; in (4c) and (4d) it is an adjective denoting 'short, low, etc.'; and in (4e), it is a preposition denoting 'under'. It is interesting to note that when the word is used as a lexical form it behaves differently from when it is used as the preposition, i.e., it inflects for number when it is a noun (i.e., *bajo* and *bajos* in (4a) and (4b)) and further for gender when it is an adjective (i.e., *bajo* and *baja* in (4c) and (4d)), following the general rule of Spanish grammar. On the other hand, when it is used as a preposition, also following the general rule about prepositions, does not inflect for number or gender, a clear case of decategorialization.

In this context of divergence, our tripartite classification of primary, composite, and complex adpositions is particularly useful. In other words, divergence may not be easily recognizable in primary adpositions; it becomes relatively easier in the case of composite adpositions; and it is nearly always possible in the case of complex adpositions. Evidently, the gradient levels of ease of recognizing divergence are due to their differential extent of grammaticalization, i.e., as grammaticalization proceeds, the level of formal transparency decreases, and in extreme cases, the older lexical use may eventually become defunct in the contemporary speech community. This is straightforward with complex adpositions. For instance, Spanish and English complex prepositions in the form of P(D)NP contain N (the noun), which is itself a full-fledged noun in common use, e.g., the English *top* displays divergence with n. *top* and prep. *on top of.*

9.2 Persistence

Persistence refers to the phenomenon in which grammaticalized forms reflect their earlier lexical characteristics (Hopper 1991). Even though desemanticization is robust in grammaticalization (nearly to the point of being a necessary condition for grammaticalization), original lexical meanings tend to linger and impose constraints on the way the grammaticalized form behaves. This is well illustrated by Lord (1993), who, in her discussion of grammaticalization of serialized verbs into Accusatives in West African languages, notes that a verb denoting 'take' (*kɛ̀*) has grammaticalized into an object marker (Accusative), as shown in (5) of a Benue-Kwa language Gã:

(5)   a. *È* *kɛ̀*   wòlò ŋmè-sĩ
            she **ACC** book lay-down
            'She put down a book.'

b. *È   ***kὲ***   wɔ̀lɔ̀   ŋmὲ
    she **ACC** egg   lay
    'She laid an egg.'

(Lord 1993: 120, as cited in Hopper and Traugott 2003: 96)

In (5a) *kὲ* is the Accusative that originated from v. *kὲ* 'take'. Because of this lexical meaning of physical handling (i.e., prehension), *kὲ* cannot be used in a sentence in which the object is not 'affected' (e.g., a book put down) but 'effected' (an egg laid). Considering the verb semantics, the Chinese Accusative *bǎ* (把), which developed from *bǎ* (把) v. 'hold, take', is expected to behave similarly to the Gã Accusative *kὲ*. However, as we noted 7.4.3.2, the Chinese Accusative *bǎ* (把) does not discriminate objects as to whether they are affected or effected. This is a good example that shows that grammaticalization is not uniformly deterministic but shows great variability across languages.

Grammaticalization scenarios of adpositions in the six languages show instances of persistence in a number of ways. Since persistence can be best observed from the macroscopic point of views (contra microscopic views, Lessau 1994), only historically well-documented instances of grammaticalization can show persistence with clarity. In the present study addressing a large number of adpositions, individual instances of persistence are not given much focus. However, there are a number of good examples of persistence, well observed in specialization patterns, as exemplified by the Korean Allatives below (as we briefly noted in 3.4.2):

(6)   Lexical source   Allative
      'edge'   *-kkaci, -eykkaci, -lokkaci*
      '(one) place'   *-hanthey(se), -hantheyta(ka(tayko(se))), -eykey*
      'that place'   *-kkey*
      'see'   *-(ul) poko(se)*
      'be accompanied by'   *-(ul)tele*
      'touch'   *-(ey) tayko(se), -hantheyta(tayko(se)),*
                             -(ey)ta(ka(tayko(se)))
      'approach'   *-lotaka, -hantheyta(ka(tayko(se))), -hantheyta(tayko(se)),*
                             -(ey)ta(ka(tayko(se)))

We already noted in 3.4.2 that these multiple Allatives have differential specialization, depending on register, honorification, pejoration, etc. The Allatives based on 'edge' (*kkaci* (까지) 〈 *kAs* (ㅈ), S Rhee 2020c, 2021a) tend to signal surprise, attributable to their relation to the source meaning 'edge, boundary', hence the overtone of 'extreme'. The use of the Allative that developed from 'that place' *-kkey* (-께) is restricted to marking an honorable person, evidently due to the distal demonstrative (*ku* 그 'that') metaphorically indexing psychological distance (i.e., negative politeness) by means of spatial distance. The use of the Allative *-(ul)tele* (-(을)더러), which developed from the verb *tAli-* (드리-) 'be accompanied by', is restricted to marking someone who is lower in status than the sentential subject (e.g., father to son), because a socially superior person is accompanied by an inferior person, not vice versa.[1] The Allatives that developed from the verbs 'touch' and 'approach' are used in emphatic contexts and often register the speaker's negative attitude (i.e., pejorative). This is likely to be due to the influence of the culture, where 'touching' is best avoided and 'approaching' is to be done with caution. Encoding pejoration with culture-specific means is indeed widespread in Korean (see Koo and Rhee 2016).

There are many subtle cases as well. For instance, the Thai primary preposition *hây* 'for, to', which developed from the verb 'give', presents a sophisticated case of persistence. The source characteristics place a constraint in use, as shown in the following constructed examples (Kultida Khammee, p.c.):

(7) a. ฉัน ซื้อ ดอกไม้นี้ ให้ คุณ

chăn	*súu*	*dɔ̀ɔkmáay*	*nî*	**_hây_**	*khun*
I	buy	flower	this	**for**	you

'I bought this flower for you.'

---

[1] This restriction is being eased in contemporary Korean, especially in children's or colloquial speech.

b. เขา สร้าง ปัญหา ให้ ฉัน มากมาย

   *khǎw sâaŋ   panhǎa **hây** chǎn mâakmaay*

   he   create trouble   **to**   me   lots.of

   'He gave me lots of trouble.'

c. เขา สั่ง ให้ ฉัน ทำ มัน

   *khǎw sàŋ   **hây** chǎn tham man*

   he   command   **to**   I   do   it

   'He commanded me to do it (even though I didn't want to do it).'

d. *ฉัน ถาม คำถาม ให้ คุณครู

   chǎn thǎam khamthǎam **hây khunkhruu*

   I   ask   question   **to**   teacher

   (intended) 'I asked a question to the teacher.'

As shown in the above, the preposition *hây* 'for', originating from the verb of transfer *hây* 'give', marks the target of an action or the end-point of transfer. The common semantic features associated with 'give' across languages (Kuteva et al. 2019) include benefaction and transfer, among others. Example (7a) shows the goal and benefaction, but as shown in (7b,c), the benefaction feature is no longer a constraint (cf. *Smoking is bad 'for' you.* in English, S Rhee 2007b, see also H Koo 2003 for Korean). The semantic feature of transfer still survives as shown in (7a,b,c). However, unlike (7c) which signals a burden being imposed, (7d) shows that a verb that merely designating the direction is not licensed by the preposition *hây* 'for'. In this case the preposition *kàp* (กับ) 'with, to' should be used instead (note that in comparison with 'to/for', the transfer sense is much weaker or non-existent with 'with'). This shows that semantic residue can effect diverse and very subtle selectional restrictions even after grammaticalization.

Even though it will need more research for confirmation, an impressionistic generalization is that primary adpositions are less likely to show divergence than composite adpositions, which, in turn, are less so than complex adpositions. For instance, even at a cursory look at the primary prepositions in English, the 10 most frequent prepositions, i.e., *of, in, to, for, with, on, at, from, by,* and *about,* do not have heteronyms in the primary category in contemporary English, whereas all complex prepositions, e.g., *at the top of, in the face of, in the back of,* etc., have their heteronymous nouns, from which they diverged, in common use in contemporary English.[2]

9.3 Source Determination

Bybee et al. (1994: 9), in their excellent analysis of tense, aspect, and modality systems across languages, present a hypothesis that the actual meaning of the construction that enters into grammaticalization uniquely determines the path that grammaticalization follows and, consequently, the resulting grammatical meaning. This is intuitively appealing since grammaticalization begins with a lexical item or a construction consisting of multiple lexical and grammatical items, and grammaticalization goes through diverse conceptual and discourse-pragmatic operations, e.g., metaphor, metonymy, inference, reinterpretation, etc., in the course of meaning negotiation between interlocutors. As these operations are based on given form and meaning at all times, human conceptual adjustments are constrained by the bounds of shared cognitive capabilities; and, further, the needs of grammatical concepts to be expressed are, though variable in detail, by and large similar, the paths and results of grammaticalization necessarily reflect the source semantics.

In this study of the same grammatical category, i.e., adpositions, in multiple languages, the source determination hypothesis deserves attention to see if it is upheld by the six languages addressed here. Since detailed diachronic paths have not been individually traced, our discussion will be limited to the comparison between source concepts and the final grammaticalized adpositional concepts. The sources and the targets are presented in Table 9.1. Based on the table we will review briefly to

---

[2] A low frequency usage of the noun *fore* (as in 'come to the fore') and the preposition *for* may be an instance of divergence (see S Rhee 2007b, for grammaticalization of *fore/for*).

what extent the development of targets from the given sources is motivated. Those that have unestablished sources are excluded in the Table (note that the applicable languages are indicated by their initials).

Category	Grammaticalization Sources (Language)			
REGIONAL 'at'	v. exist	(KCT)		
	n. place	(CT)		
	v. do	(J)		
DIRECTIONAL 'to' 'toward(s)' 'in the direction of'	n. direction	(ESC)	v. face	(KJC)
	n. course	(S)	v. go (up/down)	(CT)
	n. passage	(S)	v. turn towards	(J)
	n. way	(T)	v. move to	(T)
	a. through	(S)	v. enter	(T)
			v. give	(C)
	n. front	(S)	v. result	(T)
	n. face	(S)		
			v. shine	(C)
	n. place	(KJ)		
SOURCE 'of' 'from'	n. self	(C)	v. depend on	(C)
	n. nature, essence	(J)	v. accord	(T)
	n. cause/reason	(C)	v. take	(C)
			v. adhere	(K)
	n. (a)way	(E)	v. follow	(C)
	v. divide, part	(S)	v. strike	(C)
	v. leave	(T)		
			v. exist	(K)
PATH 'through' 'via' 'on the way to'	n. way	(EST)	n. half	(S)
	n. route	(ES)	n. middle	(S)
	n. passage	(S)	v. mediate	(S)
	n. conduit	(S)		
	v. go through	(KJ)	n. deviation	(S)
	v. pass (by)	(T)		
	v. follow	(K)	n. cause/reason	(C)
	v. cross	(K)		
	v. extend	(J)		
	a. thorough	(T)		
	a. throughout	(T)		

GOAL	v. arrive at	(CT)	n. edge	(K)
'to'	v. do-stop	(CT)	n. place	(K)
'up to'	v. accompany	(K)	n. destination	(S)
	v. approach	(K)		
	v. go to, take	(C)	n. both hands	(J)
	v. give	(C)		
	v. see	(K)		
MEDIAL	n. center	(SC)	n. two	(E)
'between'	n. interval	(KJ)		
'among'	n. middle	(ET)	n. way	(S)
	n. half	(S)	n. course	(E)
	n. midst	(E)		
	n. midpoint	(C)		
	n. interim	(T)		
	n. heart	(E)		
	n. inside	(J)		
	n. company	(E)		
ULTERIOR	v. go over	(K)	n. outside	(C)
'over'	v. cross	(K)	pro. that	(E)
'beyond'	v. extend over	(J)	ad. over	(E)
	v. surpass	(T)	ad beyond	(S)
	v. pass by	(T)		
ASSOCIATION	n. company	(ES)	v. follow	(KCT)
'with'	n. connection	(E)	v. go along	(C)
'along with'	n. conjunction	(E)	v. accord	(T)
'together with'	n. combination	(E)	v. accompany	(J)
	n. union	(S)	v. join	(T)
	n. association	(E)	v. attend	(T)
	n. agreement	(E)	v. take	(T)
	n. harmony	(C)	v. hitch	(T)
	n. trap	(T)	v. collect	(E)
	n. property	(T)	v. give	(C)
	n. breast	(E)		
	n. side	(T)	v. be together	(KT)
	n. rim	(T)	a. near	(ST)
			v. be like	(K)
	n. place	(KT)	a. same	(C)
	n. line	(ET)		
	n. way	(T)	v. measure	(T)
	n. round, ring	(T)		
	v. detour	(T)		

Category	Term	Code	Term	Code
ADJACENCY 'by' 'beside' 'near' 'around'	n. side, loin	(KJEST)	a. near	(KEST)
	n. left–right	(C)	a. next	(S)
	n. top–bottom	(C)	a. close	(E)
	n. horizontal side	(J)	v. bring close	(S)
	n. environment	(K)		
	n. circumference	(K)	n. edge, rim	(ET)
	n. ring	(E)	n. point	(E)
	n. round	(T)	n. brink, verge	(E)
	a. around	(S)		
	n. turn	(S)	n. inch	(E)
	v. detour	(T)	n. mile	(E)
	n. neighborhood	(E)	n. doorstep	(E)
	n. vicinity	(E)	n. nose	(E)
	n. proximity	(E)	v. throw	(S)
	n. reach	(E)	n. area	(E)
	n. sight	(E)		
	n. trail	(E)	n. flower	(S)
	n. line	(T)	n. love	(S)
	n. course	(E)		
SEPARATION 'off' 'apart from' 'far from'	a. far	(EST)	v. stop	(K)
	a. far	(S)	v. be separated	(K)
	a. distant	(S)	n. exception	(E)
	pro. that	(E)	n. exclusion	(E)
			v. exclude	(K)
	n. side	(E)	v. isolate	(S)
	n. place, side	(E)	v. pass	(E)
	n. margin	(S)	ad. apart	(S)
CONTIGUITY 'next to' 'in contact with'	v. be connected	(K)	n. tip	(S)
	v. stick (with)	(T)	n. base, root	(S)
	n. continuation	(S)	n. side, edge	(C)
	a. next	(E)		
	n. touch	(E)		
	n. contact	(E)		
	a. near	(S)		
OPPOSITE 'against' 'opposite'	v. face	(KJ)	v. connect	(T)
	a opposite	(E)	v. extend over	(J)
	n. opposition	(S)	v. pass way	(T)
	n. other side	(S)		
	v. return	(T)	ad. adversely	(E)
	n. cross	(E)	v. stab, pierce	(T)
	v. cross	(T)		
	v. cross straight	(T)		

INTERIOR 'in(side)' 'within'	n. inside	(KJESCT)	n. area	(E)
	n. center	(KJC)	n. region	(E)
	n. interior	(S)	n. space	(E)
	n. middle	(K)	n. sphere	(E)
			n. premises	(E)
			n. scope	(E)
			n. realm(s)	(E)
			n. limits	(E)
			n. boundaries	(E)
			n. range	(E)
			n. bounds	(E)
			n. field	(E)
			n. span	(E)
			n. orbit	(E)
			n. circumference	(E)
			n. distance	(E)
EXTERIOR 'out' 'outside (of)'	n. outside	(KESCT)	v. exit	(T)
	n. backside	(J)	a. out	(T)
	n. exterior	(S)	adv. away from	(E)
			pro. that	(E)
	n. limits	(E)		
	n. boundary	(E)		
	n. range	(E)		
	n. reach	(E)		
	n. field	(E)		
SUPERIOR 'on' 'on top of'	n. top	(KJESC)	adv. up	(ES)
	n. head	(ES)	adv. above	(ET)
	n. summit	(C)	a. high	(S)
INFERIOR 'under' 'down' 'below' 'beneath'	n. bottom	(KESC)	n. foot	(ES)
	n. base	(ES)	n. heel	(E)
	n. below	(KT)		
	n. underside	(ET)	n. ground	(J)
	a. low	(E)	n. hill	(E)
	a. lower	(T)		
	a. inferior	(S)	n. back side	(T)

ANTERIOR	n. front	(KJESC)	n. eye location	(J)
'before'	n. forefront	(E)	n. face	(T)
'in front of'	n. foreground	(E)	n. head	(E)

POSTERIOR	n. back	(KESCT)	v. follow	(KET)
'behind'	a. posterior	(S)	ad. subsequent	(E)
'in back of'	n. back buttocks	(J)		
	n. heels	(E)	n. wake	(E)
	n. base, root	(S)	n. track	(E)
	n. background	(E)		

LATERAL	n. side	(JESCT)	n. right	(JEST)
'on the side of'	n. horizontal side	(JS)	a. right, correct	(K)
'right to'	n. side, loin	(K)	n. right hand	(T)
'left to'	n. flank	(ET)		
	n. side, edge	(C)	n. left	(ESCT)
	n. edge, rim	(T)	a. left, wrong	(K)
			n. left hand	(T)
			n. sun down place	(J)

Table 9.1 Grammaticalization sources by functional categories

[Regional]

Regionals develop from the verb 'exist' in Korean, Chinese, and Thai and from the noun 'place' in Chinese and Thai. Since 'place' explicitly designates a location, and 'exist' designates the presence of an entity, the development of these two lexemes into Regional is well motivated. Japanese is the only language using the verb 'do'. This may look peculiar but the source structure involves -ni 'at, to' and the verb s- 'do' is not an action verb but a light verb (like the Korean ha-), performing diverse lexical and grammatical functions without contributing much in meaning. Thus, the meaning of the source construction is simply 'be/do at/to', a good candidate for Regional in terms of meaning.

[Directional]

Directionals (Allatives) develop from a number of different concepts. There are many Directionals that originate from specific 'direction'- and 'passage'-related nouns (e.g., 'direction', 'course', 'passage', 'way') in many languages (ESCT) and from the verbs of directed motion (e.g., 'go (up/down)', 'face', 'turn towards', 'move to', 'enter', 'give', 'result in') (KJCT). Other lexemes such as the nouns 'front' and 'face' (S) imply directionality, and thus the conceptual motivation behind the development of 'to' from them is straightforwardly clear. The Chinese verb *zhào* 'towards' (《 'shine') stands out in this regard in that there is no movement involved but only the travel of the light to the focused entity.

The noun 'place' (KJ) is a little different. The word itself is direction-neutral, thus, a phrase 'place-school', in principle, could be interpreted as 'to school' or 'from school' as well as 'at school'. The emergence of 'to' (instead of 'to', 'from', etc.) from 'place' seems to have been enabled from pragmatic inferences at the moment of interaction.[3] Furthermore, there is a source-goal asymmetry across languages, i.e., languages use more goal markers than source markers, reflecting the human propensity of goal-orientedness (see Stefanowitsch and Rohde 2004, Lakusta and Landau 2005, S Rhee 2006a, Kabata 2012, Zanchi 2017, Fagard and Kopecka 2021, Kopecka and Vuillermet (eds.) 2021 and works therein, among many others).

[Source]

Sources (Ablatives) develop from nouns designating the origin or basis (in contrast with derivatives), such as 'self', 'essence', 'cause' (JC), and from lexemes denoting separation, e.g., '(a)way', 'divide', 'leave' (EST), the motivation of which is obvious as they denote departure or a point of departure.

A less straightforward semantic category is that of dependence or contact, e.g., 'depend on', 'accord', 'adhere', 'follow', 'take', and 'strike' (KCT). The development of 'from' from these sources, at first sight, may seem counterintuitive because these

---

[3] It is notable that according to Blake's (1977) crosslinguistic study, a Locative-Allative syncretism is a very common phenomenon (p. 60) (see also Andrews 2007[1985], Pantcheva 2010). See also S Rhee (2004d, 2006a) for discussion on Location-Direction-Movement connection.

verbs involve an action, actual or imagined, "toward" the referenced theme. In other word, the source construction [(A) follows B], for example, developing into [(A) to B] would seem more plausible than into [(A) from B]. However, when A follows B and then performs an action, the action is 'based on' A's following B. For instance, [He follows rules and joins the army], can engender the meaning [Following the rules, he joins the army]; and [He follows curiosity and asks a question] can develop into the meaning [He asks a question from curiosity]. The same applies to the contact verbs; one establishes a contact with a reference point, then the reference point functions as the source of subsequent action. This type of apparent schematic change has been observed with 'adhere' (K), in 3.3.3.2. The verb of existence 'exist' (K) presents a similar picture largely aided by the converb particle -se 'and then', a marker of sequence, which establishes the existence of an entity or state and turns the existence as the starting point (see S Rhee 1996, 2000a, for more discussion on schematic shift in grammaticalization).

[Path]

The sources of Paths (Perlatives, Prolatives) are less variegated as compared to most other categories. They are mostly the lexemes that denote a path or a passing event explicitly, e.g., nouns 'way', route', 'passage', 'conduit'; adjectives 'thorough', 'throughout' (EST); and verbs 'pass', 'go through', 'follow', 'cross', 'extend' (KJT). The lexemes indicating the medial location or an action occurring between two entities, e.g., 'half', 'middle', 'mediate' (S), are also close to the first category, though these are more specific in semantics than the first group. Of these, the noun 'way/route' (EST) and the verb 'go through' (KJT) surface most productively.

The nouns 'deviation' (S) and 'cause/reason' (C) are less straightforward with respect to their motivation of grammaticalization into Path. The Spanish noun *través* 'deviation' in *a través de* 'through' seems to indicate that the referenced noun is not the terminus but a medial point which the trajector passes (i.e., 'deviates'). The Chinese noun *yóu* 'cause, reason' that grammaticalized into the Path marker *yóu* 'through' (also into Ablative 'from') evidently marks the enabling or causative force of an action or state (e.g., *An interruption of work through illness* in English), in which case the cause can be interpreted as the path.

[Goal]

The markers of Goal (Dative) are similar in function to Directionals, the only difference being the former designating the end-point whereas the latter merely indicating orientation (cf. 6.3.1). These two markers are often inseparable in language. The sources of Goal are also relatively simple. They include the verbs denoting a motion towards (and eventually reaching) a target or the target itself, e.g., 'arrive at', 'do and stop', 'accompany', 'approach', 'go to, take', 'give', and 'see' (KCT); or 'place', 'edge', and 'destination' (KS). The conceptual motivation behind their development is plainly obvious. The only outlier is *-made* 'both hands' (J), of which the syntagmatic collocation pattern for grammaticalization of Goal is not available. Narrog and Rhee (2013: 296) indicate that even the hypothesized source 'both hands' is not firmly established yet (see also 4.3.3.2). This should await further research.

[Medial]

The markers of Medial denote the spatial relationship that the trajector is in the medial position between two or more landmark entities, i.e., 'between', 'among'. It is different from Interior in that it does not require an axial contrast, e.g., in-out, top-down, front-back, etc. (cf. Medial '<u>between</u> you' and Interior '<u>inside</u> the house'). The source lexemes of Medials are those that clearly mark the medial position of, association with, or inclusion in multiple entities. The lexemes attested in the six languages are all nouns with such meanings, e.g., 'center', 'interval', 'middle', 'half', 'midst', 'midpoint', 'interim', 'heart' 'inside', and 'company' (KJESCT). The nouns 'way' and 'course' denote a wider spectrum than 'between' and 'among', but the development involving semantic narrowing (e.g., from a whole course to a midpoint) is not counter-intuitive, considering that a 'way' lies between the source and the goal.

The noun *two* (E) in *between* has been enabled by the presence of the prefix *be-* denoting 'around' (cf. *OED*, entry of *between*) (see J. Lee 2013). The development of the initial 'around two' meaning into the prepositional meaning 'in the medial position of two' involves subjectification in that it involves rearrangements of the landmark entities in a linear configuration (S Rhee 2002b: 159).

[Ulterior]

The markers of Ulterior in spatial positions, i.e., those designating the 'beyond'-relationship, are relatively fewer in number as compared to other conceptual categories, even though all six languages surveyed here have them. The source lexemes are typically those that denote surpassing, e.g., 'go over', 'cross', 'extend over', 'surpass', 'pass by' (KJT) or those that explicitly mark ulteriority, e.g., 'outside' (C), 'over, beyond' (ES), and 'that' (distal) (E).

[Association]

The markers of Association (Comitatives, Associatives) are among those that have a large number of source lexemes. Despite their multiplicity of source lexemes, however, their source semantics is largely uniform, e.g., those that signify association, e.g., nouns 'company', 'connection', 'conjunction', 'combination', 'union', 'association', 'agreement', 'harmony' (ESC); or those that denote belonging by possession, acquisition, or by synecdoche (part-whole), e.g., 'property', 'trap', 'breast', 'side', 'rim' (ET); or those that denote location where the trajector and the landmark coexist or are associated, e.g., 'place', 'line', 'way', 'round', 'detour' (KET). The source verbs also designate an action through which association is obtained in diverse manners, e.g., 'follow', 'go along', 'accord', 'accompany', 'join', 'attend', 'take', 'hitch', 'collect', 'give' (KJECT); or a state whereby the trajector and the landmark remain in static association, e.g., 'be together', 'near', 'be like', 'same' (KSCT).

The conceptual motivation behind the development of Association 'with' from 'measure' (T) is unclear. We noted that in Japanese, the lexemes with the same semantics, i.e., *hakari* v.n. 'measure' and *take* n. 'length, measure', developed into the Focus-marking postpositions *-bakari* 'only, just' and *-dake* 'only' (4.4.4), and that in Spanish *medida* 'measure' developed into the complex preposition *a (la) medida de* 'to the measure of', marking a specific point on a scale (6.4.3.3). These developments are relatively clear with respect to their conceptual connection. The clue to the Thai puzzle, as it seems, is that the Thai lexeme *thǽæw* (แถว) has undergone semantic generalization from 'measure' to 'line', 'row', 'area', 'locality', 'vicinity', etc. (*HUFS-TK Dictionary*). The Association sense from 'vicinity' is then clearer. This shows that the original meaning may not present a clear connection but the later meanings do and, thus, in order to determine the immediate source meaning for a grammatical form we need to consider not only the ultimate source but also its diachronic semantic development, a point addressed in 7.3.3.

[Adjacency]

The markers of Adjacency (Proximatives) also have numerous source lexemes, as do their functional relatives Associatives (Comitatives), discussed above. They are predominantly nominal and consist of a few semantics-based subcategories. Most languages (KJEST) make use of 'side, loin' for the development of Proximative and combining directional nouns as 'left and right' and 'top and bottom' (C). There are also a number of nouns denoting locational adjacency, e.g., 'environment', 'circumference', 'neighborhood', 'vicinity', 'proximity', 'ring', 'round', 'around', and 'turn' (KEST). Another group of nouns refers to accessibility or means thereof, e.g., 'reach', 'sight', 'trail', 'line', and 'course' (ET). Also common are the adjectives denoting adjacency, e.g., 'near', 'next', 'close' (KEST). Needless to say, the conceptual motivation behind grammaticalization of these lexemes is very direct.

The partitive nouns designating a specific part of the landmark, often denoting extremity, e.g., 'edge', 'rim', 'point', 'brink', 'verge' (ET), are also common and the motivation behind the development is also clear, in that the referenced entity is located at the extreme end of the first referent, thus the two are not disconnected, thus schematically moving from [A-edge-B] to [A near B].

Still another category refers to a (potentially scalar) location, e.g., 'inch', 'mile', 'doorstep', 'nose', 'throw', 'area' (ES), which are used subjectively to delimit the boundary of the location of a referenced entity. Depending on the scale being invoked, various scalar units are recruited. These nominals, however, are used to intensify the locational perimeter in the form of complex prepositions, e.g., *within an inch of* (E), *within a stone's throw of* (E), *a tiro de* 'within the range of' (‹ *tiro* n. 'throw') (S).

The two remaining sources are 'flower' and 'love' (S), i.e., *a flor de* 'on surface of', and *al amor de* 'near' (‹ *flor* n. 'flower'; *amor* n. 'love'). It is not clear how these lexemes served as the source lexemes of Adjacency. We can only hypothesize the motivations, i.e., that a flower is the most noticeable manifestation of the spectacular point in a plant's life-cycle to which humans are irresistably attracted (thus, the inseparable flower-attraction relationship) and that love is the strongest motivation for being together (thus, the inseparable love-union relationship) (Kyunghee Kim, p.c.). However, these hypotheses require further investigation with reference to the usage patterns at the incipient stages of the grammaticalization of the lexemes, in order to validate them.

[Separation]

The markers of Separation (Separatives, Abessives, Caritives) denote the opposite of Association. It indicates separation, exclusion, or absence, typically marked by the adpositions developed from the lexemes with the meaning of distance, e.g., 'far', 'distant', 'that' (EST) or those of withdrawal or exclusion in one way or another, e.g., 'stop', 'be separated', 'exception', 'exclusion', 'exclude', 'isolate', 'pass', 'apart' (KES). Another group consists of nouns denoting a place, either the whole or a part thereof, e.g., 'side', 'place', 'margin' (ES).

The English *besides* and *aside* both developed from the lexical noun *side* and, similarly, the Spanish *al margen de* 'apart from', from the lexical noun *margen* 'margin'. The conceptualization involved in the semantic change of these nouns is somewhat peculiar, because these very concepts, as we have seen above, are the sources of Association, the conceptual opposite of Separation. The Association meaning, evidently, is based on the reasoning, [X is at the side of Y], thus, [X is connected to Y], therefore, [X is near Y]; whereas the Separation meaning is based on the reasoning, [X is at the side of Y], thus, [X is not at the central part of Y], therefore, [X is separate from Y], in the last stage of which there occurred strongly evaluative subjectification that non-central members are "not" true members. This strongly suggests that human conceptualization is quite fluid due to its subjective nature (see S Rhee 2000a for variable conceptualization of an event with frame-of-focus variation, through which seemingly antonymous meanings emerge from the identical lexeme).

[Contiguity]

The markers of Contiguity (Contiguitive) are similar in function to markers of

Association and Adjacency (see 6.3.1 and 8.2). Because of their functional affinity, their lexical sources are nearly identical. They develop from the lexemes that clearly denote connection, e.g., 'be connected', 'stick (with)', 'continuation', 'next', 'touch', 'contact', and 'near' (KEST), thus the motivating conceptualization is clear. They also develop from such partitive nouns, e.g., 'tip', 'base, root', 'side, edge' (SC). Their connection to Contiguity is also straightforward, as was discussed in Adjacency above.

[Opposite]

The markers of Opposite (Oppositives) mark the 'against' relationship between two entities. In spatial relationships, Oppositives mark an entity in a position facing the landmark. Since the two entities being referred to are largely static, the 'opposite' relationship is the result of subjective construal of spatial alignment of two entities in such a way that they are 'facing' each other. In other words, when A and B are seated at a table, describing their spatial configuration as 'A sitting opposite B' is possible only when their positions are placed in a linear alignment and the conceptualizer adopts B's position as the vantage point of description. The 'against' construal is even more subjective since it involves some form of dynamism between the entities (cf. S Rhee 2002c). The markers of this 'across' and 'against' relationship develop from the lexemes clearly denoting opposing or facing, e.g., 'face' (v.), 'opposite', 'opposition', 'return', 'other side', 'cross' (n.), 'cross' (v.), and 'cross straight' (KJEST), or those that denote connection, e.g., 'connect', 'extend over', 'pass the way' (JT), to which the subjective oppositional meaning is added.

There are also two source lexemes that explicitly encode adversity, e.g., 'adversely' and 'stab, pierce' (ET). Since these are highly specific in meaning, it is a puzzle that they grammaticalized into prepositions, in view of the fact that semantic generality of the source lexeme has been often considered as a prerequisite of grammaticalization (Hopper and Traugott 2003[1993]: 101-103, Bybee et al. 1994: 130). However, when the target function is semantically specific, recruiting a semantically specific lexeme as a grammaticalization source is not uncommon (S Rhee 1996, K Ahn 2005, Bybee et al. 1994: 130). The present case is an addition to these previous studies that show the general requirement of semantic generality of the source lexemes is not inviolable.

[Interiority]

The markers of Interiority (Interiors) designate the trajector's location being 'inside' the landmark in the axial relationship of two polar concepts inside-outside. They typically develop from the nouns explicitly denoting interiority, e.g., 'inside', 'center', 'interior', 'middle' (KJESCT), or the nouns denoting general location or boundaries, e.g., 'area', 'region', 'space', 'sphere', 'premises', 'scope', realm(s)', 'limits', 'boundaries', 'range', 'bounds', 'field', 'span', 'orbit', 'circumference', 'distance', all occurring in English only, in the form of complex prepositions. However, one caveat is that these general nouns do not designate the Interiority by themselves; instead, they involve a primary preposition of Interiority, such as 'in' and 'within'. Therefore, the meaning of inclusion is primarily marked by these prepositions and the nouns listed here are only delimiting the boundary of the 'within'-relationship. The crucial role of these primary prepositions is evident that the same nouns can be used to express Exteriority (the conceptual opposite of Interiority) by occurring with *outside* or *beyond* (see below).

[Exteriority]

The markers of Exteriority (Exteriors) develop from the lexemes that bear a straightforward relationship with the 'outside' notion, e.g., 'outside', 'backside', 'exterior', 'out', 'away from', 'that' (distal), 'away from' (KJESCT), or those that denote a bounded spatial entity, e.g., 'limits', 'boundary', 'range', 'reach', 'field', all occurring in English only, in the form of complex prepositions. As is the case with Interiors, discussed above, these nouns only delimit the boundary and the exclusion relationship is marked by the primary prepositions *outside* and *beyond*.

[Superiority]

The markers of Superiority (Superiors) develop from the lexemes denoting the trajector's 'on'-relationship with the landmark. The relationship between the grammatical notion and the source semantics is straightforwardly clear, as can be seen in 'top', 'head', 'summit', 'up', 'above', and 'high' (KJESCT).

[Inferiority]

The markers of Inferiority (Inferiors) mark the trajector's relationship in the 'under/below'-relationship with the landmark. They develop from the lexemes directly related to these inferiority meanings, such as 'bottom', 'base', 'below (region)', 'underside', 'low', 'lower', 'inferior' (KESCT); from those that denote the lower part of the body, e.g., 'foot', 'heel' (ES); and from those that denote the landmark typically associated with the lower region, e.g., 'ground' (J), 'hill' (E), or with the posterior region, e.g., 'back side' (T). The fact that the mixed sources denoting 'low', 'lower body part', and 'back' are used in the development of Inferiors reflects the fact that a number of different reference models are being used, i.e., the anthropomorphic model (human body), the zoomorphic model (animal body), and the landmark model (Heine 1997: 40-49, S Rhee 2016[1998]: 94-98, K Park 2017, Park and Rhee 2018). It is to be noted that 'back' typically develops into Posterior in the anthropomorphic model and into Superior and Posterior in the zoomorphic model, and further that the development of 'back' to Inferior is available in the Western Nilotic model of anthropomorphic model, Heine 1997: 49).

[Anteriority]

The markers of Anteriority (Anteriors) signal that the trajector is 'before' the landmark. The lexical sources of this conceptual category are all nouns denoting the frontal area, e.g., 'front', 'forefront', 'foreground' (KJESC), or those denoting the frontal part of the body, e.g., 'eye location', 'face', and 'head' (JTE). It is also notable that 'head'-'front' relationship is typically due to the zoomorphic model, whereas 'face'-'front' and 'eye'-'front' relationships are available in the anthropomorphic model.

[Posteriority]

The markers of Posteriority (Posteriors) signal that the trajector is 'behind' the landmark. The most common source is 'back' (KESCT), and if we include 'back buttocks' (J) in this broader category 'back', in all six languages Posterior developed from 'back'. Closely related 'back'-nouns are 'posterior', 'heels', 'base, root', 'background' (JES). Another interesting group consists of 'wake' and 'track' (E), which are left 'behind' a moving object or an animal. Even though 'wake' has not been mentioned as a source lexeme for Posterior in the extant literature, 'track' and 'trace' are among the common sources developed from the landmark model (Svorou 1994: 80ff, Heine 1997: 39). Still another group concerns those that mark an activity in the back region, e.g., 'follow' (KET), or designating the 'behind'-relationship in sequence, e.g., 'subsequent' (E), which originally made "reference to succession in both place and time" (*OED*, entry of *subsequent*).

[Laterality]

The final category is the markers of Laterality (Laterals). Laterals designate the location of the trajector as being 'on the side of', 'left to', or 'right to' the landmark. Even though Laterals do not occur frequently in everyday language, there are subgroups in this conceptual category as indicated above, i.e., 'general side' (Lateral), 'right side' (Lateral-Dextravus), and 'left side' (Lateral-Laevus). Lexical sources differ according to these subcategories. The general-side markers develop from 'side' lexemes, e.g., 'side', 'horizontal side', 'loin', 'flank', 'edge', and 'rim' (KJESCT); the right-side markers from 'right', 'right hand', 'correct' (KJEST); and the left-side markers from 'left', 'left hand', and 'wrong' (KESCT). It is to be noted that the association of 'correct-right' and 'wrong-left' has been frequently observed across languages (Foolen 2017, 2019), but this common association does not necessarily mean that diachronically 'wrong' gave rise to 'left' and 'correct' gave rise to 'right'; rather, the reverse seems to be the case.

An outlier is 'where the sun goes down' (J) (*-no hidari*) for 'left' (4.3.3.2). This suggests that Japanese made use of an orientation model, according to which the human is facing the north. Incidentally, the orientation models for cardinal directions mentioned in the preceding exposition are the south-facing model (Korean, see 3.3.3.1), and the 'top-north' model, possibly an influence of Western cartographic tradition (Thai, see 8.3.3.1).

From the foregoing discussion by conceptual categories, one important generalization arises, i.e., there is a strong conceptual relatedness between the sources and the targets in the grammaticalization of adpositions, even though there are a few inconclusive cases as to their relationship. It is particularly prominent that the relationship is transparent in the cases of complex adpositions.[4] This again points to the fact that periphrastic constructions have transparent concatenative meanings and have not advanced extensively in grammaticalization, whereas the more grammaticalized adpositions, such as composite adpositions and further primary adpositions, have been reduced in form, have become relatively opaque as to their compositional meanings, and have undergone a greater extent of grammaticalization. This generalization is also applicable at a global level to the Parallel Reduction Hypothesis (Bybee et al. 1994). Overall, the source-target correlation is strong and the Source Determination Hypothesis is upheld by the grammaticalization scenarios of adpositions, even though the individual paths of change could not be traced.

9.4 Unidirectionality

Among numerous defining characteristics of grammaticalization processes, the most prominent one is arguably the unidirectionality of the change (Hopper and Traugott 2003[1993], Bybee et al. 1994, Traugott and Dasher 2002, Company 2008, Börjars and Vincent 2011, Hilpert and Saavedra 2016, Kuteva et al. 2019). Despite some criticisms as presented by Campbell (2001), Janda (2001), and others, unidirectionality is generally accepted as a robust statistical tendency in grammaticalization.

Unidirectionality occurs at a number of planes of grammar, and the changes at multiple planes seem to go in tandem through a mutual feeding relationship. The diverse levels of language and the characteristic changes can be presented in a simplified form as follows:

(8) a. Word class: Open   〉 Closed
     b. Function: Lexical   〉 Grammatical

---

4) N.B., however, that *a flor de* 'on the surface of, near' (〈 *flor* 'flower') and *al amor de* 'near' (〈 *amor* 'love') in Spanish are notable exceptions.

c.	Sound:	Long/Strong	⟩	Short/Weak
d.	Structure:	Periphrastic	⟩	Morphological
e.	Position:	Free	⟩	Fixed
f.	Prominence:	High	⟩	Low
g.	Meaning:	Content	⟩	Abstract

Of these diverse planes of language, (8a) and (8b) do not concern us in the discussion of grammaticalization of adpositions, because it is beyond question that adpositions belong to a closed class and carry a grammatical function, the assumptions that served as the starting point of discussion. The patterns in (8c) through (8e) are concerned with the formal aspects, and those in (8f) and (8g) are concerned with the semasiological aspects. Thus, in the following, we will discuss form and meaning with reference to unidirectionality.

9.4.1 Form

Unidirectionality in formal domains, as shown in (8) above, will be realized in a number of ways. The phonetic volume will become smaller; the phonetic salience will be weakened; the longer structures will become shorter (often leading from periphrastic to morphological forms); and the freedom of occurring at syntagmatic positions will be lost (thus losing autonomy). The loss of the syntagmatic freedom of the source lexemes, mostly nouns and verbs, participating in grammaticalization of adpositions is obvious because adpositions are bound to their host nominals, thus are placed in front or back of their hosts, a process labeled as 'fixation' by Lehmann (2015[1982]). Since nouns and verbs are autonomous forms, their development into adpositions necessarily involves loss of syntactic freedom. Thus, leaving these obvious aspects aside, we will focus on the loss of phonetic volume in the following discussion.

The loss of phonetic volume has been discussed in each chapter for the six languages under the grammaticalization mechanism of erosion. Thus, it is not necessary to discuss the issue in full detail again here. Suffice it to summarily reiterate the findings. We focus on the loss of form that occurs through structural simplification.

In Korean, among noun-based postpositions such reduction of the sound and structure typically involve the deletion of postpositions, e.g., P_1 -*uy* Genitive and P_2 -*ey* Locative in [NP-*uy* N-*ey*], in most cases. There are instances of phonetic weakening that occur to lexemes, as well (3.4.3.4). In verb-based postpositions the reduction also involves P_1, typically Accusative -*ul* or Locative -*ey*. There are no observed instances, in which phonetic volume is increased or morphosyntactic complexity is increased.

In Japanese, phonetic and structural reduction has been observed with respect to some primary postpositions by historical linguists, even though their reductive processes have not been clearly mapped along the timeline. However, as Narrog and Rhee (2013) note, the verb-based complex postpositions, typically occurring in the form of [-*ni/o* V-*te*] (LOC/ACC V-NF), are remarkably well preserved, i.e., without deletion of P_1 (LOC/ACC) (4.4.3.4). Thus, Japanese clearly shows formal reduction with primary postpositions, but the complex postpositions do not offer traces of such reductive processes. However, unidirectionality has not been violated in the grammaticalization scenarios of postpositions in Japanese.

In English, phonetic and structural reduction is common. The most common case is the deletion of the definite article in the complex prepositions, i.e., from PDNP to PNP. According to a quantitative analysis, the directionality of gradual change is manifested clearly; the complex prepositions do not occur in the High frequency range, i.e., 33.3% of the time, whereas in the Very Low frequency range, the article is lost only 20.2% of the time (see Table 5.7) (5.4.3.4). There are no observed cases in which this reductive directionality is violated.

In Spanish, reductive processes are commonly observed as well. The processes occur not only in individual cases, i.e., when a form is fluctuating between the PDNP and PNP structures, but also across the prepositional categories, i.e., primary, composite, and complex prepositions. For instance, certain forms show full, reduced, and intermediate forms on the way, e.g., *por debajo de* 'below', *por bajo de* 'below', *abajo de* 'under', *debajo de* 'under', *bajo de* 'under', *bajo* 'below, under' (see 6.4.2). Across the subcategory of complex prepositions, it has been shown that high frequency forms (with an advanced level of grammaticalization) tend to lack the definite article, whereas the low frequency forms (with a limited level of grammaticalization) tend to retain it (6.4.3.4). Formal reduction also occurs, though less frequently, by way of losing P$_1$ (as in *a orillas de* 〉 *orillas de* 'at the edge of') or P$_2$ (*no obstante a/de* 〉 *no obstante* 'notwithstanding') in a few complex prepositions (6.4.3.4). Based on the observations, it is reasonable to argue that unidirectionality of reductive processes is well manifested in the grammaticalization of Spanish prepositions.

In Chinese, reductive processes are much more limited as compared to other languages. We noted that due to the typological characteristics of a isolating language, structural reduction and reductive pronunciation are rare. However, there are still instances where the Genitive linker *zhī* (之) may have been deleted. Further, some historical studies (e.g., Peyraube 2015) present examples of bonding that occurred in the history of Chinese, even though such established cases have not been reported with respect to the grammaticalization of adpositions. We also noted that phonological change (such as tone sandhi) is similarly rare, but has been observed in Duanmu (2005). Thus, there are no reported instances in which the change supposedly occurred in the opposite direction of reductive change, but unidirectionality of formal reduction is not strongly manifested in Chinese.

In Thai, also an isolating language, we noted that formal reduction is not frequently observed. Even though reduction has been reported in some instances (Matisoff 1991a, see 8.2), the reductive processes are not prominent. Instead, it seems that prepositions are often reinforced by other forms with similar functions or even by reduplicating the identical forms as shown in such pairs as *phrɔ́ɔm* 'with, together with' and *phrɔ́ɔm kàp* 'with' (note that *phrɔ́ɔm* and *kàp* both mean 'with'), *ʔɔ́ɔm* 'around' 〉 *ʔɔ́ɔm ʔɔ́ɔm* 'around', etc. Evidently, these are instances of innovation for emphasis and do not constitute a counterexample. From the observations, however, we conclude that unidirectionality of reductive change, though not violated, is not strongly supported in Thai.

The foregoing exposition of reductive changes in form in individual languages leads to a conclusion that isolating languages do not present clear instances of unidirectional formal reduction but that there are no reported instances of the change occurring in the opposite direction. Thus, unidirectionality can be said to be a valid hypothesis in the cases of grammaticalization of the six languages discussed in this book.

9.4.2 Meaning

Unidirectionality in the semantic domains, as shown in (8) above, is realized in a number of ways. The form's prominence will be weakened, and the meanings will become more abstract as grammaticalization proceeds. The weakening of the form's perceptual and conceptual prominence is directly related to the weakening of its sound and the loss of meaning. In other words, as the form loses phonetic volume and as the meaning becomes more abstract, grammatical meaning, the form is not attended to by the language users (see Harder and Boye 2011: 60-65, who characterize grammaticalization as a process whereby forms lose in their competition for prominence and become discursively secondary).

Meanings of grammatical forms are necessarily abstract because grammatical notions are highly schematic (Talmy 1985, Heine 1992a,b, 1993, 1994a,b, 1997, S Rhee 1996). Therefore, a discussion on the unidirectionality in semantic change that occurs in the scenarios of grammaticalization of adpositions needs to focus on the semantics of source lexemes, especially on examining if the source semantics is sufficiently concrete. It is beyond our immediate interest in this macroscopic study to investigate all individual lexemes that participated in grammaticalization of adpositions. Thus we will focus on the general pattern to prove or disprove the hypothesis that meanings of the source lexemes are more concrete and thus they are reduced en route to grammaticalization of adpositions.

It is widely accepted that the process of semantic generalization involves semantic shift that can be characterized as abstraction or metaphorization along the continuum of ontological categories ('categorial metaphor') that form a chain, as proposed by Heine et al. (1991a: 48) (see also Genetti 1991):

(9)   PERSON > OBJECT > ACTIVITY > SPACE > TIME > QUALITY

Since adpositions, especially spatial adpositions, belong to the fourth ontological category SPACE, we will examine if the source lexemes are indeed those that denote the concepts left to it, i.e., PERSON, OBJECT, and ACTIVITY (note that the same authors also use PROCESS in place of the term ACTIVITY (Heine et al. 1991b: 157)). The conceptual categories of the identified source lexemes of spatial adpositions are listed in Table 9.1. Some classifications may be debatable. For instance, 'side' can be in the PERSON, OBJECT, or SPACE categories. When it refers to 'loin' as well, it is placed in PERSON; if it is to refer to the side part in general, it is placed in OBJECT; and if it is combined with '-side' and designates the spatial location, it is placed in SPACE. However, the distinction may not be always clear because of the lack of historical data. Similarly, if 'back' refers to the body part, it is placed under PERSON, even though it may also refer to an animal body part, because when body-part names are shared by humans and non-humans, the situation is likely to be due to personification. The lexemes 'way', 'road', 'route' can be members of the OBJECT or SPACE categories, but despite the possibility of dual membership, they are treated as OBJECT category members, because they are primarily objects (though occupying a space), unlike 'middle', 'near', etc. Some nouns involving actions or processes, e.g., 'association', 'combination', etc., are also placed in the ACTIVITY category. The categorization shown in Table 9.2 is subject to further refinement, but the list as is can suit the purpose of a broad characterization.

	PERSON	OBJECT	ACTIVITY (PROCESS)	SPACE	TIME	QUALITY
	side (loin)	edge	accompany	back		be like
		side	adhere	bottom		
			approach	center		
			be connected	circumference		
			be separated	environment		
			be together	front		
			cross (v.)	inside		
			exceed	interval, gap		
Korean			exclude	middle		
			exist	near		
			face (v.)	outside		
			follow	place		
			go through	top		
			see			
			stop			
			touch (v.)			

Japanese	back, buttocks both hands eyes (location of)	horizontal side side	accompany do extend over face (v.) go through turn towards	back side center front ground inside interval place place of sunset top	essence
English	breast foot head heart nose heel flank	brink company course cross (n.) doorstep edge hill inch line mile point ring side track trail two verge wake way, road	agreement association collect combination contact exception exclusion follow pass reach sight touch	area background base boundaries bottom bounds circumference close direction distance far field (fore)front foreground inside left limits middle near, vicinity neighborhood next opposite orbit outside premises proximity range (n.) realm(s) region right scope space span sphere subsequent that (distant) top underside	

Spanish	face (n.) foot head heart	base bottom company conduit course flower half love passage road road, way root side tip top union	bring close continuation deviate divide isolate mediate opposition throw turn	apart beyond center destination direction exterior far, distant front front high (place) inferior (place) inside, interior lateral left middle near next other side outside posterior (place) right	
Chinese		bottom cause, reason edge self side summit	arrive consent do-stop exist face (v.) follow follow (a course) give go go along go through shine strike take	back center direction front inside left-right midpoint outside outside place top-bottom	harmony same
Thai	back face side, flank	edge line property rim round (object) side trap way	accord (v.) arrive attend (with) connect cross (v.) cross straight descend detour (v.) enter exist exit follow follow behind	above back side below everywhere far inside interim left lower middle near out outside	

go	place
go up	right
hitch	under side
join	upper side
leave (v.)	
maintain	
measure (v.)	
move to	
pass	
pass (a way)	
pass (by)	
result (v.)	
return	
stab, pierce	
stick (with)	
stop	
surpass	
take	
together	

Table 9.2 Ontological categories of source lexemes of adpositions

Evident from the list in Table 9.2 are that there are no TIME-category nouns that developed into adpositions (note that the English *subsequent* was originally referring to spatial order as well as temporal order; *OED*), and that QUALITY-category nouns are extremely few as well. There are only three items, 'essence' (J), 'harmony' (C), and 'same' (C). The lexeme 'essence', the source of Japanese Ablative *-kara* 'from', also had the meaning 'nature', thus the source seems to have meant 'essential part' of an object. This meaning then opens the possibility that it was simply referring to an intangible object, thus, belonging to the OBJECT category. The Chinese Comitative prepositions *hé* 'with' (< 'harmony') and *tóng* 'with' (< 'same') may fit in the QUALITY category. Out of many source lexemes, the proportion of the lexemes in the two categories (TIME and QUALITY), more abstract than SPACE, is negligible, thus supporting the directionality of abstraction in grammaticalization.

Also notable from the list is that there are a large number of spatial lexemes (mostly nouns). A closer look shows that the majority of these spatial lexemes are members of complex adpositions, which suggests that they have not undergone grammaticalization to a substantial extent. In encoding a spatial relationship, language users tend to use spatial nouns in a given template, such as P(D)NP in English and Spanish, and PNP in Korean and Japanese.

Another noteworthy aspect of source lexeme categories is that there are numerous verbs (and verbal nouns) that denote an activity or process (note, however, that English and Spanish do not have many verbal sources). As has been pointed out (Heine et al. 1991a, Y Matsumoto 1998, see 3.3.3.2), most lexemes in this category are transitive verbs. The notion of 'transitivity' as applied to English might be unsuitable for other languages, because the use of a case marker cannot be the criterion of transitive-intransitive distinction. For instance, the Korean verb of locomotion *ka-*'go' often occurs with an Accusative-marked spatial entity as the goal of movement, instead of Locative-marked entity (which is also possible), as in [school-Acc go], a configuration for a transitive verb. Thus, the important characterization here is whether the verb involves an object as a target or theme of the activity, instead of what types of grammatical markers are used for the object.

A final point is that PERSON-category lexemes are not a frequently exploited category in the grammaticalization of adpositions.[5] There may be a couple of reasons for this. There are not many human body-part nouns in language in the first place, and out of the small number of nouns, those that can constitute a good reference point in a schema (e.g., head, face, back, heart, etc.) are even smaller in number. This is plainly true considering that 'elbow', 'finger', 'wrist', 'cheek', etc. cannot be easily recruited in encoding a general spatial relationship. Another possibility is that general nouns are vast in number and there is no lack of lexemes that can express the profiled spatial relationship, sharply contrasting with human body-part nouns. For instance, such nouns as 'edge', 'hill', 'course', 'root' etc. do not have good counterparts among the human corporeal terms.

From the foregoing discussion, it is clear that the lexemes involved in the grammaticalization of spatial adpositions are at the level of SPACE or below in the

---

[5] This is an interesting aspect considering that Bowden (1992) and Esseesy (2010) report that body-part terms are among the most common sources of prepositions in Oceanic languages and Arabic (see 5.3.3.1). See also Brugman (1983) and MacLaury (1989) for common use of corporeal-metaphorization in the development of spatial grams.

ontological chain, which points to the fact that grammaticalizing forms generally undergo semantic reduction ('bleaching') or abstraction, supporting the unidirectionality hypothesis.

9.5 Universal Path

We have seen in the above that grammaticalization scenarios of adpositions in the six languages surveyed in this book are largely consonant with the source determination and unidirectionality hypotheses. As Bybee et al. (1994: 14) state, these two hypotheses predict that there will be crosslinguistically similar paths for the development of grammatical meaning, labeled as the 'universal path' hypothesis. In other words, any instances of grammaticalization "that begin with the same or similar source meaning can be expected to follow the same course of change" (Bybee et al. 1994: 14; see also Heine and Reh 1984, Dahl 1985, Bybee and Dahl 1989, Heine et al. 1991a). A serious and ideal discussion on the universal path hypothesis should draw upon the analyses of an individual gram's developmental paths and adjacent grammatical categories, but our discussion will be limited to the patterns displayed by the nominal and verbal sources.

9.5.1 The Noun Channel

We have noted in the above that source lexemes bear a great level of similarity with the target, i.e., spatial adpositions, and that this is particularly prominent in the cases of complex adpositions. The channels necessarily involve the meaning and form of grammaticalizing forms. Since the semantic affinity of source lexemes has been already discussed above, we will pay more attention to their structural properties and examine how similar they are across languages. The structural properties of those involving a noun, disregarding unidentified or idiosyncratic patterns, are as follows, in which NP is the host noun and the rest is the source of the adposition:

(10) Korean: NP-uy RN-(ey/...)   [NP-Gen RN-LOC]   'at/... RN of NP'
      Japanese: NP-no RN-(ni/...)   [NP-Gen RN-LOC]   'at/... RN of NP'
      English: in/... (the) N of NP   [LOC (D) N of NP]   'in/... N of NP'
                 in/... (the) RN of NP   [LOC (D) RN of NP]   'in/... RN of NP'
      Spanish: en/... (el/la...) N de NP   [LOC (D) N of NP]   'in/... N of NP'
                 en/... (el/la...) RN de NP   [LOC (D) RN of NP]   'in/.. RN of NP'
      Chinese: N NP   [N NP]   'Prep NP'
                 NP-de/zhī... RN   [NP-GEN RN]   'Post NP'
      Thai: N NP   [N NP]   'Prep NP'

The summarized structural patterns of adpositional source constructions in (10) clearly show a few intriguing structural aspects of the source constructions entering into the grammaticalization paths. First of all, typologically similar languages show a greater level of similarities, e.g., Korean and Japanese, English and Spanish, and Chinese and Thai.

There is a mirror-image relationship between Korean and Japanese on the one hand (postpositional) and English and Spanish on the other (prepositional). The major differences include the presence and absence of definite articles (a natural consequence of their being article and article-less languages, respectively). And another difference is the omissibility or erosion of Locatives in the two groups. If we consider the older grams, e.g., primary and composite prepositions in English and Spanish, the presence of *across* (< *a-cross* 'on/at cross'), *atop* (< *a-top* 'on top') in English (see 5.2) and *bajo* 'under' (< *bajo* n. 'base', cf. *bajo de* (< *bajo de* 'base of')) (see 6.4.2), the omission of the final linker (e.g., *of* or *de*) is likely to have happened in English and Spanish.

In case of English, the linker could have been not an independent linker but the inflection of the nominal, as can be seen in *besides, amongst, amidst*, etc., which include *-(e)s*, the adverbial Genitive, similar to the Korean *-uy* and the Japanese *-no* (see 5.3.2), and *admid(st)* (< *on middan* 'in middle' in which *middan* is Dative marked) (see 5.2). The difference between Spanish and English in this respect is due to the fact that Spanish non-pronominal nouns do not case-inflect (a general feature in Romance languages, sharply contrasting with their ancestral Latin which was heavily case-inflected with seven cases), whereas English did case-inflect prior to Modern English times.

The patterns in Chinese and Thai are similar to each other, except that Chinese has both prepositions and postpositions, whereas Thai has prepositions only. These two languages stand out among the surveyed languages in that there are no complex structures involved, which is in line with the general characteristics of isolating languages. A simple juxtaposition of a noun and another noun, in which one that has the potential of designating a spatial relationship becomes reinterpreted as an adposition (see 9.6 for more discussion).

9.5.2 The Verb Channel

Just as is the case with noun-based adpositions, verb-based adpositions also have specific source structures. The structural properties of those involving a verb, disregarding unidentified or idiosyncratic patterns, are as follows, in which NP is the host noun and the rest is the source of the adposition (note that Korean and Japanese verbal inflections for linking, i.e., -e and -te, are both glossed as a non-finite marker, NF):

(11) Korean: NP-ul/ey/lo.. V-e   [NP-ACC/ALL... V-NF]   'Verbing NP'
      Japanese: NP-o/ni... V-te   [NP-ACC/ALL... V-NF]   'Verbing NP'
      English: V-ing NP   [V-prp NP]   'Verbing NP'
      Spanish: V-ando/iendo NP   [V-Prp NP]   'Verbing NP'
                 a V de NP   [to V from NP]   'to V from NP'
                 V-mente a/de NP   [V-Adv to NP]   'in a Verbing manner to'
      Chinese: V NP   [V NP]   'Prep NP'
      Thai: V NP   [V NP]   'Prep NP'

The patterns shown in (11) are very similar to those of the noun-based adpositions, shown in (10) above. Typologically paired languages have similar patterns, and the agglutinative languages (Korean and Japanese) and inflecting languages (English and Spanish) have comparable patterns that are mirror images in linear configuration, as expected from the difference of postpositional and prepositional languages. The first linking element in Korean and Japanese is the Accusative or Allative and the final linking element hosted by the source verb is *-e* and *-te* (non-finite markers, also broadly defined as Connectives, but are known by various other names including converbs, etc.; see 3.3.3.2 and 4.3.3.3).

The linking devices in English and Spanish comparable to the Korean *-e* and the Japanese *-te* are the participial inflection of the verb, *-ing* in English and *-ando/iendo* (also often called gerundive in Spanish), of which the functions are nearly identical with the linkers in Korean and Japanese. One unique type in Spanish is the use of adverbial forms, in which case an additional linker, the preposition *a* 'to' or *de* 'of' is also needed (see 6.3.3.3 and 6.3.3.4).[6]

The Chinese and Thai patterns are again very simple and similar to each other. The participating verbs, typically transitive verbs or those that frequently occur with a nominal having a conceptual relationship with the verb (see 9.4 above), occur before a noun, and the relationship between these two adjacent forms [V–NP] triggers the reinterpretation of the function of the verb, as that of a preposition (see 9.6 for more discussion).

9.6 Analogy, Reanalysis, and Reinterpretation

Even though analogy and reanalysis have been widely recognized as significant processes involved in language change in general (Hopper and Traugott 2003[1993]: 39), from the early days of grammaticalization studies, analogy has often been contrasted with reanalysis, and its role in grammaticalization has been largely disregarded (e.g., Meillet 1912: 133, see also Givón 1991b). The recognized role of analogy was the contribution to rule spread, whereas the role of reanalysis is regarded as innovation of a new rule, i.e., the primary source of grammaticalization

---

6) Since many adverbial forms that serve as the adpositional source in Spanish are not directly derived from verbs, their patterns are not included in the present discusson (see 6.3.3.4).

(Hopper and Traugott 2003[1993]: 39-40, 46-58).

However, recent case studies (De Smet 2009, 2012, 2014, Fischer 2007, 2008, 2011, 2012, 2013, M Ahn 2009a,b, H Lee 2011, Rhee and Koo 2015, K Ahn 2015, Traugott and Trousdale 2013: 37-38, Yae 2018, among numerous others) present proposals in favor of analogy as a trigger of structural reanalysis leading to grammaticalization. Further, Delbecque and Verveckken (2014: 639) propose to describe the type of analogy operative in grammaticalization with 'conceptual persistence' as analogous to Hopper's (1991) notion of 'lexical persistence.' With respect to grammaticalization in Korean, H Koo (2010) and S Rhee (2014) propose 'structural analogy' as a crucial mechanism of grammaticalization, especially when new paradigms arise from older ones (see also M Kim, 2010 for discussion of the development of the Korean connective *siphi* per analogy based on formal and functional similarity). Indeed language is replete with cases in which similar yet diverse functions arise from context-induced reinterpretation (Heine et al., 1991a), in which contexts provide analogical bases for extension.

With respect to the grammaticalization of adpositions, Hoffmann (2005), in his analysis of the grammaticalization of English complex prepositions, notes that some of them, e.g., *by reference to, in accordance with, in addition to*, etc., do not exhibit noticeable processes of grammaticalization, and are likely to have developed based on structural and functional analogy from the well-established complex prepositions, e.g., *in favor of, in view of*, etc. (of the PNP structure), which he calls 'structural relatives' (p. 153). He argues that certain aspects of grammaticalization rely much less on the nature and context-dependent use of individual content words, contra common belief, and concludes that grammaticalization may result in the establishment of constructional schemas, which will be utilized by other lexical items, whose grammaticalization will be not gradual but abrupt (see also M Ahn 2009, H Lee 2011, Rhee and Koo 2015, K Ahn 2015 for similar analyses).

A look at the patterns of adpositional grammaticalization indeed suggests that structural analogy seems to be at work. As has been noted in the above, most languages, Korean, Japanese, English, and Thai, in particular, have complex structural patterns that are likely to function as constructional schemas, since there are already well-established forms in that configuration, especially those involving nouns and verbs. We also noted that the source lexemes tend to belong to similar conceptual categories in meaning, such as relational nouns, spatial nouns, transitive verbs (or those denoting some forms of interaction or relation with a nominal). This semantic affinity, coupled with the structural affinity with the easily accessible templates, seems to have prompted or at least contributed to the development of complex adpositions (and composite adpositions to a lesser extent). Such possibility can be illustrated in the following:

(11) Korean

a. *kang-ul   pwuth-e*   〉〉   *kang-pwuthe*
   river-ACC   adhere-NF   river-ABL
   'adhere to the river and'   'from the river'

b. *kang-ul   ttal-a*   〉〉   *kang-ttala*
   river-ACC   follow-NF   river-PROL
   'follow the river and'   'along the river'

c. *kang-ul   nem-e*   〉〉   *kang-neme*
   river-ACC   cross-NF   river-ULT
   'cross the river and'   'across the river'

The Ablative postposition *-pwuthe* has a long history, attested in Late Middle Korean (15th~16th centuries). The verb of movement *pwuth-* 'adhere', as a transitive verb, takes the noun complement *kang* 'river' marked by an Accusative *-ul* (see 3.3.3.2), in the structural template of [NP-ACC V-NF]. It is quite plausible to hypothesize that the Prolative *-ttala* and the Ulterior *-neme,* which developed at a later time, were triggered or aided by the meaning of the source verbs (i.e., all making reference to an action with respect to a theme landmark), thus adopting the structural template [NP-ACC V-NF]. A more fine-grained analysis, however, should await in-depth research with respect to their motivation.

   In the process of grammaticalization, there occur structural reanalysis and functional reinterpretation. This can be illustrated with the example given above, repeated here as (12):

(12) Syntactic   **Reanalysis/Reinterpretation**   Morphological

kang-ul   *pwuth-e* ⟩⟩   *kang-[ul pwuth-e]*   ⟩⟩   *kang-pwuthe*

river-ACC   adhere-NF   river-[ABL]   river-ABL

'adhere to the river and'   'from the river'   'from the river'

In (12), the syntactic construction becomes a morphological unit through reanalysis and reinterpretation. In other words, at the intermediate stage, there is no change in surface manifestation but the complex unit of [ACC adhere-NF] is regarded as a single unit (i.e., reanalysis), and the function of the unit is regarded not as [adhere N and] but as [from] (i.e., reinterpretation). It is also notable that when the internal structure is 'ignored', the unit is subject to further reductive change, which, in this case, is the loss of the Accusative *-ul*. This type of change seems to have occurred to most primary and composite postpositions in Korean, and analogous changes seem to have occurred in other languages as well, in which structural simplification is visible in primary and composite adpositions.

In languages that relatively lack established morphosyntactic trappings, such as Chinese and Thai, the developmental patterns of adpositions largely depend on reanalysis of the structure and reinterpretation of the function, without much structural change. This can be illustrated with the following Thai examples:

(13) นี่ หนังสือ ของ เพื่อน

    a. *ni*   *náŋsŭu* ***khong***   *phuan*   b. *ni náŋsŭu*   ***khong***   *phuan*

    this   book   **property**   friend   this book   **of**   friend

    'this book friend's property'   'This is (my) friend's book.'

(14) พบ กัน ที่ บ้าน เพื่อน

    a. *phop kan*   ***thii*** *baan phuan*   b. *phop kan*   ***thii*** *baan phuan*

    meet together **place** house friend   meet together **at**   house friend

    'meet place friend's house'   'We met at a friend's house'

(15)   แม่ ขาย ของ จาก เช้า ถึง ค่ำ

    a.   *mae*   *khai* *khong* **_caak_**   *chaw*   **_thung_** *kham*
        mother sell   thing   **depart** morning **arrive**   evening
        'mother sell thing depart morning arrive evening'

    b.   *mae*   *khai* *khong* **_caak_** *chaw*   **_thung_** *kham*
        mother sell   thing   **from** morning **till**   evening
        'Mother sold things from morning till evening.'

In the examples above, the (a) examples are given with the lexical meaning in glossing, and the (b) examples are with the prepositional meaning. Since the grammaticalization processes do not involve any structural change, the source structures are simply reanalyzed and reinterpreted. For instance, in (13), 'property' in the string of [book property friend] (or [book friend's property]; note that juxtaposed 'property friend' (*khong phuan*) is a regular expression for 'friend's property' in Thai) is simply functionally reinterpreted as a marker of possession, i.e., Genitive. Accordingly the string is reanalyzed from [book property friend] to [book [of friend]], in which 'property' is the Genitive marker. This reinterpretation must have been based on the facts that in [[book] [property] [friend]] the three nominals occur independently without conceptual cohesion; that the interlocutors have the desire to encode/decode the structure with reasonable cohesion; and that the (re)interpretation of [book property friend] as [friend's book] is the most suitable option.

    Similarly, in (14a), the string [meet together place house friend] does not show syntactic and conceptual cohesion (not even in a more natural interpretation [meet together place friend's house]), because 'place' (*thii*) is a noun without any linking function with adjacent forms syntactically, and at the same time its presence is superfluous semantically because there is another place noun, i.e., 'friend's house'. In this circumstance, when the event predicate '(we) meet together' (note that Thai is a pro-drop language) and the locative noun phrase 'friend's house' are juxtaposed, the best functional (re)interpretation of the intervening locative noun 'place' (*thii*) is attributing the Locative prepositional function to it, as a linking device for the two syntactic units.

Example (15) is a little more complex, but the situation is largely the same. The source structure is [mother sell thing depart morning leave evening] with three potential predicates 'mother sells', 'mother leaves', and 'mother arrives'. The prompts for reinterpretation are that leaving and arriving mark two end-point events of a journey; that morning and evening are not places of departure or arrival, but, instead, are designators of temporal points; and that the three events, selling, leaving, and arriving cannot be coherently aligned as a sequence of events. In this case, leaving and arriving can be paired as markers of the beginning and the end, which will naturally lead to their reinterpretation as Ablative and Allative, i.e., 'from' and 'to'. Evidently, this type of paired functions of temporal points must have followed the functions of locative-point marking, e.g., *caak Seoul thung Krung Thep* (จาก โซล ถึง กรุงเทพ) 'from Seoul to Bangkok'.

The cognitive operations of reinterpretation, reanalysis, and analogy bear special significance in grammaticalization studies (cf. Abraham 2004). Since language users are in constant search of meanings and patterns in language use, meanings are constantly extended through reinterpretation; the units are accordingly reanalyzed; and the constructions are applied to novel structures for experiment (perhaps prompted by the desire for novelty or creativity, Heine and Stolz 2008, see 10.1.1 for further discussion). In this experimental process, there is bound to be an individual variation. For instance, when a conservative structure becomes a fully grammatical form, going through an extensive erosion, e.g., [por vía de] > [vía], [de bajo de] > [bajo], etc. in Spanish, the result is the bare nominals *vía* and *bajo* functioning as prepositions. In extreme situations, this may potentially serve as a template for directly using nouns as prepositions (cf. 'conversion'). Attribution of a linking function to a noun can be interpreted as an instance of 'absorption' (cf. Bybee et al. 1994). This is radical and has not been reported to date in Spanish, perhaps due to typological constraints in Spanish.

However, this kind of scenario seems to manifest more easily with isolating languages. For instance, the Thai verb of locomotion *pay* (ไป) 'go' occurs with the preposition *yang* (ยัง) 'to'. In such cases, both of them encode directionality in common, and their cooccurrence is naturally frequent because 'going' typically involves a destination. Based on this state of affairs, the conceptual and syntagmatic cohesion increases, and eventually some authors list the polylexemic *pay yang* (ไปยัง) as a single preposition. When this conceptual consolidation in the string becomes further strengthened, *pay* 'absorbs' the direction-marking function and can increasingly host other forms forming the template [X-pay]. Through entrenchment of this template, other strings in the similar configuration may also begin to be regarded as univerbated prepositions, e.g., *khâw pay* (เข้าไป) [into-go], *khûn pay* (ขึ้นไป) [up-go], *thàt pay* (ถัดไป) [next-go], etc. (see 8.2; note that these are not included in our list because Thai consultants consider them as non-grammaticalized syntactic constructions). These instances strongly suggest that formation of a template, absorption of a function, and analogical extension are intertwined in the grammaticalization of polylexemic constructions.

9.7 Summary

In this chapter, we have looked at a number of principles and hypotheses in view of the grammaticalization scenarios of the adpositions in the six languages, e.g., divergence, persistence, source determination, unidirectionality, universal path, analogy, reanalysis, and reinterpretation.

Divergence is well observed in the vast majority of the adpositions in the six languages. In particular, in isolating languages, in which a form typically carries diverse functions across grammatical categories, identifiable divergence is a norm. In other words, with very few exceptions, all adpositions in Chinese and Thai have their lexical origins which are fully functioning as such contemporarily. Agglutinating languages, Korean and Japanese, also display divergence but to a lesser degree due to the inability to identify historical sources of some old, primary postpositions, contemporarily. Divergence in inflecting languages is also numerous, but identifiability increases along the tripartite classification of primary, composite, and complex prepositions.

Persistence, reflecting the source characteristics in the behavior of a grammaticalized form, is widely attested, though its gradual diminution of meaning and resultant complete desemanticization needs to be confirmed by historical documentation, because semantic emptying does not occur abruptly nor completely over a short period of time. Persistence is particularly noticeable in the adpositions that have not yet advanced to a great extent of grammaticalization, i.e., more easily observable in composite and complex adpositions rather than in primary adpositions.

Through a detailed analysis of grammaticalization sources, the source-target relationship was examined, whereby the source determination hypothesis is largely upheld. For instance, Directionals typically develop from 'direction'- and 'passage'-related nouns and verbs of directed motion; Sources develop from nouns designating origin, basis, etc.; Paths develop from the lexemes denoting path or passing event, etc. There are a few exceptions, the motivation of which is not immediately clear, but most adpositions of the 19 grammatical concepts of space in the six languages present a relatively clear conceptual relationship with their source lexemes, thus, upholding source determination, even though their small-step developmental paths could not be confirmed due to limitations in data and space.

Unidirectionality is supposedly the strongest tendency in, and a defining characteristic of, grammaticalization processes. Among diverse planes of grammar, we reviewed the directionality in form and meaning. Formal reduction is typically a result of pursuing simplification of articulatory gestures (for ease of utterance), and syntagmatic fixation is due to the lexemes' movement from being autonomous (as nouns or verbs) to being dependent (as adpositions). Semantic reduction occurs in tandem with formal reduction, and is inevitable because grammatical concepts are more abstract than source lexemes in meaning. In the ontological continuum of PERSON ⟩ OBJECT ⟩ ACTIVITY/PROCESS ⟩ SPACE ⟩ TIME ⟩ QUALITY, spatial grams tend to develop from space-denoting lexemes or those related to the concepts left of SPACE, and nearly never from those related to the concepts right of it, i.e., TIME and QUALITY.

The paths of grammaticalization of adpositions are investigated, in the two categories of the noun channel and the verb channel. We could confirm that there are a large number of adpositions that developed through the use of templates. The templates serve as linkers to embed a nominal, but there are other types of linkers, such as inflections (in English, which was formerly a fully inflectional language), prepositions (in Spanish), converbs (Korean and Japanese), participial forms of verbs (in Spanish and English), among others.

We have also reviewed the grammaticalization scenarios with theoretically important notions, e.g., analogy, reanalysis, and reinterpretation, which are closely interrelated. We noted that analogical processes, especially manifest in template formation and application, constitute, contrary to the common belief, a common and powerful mechanism of grammaticalization of adpositions. These processes are triggered by formal similarity (e.g., templates) or semantic affinity (e.g., synonyms, near-synonyms, or antonyms, etc.). We also noted that there are cases of 'absorption', whereby a form absorbs the function of an adjacent form that commonly cooccurs. The adjacent forms that once provided the meaning, after the absorption, disappear. These complex scenarios are the results of an intricate interaction of analogy, reanalysis, and reinterpretation.

10

Typology and Beyond

In the description of grammaticalization scenarios in six languages in the preceding chapters, a number of significant aspects have surfaced. In this chapter we will discuss some notable commonalities and differences displayed by the surveyed languages from a typological perspective and, further, from a contact-induced grammaticalization perspective.

10.1 Commonalities

Even though the surveyed languages are used by different people in different cultures, the grammaticalization scenarios of adpositions display commonalities to a great extent. Many or most of these can be attributed to human propensities shared by people regardless of their language types or cultures. We have already briefly discussed some of them, but we will look into them more in detail.

10.1.1 Restrictive Determinants and Expansive Motivations

In chapter 9, we reviewed a number of principles and hypotheses and concluded that even though the extent may be variable by the language, the principles and hypotheses were largely well supported by the grammaticalization patterns displayed in the six languages. The most prominent aspects are that there is a remarkably common pattern in the selection of source lexemes for grammaticalization of spatial adpositions, i.e., those that denote a spatial entity (noun) or an activity involving an object (verb); and that the directions of change are also remarkably similar, i.e., from the ontological categories of PERSON, OBJECT, and PROCESS to SPACE, instead of the reversed direction of metaphorization such as from TIME or QUALITY to SPACE. We noted that this directionality is in line with source determination hypothesis and the universal path hypothesis.

These patterns are manifestations of restrictive mechanisms that operate behind the grammaticalization in the sense that source lexemes are not randomly selected nor are the grammaticalization paths allowed to diverge randomly. In other words, only those lexemes that are deemed appropriate for the particular spatial encoding are selected, and only those extensions that are deemed inferrable with relative ease in a given context are allowed in the progression of change.

Though as powerful as these restrictive mechanisms are, there are also impetuses that push the change in the reverse direction, i.e., expansive motivations. There are two major forces, i.e., creativity and psychological congruity, to which we turn for more elaboration.

[Creativity]
As we briefly alluded to in 9.6, language users reanalyze the existing string of language material, reinterpret the function of the reanalyzed unit, and apply the new constructional unit to novel structures for experiment, which, perhaps is prompted by the desire for novelty or creativity. Heine and Stolz (2008: 332), following Croce (1912[1902: 172-174), note that language is essentially creative activity. Lehmann (1987) also asserts that the desire to be original, to say something that has not been uttered before, and to give one's thoughts an imposing expression are an essential part of linguistic activity, and further considers creativity not to be confined to the lexicon but to concern the grammatical-structural domain of linguistic signs as well (as cited in Heine and Stolz 2008: 335).

This is indeed true when we consider the grammaticalization of forms for a certain function when there already exist one or more grammatical markers for the same function. We noted in all six languages that there are multiple sources from which grammatical forms arise and that consequently there are multiple forms creating chronologically variegated layers within the functional domain. These functionally similar forms may be differentially specialized, or some forms may fall into disuse eventually. This is well illustrated in the following example in Korean:

(1) 迦毗羅國에 가아 淨飯王끽 安否 숣더니

   a. *KAPILAKWUK-ey ka-a   CENGPANWANG-**skuy**   ANPWU sAlp-te-ni*
      Kapilavastu-ALL   go-NF   pure.rice.king.-**HON:DAT** greetings say-PST-CONN
      '(Buddha) went to the Kapilavastu Kingdom and said greetings to (his father) Cengpan King (Pure Rice King; Suddhodana), and...'

                                        (1447 *Sekposangcel* 6:2)

   b. 그 쑬 드려 무로듸
      *ku   stAl-**tAlye**   mwul-otAy*
      that   daughter-**DAT**   ask-CONN
      'as (he) asked his daughter, (saying)...'

                                       (1447 *Sekposangcel* 6:14)

   c. 길 녈 한 사ㄹ믈 보고 무로듸
      *kil nye-l   han   salAm-**Al.poko** mwul-otAy*
      way go-ADN many   person-**DAT**   ask-CONN
      '(I) asked many people who were walking on the way, (saying)...'

                                       (1447 *Welinsekpo* 10:25b)

   d. 쥐싀기가 어미 흔테 와셔 말흥되
      *cwisAykki-ka   emi-**hAnthey**   w-asye   malhA-toy*
      mouse-NOM   mother-**to/one.place**   come-SEQ   talk-as
      'A mouse comes to its mother and says that...'

                                  (1896 *Sinceng Simsangsohak* 1: L17)

The examples in (1a)-(1c) are taken from the commentaries of the Buddhist scriptures dated from the 15th century (Late Middle Korean). Example (1a) has two directional markers, the Allative *-ey* and the honorific Dative *-skuy*. These were relatively well-established directional markers in the 15th century and even in the earlier period. However, in the same period a new Dative *-tAlye* (the predecessor of the modern-day *-tele*) in (1b) began to emerge, based on the lexical meaning 'be accompanied by'. Since a social superior is accompanied by an inferior (not the reverse), the Dative *-tAlye* tended to occur in the context when a social superior was addressing an inferior, a cooccurrence restriction still in effect, though being eased, in Modern Korean. The sense of accompaniment is weakened to association, allowing even very brief association as in asking a question to a passerby. Example (1c) is unclear if it is the instance of the Dative use of *-(Al/ul).poko* or simply a syntactic construction, i.e., X-*Al/ul po-ko* [Acc see-and], denoting 'see X and' or 'seeing X'. The syntactic-construction interpretation of (1c) is '(I) saw a lot of people coming and going in the street and asked (them)...' and the Dative interpretation is 'I asked a question to a lot of people coming and going in the street, saying...'. The status is unclear, but it certainly constitutes the 'bridging context' (Heine 2002), in which both the older and newer functional interpretations are available. In Modern Korean, the Accusative *-Al* disappeared and has been replaced by *-ul*, which also occurs at a very low frequency, thus, *-poko* functioning as a productive Dative. Example (1d), taken from a fairy tale in a 19th century textbook, contains the Dative *-hAnthey* (the predecessor of the modern *-hanthey*). This Dative developed from the noun phrase *han tey* [one place], which, by virtue of two animate entities being located at 'one' place, came to mark the end-point of locomotion or transfer (see 3.4.4.2 for more discussion). The Dative *-hanthey* is a productive grammatical marker in Modern Korean.

All these recurrent innovations, leading to multiple layers within a single functional domain, can be accounted for by resorting to the language users' desire for creative language use. At the time of innovation, some particular aspects of the lexical meanings of the source construction could have been the major attraction for the innovator. For instance, in a situation where the old gram *-ey* 'to' could be used, the innovator of the Dative *-tAlye* 'to' (< 'be accompanied by') may have felt, in the spirit of creativity, that stating that the social superior created association with the inferior and thus the speaker and the addressee were together when the action (locution or transfer) was taking place would be a more expressive and novel way of marking the directionality. Similarly, another innovator of *-Al/ul.poko* (< 'see') may have felt that stating that the agent of the action (locution or transfer) first looked at the addressee or target and then performed the action would create a more vivid image of the interactive scene and locational and temporal immediacy between the agent and the recipient. Still another innovator of *-hanthey,* despite the fact that there were already many Dative, Allative, Directional markers available, may have felt the desire to indicate that certain actions (e.g., locomotion) led to the arrival at 'one place' at which two persons became associated, as the expression, like *-Al/ul.poko,* created the sense of locational immediacy.

A similar state of affairs can be exemplified with English Interiors, the marker signaling that the trajector is located inside the landmark. The following are taken from the *Oxford English Dictionary* (with translations added):

(2) a. eOE (Mercian) Vespasian Psalter (1965) viii. 1 (2) *Domine dominus noster, quam ammirabile est nomen tuum in uniuersa terra: dryhten dryhten ur hu wundurlic is noma ðin <u>in</u> alre eorðan.*
'Lord our lord, how amazing is your name <u>in</u> the whole earth'

   b. c1175 Lamb. Hom. 89 *Þa weren þer igedered <u>wiðinne</u> þere buruh of ierusalem trowfeste men.*
'Then there were gathered <u>within</u> the city of Jerusalem true men.'

   c. 1504 in Eng. Gilds 327 *A tabell yn the syde of the halle..a bynch <u>yn the yn-syde of</u> the tabell.*
'A table in the side of the hall... a bench <u>in the inside of</u> the table.'

   d. 1791 J. Lackington Mem. (1792) 212 *The coachman put me <u>inside</u> the carriage.*

   e. 1839 C. Darwin in R. Fitzroy & C. Darwin Narr. Surv. Voy. H.M.S. Adventure & Beagle III. xxii. 567 *All the active volcanoes occur <u>within the areas of</u> elevation.*

   f. 1964 Internat. Affairs 40 198 *It is important for United Nations forces to have full freedom of movement <u>within the area of</u> operations.*

As indicated in Table 5.4, English has a number of Interiors, among which *in* is the oldest form attested in Old English as exemplified in (2a). Incidentally, in Old English, there was another Interior, now defunct, *binnan* 'within, inside of, in', etymologically composed of *bi-in-ana* [around-in-Advz], for which *OED* gives citations dated from c.1000 through c.1400. In the Middle English period, a new Interior preposition *within* appeared. According to *OED* (entry for *within*, prep.), it denoted 'in the inner part of, interior of, inside of, in' as "a mere synonym of *in*". The preposition *within* is composed of *with* and *inne*; *with* beginning with the opposition meaning and then extended to various kinds of relations (*OED*, see also S Rhee 2004a) and *inne* indicating 'inside, indoors, on the inside'. The innovation of this new Interior, despite the presence of already well-established Interior *in*, is due to its more expressive quality, though not available in Modern English, of the 'contrast' meaning associated with *with*. In other words, *within* highlights the trajector being inside 'in contrast with' being outside. In Early Modern English, still another Interior is innovated, *in the inside of* in (2c). Undoubtedly, due to its highly periphrastic and compositional nature, the meaning as well as the form must have been perceptually salient. This periphrastic form became substantially reduced by Modern English, i.e., *inside (of)*, in (2d). In Modern English still another periphrastic form was innovated, i.e., *within the area(s) of*. Being compositional, it could highlight the locational notion of 'area' more explicitly, as shown in (2e) and (2f). It is not clear if *(with)in the area of* was the trail-blazer but when the [(with)in LN of] (LN standing for locative noun) is established as a template, a large number of locative nouns seem to have followed the pattern, e.g., *region, space, sphere, premises, scope, realm(s), limits, boundaries, range, bounds, field, space, span, orbit, radius, circumference, distance*, etc. (see Table 5.4). Since these complex prepositions are periphrastic involving lexical nouns, their meaning must have been, especially at the time of innovation, very salient and emphatic as compared with their older and more plain competitors. All these instances of continual innovation can be interpreted as the manifestation of the desire for creativity and expressivity.

[Cognitive Congruity]

There is another factor that functions as an expansive mechanism, i.e., cognitive congruity. Cognitive congruity refers to the aspects of language use being congruous with the cognitive state variable with the situational context. For instance, in a situation when the speaker is casually interacting with an interlocutor their cognitive state is also casual and thus they are led to the use of casual speech congruous with the cognitive state.

What is significant in this context is what Rohdenburg (1996: 151) labels 'the complexity principle' (and 'transparency principle'), which states that when more or less explicit grammatical options are available, the more explicit one(s) will tend to be favored in cognitively more complex environment. Rohdenburg further notes that the more explicit variant is generally represented by the bulkier element or construction (p. 152). For instance, when there are seemingly equivalent prepositions, e.g., *on* and *upon*, they occur in different use contexts, e.g., *upon*, the formal and more explicit variant of the general *on*, tends to occur in more abstract and complex contexts with respect to complementation, voice, object modification, etc. (pp. 170-171), as exemplified in part in the following example (p. 170):

(3)   ... *I then prevailed upon the editor of the newspaper I then wrote for, the Daily Mail, to send me...* (*The Times* or *The Sunday Times* 1991)

Example (3) involves the preposition *upon* accompanying the verb *prevail*. Rohdenburg (1996) states that this type of *on-upon* variation occurs with such verbs as *call, count, depend, prevail*, and *rely*. Thus, according to the complexity principle the choice of a form out of multiple options is correlated with processing complexity.

When the complexity principle is applied to the use of adpositions, as exemplified by the contrast of *on* and *upon* in English by Rohdenburg (1996: 170-171), we can reasonably assume that when language users are in a cognitively complex context but do not have many options available, they are likely to feel the need to "invent" a complex and more explicit (but reasonably understandable) alternative by making use of the existing pattern. It is plausible then that a large number of complex prepositions in English and Spanish may have been the result of such an expansive cognitive mechanism. This can be exemplified in part with the following examples in Spanish:

(4) a. *Hay comida ya preparada <u>en</u> el supermercado.*
        'There's ready-made food <u>in</u> the supermarket.' (*SpanishDict*)

    b. *Situadas <u>en el interior de</u> la isla, las casas salesianas no han sido afectadas*
        directamente por el reciente maremoto.
        'Located <u>in the interior part of</u> the island, the Salesian missions were not
        struck directly by the recent tsunami. (missionidonbosco.org; *Linguee*)

As indicated in Table 6.4 and 6.3.3.1, *en* 'in' is among the top frequency prepositions
in Spanish inherited from Latin, i.e., from the Latin preposition *in* to the Spanish
preposition *en*. Thus, *en* is among those that have the longest history and,
accordingly, the most general meaning. Occurring at the 23,944 pmw frequency, it is
the second most frequent preposition, following *de* 'of', which is also an inherited
preposition from Latin. Its usage is so general that it occurs across all genres or
registers, as in examples shown in (4). It needs to be confirmed by a careful text
analysis, but it is reasonable to assume that creating a new alternative, more specific
in meaning, by way of using the lexeme *interior* and the PDNP template, i.e., *en el*
interior de, is likely to have been prompted by the desire to be more explicit and
more informative, especially in the context of higher cognitive complexity as in the
discussion of the natural disaster as in (4b).

10.1.2 Propensity for Positivity

Another common feature of all the surveyed languages is the presence of the
phenomenon of favoring 'positive sides' and 'positive directions' (Andersen 1978:
343; Heine 1997). We already noted this briefly with respect to Korean (3.4.2) and
Japanese (4.3.2), English (5.3.3.1), and Chinese (7.2). Since this propensity for
positivity seems to be among the robust commonalities, we will discuss the issue in a
little more detail.

[Top over Bottom]
Spatial adpositions may belong to one or the other of the broad categories of

non-axial or axial adpositions. In the top-down axial domains (Superiors and Inferiors), the top region is favored over the bottom region. The preference is so strong that even the locational terms 'superior' and 'inferior' carry an evaluative meaning. We have already seen 'top' and 'bottom' adpositions in individual languages in preceding chapters and now we will look at the global picture. The propensity for the top over the bottom, and in any axis in general, should be manifest in occurrence frequency. Table 10.1 shows the number of markers and the aggregate per-million token frequencies of Superiors and Inferiors.

Language	Number of Superiors	Aggregate Tokens (pmw)	Axial Proportion	Number of Inferiors	Aggregate Tokens (pmw)	Axial Proportion
Korean	2	156	65.5%	4	82	34.5%
Japanese	1	109	60.9%	1	70	39.1%
English	8	6,574	92.4%	11	541	7.6%
Spanish	7	1,809	87.3%	12	264	12.7%
Chinese	4	1,386	85.2%	2	241	14.8%
Thai	3	929	73.2%	4	340	26.8%

Table 10.1 Frequencies of top-down spatial adpositions

As shown in Table 10.1, Superiors by far exceed Inferiors in frequency, accounting for more than 60% of all tokens of adpositions of the top-bottom axis. The highest level of asymmetry is observed with English where Superiors account for as much as 92.4%, whereas Inferiors account for a low as 7.6%. Another noteworthy aspect is that the number of markers do not show such asymmetry.[1]

[Inside over Outside]
Another type of asymmetry is observed with the inside-outside axis. The Interiors

---

[1] It is to be noted that in calculating the number of Korean postpositions, the variants as a result of variable degrees of reduction, e.g., *hanthey(ta(ka(tayko)))*, *ey(ta(ka(tayko(se))))*, etc., are not separately counted. Thus, the number of adpositions in Korean may be different depending on the way the variants are counted.

and Exteriors in the six languages show the distributional patterns, as in Table 10.2.

Language	Number of Interiors	Aggregate Tokens (pmw)	Axial Proportion	Number of Exteriors	Aggregate Tokens (pmw)	Axial Proportion
Korean	5	343	73.1%	2	126	26.9%
Japanese	3	13,298	99.9%	1	10	0.1%
English	24	16,009	99.1%	10	142	0.9%
Spanish	6	24,163	99.6%	5	89	0.4%
Chinese	3	3,255	89.7%	3	375	10.3%
Thai	4	16,473	97.5%	6	418	2.5%

Table 10.2 Frequencies of inside-outside spatial adpositions

Table 10.2 shows that the inside-outside asymmetry is even greater than the top-down asymmetry. Exteriors in half the languages surveyed have less than 1% of the inside-outside total tokens. Korean shows the least level of asymmetry but still Interiors account for about three quarters of all inside-outside adpositional tokens. As is the case with the top-down axis, the numbers of adpositions in the languages do not exhibit asymmetry, i.e., the number of Interiors is not always greater than that of the Exteriors.

[Front over Back]
Adpositions in the front-back axis show a general pattern of asymmetry, but the patterns are not uniform, as shown in Table 10.3.

Language	Number of Anteriors	Aggregate Tokens (pmw)	Axial Proportion	Number of Posteriors	Aggregate Tokens (pmw)	Axial Proportion
Korean	2	538	84.2%	3	101	15.8%
Japanese	2	92	89.3%	1	11	10.7%
English	7	144	33.0%	13	292	67.0%
Spanish	10	548	60.4%	8	360	39.6%
Chinese	3	527	78.5%	4	144	21.5%
Thai	3	167	35.7%	4	301	64.3%

Table 10.3 Frequencies of front-back spatial adpositions

Table 10.3 shows quantitative asymmetry of front and back adpositions, but unlike the top-down and inside-outside asymmetry, in which top and inside are favored in all languages, the asymmetry in the front-back axis is not uniform. English adpositions deviate in that Anteriors occur at a lower frequency than the Posteriors (33% vs. 67%). These figures are based on the count of the prepositions of spatial marking, thus, only those instants that denote spatial relationship are counted, e.g., *come true before our eyes; speak before the Senate; go after the powerful; piece of furniture after piece of furniture, etc.* (all taken from COCA), thus excluding purely temporal usage. Even counting attested tokens including those of temporal usage, the pattern is not dissimilar, i.e., 519 tokens vs. 985 tokens (34.5% vs. 65.5%).[2] The reasons for the deviation of English front-back adpositions is not immediately clear, and need further in-depth research.

[Right over Left]

The right-left axis is slightly peculiar as compared with the others in that the distinction is not binary but ternary, i.e., lateral-general, lateral-right, and lateral-left. Their token frequencies are shown in Table 10.4.

Language	Number of Lateral-General	Aggregate Tokens (pmw)	Axial Proportion	Number of Lateral-Right	Aggregate Tokens (pmw)	Axial Proportion	Number of Lateral-Left	Aggregate Tokens (pmw)	Axial Proportion
Korean	3	168	99.4%	3	0	0%	2	1	0.6%
Japanese	2	38	86.4%	1	3	6.8%	1	3	6.8%
English	5	43	56.6%	4	23	30.3%	4	10	13.1%
Spanish	3	23	88.5%	2	2	7.7%	1	1	3.8%
Chinese	3	158	100%	0	0	0%	0	0	0%
Thai	3	297	100%	4	0	0%	4	0	0%

Table 10.4 Frequencies of right-left spatial adpositions

Table 10.4 shows that, in most languages, lateral axis is not divided by polar

---

[2] In random sampling of Anterior and Posterior attestations of *before* and *after*, spatial usage accounted for 7.0% of all tokens for both prepositions.

opposition, i.e., right vs. left, but spatial location along the axis is expressed by the general terms equivalent to 'beside, at the side of' in English. Notable exceptions are English and Spanish in which 'right' and 'left' do occur, with 'right' more frequently than 'left'. In Japanese 'right' and 'left' are attested at the same proportion but the total occurrence is negligible. Even though three languages, i.e., Korean, Chinese, and Thai, show 0 pmw for 'right' and 'left', it does not necessarily mean that they are unattested; it is only that the number is too small. It is widely known that across many languages 'right' is a positive and favored side as compared to 'left' (Werner 1904, Heine 1997, Cienki 1999, Foolen 2017, 2019, see also 3.3.3.1), this asymmetry is not prominently manifested in the six languages we surveyed. Rather, most languages use the general lateral term far more frequently than with the distinction of 'right' and 'left'. In conclusion, when the polar lateral concepts are expressed, there is asymmetry of favoring 'right' but only weakly.

[Goal over Source]

A large body of literature has demonstrated that there exists asymmetry between the sources and goals of motion events, with goals being mentioned more frequently than sources in motion descriptions (Ikegami 1987, Ungerer and Schmid 1996, Bourdin 1997, Dirven and Verspoor (eds.) 1998, Stefanowitsch and Rohde 2004, Papafragou 2010, Verkerk 2017, Zanchi 2017, Luraghi 2017, works in Luraghi et al. (eds.) 2017, Stefanowitsch 2018, Georgakopoulos 2018, Johanson et al. 2019, Fagard and Kopecka 2021, works in Kopecka and Vuillermet 2021b (eds.), among others). This preference toward the Goal is so robust that it has been labeled 'the goal-over-source principle' or 'the goal bias' (Ungerer and Schmid 1996, Dirven and Verspoor (eds.) 1998, Fagard and Kopecka 2020, inter alia). The preference has often been attributed to the cognitive and pragmatic salience of goal (e.g. Lakusta and Landau 2005, 2012, Regier and Zheng 2007, as cited in Fagard and Kopecka 2020). The frequency of the markers of source (Ablatives) and goal (Directionals/Allatives/Datives) by means of adpositions in the six languages is shown in Table 10.5.3) The literature addressing

---

3) The frequency of spatial functions of polyfunctional adpositions is based on the proportions found in random samples taken from the corpora. Korean -ey has the goal-marking function 34% of the

the asymmetry in multiple, and often typologically different, languages (Johanson et al. 2019, Kopecka and Vuillermet 2021a and works therein) shows that the bias for goal, as opposed to source, is robust in language use of both children and adults.

Language	Number of Allatives/ Directional	Aggregate Tokens (pmw)	Axial Proportion	Number of Ablatives	Aggregate Tokens (pmw)	Axial Proportion
Korean	12	7,098	80.0%	6	1,773	20.0%
Japanese	2	23,220	76.8%	2	7,004	23.2%
English	10	11,408	59.6%	11	7,744	40.4%
Spanish	14	7,744	68.6%	3	3,551	31.4%
Chinese	9	2,030	43.7%	6	2,616	56.3%
Thai	11	7,366	58.7%	2	5,174	41.3%

Table 10.5 Frequency of source- and goal-marking adpositions

If we expect that goal-marking adpositions to occur more frequently than source-marking adpositions, Table 10.5 confirms the expectation in most languages. However, the table also shows that Chinese exhibits a slightly different pattern in that regard, i.e., the frequency of source adpositions exceeds that of goal adpositions, even though the actual proportion is not overwhelming (56.3% vs. 43.7%). This deviance deserves our attention, though the answer to the puzzle is not immediately available.

As indicated, the goal-over-source principle is a crosslinguistically robust tendency but it needs to be examined with caution, because languages have different means of encoding motion. For instance, Johanson et al. (2019) point out that the source-goal asymmetry does not surface uniformly across different morphosyntactic

---

time, *-lo* has the direction-marking function 34.2% of the time, and *-eyse* has the source marking function 37% of the time. English *of* has the source-marking function 14% of the time. Spanish *de* has the source-marking function 4% of the time. Chinese *yú* has the direction-marking function 7% of the time and the source-marking function 3% of the time, and *yǐ* marks the source 2% of the time. Special thanks go to Heeran Lee and Lin Zhang for their assistance in statistical analyses of Spanish and Chinese data, respectively.

devices (e.g., verbs vs. adpositions) used to encode motion across languages. Therefore, it would be wrong to assume that the frequency of adpositions would straightforwardly reveal the bias. In other words, the goal or source indication may be realized by means of verbs instead of adpositions in some languages (cf. satellite-framed vs. verb-framed languages, Talmy 1985, 2000, see also Zlatev and Yangklang 2004, Slobin 2004, 2006).

According to typological analysis, Chinese is a satellite-framing language, encoding the path of movement outside the verb, in things such as particles. Since Thai is also a satellite-framing language, however, if this typological division is the only determinant, the difference between Thai and Chinese cannot be accounted for. Therefore, we can hypothesize that the typological difference in verb-framing vs. satellite-framing is important in preposition and adverbial productivity but its effect is not uniform. Indeed, languages vary depending on their framing types in lexicalization and even among the languages of the same type may exhibit different levels of asymmetry (cf. Fagard and Kopecka 2021). Furthermore, the adposition statistics does not include adverbials, a close functional relative of adpositions. Since satellite languages may indicate the path either with adverbs or adpositions, this omission may have made an impact. Thus, a cogent explanation on the reversed asymmetry of source-goal in Chinese should await more research on verb inventories and the verb-particle combination patterns.

10.2 Word order

From the seminal work by Greenberg (1963) based on a crosslinguistic investigation involving as many as 142 languages, studies of word-order universals have made great impact in modern linguistics. The language sample was further expanded to 350 languages in Hawkins (1983). Subsequent studies (Rijkhoff 1986, Campbell et al. 1988, Hahn et al. 2020) elaborated and refined the previous findings.

Greenberg's (1963) study presents 45 universals of language, of which some relate to adpositions, as exemplified in (5):

(5) a. UNIVERSAL 2. In languages with prepositions the genitive almost always follows the governing noun, while in languages with postpositions it almost always precedes.

   b. UNIVERSAL 4. With overwhelmingly greater than chance frequency languages with normal SOV order are postpositional.

With respect to (5a), it is evident that the adpositional patterns and word orders are correlated, as shown in (6):

(6) 'the playground of the school'

   a. Korean (Postposition)
      hakkyo uy _wuntongcang_ (학교 의 운동장)
      [**school of** playground]

   b. Japanese (Postposition)
      gakkō no _asobiba_ (学校 の 遊び場)
      [**school of** playground]

   c. Chinese (Postposition)
      xuéxiào de _cāochǎng_ (学校 的 操场)
      [**school of** playground]

   d. English (Preposition)
      the playground **_of the school_**
      [the playground **of the school**]

   e. Spanish (Preposition)
      el patio **_de la escuela_**
      [the playground **of the school**]

   f. Thai (Preposition)
      sanǎamdèklên **_khɔ̌ɔŋ rooŋrian_** (สนามเด็กเล่น ของ โรงเรียน)
      [playground **of school**]

As is contrasted between the postpositional and prepositional languages, i.e., (6a~c) and (6d~f), the governing noun 'school' is placed before and after the Genitive marker, respectively (i.e., 'school-of' or 'of-school'). This is in consonance with the observed generalization of the word order by Greenberg (1963).

With respect to Universal 4, in (5b), among the six languages that we have surveyed in this book, only two languages are with "normal SOV" order, i.e., Korean and Japanese. As we have noted, these two languages are postpositional languages. Thus, Universal 4 is upheld. We also noted in chapter 7 that Chinese has both prepositions and postpositions, with prepositions more dominant and postpositions typically older and restricted to relational nouns. Chinese is known to be primarily of SVO word order with SOV word order in special constructions (see also 7.4.3.2 for the the discussion on *bǎ*-constructions involving word-order change).

The impact of word-order in grammaticalization of adpositions is crucial because it is the key feature of preposition-postposition divergence (see Comrie 1989[1981]: 90-92). For instance, in the preceding chapters, we have seen how complex adpositions arise by way of templates, notably those involving relational nouns. This is illustrated in the following:

(7) a. Korean (SOV)

(학교의 뒤에 산이 있다.)

*hakkyo-***uy**	***twi-ey***	*san-i*	*iss-ta*
school-**GEN**	**back-LOC**	mountain-NOM	exist-DEC

'There is a mountain behind the school.'

(lit. Mountain exists at the back of the school.)

b. Spanish (SVO)

La	*universidad*	*está*	***en***	***el***	***medio***	***de***	*la*	*ciudad.*
the	university	is	**in**	**the**	**middle**	**of**	the	city

'The university is in the middle of the city.'

In the source structure of the adposition in a SOV language (like Korean), the original head noun in (7a) is *twi* 'back', thus bracketed as [hakkyo-uy [[twi]-ey]]], i.e., the central element is 'at the back' and *hakkyo-uy* 'of school' is only a modifier of the head noun 'back'. Since 'school' is the more salient entity in normal discourse situations than 'back', the discursive focus shifts from 'back' to 'school', and accordingly the reanalysis from [hakkyo-uy [[twi]-ey]] to [[hakkyo]-uy.twi.ey] and also the reinterpretation from [school-of back-at] to [school-behind] occurs. The final product of the reanalysis and reinterpretation is the conceptually consolidated postposition *-uy.twi.ey* 'behind'. This is largely due to the configurational characteristic of Korean, i.e., Genitive (*-uy* 'of') preceding the governing noun (*twi* 'back'), as in *-uy twi*.

On the other hand, in the source structure of the adposition in a SVO language (like Spanish), the head noun is *el medio* 'the middle' in (7b), and the initially focused phrase is *en el medio* 'in the middle'. The phrase *de la ciudad* 'of the city' is only performing a modifier function. Since 'city' is the more salient entity in normal discourse situations than 'middle', the discursive focus shifts from 'middle' to 'city', and accordingly the reanalysis from [in [the middle] [of [the city]]] to [in the middle of [the city]] and also the reinterpretation from [in the middle of the city] to [in.the.middle.of the city] occurs. The final product of the reanalysis and reinterpretation is the conceptually consolidated preposition *en.el.medio.de* 'in the middle of'. This is largely due to the configurational characteristic of Spanish, i.e., Genitive (*de* 'of') follows the governing noun (*el medio* 'the middle'), i.e., *el medio de*.

From the illustration, it is obvious that the morphosyntactic reanalysis and functional reinterpretation occur on the basis of the configuration of existing strings. This is consonant with the general states of affairs of grammaticalization that grammaticalization is fundamentally gradient, always retaining older characteristics in form and meaning, as is reflected in the axiomatic slogan "Today's morphology is yesterday's syntax" (Givón 1971: 413), one that highlights vestiges of the old configuration lingering in the new innovated forms despite (often extensively) reductive changes. For more illustration of word order and grammaticalization of prepositions and postpositions, see Hopper and Traugott (2003[1993]: 59-63).

10.3 Inflection vs. Agglutination vs. Isolation

Another significant typological issue concerns the morphological typology. The six languages surveyed in this book have various morphological types, as briefly illustrated in chapter 1. Korean and Japanese are synthetic and agglutinative languages often allowing multiple bound morphemes to occur stacked together. English and Spanish are synthetic and inflecting languages (fusional), even though English is only weakly inflectional in modern times due to extensive loss of inflection and is often classified as an analytic language. Chinese and Thai are analytic, isolating languages, in which grammatical relations are expressed by separate words, the major characteristic that often leads to the debates on status of those words as to whether they are grammaticalized or not. Despite the fact that English in modern times has the features of a strong analytic language, it is quite different from Chinese and Thai in that it has well-partitioned word classes, unlike Chinese and Thai, where word classes are often flexible and thus a form may be categorized under multiple word classes (see 7.4.4.2 and 8.4.2).

These typological differences present interesting and unique aspects of grammaticalization of adpositions in the six languages. There are multiple aspects that deserve attention, but we will limit our discussion to two significant issues, i.e., transparency of form and meaning and productivity of morphosyntactic operations.

[Transparency of Form and Meaning]
The most striking aspect of adpositions variable with morphological types is the transparency in form and meaning. Words in isolating languages like Chinese and Thai do not change their slot in the strings of words (i.e., sentences) nor do they change in formal shapes to a significant level, in line with the observation by Bisang (1996), who states that the oft-cited form-meaning coevolution (Bybee et al. 1994) is not observed in isolating languages for their conservative tendency to resist formal change (see also Matisoff 1991a,b,c, Bisang 2011, Ansaldo et al. 2018 for EMSEA (East and Mainland Southeast Asian) languages). Therefore, even grammaticalized forms tend to retain the old shape, occurring in the same morphosyntactic position, thus providing clues for the older meaning. This has two major effects: (i) the origin of the

grammaticalized forms is often straightforwardly clear, and (ii) the grammatical status of these forms can be controversial (as noted in the discussion of Thai in 8.2). This is exemplified with simple examples in (8):

(8) a. Chinese (Isolating)

我 给 你 买了 一 支 笔。

*Wǒ **gěi** nǐ mǎi-le yī zhī bǐ.*

I **for** you bought one CLS pen

'I bought a pen for you.'

b. Thai (Isolating)

ผม ซื้อ ปากกา ให้ คุณ

*phom suu bakka **hây** khun*

I   buy pen   **for** you

'I bought a pen for you.'

In example (8), the donative verb 'give' occurs as a benefactive preposition 'for'. The prepositions *gěi* (给) and *hây* (ให้) have their heteronyms *gěi* (给) and *hây* (ให้), respectively, fully functioning as lexical verbs with the 'give' meaning. Syntactically, the full verb will occur in the same slot as the preposition, i.e., *Wǒ gěi nǐ* 'I give you' and *Phom hây khun* 'I give you'. The give-Benefactive connection is conceptually well-motivated and crosslinguistically common, perhaps due to the pragmatic inference and subjectification, e.g., ["A gives x to B", therefore, "x is for B"]. Based on this conceptual relation and pragmatic relevance, *gěi nǐ* and *hây khun* can be easily reinterpreted as to mean 'for you'.

On the other hand, Japanese and Korean are agglutinative languages, in which morpho-phonological reduction is common. When the reduction occurs to the grammatical markers like the particles signaling syntactic relations (which is common especially in Korean), the relationship between the host noun and the grammatical marker becomes unclear. This is illustrated with the Korean examples in (9), adapted from S Rhee (1996: 238):

(9) Korean (Agglutinative)

a. (書生이 보ᅀᆞ바 同志ᄅᆞᆯ 브터 오니)

SESAYNG-i	*po-zAv-a*	*TONGCI-lAl*	**_puthe_**	*o-ni*
scholar-NOM	see-HON-CONN	same.aspiration-ACC	**adhering/ABL**	come-as

'When the scholar saw (King Taejong's great caliber), he joined him out of kindred aspirations, and...' (1447, *Yongpiechenka* 97)

b. (젼년브터 하ᄂᆞᆯ히 ᄀᆞ므라)

*cyennyen-**puthe***	*hanAlh-i*	*kAmAl-a*
last.year-**ABL**	heaven-NOM	dry-CONN

'As it has been dry since last year, ⋯' (1517, *Penyek Nokeltay* 1:27a)

The Modern Korean spatio-temporal Ablative *-pwuthe* began its life as a verb inflected with a converb marker (i.e., *puth-e* [adhere-Conv] 'adhering, adhere and' (3.3.3.2). The source construction (9a) is an instance in which the transitive verb *puth-* 'adhere to' takes a noun phrase marked by the Accusative (*-lAl*) as its object, thus giving the meaning 'adhering to the kindred aspirations'. However, when the Accusative is deleted, which is common in this language, as in (9b), the former relationship of NP complement and the transitive verb in *cyennyen-puthe* becomes quite opaque. In other words, the cue for the interpretation of *puthe* as having the verbal source is lost when the Accusative marker is not present on the surface.

A more complex example is found in the Dative *-hantheytakatayko* 'to' (briefly mentioned in 3.3.3.4), a multiply-agglutinated marker of goal, exemplified in (10):

(10) Korean (Agglutinative)

(어린아이한테다가대고 욕을 했다.)

*elinai-**hantheytakatayko***	*yok-ul*	*ha-n-ta*
child-**DAT**	curse-ACC	do-PRES-DEC

'(He) cursed a child.'

The emphatic and pejorative Dative *-hantheytakatayko* can be decomposed as *han tey tak-a tay-ko* [one place approach-Conv touch-Conn] 'approach and touch one place and'. The noun phrase *han tey* 'one place' designates the location being referred to, but the change of the form from *han tey* to *hanthey* (i.e., coalescence and aspiration) makes the origin opaque. The verb *tak-* 'approach, draw near' is a transitive verb normally requiring an Accusative- or Allative-marked noun phrase complement, but the noun phrase *han tey* (which is now *hanthey*) occurs without the Accusative or Allative, which further increases opacity to the already-opaque origin. Furthermore, the converb form *taka-* often occurs in its eroded from *ta-* (i.e., *-hantheytatayko*), in which case the connection becomes even more unclear. Similarly, the verb *tay-* 'touch' is a transitive verb normally requiring an Accusative- or Allative-marked noun phrase complement, but there is no candidate for the noun phrase complement; *han tey* 'one place' is already unavailable due to the intervening verb *tak-* 'approach'. All this complicated situation makes it very difficult for language users to identify the source construction of the Dative *-hantheytakatayko*. When new postpositions are coined by means of the existing templates, the sources are largely very clear, and the case of *-hantheytakatayko* is admittedly a rather extreme case, but agglutination of multiple forms and erosion of involved forms make the sources of grammaticalized forms in agglutinative languages very low in transparency in terms of form and meaning.

Old adpositions in inflectional (fusional) languages such as English and Spanish are similarly opaque with respect to their formal and semantic transparency. For instance, the following English prepositions contain inflected forms, reflecting the historical fact that the language was an inflecting language at the time of formation of those prepositions (information has been adapted from the *Oxford English Dictionary*).

(11)   a.   *between* ⟨ *bi-twéonum* (cf. ⟨ OE Dative **twîhnum, *tweohnum*) 'by two'

        b.   *betwixt* ⟨ probably shortened from the dative form **be-tweoxum, -tweox(a)n*

        c.   *near* ⟨ *neah-r* 'near-Comparative'

        d.   *next to* ⟨ *next*: superlative 'nearest'

        e.   *against* ⟨ *again-s-t* (cf. excrescent final *-t*, probably reinforced by association with superlatives in *-st*; cf. *alongst* prep., *amidst* adv., *betwixt*, etc.)

The information in (11) is in simplification glossing over great historical complexities. But what is clear is that their historical morphological operations are nearly completely opaque to contemporary English speakers. Thus, the morphosyntactically motivated features, such as inflection, are absent, and consequently, individual forms are regarded as uninflected basic forms. This process of 'de-morphologization' (Joseph and Janda 1988) has been labeled as 'phonogenesis' by Hopper (1990, 1994). Contemporary speakers of English need to learn these forms as single lexemes, a situation well suiting Givón's (1979: 209) point that as grammaticalization proceeds, the syntactic structure erodes, via processes of morphologization and 'lexicalization'.[4] Lessau (1994: 336) also notes that when forms are fossilized and become unobtainable through the rules of grammar, they must be listed in the lexicon (cf. Lehmann 2015[1982]: 145).

From the foregoing discussion, it is evident that the transparency of form and meaning is high in isolating languages, largely due to their conservative nature toward formal change, whereas agglutinative and inflectional languages are low in transparency, largely due to their susceptibility to erosion in the course of grammaticalization.

[Productivity of Morphosyntactic Operations]

The next issue concerns productivity of morphosyntactic operations in innovating adpositions. The adpositions of all functions, spatial adpositions, and grammaticalizing adpositions are presented by the three categories of primary (PRIM), composite (CMST), and complex (CMPX) adpositions in Table 10.6.

---

4) For a similar observation in Korean, see Y Ko (1995).

	ALL				SPATIAL				GRAMMATICALIZING		
	PRIM	CMST	CMPX	TOT	PRIM	CMST	CMPX	TOT	CMST	CMPX	TOT
Korean	24	15	165	**204**	7	15	115	**137**	15	27	**42**
Japanese	33	4	42	**79**	7	0	21	**28**	0	15	**15**
English	97	64	523	**684**	61	32	120	**213**	19	6	**25**
Spanish	25	136	690	**851**	19	51	99	**169**	13	20	**33**
Chinese	60	21	10	**91**	34	7	5	**46**	3	4	**7**
Thai	101	71	9	**181**	55	31	5	**91**	16	0	**16**

Table 10.6 Adpositions by types and categories

A few noteworthy aspects present themselves in Table 10.6. For reasons unclear, Japanese has relatively very few postpositions in all three categories. In particular, it does not have as many complex postpositions as Korean, its typologically similar language. It has often been observed that Korean and Japanese have striking similarities in structure and patterns of expression, though the overlap in lexical sources of concrete expressions is limited (Narrog and Rhee 2013, Narrog et al. 2018). The overall similarity between Korean and Japanese makes the difference in postpositional systems even more prominent.

One related factor, though not conclusive, is that unlike Korean, in which a large number of general nouns are recruited into the structural template [P-N-P] and a large number of verbs are recruited into the structural template [P-V-Conv] (see Appendix 1), Japanese does not productively utilize these structures, even though it does have them. The use of nominal template [P-N-P] in Japanese is largely restricted to the relational nouns in the N slot, but relational nouns constitute a rather limited set, because human cognition does not seem to partition space in more than a few categories. Likewise, the verbs used in the verbal template [P-V-Conv] in Japanese are much more limited than those in Korean. This may simply be an idiosyncrasy of the Japanese language, but more comprehensive studies are required to satisfactorily explain this austerity.

Another notable aspect observable in Table 10.6 is that English and Spanish have a large number of complex prepositions. As we have noted in the discussion of these two languages separately, the prolificity of complex prepositions in these languages is due to their productive use of the nominal template [P-(D)-N-P]. Not only relational nouns or spatial nouns but also diverse nouns are recruited to fill in the N slot, for the sake of cognitive congruency in formal contexts. The fact that English and Spanish have numerous primary prepositions and many of them may occur in P_1 and P_2 positions (even though there exist preferences, e.g., *in N of* for English and *en N de* in Spanish) may have contributed to multiplying the number of prepositions to a great extent.

The contributive role of the templates to multiplicity of adpositions seems to be responsible for the relative paucity of complex adpositions in the isolating languages, Thai and Chinese. As we have seen Thai has very few complex prepositions, i.e., nine of them, the smallest in number among the six surveyed languages, making a sharp contrast with primary prepositions, numbering as many as 101, the largest among the six languages. Chinese, similarly, has only ten complex postpositions, whereas it has as many as 60 primary adpositions (42 prepositions and 18 postpositions).[5]

We have noted that Thai has a number of prepositions developed from nouns (see Table 8.7), many of which are relational nouns, and similarly, a number prepositions developed from verbs (see Table 8.8), many of which are verbs of locomotion. But there is no fixed structural pattern in composite and complex prepositions, even though Smyth (2002) presents a few combinatory patterns, which involve such nouns as 'side' and 'way' (see 8.2). Chinese has a relatively large number of prepositions developing from diverse sources, but noun-based prepositions are very small in number. The source nouns are seemingly from random conceptual categories. Verb-based prepositions, on the other hand, are larger in number but the sources of the verbs, though mostly transitive verbs, also seem to be from various conceptual categories. Postpositions are nearly entirely restricted to relational

---

[5] As has been noted, Chinese lacks rigid templates, usually having the plain [P-N] configuration for prepositions. However, the configuration may be optionally elaborated with another P as [P-N-P] (see H Wu 2015: 213-222). In the examples given by H Wu (2015: 214), however, the second P is a postposition in our analysis, e.g., *zai shugui shang* [at-bookshelf-on] 'on the shelf', *zai shugui li* [at-bookshelf-in] 'in the shelf', etc.

notions, which, as noted above, constitute a restricted set. Complex postpositions in Chinese have one template, i.e., [P N], in which P is either *zhī* 'of' or *yǐ* 'with' and N is invariably a relational noun. It is notable that this unproductive template is used only in postpositions, and that Chinese, an SVO-dominant language, does not favor postpositions. Thus, the role of the template in Chinese is extremely limited (note that there are only 10 complex postpositions).

The most prominent feature of Chinese and Thai, therefore, is that these languages do not make use of the structural templates for creating adpositions, most likely due to their preference of monosyllabic word forms instead of templates (Post 2007, citing Norman 1988: 8-10, Matisoff 1991a,b,c, see also 10.5 below). This points to the significance of prefabricated template in production of novel forms, including coining new adpositions. The notion of 'attractor position' by Bisang (1996) seems to be relevant in this context as well. Bisang (1996: 523) states that attractor positions, which occur to the left of to the right of the head noun or the main verb, are the slots which attract linguistic items in order to grammaticalize them. Since adpositions are nominal morphology, the existence of ready-made templates at these attractor positions will undoubtedly trigger or facilitate the process of grammaticalization. And conversely, the absence of such convenient devices may be a disadvantageous feature from the perspective of grammaticalization.

This situation is consonant with Bybee et al. (1994: 118), who state, with reference to constraints of linguistic typology, that isolating languages do not carry grammaticalization as far as fusional or agglutinating languages do, and that such languages not only do not affix but also they do not have grams with meaning as abstract and generalized as synthetic languages do.

10.4 Language Contact

Grammaticalization, or language change in general, may be categorized into two broad types. One type arises as a 'natural' (Thomason and Kaufman 1988) or 'evolutive' (Paul 1920[1880], Andersen 1973) process, largely based on cognition and discursive needs, thus an 'internally-motivated' grammaticalization (Heine and

Kuteva 2005), and the other arises from contact with a different language, thus, a 'contact-induced' grammaticalization (Heine and Kuteva 2005, 2008). Despite some claims that 'any linguistic feature' can be borrowed (Thomason and Kaufman 1988: 14, Curnow 2001: 434, Campbell 1993: 104, among others), Heine and Kuteva (2008) refute them by showing that there indeed are constraints. Some of the six languages addressed in this book share with other language(s) certain typological features and genetic relations, and certain grammaticalization scenarios seem to have been influenced by contact. We will address the contact-induced grammaticalization and areal influence briefly here.

As Heine and Kuteva (2005: 5) note, contact-induced language change is a complex process that not infrequently extends over centuries, or even millennia. Research on contact-induced grammaticalization is often faced, among others, with the problem of data sources, i.e., not much information is available. Notwithstanding such obstacles, we will look into the issue, though necessarily briefly.

Korean and Japanese, as noted above, share structural features to a great extent, but they also show much difference especially with respect to grammaticalization of postpositions. In this regard, Narrog and Rhee (2013) and Narrog et al. (2018) note that the differences may be due to the fact that the large majority of structures used in spatial postpositions are recent historical developments and that there seems to have been the high degree of grammatical renewal in both languages over a limited period of time. Even though the two languages are spoken in close proximity in distance, there was no protracted intensive language contact between Korean and Japanese during historical times, largely due to the separation by sea and largely hostile nature of the relationship (with frequent warfare) between the two countries.

However, Japanese and Korean share the same influence from Sinitic, with the same patterns of borrowing, largely based on the same lexical sources. Thus, during historical times, the influence of Chinese on both languages was clearly much stronger than the influence of the two languages on each other (Narrog and Rhee 2013, Narrog et al. 2018). Interestingly, the language contact with Chinese is mainly through written language, largely texts of religion, philosophy, literature, science and technology. As noted in 3.4.4.1 and 4.3.3.4, Korean and Japanese make use of Chinese relational nouns in the structural template for complex postpositions. This strategy was so common in the history of Japanese that some of the complex postpositions in Japanese are likely to be complete calques, e.g., *-o motte* (を以して) 'with', *-ni oite* (に 於して) 'at, concerning' (Yamada 1935, Chen 2005, Narrog and Rhee 2013, see 4.3.3.4 above). The use of Sino-Korean lexemes and even set phrases has long been revered as a sign of erudition in Korea because previously high-register Chinese texts were available only to the intellectual class (see S Rhee 2020a, 2021 in press, Eom and Rhee 2021 in press). Heavy use of Sino-Korean lexemes and phrases was typically in the written register, but recent government-led language purification initiatives discourage the use of certain types of Sino-Korean phrases, especially those that belong to the level beyond lexemes (Eom and Rhee 2021 in press). Thus, Korean and Japanese complex postpositions show borrowing from written texts and its resultant grammaticalization. This is a unique situation because contact-induced change generally occurs in the spoken use of a language (Heine and Kuteva 2005: 250).

Another notable language contact incidence is that of English with French. Even though French is not included in the six languages under consideration, it is well-known that French made a significant impact on English from the Norman Conquest (1066 AD) and subsequent dominion of England by French-speaking rulers. Among many important consequences is the nearly total elimination of the old English aristocracy and its replacement with French-speaking rulers, thus French becoming the language of the powerful and English the language of the powerless. The massive French influence on English is obvious not only in the lexicon but also in the grammar of English, and borrowing and calquing of complex prepositions from French are notable, as extensively discussed in Hoffmann (2005). When English borrowed the then-French template [P(D)NP], e.g., [en N de], and productively used it in the form of [P(D)NP], e.g., [in N of], proliferation of complex prepositions ensued. This may have to do with the fact that grammatical replication is a creative activity (Heine and Kuteva 2005), and the frequent use of the template may have satisfied diverse socio-pragmatic needs of the speakers. Since the French template [en N de] is identical with the Spanish [en N de], the result is a great level of resemblance between English complex prepositions and Spanish complex prepositions. Furthermore, since the high-register lexemes in English tend to be of Latinate origin, a great proportion of English complex prepositions share the same nominal with

Spanish complex prepositions (cf. Appendices 2 and 3).

Thai and Chinese belong to different language families, i.e., Sino-Tibetan and Kra-Dai (Tai-Kadai), respectively. Despite the fact that the two languages are not genealogically connected, they share a number of typological features including analytic, isolating morphology. They share similar segment inventories, tone systems, and syllable structure (Brown 1965, Matisoff 1973, as cited in Post 2007). Researchers also note that the two languages share, or have historically shared, an extreme isolating morphosyntax in which "a basic unity syllable = morpheme = word predominates, and in which affixation generally does not occur" (Post 2007, citing Norman 1988: 8-10, Matisoff 1991c). This propensity may be responsible for the relative paucity of polysyllabic, polymorphemic forms in the lexicon and the grammar, such as templates for complex adpositions, as we have noted in the above.

Many features shared by Chinese and Thai may be an areal effect, since some of them are also shared in East and mainland South East Asian languages like Hmong, Vietnamese, Cambodian, etc. (Bisang 1996). Further, some authors have shown the contact with and influence of Austroasiatic and Austronesian languages on Thai (Varasarin 1984, Suthiwan 1992, Khanittanan 2001, Diller 2008, among others). Many languages in Southeast Asia, e.g., Thai, Khmer, Vietnamese, Hmong, and Mandarin, have locus verbs that grammaticalized into prepositions, as well, e.g., from 'be at', 'reach to', 'give to', 'go to', etc. (*Ɂùu, thɯ̌ŋ, hây, pay*, etc. in Thai) to Benefactive, Temporal and other abstract relation markers (Clark and Prasithrathsint 1995). Similarly, many Southeast Asian languages have relational nouns that gain grammatical functions, e.g., *nay* 'inside', *nɔ̂ɔk* 'outside', *bon* 'top', *nǔa* 'top', *lǎŋ* 'back', *tâay* 'bottom', *nâa* 'front', *lâaŋ* 'bottom', *klaaŋ* 'middle', *thîi* 'place' in Thai (Clark and Prasithrathsint 1995).

The language communities of Chinese and Thai are geographically connected, and according to certain sources, Thai had strong Chinese influence until the 13th century, when the use of Chinese characters was abandoned and replaced by Sanskrit and Pali scripts, but Thai still retains many words borrowed from Middle Chinese (Haarmann 2012[1986]: 165, Haspelmath and Tadmor 2009: 611, among others).

In the category of adpositions, however, Chinese influence on Thai seems marginal. For instance, only the prepositions *nay* (ใน) 'inside' (≺ Ch. *nèi* 內 'inside') and *kwàa* (กว่า) 'than' (《 Ch. *guò* 過 'exceed, pass') seem to be among the few prepositions developed from Sino-Thai lexemes. Considering the supposed high level of Chinese influence, this relative paucity of grammatical borrowing or replication is a little unexpected. However, this may be partly due to the conservative typological characteristics of Thai, favoring monosyllabic and monomorphemic words, thus not enthusiastically embracing the polymorphemic templates for complex prepositions (also note that Chinese does not have well-developed complex adpositional templates). Another possibility is the early grammaticalization of primary prepositions in history, and the entrenchment of these robust forms may have resisted replacive borrowing at a later time. A more conclusive answer to this puzzle of minimal impact on prepositions should await further diachronic research.

10.5 Summary

In this chapter, we discussed diverse issues with respect to the grammaticalization of adpositions from a typological perspective. Since the six languages discussed in this book are deliberately chosen to diversify the typological characteristics, we could discuss the issues more comprehensively than we would have been able with only one or two languages.

Despite the typological differences, those surveyed languages exhibit a high level of similarity, due to the common restrictive mechanisms behind grammaticalization. For instance, source lexemes are not randomly selected nor do the grammaticalization paths diverge randomly. It is due to the fact that functional innovators are necessarily constrained by the inferences that are deemed to be available to the interlocutors for the sake of avoiding communicative breakdown. There are, however, expansive motivations as well, e.g., creativity and cognitive congruity. By creativity, language users innovate new forms despite the forms already existing for the same function. By cognitive congruity, language users activate more complex, abstract, and more specific forms to suit the cognitively-complex contexts of speech. These expansive mechanisms may thus push the boundary set by the restrictive operational mechanisms.

We also noted that there is propensity for positivity commonly observed in the languages surveyed. The positivity is usually in the form of polar opposition, i.e., top over bottom, inside over outside, front over back, right over left, and goal over source. From a quantitative analysis, we could confirm that the positivity propensity appears in an asymmetrical distribution in discourse, but not without exceptions.

As for word order, we reviewed the two language universals by Greenberg (1963), related to adpositions. The observed patterns in the six languages confirm those two universals. We suggested that morphosyntactic reanalysis and functional reinterpretation occur on the basis of the configuration of existing strings. Since reanalysis and reinterpretation occur only gradually, the original word order is reflected in the final grammaticalized adpositions.

With respect to typological characteristics of inflection, agglutination, and isolation, we observed that there are two prominent issues, i.e., transparency of form and meaning and productivity of morphosyntactic operations. In isolating languages, due to their conservative tendency to resist formal change, adpositions show a high level of transparency of form and meaning. In agglutinative languages, the transparency is lower due to frequent stacking of multiple forms and erosion of parts thereof. In inflectional languages, the transparency is often very low. In English, which has now lost most of its inflection, the formal and semantic transparency has been greatly obscured through the loss of inflection and fossilization of certain grammatical morphemes.

In the discussion of productivity of morphosyntactic operations, we presented some noteworthy aspects of adpositions. Japanese has a particularly small number of adpositions as compared to others, the reason for which is unclear. Most languages utilizing structural templates have a large number of adpositions through prolific use of the templates. Isolating languages do not use structural templates productively, perhaps due to their preference for monosyllabic word forms over templates.

We also briefly discussed language contact. We noted the strong influence of written Chinese on the development of Korean and Japanese postpositional systems. Grammaticalization induced by written language is not commonly attested, and the postpositions that developed from Chinese origins tend to specialize in marking abstract notions as compared to their native counterparts in these two languages.

English also shows a heavy influence of French (and of Latin) for socio-political reasons in history and bears much resemblance with Spanish, in such a way that many complex prepositions in the two languages have shared etyma. Thai has supposedly been heavily influenced by Chinese and the two languages share many typological features. However, our investigation shows only a minimal level of Chinese influence on Thai prepositions.

11

Conclusion

Adpositions constitute an interesting grammatical category as they provide a linking device for a noun phrase that would be syntactically isolated otherwise. We have looked at adpositions in six languages, Korean, Japanese, English, Spanish, Chinese, and Thai. These languages have prepositions or postpositions, or both. These languages are selected for their typological features and characteristics of adpositional systems: Korean and Japanese are synthetic, agglutinative languages with postpositions only; English and Spanish have prepositions (even though English has a few postpositions as well) and are synthetic, inflectional languages (even though English has become very weakly inflectional); and Chinese and Thai are analytic, isolating languages. Chinese has a large number of prepositions and some postpositions, whereas Thai has prepositions only.

In order to differentiate their compositional complexity, we classified the adpositions into three groups, i.e., primary, composite, and complex adpositions. Primary adpositions are short and monomorphemic. If they are historically polymorphemic but their internal composition is synchronically opaque, even though opacity may be variable depending on individual sensitivity to linguistic features and extent of historical knowledge, they are grouped into the primary adpositions. Composite adpositions are typically bimorphemic or trimorphemic forms but do not involve syntactic operations for creation. Complex adpositions tend to involve syntactic operations, and thus are long in form. In languages where no clear syntactic operations are clearly visible, we classified the prepositions purely based on the number of morphemes/words, i.e., monomorphemic/monolexemic forms as primary, bimorphemic/bilexemic forms as composite, and trimorphemic/trilexemic forms and those with more than three morphemes or words as complex prepositions. Since grammaticalization is largely a reductive process, we hypothesized that this tripartite classification corresponds to the degree of grammaticalization as well.

We also focused on spatial adpositions because spatial marking is presumably the most prominent function of adpositions and is the basis of further abstraction by means of metaphorization or other cognitive extensional processes. Non-spatial adpositions tend to be diverse in function, often carrying subjective functions in information structuring or marking scalarity. Our discussion also focused on composite and complex adpositions because these, unlike the primary adpositions, have not yet reached a high level of grammaticalization and exhibit various aspects of on-going grammaticalization. Further, we selected those that occur at the frequency of 10 pmw or higher, to ensure that they are viable forms in the category of adposition. These adpositions are in functional competition with their more frequent counterparts, i.e., primary adpositions, which have a longer history, generalized functions, and a high token frequency in corpora. These adpositions undergoing grammaticalization with reasonable viability also have competitors in the lower spectrum of grammaticalization, i.e., below 10 pmw, which are nearly invariably complex adpositions. We analyzed their competition scenarios and tried to identify the reasons of being relatively unsuccessful as compared to their stronger competitors and of being relatively successful as compared to their weaker competitors. We could confirm time and again that semantic generality, formal complexity, degree of grammaticalization, and extent of circulation (token frequency) are coextensive.

We addressed Korean postpositions in Chapter 3. Korean postpositions are large in number and heterogeneous in function and formal makeup. Out of a total 204 postpositions in Modern Korean, 137 postpositions mark spatial relationship. The spatial postpositions develop predominantly from nominal sources, mostly relational nouns of native Korean and Sino-Korean origins, and a relatively smaller number of them develop from verbal sources. In terms of form-function mapping, there are multiple forms marking an identical or nearly identical grammatical concept, especially in the categories of Allative, Ablative, etc., where forms have differential specialization. When we analyzed the spatial postpositions that are in the process of active grammaticalization, we could identify the two common determinants of viability, i.e., formal shape (simplicity preferred) and semantics (generality preferred). One prominent aspect is the grammaticalization of Sino-Korean relational nouns. The postpositions of Sino-Korean origin are, as compared to those of native Korean semantic counterparts, lower in frequency, but are higher in the degree of abstraction.

With respect to grammaticalization mechanisms, the grammaticalizing postpositions show extension of use context, which is closely tied to desemanticization, i.e., generalization of meanings and decategorialization. However, we observed that they are still relatively transparent with respect to their source constructions, mainly due to the presence of relational nouns in most of them. Erosion is also prominent but to a variable extent. Noun-based postpositions show a high level of Genitive -uy (의) deletion, but most of them tend to retain the Locative -ey (에). Our analysis suggests that the Locative particle deletion may be influenced by the syllable structure of the preceding relational noun.

Korean spatial postpositions typically show functional extension, mostly from spatial meaning to temporal meaning, a common direction widely attested across languages. In addition to such changes, there are instances in which forms denoting location, neutral with respect to directionality of motion, acquired the directionality meaning, e.g., Allative, Ablative, etc., through pragmatic enrichment prompted by the context.

We addressed Japanese postpositions in Chapter 4. Japanese is unique in a number of ways. It has a total of 79 postpositions, the smallest inventory among the six languages surveyed in this book. The inventory of spatial postpositions has only 28 of them, also the smallest in the sampled languages. Japanese postpositions are generally evenly spread across conceptual domains rather than being concentrated in a large number in a small number of domains. This is also a unique situation as compared with other languages.

Japanese complex postpositions develop from established templates, i.e., noun-based postpositions typically in the form of [P N(-P)], whereas verb-based postpositions typically in the form of [P V-*te*]. Also notable is the fact that there are a large number of postpositions developed from Sino-Japanese sources, an indication of the influence of contact with written Chinese. When there exist both of the paired forms of Sino-Japanese and native Japanese denoting the same relational concepts, they tend to have differential specialization of functions, with native Japanese typically for spatial meaning and Sino-Japanese for temporal or other abstract meanings, even though the division is not sharply delineated. This situation is similar to that of Korean.

About 15 postpositions are deemed to be actively undergoing grammaticalization. Just as is the case with Korean, those undergoing grammaticalization show that semantic generality is closely tied to frequency and consequently to the extent of grammaticalization. The development of Japanese postpositions is generally consonant with the mechanisms of extension, desemanticization, decategorialization, and erosion. However, there are a large number of postpositions that do not prominently exhibit such phenomena. This is largely due to the fact that they have a shallow temporal depth of grammaticalization. A unique situation of Japanese postpositions is that there are a few old primary postpositions used at a very high frequency and a few complex postpositions that are spread across diverse conceptual domains without having numerous functional competitors of variable strengths.

We addressed English prepositions in Chapter 5. English has a large number of prepositions that belong to primary, composite, and complex prepositional categories. English has a large number of primary prepositions, numbering 97, which sharply contrasts with Spanish, which has only 25 of them. We catalogued a total of 523 complex prepositions but the number is inconclusive due to the fuzzy boundary between complex prepositions with the PDNP template and syntactic constructions. This situation is similar to that of Spanish. Their strengths are widely variable, and many of them (about 71) are attested for 0 pwm in the corpus. Important sources of prepositions are nouns, whereas verbs are very few. An idiosyncrasy is the large number of borrowings from French, many of which are also related to Latin. The borrowed nouns are put into the noun slot of the well-established PDNP structural template.

We selected 25 spatial prepositions, which are regarded as actively undergoing grammaticalization with a degree of viability. Our analysis led to a conclusion that semantic generality/specificity is among the most important determinants of grammaticalization, confirming the hypothesis that frequency plays a critical role in grammaticalization. We also noted that a defining characteristic of grammaticalization is the directionality in a number of domains, and that the changes in form, meaning, and function occur in tandem. The development of English prepositions is consonant with the notions, such as extension, desemanticization, decategorialization, and erosion.

English spatial prepositions often develop into prepositions for more abstract notions, such as time, quality, etc. More importantly, many prepositions also function as adverbs (thus, 'intransitive prepositions'), as conjunctions, and some as discourse markers. Also notable is that, though not significant in number, there are postpositions, a unique situation not observed in Spanish.

We addressed Spanish prepositions in Chapter 6. Spanish has a large number of prepositions. Even though primary prepositions are relatively fewer, numbering about 25, composite prepositions and complex prepositions are great in number, with 136 and 690, respectively, thus 851 all combined. Just as is the case in English, these numbers are inconclusive for the fuzzy boundary between complex prepositions with the P(D)NP template and syntactic constructions. Spanish prepositions have developed through a few common paths, such as inheritance from Latin, borrowing, and language-internal evolution, the last constituting the vast majority. Complex prepositions develop predominantly from the nominal sources, by virtue of having the P(D)NP structure. Prepositions from the verbal sources typically develop from participial forms, and such prepositions are nearly non-existent in the complex preposition group. Another common source is adverbs, of which the -mente-suffixed forms constitute a large group with 58 members.

A particularly notable aspect of prepositions in Spanish is that a single function may be carried by multiple forms, thus, creating multiple layers, which also come from diverse sources. Some of the multiple layers are in fact those that developed from the same source but with variable degrees of erosion.

On the basis of the given criteria, we selected 33 prepositions that are thought to be actively undergoing grammaticalization. When these prepositions are compared with their functional competitors, we could identify an effect of formal complexity, i.e., a tendency that the simpler a form is, the higher its frequency (and more advanced grammaticalization).

The mechanisms of grammaticalization are found to be effective in capturing the gradual nature of grammaticalization of prepositions in Spanish. Further, we could confirm that differential degrees of structural variability is largely coextensive with the use frequency and degrees of grammaticalization.

Spanish spatial prepositions typically carry extended functions in other semantic domains, such as temporal and other abstract domains, a pattern found in all surveyed languages. Spanish is the only language among the sampled languages that has ambipositions, i.e., those that can function as both a preposition and a postposition.

We looked at Chinese adpositions in Chapter 7. Chinese is the only language that has both prepositions and postpositions in a reasonable number (note that English also has a few postpositions and Spanish has a few ambipositions). In Chinese linguistics, whether a particular word is an adposition or not is often debatable due to the conservative nature of Chinese morphosyntax and the gradient nature of grammaticalization, and consequently, the adposition inventory is controversial. We catalogued 56 prepositions and 35 postpositions, totaling 91. Chinese adpositions are diverse in their grammatical meanings, but postpositions tend to encode spatial (and more abstract, but space-derived) relationships because most of them involve relational nouns.

Spatial prepositions encoding non-axial notions tend to be largely primary prepositions, whereas the domain of axial spatial notions is occupied entirely by postpositions. Nominal sources are more strongly associated with the postpositions than with the prepositions, and conversely, prepositions are predominantly associated with verbal sources. As is usually the case, many adpositions, each from different sources, develop into identical or nearly identical functions, thus creating multiple layers.

One noticeable aspect of Chinese adpositions is that there are only a few of them that fall into the category of grammaticalizing forms with reasonable viability, i.e., only two prepositions and five postpositions. This situation, as we interpret it, is that spatial prepositions in Chinese are relatively well established, despite much intercategorial fluidity. Further, we argued that individual forms' strengths are directly related to the level of their formal complexity.

When the grammaticalization scenarios are reviewed with respect to mechanisms, extension is the only mechanism that is well attested. Desemanticization, often deemed to be robust, is not prominent in Chinese because they mostly developed from relational nouns and still retain such relational meanings. Decategorialization is only weakly manifested, largely due to the fact that adpositions often retain verbal characteristics in terms of morphosyntax. Similarly, erosion is not prominent, also due to the language's conservative morphosyntactic behavior.

We looked at Thai prepositions in Chapter 8. Thai prepositions develop prominently from such primary categories as nouns and verbs but also from other categories such as adjectives and adverbs. As is the case with Chinese, Thai prepositions are subject to scholarly debate as to their grammatical status partly because they do not exhibit formal departure from their source lexemes and partly because they still retain their source characteristics in terms of morphosyntax and semantics. There are, however, a few noun-based prepositions whose etymon is no longer used in the nominal function.

Despite the debate, we, adopting a more fluid perspective on grammar, catalogued as many as 181 prepositions, about a half of which are spatial prepositions. It is particularly noteworthy that as many as 28 primary and composite prepositions mark Association, an extreme case of layering. Thai is also unique in that there are no complex prepositions in the group of actively grammaticalizing prepositions; all in that group are composite prepositions. When the formal structures of composite and complex prepositions are seen closely, Thai prepositions, unlike any other language, are heavily built on primary prepositions by recycling them. In other words, many composite and complex prepositions are formed by combining two or more prepositions that are semantically similar, thus making them look functionally superfluous or redundant.

When the grammaticalization processes of Thai prepositions are viewed with respect to grammaticalization mechanisms, formal erosion is not prominently observable whereas desemanticization, decategorialization, and extension are relatively more readily identified. This is a general characteristic of an isolating language as we have observed with Chinese. But as we noted above, desemanticization is not prominent in Chinese because they mostly developed from relational nouns and still retain such relational meanings. In this respect, Thai and Chinese show some contrast.

In Chapter 9, we looked at a number of principles and hypotheses in view of the grammaticalization scenarios of the adpositions in the six languages, e.g., divergence, persistence, source determination, unidirectionality, universal path, analogy, reanalysis, and reinterpretation.

Divergence is well observed in the vast majority of the adpositions in the six languages. In isolating languages, identifiable divergence is a norm, i.e., with very few exceptions, all adpositions in Chinese and Thai have their lexical origins which are fully functioning as such contemporarily. Agglutinating languages, Korean and Japanese, also display divergence but to a lesser degree due to inability to identify historical sources of some old, primary postpositions, contemporarily. Inflecting languages also show numerous instances of divergence, particularly in complex prepositions. Persistence is also widely attested and is particularly noticeable in the adpositions that have not yet advanced to a great extent of grammaticalization.

We also examined the source determination hypothesis by means of source-target analysis, and concluded that the hypothesis is largely upheld. There are a few exceptions, the motivation of which is not immediately clear, but most adpositions of the 19 grammatical concepts of space in the six languages present relatively clear conceptual relationship with their source lexemes.

Unidirectionality, supposedly the strongest tendency in grammaticalization processes, is also confirmed in the change patterns of form and meaning. Formal reduction is typically a result of pursuing simplification of articulatory gestures, and syntagmatic fixation is due to the lexemes' movement from being autonomous to being dependent. Semantic reduction or abstraction occurs along the ontological continuum of PERSON > OBJECT > ACTIVITY/PROCESS > SPACE > TIME > QUALITY. We observed from a statistical analysis that spatial grams tend to develop from space-denoting lexemes or those related to the concepts to the left of SPACE, and nearly never from those related to the concepts right of it, i.e., TIME and QUALITY. The paths of grammaticalization of adpositions were investigated, and we could confirm that there are a large number of adpositions that developed through the use of language-specific templates and linkers.

We also reviewed the grammaticalization scenarios with respect to analogy, reanalysis, and reinterpretation, which are closely interrelated. We noted that analogical processes, especially manifest in template formation and application, constitute, contrary to the common belief, a common and powerful mechanism of grammaticalization of adpositions. Also noteworthy is that there are cases of 'absorption', whereby a form absorbs the function of an adjacent form that commonly cooccurs. These complex scenarios are the results of an intricate interaction of analogy, reanalysis, and reinterpretation.

In Chapter 10, we discussed diverse issues from a typological perspective. Despite the typological differences, the six languages exhibit a high level of similarity, due to the common restrictive mechanisms behind grammaticalization. Restrictive mechanisms concern selection of source lexemes and the developmental patterns. Expansive motivations, on the other hand, concern creativity and cognitive congruity. Language users, motivated by creativity, innovate new forms despite the forms already existing for the same function. They also activate, for the sake of cognitive congruity, more complex, abstract, and more specific forms to suit the cognitively-complex contexts of speech.

We also discussed the propensity for positivity, which usually occurs in the form of polar opposition, i.e., top over bottom, inside over outside, front over back, right over left, and goal over source. From a quantitative analysis, we could confirm that the positivity propensity appears in asymmetrical distribution in discourse, but not without exceptions.

We reviewed the two word-order language universals by Greenberg (1963), related to adpositions. The observed patterns in the six languages confirm those two universals. We suggested that the universals are the result of two facts that morphosyntactic reanalysis and functional reinterpretation occur on the basis of the configuration of existing strings, and that since reanalysis and reinterpretation occur only gradually, the original word order is reflected in the final grammaticalized adpositions.

When the typological characteristics of inflection, agglutination, and isolation are considered, there appear two prominent issues, i.e., transparency of form and meaning and productivity of morphosyntactic operations. In isolating languages, due to their conservative tendency to resist formal change, adpositions show a high level of transparency of form and meaning. In agglutinative languages, the transparency is lower due to frequent stacking of multiple forms and erosion of parts thereof. In inflectional languages, the transparency is often very low. In English, which has now lost most of its inflection, formal and semantic transparency has been greatly obscured through the loss of inflection and fossilization of certain grammatical morphemes. As for productivity of morphosyntactic operations, we noted a puzzle in Japanese in that it has a particularly small number of adpositions as compared to others, the reason of which is unclear. Most languages utilizing structural templates have a large number of adpositions through prolific use of the templates. Isolating languages do not use structural templates productively, perhaps due to their preference of monosyllabic word forms over templates.

We also discussed language contact and noted the strong influence of written Chinese on the development of Korean and Japanese postpositional systems. This is unique in that grammaticalization induced by written language is not commonly attested. English also shows a heavy influence of French for socio-political reasons in history and bears much resemblance with Spanish, in such a way that many complex prepositions in the two languages have shared etyma. Thai, despite the supposed high level of influence of Chinese until the 13th century and many typological features shared with Chinese, shows only a minimal level of Chinese influence on Thai prepositions.

In the foregoing chapters, we noted the presence of a number of puzzles for which no immediate answers could be provided. This is partly due to the absence of relevant historical data and partly due to the nature of such issues going beyond the scope of this macroscopic study. However, they constitute important research topics in the future, and the findings from more microscopic, exemplar-based research will complement the many gaps that occur in the present volume, and help us better understand the grammaticalization of adpositional systems across languages.

Appendix 1. Korean Complex Postpositions

-(ey) myenhay	'facing'		-(ul) poko	'to'
-(ey) myenhayse	'facing'		-(ul) pokose	'to'
-(ey) tayko	'to, unto'		-(ul) thonghay	'through'
-(ey) taykose	'to, unto'		-(ul) ttala	'along, through'
-(ey) ttala	'following'		-(ul) ttala	'following'
-(ey) ttalase	'following'		-(ul) ttalase	'along, through'
-(ey) yenhay	'contiguous to'		-(ul) ttalase	'following'
-(ey) yenhayse	'contiguous to'		-(ul) yenhay	'contiguous to'
-(ey)ta tayko	'to'		-(ul) yenhayse	'contiguous to'
-(ey)ta taykose	'to'		-(uy) alay	'below, under'
-(ul) ceyhako	'except'		-(uy) alayey	'below, under'
-(ul) ceyoyhako	'except'		-(uy) alayeyse	'below, under'
-(ul) ceyoyhakose	'except'		-(uy) alayse	'below, under'
-(ul) hyanghay	'toward'		-(uy) aney	'in, within'
-(ul) hyanghaye	'toward'		-(uy) aneyse	'in, within'
-(ul) hyanghayse	'toward'		-(uy) aphey	'before'
-(ul) kaciko	'with'		-(uy) apheyse	'before'
-(ul) kacko	'with'		-(uy) chukmyeney	'beside'
-(ul) kalocille	'across'		-(uy) chukmyeneyse	'beside'
-(ul) kalocillese	'across'		-(uy) cwachukey	'left to'
-(ul) kenne	'across'		-(uy) cwachukeyse	'left to'
-(ul) kennese	'across'		-(uy) cwupyeney	'around'
-(ul) kwanthonghaye	'through'		-(uy) cwupyeneyse	'around'
-(ul) kwanthonghayse	'through'		-(uy) cwuwiey	'around'
-(ul) kyekhay	'apart from'		-(uy) cwuwieyse	'around'
-(ul) kyekhaye	'apart from'		-(uy) kawuntey	'in, among'
-(ul) kyekhayse	'apart from'		-(uy) kawunteyey	'in, among'
-(ul) ne.me	'over'		-(uy) kawunteyse	'in, among'
-(ul) ne.mese	'over'		-(uy) kyethey	'beside, by'
-(ul) nem.e	'over'		-(uy) kyetheyse	'beside, by'
-(ul) nem.ese	'over'		-(uy) mithey	'below, under'

-(uy) mitheyse	'below, under'	-ey cwunhayse	'following, with reference to'
-(uy) olunccokey	'right to'		
-(uy) olunccokeyse	'right to'	-ey hanhay	'limited to'
-(uy) oynccokey	'left to'	-ey hanhaye	'limited to'
-(uy) oynccokeyse	'left to'	-ey hanhayse	'limited to'
-(uy) pakkey	'outside, except'	-ey kwanhay	'about'
-(uy) pakkeyse	'outside'	-ey kwanhaye	'about'
-(uy) palunccokey	'right to'	-ey kwanhayse	'about'
-(uy) palunccokeyse	'right to'	-ey panhay	'against, contra'
-(uy) saiey	'between'	-ey panhaye	'against, contra'
-(uy) saieyse	'between'	-ey panhayse	'against, contra'
-(uy) sayey	'between'	-ey pihay	'compared to'
-(uy) sayeyse	'between'	-ey pihaye	'compared to'
-(uy) sokey	'in, within'	-ey pihayse	'compared to'
-(uy) sokeyse	'in, within'	-ey taka tayko	'to, unto'
-(uy) thumey	'between'	-ey taka taykose	'to, unto'
-(uy) thumeyse	'between'	-ey taka	'to, unto'
-(uy) twiey	'behind, after'	-ey tayhay	'about'
-(uy) twieyse	'behind'	-ey tayhaye	'about'
-(uy) wiey	'on, above, over'	-ey tayhayse	'about'
-(uy) wieyse	'on, above, over'	-ey tayko	'to'
-(uy) wuchukey	'right to'	-ey taykose	'to'
-(uy) wuchukeyse	'right to'	-ey uyhay	'by'
-(uy) yephey	'beside, by'	-ey uyhaye	'by'
-(uy) yepheyse	'beside, by'	-ey uyhayse	'by'
-(wa) hamkkey	'(together) with'	-ey(to) pwulkwuhako	'despite'
-(wa) ttelecye	'apart from'	-ey(to) pwulkwuhakose	'despite'
-(wa) ttelecyese	'apart from'	-haey	'under'
-ceney	'before'	-haeyse	'under'
-cwungey	'in, among'	-hako hamkkey	'(together) with'
-cwungeyse	'in, among'	-hako kathi	'(together) with'
-ey cwunhay	'following, with reference to'	-hanthey taka tayko	'to'
		-hanthey taka taykose	'to'
-ey cwunhaye	'following, with reference to'	-hanthey taka	'to'
		-hanthey tayko	'to'

-hanthey taykose	'to'	-ul inhaye	'due to'
-hwuey	'after'	-ul inhayse	'due to'
-kaney	'between'	-ul kihay	'as of, starting at'
-lo hyanghay	'toward'	-ul kihaye	'as of, starting at'
-lo hyanghaye	'toward'	-ul kihayse	'as of, starting at'
-lo inhay	'due to'	-ul kyemhay	'along with, cum'
-lo inhaye	'due to'	-ul kyemhaye	'along with, cum'
-lo inhayse	'due to'	-ul kyemhayse	'along with, cum'
-lo taka	'to, unto'	-ul nohko	'about, over'
-nayey	'in, within'	-ul nohkose	'about, over'
-nayeyse	'in, within'	-ul tele	'to'
-oyey	'outside, except'	-ul twuko	'about, over'
-sangey	'on'	-ul twukose	'about, over'
-tekpwuney	'thanks to'	-ul wihay	'for, for the benefit of'
-ul chokwahay	'exceeding, surpassing'	-ul wihaye	'for, for the benefit of'
-ul chokwahaye	'exceeding, surpassing'	-ul wihayse	'for, for the benefit of'
-ul chokwahayse	'exceeding, surpassing'	-wa kathi	'(together) with'
-ul inhay	'due to'	-wa tepwule	'(together) with'

Appendix 2: English Complex Prepositions

after the conclusion of
after the fashion of
after the period of
against the background of
against the perils of
all of a piece with
along the side of
among the ranks of
as a consequence of
as a pledge of
as a reason for
as a replacement for
as a representative of
as a result of
as a reward for
as a sign of
as a substitute for
as an alternative to
as far as
as part of
as proxy for
at a distance from
at a distance of
at a height of
at cross purposes with
at odds over
at odds with
at the back of
at the base of
at the behest of
at the bottom of

at the break of
at the command of
at the conclusion of
at the cost of
at the discretion of
at the doorstep of
at the expense of
at the feet of
at the foot of
at the forefront of
at the hand of
at the hands of
at the head of
at the heels of
at the helm of
at the instance of
at the mercy of
at the pleasure of
at the price of
at the request of
at the reverence of
at the risk of
at the sacrifice of
at the suggestion of
at the threshold of
at the time of
at the top of
at the turn of
at the wheel of
at the whim of
at the wish of

at variance with
beyond the bounds of
beyond the field of
beyond the limits of
beyond the range of
beyond the reach of
beyond the scope of
beyond the shadow of
by a decree of
by a margin of
by analogy with
by benefit of
by comparison with
by courtesy of
by decree of
by dint of
by means of
by reason of
by right of
by the act of
by the action of
by the agency of
by the aid of
by the combination of
by the decree of
by the good offices of
by the mechanism of
by the operation of
by the side of
by use of
by virtue of
by way of
during the period of
during the reign of
during the time of

en route from
en route to
for a period of
for behalf of
for dint of
for fear of
for lack of
for purposes of
for sake of
for the advantage of
for the benefit of
for the duration of
for the object of
for the period of
for the price of
for the purpose of
for the purposes of
for the sake of
for want of
from a position of
from the point of view of
from the position of
from the standpoint of
from the viewpoint of
from want of
in a case of
in a fit of
in a state of
in accord with
in accordance with
in acknowledg(e)ment of
in addition to
in advance of
in agreement with
in aid of

in alliance with
in alternation with
in anticipation of
in approximation to
in association with
in back of
in behalf of
in cahoots with
in case of
in charge of
in collaboration with
in collusion with
in combination with
in combinations with
in commemoration of
in common with
in company with
in comparison with
in compensation for
in compliance with
in concert with
in concordance with
in conflict with
in conformity with
in conjunction with
in connection with
in consequence of
in consideration of
in consort with
in contact with
in contemplation of
in contempt of
in contradiction to
in contradistinction to
in contrast with

in contravention of
in cooperation with
in coordination with
in correspondence with
in default of
in defence/defense of
in deference to
in defiance of
in dependence of
in despite of
in disagreement with
in disregard of
in evidence of
in excess of
in exchange for
in exchange of
in expectation of
in extenuation of
in face of
in favo(u)r of
in freedom of
in front of
in gratitude for
in gratitude to
in gratitude unto
in harmony with
in hono(u)r of
in hope of
in imitation of
in keeping with
in lieu of
in light of
in line for
in line with
in lockstep with

in memory of
in need to
in obedience to
in observance of
in opposition to
in order of
in parallel with
in payment of
in place of
in pledge for
in point of
in praise of
in precedence of
in preference to
in preparation for
in process of
in proof of
in proportion to
in protest against
in provision for
in proximity to
in punishment for
in pursuance of
in pursuit of
in quest of
in questions of
in reaction to
in reaction with
in recognition of
in recompense for
in reference to
in regard to
in relation to
in relation with
in respect of

in respect to
in retaliation for
in retribution for
in return for
in rows of
in satisfaction of
in search of
in settlement of
in spite of
in step with
in substitution for
in support of
in sympathy with
in sync with
in terms of
in testimony of
in the absence of
in the act of
in the aftermath of
in the age of
in the area of
in the back of
in the bosom of
in the case of
in the cases of
in the company of
in the context of
in the core of
in the course of
in the direction of
in the era of
in the event of
in the eyes of
in the face of
in the field of

in the forefront of

in the foreground of

in the form of

in the furtherance of

in the grip of

in the hands of

in the heart of

in the heat of

in the hollow of

in the hope of

in the interest of

in the interests of

in the light of

in the line of

in the manner of

in the matter of

in the middle of

in the midst of

in the name of

in the nature of

in the neighbo(u)rhood of

in the order of

in the period of

in the person of

in the place of

in the presence of

in the process of

in the pursuance of

in the question of

in the region of

in the reign of

in the safety of

in the semblance of

in the sense of

in the service of

in the shadow of

in the shape of

in the sight of

in the space of

in the sphere of

in the stead of

in the style of

in the teeth of

in the thick of

in the throes of

in the time of

in the tradition of

in the train of

in the transition to

in the vicinity of

in the wake of

in the way of

in times of

in token of

in touch with

in transit to

in tune with

in unison with

in unity with

in view of

in virtue of

of the order of

on a background of

on a par with

on a scale of

on account of

on authority of

on behalf of

on board of

on course for

on ground of
on grounds of
on pain of
on penalty of
on peril of
on route from
on route to
on security of
on terms of
on the advice of
on the allowance of
on the authority of
on the back of
on the basis of
on the brink of
on the character of
on the conclusion of
on the confines of
on the edge of
on the eve of
on the flank of
on the ground of
on the grounds of
on the heels of
on the high road to
on the left of
on the left side of
on the matter of
on the matters of
on the model of
on the occasion of
on the outskirts of
on the part of
on the point of
on the premises of

on the pretext of
on the principle of
on the question of
on the right of
on the right side of
on the road to
on the score of
on the side of
on the strength of
on the subject of
on the theme of
on the topic of
on the track of
on the trail of
on the underside of
on the verge of
on the very point of
on the way to
on top of
out of a sense of
out of alignment with
out of all proportion to
out of consideration for
out of courtesy to
out of deference to
out of keeping with
out of line with
out of proportion to
out of respect for
out of respect to
out of sight of
out of step with
out of sympathy for
out of sync with
out of tune with

outside the boundaries of
outside the limits of
outside the range of
outside the reach of
since the time of
through a series of
through the agency of
through the good offices of
through the instrumentality of
through the intercession of
through the intermediation of
through the intervention of
through the mediation of
through the medium of
through the midst of
through the operation of
through the working of
throughout the course of
till the time of
to the accompaniment of
to the amount of
to the cause of
to the detriment of
to the exclusion of
to the extent of
to the front of
to the left of
to the memory of
to the point of
to the right of
to the tune of
to the verge of
under authority of
under cover of
under pain of

under penalty of
under the aegis of
under the auspices of
under the authority of
under the cloak of
under the condition of
under the eyes of
under the heel of
under the name of
under the nose of
under the patronage of
under the pretext of
under the protection of
under the supervision of
under the threat of
under the title of
under threat of
upon pain of
with a view to
with an eye to
with benefit of
with reference to
with regard to
with relation to
with respect to
with the addition of
with the aid of
with the aim of
with the assistance of
with the exception of
with the help of
with the intention of
with the object of
with the objective of
with the permission of

with the purpose of
within a area of
within a circumference of
within a distance of
within a hair's breadth of
within a mile of
within a small area of
within a stone's throw from
within a stone's throw of
within an ace of
within an inch of
within hail of
within reach of
within sight of
within the ambit of
within the bosom of
within the boundaries of
within the bounds of
within the compass of
within the field of
within the framework of

within the limits of
within the orbit of
within the period of
within the radius of
within the range of
within the ranks of
within the realm of
within the realms of
within the scope of
within the space of
within the span of
within the sweep of
within the verge of
without detriment to
without reference to
without regard to
without respect to
without the aid of
without the assistance of
without the peril of

Appendix 3: Composite and Complex Prepositions in Spanish

a ambos lados de	'on both sides of'
a base de	'based on'
a beneficio de	'for the benefit of'
a bordo de	'aboard'
a cambio de	'in exchange of'
a cargo de	'in charge of'
a causa de	'due, by the cause of'
a cobijo de	'in the shelter of'
a colación de	'in collation of'
a comienzo de	'at the beginning of'
a comienzos de	'at the beginnings of'
a condición de	'on condition of'
a consecuencia de	'as a result of'
a continuación de	'in continuation of'
a contra de	'against'
a costa de	'at the expense of'
a criterio de	'at the discretion of'
a cubierto de	'under cover of'
a cuenta de	'on account of'
a cuento de	'on account of'
a demanda de	'at the request of'
a despecho de	'in spite of'
a diferencia de	'unlike'
a disposición de	'at the disposal of'
a distinción de	'unlike'
a efectos de	'for the purposes of'
a ejemplo de	'as an example of'
a escondidas de	'in secret from'
a eso de	'around'
a espaldas de	'behind'
a excepción de	'except for'

a excusa de	'to excuse of'
a expensas de	'at the expense of'
a falta de	'in the absence of'
a favor de	'in favor of'
a fe de	'in faith of'
a filo de	'on the edge of'
a fin de	'for the purpose of, at the end of'
a final de	'at the end of'
a finales de	'at the end of'
a fines de	'at the end of'
a flor de	'on the surface of, around'
a fuer de	'in the capacity of'
a fuerza de	'by dint of'
a golpe de	'at the stroke of'
a golpes de	'at the strokes of'
a guisa de	'by way of'
a gusto de	'at the pleasure of'
a hombros de	'on the shoulders of'
a imitación de	'in imitation of'
a impulsos de	'at the impulse of'
a instancias de	'at the behest of'
a juicio de	'in the opinion of'
a juzgar por	'judging by'
a la altur de	'at the height of'
a la busca de	'in search of'
a la búsqueda de	'in search of'
a la cabeza de	'at the head of'
a la carga de	'to the load of'
a la caza de	'on the hunt for'
a la derecha de	'to the right of'
a la edad de	'at the age of'
a la espera de	'waiting for'
a la hora de	'at the time of'
a la izquierda de	'to the left of'
a la ley de	'to the law of'

a la luz de	'in the light of'
a la manera de	'in the way of'
a la medida de	'to the measure of'
a la memoria de	'to the memory of'
a la merced de	'at the mercy of'
a la mira de	'in the sights of'
a la par de	'on par with'
a la sombra de	'in the shadow of'
a la usanza de	'in the style of'
a la utilización de	'to the use of'
a la vera de	'next to'
a la vista de	'in sight of'
a la vuelta de	'around'
a las órdenes de	'at the orders of'
a ley de	'to law of'
a lo ancho de	'across'
a lo largo de	'along'
a manera de	'by way of'
a mano de	'by hand of'
a manos de	'at the hands of'
a más de	'over'
a mediados de	'in the middle of'
a medida de	'to the measure of'
a medio a	'half to'
a medio de	'in the middle of'
a menos de	'less than'
a merced de	'at the mercy of'
a mitad de	'in the middle of'
a modo de	'by way of'
a nivel de	'at the level of'
a nombre de	'on behalf of'
a orillas de	'on the shores of'
a partir de	'from, apart from'
a pesar de	'despite'
a petición de	'at the request of'

a poco de	'shortly after'
a pretexto de	'under the pretext of'
a principios de	'at the beginning of'
a proporción de	'at the proportion of'
a propósito de	'about'
a propuesta de	'at the proposal of'
a prueba de	'at the proof of'
a punta de	'at the point of'
a punto a	'about to'
a punto de	'about to'
a raíz de	'because of, next to'
a ras de	'at the level of'
a razón de	'at the rate of'
a remolque de	'in tow of'
a requerimiento de	'at the request of'
a reservas de	'at reserves of'
a resguardo de	'to the protection of'
a resultas de	'as a result of'
a riesgo de	'at risk of'
a ruegos de	'at the request of'
a salvo de	'safe from'
a satisfacción de	'to the satisfaction of'
a semejanza de	'like'
a servicio de	'at the service of'
a solas con	'alone with'
a solicitud de	'at the request of'
a son de	'at the sound of'
a tenor de	'according to'
a título de	'by title of'
a través de	'via'
a virtud de	'by virtue of'
a vista de	'in view of'
abajo de	'under'
acerca de	'about'
acorde con	'according to'

adecuadamente a	'appropriately to'
adecuadamente con	'appropriately with'
adelante de	'ahead of'
además de	'in addition to'
adentro de	'inside'
afuera de	'outside of'
aisladamente a	'in isolation to'
al abrigo de	'sheltered from'
al alcance de	'in the reach of'
al amor de	'to the love of, near'
al amparo de	'to protection of'
al arrimo de	'at the vicinity of, with the help of'
al borde de	'at the edge of'
al cabo de	'after'
al calor de	'in the heat of'
al comienzo de	'at the beginning of'
al compás de	'to the beat of'
al contacto con	'to contact with'
al contacto de	'to the contact of'
al contrario de	'contrary to'
al corriente de	'aware of'
al cuidado de	'in the care of'
al empleo de	'to the use of'
al encuentro de	'to the meeting of'
al estilo de	'in the style of'
al exterior de	'outside'
al extremo de	'to the extreme of'
al filo de	'on the edge of'
al final de	'at the end of'
al final de	'at the end of'
al finales de	'at the end of'
al fondo de	'at the bottom of'
al frente de	'in front of'
al habla con	'in speaking with'
al instante de	'at the instant of'

al interior de	'inside'
al lado de	'next to'
al mando de	'in command of'
al margen de	'at the margin of, outside of, apart from'
al modo de	'in the manner of'
al momento de	'at the time of'
al nivel de	'at the level of'
al objeto de	'to the object of'
al otro lado de	'at the other side of'
al par de	'in a pair with, on a par with, next to'
al pie de	'at the foot of'
al precio de	'at the price of'
al principio de	'at the beginning of'
al punto de	'to the point of'
al revés de	'in reverse of'
al revés que	'the other way around of'
al servicio de	'at the service of'
al socaire de	'in the wake of'
al son de	'to the sound of'
al tanto de	'aware of'
al término de	'at the end of'
al trato de	'to deal with'
al uso de	'to the use of'
allende de	'beyond'
alrededor de	'about, around'
alternativamente a	'alternatively to'
análogamente a	'analogously to'
análogo a	'analogous to'
angularmente a	'angularly to'
anteriormente a	'prior to'
antes de	'prior to'
apartdamente de	'apart from'
aparte de	'apart from'
apegadamente a	'attached to'
arriba de	'above'

atentamente a	'attentively to'
atrás de	'behind of'
ávidamente de	'eagerly of'
bajo capa de	'under layer of'
bajo de	'under'
bajo la protección de	'under the protection of'
bajo las órdenes de	'under the orders of'
bajo pena de	'on pain of'
bajo pretexto de	'under the pretext of'
cabe a	'fitting'
camino a	'on the way to'
camino de	'on the way of'
cara a	'facing'
casi a	'almost to'
caso de	'in case of'
cerca de	'near'
cercanamente a	'closely to'
cercano a	'close to'
cercano de	'close to'
circularmente a	'circularly to'
como a	'like'
como adelanto de	'as a preview of'
como comprensción a	'as understanding to'
como consecuencia de	'as a consequence of'
como de	'like'
como demostración a	'as a demonstration to'
como en	'like in'
como expresión de	'as an expression of'
como muestra de	'as a sample of'
como preparación a	'in preparation for'
como preparación de	'as preparation of'
como prueba de	'as proof of'
como respuensta a	'as a result of'
como respuesta a	'in response to'
como resultado de	'as a result of'

como señal de	'as a sign of'
como testimonio de	'as a testimony of'
con ánimo de	'with the spirit of'
con anterioridad a	'prior to'
con arreglo a	'according to'
con ayuda de	'with the help of'
con base a	'based on'
con base de	'based on'
con base en	'based on'
con cargo a	'under'
con cuidado de	'with care of'
con destino a	'bound for'
con diferencia de	'with difference of'
con dirección a	'with direction to'
con efectos de	'with effects of'
con el fin de	'with the purpose of'
con el mando de	'with the command of'
con el nombre de	'with the name of'
con el objeto de	'with the objective of'
con el parecer de	'with the opinion of'
con el pretexto de	'under the pretext of'
con el propósito de	'with the purpose of'
con emisión de	'with issuance of'
con esperanza de	'with hope of'
con excepción de	'with the exception of'
con experiencia de	'with experience of'
con ganas de	'in the mood for'
con honores de	'with honors of'
con idea de	'with idea of'
con intención de	'with intention of'
con la disculpa de	'with the apology of'
con la esperanza de	'hoping for'
con la intención de	'with the intention of'
con la mira de	'with the sights of'
con la probabilidad de	'with the probability of'

con menoscabo de	'with the detriment of'
con miras a	'to look at'
con motivo a	'on the occasion of'
con motivo de	'because of'
con objeto de	'with the object of'
con ocasión de	'on the occasion of'
con peligro de	'with danger of'
con perjuicio de	'to the detriment of'
con posibilidad de	'with the possibility of'
con posterioridad a	'after'
con pretensión de	'with pretense of'
con razón a	'with reason of'
con razón de	'with reason of'
con referencia a	'with reference to'
con relación a	'in relation to'
con relación con	'in relation to'
con respecto a	'with respect to'
con riesgo de	'at risk of'
con rumbo a	'bound for'
con tal de	'with the provision of'
con todo de	'with all of'
con visos de	'with hints of'
con vistas a	'with views to'
confiadamente con	'confidently with'
conforme a	'according to'
conforme con	'agreeing with'
conjuntamente a	'jointly to'
conjuntamente con	'jointly with'
conscientemente de	'consciously of'
consecuentemente a	'consequently to'
consecuentemente con	'consequently with'
consecutivamente a	'consecutively to'
contra la voluntad de	'against the will of'
contradictoriamente a	'contradictorily to'
contradictoriamente con	'contradictorily with'

contrariamente a	'contrary to'
correlativamente a	'correlatively to'
cuanto a	'as for'
cuestión de	'in the matter of'
cuidadosamente de	'carefully of'
de acuerdo a	'according to'
de acuerdo con	'in accordance with'
de acuerdo en	'according to'
de boca de	'from the mouth of'
de cara a	'facing'
de conformidad con	'in accordance with'
de espaldas a	'back to'
de frente a	'in front of'
de la mano de	'from the hand of'
de la vista de	'from the sight of'
de parte de	'from'
de paso a	'on the way to'
de paso hacia	'on the way to'
de paso para	'on the way to'
de regreso a	'back to'
de regreso de	'back from'
de resultas de	'as a result of'
de través a	'through'
de vuelta a	'back to'
de vuelta de	'back from'
debajo de	'under'
debido a	'because of'
del lado de	'on the side of'
del otro lado de	'on the other side of'
delante de	'in front of'
dentro de	'within'
desagradablemente a	'unpleasantly to'
desconfiadamente de	'distrustfully of'
desde comienzo de	'from the beginning of'
desde la perspectiva de	'from the perspective of'

después de	'after'
detrás de	'in back of'
diagonalmente a	'diagonally to'
diferentemente de	'differently from'
distante de	'distant from'
distintamente de	'distinctly from'
en abono de	'in subscription of'
en achaque de	'in fault of'
en actitud de	'in attitude of'
en ademán de	'in the appearance of'
en agradecimiento a	'in gratitude to'
en agradecimiento por	'in gratitude for'
en alabanza de	'in praise of'
en alusión a	'in allusion to'
en apariencia de	'in appearance of'
en apoyo de	'in support of'
en aras a	'for the sake of'
en aras de	'for the sake of'
en armonía con	'in keeping with'
en asuntos de	'in matters of'
en atención a	'in attention to'
en ausencia de	'in absence of'
en auxilio de	'in aid of'
en ayuda de	'in aid of'
en base a	'based on'
en base de	'in base of'
en beneficio de	'in benefit of'
en bien de	'for the good of'
en boca de	'in wide circulation in/among'
en brazos de	'in the arms of'
en busca de	'in search of'
en búsqueda de	'in search of'
en cabeza de	'at the head of'
en calidad de	'as'
en cambio de	'instead of'

en camino de	'on the way to'
en caso de	'in case of'
en combinación con	'in combination with'
en compañía de	'in company of'
en comparación a	'in comparison to'
en comparación con	'in comparison with'
en compensación a	'in compensation to'
en compensación con	'in compensation with'
en compensación de	'in compensation of'
en compensación por	'in compensation for'
en competencia con	'in competition with'
en comunicación con	'in communication with'
en concepto de	'in concept of'
en conexión con	'in connection with'
en conformidad con	'in accordance with'
en connivencia con	'in collusion with'
en conocimiento de	'in the knowledge of'
en conquista de	'in conquest of'
en consecuencia con	'in accordance with'
en consideración a	'considering'
en consonancia con	'consistent with'
en contacto con	'in contact with'
en contestación a	'in reply to'
en contra de	'against'
en contradicción con	'in contradiction to'
en contraste con	'in contrast with'
en convergenicia con	'in convergence with'
en conversación con	'in conversation with'
en correlación con	'in correlation with'
en correspondencia con	'in correspondence with'
en cuanto a	'as to'
en cuestión de	'in a matter of'
en cumplimiento de	'in pursuance of'
en defensa de	'in defense of'
en deferencia a	'in deference to'

en demanda de	'in demand of'
en demonstración de	'in demonstration of'
en derredor de	'around'
en descargo de	'in discharge of'
en descrédito de	'in discredit of'
en desdoro de	'in disdain of'
en detrimento de	'to the detriment of'
en dirección a	'in direction to'
en disposición de	'in disposition of'
en disputa con	'in dispute with'
en divergencia con	'in divergence with'
en el calor de	'in the heat of'
en el caso de	'in the case of'
en el centro de	'in the center of'
en el comienzo de	'in the beginning of'
en el corazón de	'in the heart of'
en el exterior de	'outside of'
en el fondo de	'at the bottom of'
en el interior de	'inside of'
en el momento de	'in the moment of'
en el plano de	'at the level of, in the area of'
en el término de	'in the term of'
en elogio de	'in praise of'
en espera de	'waiting for'
en evitación de	'in avoidance of'
en expresión de	'in expression of'
en favor de	'in favor of'
en fe de	'in faith of'
en forma de	'in form of'
en fuerza de	'in force of'
en función a	'based on'
en función de	'in function of'
en gracia a	'in favor of'
en gracia de	'in grace of'
en guisa de	'in the guise of'

en harmonía con	'in harmony with'
en homenaje a	'in homage to'
en honor a	'in honor to'
en honor de	'in honor of'
en interés de	'in the interest of'
en íntimo contacto con	'in intimate contact with'
en la medida de	'to the extent of'
en la necesidad de	'in need of'
en la obligación de	'in the obligation of'
en la urgencia de	'in the urgency of'
en la víspera de	'on the eve of'
en las barbas de	'in the beards of'
en las vísperas de	'on the eve of'
en ley de	'in law of'
en lo alto de	'on top of'
en lo profundo de	'in the depth of'
en lo que afecta a	'in what affects'
en lo que concierne a	'with respect to'
en lo que respecta a	'as regards'
en lo que se refiere a	'as regards'
en lo que tiene que ver con	'in what has to do with
en lo que toca a	'regarding'
en lo referente a	'regarding'
en lo relacionado con	'in relation to'
en lo relativo a	'regarding'
en lo tocante a	'in relation to'
en los alrededores de	'around'
en lugar de	'instead of'
en manos de	'in hands of'
en materia de	'in matters of'
en medio a	'in the middle of'
en medio de	'between'
en memoria de	'in memory of'
en mitad de	'in the middle of'
en muestra de	'in sample of'

en nombre de	'on behalf of'
en número de	'in number of'
en obligación de	'in obligation of'
en obra de	'in work of'
en obsequio a	'as a gift to'
en obsequio de	'as a gift of'
en observancia de	'in observance of'
en ocasión de	'on the occasion of'
en opinión de	'in the opinion of'
en oposición a	'in opposition to'
en orden a	'in order to'
en pago a	'in payment to'
en pago de	'in payment of'
en pago por	'in payment for'
en paralelo a	'parallel to'
en paralelo con	'in parallel with'
en peligro de	'in danger of'
en perjuicio de	'in prejudice of'
en petición de	'at the request of'
en plan de	'in plan of'
en poder de	'in power of'
en pos de	'in pursuit of'
en posesión de	'in possession of'
en presencia de	'in the presence of'
en prevención de	'in prevention of'
en previsión de	'in anticipation of'
en pro de	'in favor of'
en proporción a	'in proportion to'
en proporción con	'in proportion to'
en protesta por	'in protest for'
en provecho de	'for the benefit of'
en prueba de	'in proof of'
en puesto de	'in position of'
en pugna por	'fighting for'
en razón a	'in reason to'

en razón de	'on account of'
en rechazo de	'in rejection of'
en recompensa a	'in reward to'
en recompensa por	'in reward for'
en reconocimiento a	'in recognition of'
en reconocimiento de	'in recognition of'
en recuerdo de	'in memory of'
en referencia a	'in reference to'
en relación a	'regarding'
en relación con	'regarding'
en representación de	'representing'
en repulsa por	'in disgust for'
en respuesta a	'in response to'
en riesgo de	'at risk of'
en señal de	'in token of'
en servicio de	'in service of'
en solicitud de	'at the request of'
en son de	'at the sound of'
en sustitución de	'replacing'
en términos de	'in terms of'
en testimonio de	'in testimony of'
en tiempo de	'in time of'
en tocante a	'regarding'
en torno a	'around'
en torno de	'around'
en trance de	'in a trance of'
en un tris de	'at the very instant of'
en unión con	'in conjunction with'
en unión de	'in union of'
en uso de	'in use of'
en utilidad de	'in the utility of'
en vez de	'instead of'
en vías de	'in the process of'
en vinculación con	'in connection with'
en virtud de	'in virtue of'

en vísperas de	'on the eve of'
en vista de	'in view of'
encima de	'above'
enfrente de	'in front of'
entremedias de	'in between'
esquina a	'at the corner of'
excepto en	'except in'
exteriormente a	'outwardly to'
favorablemente a	'favorably to'
frente a	'versus'
frente de	'in front of'
frontero a	'frontier to'
fuera de	'outside'
gracias a	'thanks to'
gratamente a	'pleasantly to'
hostilmente a	'hostilely to'
hostilmente con	'hostilely with'
hostilmente contra	'hostilely against'
idénticamente a	'identically to'
incluso en	'even in'
incongruentemente con	'incongruously with'
independientemente de	'independently of'
indiferentemente a	'indifferently to'
indistintamente de	'indistinctly from'
inferiormente a	'inferior to'
inversamente a	'inversely to'
junto a	'next to'
junto con	'with'
junto de	'together with'
lateralmente a	'laterally to'
lejos de	'far from'
longitudinalmente a	'longitudinally to'
luego de	'after'
menos en	'less in'
merced a	'thanks to'

motivado a	'motivated to'
no obstante	'notwithstanding'
no obstante a	'notwithstanding'
no obstante de	'notwithstanding'
oblicuamente a	'obliquely to'
oblicuo a	'oblique to'
orilla a	'at the shore to'
orilla de	'at the shore of'
orillas de	'at the shores of'
para benficio de	'for the benefit of'
para bien de	'for the good of'
paralelamente a	'in parallel to'
paralelo a	'in parallel to'
pendiente de	'pending'
perpendicular a	'in perpendicular to'
perpendicularmente a	'in perpendicular to'
pese a	'despite'
por amor a	'for love of'
por bajo de	'below'
por boca de	'through the mouth of, in agreement with'
por causa de	'because of'
por cima de	'above'
por concepto de	'by concept of'
por condescendencia con	'by condescension with'
por conducto de	'through'
por consideración a	'out of consideration for'
por contra de	'against'
por cuenta de	'on behalf of'
por culpa de	'because of'
por debajo de	'below'
por deferencia a	'out of deference to'
por delante de	'in front of'
por dentro de	'inside'
por derecho de	'by right of'
por despecho a	'out of spite to'

por detrás de	'behind of'
por efecto de	'by effect of'
por el contrario de	'on the contrary of'
por encargo de	'commissioned by'
por encima de	'above'
por entremedias de	'in between'
por espacio de	'by space of'
por falta de	'for lack of'
por favor de	'for favor of'
por indicación de	'by indication of'
por influencia de	'by influence of'
por intermedio de	'through'
por intervención de	'by intervention of'
por lo que respecta a	'with respect to'
por lo que se refiere a	'as regards'
por mandado de	'by command of'
por mandato de	'by mandate of'
por medicación de	'by medication of'
por medio de	'through'
por miedo a	'for fear of'
por mitad de	'by half of'
por mor a	'for the sake of'
por motivo de	'because of'
por obra de	'by work of'
por orden de	'in order of'
por parte de	'by'
por razón a	'for reason to'
por razón de	'by reason of'
por recomendación de	'on the recommendation of'
por respeto a	'out of respect for'
por temor a	'for fear of'
por temor de	'for fear of'
por vía de	'by way of'
por virtud de	'by virtue of'
por voluntad de	'by the will of'

posteriormente a	'later to, subsequently to'
preferentemente a	'preferably to'
preferiblemente a	'preferably to'
previamente a	'prior to'
proporcionalmente a	'proportionally to'
próximamente a	'close to'
próximo a	'next to'
referente a	'relating to'
relativo a	'relative to'
respecto a	'about'
respecto de	'in respect of'
rumbo a	'toward'
salvo en	'except in'
semejante a	'similar to'
semejantemente a	'similarly to'
separadamente de	'separately from'
simétricamente a	'symmetrically to'
simultáneamente a	'simultaneously to'
sin distinción de	'without distinction of'
sin perjuicio de	'without prejudice to'
so capa de	'under the layer of'
so color de	'under the color of'
so pena de	'under penalty of'
so pretexto de	'under the pretext of'
sumisamente a	'submissively to'
subordinadamente a	'subordinate to'
tocante a	'regarding'
tras de	'behind'
ulteriormente a	'subsequently to'

Bibliography

Abney, Steven. 1987. The English noun phrase in its sentential aspect. Ph.D. dissertation, MIT.

Abraham, Werner. 2004. The grammaticalization of the infinitival preposition: Toward a theory of 'grammaticalizing reanalysis'. *Journal of Comparative Germanic Linguistics* 7: 111-170.

Ahn, Byung Hee (안병희). 1967. *Mwunpepsa* [History of grammar] (*Enemwunhaksa*, Vol. 5 of *Hankwukmwunhwasa Taykyey*). Seoul: Research Institute of Korean Studies, Korea University.

Ahn, Joo Hoh (안주호). 1997. *Hankwuke Myengsauy Mwunpephwa Yenkwu* [A study of the phenomena of grammaticalization in the Korean noun]. Ph.D. dissertation, Yonsei University, Seoul: Hankook Publisher. (in Korean)

Ahn, Key-Seob and Jinhee Song (안기섭 송진희). 2008. Cwungkwukeuy pwuchisa [Adpositions in Chinese]. In: Kyung-An Song and Ki-Gap Lee (송경안 이기갑) (eds.), *Eneyuhyenglon* [Linguistic Typology] vol. 2: 246-257. (in Korean)

Ahn, Kyou-Dong (안규동). 2005. Semantic generality dilemma in grammaticalization: A case of 'cappacita'. *The Journal of Linguistic Science* (언어과학연구) 32: 159-178. (in Korean)

Ahn, Kyou-Dong (안규동). 2015. A usage-based approach to complex prepositions in English: With special reference to analogy-driven grammaticalization. Ph.D. dissertation, Hankuk University of Foreign Studies, Korea.

Ahn, Mikyung (안미경). 2009a. English causal complex prepositions: A grammaticalization perspective. Ph.D. dissertation, Hankuk University of Foreign Studies, Korea.

Ahn, Mikyung (안미경). 2009b. Synchronic consequences of diachronic changes: With reference to English causal complex prepositions. *Journal of Linguistic Science* (언어과학연구) 49: 141-158.

Ahn, So-Min (안소민). 2012. Aspects and mechanisms of grammaticalization of *gei*. *Language & Information Society* 17: 147-174. (in Korean)

Alarcos Llorach, Emilio. 1994. *Gramatica de la Lengua Española*. Barcelona: Planeta.

Allen, Cynthia L. 2006. Case syncretism and word order change. In: Ans van Kemenade and Bettelou Los (eds.), *The Handbook of the History of English*, 201-223.

Oxford: Blackwell.

Andersen, Elaine S. 1978. Lexical universals of body-part terminology. In: Joseph Greenberg (ed.), *Universals of Human Language, vol. 3, Word Structure*, 335-368. Stanford: Stanford University Press.

Andersen, Henning. 1973. Abductive and deductive change. *Language* 49: 765-793.

Andrews, Avery D. 2007[1985]. The major functions of the noun phrase. In: Timothy Shopen (ed.), *Language Typology and Syntactic Description* vol. 1: *Clause Structure* (2nd ed.), 132-223. Cambridge: Cambridge University Press.

Ansaldo, Umberto. 2006. Serial verb constructions. In: Keith Brown (ed.), *Encyclopedia of Language and Linguistics,* (2nd edition.) Amsterdam: Elsevier. Vol. 11, 260-64.

Ansaldo, Umberto, Walter Bisang, and Pui Yiu Szeto. 2018. Grammaticalization in isolating languages and the notion of complexity. In: Heiko Narrog and Bernd Heine (eds.), *Grammaticalization from a Typological Perspective* (Oxford Studies in Diachronic & Historical Linguistics 31), 219-234. Oxford: Oxford University Press.

Baik, Junghye (백정혜). 2004. Semantic changes of relational nouns into prepositions of English from a grammaticalization perspective. Paper presented at 2004 Summer Conference, Language Science Society, Aug. 21, 2004. Catholic University of Daegu.

Baik, Junghye (백정혜). 2005. Grammaticalization of spatial nouns. Paper presented at 2005 KASELL International Conference, June 21-22, 2005. Seoul.

Baik, Junghye (백정혜). 2006. Grammaticalization of English spatial prepositions and its Educational implications. Ph.D. dissertation, Hankuk University of Foreign Studies, Korea.

Bailblé, Olivier. 2015. History of the dative markers in Korean language: From old Korean to contemporary Korean. *International Journal of Korean Humanities and Social Sciences* 1: 119-136.

Barlow, Michael and Suzanne Kemmer (eds.) 2000. *Usage Based Models of Language.* Stanford: CSLI Publications.

Barrie, Michael and Audrey Li. 2015. Analysis versus synthesis: Objects. In: Audrey Li, Andrew Simpson, and Wei-Tien Dylan Tsai (eds.), *Chinese Syntax in a Cross-Linguistic Perspective* (Oxford Studies in Comparative Syntax), 179-206. Oxford: Oxford University Press.

Bello, Andrés. 1847. Gramática de la Lengua Castellana Destinada al Uso de los

Americanos. Reprinted in: Ramón Trujillo (1981) (ed.), Litografía A. Romero, S.A.

Bennett, David. 1975. *Spatial and Temporal Uses of English Prepositions: An Essay in Stratificational Semantics*. London: Longman.

Bentley, John. 2008. *A Linguistic History of the Forgotten Islands: A Reconstruction of the Proto-Language of the Southern Ryukyus* (Languages of Asia 7). Folkestone: Global Oriental.

Bergsland, Knut. 1997. *Aleut Grammar: Unangam Tunuganaan Achixaasix*. Fairbanks: ANLC (Alaska Native Language Center).

Bisang, Walter. 1995. Verb serialization and converbs – differences and similarities. In: Martin Haspelmath and Ekkehard König (eds.), *Converbs in Cross-Linguistic Perspective. Structure and Meaning of Adverbial Verb Forms – Adverbial Participles, Gerunds*. Berlin: Mouton de Gruyter, 137–88.

Bisang, Walter. 1996. Areal typology and grammaticalization: Processes of grammaticalization based on nouns and verbs in Mainland South East Asian languages. *Studies in Language* 20.3: 519–97.

Bisang, Walter. 2011. Grammaticalization and typology. In: Heiko Narrog and Bernd Heine (eds.), *The Oxford Handbook of Grammaticalization*, 105–117. Oxford: Oxford University Press.

Bisang, Walter. 2020. Grammaticalization in Chinese – A cross-linguistic perspective. In: Janet Zhiqun Xing (ed.). *A Typological Approach to Grammaticalization and Lexicalization: East Meets West* (Trends in Linguistics Studies and Monographs 327), 17–54. Berlin: Mouton de Gruyter.

Bisang, Walter and Andrej Malchukov. 2020a. *Grammaticalization Scenarios: Cross-Linguistic Variation and Universal Tendencies*, Vol. 1, *Grammaticalization Scenarios from Europe and Asia* (Comparative Handbooks of Linguistics). Berlin: Mouton de Gruyter.

Bisang, Walter and Andrej Malchukov. 2020b. *Grammaticalization Scenarios: Cross-Linguistic Variation and Universal Tendencies*, Vol. 2, *Grammaticalization Scenarios from Africa, the Americas, and the Pacific* (Comparative Handbooks of Linguistics). Berlin: Mouton de Gruyter.

Blake, Barry J. 1977. *Case Marking in Australian Languages* (Linguistic Series 23). Canberra: Australian Institute of Aboriginal Studies.

Blake, Barry J. 2004[1994]. *Case* (2nd ed.). Cambridge: Cambridge University Press.

Bloom, Paul, Mary A. Peterson, Lynn Nadel, and Merrill F. Garrett (eds.) 1999[1996]. *Language and Space.* Cambridge, MA: MIT Press.

Bolinger, Dwight. 1971. *The Phrasal Verb in English.* Cambridge: Harvard University Press.

Bolinger, Dwight. 1977. *Meaning and Form.* London: Longman.

Bolinger, Dwight. 1988. Reiconization. *World Englishes* 7.3: 237-242.

Börjars, Kersti and Nigel Vincent. 2011. Grammaticalization and directionality. In: Bernd Heine and Heiko Narrog (eds.), *The Oxford Handbook of Grammaticalization,* 162-176. Oxford: Oxford University Press.

Bourdin, Philippe. 1997. On goal-bias across languages: modal, configurational and orientational parameters. *Proceedings of LP '96: Typology: Prototypes, Item Orderings and Universals, Proceedings of the Conference Held in Prague, August 20-22, 1996,* 185-216.

Bowden, John. 1992. *Behind the Prepositions: Grammaticalisation of Locatives in Oceanic Languages* (Pacific Linguistics Series B-107). Canberra: Australian National University.

Bowerman, Melissa and Soonja Choi. 2001. Shaping meanings for language: Universal and language-specific in the acquisition of spatial semantic categories. In: Melissa Bowerman and Stephen C. Levinson (eds.), *Language Acquisition and Conceptual Development,* 475-511. Cambridge: Cambridge University Press.

Brinton, Laurel J. 1988. *The Development of English Aspectual Systems: Aspectualizers and Post-Verbal Particles.* Cambridge: Cambridge University Press.

Brisard, Frank. 1991. *The Problem of Temporality: Tense and Time in Cognitive Grammar* (Antwerp Papers in Linguistics 67). Wilrijk: Universiteit Antwerpen.

British National Corpus, the (BNC). https://www.english-corpora.org/bnc/

Broschart, Jürgen. 1992. *Raum und Grammatik oder: Wie berechenbar ist Sprache? (Mit Beispielen zu Kasusmarkierung, Aspekt, Tempus und Modus)* AKUP - Arbeiten des Kölner Universalien - Projekts 89. Studien zur Lokalisation 3. Köln: Universität zu Köln. (in German)

Brown, Cecil H. 1983. Where do cardinal direction terms come from? *Anthropological Linguistics* 25.2: 121-61.

Brown, J. Marvin. 1965. *From Ancient Thai to Modern Dialects.* Bangkok: Social Science Foundation Press of Thailand.

Brown, Penelope and Stephen Levinson. 1987. *Politeness: Some Universals in Language*

Usage. Cambridge: Cambridge University Press.

Brown, Penelope. 1994. The INs and ONs of Tzeltal locative expressions: The semantics of static descriptions of location. *Space in Mayan Languages,* Special issue of *Linguistics* 32.4/5: 743-790.

Brugman, Claudia. 1983. The use of body-part terms as locatives in Chalcatongo Mixtec. *Survey of California and Other Indian Languages* 4: 235-90.

Bugaeva, Anna. 2013. Mermaid constructions in Ainu. In: Tasaku Tsunoda (ed.), *Adnominal Clauses and the 'Mermaid Construction': Grammaticalization of Nouns,* 667-675. NINJAL Collaborative Research Project Reports 13-01.

Burton-Roberts, Noel. 1991. Prepositions, adverbs, and adverbials. In: Ingrid Tieken, Boon van Ostade, and John Frankis (eds.), *Language: Usage and Description,* 159-172. Amsterdam: Rodopi.

Bussmann, Hadumod. 1996. *Routledge Dictionary of Language and Linguistics.* Translated and edited by Gregory P. Trauth and Kerstin Kazzazi. London: Routledge.

Bybee, Joan L. 1985. *Morphology: A Study of the Relation Between Meaning and Form.* (Typological Studies in Language 9). Amsterdam: John Benjamins.

Bybee, Joan L. 2003. Mechanisms of change in grammaticization: the role of frequency. In: Brian D. Joseph and Richard D. Janda (eds.), *The Handbook of Historical Linguistics,* 602-23. Oxford: Blackwell.

Bybee, Joan L. 2006. From usage to grammar: the mind's response to repetition. *Language* 82.4: 711-33.

Bybee, Joan L. 2011. Usage-based theory and grammaticalization. In: Heiko Narrog and Bernd Heine (eds), *The Oxford Handbook of Grammaticalization,* 69-78. Oxford: Oxford University Press.

Bybee, Joan L. and Östen Dahl. 1989. The creation of tense and aspect systems in the languages of the world. *Studies in Language* 13: 51-103.

Bybee, Joan L. and Paul J. Hopper. 2001. *Frequency and the Emergence of Linguistic Structure.* (Typological Studies in Language 45). Amsterdam and Philadelphia. John Benjamins.

Bybee, Joan L., William Pagliuca and Revere D. Perkins. 1994. *The Evolution of Grammar: Tense, Aspect, and Modality in the Languages of the World.* Chicago: The University of Chicago Press.

Camacho Becerra, Heriberto, Juan José Comparán Rizo, and Felipe Castillo. 2004[1998].

Manual de Etimologías Grecolatinas (3rd ed.). México: Limusa. (in Spanish)

Campbell, Lyle. 1993. On proposed universals of grammatical borrowing. In: Robert Jeffers (ed.), *Selected Papers of the Ninth International Conference on Historical Linguistics*, 91-109. Amsterdam: John Benjamins.

Campbell, Lyle. 2001. What's wrong with grammaticalization? *Language Sciences* 23: 113-161.

Campbell, Lyle, Vit Bubenik, and Leslie Saxon. 1988. Word order universals: Refinements and clarifications. *Canadian Journal of Linguistics* 33.3: 209-230.

Center for Chinese Linguistics at Peking University Corpus, the (CCL-Corpus). http://ccl.pku.edu.cn:8080/ccl_corpus/

Chae, Hee-Rahk (채희락). 2020. *Korean Morphosyntax: Focusing on Clitics and Their Roles in Syntax*. London: Routledge.

Chae, Wan (채완). 1990. Thukswucosa [Special particles]. In: Korean Language Research Group of Seoul National University Graduate School (ed.) *Kwukeyenkwu Etikkayci Wassna* [How far Korean language studies have advanced], 263-70. Seoul: Dong-A Publishing. (in Korean)

Chamniyom, Ratree. 2003. A study of prepositions converted from verbs in Thai. MA thesis, Silapakorn University, Thailand.

Chappell, Hilary M. and Alain Peyraube. 2008. Chinese localizers: Diachrony and some typological considerations. In: Dan Xu (ed.), *Space in Languages of China: Cross-linguistic, Synchronic and Diachronic Perspectives*, 15-37. Dordrecht: Springer.

Chappell, Hilary M., Alain Peyraube, and Yunji Wu. 2011. A comitative source for object markers in Sinitic languages: 跟 *kai*[55] in Waxiang and 共 *kang*[7] in Southern Min. *Journal of East Asian Linguistics* 20: 291-338.

Chen, Changlai (陈昌来). 2004. *Jiècí yǔ Jièyǐn Gōngnéng* (介词与介引功能) [Prepositions and Introduction Functions]. Anhui: Anhui Education Press. (in Chinese)

Chen, Chun-hui. 2005. Bunpōka to shakuyō – Nihongo ni okeru dōshi no chūshikei o fukunda kōchishi ni tsuite [Grammaticalization and borrowing: postpositions in Japanese composed from verbs in *ren'yō* or *-te* forms] *Nihongo no Kenkyū* 1/3, 123-138.

Chino, Naoko. 1991. *All about Particles: A Handbook of Japanese Function Words*. Tokyo: Kodansha International.

Cho, Young-Eon (조영언). 2004. *Hankwuke Ewensacen* [A Korean Etymology

Dictionary]. Seoul: Dasom Publishing.

Choe, Hyun-Bae (최현배). 1989[1929]. *Wulimalpon* [Korean grammar]. Seoul: Jungeum Publishing.

Choe, Jae-Woong, Sang houn Song, Jieun Jeon (최재웅 송상헌 전지은). 2008. Probabilistic context-free grammar rules based on Sejong Korean Treebank. *Language Information* 9: 87-139. (in Korean)

Choi, Ae Jung (최애정). 2001. A study on preposition of Modern Chinese. MA thesis, Kyungsung University, Korea. (in Korean)

Choi, Dong Ju (최동주). 1996. Cwungsey kwuke mwunpep [Middle Korean grammar]. In: Kwuklipkwukewen [The National Institute of the Korean Language] (ed.), *Kwukeuy Sitaypyel Pyenchen Yenkwu 1, Cwungsey Kwuke* [A Historical Study of Korean 1, Middle Korean], 152-209. Seoul: Kwuklipkwukewen [The National Institute of the Korean Language]. (in Korean)

Choi, In Young (최인영). 2021. On grammaticalization of *near, around* and *by* in English. MA thesis, Hankuk University of Foreign Studies, Korea.

Choi, Jaeyoung (최재영). 2003. The research on BEI-construction's word class. *Korea Journal of Chinese Linguistics* (中國言語研究) 17: 183-198. (in Korean)

Choi, Jaeyoung (최재영). 2004. The research of special BEI-construction in Early Modern Chinese. *Journal of Chinese Studies* (中國學研究) 28: 351-369. (in Korean)

Choi, Jaeyoung (최재영). 2007. Study on the grammaticalization of *give*-category verbs in Chinese. *Journal of Chinese Studies* (中國學研究) 41: 49-72. (in Korean)

Choi, Jaeyoung (최재영). 2009. '有'-uy phwumsa cacil kochal [An analysis of categorial properties of '有', *Journal of Chinese Studies* (中國學研究) 50: 302-325, (in Korean)

Choi, Jaeyoung and Yeon Jin Ahn (최재영 안연진). 2013. A contrastive study on passive sentence in Chinese and Korean. *Korea Journal of Chinese Language and Literature* (中語中文學) 54: 527-562. (in Korean)

Choi, Jae-Young and Seon-A Kwun (최재영 권선아). 2012. Cenchisa '趁(着)'-uy mwunpephwa soko [Thoughts on the grammaticalization of '趁(着)']. *Journal of Chinese Language, Literature and Translation* (中國語文論譯叢刊) 30: 467-496. (in Korean)

Choi, Jae-Young and Seon-A Kwun (최재영 권선아). 2013. A study on the grammaticalization of preposition *dui. Journal of Chinese Language, Literature and Translation* (中國語文論譯叢刊) 32: 143-171. (in Korean)

Choi, Jae-Young and Seon-A Kwun (최재영 권선아). 2014. Pokhapcenchisa 为了/为着 yenkwu: Myengcheng sikiwa hyentaysikiuy cakphwumpwunsekul kipanulo [A study of 为了/为着 – Based on the literature analysis of Ming and Ching Dynasties and Modern China]. *Journal of Chinese Cultural Research* (中國文化研究) 25: 331-357. (in Korean)

Choi, Jae-Young and Seon-A Kwun (최재영 권선아). 2017. Cenchisa 除(了)-uy mwunpephwa yenkwu [A study on the grammaticalization of 除(了)]. *Proceedings of the 2017 Conference of the Discourse and Cognitive Linguistics Society of Korea*, 253-268. (in Korean)

Choi, Seonggyu (최성규). 2016. A historical study of Korean case markers: Focusing on the period from the Three Kingdoms to the Goryeo Dynasty. Ph.D. dissertation, Seoul National University, Korea. (in Korean)

Choi-Jonin, Injoo. 2008. Particles and postpositions in Korean. In: Dennis Kurzon and Silvia Adler (eds.), *Adpositions: Pragmatic, Semantic and Syntactic Perspectives* (Typological Studies in Language 74), 133-170. Amsterdam: John Benjamins.

Choonharuangdej, Suree. 2003. *Ba* and *Bei* constructions in Chinese: Implications of development and usage in comparison with Thai. Ph.D. dissertation, University of Wisconsin-Madison, Wisconsin.

Chung, Jaeyoung (정재영). 1996. *A study on the grammaticalization of dA syntagma in Middle Korean.* Ph.D. dissertation, Hankuk University of Foreign Studies, Korea. Seoul: Kwukehakhoy. (in Korean)

Chung, Taegoo (정태구). 1993. Argument structure and serial verbs in Korean, PhD dissertation, University of Texas at Austin.

Cienki, Alan. 1998. STRAIGHT: An image schema and its metaphorical extensions. *Cognitive Linguistics* 9.2: 107–149.

Cienki, Alan. 1999. The strengths and weaknesses of the left/right polarity in Russian: Diachronic and synchronic semantic analyses. In: Leon de Stadler and Christoph Eyrich (eds.), *Issues in Cognitive Linguistics: 1993 Proceedings of the International Cognitive Linguistics Conference*, 299-329. Berlin: Mouton de Gruyter.

Cifuentes, Jose Luis. 2003. *Locuciones prepositivas. Sobre la gramaticalización preposicional en español.* Alicante: Publicaciones de la Universidad de Alicante. (in Spanish)

Clark, Herbert H. 1973. Space, time, semantics, and the child. In: Timothy E. Moore (ed.), *Cognitive Development and the Acquisition of Language*, 28-64. New York: Academic Press.

Clark, Marybeth. 1975. Coverbs and case in Vietnamese. Ph.D. dissertation, University of Hawai'i.

Clark, Marybeth and Amara Prasithrathsint. 1985. Synchronic lexical derivation in Southeast Asian languages In: Suriya Ratanakul, David Thomas, and Suwilai Premsrirat (eds.), *Southeast Asian Linguistic Studies Presented to Andre-G Haudricourt,* 34-81. Nakhon Pathom, Thailand: Institute of Language and Culture for Rural Development, Mahidol University.

Claudi, Ulrike and Bernd Heine. 1986. On the metaphorical base of grammar. *Studies in Language* 10: 297-335.

Colleman, Timothy and Bernard De Clerck. 2011. Constructional semantics on the move. On semantic specialization in the English double object construction. *Cognitive Linguistics* 22: 183-209.

Company, Concepción. 2008. The directionality of grammaticalization in Spanish. *Journal of Historical Pragmatics* 9.2: 200-224.

Comparán Rizo, Juan José. 2006. *Raíces Griegas y Latinas de la Lengua Española.* Jalisco, México: Ediciones Umbral. (in Spanish)

Comrie, Bernard. 1989[1981]. *Language Universals and Linguistic Typology* (2nd ed.). Chicago: The University of Chicago Press.

Cordes, von Ruth. 2014. Language change in 20th century written Chinese: The claim for Europeanization. Ph.D. dissertation, Universität Hamburg, Germany.

Corominas, Joan and José Pascual. 1981. *Diccionario Crítico Etimológico Castellano e Hispánico.* Gredos.

Corpus de Referencia de Español (CREA). https://corpus.rae.es/creanet.html

Corpus of Contemporary American English, the (COCA). n.d. Web-searchable corpus. english-corpora.org/coca/

Corpus of Spontaneous Japanese, the (CSJ). https://ccd.ninjal.ac.jp/csj/

Coventry, Kenny R., Richard Carmichael, and Simon C. Garrod. 1994. Spatial prepositions, object-specific function, and task requirements. *Journal of Semantics* 11.4: 289-309.

Craig, Collette. 1991. Ways to go in Rama: a case study in polygrammaticalization. In: Elizabeth Closs Traugott and Bernd Heine (eds.), *Approaches to Grammaticalization.* 2 vols. (Typological Studies in Language 19), vol. 2: 455-492. Amsterdam: John Benjamins.

Creissels, Denis. 2006. Encoding the distinction between location, source and destination: A typological study. In: Maya Hickmann and Stéphane Robert (eds.), *Space in Languages: Linguistic Systems and Cognitive Categories*

(Typological Studies in Language 66), 19-28. Amsterdam: John Benjamins.

Creissels, Denis. 2009. Spatial cases. In: Andrej Malchukov and Andrew Spencer (eds.), *The Oxford Handbook of Case*, 609-625. Oxford: Oxford University Press.

Croce, Benedetto. 1912[1902]. *Estetica come scienza dell'espressione e linguistica generale. Teoria e storia.* (4th edition). Bari: Laterza & Figli.

Curme, George O. 1947. *English Grammar.* New York: Barnes & Noble.

Curnow, Timothy Jowan. 2001. What language features can be 'borrowed'? In: Alexandra Y. Aikhenvald and Robert M. W. Dixon (eds.), *Areal Diffusion and Genetic Inheritance: Problems in Comparative Linguistics*, 412-36. Oxford: Oxford University Press.

Dahl, Östen. 1985. *Tense and Aspect Systems.* Oxford: Blackwell.

Davidse, Kristin, Lieven Vandelanotte, and Hubert Cuyckens (eds.) 2010. *Subjectification, Intersubjectification and Grammaticalization* (Topics in English Linguistics 66). Berlin: Mouton de Gruyter.

Davy, Belinda Lee. 2000. A cognitive-semantic approach to the acquisition of English prepositions. Ph.D. dissertation. University of Oregon.

De Mulder, Walter. 2003. La préposition "au-dessus de": Un cas de Grammaticalisation? *La Grammaticalisation en Français - Première Partie,* vol. 3, 291-305. (Verbum Tome 25). (in French)

De Silva, G. Gómez. 1985. *Elsevier's Concise Spanish Etymological Dictionary.* Amsterdam: Elsevier.

De Smet, Hendrik. 2009. Analysing reanalysis. *Lingua* 119: 1728-1755.

De Smet, Hendrik. 2012. The course of actualization. *Language* 88.3: 601-633.

De Smet, Hendrik. 2014. Does innovation need reanalysis? In: Evie Coussé and Ferdinand von Mengden (eds.), *Usage-Based Approaches to Language Change*, 23-48. Amsterdam: John Benjamins.

Debecque, Nicole, Karen Lahousse, and Willy Van Langendonck (eds.). 2014. *Non-Nuclear Cases: Case and Grammatical Relations across Languages* (Case and Grammatical Relations Across Languages 6). Amsterdam: John Benjamins.

Dejthamrong, Orathai. 1970. Nathi khong khamwa 'hai' nai pasa Thai [Grammatical functions of the word *hai* in Thai language]. Master thesis, Chulalongkorn University. (in Thai)

DeLancey, Scott. 2004. Grammaticalization: from syntax to morphology. In: Geert Booij, Christian Lehmann, Joachim Mugdan, unter Mitarbeit von Wolfgang

Kesselheim und Stavros Skopeteas (eds.), *Morphologie/Morphology. Ein internationales Handbuch zur Flexion und Wortbildung*, 1590-1599. Berlin: Mouton de Gruyter.

DeLancey, Scott. 2011. Grammaticalization and syntax: a functional view. In: Heiko Narrog and Bernd Heine (eds.), *The Oxford Handbook of Grammaticalization*, 365-377. Oxford: Oxford University Press.

Delbecque, Nicole and Katrien Verveckken. 2014. Conceptually-driven analogy in the grammaticalization of Spanish binominal quantifiers. *Linguistics* 52.3: 637-684.

Detges, Ulrich and Richard Waltereit. 2002. Grammaticalization vs. Reanalysis: A semantic-pragmatic account of functional change in grammar. *Zeitschrift für Sprachwissenschaft* 21.2: 151-195.

Di Meola, Claudio. 2000. *Die Grammatikalisierung deutscher Präpositionen*. Tübingen: Stauffenburg. (in German)

Di Meola, Claudio. 2003. Grammaticalization of postpositions in German. In: Hubert Cuyckens, Thomas Ber, René Dirven, and Klaus-Uwe Panther (eds.), *Motivation in Language: Studies in honor of Günter Radden*, 203-222. Amsterdam: John Benjamins.

Diller, Anthony V. N. 1994. Thai. In: Cliff Goddard and Anna Wierzbicka (eds.), *Semantic and Lexical Universals* (Studies in Language Companion Series 25), 149-170. Amsterdam: John Benjamins.

Diller, Anthony V. N. 2008. Resources for Thai language research. In: Anthony V. N. Diller, Jerold A. Edmondson, and Yongxian Luo (eds.), *The Tai-Kadai Languages*, 31-82. London: Routledge.

Ding, Shengshu (丁声树). 1952. *Zhōngguóyǔwén* (中國語文) [Chinese Language]. Beijing: Shangwuyinshuguan. (in Chinese)

Ding, Shengshu (丁声树). 1961. *Xiàndài Hànyǔ Yǔfǎ Jiǎnghuà* (现代汉语语法讲话) [Lectures on Modern Chinese Grammar]. Beijing: Shangwuyinshuguan. (in Chinese)

Dirven, René. 1995. The construal of cause: The case of cause prepositions. In: John R. Taylor and Robert E. Maclaury (eds.), *Language and the Cognitive Construal of the World*, 82-95. Berlin: Mouton de Gruyter.

Dirven, René. 1997. Emotions as cause and the cause of emotions. In: Susanne Niemeier and René Dirven (eds.), *The Language of Emotions*, 55-86. Amsterdam: John Benjamins.

Dirven, René and Marjolijn Verspoor (eds.). 1998. *Cognitive Exploration of Language and Linguistics*. Amsterdam: John Benjamins.

Djamouri, Redouane and Waltraud Paul. 2009. Verb-to-preposition reanalysis in Chinese. In: Paola Crisma and Giuseppe Longobardi (eds.), *Historical Syntax and Linguistic Theory*, 194-211. Oxford: Oxford University Press.

Duanmu, San. 2005. the tone-syntax interface in Chinese: Some recent controversies. *Proceedings of the Symposium: Cross-Linguistic Studies of Tonal Phenomena*, 221-254. Tokyo: Institute for the Study of Languages and Cultures of Asia and Africa, Tokyo University of Foreign Studies.

Eberhard, David M., Gary F. Simons, and Charles D. Fennig (eds.), 2021. *Ethnologue: Languages of the World* (23rd ed.). Dallas, Texas: SIL International.

Ellis, Nick C. 1998. Emergentism, connectionism and language learning. *Language Learning* 48: 631-664.

Elman, Jeffrey L. 1999. The emergence of language: A conspiracy theory. In: Brian MacWhinney (ed.), *The Emergence of Language*, 1-27. Mahwah, NJ: Erlbaum.

Enfield, Nicholas J. 2006. Heterosemy and the grammar-lexicon trade-off. In: Felix K. Ameka, Alan Dench and Nicholas J. Evans (eds.), *Catching Language: the Standing Challenge of Grammar Writing* (Trends in Linguistics Monographs 167), 297-320. Berlin: Mouton de Gruyter.

Enfield, Nicholas J. 2009. 'Case relations' in Lao, A radically isolating language. In: Andrej Malchukov and Andrew Spencer (eds.), *The Oxford Handbook of Case*, 808-819. Oxford: Oxford University Press.

Eom, Sujin (엄수진). 2005. Making sense out of five senses: Body-mediated cognition. Paper presented at 2005 KASELL International Conference, June 21-22, 2005. Seoul.

Eom, Sujin (엄수진). 2018. At the borderland of prepositions: English complex prepositions at incipient grammaticalization. *Journal of Linguistic Science* (언어과학연구) 86: 123-141.

Eom, Sujin (엄수진). 2020. Body-mediated cognition and its linguistic representation in English: The development of visual and auditory perception terms from a grammaticalization perspective. Ph.D. dissertation, Hankuk University of Foreign Studies, Korea.

Eom, Sujin and Seongha Rhee (엄수진 이성하). 2021-in press. The rise and fall of a discourse marker: The case of *kisil* in Korean. *East Asian Pragmatics*, Special issue.

Esseesy, Mohssen. 2010. *Grammaticalization of Arabic Prepositions and Subordinators:*

A Corpus-Based Study (Studies in Semitic Languages and Linguistics 59). Leiden: Brill.

Evans, Nicholas. 2007. Insubordination and its uses. In: Irina Nikolaeva (ed.), *Finiteness: Theoretical and Empirical Foundations*, 366-431. Oxford: Oxford University Press.

Everbroeck, Rene van. 1958. *Grammaire et Exercises Lingala*. Anvers-Leopoldville: Standaard-Boekhandel S. A. (in French)

Fagard, Benjamin. 2006. Evolution sémantique des prépositions dans les langues romanes: Illustrations ou contre-exemples de la primauté du spatial. Thèse, Université Paris 7/Università Roma 3. (in French)

Fagard, Benjamin. 2008. "Côté" dégrammaticalisation – le cas des prépositions. *Evolutions en Français*, 87-104. Frankfurt am Mein: Peter Lang. (in French)

Fagard, Benjamin and Anetta Kopecka. 2020. Source/goal (a)symmetry. *Studies in Language* 45.1: 130-171. Amsterdam: John Benjamins.

Fagard, Benjamin and Anetta Kopecka. 2021. Source/goal (a)symmetry: A comparative study of German and Polish. *Studies in Language* 45.1: 130-171.

Fagard, Benjamin and Alexandru Mardale. 2012. The pace of grammaticalization and the evolution of prepositional systems: Data from Romance. *Folia Linguistica* 46.2: 303-340.

Fagard, Benjamin and Walter De Mulder. 2007. La formation des prépositions complexes: Grammaticalisation ou lexicalisation? *Langue Française* 156.4: 9-29. (in French)

FDMC. 1986. *Xiàndài Hànyǔ Pínlǜ Cídiǎn* (现代汉语频率词典) [Frequency Dictionary of Modern Chinese]. Beijing: Language Institute Press. (in Chinese)

Fillmore, Charles. 1971. Towards a theory of deixis. Paper presented at the Pacific Conference on Contrastive Linguistics and Language Universals, January 1971, University of Hawaii.

Fischer, Olga. 2007. *Morphosyntactic Change: Functional and Formal*. Oxford University Press, Oxford.

Fischer, Olga. 2008. On analogy as the motivation for grammaticalization. *Studies in Language* 32.2: 336-382.

Fischer, Olga. 2011. Grammaticalization as analogically driven change? In: Heiko Narrog and Bernd Heine (eds.), *The Oxford Handbook of Grammaticalization*, 31-42. Oxford: Oxford University Press.

Fischer, Olga. 2012. On mechanisms of language change: What role does analogy play?

Plenary paper at the 45th annual meeting of the Societas Linguistica Europaea, Stockholm University, August 29-September 1, 2012.

Fischer, Olga. 2013. An inquiry into unidirectionality as a foundational element of grammaticalization: On the role played by analogy and the synchronic grammar system in processes of language change. *Studies in Language* 37.3: 515-533.

Fischer, Susann. 2010. *Word-order Change as a Source of Grammaticalisation*. Amsterdam: John Benjamins.

Foolen, Ad. 2017. The hand in figurative thought and language. In: Angeliki Athanasiadou (ed.), *Studies in Figurative Thought and Language*, 179-198. Amsterdam: John Benjamins. doi: 10.1075/hcp.56.07foo.

Foolen, Ad. 2019. The value of left and right. In: J. Lachlan Mackenzie and Laura Alba-Juez (eds.), *Emotion in Discourse*, 139-158. Amsterdam: John Benjamins.

Francis-Ratte, Alexander Takenobu. 2016. Proto-Korean-Japanese: A new reconstruction of the common origin of the Japanese and Korean languages. Ph.D. dissertation, The Ohio State University.

Freed, Alice F. 1979. *The Semantics of English Aspectual Complementation*. Dordrecht: Reidel.

Frellesvig, Bjarke. 2005. Old Japanese particles. *Proceedings of the Cornell Japanese Historical Linguistics*, 1-10. Available at https://conf.ling.cornell.edu/japanese_historical_linguistics/3.3%20Particles.pdf.

Frellesvig, Bjarke. 2010. *A History of the Japanese Language*. Cambridge: Cambridge University Press.

Frellesvig, Bjarke, Stephen Horn, Kerri Russell, and Peter Sells. 2010. Verb semantics and argument realization in Pre-Modern Japanese: A preliminary study of compound verbs in Old Japanese. *Gengo Kenkyu* 138: 25-65.

Frellesvig, Bjarke and John Whitman. 2008. Evidence for seven vowels in Proto-Japanese. In: Bjarke Frellesvig and John Whitman (eds.), *Proto-Japanese. Issues and Prospects*, 15-41. Amsterdam: Benjamins.

Frequency Dictionary of Modern Chinese (FDMC 1986). Beijing: Beijing Language Institute Press.

Fries, Charles Carpenter. 1952. *The Structure of English*. New York: Hartcourt Brace.

Fu, Yuxian and Xiaobing Zhou (傅雨贤 周小兵) 1997. *Xiàndài Hànyǔ jiècí yánjiū* (现代汉语介词研究) [Research on Prepositions in Modern Chinese]. Guangzhou: Sun Yat-sen University Press. (in Chinese)

Fung, Pascale and Dekai Wu. 1994. Statistical augmentation of a Chinese machine-readable dictionary. *WVLC-2: Second Annual Workshop on Very Large Corpora (COLING-94), Kyoto, August 1994*, 1-17.

Gabain, Annemarie von. 1950. *Alttürkische Grammatik.* Wiesbaden: Otto Harrassowitz. (in German)

Gabelentz, Georg von der. 1901[1891]. *Die Sprachwissenschaft: Ihre Aufgaben, Methoden und Bisherigen Ergebnisse* (2nd ed.). Leipzig: Weigel Nachf. (in German)

Gao, Mingkai (高明凯) 1948. *Hànyǔ Yǔfǎlùn* (汉语语法论) [Chinese Grammar]. Shanghai: Kaiming Publisher. (in Chinese)

Genetti, Carol. 1991. From postposition to subordination in Newari. In: Elizabeth Closs Traugott and Bernd Heine (eds.), *Approaches to Grammaticalization.* 2 vols. (Typological Studies in Language 19), vol. 2: 227-255. Amsterdam: John Benjamins.

Georgakopoulos, Thanasis. 2018. A frame-based approach to the source-goal asymmetry: Synchronic and diachronic evidence from Ancient Greek. *Constructions and Frames* 10.1: 61-97.

Giacalone Ramat, Anna. 1994. Fonti di grammaticalizzazione. Sulla ricategorizzazione di verbi e nomi come preposizioni. In: Palmira Cipriano, Paolo Di Giovine, and Marco Mancini (eds.), *Miscellanea di Studi Linguistici in onore di Walter Belardi,* 877-896. Fome: Il Calamo. (in Italian)

Givón, Talmy. 1971. Historical syntax and synchronic morphology: An archaeologist's field trip. *Chicago Linguistic Society* 7: 394-415.

Givón, Talmy. 1979. *On Understanding Grammar.* New York: Academic Press.

Givón, Talmy. 1981. On the development of the numeral 'one' as an indefinite marker. *Folia Linguistica Historica* 2.1: 35-54.

Givón, Talmy. 1991a. Serial verbs and the mental reality of 'event': Grammatical vs. cognitive packaging. In: Elizabeth Closs Traugott and Bernd Heine (eds.), *Approaches to Grammaticalization.* 2 vols. (Typological Studies in Language 19), vol. 1: 81-127. Amsterdam: John Benjamins.

Givón, Talmy. 1991b. The evolution of dependent clause morpho-syntax in Biblical Hebrew. In: Elizabeth Closs Traugott and Bernd Heine (eds.), *Approaches to Grammaticalization.* 2 vols. (Typological Studies in Language 19), vol. 2: 257-310. Amsterdam: John Benjamins.

Givón, Talmy. 2021. *The Life Cycle of Adpositions.* Amsterdam: John Benjamins.

Greenberg, Joseph H. 1963. Some universals of grammar with particular reference to the order of meaningful elements. In: Joseph H. Greenberg (ed.), *Universals of Language,* 73-113. Cambridge, MA: MIT Press.

Grimshaw, Jane. 1991. Extended projection. ms. Brandeis University.

Grünthal, Riho. 2003. *Finnic Adpositions and Cases in Change.* Helsinki: Société Finno-Ougrienne.

Gruntov, Ilya and Olga Mazo. 2020. A comparative approach to nominal morphology in Transeurasian: Case and plurality. In: Martine Robbeets and Alexander Savelyev. (eds.), *The Oxford Guide to the Transeurasian Languages* (Oxford Guides to the World's Languages), 522-553. Oxford: Oxford University Press.

Ha, Jaephil (하재필). 2018. Grammaticalized postposition of conditional verb form in Modern Japanese. *Language and Linguistics* (언어와 언어학) 81: 169-192. (in Korean)

Ha, Young-Sam (하영삼). 2014. *Hanca Ewen Sacen* [An Etymological Dictionary of Chinese Characters]. Seoul: Tosechwulphan 3. (in Korean)

Haarmann, Harald. 2012[1986]. *Language in Ethnicity: A View of Basic Ecological Relations.* Berlin: Mouton de Gruyter.

Hagège, Claude. 2010. *Adpositions* (Oxford Studies in Typological and Linguistic Theory). Oxford: Oxford University Press.

Hahn, Michael, Dan Jurafsky, and Richard Futrell. 2020. Universals of word order reflect optimization of grammars for efficient communication. *PNAS (Proceedings of the National Academy of Sciences of the United States of America)* 117.5: 2347-2353.

Haiman, John. 1994. Ritualization and the development of language. In: William Pagliuca (ed.), *Perspectives on Grammaticalization,* 3-28. Amsterdam: John Benjamins.

Handian. n.d. Online etymological dictionary. www.zdic.net/hans.

Harder, Peter and Kasper Boye. 2011. Grammaticalization and functional linguistics. In: Heiko Narrog and Bernd Heine (eds.), *The Oxford Handbook of Grammaticalization,* 60-65. Oxford: Oxford University Press.

Haspelmath, Martin. 1995. The converb as a cross-linguistically valid category. In: Martin Haspelmath and Ekkehard König (eds.) *Converbs in Cross-Linguistic Perspective. Structure and Meaning of Adverbial Verb Forms: Adverbial Participles, Gerunds,* 1-55. Berlin: Mouton de Gruyter.

Haspelmath, Martin. 1997. *From Space to Time: Temporal Adverbials in the World's Languages* (LINCOM Studies in Theoretical Linguistics 3). München: LINCOM Europa.

Haspelmath, Martin. 2003. Adpositions. In: William J. Frawley (ed.), *International Encyclopedia of Linguistics* (2nd ed.). Oxford: Oxford University Press.

Haspelmath, Martin. 2009. Terminology of case. In: Andrej Malchukov and Andrew Spencer (eds.), *The Oxford Handbook of Case*, 505-517. Oxford: Oxford University Press.

Haspelmath, Martin. 2011. The gradual coalescence into 'words' in grammaticalization. In: Heiko Narrog and Bernd Heine (eds.), *The Oxford Handbook of Grammaticalization*, 342-355. Oxford: Oxford University Press.

Haspelmath, Martin, Matthew S. Dryer, David Gil, and Bernard Comrie (eds.). 2005. *The World Atlas of Language Structures (WALS)*. Oxford: Oxford University Press.

Haspelmath, Martin and Ekkehard König (eds.), 1995. *Converbs in Cross-Linguistic Perspective. Structure and Meaning of Adverbial Verb Forms: Adverbial Participles, Gerunds*. Berlin: Mouton de Gruyter.

Haspelmath, Martin and Uri Tadmor. 2009. *Loanwords in the World's Languages: A Comparative Handbook*. Berlin: Mouton de Gruyter.

Haviland, John B. 1992. Anchoring, iconicity, and orientation in Guugu Yimithirr pointing gestures. *Journal of Linguistic Anthropology* 3.1: 3-45.

Hawkins, John A. 1983. *Word Order Universals*. New York: Academic Press.

He, Xiaomei (하효미; 何晓媚) 2016. Hankwuke cosawa cwungkwuke kaysauy mwunpephwa tayco yenkwu: *eyse, lo*-wa *zai, yu, you, cong*-ul cwungsimulo [A contrastive study of Korean postpositions and Chinese prepositions: With a special focus on *eyse* and *lo* and *zai, yu, you,* and *cong*]. MA thesis, University of Seoul, Korea. (in Korean)

Heine, Bernd. 1981. (collection of manuscripts, consisting of:). The morphological cycle; Nominal number inflections, prepositions, complementizer, etc.; Some basic processes; Tense and aspect. Köln: Institut für Afrikanistik, Universität zu Köln.

Heine, Bernd. 1989. Adpositions in African languages. *Linguistique Africaine* 2: 77-127.

Heine, Bernd. 1992a. Grammaticalization chains. *Studies in Language* 16.2: 335-368.

Heine, Bernd. 1992b. *Some Principles of Grammaticalization*. Lecture handout for 1992 Stanford/Berkeley grammaticalization workshop.

Heine, Bernd. 1993. *Auxiliaries: Cognitive Forces and Grammaticalization*. Oxford: Oxford University Press.

Heine, Bernd. 1994a. Areal influence on grammaticalization. In: Martin Pütz (ed.), *Language Contact and Language Conflict*, 55-68. Amsterdam: John Benjamins.

Heine, Bernd. 1994b. Grammaticalization as an explanatory parameter. In: William Pagliuca (ed.), *Perspectives of Grammaticalization*, 255-287. Amsterdam: John Benjamins.

Heine, Bernd. 1997. *Cognitive Foundations of Grammar*. Oxford: Oxford University Press.

Heine, Bernd. 2002. On the role of context in grammaticalization. In: Ilse Wischer and Gabriele Diewald (eds.), *New Reflections on Grammaticalization*, 83-101. Amsterdam: John Benjamins.

Heine, Bernd, Ulrike Claudi, and Friederike Hünnemeyer. 1991a. *Grammaticalization: A Conceptual Framework*. Chicago: The University of Chicago Press.

Heine, Bernd, Ulrike Claudi, and Friederike Hünnemeyer. 1991b. From cognition to grammar. In: Elizabeth Closs Traugott and Bernd Heine (eds.), *Approaches to Grammaticalization*. 2 vols. (Typological Studies in Language 19), vol. 1: 149-187. Amsterdam: John Benjamins.

Heine, Bernd, Tom Güldermann, Christa Kilian-Hatz, Donald A. Lessau, Heinz Roberg, Mathias Schladt, and Thomas Stolz. 1993. *Conceptual Shift: A Lexicon of Grammaticalization Processes in African Languages*. Köln: Universität zu Köln.

Heine, Bernd., Gunther Kaltenböck, and Tania Kuteva. 2011. Accounting for insubordinated clauses. Typescript.

Heine, Bernd and Tania Kuteva. 2002. *World Lexicon of Grammaticalization*. Cambridge: Cambridge University Press. (Revised as Kuteva et al. 2019)

Heine, Bernd and Tania Kuteva. 2005. *Language Contact and Grammatical Change* (Cambridge Approaches to Language Contact). Cambridge: Cambridge University Press.

Heine, Bernd and Tania Kuteva. 2007. *The Genesis of Grammar: A Reconstruction* (Studies in the Evolution of Language). Oxford: Oxford University Press.

Heine, Bernd and Tania Kuteva. 2008. Constraints on contact-induced linguistic change. *Journal of Language Contact - THEMA 2*: 57-90.

Heine, Bernd and Mechthild Reh. 1984. *Grammaticalization and Reanalysis in African Languages*. Hamburg: Helmut Buske.

Heine, Bernd and Thomas Stolz. 2008. Grammaticalization as a creative process.

Language Typology and Universals (STUF) 61: 326-357.

Heo, Seongdo (허성도). 2005. *Hyentay Cwungkwuke Epepuy Ihay* [Understanding Modern Chinese Grammar]. Seoul: Yeklak. (in Korean)

Her, One-Soon. 2006. Justifying part-of-speech assignments for Mandarin *gei*. *Lingua* 116: 1274-1302. doi: 10.1016/j.lingua.2005.06.003.

Herslund, Michael. 2012. Grammaticalization and the internal logic of the indefinite article. *Folia Linguistica* 46.2: 341-358.

Hickmann, Maya and Stéphane Robert. 2006a. Introduction: Space, language, and cognition: Some new challenges. In: Maya Hickmann and Stéphane Robert (eds.), *Space in Languages: Linguistic Systems and Cognitive Categories* (Typological Studies in Language 66), 1-15. Amsterdam: John Benjamins.

Hickmann, Maya and Stéphane Robert (eds.). 2006b. *Space in Languages: Linguistic Systems and Cognitive Categories* (Typological Studies in Language 66). Amsterdam: John Benjamins.

Hilpert, Martin and David Correia Saavedra. 2016. The unidirectionality of semantic changes in grammaticalization: An experimental approach to the asymmetric priming hypothesis. *English Language and Linguistics,* 22.3: 357-380.

Hino, Sukenari. 2000. Grammaticalization of Japanese pseudonouns and auxiliary verbs: A morphosyntactic and semantic approach. Ph.D. dissertation, The University of Hawai'i.

Hock, Hans Henrich and Brian D. Joseph. 1996. *Language History, Language Change, and Language Relationship: An Introduction to Historical and Comparative Linguistics.* Berlin: Mouton de Gruyter.

Hoelbeek, Thomas. 2017. *The Evolution of Complex Spatial Expressions within the Romance Family: A Corpus-Based Study of French and Italian* (Brill's Studies in Historical Linguistics). Leiden: Brill.

Hoffmann, Sebastian. 2005. *Grammaticalization and English Complex Prepositions: A Corpus-based Study.* London: Routledge.

Honda, Akira. 1998. Further notes on deverbal postpositions: A commentary on Matsumoto's paper. In: Toshio Ohori (ed.), *Studies in Japanese Grammaticalization: Cognitive and Discourse Perspectives,* 61-65. Tokyo: Kurosio Publishers.

Hong, Yoon-Pyo (홍윤표). 1990. Kyekcosa [Case particles]. In: Korean Language Research Group of Seoul National University Graduate School (ed.), *Kwukeyenkwu Etikkayci Wassna* [How far Korean language studies have advanced], 221-32. Seoul: Dong-A Publishing. (in Korean)

Hong, Yunpyo (홍윤표). 1994. *Kuntay Kwuke Yenkwu I* [A study of Early Modern Korean I]. Seoul: Thayhaksa. (in Korean)

Hook, Peter. 1991. The emergence of perfective aspect in Indo-Aryan languages. In: Elizabeth C. Traugott and Bernd Heine (eds.), *Approaches to Grammaticalization,* 2 vols. (Typological Studies in Language 19), Vol. 2, 59-89. Amsterdam: John Benjamins.

Hopper, Paul J. 1987. Emergent grammar. *Berkeley Linguistics Society* 13: 139-157.

Hopper, Paul J. 1990. Where do words come from? In: William Croft, Keith Denning, and Suzanne Kemmer (eds.), *Studies in Typology and Diachrony: Papers Presented to Joseph Greenberg on his 75th Birthday,* 151-160. Amsterdam: Benjamins.

Hopper, Paul J. 1991. On some principles of grammaticalization. In: Elizabeth Traugott and Paul J. Hopper (eds.), *Approaches to Grammaticalization,* 2 vols. (Typological Studies in Language 19), Vol. 1: 17-35. Amsterdam: John Benjamins.

Hopper, Paul J. 1994. Phonogenesis. In: William Pagliuca (ed.), *Perspectives on Grammaticalization,* 29-49. Amsterdam: John Benjamins.

Hopper, Paul J. and Elizabeth Closs Traugott. 2003[1993]. *Grammaticalization.* Cambridge: Cambridge University Press.

Horie, Kaoru. 1998. On the polyfunctionality of the Japanese particle *no*: From the perspective of ontology and grammaticalization. In: Toshio Ohori (ed.), *Studies in Japanese Grammaticalization: Cognitive and Discourse Perspectives,* 169-192. Tokyo: Kurosio Publishers.

Horie, Kaoru. 2001. Kōchakugo ni okeru bunpōka no tokuchō ni kansuru ninchigengogakuteki kōsatsu [Cognitive linguistic considerations on the features of grammaticalization in agglutinative languages]. *Ninchi Gengogaku Ronkō* 1, 185-227. (in Japanese)

Hu, Jianhua. 2007. Tiyuan lunyun he yufa gongneng xiang - gebiao xiangying yu yuyan chayi [Thematic roles, arguments, and GF - Case-marking effect and language variation]. *Foreign Language Teaching and Research* 3: 163-168. (in Chinese)

Hu, Mingyang (胡明揚). 1996. *Cílèi Wèntí Kǎochá* (詞類問題考察) [An Investigation of Parts of Speech]. Beijing: Beijing Language Institute Press. (in Chinese)

Huang, C.-T. James. 2009. Lexical decomposition, silent categories and the localizer phrase. *Yuyanxue Luncong* (语言学论丛) 39: 86-122.

Huddleston, Rodney and Geoffrey K. Pullum. 2002. *The Cambridge Grammar of the*

English Language. Cambridge: Cambridge University Press.

Huddleston, Rodney and Geoffrey K. Pullum. 2005. *A Student's Introduction to English Grammar.* New York: Cambridge University Press.

HUFS Korean-Thai Dictionary (한국어-태국어사전). 2006. Seoul: HUFS Press.

Iggesen, Oliver A. 2005. Asymmetrical case marking. In: Martin Haspelmath, Matthew S. Dryer, David Gil, and Bernard Comrie (eds.), *The World Atlas of Language Structures,* 206-209. Oxford: Oxford University Press.

Iggesen, Oliver A. 2008. Asymmetry in case marking: Nominal vs. pronominal systems. In: Andrej L. Malchukov and Andrew Spencer (eds.), *The Oxford Handbook of Case,* 246-257. Oxford: Oxford University Press.

Ikegami, Motoko. 2006. "Kaku joshi + dōshi" kōzō o motu joshi sōtō ku o megutte: *-te* kei to ren'yō tyūshi no sai' [On postpositional phrase equivalents with the structure "case particle + verb": Differences between the *-te* form and the infinitive], *Hokkaido University Ryūgakusei Center Kiyō* 10: 1-17.

Ikegami, Yoshihiko. 1987. 'Source' vs. 'Goal': A case of linguistic dissymmetry. In: René Dirven and Günter Radden (eds.), *Concept of Case,* 122-146. Tübingen: Günter Narr Verlag.

Indrambarya, Kitima. 1992. The grammatical function of *hay* in Thai. *Pan-Asiatic Linguistics (PAL)* 3.1: 1163-1236.

Indrambarya, Kitima. 1995. Are there prepositions in Thai? In: Mark Alves (ed.), *Papers from the Third Annual Meeting of the Southeast Asian Linguistics Society (1993),* 101-117. Tempe: Arizona State University Program for Southeast Asian Studies.

Indrambarya, Kitima. 2008. Prepositions in Thai: A Reanalysis. Paper presented at the 18th Southeast Asian Linguistic Conference, Bangi, Malaysia, May 21-22, 2008.

Inglis, Douglas. 2003. Conceptual structure of numeral classifiers in Thai. In: Eugene H. Casad and Gary B. Palmer (eds.), *Cognitive Linguistics and Non-Indo-European Languages,* 223-246. Berlin: Mouton de Gruyter.

Intratat, Charatdao. 1996. Grammaticalization of verbs into prepositions in Thai. Ph.D. dissertation, Chulalongkorn University, Thailand.

Intratat, Charatdao. 1998. Grammaticalization of verbs in to prepositions in Thai. MA thesis, Chulalongkorn University, Thailand. (in Thai)

Iwasaki, Shoichi. 2004. Discourse and cognitive resources for grammaticalization in Thai. 343-357. In: Somsonge Burusphat (ed.), *Papers from the Eleventh Annual*

Meeting of the Southeast Asian Linguistics Society, Tempe, Arizona, 343-357. Arizona State University, Program for Southeast Asian Studies.

Iwasaki, Shoichi and Preeya Ingkaphirom. 2005. *A Reference Grammar of Thai.* Cambridge, UK: Cambridge University Press.

Iwasaki, Shoichi and Foong Ha Yap. 1998. 'Give' constructions in Thai and beyond: A cognitive and grammaticalization perspective. In: Somsonge et al., (eds.), *Proceedings of the International Conference on Tai Studies, July 29-31, 1998,* Bangkok: Institute of Language and Culture for Rural Development, Mahidol University.

Jackendoff, Ray. 1973. The base rules for prepositional phrases. In: Stephen R. Anderson and Paul Kiparsky (eds.), *A Festschrift for Morris Halle,* 345-366. New York: Holt, Rinehart and Winston.

Jackendoff, Ray. 1999. The architecture of the linguistic-spatial interface. In: Paul Bloom, Mary A. Peterson, Lynn Nadel, and Merrill F. Garrett (eds.). 1999. *Language and Space,* 1-30. Cambridge, Mass.: The MIT Press.

Janda, Richard D. 2001. Beyond 'pathways' and 'unidirectionality': on the discontinuity of language transmission and the counterability of grammaticalization. *Language Sciences* 23.2-3: 265-340.

Jang, Yo-Han (장요한). 2010, Grammatical property of locative case marker *-tAlye, -tepule, -Ay/ssontAy* in Middle Korean. *Hanmincokemwunhak* (한민족어문학) 56: 5-43. (in Korean)

Janhunen, Juha. 1996. *Manchuria: An Ethnic History.* Mémoires de la Société Finno-Ougrienne 222. Helsinki: Suomalais-Ugrilainen Seura.

Janhunen, Juha. 1999. A contextual approach to the convergence and divergence of Korean and Japanese. *Central Asiatic Journal* 43: 1-23.

Janhunen, Juha. 2000. Grammatical genders from east to west. In: Barbara Unterbeck (ed.), *Gender in Grammar and Cognition,* 689-707. Berlin: Mouton de Gruyter.

Jaratjarungkiat, Sureenate. 2019. Is the copula 'pen' in Thai meaningless? *Journal of Mekong Societies* 15.2: 1-17.

Jespersen, Otto. 1924. *The Philosophy of Grammar.* London: George Allen & Unwin.

Jidaibetsu Kokugo Daijiten. Jōdaihen (JKD). [Great Dictionary of the National Language by Periods. Old Japanese]. 1967. Edited by the Jōdaigo Jiten Henshū Iinkai. Tōkyō: Sanseidō.

Jin, Changji (金昌吉). 1996. *Hànyǔ Jiècí hé Jiècí Duǎnyǔ* (汉语介词和介词短语) [Chinese

Prepositions and Prepositional Phrases], Tianjin: Nankai University Press. (in Chinese)

Johanson, Lars. 1995. On Turkic converb clauses. In: Martin Haspelmath and Ekkehard König (eds.), *Converbs in Cross-Linguistic Perspective. Structure and Meaning of Adverbial Verb Forms - Adverbial Participles, Gerunds*, 313-47. Berlin: Mouton de Gruyter.

Johanson, Lars and Martine Robbeets. 2010. *Transeurasian Verbal Morphology in a Comparative Perspective: Genealogy, Contact, Chance*. Wiesbaden: Harrassowiz.

Johanson, Megan, Stathis Selimis, and Anna Papafragou. 2019. The source-goal asymmetry in spatial language: Language-general vs. language-specific aspects. *Language Cognition and Neuroscience* 34.7: 1-15.

Johansson, Stig and Knut Hofland. 1989. *Frequency Analysis of English Vocabulary and Grammar Based on LOB Corpus*. 2 vols. Oxford: Clarendon Press.

Johnson-Laird, Philip N. 1983. *Mental Models: Toward a Cognitive Science of Language, Inference, and Consciousness*. Cambridge: Harvard University Press.

Johnston, Judith R. and Dan I. Slobin. 1979. The development of locative expressions in English, Italian, Serbo-Croatian and Turkish. *Journal of Child Language* 6: 529-545.

Joseph, Brian D. and Richard D. Janda. 1988. The how and why of diachronic morphologization and de-morphologization. In: Michael T. Hammond and Michael P. Noonan (eds.), *Theoretical Morphology*, 193-210. New York: Academic Press.

Jung, Hwan-seung (정환승). 2004. Thaykwukeuy pwutongsaey kwanhan yenkwu [A study on Thai coverbs]. *Journal of Korean Association of Thai Studies* (한국태국학회논총) 11: 1-30. (in Korean)

Jung, Hwan-seung (정환승). 2006. A study on grammaticalization of /cak/ and /theung/ in Thai. *Language and Linguistics* 38: 109-133. (in Korean)

Jung, Yonhee (정연희). 2018. Semantic change and grammaticalization of the Korean locomotion verb *ttaluta*: From *ttluta* to *ttala*. *Language and Linguistics* (언어와 언어학) 81: 149-168.

Kabata, Kaori. 2012. Goal-source asymmetry and crosslinguistic grammaticalization patterns: A cognitive-typological approach. *Language Sciences* 36: 78-89.

Kahr, Joan Casper. 1976. The renewal of case morphology: sources and constraints.

Working Papers on Language Universals (Stanford) 20: 107-151.

KAIST KORTERM Corpus. http://morph.kaist.ac.kr/kcp/

Kang, Kil-Woon (강길운). 2010. *Pikyoenehakcek Ewensacen* [A comparative linguistic etymology dictionary]. Seoul: Hankook Publishing. (in Korean)

Karaman, Burcu I. 2008. On contronymy. *International Journal of Lexicography* 21.2: 173-192.

Katsuki-Pestemer, Noriko. 2003. *Japanese Postpositions: Theory and Practice.* München: LINCOM Europa.

Khanittanan, Wilaiwan. 2001. Khmero-Thai: the great change in the history of the language of the Chao Phraya Basin. Paper presented at the Ninth Annual Meeting of the Southeast Asian Linguistic Society, Bangkok.

Khokhlova, Natalia. 2014. Understanding of abstract nouns in linguistic disciplines. *Procedia-Social and Behavioral Sciences* 136: 8-11.

Kim, Dong-So (김동소). 2002. *Cwungsey Hankwuke Kaysel* [An introduction to Middle Korean]. Seoul: Hankook Publisher. (in Korean)

Kim, Eunmi (김은미). 2011. Grammaticalization of *like* in English. MA thesis, Hankuk University of Foreign Studies, Korea.

Kim, Eunmi (김은미). 2015. Diachronic and synchronic properties of English prepositions in emotion constructions: From a grammaticalization perspective. Ph.D. dissertation, Hankuk University of Foreign Studies, Korea.

Kim, Eunmi (김은미). 2018. Persistence of spatial meanings in the conceptualization of causality: *At, by, with* and *about* in emotion constructions. *Poznan Studies in Contemporary Linguistics* 54.2: 223-254.

Kim, Hansaem (김한샘). 2005. *Hyentay Kwuke Sayong Pinto Cosa 2* [An Analysis of Use Frequency in Modern Korean]. Seoul: The National Institute of the Korean Language. (in Korean)

Kim, Hyung-Chul (김형철). 1981. 3-inching taymyengsaey tayhaye - *tye, ku*-lul cwungsimulo [On the 3rd personal pronoun: With a focus on *tye* and *ku*]. *Journal of Korean Language and Literature* (문학과 언어) 2.1: 3-14. (in Korean)

Kim, In Soon (김인순). 2010. A study on the grammaticalization of *Bei* constructions. *Journal of Chinese Studies* (中國學論叢) 29: 1-20. doi: 10.26585/chlab.2010..29. 001 (in Korean)

Kim, In Soon (김인순). 2011. The unaccusative hypothesis and passive constructions. *Journal of Chinese Studies* (中國學論叢) 31: 43-65. doi: 10.26585/chlab.2011..31. 002 (in Korean)

Kim, Jae-Hoon (김재훈). 2005. Kwumwunkwuco pwuchak malmwungchi kwuchuk [Construction of structure-tagged corpus]. A project report for Mobico & Sysmeta. (in Korean)

Kim, Jong Do (김종도). 1986. Uymi cwungsimuy cenchisa kyoyuk -at-lul cwungsimulo. [Meaning-centered preposition education: with particular emphasis on *at*]. *English Education* 31: 95-117. (in Korean)

Kim, Joungmin (김정민). 2013. Mermaid construction in Korean. In: Tasaku Tsunoda (ed.), *Adnominal Clauses and the 'Mermaid Construction': Grammaticalization of Nouns*, 249-296. *Tokyo: National Institute for Japanese Language and Linguistics.*

Kim, Joungmin (김정민). 2020. Korean. In: Tasaku Tsunoda (ed.), *Mermaid Construction: A Compound-Predicate Construction with Biclausal Appearance* (Comparative Handbooks of Linguistics), 283-331. Berlin: Mouton de Gruyter.

Kim, Jungmin (김정민). 2020. Lexical and grammatical contronomy in English: A cognitive linguistic approach. Ph.D. dissertation, Hankuk University of Foreign Studies, Korea.

Kim, Kyunghee (김경희). 2018. A contrastive analysis of the grammaticalization of Spanish prepositions *hacia* and *de cara a. Estudios Hispanicos* (스페인어문학) 88: 9-35. doi: 10.21811/EH.88.9.

Kim, Kyunghee (김경희). 2019. Subtypes of Spanish complex prepositions and grammaticalization. *Estudios Hispanicos* (스페인어문학) 91: 9-37. doi: 10.21811/EH.91.9. (in Korean)

Kim, Kyunghee and Seongha Rhee (김경희 이성하). 2018. Grammaticalization of prepositions in Spanish. *Language and Linguistics* (언어와 언어학) 81: 21-50. doi: 10.20865/20188102. (in Korean)

Kim, Minju (김민주). 2010. The historical development of Korean *siph-* 'to think' into markers of desire, inference, and similarity. *Journal of Pragmatics* 42: 1000-1016.

Kim, Minju (김민주). 2011. *Grammaticalization in Korean: The Evolution of the Existential Verb* (Saffron Korean Linguistics Series 5). London: Saffron.

Kim, Nam-Kil (김남길). 1992. Korean. In: William Bright (ed.), *International encyclopedia of linguistics*, 282-286. Oxford: Oxford University Press.

Kim, Seon-A (김선아). 2004. Hyentay cwungkwuke tongsauy mwupephwa [Grammaticalization of Modern Chinese]. *Korea Journal of Chinese Linguistics*

(中國言語研究) 19: 113-133.

Kim, Seung-Gon (김승곤). 1989. *Wulimal Thossi Yenkwu* [A study on Korean particles]. Seoul: Konkuk University Press. (in Korean)

Kim, Seung-Gon (김승곤). 1992. *Kwuke Thossi Yenkwu* [A study on Korean particles]. Seoul: Suhkwang Academic Press. (in Korean)

Kim, Seung-Gon (김승곤). 1995. *Wulimal thossiyenkwu* [Particles in Korean]. Seoul: Konkuk University Press. (In Korean)

Kim, Seung-Gon (김승곤). 2004. *Kwuke Thossi Ewenkwa Yongpep* [Etymology and usage of Korean particles]. Seoul: Youkrak Publishing. (in Korean)

Kim, Sheon-Gi (김선기). 1975. *Ing, kung, tyeng*: Kalukhim (kalommal)-uy say kkaychim (cisi taymengsauy say insik) [*Ing, kung and tyeng*: New understanding of demonstrative expressions]. *Myungji University Journal* (명대논문) 8: 9-22. (in Korean)

Kim, Somin (김소민). 2015. Grammaticalization of English prepositions of temporal duration: With focus on *during, for,* and *over*. MA thesis, Hankuk University of Foreign Studies, Korea.

Kim, Yoonjeong (김윤정). 2008. A study on the grammaticalization of *bèi*. *Journal of Linguistic Science* (언어과학연구) 46: 201-219. (in Korean)

Kinsui, Satoshi. 1992. 'Ōbunyaku to judōbun. Edo jidai o chūshin ni' [Western translations and the passive: focus on the Edo period], in Bunka Gengogaku Henshū Iinkai (eds.), *Bunka Gengogaku: Sono Teigen to Kenchiku*. Tokyo: Sanseidō, 1-15. (in Japanese)

Kittilä, Seppo and Jussi Ylikoski. 2011. Remarks on the coding of Goal, Recipient and Vicinal Goal in European Uralic. In: Seppo Kittilä, Katja Västi, and Jussi Ylikoski (eds.), *Case, Animacy and Semantic Roles,* 29-64. Amsterdam: John Benjamins.

Klégr, Aleš. 1997. English complex prepositions of the prepositional phrase type. *Acta Universitatis Carolinae - Philologica 5. Prague Studies in English* 22: 51-78.

Klégr, Aleš. 2002. *English Complex Prepositions of the Type in spite of and Analogous Sequences: A Study and Dictionary*. Univerzita Karlova V Praze: Nakladatelstvi Karolinum.

Ko, Seongyeon, Andrew Joseph, and John Whitman. 2014. Comparative consequences of the tongue root harmony analysis for proto-Tungusic, proto-Mongolic, and proto-Korean. In: Martine Robbeets and Walter Bisang (eds.), *Paradigm Change in the Transeurasian Languages and Beyond,* 141-76. Amsterdam: John

Benjamins.

Ko, Yong-Kun (고영근). 2012. A study on case-markers, adpositions and particles, and in Korean and their typological implication. *Journal of Korean Linguistics* (국어학) 65: 73-108. (in Korean)

Ko, Yong-Kun (고영근). 2013. A study of Korean verbal morphology and its typological implications. *Hyengthaylon/Morphology* (형태론) 15.1: 1-34. (in Korean)

Ko, Young Chin (고영진). 1995. *A Study of the Processes of Grammaticalization in Korean Predicates: From Syntactic Constructions to Morphological Constructions.* Ph.D. dissertation, Yonsei University, Korea. Published 1997, *Hankwukeuy Mwunpephwa Kwaceng* [Grammaticalization Processes in Korean]. Seoul: Kwukhakcalyowen. (in Korean)

Koelle, Sigismund Wilhelm. 1968[1854]. *Outlines of a Grammar of the Vei Language: Together with a Vei-English Vocabulary and an Account of the Discovery of the Vei Mode of Syllabic Writing.* London: Church Missionary House. Reprinted: Farnborou: Gregg International Publishers.

Kohler, Klaus J. 1995. *Einführung in die Phonetik des Deutschen* (2. neubearbeitete Auflage) [Grundlagen der Germanistik 20]. Berlin: Schmidt. (in German)

Koike, Kazumi. 1997. Valores funcionales de las locuciones prepositivas en español. *Onomazein* 2: 151-179. (in Spanish)

Kölver, Ulrike. 1984. *Local Prepositions and Serial Verb Constructions in Thai.* AKUP: Arbeiten des Kölner Universalien – Projekts 56. Cologne: University of Cologne.

Komin, Suntaree. 1990. *Psychology of the Thai People: Values and Behavioral Patterns.* Bangkok, Thailand: National Institute of Development Administration (NIDA).

König, Christa. 2004. Case in Africa. Paper presented at the Language Typology Workshop, Chonnam National University, October 18-21, 2004.

König, Ekkehard. 1995. The meaning of converb constructions. In: Martin Haspelmath and Ekkehard König (eds.), *Converbs in Cross-Linguistic Perspective. Structure and Meaning of Adverbial Verb Forms – Adverbial Participles, Gerunds,* 57-95. Berlin: Mouton de Gruyter.

Koo, Hyun Jung (구현정). 1987. Ssikkuth *-a, -key, -ci, -ko*-uy ssuimkwa uymi [The usage and semantics of suffixes, *-a, -key, -ci,* and *-ko*]. *Konkuk Emwunhak* (건국어문학) 11-12: 167-188. (in Korean)

Koo, Hyun Jung (구현정). 1998. Grammaticalization of conditional markers in Modern Korean. *Journal of Sangmyung Language and Literature* (어문학연구, 상명대학교

어문학연구소) 8: 1-13. (in Korean)

Koo, Hyun Jung (구현정). 2003. On aspects of grammaticalization of 'giving' verbs in Korean. *Eoneohag* (언어학) 37: 3-24. (in Korean)

Koo, Hyun Jung (구현정). 2004. A cognitive analysis of lexicalization patterns of (dis-)honorification in Korean. *Korean Semantics* (한국어 의미학) 14: 97-120. (in Korean)

Koo, Hyun Jung (구현정). 2009. Body in the language: A case with Korean body-part term 'head'. *Language and Linguistics* (언어와 언어학) 46: 1-27. (in Korean)

Koo, Hyun Jung (구현정). 2010. Fused paradigms: Grammaticalization approach to extension of conditional markers. *Han-Geul* (한글) 287: 45-71. (in Korean)

Koo, Hyun Jung (구현정). 2016. On change of the terms of address between couples during the 70 years of post-colonization as reflected in mass media. *Korean Semantics* (한국어 의미학) 51: 85-110. doi: 10.19033/sks.2016.03.51.85.

Koo, Hyun Jung (구현정). 2019. A study on the grammatical competence of the extension of '-eum' nominal sentences. *Han-Geul* (한글) 80.4: 863-890.

Koo, Hyun Jung (구현정). 2020. Aspect of emergent grammar of Modern Korean reflected in sentence-final dependent noun construction. *Korea Language Research* (한 말연구) 58: 5-34. doi: 10.16876/klrc.2020.58.5.

Koo, Hyun Jung and Seongha Rhee (구현정 이성하). 2001. Grammaticalization of a sentential end marker from a conditional marker. *Discourse and Cognition* (담화와 인지) 8.1: 1-19.

Koo, Hyun Jung and Seongha Rhee (구현정 이성하). 2006. Cognitive-semantic network: The case of Korean instrumental. *The Journal of Linguistic Science* (언어과학연구) 38: 93-119.

Koo, Hyun Jung and Seongha Rhee (구현정 이성하). 2013. "I will do it… but I'm asking you to do it": On the Emergence of Polite Imperative from Promissive. *Procedia - Social and Behavioral Sciences* 97: 487-494.

Koo, Hyun Jung and Seongha Rhee (구현정 이성하). 2016. Pejoratives in Korean. In: Rita Finkbeiner, Jörg Meibauer and Heike Wiese (eds.), *Pejoration,* 301-323. Amsterdam: John Benjamins.

Koo, Hyun Jung and Seongha Rhee (구현정 이성하). 2018. Ideophones and attenuatives in Korean. Paper presented at the 51st Societas Linguistica Europaea (SLE) Conference, University of Tallinn, Estonia, 29 August - 1 September 2018.

Koo, Hyun Jung and Seongha Rhee (구현정 이성하). 2019. From self-talk to grammar: The emergence of multiple paradigms from self-quoted questions in Korean. *Lingue e Linguaggi* 31: 255-278. doi: 10.1285/i22390359v31p255.

Koopman, Hilda. 2000. *The Syntax of Specifiers and Heads: Collected Essays of Hilda J. Koopman*. London: Routledge.

Kopecka, Anetta and Marine Vuillermet. 2021a. Introduction: Source-goal (a)symmetries across languages. Special issue of *Studies in Language* 45.1: 2-35.

Kopecka, Anetta and Marine Vuillermet (eds.) 2021b. Source-Goal (a)symmetries across languages. Special issue of *Studies in Language* 45.1.

Kortmann, Bernd and Ekkehard König. 1992. Categorial reanalysis: The case of deverbal prepositions. *Linguistics* 30: 671-697.

KU-CKD (Korea University Chinese-Korean Dictionary) 1995. *Cwunghan Taysacen* [A Comprehensive Dictionary of Chinese-Korean]. Seoul: Research Institute of Korean Studies, Korea University.

Kullavanijaya, Pranee. 1974. Transitive verbs in Thai. Ph.D. thesis, University of Hawaii at Manoa.

Kullavanijaya, Pranee. 2003. A historical study of time markers in Thai. In: Shoichi Iwasaki, Andrew Simpson, Karen Adams and Paul Sidwell (eds.), *SEALS-XIII: Papers from the 13th Meeting of the Southeast Asian Linguistics Society (2003)*, 105-124. Canberra, Pacific Linguistics.

Kullavanijaya, Pranee. 2008. A historical study of /thîi/ in Thai. In: Anthony V. N. Diller, Jerold A. Edmondson, and Yongxian Luo (eds.), *The Tai-Kadai Languages* (Routledge Language Family Series), 445-467. London: Routledge.

Khammee, Kultida and Seongha Rhee. 2021. Diminutive Small and cute? Small and bad?: Semantic network of diminutives in Thai and Korean. Paper presented at the 54th Societas Linguistica Europaea Conference, National and Kapodistrian University of Athens (online platform), August 31 - September 3, 2021.

Kuryłowicz, Jerzy. 1975[1965]. The evolution of grammatical categories. In: Eugenio Coseriu (ed.), *Esquisses Linguistiques II,* 38-54. Munich: Fink.

Kurzon, Dennis. 2008. 'Ago' and its grammatical status in English and other languages. In: Dennis Kurzon and Silvia Adler (eds.), *Adpositions: Pragmatic, Semantic and Syntactic Perspectives* (Typological Studies in Language 74), 209-227. Amsterdam: John Benjamins.

Kurzon, Dennis and Silvia Adler (eds.). 2008. *Adpositions: Pragmatic, Semantic and Syntactic Perspectives* (Typological Studies in Language 74). Amsterdam: John Benjamins.

Kuteva, Tania, Bernd Heine, Bo Hong, Haiping Long, Heiko Narrog, and Seongha Rhee. 2019. *World Lexicon of Grammaticalization* (2nd ed.) Cambridge: Cambridge University Press.

Kuteva, Tania and Chris Sinha. 1994. Spatial and non-spatial uses of prepositions: Conceptual integrity across semantic domains. In: Monika Schwarz (ed.), *Kognitive Semantik/Cognitive Semantics. Ergebnisse, Probleme, Perspektiven,* 215-237. Tübingen: Gunter Narr Verlag.

Kwon, Jae-il (권재일). 1985. Hyentaykwukeuy uyconmyengsa yenkwu [A study of dependent nouns in Modern Korean], in Festschrift publication committee (ed.), *Sotang Chensikwen paksa hwakapkinyem kwukehak nonchong* [Papers on Korean linguistics, Festschrift for Dr. Sodang Chun Si-kwon]. Seoul: Hyungseol Publishing, 89-112. (in Korean)

Kwun, Seon-A (권선아). 2010. '都'-uy mwunpephwa yenkwu. MA thesis, Hankuk University of Foreign Studies, Korea. (in Korean)

Lakoff, George and Mark Johnson. 2003[1980]. *Metaphors We Live By.* (2nd ed.). Chicago: University of Chicago Press.

Lakusta, Laura and Barbara Landau. 2005. Starting at the end: The importance of goals in spatial language. *Cognition* 96.1: 1-33.

Lakusta, Laura and Barbara Landau. 2012. Language and memory for motion events: Origins of the asymmetry between source and goal paths. *Cognitive Science* 36.3: 517-544.

Langacker, Ronald W. 1987. *Foundations of Cognitive Grammar,* vol. 1: *Theoretical Prerequisites.* Stanford, CA: Stanford University Press.

Langacker, Ronald W. 1991. *Foundations of Cognitive Grammar,* vol. 2: *Descriptive Application.* Stanford, CA: Stanford University Press.

Langacker, Ronald W. 2000. A dynamic usage-based model. In: Michael Barlow and Suzanne Kemmer (eds.), *Usage Based Models of Language,* 1-63. Stanford, CA: CSLI Publications.

Langacker, Ronald W. 2008. *Cognitive Grammar – A Basic Introduction.* Oxford: Oxford University Press.

LaPolla, Randy J. 2021. Grammatical relations. In: Robert D. Van Valin Jr, Delia Bentley, Ricardo Mairal, and Wataru Nakamura (eds.), *The Cambridge Handbook of Role and Reference Grammar.* Cambridge: Cambridge University Press.

Lee, Heeran (이희란). 2019. A study on subtypes of spatial complex prepositions in Spanish and their semantic extension. MA thesis, Hankuk University of Foreign

Studies, Seoul. (in Korean)

Lee, Hee-Seung (이희승). 1949. *Chokup Kwuke Mwunpep* [Korean Grammar for Beginners]. Seoul: Pakmwunsa. (in Korean)

Lee, Hyun Sook (이현숙). 2011. Grammaticalization of concessive markers in English from verbal and nominal sources. Ph.D. dissertation, Hankuk University of Foreign Studies, Korea.

Lee, Jae-Sun (이제선). 2000. A study on prepositional usage of Thai verbs. MA thesis, Hankuk University of Foreign Studies, Seoul. (in Korean)

Lee, Jung Eun (이정은). 2013. Convergence and divergence in grammaticalization: The case of *between* and *among*. MA thesis, Hankuk University of Foreign Studies, Korea.

Lee, Kee-dong (이기동). 1981a. Cenchisa *on*-uy uymi [Meaning of the preposition *on*]. *English Education* (영어교육) 22: 31-42. (in Korean)

Lee, Kee-dong (이기동). 1981b. *On*-uy uymi [Meaning of *on*]. *Language Research* (어학연구) 17.2: 199-214. (in Korean)

Lee, Kee-dong (이기동). 1982a. *In*-uy uymi [Meaning of *in*]. *Modern English Linguistics* (현대영어학) 169-189. (in Korean)

Lee, Kee-dong (이기동). 1982b. *About*-uy uymi [Meaning of *about*]. *English Education* (영어교육) 23: 193-204. (in Korean)

Lee, Ki-Moon (이기문). 1998 [1961]. *Kwukesa Kaysel* [An introduction to Korean historical linguistics] (revised ed.). Seoul: Thayhaksa. (in Korean)

Lee, Kyung Kyu (이경규). 2011. *Komwun Hesa Sacen* [A Dictionary of Function Words in Ancient Literature]. Seoul: J&C Publishing. (in Korean)

Lee, Sang Oak (이상억). 2021. Morphological analysis of the Sino-Korean words: Comparison to the functional loads of phonetic/phonological constraints and syntactic rule. Plenary lecture at ICKL-2021. *The Proceedings of the 22nd Biennial Meeting of the International Circle of Korean Linguistics (ICKL-2021), August 17-18, 2021, Seoul, Korea (online platform)*, 38-50.

Lee, Soong-Nyeong (이숭녕). 1992[1961]. *Cwungseykwuke Mwunpep* [Middle Korean grammar] (Revised edition). Seoul: Eulyu Munhwasa. (in Korean)

Lee, Woon Young (이운영). 2002. Phyocwunkwuketaysacen Yenkwu Pwunsek [An analysis of *Phyocwunkwuketaysacen*]. Seoul: The National Institute of the Korean Language. (in Korean)

Leech, Geoffrey. 1969. *Towards a Semantic Description of English*. London: Longmans.

Lehmann, Christian. 1978. On measuring semantic complexity: A contribution to a rapprochement of semantics and statistical linguistics. *Georgetown University Papers in Languages and Linguistics* 14: 83-120.

Lehmann, Christian. 1985. Grammaticalization: Synchronic variation and diachronic change. *Lingua e Stile* 20: 303-318.

Lehmann, Christian. 1987. Sprachwandel und Typologie. In: Norbert Boretzky, Werner Enninger, and Thomas Stolz (eds.), *Beiträge zum 3. Essener Kolloquium über Sprachwandel und seine bestimmenden Faktoren vom 30. 9. bis 2. 10. 1987 [recte 1986] an der Universität Essen.* (Bochum-Essener Beiträge zur Sprachwandelforschung 4), 201-225. Bochum: Brockmeyer. (in German)

Lehmann, Christian. 2004. Interlinear morphemic glossing. In: Herbert Ernst Wiegand (ed.), *Morphologie: Handbucher zur Sprach- und Kommunikations-wissenschaft,* Band 172, 1834-57. Berlin: Walter de Gruyter.

Lehmann, Christian. 2015[1982]. *Thoughts on Grammaticalization* (3rd ed.). (Classics in Linguistics 1). Berlin: Language Science Press.

Lessau, Donald A. 1994. *A Dictionary of Grammaticalization.* 3 vols. Bochum: Universitätsverlag Dr. N. Brockmeyer.

Levinson, Stephen C. 1992. Language and cognition: The cognitive consequences of spatial descriptions in Guugu Yimithirr. *Working Paper* 13, Cognitive Anthropology Research Group, Max Planck Institute for Psycholinguistics, Nijmegen.

Levinson, Stephen C. 1994. Vision, shape and linguistic description: Tzeltal body-part terminology and object description. In: John B. Haviland and Stephen C. Levinson (eds.), *Space in Mayan Languages,* Special issue of *Linguistics* 32.4: 791-855.

Levinson, Stephen C. 1996a. Frames of reference and Molyneux's question: crosslinguistic evidence. In: Paul Bloom, Mary A. Peterson, Lynn Nadel, and Merrill F. Garrett (eds.), *Language and Space,* 109-169. Cambridge, Mass.: MIT Press.

Levinson, Stephen C. 1996b. Language and space. *Annual Review of Anthropology* 25: 353-382.

Levinson, Stephen C. 1997. Language and cognition: The cognitive consequences of spatial description in Guugu Yimithirr. *Journal of Linguistic Anthropology* 7.1: 98-131.

Levinson, Stephen C. 2002. The body in space: Cultural differences in the use of body-schema for spatial thinking and gesture. In: G. Lewis and F. Sigaut (eds.), *Culture and Uses of the Body*. Oxford: Oxford University Press.

Levinson, Stephen C. 2004[2003]. *Space in Language and Cognition: Explorations in Cognitive Diversity*. Cambridge: Cambridge University Press.

Levinson, Stephen C. and David P. Wilkins (eds.). 2006. *Grammars of Space: Explorations in Cognitive Diversity*. Cambridge: Cambridge University Press.

Li, Audrey, Andrew Simpson, and Wei-Tien Dylan Tsai (eds.). 2015. *Chinese Syntax in a Cross-Linguistic Perspective* (Oxford Studies in Comparative Syntax). Oxford: Oxford University Press.

Li, Changbo. 2002. *Nihongo Shiji Taikei no Rekishi* [History of the Japanese Demonstrative System] Kyōto: Kyōto Daigaku Shuppankai. (in Japanese)

Li, Charles N. and Sandra A. Thompson. 1974a. Co-verbs in Mandarin Chinese: Verbs or prepositions? *Journal of Chinese Linguistics* 2.3: 257-278.

Li, Charles N. and Sandra A. Thompson. 1974b. An explanation of word order change SVO 〉 SOV. *Foundations of Language* 12.2: 201-214.

Li, Charles N. and Sandra A. Thompson. 1976. Development of the causative in Mandarin Chinese: Interaction of diachronic processes in syntax. In: Masayoshi Shibatani (ed.), *The Grammar of Causative Constructions*, 477-492. New York: Academic Press.

Li, Charles N., Thompson, Sandra A., 1981. *Mandarin Chinese. A Functional Reference Grammar*. Berkeley: University of California Press.

Li, Jinxi (黎锦熙). 1933[1924]. *Xīnzhù Guóyǔ Wénfǎ* (新著国语文法) [New Chinese Grammar]. Beijing: Shāngwùyìnshūguǎn. (in Chinese)

Li, Yimin (李忆民). 1995. *Xiàndài Hànyǔ Chángyòngcí Yòngfǎ Cídiǎn* (现代汉语常用词用法词典) [A Dictionary of Practical Usage of Modern Chinese]. Beijing: Beijing Language and Culture University Press. (in Chinese)

Libert, Alan Reed. 2006. *Ambipositions*. (LINCOM studies in language typology No. 13). Newcastle: Lincom Europa.

Libert, Alan Reed. 2013. *Adpositions and Other Parts of Speech*. Frankfurt am Main: Peter Lang.

Libert, Alan Reed. 2017. *Conjunctions and Other Parts of Speech*. Frankfurt am Main: Peter Lang.

Lichtenberk, Frantisek. 1991. Semantic change and heterosemy in grammaticalization. *Language* 67.3: 475-509. doi:10.1353/lan.1991.0009

Lin, Hai Tao (임해도 林海濤). 2014. A contrastive study of adpositions in Korean and Chinese for Korean as Second Language. MA thesis, Chonnam National University, Korea. (in Korean)

Liu, Danqing (刘丹青). 2002. *Hanyu-li de kuangshi jieci* (汉语中的框式介词) [Circumpositions in Chinese]. *Contemporary Linguistics* (当代语言学) 4: 241-253.

Liu, Danqing (刘丹青). 2004. *Yǔxù Lèixíngxué Yǔ Jiècí Lǐlùn* (语序类型学与介词理论) [Word Order Typology and Theory of Adposition]. Beijing: Shangwuyinshuguan. (in Chinese), Korean translation by Ki Hyuk Kim and Jin-qiu Sun (김기혁 손금추), 2011. Seoul: Bogosa.

Liu, Danqing (刘丹青). 2008. *Yǔfǎ Diàochá Yánjiū Shǒucè* (语法调查研究手册) [A Handbook of Grammar Investigation and Research]. Jinan: Shanghai Education Press. (in Chinese)

Liu, Feng-Hsi. 2006. Dative constructions in Chinese. *Language and Linguistics* 7: 863-904.

Liu, Hsiuying. 2016. Degree adverb *zhī* (之) in Modern Chinese. *Journal of Applied Linguistics and Language Research* 3.3: 14-41.

Liu, Yongquan (刘涌泉). 1987. New advances in computers and natural language processing in China. *Information Science* 8.1: 64-70. (in Chinese)

Liu, Yuehua, Wenyu Pan, Weizhe Gu (刘月华·潘文娱·故韡). 2005. *Shíyòng Xiàndài Hànyǔ Yǔfǎ* (实用现代汉语语法) [Practical Modern Chinese Grammar]. Korean translation by Hyun-Chul Kim, Jung-Goo Park, Moon-Eui Oh, and Kyu-Bal Choi (김현철 박정수 오문의 최규발), *Silyong Hyentay Hane Epep*. Seoul: Songsan Publisher.

Lord, Carol. 1993. *Historical Change in Serial Verb Constructions* (Typological Studies in Language 26). Amsterdam: John Benjamins.

Loss, Daniel Peter. 2017. A comparison of grammaticalization in Shan and Thai. MA thesis, Payap University.

Lu, Na (여나). 2015. A contrastive analysis between Korean auxiliary words and Chinese prepositions in grammatical perspectives. Ph.D. dissertation, Hannam University, Korea. (in Korean)

Lu, Shuxiang (吕淑湘) (ed.) 1980. *Xiàndài Hànyǔ Bābǎicí* (现代汉语八百词) [800 Words of Modern Chinese], Beijing: Shangwuyinshuguan. (in Chinese)

Lu, Shuxiang (吕淑湘) 1984. *Hànyǔ Yǔfǎ Lùnwénjí* (汉语语法論文集) [Collection of Essays on Chinese Grammar]. Beijing: Shangwuyinshuguan. (in Chinese)

Lu, Shuxiang (吕淑湘). 1965. Fāngwèicí Shǐyòng Qíngkuàng de Chūbù Kǎochá (方位词使用情况的初步考察) [A Preliminary Investigation on the Usage of Location Words]. *Zhōngguó Yǔwén* (中國語文) 3. (Reprinted in Shuxiang Lu 1984). (in Chinese)

Luraghi, Silvia. 2003. *On the Meaning of Prepositions and Cases. The Expression of Semantic Roles in Ancient Greek.* (Studies in Language Companion Series 67). Amsterdam: Benjamins.

Luraghi, Sylvia. 2017. Differential goal marking vs. differential source marking in Ancient Greek. In: Sylvia Luraghi, Tatiana Nikitina, and Chiara Zanchi (eds.), *Space in Diachrony,* 119-146. Amsterdam: John Benjamins.

Luraghi, Sylvia, Tatiana Nikitina, and Chiara Zanchi (eds.). 2017. *Space in Diachrony.* Amsterdam: John Benjamins.

Lyons, Christopher. 1999. *Definiteness.* Cambridge: Cambridge University Press.

Lyons, John. 1968. *Introduction to Theoretical Linguistics.* Cambridge: Cambridge University Press.

Lyons, John. 1977, *Semantics,* Vols. I and II, Cambridge: Cambridge University Press.

Ma, Beijia (马贝加). 2002. *Jìndài Hànyǔ Jiècí* (近代汉语介词) [Modern Chinese Prepositions]. Beijing: Zhonghua Book Co. (in Chinese)

Ma, Beijia (马贝加). 2014. *Hànyǔ Dòngcí Yǔfǎhuà* (汉语动词语法化) [Grammaticalization of Chinese Verbs]. Vol. 1. Beijing: Zhonghua Book Co. (in Chinese)

Ma, Jianzhong (马建忠). 2003[1898]. *Mǎshì Wéntōng* (马氏文通) [Mr. Ma's Key to Mastering Written Language], Shanghai: Shangwuyinshuguan. (in Chinese)

MacLaury, Robert E. 1989. Zapotec body-part locatives: Prototypes and metaphoric extensions. *International Journal of American Linguistics* 55.2: 119-154.

MacWhinney, Brian. 1999. Preface. In: Brian MacWhinney (ed.), *The Emergence of Language,* ix-xviii. Mahwah, NJ: Erlbaum.

Maeng, Joo-Oeck and Seon-A Kwun (맹주억 권선아) 2009. The analysis of *dou* (都)'s semantic extension in cognitive linguistics. *Journal of Chinese Language, Literature and Translation* (中國語文論譯叢刊) 25: 143-167. (in Korean)

Malchukov, Andrej. 2009. Rare and 'exotic' cases. In: Andrej Malchukov and Andrew Spencer (eds.), *The Oxford Handbook of Case,* 635-648. Oxford: Oxford University Press.

Malchukov, Andrej and Heiko Narrog. 2009. Case polysemy. In: Andrej Malchukov and Andrew Spencer (eds.), *The Oxford Handbook of Case,* 518-534. Oxford:

Oxford University Press.

Malchukov, Andrej and Andrew Spencer (eds.). 2009. *The Oxford Handbook of Case*. Oxford: Oxford University Press.

Markman, Vita. 2009. On the parametric variation of case and agreement. *Natural Language & Linguistic Theory* 27.2: 379-429.

Martin, Samuel. 1987. *The Japanese Language through Time*. New Haven, Connecticut: Yale University Press.

Martin, Samuel. 1993. *A Reference Grammar of Korean*. Rutland, Vermont: Charles E. Tuttle.

Martin, Samuel. 1997. Unaltaic features of the Korean verb. *Japanese/Korean Linguistics* 6: 3-40.

Maslova, Elena. 2003. *A Grammar of Kolyma Yukaghir*. Berlin: Mouton de Gruyter.

Matisoff, James A. 1969. Verb concatenation in Lahu: The syntax and semantics of 'simple' juxtaposition. *Acta Linguistica Hafniensia* 12: 69-120.

Matisoff, James A. 1973. Tonogenesis in Southeast Asia. In: Larry M. Hyman (ed.), *Consonant Types and Tone*, 73-95. Los Angeles: UCLA.

Matisoff, James A. 1991a. Areal and universal dimensions of grammatization in Lahu. In: Elizabeth C. Traugott and Bernd Heine (eds.), *Approaches to Grammaticalization*, 2 vols. (Typological Studies in Language 19), vol. 1: 383-453. Amsterdam: John Benjamins.

Matisoff, James A. 1991b. Endangered languages of Mainland Southeast Asia. In: Robert H. Robins and Eugenius M. Uhlenbeck (eds.), *Endangered Languages*, 189-228. Oxford: Berg.

Matisoff, James A. 1991c. Sino-Tibetan linguistics: present state and future prospects. *Annual Review of Anthropology* 20: 469-504.

Matsumoto, Katsumi. 1998. Yuurashia ni okeru boin chōwa no futatsu no taipu [Two types of vowel harmony in Eurasia], *Gengo kenkyū* 114: 1-34. (in Japanese)

Matsumoto, Yo. 1988. From bound grammatical markers to free discourse markers: History of some Japanese connectives. *Berkeley Linguistics Society* 14: 340-351.

Matsumoto, Yo. 1996. *Complex Predicates in Japanese: A Syntactic and Semantic Study of the Notion 'Word'*. Stanford, CA: CSLI Publications.

Matsumoto, Yo. 1998. Semantic change in the grammaticalization of verbs into postposition in Japanese. In: Toshio Ohori (ed.), *Studies in Japanese*

Grammaticalization: Cognitive and Discourse Perspectives, 25-60. Tokyo: Kurosio Publishers.

Matthews, Stephen and Virginia Yip. 2011[1994]. *Cantonese: A Comprehensive Grammar* (2nd ed.) (Routledge Comprehensive Grammars). London: Routledge.

McClure, William and Alexander Vovin (eds.). 2018. *Studies in Japanese and Korean Historical and Theoretical Linguistics and Beyond: Festschrift Presented to John B. Whitman*. Leiden: Brill.

Meillet, Antoine. 1912. L'évolution des formes grammaticales. *Scientia* 12. (Reprinted in Meillet. 1948. *Linguistique Historique et Linguistique Générale*. 1, 130-148. Paris: Edouard Champion).

MICASE Corpus (Michigan Corpus of Academic Spoken English). Online searchable corpus, http://micase.umdl.umich.edu/m/micase/

Mithun, Marianne. 1999. *The Languages of Native North America*. Cambridge: Cambridge University Press.

Miyake, Tomohiro. 2005. Gendai nihongo ni okeru bunpōka – naiyōgo to kinōgo no renzokusei o megutte [Grammaticalization in Modern Japanese: on the continuum between content words and function words]. *Nihongo no Kenkyū* 1/3, 61-76. (in Japanese)

Muraki, Shinjiro. 1996. *Nihon-go-doshi no Shoso* (5th ed.). Tokyo: Hitsuzi-shobo. (in Japanese)

Murphy, M. Lynne. 2003. *Semantic Relations and the Lexicon: Antonymy, Synonymy, and Other Paradigms*. Cambridge: Cambridge University Press.

Nam, Kwang-Woo (남광우). 2007. *Koesacen* [A dictionary of Old Korean]. Seoul: Kyohaksa Publishing. (in Korean)

Nam, Pung-hyun (남풍현). 2012. Old Korean. In: Nicholas Tranter (ed.), *The Languages of Japan and Korea*, 41-72. Milton Park, UK: Routledge.

Nam, Seungho (남승호). 1995. The semantics of locative prepositional phrases in English. Ph.D. dissertation, The University of California, Los Angeles.

Nam, Seungho (남승호). 1996. Yenge cangsophyohyen cenchisakwuuy uymiceyyak [Semantic constraints on English locative prepositional phrases]. *Korean Journal of Linguistics* (언어) 21.1: 305-326. (in Korean)

Narrog, Heiko. 2005. Nihongo no bunpoka no keitaiteki sokumen [The morphological aspect of grammaticalization in Japanese]. *Nihongo no Kenkyu* 1.3: 108-122. (in Japanese)

Narrog, Heiko. 2010. (Inter)subjectification in the domain of modality and mood: Concepts and cross-linguistic realities. In: Kristin Davidse, Lieven Vandelanotte, and Hubert Cuyckens (eds.) 2010. *Subjectification, Intersubjectification and Grammaticalization* (Topics in English Linguistics 66), 385-429. Berlin: Mouton de Gruyter.

Narrog, Heiko. 2017. Three types of subjectivity, three types of intersubjectivity, their dynmicization and a synthesis. In: Daniel Van Olmen, Hubert Cuyckens, and Lobke Ghesquière (eds.), *Aspects of Grammaticalization: (Inter)Subjectification and Directionality* (Trends in Linguistics Studies and Monographs 305), 19-46. Berlin: Mouton de Gruyter.

Narrog, Heiko and Bernd Heine (eds.). 2011. *The Oxford Handbook of Grammaticalization.* Oxford: Oxford University Press.

Narrog, Heiko and Bernd Heine (eds.). 2018. *Grammaticalization from a Typological Perspective* (Oxford Studies in Diachronic & Historical Linguistics 31). Oxford: Oxford University Press.

Narrog, Heiko and Toshio Ohori. 2011. Grammaticalization in Japanese. In: Heiko Narrog and Bernd Heine (eds.), *The Oxford Handbook of Grammaticalization*, 775-85. Oxford: Oxford University Press.

Narrog, Heiko and Seongha Rhee. 2013. Grammaticalization of space in Korean and Japanese. In: Martine Robbeets and Hubert Cuyckens (eds.), *Shared Grammaticalization. With Special Focus on the Transeurasian Languages*, 287-315. Amsterdam: John Benjamins.

Narrog, Heiko, Seongha Rhee, and John Whitman. 2018. Grammaticalization in Japanese and Korean. In: Heiko Narrog and Bernd Heine (eds.), *Grammaticalization from a Typological Perspective* (Oxford Studies in Diachronic and Historical Linguistics), 166-188. Oxford: Oxford University Press.

Natthawan, Sinaroj (씨나롯 낫타완). 2011. Research on the Korean adverbial case particles with Thai preposition. MA thesis, Chungnam National University. (in Korean).

Navarro Melara, Gloria Noemi. 2021. Grammaticalization of numeral ONE into indefinite article in English and Spanish. MA thesis. Hankuk University of Foreign Studies, Korea.

Nebrija, Antonio de. 1989[1492]. *Gramática de la Lengua Castellana,* Estudio y edición de Antonio Quilis, 1989, Madrid: Editorial Centro de Estudios Ramón Areces. (in Spanish)

Nedjalkov, Vladmimir P. and Galina A. Otaina. 2013. *A Syntax of the Nivkh Language. The Amur Dialect.* (Translated and edited by Emma Š. Geniušienė, edited by Ekaterina Gruzdeva). Amsterdam: John Benjamins.

Nichols, Johanna and Alan Timberlake. 1991. Grammaticalization as retextualization. In: Elizabeth Closs Traugott and Bernd Heine (eds.), *Approaches to Grammaticalization.* 2 vols. (Typological Studies in Language 19), vol. 1: 129-146. Amsterdam: John Benjamins.

Nichols, Johanna. 2004. Head/Dependent Marking. In: Keith Brown (ed.), *Encyclopedia of Language and Linguistics,* vol. 5, 234-255. Amsterdam: Elsevier.

Nihon Kokugo Daijiten (NKD) [Great Dictionary of the National Language of Japan]. 2000-2002, 14 vols. (2nd edition) (Edited by the Nihon Kokugo Daijiten Henshū Iinkai). Tōkyō: Shōgakkan.

Norman, Jerry. 1988. *Chinese.* Cambridge: Cambridge University Press.

Noss, Richard B. 1964. *Thai Reference Grammar.* Washington, D.C.: US Government Printing Office.

NGLE (Nueva Gramática de la Lengua Española) 2009. Real Academia Española (RAE) and Asociación de Academias de la Lengua Española (ASALE). Madrid. (in Spanish)

O'Dowd, Elizabeth M. 1998. *Prepositions and Particles in English: A Discourse-Functional Account.* Oxford: Oxford University Press.

O'Grady, William. 2005. *Syntactic Carpentry: An Emergentist Approach to Syntax.* Mahwah, NJ: Erlbaum.

O'Grady, William. 2008. Language without grammar. In: Peter Robinson and Nick C. Ellis (eds.), *Handbook of Cognitive Linguistics and Second Language Acquisition,* 139-167. New York: Routledge.

Ohori, Toshio. 1995. Remarks on suspended clauses: a contribution to Japanese phraseology. In: Shibatani, Masayoshi and Sandra A. Thompson (eds.). *Essays in Semantics and Pragmatics in Honor of Charles J. Fillmore,* 201-218. Amsterdam: John Benjamins.

Ohori, Toshio (ed.). 1998. *Studies in Japanese Grammaticalization: Cognitive and Discourse Perspectives.* Tokyo: Kurosio Publishers.

Ohta, Tatsuo. 1958. *Chugokugo Rekishi Bumpo* [A Historical Grammar of Modern

Chinese]. Tokyo: Konan Shoin. (in Japanese)

Onodera, Noriko O. 2004. *Japanese Discourse Markers*. Amsterdam: John Benjamins.

Oxford English Dictionary (OED). 2021. Online searchable dictionary. www.oed.com. Oxford: Oxford University Press.

Pagliuca, William. 1976. PRE-fixing. ms. State University of New York, Buffalo.

Pantcheva, Marina. 2010. The syntactic structure of locations, goals and sources. *Linguistics* 48.5: 1043-1081.

Panupong, Vichin. 1989. *The Structure of Thai: Grammatical System*. Bangkok: Ramkhamhaeng University Press.

Papafragou, Anna. 2010. Source-goal asymmetries in motion representation: Implications for language production and comprehension. *Cognitive Science* 34.6: 1064-1092.

Paradis, Carita, Jean Hudson, and Ulf Magnusson (eds.). 2013. *The Construal of Spatial Meaning: Windows into Conceptual Space* (Explorations in Language and Space 7). Oxford: Oxford University Press.

Paris, Marie-Claude and Marie-Thérèse Vinet. 2010. Approximative *zuǒyòu* 'around, about' in Chinese. *Language and Linguistics* 11.4: 767-801.

Park, Hyang Lan (박향란). 2012. *Gei*-uy tacwung mwunpephwa [On polygrammaticalization of *gei*]. *Journal of Chinese Language and Literature* (中國語文學) 60: 581-601. (in Korean)

Park, Hyojin (박효진). 2018. Grammaticalization of the vision-derived complex preposition. MA thesis, Hankuk University of Foreign Studies, Korea.

Park, Jinho (박진호). 1998. Kotay kwuke mwunpep [Old Korean grammar]. In: Kwuklipkwukewen [The National Institute of the Korean Language] (ed.), *Kwukeuy Sitaypyel Pyenchen Yenkwu 3, Kotay Kwuke* [A Historical Study of Korean 3, Old Korean], 121-205. Seoul: Kwuklipkwukewen [The National Institute of the Korean Language].

Park, Jinho (박진호). 2015. A historical study of delimiters. *Journal of Korean Linguistics* (국어학) 73: 375-435.

Park, Juyang (박주양). 2014. Grammaticalization of English prepositions denoting temporal limit. MA thesis, Hankuk University of Foreign Studies, Korea.

Park, Kyungeun (박경은). 2011. A polysemy of /gada/ in Korean in comparison to /paj/ in Thai: A cogntive linguistic approach. Ph.D. dissertation, Thammasat University, Thailand.

Park, Kyungeun (박경은). 2017. Grammaticalization of /naa/ - /lang/ in Thai and its pedagogical implication. *Journal of Korean Association of Thai Studies* (태국학논총) 23.2: 31-55. (in Korean)

Park, Kyung-Eun and Seongha Rhee (박경은 이성하). 2018. A comparative study on the grammaticalization of Korean and Thai adpositions - From macroscopic and typological perspectives. *The Journal of Linguistic Science* 86: 69-95. (in Korean)

Park, Seon-ok (박선옥). 2013. Ilpone pwuchisaey tayhan yuhyengloncek kochal [A typological study on adpositions in Japanese]. *Ilponmwunhwayenkwu* (일본문화연구) 48: 203-224. (in Korean)

Park, Seongha (박성하). 2015. A study of the semantic and syntactical properties of multisyllabic words *X着* in Modern Chinese. *The Journal of Foreign Studies* (외국학연구) 33: 115-144 (Chung-Ang University). doi: 10.15755/jfs.2015.33.115. (in Korean)

Park, Won-ki (박원기). 2012. *Cwungkwukewa Mwunpephwa* [Chinese and Grammaticalization]. Seoul: Hakgobang. (in Korean)

Paul, Hermann. 1920[1880]. *Prinzipien der Sprachgeschichte* (5th ed.). Halle: Niemeyer. (in German)

Paul, Waltraud. 2015. *New Perspectives on Chinese Syntax* (Trends in Linguistics Studies and Monographs 271). Berlin: Mouton de Gruyter.

Pei, Mario. 1949. *Story of Language.* Philadelphia: J.B. Lippincott Co.

Pellard, Thomas. 2018. A (more) comparative approach to some Japanese etymologies. In: William McClure and Alexander Vovin (eds.), *Studies in Japanese and Korean Historical and Theoretical Linguistics and Beyond: Festschrift Presented to John B. Whitman,* 55-64. Leiden: Brill.

Peyaube, Alain. 1986a. *Evolution des constructions datives du 14e siècle av. J.C. au 18 siècle* (Evolution of the datives constructions from the 14th century to 18th century). Paris: Collège de France. (in French)

Peyraube, Alain. 1986b. Sur la syntaxe du chinois classique - A propos de C. Harbsmeier, Aspects of Classical Chinese syntax. *Cahiers de linguistique - Asie orientale* 15.2: 329-337. (in French)

Peyraube, Alain. 1989. History of the passive construction in Chinese until the 10th century. *Journal of Chinese Linguistics* 17.2: 335-372.

Peyraube, Alain. 1994. On the history of Chinese locative prepositions. *Chinese Language and Linguistics* 2: 361-387.

Peyraube, Alain. 1999. Historical change in Chinese grammar. *Cahiers de Linguistique - Asie Orientale* 28: 177-226.

Peyraube, Alain. 2003. On the history of place words and localizers in Chinese: A cognitive approach. In: Y.-H. Audrey Li and Andrew Simpson (eds.), *Functional Structure(s), Form and Interpretation,* 180-198. London: Routledge.

Peyraube, Alain. 2015. Syntactic and semantic change in Chinese. *Newcastle & Northumbria Working Papers in Linguistics* 2015-1: 112-129.

Phonkhunsap, Sumalee and Itsarate Dolphen. 2019. The grammaticalization of verbs in Thai. *International Journal of Management and Applied Science* 5.11: 91-98.

Phyocwun Kwuke Taysacen (표준국어대사전). 1992. [A Comprehensive Korean Dictionary].

Portilla, Mario. 2011. El origen de las preposiciones en Español. *Filogía y Lingüística* 37.1: 229-244. (in Spanish)

Post, Mark. 2007. Grammaticalization and compounding in Thai and Chinese: A text-frequency approach. *Studies in Language* 31.1: 117-176.

Prasithrathsint, Amara. 2000. Adjectives as verbs in Thai. *Linguistic Typology* 4: 251-271.

Prasithrathsint, Amara. 2001. The adversative passive marker as a prominent areal feature of Southeast Asian languages. Paper presented at the SEALS XI, May 16-18, 2001, Bangkok.

Prasithrathsint, Amara. 2003. A typological approach to the passive in Thai. *Manusya Journal of Humanities* 6: 1-17.

Prasithrathsint, Amara. 2004. Development of the /thuuk/ passive marker in Thai. Paper presented at the Workshop on Passive within the 20th Scandinavian Conference of Linguistics, January 7-9, 2004, University of Helsinki, Finland.

Prasithrathsint, Amara. 2010a. Parts of Speech in Thai. A Syntactic Approach. Bangkok: Chulalongkorn University Press. (in Thai).

Prasithrathsint, Amara. 2010b. Grammaticalization of nouns into prepositions in Thai. *Language and Linguistics* 28.2: 69-83.

Quirk, Randolph and Joan Mullenhold. 1964. Complex prepositions and related sequences. *English Studies* 45: 64-73.

Quirk, Randolph, Sidney Greenbaum, Geoffrey Leech, and Jan Svartvik. 1985. *A Comprehensive Grammar of the English Language.* London: Longman.

Qun, Fan. 2005. The grammaticalization of *gei* (給) and its pragmatics function as a focus mark in contemporary spoken Chinese. MA thesis, Shanxi University, China. (in Chinese)

Radden, Günter. 1981. The conceptualization of emotional causality by means of prepositional phrases. In: Angeliki Athanasiadou and Elzbieta Tabakowska (eds.), *Speaking of Emotions: Conceptualization and Expression*, 273-294. Berlin: Mouton de Gruyter.

Radden, Günter. 1985. Spatial metaphors underlying prepositions of causality. In: Wolf Paprotté and René Dirven (eds.), *The Ubiquity of Metaphor: Metaphor in Language and Thought*, 177-205. Amsterdam: John Benjamins.

Ramstedt, Gustaf J. 1903. *Über die Konjugation des Khalkha-Mongolischen.* Helsingfors: Société Finno-Ougrienne. (in German)

Ramstedt, Gustav John. 1997[1939]. *A Korean Grammar.* Helsinki: Suomalais-Ugrilainen Seura.

Rangkupan, Suda. 2007. The syntax and semantics of *give*-complex constructions in Thai. *Language and Linguistics* 8.1: 193-234.

Rapp, Eugen Ludwig. 1966. *Die Gurenne-Sprache in Nord-Ghana.* Leipzig: Enzyklopädie. (in German)

Ratliff, Martha. 1991. *Cov,* the underspecified noun, and syntactic flexibility in Hmong. *Journal of the American Oriental Society (JAOS)* 111.4: 694-703.

Regier, Thierry and Mingyu Zheng. 2007. Attention to endpoints: A cross-linguistic constraint on spatial meaning. *Cognitive Science* 31. 705-719.

Reindl, Donald F. 2001. Areal effects on the preservation and genesis of Slavic postpositions. In: Lj. Šarić and D. F. Reindl (eds.), *On Prepositions* (Studia Slavica Oldenburgensia 8), 85-100. Oldenburg: Carl-von-Ossietzky-Universitat Oldenburg.

Rhee, Seongha (이성하). 1996. *Semantics of Verbs and Grammaticalization: The Development in Korean from a Cross-Linguistic Perspective,* Ph.D. dissertation, The University of Texas at Austin. Seoul: Hankook Publisher (Dissertation Series 219).

Rhee, Seongha (이성하). 2000a. Frame of focus in grammaticalization. *Discourse and Cognition* (담화와 인지) 7.2: 79-104.

Rhee, Seongha (이성하). 2000b. Semantic specificity and grammaticalization: A crosslinguistic investigation. *Korean Language Research* (한말연구) 7: 223-248. (in Korean)

Rhee, Seongha (이성하). 2000c. Semantic generality and grammaticalization: With special Reference to Korean synonymous pairs. *The Journal of Linguistic Science* (언어과학연구) 18: 187-208. (in Korean)

Rhee, Seongha (이성하). 2002a. Grammaticalization of *a*-derivative prepositions in English. *The Journal of Linguistic Science* (언어과학연구) 21: 133-156.

Rhee, Seongha (이성하). 2002b. Grammaticalization of *be*-derivative prepositions in English. *Discourse and Cognition* (담화와 인지) 9.2: 147-167.

Rhee, Seongha (이성하). 2002c. Semantic changes of English preposition 'against': A grammaticalization perspective. *Language Research* (어학연구) 38.2: 563-583

Rhee, Seongha (이성하). 2003a. Semantic changes in grammaticalization of postpositionoids from movement verbs in Korean. *Language Research* (어학연구) 39.1: 50-69

Rhee, Seongha (이성하). 2003b. The parallel reduction hypothesis in grammaticalization revisited: A case of English prepositions. *Discourse and Cognition* (담화와 인지) 10.3: 187-205

Rhee, Seongha (이성하). 2004a. From opposition to cooperation: Semantic change of 'with'. *Korean Journal of English Language and Linguistics* (영어학) 42: 151-174

Rhee, Seongha (이성하). 2004b. Grammaticalization and lexicalization of rhetorical questions in Korean. *Studies in Modern Grammar* (현대문법연구) 35: 111-139

Rhee, Seongha (이성하). 2004c. Grammaticalization of spatio-temporal postpositions in Korean. *The Journal of Linguistic Science* (언어과학연구) 31: 169-188

Rhee, Seongha (이성하). 2004d. Semantic structure of English prepositions: An analysis from a grammaticalization perspective. *Language Research* (어학연구) 40.2: 397-427

Rhee, Seongha (이성하). 2005a. A comparative analysis of grammaticalization of English and Korean adpositions. *Studies in Modern Grammar* (현대문법연구) 40: 195-214

Rhee, Seongha (이성하). 2005b. How far likeness can go: Grammaticalization of *kath*- in Korean. *Berkeley Linguistics Society* 30: 391-402.

Rhee, Seongha (이성하). 2006a. A cognitive comparative analysis of spatial concepts in English and Korean. *Discourse and Cognition* (담화와 인지) 13.1: 133-161

Rhee, Seongha (이성하). 2006b. Grammaticalization of postpositional particles from spatial terms in Korean. *Japanese/Korean Linguistics* 14: 139-150.

Rhee, Seongha (이성하). 2007a. Particle selection in Korean auxiliary formation. In: Raúl

Aranovich (ed.) *Split Auxiliary Systems* (Typological Studies in Language 69), 237-254., Amsterdam: John Benjamins.

Rhee, Seongha (이성하). 2007b. What is it for if it's before me?: Subjectification and grammaticalization of English *for* and *before*. *Studies in British and American Language and Literature* (영미어문학) 84: 209-231.

Rhee, Seongha (이성하). 2007c. Different faces of equality: Grammaticalization of equative comparatives in Korean. *Japanese/Korean Linguistics* 15: 149-160.

Rhee, Seongha (이성하). 2009. Thoughts on semantic change mechanisms in grammaticalization. *The Journal of Linguistic Science* (언어과학연구) 51: 175-204.

Rhee, Seongha (이성하). 2010. Many uses of one place: Grammaticalization of *han-tey* 'one place', *Japanese/Korean Linguistics* 17: 581-593.

Rhee, Seongha (이성하). 2011. Divergent specialization in the grammaticalization of native Korean and Sino-Korean spatio-relational terms. *Language and Linguistics* (언어와 언어학) 50: 171-202.

Rhee, Seongha (이성하). 2012a. Context-induced reinterpretation and (Inter)subjectification: The case of grammaticalization of sentence-final particles. *Language Sciences* 34.3: 284-300.

Rhee, Seongha (이성하). 2012b. Persistence and division of labor in grammaticalization: The case of 'out of' and 'from' in English. *Linguistic Research* (언어연구) 29.3: 461-484.

Rhee, Seongha (이성하). 2014. Analogy-driven grammaticalization: A case of grammaticalization of sentence-final markers from concomitance-connectives. *Linguistic Research* (언어연구) 31.3: 591-614. doi: 10.17250/khisli.31.3.201412. 008.

Rhee, Seongha (이성하). 2016[1998]. *Mwunpephwauy Ihay* (문법화의 이해) [Understanding Grammaticalization] (2nd ed.). Seoul: Hankook Publisher. (in Korean)

Rhee, Seongha (이성하). 2016. From quoting to reporting to stance-marking: Rhetorical strategies and intersubjectification of reportative. *Language Sciences* 55: 36-54. doi: 10.1016/j.langsci.2016.02.003.

Rhee, Seongha (이성하). 2020a. From object to text to stance: The case of *kyelkwa* in Korean. *Papers from the 20th National Conference of the Japanese Cognitive Linguistics Association* vol. 20 (日本認知言語學會論文集 第20卷), 471-476.

Rhee, Seongha (이성하). 2020b. Grammaticalization in Korean. In: Walter Bisang and Andrej Malchukov (eds.), *Grammaticalization Scenarios: Cross-linguistic Variation and Universal Tendencies. Volume 1: Grammaticalization Scenarios from Europe and Asia*, 575-608. Berlin: Mouton De Gruyter. doi: 10.1515/9783110563146-013.

Rhee, Seongha (이성하). 2020c. Where to go at the end: Polygrammaticalization of *kAs* 'edge' in Korean. Paper presented at the 2nd Conference on Uralic, Altaic and Paleo-Asiatic Languages, The Institute for Linguistic Studies of the Russian Academy of Sciences, Saint Petersburg, Russia (online platform), October 8-10, 2020.

Rhee, Seongha (이성하). 2021. Functional competition and sociolinguistic pressure: The case of layered datives in Korean. Paper presented at the 54th Societas Linguistica Europaea Conference, National and Kapodistrian University of Athens (online platform), August 31 - September 3, 2021.

Rhee, Seongha (이성하). 2021 (in press). From truth to reality to effect: The journey of *sasilsang* in Korean. *East Asian Pragmatics*, Special issue.

Rhee, Seongha and Hyun Jung Koo (이성하 구현정). 2015. Analogy-driven inter-categorial grammaticalization and (inter)subjectification of *-na* in Korean. *Lingua* 166: 22-42. doi: 10.1016/j.lingua.2015.08.007.

Rhee, Seongha and Hyun Jung Koo (이성하 구현정). 2017. Audience-blind sentence-enders in Korean: A discourse-pragmatic perspective. *Journal of Pragmatics* 120: 101-121. doi: 10.1016/j.pragma.2017.09.002.

Rhee, Seongha and Hyun Jung Koo (이성하 구현정). 2020. From quotation to surprise: The case in Korean. *Journal of Pragmatics* 155: 83-100. doi: 10.1016/j.pragma.2019.10.006.

Rickmeyer, Jens. 1995. *Japanische Morphosyntax*. Heidelberg: Julius Groos. (in German)

Riemsdijk, Henk van. 1990. Functional prepositions. In: Harm Pinkster and Inge Genee (eds.), *Unity in Diversity: Papers presented to Simon C. Dik on his 50th Birthday*, 229-242. Dordrecht: Foris.

Rijkhoff, Jan. 1986. Word order universals revisited: The Principle of Head Proximity. *Belgian Journal of Linguistics* 1: 95-125. doi: 10.1075/bjl.1.05rij

Robbeets, Martine. 2003. Etymological index of Japanese (Appendix 2 of Is Japanese Related to the Altaic Languages?). Ph.D. dissertation, Universiteit Leiden.

Robbeets, Martine. 2005. *Is Japanese related to Korean, Tungusic, Mongolic and Turkic?* (Turcologica 64). Wiesbaden: Harrassowitz.

Robbeets, Martine. 2010. Transeurasian: Can verbal morphology end the controversy? In: Lars Johanson and Martine Robbeets (eds.), *Transeurasian Verbal Morphology in a Comparative Perspective: Genealogy, Contact, Chance* (Turcologica 78), 81-114. Wiesbaden: Harrassowitz.

Robbeets, Martine. 2015. *Diachrony of Verb Morphology: Japanese and the Transeurasian Languages.* Berlin: Mouton de Gruyter.

Robbeets, Martine. 2020. The typological heritage of the Transeurasian languages. In: Martine Robbeets and Alexander Savelyev. (eds.), *The Oxford Guide to the Transeurasian Languages* (Oxford Guides to the World's Languages), 127-144. Oxford: Oxford University Press.

Robbeets, Martine and Alexander Savelyev. (eds.) 2020. *The Oxford Guide to the Transeurasian Languages* (Oxford Guides to the World's Languages). Oxford: Oxford University Press.

Roberts, Ian (ed.). 2017. *The Oxford Handbook of Universal Grammar.* Oxford: Oxford University Press.

Rohde, Ada Ragna. 2001. Analyzing PATH: The Interplay of Verbs, Prepositions and Constructional Semantics. PhD. dissertation, Rice University.

Rohdenburg, Günter. 1996. Cognitive complexity and increased grammatical explicitness in English. *Cognitive Linguistics* 7.2: 149-82.

Rosch, Eleanor. 1973. Natural categories. *Cognitive Psychology* 4: 328-350.

Rosch, Eleanor. 1975. Cognitive representations of semantic categories. *Journal of Experimental Psychology: General* 104.3: 192-233.

Rosch, Eleanor. 1978. Principles of categorization. In: Eleanor Rosch and Barbara B. Lloyd (eds.), *Cognition and Categorization,* 27-48. Hillsdale, NJ: Lawrence Erlbaum Associates.

Ross, John. 1967. Constraints on variables in syntax. Ph.D. dissertation, Massachusetts Institute of Technology.

Rudanko, Juhani. 1996. *Prepositions and Complement Clauses: A Syntactic and Semantic Study of Verbs Governing Prepositions and Complement Clauses in Present-Day English.* Albany, NY: State University of New York Press.

Rutherford, Attapol T. and Santhawat Thanyawong. 2019. Written on leaves or in stones?: Computational evidence for the era of authorship of Old Thai prose. *Proceedings of the 1st International Workshop on Computational Approaches to Historical Language Change,* 81-85. Florence, Italy, August 2, 2019.

Sak-Humphry, Chhany, Kitima Indrambarya, and Stanley Starosta. 1997. Flying 'in' and 'out' in Khmer and Thai. In: Arthur S. Abramson (ed.), *Southeast Asian Linguistics Studies in Honor of Vichin Panupong*, 209-220. Bangkok: Chulalongkorn University Press.

Sanders, Robert and Satoshi Uehara. 2012. A syntactic classification of the synchronic use of *gĕi* in Beijing Mandarin. *Chinese Language and Discourse* 3.2: 167-199. doi: 10.1075/cld.3.2.02san.

Sanit, Samakkarn. 1975. Concerning the 'face' of Thai people: Analysis according to the anthropological linguistics approach. *NIDA Journal* 4. National Institute of Development Administration (NIDA).

Sapir, Edward. 1949. *Selected Writings of Edward Sapir in Language, Culture, and Personality.* ed. by David G. Mandelbaum. The University of California Press.

Savetamalya, Saranya. 1989. Thai nouns and noun phrases: A lexicase analysis. Ph.D. dissertation, University of Hawai'i.

Schiering, René. 2010. Reconsidering erosion in grammaticalization: Evidence from cliticization. In: Katerina Stathi, Elke Gehweiler, and Ekkehard König (eds.), *Grammaticalization: Current Views and Issues*, 73-100. Amsterdam: John Benjamins.

Schiller, Eric. 1992. Autolexical solutions to the problem of 'parts of speech' in Southeast Asian languages. *SEALS-I, Papers from the First Annual Meeting of the Southeast Asian Linguistics Society (1991)*, 397-415. Tempe, AZ: Arizona State University Program for Southeast Asian Studies.

Schwegler, Armin. 1990. *Analyticity and Syntheticity.* Berlin: Mouton de Gruyter.

Serafim, Leon A. 1985. *Shodon: The Prehistory of a Northern Ryukyuan Dialect of Japanese.* Tokyo: Hompo Shoseki.

Serafim, Leon A. 2003. When and where did the Japonic language enter the Ryukyus? A critical comparison of language, archeology and history. In: Toshiki Osada and Alexander Vovin (eds.), *Perspectives on the Origins of the Japanese Language*, 463-476. Kyoto: International Research Center for Japanese Studies.

Shen, Jiaxuan (沈家煊). 1989. *Yŭyán Gòngxìng hé Yŭyán Lèixíng* (语言共性和语言类型) [Language Universals and Linguistic Typology]. Beijing: Huaxia Publishing Co., 北京: 华夏出版社. (in Chinese). Translation of Bernard Comrie, 1989, *Language Universals and Linguistic Typology* (2nd ed.), Chicago: The University of Chicago Press.

Shin, Yong-Kwon (신용권). 2009. A study on the Han'eryanyu reflected in *Laoqida*. *Altai Hakpo* (알타이학보) 19: 185-213. (in Korean)

Sims-Williams, Helen and Matthew Baerman. 2021. A typological perspective on the loss of inflection. In: Svenja Kranich and Tine Breban (eds.), *Lost in Change: Causes and Processes in the Loss of Grammatical Elements and Constructions*, 21-49. Amsterdam: John Benjamins.

Sinha, Chris, Liz Thorseng, Mariko Hayashi and Kim Plunkett. 1994. Comparative spatial semantics and language acquisition: Evidence from Danish, English and Japanese. *Journal of Semantics* 11: 253-287.

Slater, Keith W. 2000. What is a particle? On the use and abuse of the term particle in East and Southeast Asian Languages: With some modest recommendations for improving a mildly lamentable situation. *Payap University Working Papers* 6.2: 1-18.

Slobin, Dan I. 2004. The many ways to search for a frog. Linguistic typology and the expression of motion events. In: Sven Strömqvist and Ludo Verhoeven (eds.), *Relating Events in Narrative: Typological and Contextual Perspectives*. 219-257. Mahwah NJ: Lawrence Erlbaum.

Slobin, Dan I. 2006. What makes manner of motion salient? Explorations in linguistic typology, discourse and cognition. In: Maya Hickmann and Stéphane Robert (eds.), *Space in Language: Linguistic Systems and Cognitive Categories*, 60-81. Amsterdam: John Benjamins.

Smessaert, Hans, William Van Belle, and Ingrid Van Canegem-Ardijns. 2014. In: Nicole Debecque, Karen Lahousse, and Willy Van Langendonck (eds.), *Non-Nuclear Cases: Case and Grammatical Relations across Languages* (Case and Grammatical Relations Across Languages 6). 127-171. Amsterdam: John Benjamins.

Smyth, David. 2002. *Thai: An Essential Grammar*. London: Routledge.

Sohn, Ho-min (손호민). 1976. Semantics of compound verbs in Korean. *Ene* (언어) 1.1: 142-50.

Sohn, Ho-Min (손호민). 1999. *The Korean Language* (Cambridge Language Surveys). Cambridge: Cambridge University Press.

Sohn, Sung-Ock S. (손성옥). 2002. The grammaticalization of honorific particles in Korean. In: Ilse Wischer and Gabriele Diewald (eds.), *New Reflections on Grammaticalization*, 309-25. Amsterdam: John Benjamins.

Sohn, Sung-Ock S. (손성옥). 2003. On the emergence of intersubjectivity: An analysis of the sentence-final *nikka* in Korean. *Japanese/Korean Linguistics* 12: 52-63.

Sommerer, Lotte. 2018. *Article Emergence in Old English: A Constructionalist Perspective*. Berlin: Walter de Gruyter.

Song, Jae Jung (송재정). 1997. On the development of MANNER from GIVE. In: John Newman (ed.), *The Linguistics of Giving*, 327-348. Amsterdam: John Benjamins.

Song, Jae Jung (송재정). 2005. *The Korean Language: Structure, Use and Context*. London: Routledge.

Song, Kyung-An (송경안). 2008. Kyekuy yuhyenglon [Linguistic typology of case]. In: Kyung-An Song and Ki-Gap Lee (송경안 이기갑) (eds.), *Eneyuhyenglon: Kyek, Pwuchisa, Caykwikwumwun, Cepsokphyohyen* (언어유형론: 격, 부치사, 재귀구문, 접속표현) [Linguistic Typology: Case, Adposition, Reflexive Construction, Connectives] vol. 2, 9-53. Seoul: Welin.

SpanishDict. n.d. online searchable dictionary, www.spanishdict.com

Sroka, Kazimierz A. 1972. *The Syntax of English Phrasal Verbs*. The Hague: Mouton.

Starosta, Stanley. 1985. Relator nouns as a source of case inflection. *Oceanic Linguistics Special Publications, No. 20, For Gordon H. Fairbanks*, 111-133. University of Hawai'i Press.

Starosta, Stanley. 1988, *The Case for Lexicase: An Outline of Lexicase Grammatical Theory* (Open Linguistics Series). London: Pinter Publishers.

Starosta, Stanley. 2000. The identification of word classes in Thai. In: M. R. Kalaya Tingsabadh and Arthur Abramson (eds.), *Essays in Tai Linguistics*, 63-90. Bangkok: Chulalongkorn University.

Stefanowitsch, Anatol and Ada Rodhe. 2004. The goal bias in the encoding of motion events. In: Günter Radden and Klaus-Uwe Panther (eds.), *Studies in Linguistic Motivation*, 249-267. Berlin: Mouton de Gruyter.

Stefanowitsch, Anatol. 2018. The goal bias revised: A collostructional approach. *Yearbook of the German Cognitive Linguistics Association* 6.1: 143-166.

Suh, Sang Kyu (서상규). (n.d.). Kyoyukyong kipon 1-man ehwi [10,000 basic words for education]. ms. Yonsei University, Seoul. (in Korean)

Sun, Chaofen. 1996. *Word-Order Change and Grammaticalization in the History of Chinese*. Stanford: Stanford University Press.

Sun, Chaofen. 1998. Aspectual categories that overlap: A historical and dialectal perspective of the Chinese *zhe*. *Journal of East Asian Linguistics* 7: 153-174.

Suthiwan, Titima. 1992. Malay Loanwords in Thai. *Pan-Asiatic Linguistics (PAL)* 3.1: 1358-1366.

Suzuki, Shigeyuki. 1972. *Nihongo Bunpō, Keitairon* [Japanese Grammar: Morphology]. Tokyo: Mugi Shobo. (in Japanese)

Suzuki, Tomomi (ed). 2007. *Fukugō Joshi ga Kore de Wakaru* [All about compound particles]. Tōkyō: Hitsuji Shobō. (in Japanese)

Svorou, Soteria. 1986. On the evolutionary paths of locative expressions. *Berkeley Linguistics Society* 12: 515-527.

Svorou, Soteria. 1994. *The Grammar of Space* (Typological Studies in Language 25). Amsterdam: John Benjamins.

Sylak-Glassman, John, Christo Kirov, Matt Post, Roger Que, and David Yarowsky. 2015. A Universal Feature Schema for Rich Morphological Annotation and Fine-Grained Cross-lingual Part-of-Speech Tagging. In: Cerstin Mahlow and Michael Piotrowski (eds.), *Systems and Frameworks for Computational Morphology*, 72-93. Heidelberg: Springer.

Tagashira, Yoshiko. 1999. Some aspects of relational nouns. In: Leon de Stadler and Christoph Eyrich (eds.), *Issues in Cognitive Linguistics 1993. Proceedings of the International Cognitive Linguistics Conference*, 249-276. Berlin: Mouton de Gruyter.

Takahashi, Kiyoko. 2003. Accomplishment constructions in Thai: Diverse cause-effect relationships. *Papers from the 13th Annual Meeting of the Southeast Asian Linguistics Society 2003, Los Angeles, May 2-4, 2003, 263-277*. Canberra: Pacific Linguistics (Research School of Pacific and Asian Studies, The Australian National University).

Takahashi, Kiyoko. 2005. Allative preposition in Thai. In: Paul Sidwell (ed.), *Papers from the 15th Annual Meeting of the Southeast Asian Linguistics Society 2005*, 111-120. Canberra: Pacific Linguistics (Research School of Pacific and Asian Studies, The Australian National University).

Takahashi, Kiyoko. 2008. Grammaticalization paths of the Thai verb *day*: A corpus-based study. In: Uri Tadmor and Paul Sidwell (eds.), *SEALS-XVI, Papers from the 16th Annual Meeting of the Southeast Asian Linguistics Society* (2006), 122-132. Canberra: Pacific Linguistics (Research School of Pacific and Asian Studies, The Australian National University).

Takahashi, Kiyoko. 2012. On historical semantic changes of the Thai morpheme *haj*.

JSEALS (Journal of Southeast Asian Linguistics Society) 5: 126-141.

Takahashi, Tarō. 2003. *Dōshi Kyūshō* [Nine Chapters on Verbs]. Tokyo: Hitsuji Shobō. (in Japanese)

Talmy, Leonard. 1983. How language structures space. In: Herbert L. Pick, Linda P. Acredolo, (eds.), *Spatial Orientation - Theory, Research and Application,* 225-282. New York: Plenum Press.

Talmy, Leonard. 1985. Lexicalization patterns: Semantic structure in lexical forms. In: Timothy Shopen (ed.), *Language Typology and Syntactic Description,* vol. 3: 57-149. Cambridge: Cambridge University Press.

Talmy, Leonard. 1988. Force dynamics in language and cognition. *Cognitive Science* 12: 49-100.

Talmy, Leonard. 2000. *Toward a Cognitive Semantics. Volume I: Concept Structuring Systems.* Cambridge, MA, USA: MIT Press.

Tanaka, Hiroshi. 2010. *Fukugōji kara Mita Nihongo Bunpō no Kenkyū* [Research on Japanese Grammar from the Viewpoint of Compound Morphemes]. Tōkyō: Hitsuji Shobō. (in Japanese)

Taylor, John R. 1988. Contrasting prepositional categories: English and Italian. In: Brygida Rudzka-ostyn (ed.), *Topics in Cognitive Linguistics,* 299-326. Amsterdam: John Benjamins.

Tenbrink, Thora, Jan Wiener, and Christophe Clramunt (eds.). 2013. *Representing Space in Cognition: Interrelations of Behavior, Language, and Formal Models* (Explorations in Language and Space 8). Oxford: Oxford University Press.

Thai National Corpus, the (TNC). http://www.arts.chula.ac.th/~ling/ThaiConc/

Thepkanjana, Kingkarn. 1986. Serial verb constructions in Thai. Ph.D. dissertation, University of Michigan, Ann Arbor.

Thepkanjana, Kingkarn. 2003. A cognitive account of the causative/inchoative alternation in Thai. In: Eugene H. Casad and Gary B. Palmer (eds.), *Cognitive Linguistics and Non-Indo-European Languages,* 247-274. Berlin: Mouton de Gruyter.

Thepkanjana, Kingkarn and Satoshi Uehara. 2008. The verb of giving in Thai and Mandarin Chinese as a case of polysemy: A comparative study. *Language Sciences* 30: 621-651.

Thomason, Sarah G. and Terrence Kaufman. 1988. *Language Contact, Creolization, and Genetic Linguistics.* Berkeley: University of California Press.

Thompson, Laurence A. 1965. *A Vietnamese Grammar.* Seattle: University of Washington Press.

Ting, Jen. 1998. Deriving the *bèi*-construction in Mandarin Chinese. *Journal of East Asian Linguistics* 7.4: 319-354.

Traugott, Elizabeth Closs. 1982. From propositional to textual and expressive meanings: Some semantic-pragmatic aspects of grammaticalization. In: Winfred P. Lehmann and Yakov Malkiel (eds.), *Directions for Historical Linguistics: a Symposium,* 245-271. Austin: University of Texas Press.

Traugott, Elizabeth Closs. 2003. From subjectification to intersubjectification. In: Raymond Hickey (ed.), *Motives for Language Change,* 124-139. Cambridge: Cambridge University Press.

Traugott, Elizabeth Closs. 2010. (Inter)subjectivity and (inter)subjectification: A reassessment. In: Kristin Davidse, Lieven Vandelanotte and Hubert Cuyckens (eds.), *Subjectification, Intersubjectification and Grammaticalization,* 29-71. Berlin: De Gruyter Mouton.

Traugott, Elizabeth Closs. 2011. Grammaticalization and mechanisms of change. In: Heiko Narrog and Bernd Heine (eds.), *The Oxford Handbook of Grammaticalization,* 19-30. Oxford: Oxford University Press.

Traugott, Elizabeth Closs and Richard B. Dasher. 2002. *Regularity in Semantic Change.* Cambridge: Cambridge University Press.

Traugott, Elizabeth Closs and Ekkehard König. 1991. The semantics-pragmatics of grammaticalization revisited. In: Elizabeth Closs Traugott and Bernd Heine (eds.), *Approaches to Grammaticalization.* 2 vols. (Typological Studies in Language 19), vol. 1: 189-218. Amsterdam: John Benjamins.

Traugott, Elizabeth and Graeme Trousdale. 2013. *Constructionalization and Constructional Change* (Oxford Studies in Diachronic and Historical Linguistics). Oxford: Oxford University Press.

Tsai, Wei-Tien Dylan (ed.). 2015. *The Cartography of Chinese Syntax* (The Cartography of Syntactic Structures 11). Oxford: Oxford University Press.

Tsunoda, Tasaku (ed.). 2013. *Adnominal Clauses and the 'Mermaid Construction': Grammaticalization of Nouns.* Tokyo: National Institute for Japanese Language and Linguistics.

Tsunoda, Tasaku (ed.). 2020. *Mermaid Construction: A Compound-Predicate Construction with Biclausal Appearance* (Comparative Handbooks of

Linguistics). Berlin: Mouton de Gruyter.

Tyler, Andrea, and Vyvyan Evans. 2003. *The Semantics of English Prepositions: Spatial Scenes, Embodied Meaning and Cognition.* Cambridge: Cambridge University Press.

Ueda, Hiroto. 1990. Frases prepositivas del espanol. *Revista de la Facultad de Ciencias Humanisticas de la Universidad de Tokyo* 22, 9-33. (in Spanish)

Ukosakul, Margaret. 1999. Conceptual metaphors motivating the use of Thai 'face'. MA thesis, Payap University, Thailand.

Ukosakul, Margaret. 2003. Conceptual metaphors motivating the use of Thai 'face'. In: Eugene H. Casad and Gary B. Palmer (eds.), *Cognitive Linguistics and Non-Indo-European Languages,* 275-304. Berlin: Mouton de Gruyter.

Ungerer, Friedrich and Hans-Jörg Schmid. 1996. *An Introduction to Cognitive Linguistics.* London: Longman.

Uppakitsinlapasan, Phraya. 1953. *Siamese Grammar.* Bangkok: Thai Wattana Phanich.

Vandeloise, Claude. 1991. *Spatial Prepositions: A Case Study from French* (Translated by Anna R. K. Bosch). Chicago: The University of Chicago Press.

Varasarin, Uraisi. 1984. *Les éléments khmers dans la formation de la langue siamoise* (Langues et civilizations de l'asie du sud-est et du monde insulindien, 15). Paris: SELAF. (in French)

Verkerk, Annemarie. 2017. The goal-over-source principle in European languages: Preliminary results from a parallel corpus study. In: Silvia Luraghi, Tatiana Nikitina and Chiara Zanchi (eds.), *Space in Diachrony,* 1-40. Amsterdam: John Benjamins.

Vovin, Alexander. 2008. *Koreo-Japonica: A Re-Evaluation of a Common Genetic Origin* (Center for Korean Studies Monograph). Honolulu: University of Hawai'i Press.

Wang, Jun Xiang (王君湘). 2013. Bèidòng biāojì "zhe (zhe)" de láiyuán hé yǎnbiàn (被动标记"着(著)"的来源和演变). [A study on the origin and the change process of the passive marker "zhe"(着(著)] *Journal of Chinese Studies* (中國學論叢) 41: 19-54. doi: 10.26585/chlab.2013..41.002. (in Chinese)

Wang, Jun Xiang (王君湘). 2014. Fāng suǒ jiècí "zhe (zhe)" de shǐyòng hé yǔfǎhuà (方所介词 "著(着)"的使用和语法化) [The use and grammaticalization of the locative preposition 著(着)) *Journal of Chinese Studies* (中國學論叢) 46: 177-214. (in Chinese)

Wang, Li (王力). 1984. *Zhōngguó Yǔfǎlǐlùn* (中国语法理论) [Theory of Chinese grammar]. Jinan: Shanghai Education Press (*Wang Li Wenji Di 1 Juan*; Vol. 1 or Wang Li's Articles), 1st ed. 1944-45, Chongqing: Shangwuyinshuguan. (in Chinese)

Wang, Li (王力). 1985. Zhōngguó Xiàndài Yǔfǎ (中国现代语法) [Modern Chinese Grammar]. Beijing: Shangwuyinshuguan. (*Hanyu Yufa Congshu*, 1st ed. 1943-44. Chongqing. Beijing: Shangwuyinshuguan). (in Chinese)

Warotamasikkhadit, Udom. 1988. There are no prepositions in Thai. *The International Symposium on Language and Linguistics*, 70-76.

Warotamasikkhadit, Udom. 1992. Syntactic variations in Thai poetry. In: Carol J. Compton and John F. Hartmann (eds.), *Papers on Tai Languages, Linguistics, and Literatures: In Honor of William J. Gedney's 77th Birthday, Monograph Series on Southeast Asia, Occasional Papers* 16, 293-300. DeKalb, IL: Center for Southeast Asian Studies, Northern Illinois University.

Warotamasikkhadit, Udom. 1994. Is *hay* really a benefactive-causative in Thai? *Papers from the Second Annual Meeting of the Southeast Asian Linguistics Society 1992*, 383-388. Tempe, AZ: Arizona State University.

Werner, Alice. 1904. Note on the terms used for 'right hand' and 'left hand' in the Bantu languages. *Journal of the African Society* 13: 112-16.

Westermann, Diedrich. 1924. *Die Kpelle-Sprache in Liberia: Grammatische Einführung, Texte und Wörterbuch.* (Zeitschrift für Eingeborenen-Sprachen, Beiheft 6) Berlin: Dietrich Reimer. (in German)

Whitman, John. 1985. The phonological basis for the comparison of Japanese and Korean. Ph.D. dissertation, Harvard University.

Whitman, John. 2015. Old Korean. In: Lucien Brown and Jae Hoon Yeon (eds.), *The Handbook of Korean Linguistics*, 422-38. London: Wiley-Blackwell.

Whitman, John, Miyoung Oh, Jinho Park, Valerio Luigi Alberizzi, Masayuki Tsukimoto, Teiji Kosukegawa, and Tomokazu Takada. 2010. Toward an international vocabulary for research on vernacular reading of Chinese texts (漢文訓讀 Hanwen xundu). *Scripta* 2: 61-83.

Wienold, Götz. 1995 Lexical and conceptual structures in expressions for movement and space: With reference to Japanese, Korean, Thai, and Indonesian as compared with English and German. In: Urs Egli, Peter E. Pause, Christoph Schwarze, Arnim von Stechow, and Götz Wienold (eds.), *Lexical Knowledge in the Organization of Language*, 301-340. Amsterdam: Benjamins.

Witayasakpan, Sompong. 1992. The amazing morphology of Thai. *Proceedings of the Third International Symposium on Language and Linguistics, Bangkok, Thailand*, 355-372. Bangkok: Chulalongkorn University.

Wong, May L-Y. 2009. *Gei* constructions in Mandarin Chinese and *bei* constructions in Cantonese: A corpus-driven contrastive study. *International Journal of Corpus Linguistics* 14.1: 60-80. doi: 10.1075/ijcl.14.1.04won.

Wu, Fuxiang (吴福祥). 2005. Yǔfǎhuà lǐlùn, lìshǐ jùfǎxué yǔ Hànyǔ lìshǐ yǔfǎ yánjiū (语法化理论、历史句法学与汉语历史语法研究) [Grammaticalization theory, historical syntax, and research on Chinese historical grammar]. In: Danqing Liu (刘丹青) (ed.), Yǔyánxué qiányán yǔ Hànyǔ yánjiū (语言学前沿与汉语研究) [*Frontiers of Linguistics and Chinese Studies*], chapter 10. Shanghai: Shanghai Education Press (in Chinese). Korean summary translation by Fuxiang Wu and Jaeyoung Choi (최재영). Mwunpephwa ilon, yeksathongsalonkwa cwungkwuke yeksamwunpep yenkwu. *Korea Journal of Chinese Language and Literature* (中語中文學) 44: 597-624.

Wu, Fuxiang (吴福祥). 2008. Origin and evolution of the locative term *hòu* 'back' in Chinese. In: Dan Xu (ed.), *Space in Languages of China: Cross-linguistic, Synchronic and Diachronic Perspectives*, 229-247. Dordrecht: Springer. doi: 10.1007/978-1-4020-8321-1_10.

Wu, Hsiao-Hung Iris. 2015. The fine structure of spatial PPs in Mandarin Chinese. In: Wei-Tien Dylan Tsai (ed.), *The Cartography of Chinese Syntax* (The Cartography of Syntactic Structures 11), 209-234. Oxford: Oxford University Press.

Wulimal Khunsacen [A Comprehensive Korean Dictionary]. 1996[1992]. Seoul: Emwunkak.

Xing, Janet Zhiqun. 2003. Grammaticalization of verbs in Mandarin Chinese. *Journal of Chinese Linguistics* 31.1: 101-144.

Xing, Janet Zhiqun. 2013. Semantic reanalysis in grammaticalization in Chinese. In: Zhuo Jing-Schmidt (ed.) *Increased Empiricism: Recent Advances in Chinese Linguistics* (Studies in Chinese Language and Discourse 2), 223-246. doi: 10.1075/scld.2.11xin. Amsterdam: John Benjamins.

Xing, Janet Zhiqun. (ed.). 2020. *A Typological Approach to Grammaticalization and Lexicalization: East Meets West* (Trends in Linguistics Studies and Monographs 327). Berlin: Mouton de Gruyter.

Yae, Sunhee (예선희). 2008. Grammaticalization and corpus-based study of substitutive complex prepositions *instead of* and *on behalf of*. *Studies of English Language & Literature* (영어학) 34.4: 283-300.

Yae, Sunhee (예선희). 2012. An analysis of a semantic divergence, a semantic extension, and semantic errors of verbs and an auxiliary particle derived from a Middle Korean verb *cochta* 'follow': From the perspective of grammaticalization. *The New Studies of English Language & Literature* (신영어영문학) 51: 241-256. (in Korean)

Yae, Sunhee (예선희). 2015. Grammaticalization of 'Case particle + *-taka*' in Korean. *Studies in Modern Grammar* (현대문법연구) 86: 31-46. (in Korean)

Yae, Sunhee (예선희). 2018. A corpus-based study of the *regard*-PNP. *Language and Linguistics* (언어와 언어학) 81: 105-124.

Yamada, Yoshio. 1935. *Kanbun no Kundoku ni Yorite Tutaeraretaru Gohō* [Idioms originating in Japanese readings of Chinese texts]. Tōkyō: Hōbunkan. (in Japanese)

Yao, Ruoyu. 2013. Analyse comparative synchronique et diachronique des locatifs en chinois. Ph.D. dissertation, Institut National des Langues et Civilisations Orientales (INALCO), Paris. (in French)

Yi, Hye-Won (이혜원). 2009. Semantic and functional changes of English *up*: A grammaticalization perspective to heterosemy. MA thesis, Hankuk University of Foreign Studies, Korea.

Yi, Hye-Won (이혜원). 2018. Grammaticalization of complex conjunctive adverbials. Ph.D. dissertation, Hankuk University of Foreign Studies, Korea.

Yi, Tae-Yong (이태영). 1988. A study on the grammaticalization of Korean verbs. Ph.D. dissertation, Chonbuk National University, Seoul: Hanshin Publishing. (in Korean)

Yi, Tae-Yong (이태영). 1993[1988]. *Kwuke Tongsauy Mwunpephwa Yenkwu* [A study on the grammaticalization of Korean verbs]. Seoul: Hanshin Publishing. (in Korean)

Yin, Hui. 2004. Grammaticalization of Mandarin transfer verbs *gěi* and *bèi* as passive markers. *Actes du congrès annuel de l'Association candienne de linguistique*, 1-12.

Yip, Po-Ching and Don Rimmington. 1997. *Chinese: An Essential Grammar*. London: Routledge.

Yu, Zhihong (余志鴻). 1986. *Hànyǔ Qiánhòuzhicí Hùnyòng de Shízhi* (漢語前後置詞混用的 實質) [The Essence of the Mixed Use of Chinese Prepositions and Postpositions] Yǔyán xué niánkān (語言學年刊) [Annals of Linguistics]. Zhèjiāng shěng Yǔyán xuéhuì [Zhejiang Linguistics Association]. (in Chinese)

Yu, Chang-Don (유창돈). 2000[1964]. *Icoe Sacen* [A dictionary of the Josen Dynasty language]. Seoul: Yonsei University Press. (in Korean)

Zanchi, Chiara. 2017. New evidence for the source-goal asymmetry. In: Silvia Luraghi, Tatiana Nikitina, and Chiara Zanchi (eds.), *Space in Diachrony*, 147-178. Amsterdam: John Benjamins.

Zhang, Bin (张斌). 2010. *Xiàndài Hànyǔ Miáoxiě Yǔfǎ* (现代汉语描写语法) [Modern Chinese Descriptive Grammar]. Beijing: Shangwuyinshuguan. (in Chinese)

Zhang, Hongming. 1991. The grammaticalization of *bei* as a passive marker in Chinese. Paper presented at the 2nd International Symposium on Chinese Languages and Linguistics, Taiwan.

Zhang, Ying, Ralf Brown, Robert Frederking, and Alon Lavie. 2001. Pre-processing of bilingual corpora for Mandarin-English EBMT. *Proceedings of Machine Translation Summit VIII, Santiago de Compostela, Spain, September 18-22, 2001.*

Zlatev, Jordan. 2003. Holistic spatial semantics of Thai. In: Eugene H. Casad and Gary B. Palmer (eds.), *Cognitive Linguistics and Non-Indo-European Languages*, 305-335. Berlin: Mouton de Gruyter.

Zlatev, Jordan and Peerapat Yangklang. 2004. A third way to travel: the place of Thai in the motion event typology. In: Sven Strömqvist and Ludo Verhoeven (eds.) *Relating Events in Narrative: Typological and Contextual Perspectives*, 159-190. Mahwah, NJ: Lawrence Erlbaum.

Zwarts, Joost. 1995. Lexical and functional direction. In: Marcel den Dikken and Kees Hengeveld, (eds.), *Linguistics in the Netherlands 1995*, 227-238. Amsterdam: John Benjamins.

Author Index

Abney, Steven 33

Abraham, Werner 404

Ahn, Byung Hee (안병희) 50

Ahn, Joo Hoh (안주호) 29

Ahn, Key-Seob (안기섭) 278

Ahn, Kyou-Dong (안규동) 5, 29, 159, 177, 223, 382, 400

Ahn, Mikyung (안미경) 5, 29, 177, 400

Ahn, So-Min (안소민) 281

Ahn, Yeon Jin (안연진) 5, 250, 278

Alarcos Llorach, Emilio 205,

Allen, Cynthia L. 22

Andersen, Elaine S. 75, 199, 174, 265, 415

Andersen, Henning 432

Andrews, Avery D. 19, 376

Ansaldo, Umberto 425

Baerman, Matthew 22

Baik, Junghye (백정혜) 5, 29, 194

Bailblé, Olivier 256

Barlow, Michael 21

Barrie, Michael 255

Bello, Andrés 204, 247

Bennett, David 34

Bentley, John 24

Bergsland, Knut 35

Bisang, Walter 20, 276, 299, 309, 352, 355, 357, 425, 432, 435

Blake, Barry J. 35, 36, 46, 60, 115, 310, 376

Bloom, Paul 31, 32

Bolinger, Dwight 34, 36

Börjars, Kersti 386

Bourdin, Philippe 419

Bowden, John 29, 34, 174, 395

Bowerman, Melissa 31

Boye, Kasper 390

Brinton, Laurel J. 362

Brisard, Frank 31, 32

Broschart, Jürgen 32

Brown, Cecil H. 62, 340

Brown, J. Marvin 435

Brown, Penelope 32, 67

Brugman, Claudia 395

Buakhao, Supakit 5

Burton-Roberts, Noel 195

Bussmann, Hadumod 308

Bybee, Joan L. 5, 21, 29, 64, 81, 84, 183, 194, 286, 361, 370, 382, 386, 396, 404, 425, 432

Camacho Becerra, Heriberto 26

Campbell, Lyle 386, 421, 433

Chae, Hee-Rahk (채희락) 50

Chae, Wan (채완) 61

Chamniyom, Ratree 309, 342

Chappell, Hilary M. 29, 252, 297

Chen, Changlai (陈昌来) 253, 257, 304

Chen, Chun-hui 125, 434

Chen, Xinren 5

Chin, Jungran (진정란) 5

Chino, Naoko 105, 107-109, 130

Cho, Young-Eon (조영언) 61, 122

Choe, Hyun-Bae (최현배) 35

Choe, Jae-Woong (최재웅) 43

Subject index

Benefactive, benefaction 311, 346, 369, 426, 435
Beneficiary 39, 281
bi-clausal 295
bidimensional (spatial case) 40
bigram 252-253
bilexemic 440
bimorphemic 38, 439-440
bleaching 81, 136, 278, 286, 296-297, 353, 396
body part/body-part (term, noun) 60, 62, 122, 140, 174, 187, 189-190, 330, 339, 355, 384, 391, 395
bondedness 28, 90, 141
borrowing/borrowed 95-98, 125-126, 152, 157, 172-177, 197, 201, 221-222, 248, 433-436, 442-443
bottom-south (association) 340
bridging context 295, 411
calque 125, 434
cardinal direction 62, 283-284, 340, 385
cartographic tradition 385
case inflection 20, 149
case particle 20, 149
categorial fluidity 34, 105, 150, 157, 200, 203, 253-254, 306, 342, 445
categorial metaphor 390
Causal 39
Cause/Causative 40, 45, 47
center vs. periphery 59
central-peripheral axis 275
cìdòngcí 251
circumposition 196, 251, 253, 304, 306
class noun 359
coalescence 90, 428

coexistence 208, 362
cohesion 28, 140, 214, 262, 322, 360, 403, 405
cohesive/cohesiveness 158
colloquial(ity) 49, 76, 284, 286, 368
Comitative 39, 45- 48, 100, 311, 318, 321, 332, 348, 350-352, 379-380, 394
Comparative 45, 47, 428
competition/competitor 70, 76-77, 80, 97, 101-102, 131-134, 144-145, 148, 182, 184-186, 198, 233, 236, 254, 289-291, 348, 352, 390, 413, 440, 442, 444
complexity 25, 30, 35, 80, 84, 197, 204, 234, 237, 249, 291, 306, 314, 349, 351, 388, 415, 439, 440, 444-445
complexity principle 159, 227, 414
compositional 80, 105, 143, 184-185, 386, 413, 439
conceptual chain 100
conceptual cohesion 403
conceptual connection 122, 124, 131, 379
conceptual motivation 274, 304, 350, 352, 376, 378-380
conceptual persistence 400
conceptual relationship 399, 406, 446
conceptual salience 21
conceptualization 31-32, 39, 59, 381-382
concrete case 35
configuration(al) 19, 51, 59, 173-174, 186, 310, 312, 378, 382, 395, 398, 400, 405, 424, 431, 437, 448

21, 130, 145, 177, 210, 270, 341, 346, 405, 436

Enumerative 45-48, 71, 109, 126,

erosion/erode 88ff, 142ff, 192ff, 245ff, 299ff, 355ff, 387, 397, 404, 428-429, 437, 441-448

Essive 45, 47, 53, 56, 117, 130

ethnocentric perspective 307

Ethnologue 23-27

etymology/etymologies/etymological(ly) 46, 61-62, 120-122, 133, 201, 208, 224, 273, 275-276, 291, 363, 413

etymon/etyma 24, 208, 438, 445, 448

evaluative meaning 416

evolutive (process) 220, 432

Exclusive (focus) 45, 47, 108, 109

exocentric complement 309

expansive motivation 408ff, 436, 447

Experiencer 39

expressivity 413

extension/extend 82ff, 98ff, 135ff, 187ff, 237ff, 292ff, 352ff, 400, 405, 409, 440-446

Extent Focus 108, 126

Exterior 41, 52, 93, 117, 135, 161, 163, 181, 186, 213, 261, 268, 275, 332, 348, 374, 383, 417

extrapolation/extrapolate 139

extremity 380

fading 279

fake adposition 36

fāngwèicí 252

fixation 224, 387, 406, 446

flag 36

flexible/flexibility 24, 37, 140, 243, 313,

425

fluid perspective 310, 360, 445

Focus 45-48, 107-109, 126, 145, 379

formal aspect 256, 387

formal reduction 84, 87, 89, 237, 388-389, 406

formal similarity 407

form-meaning coevolution 425

fossilization/fossilized 37, 171, 243, 271, 429, 437, 448

frame-of-focus variation 381

front over back 437, 447

fùdòngcí 251

functeme 36

functional affinity 382

functional analogy 357, 400

functional diversity/functionally diverse 135, 289

functional extension 20, 98ff, 146, 195-196, 247, 303, 357-359, 441

functional strength 21, 47, 54, 79, 101, 231, 263, 269, 289, 334, 348

functional territory 70

functor 341

functor-like status 341

fusional 22, 36-37, 425, 428, 432

fùzhìcí 251

generality 34, 76, 81, 101, 132-133, 147, 171, 183-186, 198, 219, 237, 382, 440, 441-443

Genitive 35-36, 45-49, 60, 74, 88, 91, 102, 140, 144, 261-262, 271, 282, 292, 299-300, 310, 388-389, 397, 403, 423-424, 441

Germanic 22-23, 25, 30, 35, 152, 175,

Linguistic Forms at the Border of Lexis and Grammar:
Grammaticalization of Adpositions across Languages